International Handbook on Services for the Elderly

International Handbook on Services for the Elderly

Edited by JORDAN I. KOSBERG
Foreword by ALFRED GRECH

GREENWOOD PRESS
Westport, Connecticut • London

Library of Congress Cataloging-in-Publication Data

International handbook on services for the elderly / edited by Jordan
 I. Kosberg ; foreword by Alfred Grech.
   p. cm.
 Includes bibliographical references and index.
 ISBN 0-313-28338-9 (alk. paper)
  1. Aged—Services for—Handbooks, manuals, etc. I. Kosberg,
 Jordan I., 1939– .
 HV1451.I547   1994
 361.6—dc20   93-44507

British Library Cataloguing in Publication Data is available.

Copyright © 1994 by Jordan I. Kosberg

All rights reserved. No portion of this book may be
reproduced, by any process or technique, without the
express written consent of the publisher.

Library of Congress Catalog Card Number: 93-44507
ISBN: 0-313-28338-9

First published in 1994

Greenwood Press, 88 Post Road West, Westport, CT 06881
An imprint of Greenwood Publishing Group, Inc.

Printed in the United States of America

The paper used in this book complies with the
Permanent Paper Standard issued by the National
Information Standards Organization (Z39.48–1984).

10 9 8 7 6 5 4 3 2

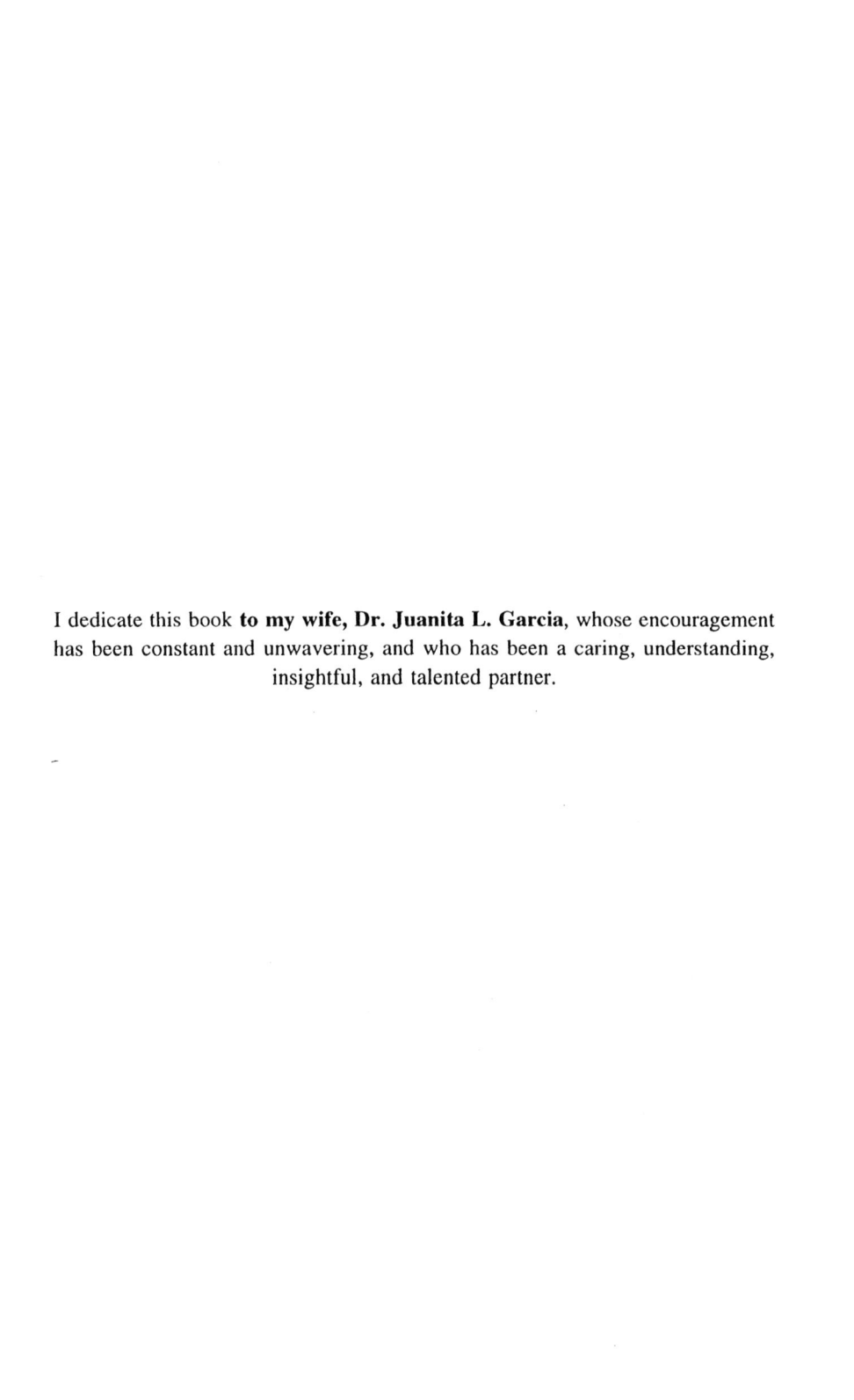

I dedicate this book **to my wife, Dr. Juanita L. Garcia**, whose encouragement has been constant and unwavering, and who has been a caring, understanding, insightful, and talented partner.

CONTENTS

	Tables	xi
	Foreword Alfred Grech	xiii
	Preface	xv
	Acknowledgments	xxv
1.	**Argentina** Roberto E. Barca	1
2.	**Australia** John McCallum	17
3.	**Austria** Josef Hörl	34
4.	**Barbados** Farley S. Brathwaite	51
5.	**Canada** Victor W. Marshall and Blossom T. Wigdor	66
6.	**China** Cai Wenmei, Song Yuhua, Luo Xiaoyui, and Jiang Leiwen	80
7.	**Czech and Slovak Federal Republic (Former)** Ladislav G. Hegyi	95

8.	**France**	104
	Jean-Claude Henrard	
9.	**Germany**	125
	Fred Karl	
10.	**Ghana**	139
	Charles K. Brown	
11.	**Great Britain**	154
	Malcolm L. Johnson	
12.	**Hong Kong**	175
	Nelson W. S. Chow	
13.	**India**	188
	S. D. Gokhale and Chandra Dave	
14.	**Israel**	198
	Howard Litwin	
15.	**Italy**	213
	Massimo Mengani, Cristina Gagliardi, Micaela Tonucci, and Giovanni Lamura	
16.	**Japan**	227
	Yutaka Shimizu and Junko Wake	
17.	**Jordan**	244
	Amal H. El-Farhan and Muhsen A. Makhamreh	
18.	**Malaysia**	252
	Cho Kah Sin and Abdullah Malim Baginda	
19.	**Malta**	270
	Marisa Scerri and Mario D. Garrett	
20.	**Netherlands**	288
	Theo N. M. Schuyt and Gerard H. van der Zanden	
21.	**New Zealand**	305
	Peggy G. Koopman-Boyden	
22.	**Norway**	321
	Eva Beverfelt	
23.	**Poland**	340
	Brunon Synak	

Contents

24.	**South Korea**	356
	Kyu-taik Sung	
25.	**Spain**	373
	Ricardo Moragas Moragas	
26.	**Sudan**	393
	Niemat A. Latiff Mursi	
27.	**Sweden**	401
	Gerdt Sundström and Mats Thorslund	
28.	**Switzerland**	415
	Hans-Dieter Schneider	
29.	**Thailand**	430
	Malinee Wongsith and Chanpen Saengtienchai	
30.	**United States**	445
	Abraham Monk	
31.	**USSR (Former)**	458
	Vladislav V. Bezrukov and Nina V. Verzhikovskaya	
32.	**Zimbabwe**	472
	Andrew C. Nyanguru	
	Selected Bibliography	483
	Index	485
	About the Editor and Contributors	495

TABLES

4.1	Health Care System Structure in Barbados	56
6.1	Monthly Income of the Elderly	82
6.2	Economic Position of the Elderly in the Family	83
8.1	Evolution of the Age Structure of the Population of Elderly People in France, 1968–2010	106
8.2	Household Structure of Elderly People by Age and Sex	107
8.3	Life Expectancy Without Disability (L.W.D.) in France in 1982 at Ages 60 and 75 According to Sex	109
8.4	Percentages of People Aged 65 and over with Loss of Mobility and/or Unable to Perform Personal Tasks, Living in Private Households in 1982	110
8.5	Main Characteristics of the Elderly Population in France	111
8.6	Levels of Pensions According to Occupation, Gender, Socioeconomic Group, Age and Marital Status	114
8.7	Labor Participation Rate of the Older Age Groups, 1962–88	115
8.8	Fiscal Income of Household with a Head Aged 60 and over in 1984	116
8.9	Extent of Main Domiciliary Services and Places for People Aged 60 and over, 1970–90	118
10.1	Estimated and Projected Population Aged 60 and Over by Sex and Age Group in Ghana, 1960, 1980, 2000, 2020, and 2025	140

10.2	Some Socioeconomic Indicators Related to the Health Delivery System in Ghana	146
11.1	Domiciliary Services for Elderly People	168
16.1	Plan of Middle-Aged Persons Aged 30–49 Years for Care of Parents When They Become Bedridden	229
16.2	Eligibility Requirements and Benefits of Major Public Pensions	232
17.1	Statistics for the Elderly in Jordan in 1990	245
17.2	Monthly Income for the Elderly in Jordan	246
17.3	Sources of Income for the Elderly	247
17.4	Sponsors of Elderly Caretaking Organizations	248
19.1	General Demographic Statistics in Malta	272
23.1	Percentage of the Elderly (65+) in Poland by Gender and Place of Residence, 1950–90	342
26.1	Distribution of the Sudanese Population According to Age and Sex, 1985	394
28.1	The Presumable Partition of the Population in Switzerland According to Age Until 2020	417
28.2	Special Living Arrangements for the Elderly in Switzerland	422
28.3	Housing for the Aged in Switzerland	423
31.1	Characteristics of Level of Amenities in Pensioners' Households	464

FOREWORD

To those skeptics who are inclined to question the imminence and inevitability of a "longevity revolution," Alfred Sauvy (1948) pointed out that demographic aging, of all contemporary phenomena, "is the least doubted, the best measured, the most regular in its effects and the easiest to forecast well ahead, as well as the most influential."[1] After all, the people involved in the eventual bulging of the age pyramid can already be accounted for, and they will strive to survive within the ever-expanding limits of human endeavor and medical technology.

This far-reaching, if quiet, demographic revolution is bound to affect the social and economic structures of all countries and to have a major impact on their developmental programs and plans. Policymakers gazing into crystal balls may well raise the specter of a crippling burden in health and welfare costs, fearing that a diminishing pool of caretakers and the growing dependency of more old people will lead to intergenerational stress and a resurgence of ageism.

But this is not the only scenario. Clearly the challenge is great, and foremost it lies in identifying and supporting the new opportunities for older persons and the benefits for society that arise from the aging of populations. Equally daunting, though ultimately rewarding, in relation to the needs of the elderly is the initiative undertaken by Jordan I. Kosberg to provide, through the collaborative efforts of highly esteemed experts, a cross-national, comparative assessment of the facilities and services, their strengths and weaknesses, currently available in thirty-two countries and, at the same time, the means to draw the proper conclusion and balance among alternative support mechanisms. This handbook sets out, eminently successfully, to achieve these goals.

In this handbook, a number of authors of international repute, painstakingly selected for their expertise in the field of aging, examine the methods by which 32 countries around the world (in Africa, Asia, North and Latin America, Europe, and Oceania) attempt to meet the needs of their elderly populations. It contains ample descriptive information that affords the reader the opportunity not only to become familiar with the services currently available to cope with such needs but also to compare and contrast the elderly's social conditions and living arrangements (e.g., housing and leisure-time resources) within different countries.

As a goal, this comprehensive, multiauthor handbook is a valuable contribution to the literature in this field and should appeal to a diverse group of readers—undergraduate students, graduates, and academics alike. Belatedly also, this handbook may promote awareness and discussion among policy developers and hopefully motivate them into critically appraising the prevailing situation in relation to the elderly in their countries and, if so indicated, into taking appropriate, even innovative, corrective measures.

My association with the editor dates back to the years when he was Professor of Gerontology at the University of South Florida in Tampa. He has been a close collaborator in an area of common interest and a friend and supporter of the International Institute on Aging (INIA) since its inception in 1988. In fact, the seed for the preparation of the *International Handbook on Services to the Elderly* was planted during his stay in Malta in 1989 as one of the key speakers at a consultative meeting on gerontology, and he was encouraged to persevere in subsequent visits when he was a regular tutor in INIA's training programs. It is therefore all the more gratifying to learn that this project has been brought to its fruition.

—*Alfred Grech*
Director
International Institute on Ageing
United Nations–Malta

NOTE

1. Alfred Sauvy, "Social and Economic Consequences of the Ageing of Western European Countries," *Population Studies* 2 (1948): 44.

PREFACE

THE CHANGING DEMOGRAPHICS OF THE WORLD

The world is aging; its countries are growing older at an unprecedented pace. The United Nations (1992) has estimated an increase in those 65 years of age and older in the world from 6% of the total population in 1985 to 9.7% of the population by the year 2025. Moreover, the oldest of the old—those aged 80 and older—will increase the fastest among all elderly. "The [old old are] the fastest growing population group in the world, projected to grow by a factor of 10 between 1950 and 2025, compared with a factor of six for those 60-and-above, and a factor of little more than three for the total population" (United Nations, 10 September 1992, p. 3). Third Age is a popularly used phrase in certain countries (synonymous with Golden Age) which refers to the last third of one's lifespan in a positive way. The term pertains to both the elderly and to services for the elderly.

"The major demographic forces that change the size of a population and its age composition are levels of fertility and mortality" (Myers, 1990, p. 28). Such forces result from improved medical technology and use of birth control, among other explanations. The demographics in different countries are also influenced by such dynamics as smaller family size, greater mobility and emigration of the younger members of society, increases in divorce and remarriage, the in-migration of populations (resulting in an increasingly heterogeneous population), and the changing role of women in societies (Kosberg and Garcia, 1991).

In the past, the number and proportion of the elderly were higher in the more developed nations of the world. This resulted from higher standards of living; better preventive, acute, and chronic health care; and a greater economic ability to care for the needs of the elderly by the aged themselves, their families, and society (Cowgill, 1986).

Yet, currently, this growth in the aging of world's population is not a phenomenon for only developed countries. Not only are there increasing numbers and proportion of elderly persons in developing nations, but the growth rates exceed those of developed nations. For example, as reported by the United Nations's *The World Ageing Situation 1991* (1991, p. 15):

In 1950, there were about 200 million people above 60 years of age in the world, evenly distributed between developed and developing regions. By 1975, there were about 350 million elderly people, with a similar distribution. Projections indicate a definite change in the pattern by the year 2000. The total world elderly population will then be 614 million, and the proportion living in developing regions will be over 62 percent. In 2025, the absolute number of the elderly will double, to 1.2 billion.

Hernandez (1992) has indicated that the projected increase in the elderly population in developed nations between 1990 and 2025 will be 67%, whereas the increase will be 205% in developing nations.

Thus, the growth of the elderly is a worldwide phenomenon. Although more developed nations (such as Sweden, Austria, and Japan) have relatively high proportions of elderly populations, less-developed countries (such as China and India) have larger populations of older persons. The aging of less-developed countries is occurring more rapidly. Finally, it is projected that the oldest of the old—those for whom care will be needed—are the fastest growing group among the aged, indeed, among all age groups in the world.

CHANGING VALUES TOWARD CARE OF THE ELDERLY

In part, a result of changing demographics is changes in the perception of the elderly and answers to the question of responsibility for a country's elderly (especially those who are the most frail, impaired, and dependent).

Historically, in most countries in the world, family care of the elderly has been the major method by which the needs of the elderly have been met (Kosberg, 1992). Indeed, family care has often been supported by tradition based upon moral and religious dictates. Yet, obvious to most, family caregiving cannot be viewed as a panacea (Kosberg and Garcia, 1991). Family members may be ill-suited and inappropriate for caregiving responsibilities (for a variety of social, psychological, physical, or economic reasons) or may be unable to provide care (due to other responsibilities at home or in employment). Many elderly have no family members (or family may be unavailable or live great distances away). Some family members may not want to provide care to an elderly relative for many reasons.

Thus, there is often the need for mechanisms, other than the individual or family, to provide needed assistance to the elderly in a country. The providers of such assistance—whether financial, social, psychological, or physical—can come from public or private sectors of society. Public resources can be provided by villages, towns, cities, or other local communities; by districts or regions; or by national or federal governments. Private resources can be based upon religious, fraternal, tribal, ethnic, or other such characteristics. Of course, countries can reflect, and often do, a combination of privately and publicly sponsored resources for those in need.

Only in welfare states or through universal programs are resources provided to all elderly on the basis of their chronological age. More often, eligibility criteria must be met to receive programs, services, and benefits. The major criteria used to determine eligibility are "need" (which might be based upon economic, health, psychological, or social conditions) and vulnerability or high risk (related not only to the present condition of older persons but also to a high probability that adversity will occur to them).

PURPOSE OF THE HANDBOOK

Different countries reflect a range of mechanisms for the care of the elderly and an array of combinations of auspices of, and eligibility criteria for, resources for the elderly—where and when they exist. Efforts to describe and compare services for the elderly in different countries have existed for many years. For example, in 1976, Kammerman provided a comparative analysis of community services for the elderly in eight countries. Teicher, Thursz, and Vigilante (1986) edited a book about social services in 44 countries.

The intent of this handbook on services for the elderly is to explore the methods by which 32 countries around the world attempt to meet the needs of their elderly populations. The handbook provides the reader with information on common areas of services for the elderly within each of the represented countries. That is, each chapter (country) addresses the same eight specific areas.

This handbook is intended to meet the needs of a diverse group. As it provides descriptive information on services for the elderly in 32 countries, it should be useful to undergraduate and graduate students by providing them with opportunities not only to learn of the resources within different countries but also to compare and contrast these opportunities for the elderly. Certainly academics should find useful information that has implications for their own teaching and research agendas in community services and/or gerontology.

Hopefully this handbook also has applied implications for those involved from many countries in policy formulations and program development for the elderly. The discussion and description of services for the elderly within 32 countries provide an opportunity to learn of differing mechanisms by which to meet the needs of the elderly. Thus, this handbook can provide policy developers, community planners, and other decision makers with useful information to consider—to reject or to accept—and with new and different methods by which to better meet the present and future needs of a country's elderly population.

ORGANIZATION OF THE HANDBOOK

There are many methods by which to subdivide services for the elderly, and there is a degree of arbitrariness to the identification of areas to be addressed in a book on social services. For example, both Wilson (1984) and Huttman (1985) wrote about social services for older persons and used different approaches by which to discuss such resources. The areas of exploration addressed in each chapter of the handbook include eight sections: (1) an introduction, (2) income maintenance and employment, (3) health care services, (4) housing resources, (5) supportive services, (6) leisure-time resources, (7) advocacy and protection, and (8) future projections.

Following is a description of the areas generally addressed by each author.

Introduction

This section provides an overview of the elderly and the mechanisms by which services are provided to the elderly.

The Role of the Elderly

A brief overview of the elderly in the country includes several areas of discussion: how old age is defined, the demographic characteristics of the elderly, the perception of the elderly (i.e., value, status, power), and history of the perceived responsibility for the care of the elderly.

The Formal Structure of Care of the Elderly

This subsection includes an overview of the role of government in the provision of services to the elderly and a discussion of the following areas: form of governmental economy supporting services to the elderly, the relationship between levels of government in meeting needs, the sponsorship of services (public or private, religious or nonsectarian), and whether services are provided on the basis of entitlement (i.e., by virtue of age) or on the basis of need.

Income Maintenance and Employment

This section includes information on income security for older persons and attention to the existence, eligibility, and use of public income security programs and policies for the elderly. Also included are discussions on any private retirement benefits and/or pensions and any financial assistance programs for the impoverished aged.

If applicable, authors address economic benefits policies for the elderly (such as tax benefits or deductions, food or food stamps, housing assistance, reduced transportation fares) and whether local, regional, state, or district economic assistance supplements are given by the national/federal government. Finally, the authors address opportunities to retain older employees in the labor force through job redesign and restructuring, and job training (and retraining) programs or employment (or reemployment) services for the elderly.

Health Care Services

In this section, authors focus upon medical (not mental) health services for the elderly. Topics discussed include the general health care system in the country, the general financing arrangement of health care (contributions by government, individual, and so on), and the existence of acute and chronic care services.

If applicable, authors discuss the availability of hospitals, clinics, hospice care, and other health care resources, as well as the use and characteristics of institutions for the elderly. Finally, authors discuss any provisions for home-based health care services within one's dwelling while living independently within the community.

Housing Resources

This section focuses upon social settings available for the elderly and assistance for maintaining them in the dwellings of their choice. There is attention to urban and rural differences.

Specific topics include the overall national housing policy/programs for the elderly. In addition, authors discuss the overall housing policy for the elderly and the development of the private housing industry to meet the housing needs of the elderly. If applicable, attention is given to the existence of congregate housing for the elderly, retirement housing or communities, and innovative housing arrangements. Community services that permit the elderly to remain in their own dwellings (e.g., friendly visitors, shopping, maintenance and home repair services) are discussed.

Supportive Services

In addition to the major areas of need for older persons (indeed, for all persons), other services help the elderly develop their full capacities in personal, social, and community relationships and maintain a quality of independent living to the best of their abilities.

The authors address, as appropriate, supportive services such as information and referral (whereby individuals can obtain information on services, benefits, and programs for the elderly) and nutrition programs that provide meals to the elderly either within their own homes (e.g., meals-on-wheels) or in settings outside their homes (e.g., congregate meals programs). Also included are programs to care for the elderly within their own (or a relative's) home (e.g., homemaker, chore and shopping assistance, respite care, friendly visitors services) or outside their homes (e.g., multiservice senior service and day-care centers, day hospitals).

Also included in this section are discussions of mental health services (both inpatient and outpatient) and counseling and social work services for the elderly.

Leisure-Time Resources

Like any other age group, the elderly desire to fill their leisure time. The majority of nonstructured time for the elderly may be spent in family-related activities (e.g., cooking for children or caring for grandchildren) or in solitary pursuits (e.g., reading, gardening, watching television). In addition to such activities, authors focus upon more formally organized leisure-time resources available for the elderly in their country.

Volunteerism is discussed—the societal value of volunteering one's time, examples of volunteer efforts, and the organization of such activities (by government, organized religion, private groups, neighbors, and so on). Also, authors discuss voluntary organizations that provide for the active involvement of elderly persons (and whether such resources are formed by religious organizations, retirement groups, or civic or fraternal associations).

This section also addresses recreational opportunities for the elderly—whether sports (as spectators or participants), hobbies, games, or other activities that are engaged in for their enjoyment. Authors discuss opportunities for socialization (bringing older persons together for companionship, the development of friendships, and the growth and maintenance of social abilities). While related to recreational activities, socialization activities can include religious study groups, dances, discussion groups, and other opportunities for those of a certain age group (and possibly from similar backgrounds) to come together for companionship.

Finally, educational resources for the elderly are addressed—whether for a specific goal (such as a diploma) or for the sake of enhancing one's knowledge (e.g., in history, philosophy, world affairs, religion, or civic affairs).

Advocacy and Protection

In some countries, the elderly (as a group) have organized to ensure the betterment of their lives. On occasion, such advocacy groups have included individuals of all ages. Also, there has been an increasing awareness of the vulnerability of elderly persons to victimization in society, whether a result of crime by strangers (on the street or within one's home), maltreatment within institutions (or within other formal service settings), and elder abuse (by family, friends, and neighbors). This section addresses organized efforts for advocacy and the protection of the elderly.

If available in their countries, authors identify opportunities for legal assistance for advice on rights pertaining to such things as wills, contracts, policies (i.e., insurance, burial), and taxes and for victim assistance (to help and represent them in the criminal justice, tribal, religious, or community systems—or wherever disputes are resolved and judgments made on issues of right or wrong).

Some countries have mechanisms (e.g., protective services) to safeguard those elderly who are especially frail, vulnerable, mentally incompetent, or otherwise unable to protect themselves or make appropriate judgments about their safety or security. While such services may be provided by public or private organizations or agencies, they may also be offered by volunteer groups, family members, and so on. Authors discuss such resources in their countries.

Finally, authors describe the advocacy organizations for the elderly that can be found in some countries. Some of these groups seek to ensure a better quality of life for all elderly and equity in opportunities for them; others seek to represent specific groups of elderly persons (i.e., impoverished, institutionalized, women, minority groups).

Future Projections

A final section provides general conclusions regarding the unique features and overall effectiveness of services for the elderly that currently exist in a country. Authors address unmet needs of the elderly, as well as emerging needs of the elderly in the near and distant future that have implications for new or expanded services for the elderly (and those who care for the elderly). Final thoughts appear about methods to improve the quality of life for elderly persons.

PROCESS BY WHICH AUTHORS/COUNTRIES WERE SELECTED

From the beginning, the process by which countries in the world would be included in this handbook was rather arbitrary. To be certain, because of the long history of services provision to the elderly and the characteristics of such services, some countries seemed to be especially important for a book describing programs and services for the elderly. Aside from these countries, the handbook needed to include chapters from countries that represented, as best as possible, all the world's continents and a fair representation of stages of development, forms of government/economies, and values and philosophies.

In the effort to identify potential authors (from various countries) for the handbook, individuals were contacted who were personally known to the editor (or to friends and colleagues) or who had written (or who could write) on the resources for the elderly in their countries. In addition, persons from other countries whose work had been read in the past—but were neither known to the editor nor recommended by others—were contacted. The list of potential authors included individuals from academe, government, and health and social service agencies and research centers. All were involved—directly or indirectly—in the study of, or service to, the elderly in their countries.

These individuals were informed of the purpose of the handbook and invited to author (or coauthor) a chapter on their country. The policy was set that authors and coauthors must be living and working in their countries; thus excluded were individuals no longer living in their native countries and experts on countries who were living elsewhere.

In the letter of invitation were the expectations for a chapter, sections to be included, and deadlines for manuscripts. In all but one case, an affirmative reply resulted from the letter of invitation. Given the publisher's total page expectations and determination of the average page length for each chapter, it was concluded that about 30 countries could be included in the handbook.

Thirty-two countries are represented in this handbook, and the following are the locations of these countries (as defined by the Population Reference Bureau, 1990): Three countries are from Africa: Ghana (from Western Africa), Sudan (from Northern Africa), and Zimbabwe (from Eastern Africa). Nine countries are from Asia: Israel and Jordan (from Western Asia), India (from Southern Asia), Malaysia and Thailand (from Southeast Asia), and China, Hong Kong, Japan, and South Korea (from East Asia). Two countries are from North America: Canada and the United States. From Latin America, one country (Barbados) is from the Caribbean, and one country (Argentina) is from South America. Thirteen countries are from Europe: Norway, Sweden, and Great Britain (from Northern Europe); Austria, France, Germany, the Netherlands, and Switzerland (from Western Europe); the former Czechoslovakia (now the Czech Republic and Slovakia) and Poland (from Eastern Europe); and Italy, Malta, and Spain (from Southern Europe). Two countries are from Oceania: Australia and New Zealand. Finally, a chapter is written on the former USSR (by coauthors from the Ukraine).

The countries represented in this handbook are not meant, in any way, to be the most significant ones nor representative of other countries in the world. The initial intent was to seek a general worldwide balance and representation, but the inclusion of countries resulted from the editor's familiarity with individuals, recommendations made to him, and random letters of invitation to individuals who had written in the area of the handbook. Nonetheless, the countries represented in this volume do reflect the desired degree of heterogeneity and diversity of countries from around the world.

The editor thanks the authors of this handbook for their willingness to write a chapter in English, with attention to sections pre-determined by the editor. English was not the primary language for the majority of authors, and many struggled heroically with a language little used by them in their country.

On some occasions, the editor translated into more understandable language the manuscript provided to him, and, on other occasions, revisions had to be made in chapters so as to make the text, structure, and grammar congruent with those of the other chapters. Finally, editing changes were occasionally required to shorten chapters to a maximum length set for all. The editor apologizes to authors for any inadvertent errors resulting from the translation of terms or meanings or the editing of chapters.

BIBLIOGRAPHY

Cowgill, D. O. (1986). *Aging Around the World.* Belmont, CA: Wadsworth.
Hernandez, R. (1992). Demography of aging. *Bold* (International Institute on Aging, United Nations, Malta), 2(4), 8–12.
Huttman, E. D. (1985). *Social Services for the Elderly.* New York: Free Press.
Kammerman, S. B. (1976). Community services for the aged: The view from eight countries. *Gerontologist,* 16, 529–537.
Kosberg, J. I., ed. (1992). *Family Care of the Elderly: Social and Cultural Changes.* Beverly Hills, CA: Sage.
Kosberg, J. I., and J. L. Garcia. (1991). Social changes affecting family care of the elderly. *Bold* (International Institute on Aging, United Nations, Malta), 1 (2), 2–5.
Myers, G. C. (1990). Geography of aging. In R. H. Binstock and L. K. George, eds., *Handbook of Aging and the Social Sciences,* 3d ed. New York: Academic Press, 19–44.
Population Reference Bureau, Inc. (1990). *1990 World Population Data Sheet.* Washington, DC: Population Reference Bureau.
Teicher, M., D. Thursz, and J. Vigilante, eds. (1986). *Reaching the Aged: Social Services in Forty-Four Countries.* Beverly Hills, CA: Sage.
United Nations. (1991). *The World Ageing Situation 1991.* New York: Centre for Social Development and Humanitarian Affairs.
―――. (10 September 1992). *Global Targets on Ageing for the Year 2001: A Practical Strategy.* General Assembly (A/47/339).
―――. (17 September 1992). *Implementation of the International Plan of Action on Ageing.* General Assembly (A/47/369).
Wilson, A.J.E., III. (1984). *Social Services for Older Persons.* Boston: Little, Brown.

ACKNOWLEDGMENTS

Change in the world is ongoing. Between the time of signing the contract to edit this handbook and its publication, several changes in persons and events have occurred which I would like to acknowledge.

Editing this international handbook on services to the elderly from 32 countries could not have come at a more tumultuous time in my career. After signing the contract with Greenwood Publishing Group and contacting individuals who had agreed to write chapters on their countries, I decided to accept a position at McGill University in Montreal, Quebec and relocate from my position at the University of South Florida in Tampa. My new appointment in Canada began, and I was in the process of moving and adjusting to a new position, new university, new city, and new country while the contributors were sending their chapters to me to edit and return to them. Things could not have been more chaotic. I mention this because I want to acknowledge the patience of the authors during my "settling in" period.

In the time between the initial agreement by individuals to write chapters and the actual deadline, there were several dramatic historical changes in the world which influenced the existence of old, and creation of new, nations and national boundaries. Two chapters here—two countries—were affected by the passage of time. One chapter was to be written about USSR services for the elderly. And while the title for a chapter on USSR continues to exist, the chapter emphasizes Ukraine (where both co-authors live and work). The second chapter (country) affected by the passage of time was that of Czechoslovakia (or Czech and Slovak Republic). While the book was under development, the country divided and the chapter now focuses upon the Slovak Republic. I would like to acknowledge the special challenges to the authors of these two chapters.

I want to acknowledge the cooperation of the authors who complied with my inquiries in a generally prompt and responsive manner. I thank them for this. For many of the authors, English is not their first (or familiar) language and many made heoric efforts to turn in manuscripts that would be understandable to an English-speaking editor. I would like to acknowledge that there will be inadvertent misinterpretations of certain concepts and phrases in some chapters, due to differences in language and terminologies. Let all know, any inaccuracies are regretted. Also, it should be noted that when financial figures are given in foreign amounts, they are either converted into U.S. dollars or given in U.S. dollar amounts.

There have also been changes among individuals at Greenwood Publishing Group who worked with me in putting the book through to publication and whose help I would like to acknowledge. First I thank Dr. George Knight, who initially asked me to edit an international handbook on services for the elderly. I would like to acknowledge the assistance of Mildred Vasan, Senior Editor; Maureen Melino, Coordinating Editor; and Margaret Hogan and Sasha Kintzler, Production Editors.

I would like to thank my friends and colleagues in Tampa and Montreal. The fact that I was leaving one institution, and was new at another, did not adversely influence their support and encouragement of my work on this project. In a way, my move merely underscored in a personal way the interrelationship between nations and the importance of the handbook. Finally, I would like to thank my Research Assistant at McGill University, Iryna Dulka, for her cheerful and competent assistance during my work on the completion of the handbook.

1

ARGENTINA

Roberto E. Barca

INTRODUCTION

The Role of the Elderly

Since the beginning of the Argentine independence, the elderly in Argentina have been seen as deserving help because of their inability to work (Informe Argentino, 1982). The Social Security system was developed very early. In 1904, the first laws concerning pensions were passed, and by 1954 all the workers had preventive coverage. A "Declaration of the Rights of the Elderly" was proposed in the third general assembly of the United Nations and was then adopted (Resolution 213) (United Nations [UN], 1948).

With the creation of the National Institute of Social Services for Retirees and Pensioners (INSSJP) in 1971, the elderly were viewed as consumers of services. Long-term care and residential facilities have increased, as has the number of professionals working in direct and indirect relationship with the elderly population. Argentina has participated in the World Assembly on Aging and officially adopted the arbitrary definition that 60 is the beginning of old age. The country has been represented at international meetings in aging and at important Latin American and Caribbean conferences (Barca, 1986; Tout, 1989) and established the Argentinian Gerontological Conference in 1989.

Beginning in 1984, the elderly have been seen as active participants and voters. The organization of the retirees and the elderly participating in official organizations and autonomous associations is encouraged and is increasing. The traditional parties contend for the votes of the elderly, who constitute 30% of the electorate, and in 1987 the party of the retirees (White) was founded.

Demographic Characteristics

Argentina has a large percentage of elderly and is one of the countries with a type II pattern of aging population (in number and proportion) (UN, 1984). Argentina, jointly with Uruguay, has had a marked demographic transition (with respect to other Latin American countries) that has resulted in an increase in the absolute number of elderly and in their proportion to the general population.

While the estimated growth of the general population is 22% between 1980 and 2000 and 17.5% between 2000 and 2025, the population of 60 and older will increase by 41.3% and 40.3%, respectively, during the same periods. While, in 1947, 6.6% of all Argentinians were 60 years of age and older, by 2025 the proportion will increase to 15.8% (Programa Nacional de Estadistica y Censos [PNES], 1990).

The aging Argentinian population has several characteristics. First, there is a high proportion of elderly in urban areas (86.7%) and in "specified areas" of the country (Gastron, 1991). Second, there is a predominance of elderly women in all the territories. In the 60 to 64 age range, the masculine index "sex ratio" was 88.3 men to 100 women, and in the group 85 and above it reached 50.9 men to 100 women (Gastron, 1991). The greater feminine longevity signifies a greater risk of widowhood, loneliness, and possibly poverty (Muchinik, et al., 1989; Gastron and Andres, 1989). Third, there is the aging of the elderly population. The percentage of the population 75 and older, in contrast to the population of 60 or more years, shows a progressive increase. For example, while in 1950, 15.9% of all those at least 60 years of age were 75 or older, the projection for the year 2025 is for 28.6% to be 75 years of age and older (Centro Latinamericano de Demografia [CELADE], 1982).

Fourth, there is the aging of the active population. In some cities, such as Buenos Aires, the median age of the active population is rising (Barca and Muchinik, 1988). Two-fifths of the women and three-quarters of the men live with partners (spouses). Three-fourths of the women over 70 are spinsters, widows, or separated. However, 67% of the men still live with partners, and the widowers predominate only after 80 years (Instituto Nacional de Estadistica y Censo [INDEC], 1980). The percentage of the population that lives at home (or with their families) is high (98%). The majority live in their own homes, others share a dwelling with other family members, and a small number live in rented houses (Muller and Pantelides, 1991).

Between 6% and 17% of the elderly live alone in the large cities (INSSJP, 1988). The number of women who live alone is twice that of the men. Nearly 80% of the elderly live with extended families. It is not known if the families are one generation or multi-generational. The condition of the homes in regard to habitability (sanitation, heat, and so on) is good, at least in urban areas. Lacking is the telephone (Knallinsky and Pantelides, 1988). Some 50,000 persons of 60 or more years lived in collective homes in 1980 (geriatric establishments, hospitals, convents, and prisons).

Argentina has a high degree of literacy; 84% of the elderly have received an elementary school education (but one-third did not complete their studies). One of each four illiterates is more than 65 years of age. Life expectancy at birth is increasing and favors women. In 1980, the expected life at birth for men was 65.5 years, compared with 72.7 years for women (CELADE, 1989).

Health Status

Of the elderly who live in the large cities, 45.2% indicate that they have health problems (Panamerican Health Organization, [PAHO], 1989). Heart disease, malignant tumors, and cerebrovascular diseases are responsible for nearly 75% of the causes of death in the population of the third age (Balossi, Hauger, and Klevene, 1988). The indicators of damage show chronic pathologies prevalent (Balossi, 1989). The problems more frequently perceived are cardiovascular diseases, arterial hypertension, and bone pathology. Studies of the perception of disability show that almost 90% of the elderly population can travel far from home and use transportation without help (PAHO, 1989).

The major causes of hospitalization for both sexes are disease of the circulatory system, surgical problems (such as malignant tumors), and cerebrovascular and respiratory illnesses. In the group 75 years of age and older, cerebrovascular diseases and fractures gain importance (PNES, 1990). Both problems are greatly incapacitating.

Economic Characteristics

In the last 15 years, Argentina has had a deteriorating economy. Salaries in the middle-income group fell 20%, a high indication of inflation and great variation in goods and services. The indicators of employment are stable, but living expenses are increasing.

There are an impoverishment of the middle class and those with lower incomes and an especially marked pauperization of the lower middle class. The elderly, as a heterogeneous group, suffered this general process in a different way. Retirement funds dropped to half, in constant prices, from 1975 until 1991; 65% of the retirees receive the minimum allotment (US$150), and almost 30% receive between one and two minimum allotments (Secetaria de Seguridad Social, 1992).

A retiree earns almost half as much as an active worker in the same job. In 1991, 30% of the retirees and pensionists needed family help to live, and 39% had only their pensions (Scipioni, 1992). According to official statistics compiled in the metropolitan area in 1986, 88.1% of the people 60 years or over who live in single-occupancy homes make up the population with the lowest incomes. Thus, the economic conditions of the retirees in Argentina are not good (PNES, 1990).

About 20 to 30 percent of individuals 60 or over have a paid job in the large cities. The rate of activity is decreasing. However, 25% to 40% of the elderly population have expressed their need to work, and half of them would like to work (Knallinsky and Pantelides, 1988). An indeterminate number of retirees work at "temporary" jobs. Studies in 1980 showed that 20% of the population 65 and older had basic unsatisfied needs (INDEC, 1984). The elderly who live with partners without children and on only one retirement income are below the poverty level—even more than those who live alone. Elderly who live with their children add their retirement income as a strategy to survive (Redondo, 1991).

The Formal Structure of Care of the Elderly

The state has the responsibility to guarantee the common welfare and assure basic social services to all the population. These obligations to the elderly can be analyzed since the inception of Social Security and social action. The state oversees and conducts the national system of Social Security through the Ministry of Labor. In regard to old age, it does this by way of a national system. Furthermore, there are similar provincial and municipal systems, as well as systems for the armed forces. Of the total beneficiaries, 86.6% belong to the national system (13.4% provincial, municipal, and armed forces).

Retirement, through a 1968 law, is a system where the contributions of the active workers and the employers constitute the total amount of money to be distributed. This is an obligatory, not a voluntary, act. By law, since the year 1971, all the pensioners and retirees of the National Institute of Provision are beneficiaries of the medical and social services of the INSSJP. In 1990, the INSSJP took care of 4 million people and is the basis of gerontological assistance in the country. INSSJP has a central administrative structure to plan, regulate, supervise, and control the different actions and programs of the decentralized regional delegations with executive function. In this system, the private enterprises are service providers and charge according to the services rendered.

The state is organized to give coverage to the most unprotected people. The national organization in charge of exercising the protection of the needy and those lacking the means to subsist is the Direccion Nacional de Ancianidad (DNA), under the Ministry of Health. Social action includes (1) free assistance in public hospitals to those lacking means, (2) meeting the housing problems of the needy elderly (gerontological establishments, long-term care homes, subsidies), and (3) the promotion of sociocultural recreation, sports, and so on. There is no formal, permanent mechanism of coordination among the national government, provinces, and municipalities. The national government oversees all other levels. Provincial policies can be independent of national policies. Fundamentally, they have developed three solutions to confront this problem: the system of pensions (provincial), residential homes for the elderly, and some alternative systems to being institutionalized (hospital, clinic, or sanatorium) (Informe Argentino AME, 1982).

Nongovernmental organizations have been involved since the past century. The Catholic church has been providing education, helping the needy with housing, and sponsoring parish dining rooms and clubs for the elderly. Foreign groups developed systems of medical care and homes for the elderly. Outstanding among these are the numerous institutions founded and developed by the Jewish community, including long-term care centers, clubs, meals-on-wheels, hospitals, and homes for the elderly. The scientific societies began their medical activities around the middle of the century. The development of gerontological societies began 20 years later.

Social services have developed as a response to specific problems, but as the population ages, there are increasing demands for solutions to complex problems of aging. As solutions appear for this older group, they compete for resources with other groups having higher priorities, such as maternity and infant programs. The family, in spite of all its transformations, is the unit of greatest importance for the effective and economic security of the elderly in Argentina.

INCOME MAINTENANCE AND EMPLOYMENT

Argentina has a mature state system of Social Security that began in 1904 and was generalized 50 years later (Informe Argentino AME, 1982). About 62% of the population of 60 or more years had coverage in 1983 (PNES, 1990). Against the infirmities of aging, all the population remains protected by means of retirement and pension funds (whether contributory or not). An ordinary retirement is approved when one has a minimum of 10 years' affiliation with the system, having worked or having been dependent for 30 years. The age of retirement is variable for men (60–65) and for women (55–60) who have worked dependently or self-employed. There are retirement benefits at advanced age and pensions to survivors and noncontributors (Informe Argentino AME, 1982).

The retirement system substitutes the remuneration or income previously received by the worker. The law stipulates that the amount of money to which a retiree is entitled consists of 70–80% of what a person earned. Until late in the 1980s, private enterprises did not offer retirement insurance. Those individuals who do not have adequate resources or rights to retirement benefits or pensions have rights to a state pension on becoming 65. In 1988, almost 80,000 people had such noncontributory pensions. According to official data between 1982 and 1988, the number of noncontributor beneficiaries increased by 123% (PNES, 1990).

The benefits given are uniform and correspond to approximately half of the minimum retirement allotment. There are other forms of economic benefits, such as subsidies and special discounts or services. The beneficiaries of subsidized programs of the Direccion Nacional de Ancianidad (DNA) lack economic resources. The cash grant covers the basic necessities and is given monthly or in a one-time grant. There are other types of complementary subsidies in the program for those who have families under their care or as a stimulus for seeking further actions: home assistance, sheltered workshops, and so on. There is also a sum of money for provincial or municipal help (DNA, 1991). In 1991, 6.1

million pesos (or $6.1 million USD) from the National Treasury were destined for subsidies to the elderly (Diario, 1991).

In some municipalities there are tax benefits for homeowners over 60 who occupy their homes (a sum determined by a fiscal appraisal). There are reduced transportation fares at certain hours for public transportation, on trains, and in airplanes during certain times of the year. A retired person can continue working, although there will be a decrease in retirement pay. In a survey in 1987, 25% to 40% of the population expressed a need to work. Half wanted to work, but only about 6% to 20% continued to do so (Knallinsky and Pantelides, 1988). Men, if they are self-employed professionals or workers on commission, continue to work at the same tasks as before, while women who continue working are employed mainly as domestics (Knallinsky and Pantelides, 1988). An undetermined number of people work at "temporary" jobs.

HEALTH CARE SERVICES

The health system of Argentina is composed of three subsystems: the public, the private, and social works. The public sector is composed of dependent institutions of national, provincial, and municipal public health. The private sector includes independent medical involvement, diagnostic and boarding institutions, and a prepaying system. Independent practice in private offices, paid directly by the patient, is reimbursed partially by a program of deferred payment. The prepay system involves private medical assistance through voluntary affiliation by means of a monthly quota that began to function during the 1960s. In 1991, there were 119 enterprises with 2.5 million affiliated members and 3,500 doctors working in them (Diario, July 1991).

The sector of social works (Obras Sociales [OS]), a nongovernmental organization of social security, is run by groups of employees who contribute a percentage of their wages to establish and maintain a fund. According to Neri, it is "a mixed modality of Social Security, founded in the collective grouping of the people based on their occupations with the object of satisfying social needs within a philosophy of group solidarity" (1982, p. 102). This was developed in the 1940s, and coverage became universal in 1970 for all the laboring population and establishing a salary deduction. All workers must contribute from their salaries to obtain needed medical and social assistance.

In 1971, INSSJP was created. Its beneficiaries are all the retired and pensioned of the national system. It is the largest social program in Argentina. In 1990, it took care of 4 million beneficiaries. The institute has programs of medical assistance (Programa de asistencia medicas [PAMI]), social assistance (Programa de asistencia social integral [PASI]), and housing assistance (Programa de asistencia a la vivienda [PAVI]), as well as for nutrition, literacy, and microenterprises.

PAMI has a system of medical attention with three levels of assistance. The first level is diagnostic and is formed by family physicians who take care of the affiliated in their nearby offices and have the use of centers for auxiliary examinations. The second level is for the hospitalization of acutely ill patients and for consultation with different specialists. The third level is prolonged care. A program offered by PAMI is psychiatric care. In 1983, more representation was given to the beneficiaries of the system by including them in the administration of the institute. The public sector was drafted and regionalized in the 1960s. The actual tendency is to transfer the responsibilities from the national public sector to the provinces and municipalities.

Argentina has many professional medical personnel, with the exception of nurses; there are about two doctors for each nurse. The number of beds for the acutely ill in the country supposes a proportion of 4.8 beds per 1,000 inhabitants. The private sector has more than half of the residential facilities and almost one-third of the beds. The "functioning" capacity of the private sector grows proportionally 4.2% annually (Guidasio, 1991).

The sector of social works has few beds for the acutely ill because it utilizes the private system. About 93% of the medical institutions that board individuals and 80% of the beds are for acutely ill patients (Catastro Nacional, 1981).

There are specialized resources in gerontology and geriatrics. The specialty of geriatrics was officially recognized in 1978 and is conferred through accredited courses. Gerontology is taught at postgraduate and master's levels but is not recognized as a specialty. There are 200 geriatric doctors and as many gerontologists who have taken courses that began formally around 1986. In 1980, there existed 62 long-term-care facilities specializing in geriatrics, with 3,500 beds: 60% were from the public sector, 35% were private, and 4% were from the social work sector (Catastro Nacional, 1981). At the official level, some of the beds available for geriatrics are old hospices where lodging, food, and low-level medical assistance are destined for needy elderly.

The aged are hospitalized in geriatric units within general hospitals. The three geriatric units for the acutely ill in Buenos Aires were officially created in 1978, and only one existed in 1992 with its own beds and space. Also, there are general hospitals and sanatoriums. Social Security permits the elderly to use all these places. There are day geriatric hospitals. The first one commenced functioning in 1978, was private, and had space for 60 persons. The day hospital developed models for physical rehabilitation, psychosocial rehabilitation for neurotic patients, multistimulation for cerebral organic syndromes, and programs of maintenance for the physically and mentally disabled (Barca, 1983). Only one-fourth of the institutions (reviewed in one report) belong to this assistance modality (INSSJP, 1986). The geriatric day hospital is not included, as a rule, in the registry of social programs (OS) or in INSSJP.

In 1991, some 40,000 registered places (beds) existed for long-term stays in geriatric institutions; 71% of the existing institutions were private, for-profit enterprises. Of the total living quarters available, three-fourths of them housed physically and mentally disabled patients living together with ambulatory or higher-functioning individuals (INSSJP, 1986). For those in the country with the least resources, there were almost 9,000 beds for long-term stays. There remained a 90% occupancy rate (PNES, 1991).

The caregiving system of the INSSJP includes at-home medical nursing and domestic help for cleaning, preparation of foods, and so on. In 1977, Hospital Italiano of Buenos Aires created specialized homebound programs (Passanante, 1983). At the private level, homebound rehabilitation, nursing, and accompanying therapy are offered.

As to the utilization of resources, in 1990 there were 50 million consultations and 1,600,000 discharges, and 15 million outpatients were served in the official sector (PNES, 1990). One-half of the demands for admission of acutely ill patients took place through the public system (PNES, 1990). Almost 200,000 people who were 60 and older were released from public hospitals in 1985, of whom 34% were 75 or older (PNES, 1990). The INSSJP had 260,000 discharges from short-term establishments, 10.4 for each 100 beneficiaries with a mean stay of 6.3 days (INSSJP, 1991). Less than 2% of the elderly population live in collective establishments.

The public sector is financed by fiscal funds. In 1992, 3.6% of its total budget was allotted to health. The combined tax of Social Security consists of 34% of the worker's salary contributed by the employer and 15.5% contributed by the employee (this includes retirement, family subsidies, INSSJP, unemployment insurance, and Social Works).

The expenses of Social Security for the third age (including the expenses of aging, disabilities, and charges of the INSSJP) are equivalent to 5–6% of the gross national product (GNP) for the period 1981–85 and about 60% of all the expenses of Social Security (Golbert, 1988). The INSSJP utilized 85% of its budget in the Program for Integrated Medical Attention ([PAMI]) during that period.

HOUSING RESOURCES

More than two-thirds of the elderly questioned in one study have their own homes, and one out of eight lives gratuitously in the home of relatives (Knallinsky and Pantelides, 1988). The prevalent attitude of the elderly is the desire to remain in their own established homes. In the highly urban areas, the nuclear home predominates, but in reality the emotional and material supports are provided by a network of reciprocity (spontaneous or institutional) that functions as a modified extended family (Oddone, 1991). The urban family lacks the space and time for the care of the elderly; while many elderly do not live with their families, they avoid institutionalization, even in situations of dependency.

In rural areas, the elderly often live in extended families. As their children migrate, some elderly raise their grandchildren. But these rural elderly often lack collective networks (Oddone, 1991). Some people who work on the farms have few possessions and end up in provincial institutions in their old age.

The state offers lodging to the needy elderly who are fundamentally ambulatory, without infectious, contagious, or mental pathologies. There are 10 such national establishments, 93 provincial, 79 municipal, and 5 of the INSSJP. There are also 72 secular homes of public welfare and 58 of religious sponsorship that give lodging to those people who do not have access to private dwellings (INSSJP, 1986). A national program of social and economic welfare of the elderly, proposed by the DNA in 1990, prioritizes the systems of treating the elderly in the community. For the maintenance of the needy elderly at home, the program proposes various types of subsidies to encourage self-help, family or substitute family care, long-term homes, community residences, clubs, and permanent residences as a final option (DNA, 1990).

In 1988, home-delivered services for the third age was created by the Municipalidad de la Ciudad de Buenos Aires (MCBA) for people of limited resources. Grants provided for personal hygiene, food preparation, assisted feeding, companions, management of the house, and so on.

The INSSJP loan grants for the acquisition of homes were suspended, and in its place are subsidies to pay rent for homes. Rental investments by the private sector have been a most important mechanism for the creation of geriatric residences during the past decade and have led to the growth of the number of such resources for the elderly. In the last few years, protected residences (apartments with central supportive services) have been developed by the German Jewish community, a Catholic foundation, and private groups.

SUPPORTIVE SERVICES

Although the INSSJP can provide an orientation to services, there are no programs for systematic information of and referral to community resources.

The home food program (meals-on-wheels) has been developed by the Jewish community as an experiment to alleviate the needs that could result in institutionalization of the elderly. The program of free food includes the elderly and is organized through religious communities, in parishes and temples. Long-term homes include meals among their services. Other valid alternatives to resolve the problem of the indigent elderly without social coverage are homes and long-term centers. Only 21 homes and long-term centers were regulated in 1986 (INSSJP, 1986). The province of Nacion accounts for three; the majority (260) are found in the province of Cordoba (included in a provincial program of Social Security). In addition to shelter, these resources provide food, rehabilitation, therapy, nursing, and so on.

The INSSJP has developed special institutional programs in the community where people plan and generate groups of self-implementation. In this manner, long-term centers are organized and directed by the people involved. Argentina has a high percentage of professionals dedicated to this theme.

In 1970, in a center of mental health in Buenos Aires, the first service of psychogeriatrics and preventive mental health was created that produced clinical, technical, and theoretical experiences and "works" with the elderly (Salvarezza,

1988). The treatment in psychogeriatrics utilizes three modalities: psychotherapy, psychopharmacy, and family help. Individual or group psychotherapy with psychoanalysis is the prevailing therapy in mental health centers. Family help, by way of orientation or therapy, is an indispensable modality (Salvarezza, 1988).

The day geriatric hospital incorporates these techniques and offers adequate means to dispense therapy in an ambulatory center (Barca, 1983). In an eight year period (1982–90) there had been a 40% increase in interned psychiatric beds, duplicating the number of private beds. The increment has little relationship with the epidemiological facts and is linked more with professional attitudes and other factors external to mental health (Calisti, 1991).

In 1982, the INSSJP incorporated the program of psychiatric care, extending coverage to ambulatory and home and day hospital patients and seeking to shorten the period of institutionalization. This program was developed in the metropolitan area with a total cost of 4.5 million pesos (95% of which is used for institutionalization). For every three persons being seen as outpatients, one is seen in an institution. The number of those in institutions has doubled in six years (1980–86), contrary to the emphasis INSSJP intended to promote.

The growth of institutionalization is attributed to psychosocial deterioration of the elderly and the persistence of the mental health/illness model perceived by the mental health workers. This growth of institutionalization was assessed in 1989 (Calisti, 1991). There were a total of 440 places in gerontopsychiatric facilities for long-term care in the country (INSSJP, 1986). The majority of the patients with organic cerebral deterioration were cared for in common geriatric establishments without specialized help.

LEISURE-TIME RESOURCES

In Argentine society, the elderly are prone to spend the majority of their time in activities limited to the home and the family, with little community participation (Oddone, 1991). The activities of leisure time are television, radio, visiting and receiving visits, and shopping. Others read daily newspapers, take walks, go to the square (plaza), or attend religious services, and a few attend cultural events or sports (Knallinsky and Pantelides, 1988; Oddone, 1991).

In 1984, MCBA started a program to promote voluntary groupings of the third age. This was in response to the 37,000 elderly who frequented the squares in their neighborhoods and who were given sanitary facilities, recreative material, and so on. There are now municipal programs of recreation and physical activities and cultural workshops for the third age. There are also nonprofit institutions and voluntary groups involved in such activities.

In 1957, the Silver Age Club was founded, the first of 40 such clubs, by the Jewish community in Argentina. About 3,000 people attend these clubs—8–10% of the elderly population (Gutman, 1985). The Young Men's Christian Association and Young Women's Christian Association have had leisure groups since the 1970s. In some Catholic parishes, information and recreational activities have been developed, as well as the promotion of the role of the elderly within the family (Passanante, 1983).

There are not many organized volunteers, but there are individual responses in situations of necessity. With the creation of the Silver Age Clubs, the elderly participated and functioned as volunteers. Later, the Jewish community paid elderly volunteers to provide other elderly with a sense of social solidarity—and with mutual benefits. The elderly come to the institution soliciting information and offering, in exchange, other services, visits, help in domestic work, shopping, running errands, and so on. This activity is coordinated by the Social Service, which distributes and supervises the work (Passanante, 1983). There are also groups of volunteers in hospitals, residences, and so on organized by the INSSJP.

Models of growing interest are centers for retirees; in 1992, there were 2,300 centers in the country, and the number is growing. For example, in the capital, there were 75 centers in 1980, and in 1992 there were about 450. A council has been formed with participant representation from the centers.

ADVOCACY AND PROTECTION

There are no specific services for legal assistance. Although legal services exist within the INSSJP, there is no adequate, systematic method of help for the elderly. The first efforts in victim assistance in Argentina were provided to battered women and children. There is a current tendency to extend concern to the elderly and handicapped. In the National Congress, the elderly have been determined to be people who have the right to special protection by the legal system (judges, courts).

No mechanism or organization exists to protect those elderly who cannot protect themselves. The existing legislation does not refer specifically to the elderly but provides norms of protection to "people of diminished faculties." Such individuals (of any age) can be assigned a guardian to protect their birthright (e.g., possessions) and to institute a judicial act limiting their self-determination. This is an extreme measure and not necessarily permanent. The legislation considers all persons who are unable to be completely capable to act in civilian life. In actuality, no group of lawyers exists who specifically work to ensure the best quality of life for the elderly.

FUTURE PROJECTIONS

It is not believed that a major economic growth will generate the necessary income for social development in Argentina, but fiscal adjustments should not be made at the expense of vulnerable groups such as the elderly. Humanitarian gestures will not alleviate the problems of the most fragile without the necessary participation of individuals in social development.

Policy must include aging individuals, their primary groups, and their communities in the definition and structure of the future. This form of development requires a direct, participating democracy. Experiences point to social development strategies for the personal improvement efforts of the elderly (such as dining rooms in Buenos Aires, community vegetable gardens, shared housing) or experimental programs (democratic groups within geriatric institutions).

Assistance to the elderly rests upon two large axes: the family and Social Security. The family, which suffers the consequences of socioeconomic forces, has been the traditional provider of affective and material care of the elderly. In the family, the elderly can play different active roles, from being the economic mainstay of unemployed family members to raising their grandchildren. The urban family in Argentina lacks the time and space for the care of the elderly; yet, institutionalization definitely remains low.

In Argentina, there is a sense of community among family, friends, and coworkers. Nevertheless, no social forces have developed that articulate more general, more public, more common interests. The political parties became weak from military actions that interrupted their development. A fragmented society translates into a weak state that does not express any common project.

In this context, the future development of services for the elderly is not promising because policy makers respond more to private interests than to the actual needs of the elderly. The image of old age as obsolescence affects all society and future policies for the elderly. Change should be promoted by seeing the elderly in a positive way and encouraging them to assume the role of self-advocates (Barca, 1986).

Argentina is in an economic transformation, but the state will have to be concerned with avoiding the problem of increasing poverty. The associations of retirees are mobilized and will demand better economic security, because their retirement benefits are insufficient to cover their basic needs. The retirement system covers an important percentage of the elderly population but is ineffective because it promises what it cannot deliver. The government proposes a system that integrates retirement funds and pensions. It forsees that it will have to establish a basic universal tax and a mandatory retirement program (pensions) within private and voluntary sectors (Diario, 1992). Some survival strategies to combat poverty should be promoted (Tout, 1989), such as the transformation of social attitudes, promotion of small-scale industries, improvement of health resources, upgrading of housing, support of the family, and encouragement for community action. Those who have not made retirement contributions can count on a sum financed by noncontributory pensions and subsidies that are small but that can be supplemented at age 70 with the utilization of the social services of INSSJP.

Housing problems are not exclusive to the elderly. There is an absolute deficit of 350,000 dwellings, not including the existence of 3 million below-standard houses or congested multiple-living situations. Having a house has been the traditional aspiration fulfilled in the majority of cases. Those who were unable to acquire their own homes have grave difficulties with the cost of renting, which has increased at a much greater rate than their retirement pay. The problem of housing the needy tends to resolve itself by collective public housing.

The situation of the elderly who are in public housing in the metropolitan area can be described as "coexistence of the elderly of many different social and biographic origins" (Pessagno, 1988, p. 342). All have few resources, but the motives of these residents are very diverse. In some cases they have not always been poor; rather, they have become pauperized and have had to resort to these institutions because of circumstances. Such housing reflects a relative isolation from the larger community to which they belong.

The municipality of Buenos Aires has sought the participation of older residents in the functioning of their public housing (Pessagno, 1988). Further, it is increasingly indispensable to stimulate the maintenance of homes and to utilize the subsidies and long-term homes as the most economic solution to housing the elderly. Alternatively, expensive institutional care will increase.

The health system in Argentina is less than effective and efficient because it has greater expenditures and poorer results when compared with more developed countries. It is ineffective because it is a fragmented system that does not reach all the citizens because of its medical model (with a third of the total expenses being used for medication).

In this general frame, the INSSJP is utilized by an important percentage of the elderly. Objectives are to avoid hospital rejection, give personalized attention by family physicians, and provide access to better technology. Yet, although 27% of the current beneficiaries are 75 or older, consultations with geriatricians are practically nonexistent. Many elderly residing in long-term-care institutions could be discharged if only a few community resources were available. While, on one hand, the percentage of elderly institutionalized is low, prolonged internment is the dominant service in geriatrics. In some three-fourths of institutions for long-term care, ambulatory patients have to live with patients with different types of disabilities. Depersonalization and lumping together are the rule in these types of facilities. There is definitely unnecessary hospitalization, simply because the system lacks the services of rehabilitation and convalescence. An adequate and opportune change could permit a comprehensive health care system with extensive coverage and rational functioning.

Mental assistance is well covered, in determined areas, with a program of ambulatory assistance. But even then there is a high percentage of institutionalization. Health problems (such as alcoholism, isolation, and loss of mobility) need to be further investigated.

The resources formally organized for the use of leisure time are sufficient at this time. However, the degree of utilization is low because of lack of information and also because of cultural patterns and/or prejudices. The elderly do not have differential treatment in Argentine justice. Mental deterioration or loss of individual self-determination (as occurs in alcoholism) can label one as incapable or under the protection of a guardian, regardless of the age of the person.

Legal action can redress special problems in the quality of life of the elderly and should be available.

Argentina is on the way to development, but will there be enough funds to resolve the problems of the elderly (especially if preplanning involves the consideration of spending less but more reasonably)? Official politics should help families as the center of social policy, so that they can take care of themselves (from economic and social viewpoints).

To improve the quality of life of the elderly in Argentina, we should improve the conditions of everyone and give them social justice and respect for their human rights (Edwardh, 1989). There is a need for social development in which individuals—young and old—participate actively in the creation of their destiny, in order to guarantee the satisfaction of their basic needs.

BIBLIOGRAPHY

Balossi, E. C. Aspectos epidemiològicos de la morbilidad en los ancianos de la Republica Argentina. Buenos Aires: INSSJP, (National Institute of Social Services for Retired and Pensioned Persons), 1989.

Balossi, E. C., Hauger, C., and Klevene, J. N. Aspectos epidemiològicos de la mortalidad en la tercera edad en la Repùblica Argentina. Buenos Aires: INSSJP, (National Institute of Social Services for Retired and Pensioned Persons), 1988.

Barca, R. E. El hospital de dia geriatrico. Med. 3a. edad.5,3–32, 1983.

Barca, R. E. Latin American and Caribbean Conference of Gerontology, Bogotá, Colombia, 1986. CIGS. Paris, 1986.

Barca, R. E., and Muchinik, E. La vejez en la ciudad de Buenos Aires. Paper presented at conference on: "Aging, demography and well-being in Latin America," University of Florida, Gainesville, 1988.

Calisti, T. Informaciòn basica de la Gerencia de Prestaciones medicas a la Jornada de equipos de salud mental. Buenos Aires, 1991.

Catastro Nacional de recursos y servicios para la salud. Tablas bàsicas. Totales nacionales del años, 1980. Buenos Aires: M. de Salud, 1981.

Centro Latinamericano de Demografia (CELAD). Estimaciones y proyecciones de poblaciòn 1950–2025. Serie Estudios No. 15. Buenos Aires: Instituto Nacional d Estadista y Censo, 1982.

———. Aspectos demogràficos del envejecimiento de la poblaciòn. Reuniòn CELADE— Gobierno Argentino. Buenos Aires, 1989.

Diario La Naciòn. Informe de la Asociaciòn de Entidades de Medicina Prepaga. Argentina, 21 July 1991.

———. Declaraciones del Ministro de Salud Publica. Argentina, 8 September 1991.

———. Declaraciones del Ministro de Salud Publica y Acciòn Social. Argentina, 29 October 1991.

———. Argentina, 4 June 1992.

Direciòn Nacional de Ancianidad. Programa nacional de integraciòn socioeconòmica de los ancianos. Ministerio de Salud Publica, Buenos Aires, 1990.

Edwardh, J. La vejez en America Latina: Necesidad de un programa social. CEPAL IC/R. 855. Julio, 1989.

Gastròn, L. Aspectos demogràficos y sociales de la vejez en la Argentina. *Revista Argentina de Gerontologia y Geriatria* 11 (1): 14–25, January-March 1991.

Gastròn, L., and Andres, H. Los estudios sobre el envejecimiento femenino. Cuadernos de Gerontologia, AGEBA. Buenos Aires, 1989.

Golbert, L. El envejecimiento de la poblaciòn y la seguridad social. Boletin informativo de Techint, Argentina, No. 251/1988.

Guidasio, A. Presentaciòn del INSSJP. Actas del 60. Congreso Argentino de Geriatria. Buenos Aires, 1991.

Gutman, R. Recreacion en la tercera edad. In Matrimonio y familia en la Argentina actual, ed. M. L. Rovaletti. Buenos Aires: Union Carbide, 1985.

Informe Argentino para la Asamblea Mundial sobre el envejecimiento. Ministerio de Salud Publica y medio ambiente. Argentina, 1982.

Informe de la Secretaria de Estado de Seguridad Social. January 1992.

INSSJP (National Institute of Social Services for Retired and Pensioned Persons). Algunas caracteristicas de los establecimientos para la atenciòn prolongada personas mayores. Buenos Aires, 1986.

———. Encuesta de necesidades de los ancioanos. Buenos Aires, 1988.

———. Revisiòn estadistica Gerencia de Planificaciòn y control. Informe interno. Argentina, 1991.

Instituto Nacional d Estadistica y Censo. Censo Nacional de poblacion y vivienda. Buenos Aires, 1980.

———. La pobereza en la Argentina. Indicadores de necesidades bàsicas insatisfechas a partir de los datos del censo nacional de 1980. Estudios INDEC No. 1, Buenos Aires, 1984.

Knallinsky, M., and Pantelides, E. A. La encuesta a ancianos no institucionalizados. In S. Sociales para la tercera edad en el aglomerado del Gran Buenos Aires, 1988.

Muchinik, E., Daichman, L., Labriola, V., Andrès, H., and Gastròn, L. Un estudio sobre mujeres de mediana edad en la Capital Federal. Cuadernos de Gerontologia AGEBA. Buenos Aires, 1989.

Muller, M., and Pantelides, A. Aspectos demogràficos del envejecimiento. In Dimensiones de la vejez en la sociedad argentina. R. Knopoff and M. J. Oddone, Centro editor de America Latina. Buenos Aires, 1991.

Neri, A. Salud y politica social. Edit. Hachette. Buenos Aires, 1982.

Oddone, M. J. Los ancianos en la sociedad. In Dimensiones de la vejez en la sociedad argentina. R. Knopoff and M. J., Oddone, Centro Editor de America Latina. Buenos Aires, 1991.

Panamerican Health Organization. A profile of the elderly in Argentina. Technical papers No. 26. Miami, 1989.

Passanante, M. I. Politicas sociales para la tercera edad. Humanitas. Buenos Aires, 1983.

Pessagno, G. Los hogares que albergan ancianos de escasos recursos. In S. Sociales para la tercera edad en el aglomerado del Gran Buenos Aires. CENEP. Buenos Aires, 1988.

Programa Nacional de Estadistica y Censos. Indicadores de salud y condiciones de vida para el grupo de poblaciòn de 60 y mas anos. 1985–1986. Ministerio de Salud y Acciòn Social, Buenos Aires, 1990.

———. Boletin No. 61 M. Salud Publica. Buenos Aires, 1991.

Redondo, N. Ancianidad y pobreza. Humanitas. Buenos Aires, 1991.

Salvarezza, L. Psicogeriatria. Teoria y clinica. Paidos. Buenos Aires, 1988.

Scipioni, J. C. Situaciòn de los beneficiaarios del Sistema Nacional de Previsiòn Social. Anàlisis del informe Gallup. Ministerio de Trabajo. Buenos Aires, 1992.

Secretaria de Estado de Seguridad Social. Informe. Buenos Aires, January 1992.

Tout, K. *Aging in Developing Countries.* New York: Oxford University Press, 1989.

United Nations. Resoluciòn 213. Informe Argentino AME, 1948.

―――. Documentos principales de la Asamblea Mundial sobre el envejecimiento. Reeditados por el CIGS. Paris, 1984.

2

AUSTRALIA

John McCallum

INTRODUCTION

The Role of the Elderly

There is no official definition of old age in Australia, but, popularly, it is seen as beginning around men's retirement age, soon after 60 years, or at pension eligibility age, 60 years for women and 65 years for men. Only a few percent of Australians are still in paid work after age 65, and there is little participation in part-time work. Retirement is the *rite de passage* to old age for men. For women the entry is less definable. It may be at menopause or at their husband's or their own retirement.

What are the value, status, and power of the Australian elderly? Their situation is changing as trends to earlier retirement and improved income among the young old create an active "old-age" life-style. Most Australians can now expect to enjoy active leisure for a good 10 years from their early 60s to early 70s. Along with this there is increasing differentiation between the well aged and the frail aged, as well as between the low- and high-income aged. Those with higher income consume more, use expensive leisure products, and live in high-quality housing in attractive locations like beach resorts. They are still a small minority of the aged. Older Australians are characteristically not in paid employment, and increasingly they are consumers rather than producers in the public sphere. Within families most older people remain substantial contributors to family care until they are physically or mentally unable to do so.

Public opinion surveys of the Australian population consistently show tolerance of the aged and support for public benevolence toward them. Throughout the period following World War II up to the 1990s at least two-thirds of the Australian public supported the abolition of means tests on the age pension. This expresses "compassionate ageism" in assuming need or dependency simply on the basis of chronological age. In other surveys more Australians, about 40%, are opposed to compulsory retirement than Britons, Austrians, and Italians, but opposition is stronger in the United States, where two-thirds are opposed (McCallum, 1988). This shows a growing "rights culture" that is challenging older attitudes of compassionate ageism.

What are the demographic characteristics of the Australian elderly? Birth and death rate changes, along with substantial migration after World War II, created aging in the Australian population. The post–World War II baby boom, now middle-aged, will be reflected in the sharp increase in the number of persons aged 50–59 years expected in 2006 and in the large flows expected to enter the age groups 60–69 and 70–79 in 2026. The baby boom cohorts were boosted by high rates of immigration of young adults after World War II. There is also improved survival at older ages, 60 years and over, that began to occur from the 1970s. As a result of all three forces, between 1986 and 2026, the number of persons aged 60–69 years is expected to increase by 127%, from 1.3 million to 3 million, representing an average annual increase of 2.1% (McCallum, 1990).

The aging of the baby boom generation after 2010 is dramatic and highlights the need for future planning, but a current process, the growth of the "old old" group, is also important. Between 1986 and 2006 the number of persons aged 80 years and over is expected to increase by 117%, from 314,300 to 683,400, representing an average annual increase of 4.0 percent. This is expected to result in greater numbers needing services and facilities for support in older age. By contrast, the aging of the baby boomers after 2010 is expected to produce more pressure on pensions, housing, and leisure facilities than upon institutional care and community services.

A characteristic feature of Australia's aging population is the imbalance in the sex ratio, the number of males per 100 females. In 1989 the sex ratio was 99.7 for all people but 105 at birth and 73.8 for those aged 65 and over. Elderly women have lower death rates and have experienced greater improvements in life expectancy at older ages than men. The future improvements in life expectation, however, are likely to favor men more than women (McCallum, 1990).

Australia's aged population is not only growing in size but also becoming more ethnically diverse, a long-term consequence of migration (Rowland, 1991). While the Australian-born population aged 60 years and over is likely to increase by 25% between 1981 and 2001, the corresponding increase for the overseas-born is 110%. In certain birthplace groups the growth will be even higher, for example, more than 350% for persons born in Greece, Croatia, Macedonia, and Serbia. Persons from non-English-speaking countries will constitute the substantial majority of the overseas-born aged in 2001. Southern European migrants experience lower death rates than the Australian population as a whole, partly as a result of dietary advantages.

There is a direct association with patterns of migration and aging of the first generation of particular birthplace groups. In June 1990 those with the highest median age are the Soviet-born (65.4 years), the Polish-born (56.2 years), and the Italian-born (53.4 years) who arrived in Australia in the 1950s and 1960s. In contrast, the Asian-born are much younger than the European-born (a median age of 28.4 years compared with a median age of 46.7 years in 1989). The youngest ethnic groups are those born in Hong Kong/Macao (28.8 years), Vietnam (29.1 years), and Malaysia (30.1 years) who first arrived in numbers in Australia during the 1970s and 1980s (Bureau of Immigration Research, 1990).

Aborigines and Torres Strait Islanders (ATSI), the original inhabitants of the continent, have not shared in the increased longevity of the Australian population. In 1986, only 4% of the ATSI population was aged 60 years and over, compared with 15% of the nonaboriginal population. The proportion of the ATSI population 60 years and over is comparable with that of less-developed countries, such as Bangladesh, but the causes of death are quite different (ischemic heart disease and cerebrovascular and infectious diseases). These diseases, particularly coronary heart disease, cause high rates of premature death among aboriginal men (McCallum, 1990).

The Australian-born aged population has become increasingly better educated over this century. Universal primary education was established in all states by the turn of the century. The minimum leaving age also rose steadily in the early years of the century. These developments meant that the majority of the current cohort aged 80 years and over attended school to at least age 14. The extension of secondary and tertiary education is apparent in the higher proportion of the cohort aged 60 to 64 years who remained at school to later ages.

Longer life expectancy at older ages has been accompanied by shorter periods at work. At the end of World War II, more than half of a man's remaining years of life after age 60 years was spent in paid work; by the end of the 1980s, the figure was less than a third. The declines in labor force participation of older Australian men in the 1970s were at least as strong as those in European countries (McCallum, 1988).

The important issue for women is the rapidly increasing rate of widowhood with age. It rises from one-quarter of women aged 60–69 years to three-quarters of women aged 80 years and over. Approximately 80% of married Australians aged 60 years and over live with their spouse alone rather than within three- or four-generation households. As widowhood becomes more prevalent, there are increasing numbers of elderly who live alone. After age 80 years around half of women and a quarter of men live alone. While men are likely to have a spouse to care for them in later life, women are much less likely at very advanced age to have the same access to informal support. The life careers of men and women in old age are different and demand appropriate but different community and public interventions.

The Formal Structure of Care of the Elderly

First European settlers arrived in Australia in 1788, and federation of separate colonial states was achieved in 1901. As a British penal colony, the tradition of public responsibility and control over most areas of welfare became firmly established. States remained the centers for benevolent activities of care to the aged, provided mostly by voluntary organizations. Family was the mainstay of support for the elderly except in cases of destitution, but this system was put under stress in the recession of the 1890s. Consequently Australia became one of the first countries to implement age pensions for older people from 1908 in one of the first welfare decisions of the commonwealth after federation. However, other areas of care remained the province of voluntary groups at a state and local level. This tradition continues to the present, with federal and state governments now directing their funding for long-term care through such organizations.

The means-tested age pension benefit paid from general revenue set the pattern for care of the aged. Responsibility for income support was regarded, in the first instance, as a private responsibility of the older individual and the family. If this was not available or not provided, then responsibility fell to the government. This was established by means testing of older individuals but not their families. Coercion to provide care has never been part of the modern Australian tradition.

Commonwealth funding for residential care of the elderly grew much later in history, out of its interest in health care provision. The Aged Persons Homes Act of 1954 committed the commonwealth to matching funds raised by voluntary organizations to provide independent living units for the aged. In 1964 nursing home benefits were introduced into the National Health Act. This created a commonwealth tier to a system that had previously had state and benevolent organization levels of responsibility (Commonwealth Office for the Aged, 1992).

In order to redress a growing imbalance between the rapid expansion of nursing homes and limited provision of alternative forms of care, the commonwealth introduced a separate Aged and Disabled Persons Hostels Act in 1972 to provide less intensive care. But the initiative was slow to develop relative to the more expensive nursing home care.

The beginnings of public support for community care can be seen in state government assistance to domiciliary nursing organizations in the 1950s. The commonwealth government entered the field in 1956, providing matching funds to organizations supported by state governments in the Home Nursing Subsidy Scheme. The next step was not until 1969, when the commonwealth matched state contributions to senior citizens centers under the State's Grants Home Care Act. There was a lack of integration in provision of care. Home meals, for example, were provided by separate subsidy, and domiciliary paramedical services were provided under another piece of legislation, the States Grant Paramedical Services Act of 1969. Senior citizens centers failed to develop as multipurpose centers for the elderly, and growth of other services was patchy. By contrast nursing homes developed very rapidly, involving the commonwealth in increasing support for this form of care. This imbalance between community and residential care began to be redressed in reforms in the 1980s.

The commonwealth government began to be concerned about the rising public expenditures on the aged from the late 1970s. The accretion of bureaucratic structures providing support and care for the elderly from 70 years of Australian history needed reform and development. The government reintroduced the assets test into means tests on the age pension and reinstated the means testing for people aged 70 years and over in the early 1980s. In 1985–86 the Aged Care Reform Strategy addressed the development of residential and community care (long-term care). Because public expenditures on nursing homes were rising rapidly, the commonwealth government introduced a coordinating system of aged care assessment to ensure the appropriateness of care they provided. The purpose of both changes was clear: to ration scarce nursing home beds and to target pensions on the most needy.

The major innovation of the second half of the 1980s was the development of award superannuation (company pensions) for all workers under industrial awards (Kendig and McCallum, 1990). This has increased the number of people who save income for old age, but the amounts expected at retirement will be, for many, small. The government also reorganized services delivered to the elderly at home under a national Home and Community Care program.

The eight state and territory governments began to take an active interest in aging around this time and created offices for the aged and similar central agencies of government. The major innovation at the state level has been the introduction of age discrimination legislation that effectively outlaws compulsory retirement. These state government responses were as much a reaction to the growing voting power of the elderly as to the public costs of meeting their needs.

There is a growing interest in more responsive modes of provision, including private sector provision. Models of capped, flexible case-managed funding of long-term care were considered and given limited trials. Private ownership of nursing homes remains the norm while voluntary organizations and groups are the main providers of hostel accommodations. There are some ethnospecific nursing homes and a rapidly growing number of ethnic hostels servicing the rapidly increasing numbers of migrants among Australia's aged.

INCOME MAINTENANCE AND EMPLOYMENT

About three-quarters of Australians aged 65 years and over receive, whole or in part, the flat-rate age pension. This is a minimum benefit, set at about 25% of average weekly earnings, paid from general revenue but means-tested on income and assets. It is controlled by the Department of Social Security and has been paid by the commonwealth government since 1908. This type of pension is very effective in reducing poverty because it is received by all low-income elderly. Thus an increase in the flat rate will automatically move them all above official poverty lines.

There is also a significant range of "fringe benefits" available to older Australians provided by state and local governments and by private sector businesses. These concessions, such as reduced fares on public transport, land rate relief, cheap animal licenses, and reduced charges for services such as hairdressing, vary from area to area in availability. Most are accessible to age pension recipients who fall below a specified income level indicated by holding pensioner cards. Where people take advantage of these concessions, they can add around 25% to the value of the age pension.

In June 1991, 76.5% of the Australian population of pension age (74.0% of men and 76.6% of women) received the age pension, either as a Department of Social Security age pension or as an identical service pension or widows' pension paid by the Commonwealth Department of Veterans' Affairs. This is a considerable drop since 1980, when 87.1% of the population of pension age received pensions. This drop was a consequence of reintroduction of the assets test and tightening of means tests on the age pension.

Company and personal pensions (superannuation) supplement this basic support. In 1974, 32% of all employees were covered by superannuation schemes. This rose to 40% in 1984 and 52% in 1990. About two-thirds of all employees now have superannuation coverage due to its inclusion in wage bargains from 1985 (McCallum, 1992).

In 1986 about one-third of the heads of households who were aged 65 years and over had income from employment or assets. The public pension provided 57% of the total income of single men and 68% of the total income of single women. The public age pension provided 52% of the total income of couples. Superannuation provided less than 10% of the total income received by older people in 1986, while investment income, which may have originally come from lump sum superannuation, provided 25% of total income. Superannuation income as a regular payment was received by 11.3% of older people. This is due to the high prevalence of lump sum payments from private and company pensions as opposed to regular payments. About 80% of such pensions are paid out as lump sums. This is one of the factors that can be used by Australian employers to make retirement more attractive in the short term.

While about three-quarters of adult Australians were in the work force in 1987, the proportion declines very rapidly after age 45 years for women and 55 years for men. Women's rates were lower than those for men and were much lower between ages 20 and 35, when women tend to withdraw from the work force to rear children. The probability of working, for men, between ages 60 and 64 is less than 50%, and beyond age 65 it is less than 10%.

Participation rates for women show markedly different patterns from those for men. In the last 20 years adult women aged up to 55 years have increased their participation, largely due to increases in married women's work force participation. The impact of marriage and children on participation has lessened, but, contrary to the general trend, the participation of women after 55 years showed a slight decrease between 1967 and 1987 (McCallum, 1988).

Explanations of these declines propose three factors to explain why men's participation rates declined. First, the long-term trend from the 1940s is argued to be a consequence of increases in household wealth during post–World War II economic growth. The more wealth a household has, the less the need to work. However, the acceleration of rates during the 1970s was due to two other factors: the oil price recession and marginal improvements in Social Security.

The slight declines in older women's participation rates are due to a tendency for older women to choose to have the same employment status as their spouses so as to enjoy retirement leisure together or to avoid role reversal. Role reversal arises when husbands retire and women work, the opposite of sex-role expectations.

There is a growing interest in maintaining employment and reemploying for older workers. Age discrimination in employment legislation has been enacted at the state level, but the labor market impact is limited. Little appropriate training is available to the older unemployed and even less for those of retirement age. In a highly unionized and regulated labor market, it is more difficult to provide the flexible work preferred by older workers. Australians also have a well-developed taste for leisure that appears to make retirement, even on a relatively low income, an attractive option.

HEALTH CARE SERVICES

Health care services are provided to older Australians under a universal health insurance program, Medicare, since 1983 (previously called Medibank, initiated in 1975). It is funded by a 1.25% levy on taxable income above a minimum level and covers 85% of the scheduled fee for medical services and 100% of services if they are bulk-billed by the provider. Older people are unlikely to pay the levy because of an income ceiling and receive a higher number of services per person and a higher average value of benefit per person than younger people.

While the burden of health financing is borne by the Medicare levy, private health insurance is available to cover hospital and specialist visits, where they are not covered under Medicare. The highest incidence of private health insurance was among middle-aged people, 35 to 54 years. Their rates of coverage were double those for people under 25 years. This was consistent with better health status of the younger group. The level of private hospital insurance increased from 29.5% of 15- to 24-year-olds to a peak rate of 53.5% of 35- to 54-year-olds before declining to 35.5% of people aged 75 years and over. Most older people do not have private health insurance. While younger people tend to have ancillary coverage (extras such as dental and physiotherapy), older people who are covered tend to have basic hospital coverage, but not ancillary coverage (Willcox, 1991).

The existence of the Medicare system, covering the whole population, allows us to look at trends in health service usage by age in Australia from the early 1970s. From the Medibank system in 1976 to the Medicare system in 1986 there was a 47% increase in fee-adjusted cost per head of population. However, the contribution of general practice (GP) services to costs declined from 42% to 36% of the total over the 10 years. Downward trends in GP utilization were due almost entirely to declines in the number of consultations; that is, there was no drift toward more costly consultations. By contrast, specialist consultations showed high overall rates of growth.

Costs and service usage increase steadily with age. This is particularly true for specialist consultations, where the most rapid increases were for people aged 75 years and over. Men aged 80–84 years received 160% more specialist consultations in 1986 than their counterparts in 1976, an annual increase per capita of 10%. Almost all the increase came from an increased number of consultations, with only a slight drift toward higher-priced specialist consultations of about 5% increase in fee-adjusted costs. However, specialist consultations received by the aged tended to be less costly than those received by the rest of the population in both 1976 and 1986 (Barer et al., 1990).

More recently the same trends were found by analyses conducted for the National Health Strategy. In the five years 1984–85 to 1989–90, a changing composition of services and increases in specific categories were observed. For example, GP consultations accounted for 71% of services to people aged under 20 years in 1989–90 compared with only 53% of services to people aged 60 years and over. By contrast pathology contributed only 13% of services to the younger group compared with 23% of services to those aged 60 years and over.

People aged 60 years and over received 26% of all private medical services in 1989–90. At that time they were roughly 10% of the population. Nearly half of the total increase in specialist consultations between 1984–85 and 1989–90 and 35% of the increase in pathology were concentrated on this group, aged 60 years and over. Schedule fee costs per person rose 42% for those aged 20 years of age and under, 54% for those aged 20 to 59 years, and 72% for those aged 60 years and over.

Underlying these trends in service use are increasing specialist consultations and use of pathology and radiology for monitoring postacute treatment for various conditions. Total diagnostic use (pathology and radiology) increased by 57% for those aged 60 years and over compared with 15% of those under 20 years and 36% of those aged 20 to 59 years. There was also a 25% increase in operations for those 60 years and over, compared with 6.8% for the under-20s and 17% of those aged 20 to 59 years (Deeble, 1991).

The introduction of casemix measures into the hospital payment system is expected to have a major impact on the acute hospital treatment of older people. In the United States it was predicted that the result of introducing diagnosis-related groups (DRGs) would be "sicker and quicker" discharge of older people. The early evidence is that older people are being discharged more quickly but that this is not necessarily producing worse health outcomes. The introduction of DRGs in Australia will require better discharge planning and more home and community services to replace care previously provided during longer stays in the hospital. Unless this substitution is achieved, older people's acute care needs would have been better served under the old block grant system.

HOUSING RESOURCES

Two characteristic features of current housing arrangements of older Australians are the high level of homeownership and the diversity of housing arrangements and conditions. Some 63.5% of people 65 years and over own houses, and another 8.3% are purchasers. Only 5.2% are public tenants while another 7.4% are private tenants. Of the 10% of people not in private dwellings, 4.4% lived in nursing homes, 2.4% in hostels (less intensive residential care), and 3.2% in other forms of sheltered accommodation (Howe, 1992).

There is a conspicuous disadvantage for older people in private rental accommodations. Older private tenants spend around 35% of their income on housing, compared with 5% spent by older home owners. The significance of housing for older people stems from the contribution of a home to their social and psychological well-being as well as the impact of housing on physical and economic well-being. Private tenants are targeted with means-tested rental assistance.

The importance of access to services is generally similar for old and young, married and single. Services ranked as important by more than 85% of a sample of Australians were shops, public transport, hospitals, doctors and health facilities, and friends and relatives. The item that was highly valued by people of all ages (86%) but not so much by the elderly (56% of older singles) was access to parks and open spaces.

As well as being a service, housing is a major form of wealth. The largest share of Australians' wealth, about 60%, is held in house and furniture, and the second largest share, about 16%, is held in superannuation and insurance. Vehicles and other assets account for 9% each, and money assets and business assets are around 6% of net wealth overall. The pattern of mean net wealth holding by age shows a steady increase to age 45, then a rapid increase up to age 58 years; after that there is a decrease in the wealth holdings of households relative to earlier ages (McCallum and Beggs, 1991).

SUPPORTIVE SERVICES

Long-term care refers to social, residential, and health services provided to chronically disabled persons over an extended period. It includes nursing homes and old people's homes, hostels and other elderly accommodations, and some types of rehabilitation services. Government dominates institutional care, but other voluntary and private providers operate some services delivered to the home and community.

Considering nursing home care for the elderly, recent radical reform has reorganized post–World War II legislation. Under the Aged or Disabled Persons' Homes Act 1954, grants are made to religious, charitable, and other approved organizations and local government bodies to defray costs of construction, extension, or purchase of accommodation facilities for aged or disabled people ($13 million in 1989–90). Under the Nursing Homes Assistance Act 1974, the commonwealth meets the approved operating deficits of eligible nonprofit nursing homes for persons with disabilities. In addition nursing home benefits are paid under the National Health Act 1953 to a small number of nursing homes for people with disabilities. Certain approved services attached to nursing homes and previously funded under the 1974 act will be funded under annual appropriations (therapy services provided to nonnursing home residents).

Nursing homes provide beds for frail aged who require ongoing nursing care while hostels provide a base level of hostel care or more intensive personal care services. The Aged or Disabled Persons Homes Amendment Act 1988 introduced improvements to planning and approvals arrangements for hostels. The strategy is to provide 100 nursing home and hostel places per 1,000 people over 70 years of age. This will change the balance of service provision from 58 to 40 nursing home places per 1,000 people aged 70 years and over and will increase to 60 the number of hostel places to deal with current imbalances between the two levels of intensity in institutional care. It involves freezing growth in some areas and development of required services in underbedded regions (Commonwealth Office for the Aged, 1992).

At the national level all hostel beds are provided by nonprofit organizations, including local government. However, at the national level just under half of nursing home beds are provided by the private sector (48.4%) and under a quarter by nonprofit organizations (23.9%), with a further 9.5% provided by religious and charitable bodies funded under the same regime as private sector homes. The remaining 18.2% are predominantly large state government homes.

Regardless of their private ownership, nursing homes and hostels are operated subject to a range of commonwealth regulations. A system of regionally based, multidisciplinary aged care assessment services operates across Australia, using a standard form of assessment to ensure that only persons assessed as needing institutional care gain entry to homes. Admission to nursing homes was previously controlled by commonwealth medical officers. Some 60 or more assessment services are currently operating cooperatively between the commonwealth and state and territory health authorities throughout Australia. Uniform national funding levels apply for infrastructure costs (called SAM, standard aggregated module).

As of 1 July 1991 all residents of nongovernment nursing homes pay no more than 87.5% of the maximum single rate of the age pension and the full amount of rent assistance for the accommodations and care that they need. From 1 July 1988 all residents entering nursing homes were assessed to establish their need for nursing and personal care on the five levels (from most dependent to least dependent) on the Resident Classification Instrument (called RCI). Under the Care Aggregated Module payment, a higher payment is made for higher levels of dependency measured on the RCI. Legislation has been passed to allow exempt nursing homes to cater to residents who wish to pay more for a higher standard of accommodations but with a reduced commonwealth benefit.

More recently under the Home and Community Care Act 1985 the commonwealth, in conjunction with the states, provided a comprehensive range of integrated home and community care services for frail aged and younger disabled people at risk of institutionalization to help them to continue to live in their own homes. Services include:

home help and personal care
home maintenance and modification
food services
community respite care
transport services
community paramedical services
community nursing
assessment and referral
education and training for service providers/users
information and coordination

Funding is cost-shared with the states based upon respective levels of commonwealth and state outlays in the previous year. The commonwealth also provides unmatched funds to test innovative methods of delivering services targeted particularly at those people at risk of institutionalization. The Home and Community Care (HACC) Triennial Review implemented new data collection methods that will allow better assessment and evaluation.

Trends in commonwealth expenditure from 1985–86 to 1990–91 provide an indication of the changing context of aged care. There was a very substantial shift in emphasis to community care and, within residential care, from nursing home care to hostel care. Total expenditure on aged care has increased by 28% in real terms over the last five years. This overall growth compared with increases of 16% in the population aged 70 years and over and 25% in the population aged 80 years and over for the same period. The growth of the population 80 years and over is a major determinant of the scale of increase in service needs, and the growth in expenditure over the last five years has just kept pace (Commonwealth Department of Health, Housing and Community Services, 1991).

Within this overall budget context, changes in the allocation of resources among nursing home, hostel, and community care have been a key means of improving service provision and client outcomes. These changes are seen in the differences in the growth of expenditure between program areas. In real terms, expenditure of nursing home benefits increased by 8.8%, hostel subsidies by 127%, and HACC by 95%.

While the proportion of total expenditure going to nursing home benefits declined from around 81% in 1985–86 to 69% in 1990–91, expenditure on hostel benefits increased from 5% to 10%, including the expenditure on the dementia hostels program and other activities. The considerable expansion of the hostel expenditure against the containment of nursing home expenditure evidences the effects of restructuring of residential care over the last five years.

Expenditure on HACC increased from 8% to 12% of commonwealth expenditure. This increase includes commonwealth unmatched funds totaling $62 million over the four years to 1991 allocated to Community Options Projects, based upon Wisconsin models, to develop innovative models of service delivery. HACC is a cost-shared program, with commonwealth/state matching initially approximating a 50/50 basis. The progressive absorption of the unmatched funds into the commonwealth HACC base has brought the commonwealth share of expenditure to 57% in 1990–91, and this will increase to 60% in 1991–92. It is estimated that matching state expenditure reached approximately $190 million in 1990–91, and when this amount is included, combined commonwealth and state expenditure in 1990–91 reached $469 million. Total HACC expenditure accounted for 21% of this combined total expenditure on aged care (Commonwealth Department of Health, Housing and Community Services, 1991).

The lack of effective controls in government policies, rather than demographic aging, underlies the increasing costs of providing services for older people. Between 1976–77 and 1981–82 commonwealth recurrent expenditures on nursing homes increased 144% (an average annual increase of 19.5%) and became the subject of inquiries and concerted policy development. Between 1985–86 and 1990–91 the rate of increase was constrained to 59% (an average annual increase of 9.7%), about the rate of increase of age pension expenditures. At the same time the growth in the population aged 70 years and over was 18% for the second half of the 1970s and 13% for the second half of the 1980s.

The public income support for caretakers of the elderly at home is limited but growing in the area of services. The Domiciliary Nursing Home Benefit paid $42 per fortnight to some 28,000 eligible persons in 1988–89 who provided care for approved persons at home (aged 16 years or over and would otherwise justify admission to an approved nursing home) as an alternative to nursing home care. Another form of help is to allow caretakers to place their dependent spouses or parents in nursing homes or hostels so that the caretakers can take a break or a holiday. There is a long-term planning target to provide two respite beds in nursing homes per 1,000 population aged 70 years and over. New respite arrangements were introduced into hostels in June 1989 consistent with the long-term planning target. Other services to caretakers come through the HACC program.

LEISURE-TIME RESOURCES

Voluntary organizations serving the elderly now tend to receive public subsidies for their work. They operate as not-for-profit organizations, often with substantial budgets. In small country towns groups like meals-on-wheels remain an exception in voluntarily providing services to older people. Volunteerism among the elderly themselves tends to decline after retirement. Reasons for this are the competing demands of other leisure pursuits, the lack of money to subsidize travel and other expenses, and poor health. Church attendance, however, remains high among the elderly relative to younger groups because of secularization.

The hidden face of volunteerism lies in care of older people in the family or neighborhood. Spouses are around 90% of all caretakers of severely disabled persons aged 60–69, declining to about 50% of caretakers of persons aged 75 years and over. At the older ages daughters and sons become caretakers, accounting for around 40% of caretakers of severely disabled people aged 75 years and over (Australian Bureau of Statistics, 1990).

Activity surveys of Australians show statistically significant decreases in social, outdoor, and sporting activities after age 60 years. There are parallel increases in in-home activities and passive leisure, like watching television, after age 60 years for both men and women. One interesting question is, What do men do in the extra time gained from earlier retirement from work? Time use surveys covering the period 1974 to 1987, when older men's work force participation declined dramatically, show that there were compensating increases in men's time spent on domestic tasks, shopping, and personal care. Older women's time spent in these activities declined, presumably to accommodate men's reentry into the household. Older women increased time spent in active and passive leisure (McCallum, 1989). These activity redistributions are driven by declining work force participation rather than "feminization" of men's roles in later life.

One remarkable area of growth has been in self-financing universities of the third age (U3As). These now flourish throughout Australia but particularly in capital cities. No fees are charged, and lectures are provided by volunteer specialists.

Leisure and activity services for older people received a boost in the National Better Health Program of 1987. Among five targets, like lowering preventable hypertension and improving nutrition, was "the health of the elderly." One of the most implemented types of programs was for activity and exercise. The state of Victoria has conducted a major social marketing campaign, "Active at Any Age," which uses billboards and television to promote exercise, backed by developing local exercise and activity programs. There is a growing professional interest in the leisure of the elderly that particularly comes from health promotion interests.

ADVOCACY AND PROTECTION

While earlier policy was driven by a compassionate "ageism," major advances in advocacy for the elderly have been made in recent years. Standards monitoring teams check and report on the 31 outcome standards for quality of care provided to residents (published 1 July 1987). For example, nursing home operators are required to form resident committees. Nursing homes are checked every two years by an inspection team comprising a registered nurse, an administrative officer, and others. This inspection is followed by a compliance discussion in which ratings are discussed and action plans formulated. A formal report is provided to the home in two weeks, and it has six weeks to respond. Continual failure to meet standards results in listing it as a home of concern, with regular inspection and withdrawal of commonwealth subsidies when improvements are not made.

For the broader community, Consumer Forums for the Aged were established by the commonwealth minister for Aged, Family, and Health Services in 1989 to advise him on issues of concern to older consumers. State and territory forums comprised up to 12 members who represent the views of older Australians and provide input to the policy-making process. State and territory forums meet quarterly, and members are appointed for two years. A national forum meets biannually and has established an Information Working Party and a Carers Working Group. Examples of input into policymaking have been with the recently conducted Mid-Term Review of the Aged Care Reform Strategy. The forums also played a major role in consideration of the content of a new User Rights Package and its dissemination to older consumers.

Protective services exist through guardianship legislation in various states. In New South Wales, Australia's most populous state, the Disability Services and Guardianship Act 1987 established the Guardianship Board. The board is able to make orders in relation to a "person with a disability," which includes people of advanced age and those mentally ill or incapable of managing their own affairs. Guardianship and financial management provide options for people who require others to make important decisions for them in their own best interests. Where people are at risk of abuse, exploitation, or neglect, protective orders and alternative accommodation orders are possible. Where domestic violence is involved, the Family Law Act may be used to obtain protective orders.

Extreme cases of assault or theft can be pursued under the Crimes Act. Many victims of assault, intimidation, theft, extortion, fraud, and abuse, however, are reluctant to involve police. An alternative is to obtain an Apprehended Violence Order, which restricts or prohibits the conduct of the offender in order to ensure the victim's safety. To commence proceedings, the person needs to approach the chamber magistrate at a local court and advise of the details of the situation to establish that there are reasonable grounds to fear further violence or harassment from "the defendant." A summons will be issued, and, on an appointed date, the complainant and the defendant will be required to attend court for a magistrate to determine the matter. Once an order is made, it is enforceable by the police, and any breach is a criminal offense.

In addition, age discrimination legislation is enacted in two states and coming in others. Advance notice legislation is enacted in one state and under discussion in others. The elderly are being given voice in a service system and community that previously excluded them.

FUTURE PROJECTIONS

Australian Bureau of Statistics projections spanning the period 1991 to 2031 indicate that the "graying" of Australia will continue. The aged segment of the Australian population will experience particularly marked growth after the turn of the century, after 2011. Over the next four decades the proportion of the population aged 0–14 years will continue to decline (from 22% in 1990 to 17% in 2031), and the proportion of the aged will increase. By 2031 the number of aged Australians (65 and over) will have trebled from about 1.9 million (11% of the population) in 1990 to 5.2 million (20% of the population) in 2031 (McCallum, 1990).

This means that the development of private sources of retirement income will continue to be encouraged by the commonwealth government. This will have the dual purpose of relieving pressures on the publicly funded age pension as well as increasing the adequacy of the retirement income for new generations of retirees.

One negative effect may be to decrease work participation even more. Unpublished projections from the Commonwealth Department of Employment Education and Training show that the pace of these declines will slow for men over age 60 years but that younger men 55–59 years are expected to reduce their participation rate from 70% in 1996 to 66% in 2001.

In housing, wider concepts of social housing are being developed, including retirement villages; however, the proportions of older people taking up such options are relatively small. Linkages are important among housing, supportive environments, and delivery of care services. Areas that need improved data include consumer preferences, the quality and standard of some forms of private rental housing, and local and regional variations in older persons' housing conditions. Urban planning issues, like links between housing and transport, also need to be addressed.

Health care service costs are problematic because of the unpredictability of improvements in health technologies, labor costs, and tastes of older people. We expect cost trends to continue as operations like hip replacements become more common and total knee replacement follows the same growth path. Osteoporosis may be countered by drugs that rebuild bone, but this and similar targets are as yet future goals rather than reality. We already have antihypertensive drugs, beta blockers, and the much more expensive ace inhibitors, with significant market penetration, and cholesterol-lowering drugs can follow the same growth trend.

We can add to this the so-called smart drugs, which improve mental function and are already showing effects for the mildly demented. A wonder drug for the prostate is undergoing final tests. Nonsteroidal anti-inflammatory drugs are available for arthritis and rheumatic conditions.

The need to prevent disability by primary prevention, rather than tertiary prevention or so-called late-life heroics, is likely to develop into mass screening from age 40 or thereabouts, which potentially may lead to overservicing and excess drug use. The multiple chronic illnesses and conditions of old age lead to the questions: Will there be any end to endless medical technological development? How valuable is it to marginally extend life at substantial public expense? These questions have led to a growing interest in health promotion and prevention of disease and accidents among the elderly. In more immediate responses there is a concern to constrain the growing health costs occurring in an aging Australia.

BIBLIOGRAPHY

Australian Bureau of Statistics. (1990). *Carers of the Handicapped at Home, Australia 1988.* Canberra: Australian Government Publishing Service.

Barer, M., Nichol, M., Diesendorf, M., and Harvey, R. (1990). *Australian Private Medical Care Costs and Use, 1976 and 1986.* Canberra: Australian Government Publishing Service.

Bureau of Immigration Research. (1990). *Australia's Population Trends and Prospects 1990.* Canberra: Australian Government Publishing Service.

Commonwealth Department of Health, Housing and Community Services. (1991). *Aged Care Reform Strategy: Mid Term Review 1990–91.* Canberra: Australian Government Publishing Service.

Commonwealth Office for the Aged. (1992). *Australian National Report to the OECD Project—The Care of the Frail Elderly.* Canberra: Commonwealth Department of Health, Housing, and Community Services.

Deeble, J. (1991). *Medical Services Through Medicare.* National Health Strategy Background Paper No. 2. Melbourne: National Health Strategy.

Howe, A. L. (1992). *Housing for Older Australians: Affordability, Adjustments and Care.* Canberra: Australian Government Publishing Service.

Kendig, H. L., and McCallum, J. (eds.). (1990). *Grey Policy: Australian Policies for an Ageing Society.* Sydney: Allen and Unwin.

McCallum, J. (1988). Technology and Social Change in the Ageing Lifecourse. In Australian Association of Gerontology, *Proceedings of the 23rd Annual Conference of the Australian Association of Gerontology, Brisbane 1988.* Perth: Lamb Printers: 17–21.

———. (1989). *The Dynamics of Community Involvement in Old Age: The Syndrome of Underuse.* Working Paper No. 9. Canberra: National Center for Epidemiology and Population Health.

———. (1992). *The Superannuation System in Australia.* Report to the Organization for Economic Cooperation and Development (OECD), Directorate for Education, Employment, Labour, and Social Affairs.

———. (ed.). (1990). Health: The Quality of Survival in Older Age. In Australian Institute of Health, *Australia's Health 1990: The Second Biennial Report of the Australian Institute of Health.* Canberra: Australian Government Publishing Service: 195–240.

McCallum, J., and Beggs, J. (1991). Determinants of Household Wealth: Assets of Divorcing Couples in Australia. *Australian Economic Review* 4th Quarter: 57–66.

Rowland, D. T. (1991). *Pioneers Again: Immigrants and Ageing in Australia.* Canberra: Australian Government Publishing Service.

Willcox, S. (1991). *A Health Risk?: Use of Private Insurance.* Background Paper No. 4. Melbourne: National Health Strategy.

3

AUSTRIA

Josef Hörl

INTRODUCTION

The Role of the Elderly

The World Assembly on Aging adopted the population in the 60+ age group as its main focus of concern (*Report,* 1982). Therefore, throughout this chapter the terms *the aged* or *the elderly* refer to the segment of the population aged 60 years and over. It should be clear, however, that the elderly must not be considered a monolithic group: the "very old" (over 75 or 80 years)—especially the women among them—are frequently entirely unattached and live in one-person households. Furthermore, the very old are primarily at risk for multi-morbidity or chronic health defects. They require much more help from service organizations or residential care than the "young old," aged 75 or less. In fact, there is little difference between the young old and persons aged 50+ as far as subjective health status and certain life-style patterns (traveling abroad, possession of durable consumer goods, and so on) are concerned (Fessel, 1990).

The widespread view that in industrialized societies there exists a generally negative attitude toward the elderly cannot be maintained. On the contrary, surveys show a rather favorable picture (Haller and Holm, 1987; Majce, 1992). The majority of the population does not see serious public conflicts between the generations. In particular, it is common opinion that securing an adequate standard of living for the elderly is one of the government's most important responsibilities. Clearly there is a great deal of attitudinal ambiguity toward the aged: many people perceive a definite lack of understanding on the part of the elderly with regard to problems of youth and vice versa. Furthermore, the stereotype of old age is still (wrongly) associated with dependency, sickness, loneliness, depression, and social isolation.

Political power of the elderly is weak. At present in Austria, there is neither an official national statement of rights for the elderly nor a central government bureau for the elderly. Pensioners' organizations make public announcements on concrete problems and are active in commenting on legislative initiatives that are brought to their attention. However, they do not possess any formal right of veto in matters of the aged population. Postwar economic stability has been guaranteed by the two most influential power groups: employers and employees. In Austria their cooperation has become institutionalized within a system called "social partnership." It is designed to keep in check the development of wages and prices by close cooperation between these interest groups. They exercise influence on issues far beyond labor relations, for example, retirement, pension, and caring.

Demographic Overview

Since the mid-1960s every fifth Austrian has been over the age of 60. Currently, there are somewhat more than 1.5 million Austrians over the age of 60 (or 20.3% of the overall population). More than .5 million Austrians are over 75 (or 6.8% of the overall population) (Findl, 1992). It is of major significance with regard to policies in the field of health and families, as well as with regard to intergenerational relationships, that the number of the very old population has increased above the average over the past four decades and will rise even more rapidly in the future. It is projected that those 60 to 79 years old will increase by 64% between 1990 and 2030, but those aged 80 or more will increase by 83%. The 90+ group will more than triple (Statistisches Handbuch, 1991).

Women make up 52% of the total population and there are 92 males to every 100 females. In view of the tendency for men to die sooner than women, in 1990 there were only about 53 men to every 100 women in the population aged 65+. This discrepancy in the sex ratio becomes even greater with advancing age so that for every 100 women aged 80 or more there are only about 40 men of similar age. The enormous surplus of very old women also results from the influence of the two waves of war losses, and a decrease in the proportion of very old women can be observed since 1990 (Statistisches Handbuch, 1991).

With regard to the dependency ratio, in 1991 there were 326 elderly (60+) and 280 children to every 1,000 persons of middle age (15–60 years); in 2015 only 239 children but 394 elderly to every 1,000 middle-aged persons are expected. Therefore, the total dependency rate is expected to rise from 606 (1991) to 816 (2030) (Findl, 1992; Statistisches Handbuch, 1991). This trend is interesting not only with regard to the potential economic burden of aged persons on the population of working age but also with regard to the decreasing ratio of middle-aged family members who might take over nursing responsibilities.

The development of mortality in Austria follows the worldwide phenomenon of decreasing trends during the past century, which is due to economic, social, and medical progress. In the years between 1950 and 1991 life expectancy at birth increased for males from 61.9 years to 72.6 years and for females from 67.0 years to 79.2 years. The decrease has not extended to all age groups to the same extent. Within the last 100 years, infant mortality has dropped to less than ⅟₃₀th of its original rate. Currently, the decline of mortality in older age groups gets more attention. Men aged 60 in 1991 could expect to have 18.3 more years of life ahead (3 more years than in 1950). Women of the same age had, on the average, gained 5 further years of life expectancy during this period; women aged 60 (in 1991) could expect to have 22.3 more years of life. Since 1986 life expectancy at the age of 60 improved by about 1 year for both sexes (Findl, 1992; Statistisches Handbuch, 1991).

As a result of increasing life expectancy, the length of marriages has increased, although divorce rates have risen. The proportion of singles in all age groups over 60 has dropped, although the proportion of single women is greater than that of single men for all age groups. In all age groups over 60, more men than women are married. Of those persons aged 80 and over, for instance, half the men but only 8% of the women are married (Statistisches Handbuch, 1991).

Family and Household Patterns and Help for the Elderly

In comparison with other developed countries there is a relatively frequent incidence of intergenerational living arrangements in Austria. In smaller rural communities half of all the old people live in the same house as at least one of their children; of all elderly with children, two-fifths share a common household with their children or live in the same house. Even in Vienna, every sixth person over 60 lives with one of the children in the same house (Hörl and Rosenmayr, 1992).

Results on health care show that the spouse supplies most of the aid in emergency cases, even if a child lives in the same household or same house. In health care of married women, children play a somewhat greater role than in the health care of married men; nevertheless, husbands are nominated as primary caregivers by married women as well. Most elderly people would turn to adult children only in case there is no marital partner or the partner cannot supply the aid (e.g., because of the partner's own health problems), and a substantial minority of elderly would never turn to their children for help. About 80% of all help and care is given by informal sources (Hörl and Rosenmayr, 1992; Kytir and Münz, 1992).

The history of the elderly over the last decades, in terms of the perception of responsibility for the care of the elderly in Austria, is influenced by a widespread, skeptical view on the future of the family as a potential source of support. This opinion can be corroborated by referring to the enormous increase in organized social services during the last decades. Obviously, most of these services have to be seen as functional equivalents for missing or insufficient support by family and kin. On the other side, the assumption that the family has experienced a massive reduction in caring tasks cannot withstand a closer investigation (Hörl, 1992).

Social services are expanding as a consequence of a variety of social developments:

- demographic changes resulting in a growing number of people without, or with only a reduced number of, descendants;
- closing existing service gaps, for instance, in occupational therapy or psychotherapeutic care;
- new needs that have arisen (e.g., transport systems);
- as long as federal or provincial budgets will allow, creation of new jobs for social workers and other social services workers.

Thus, there are a number of possible explanations for the expansion of organized social services without referring to the family's alleged weakened problem-solving capacity. Although the basic motivation of family caregivers seems to be unbroken, there is a certain danger in overestimating the quality of kin relationships in the lives of the elderly. For instance, empirical research shows that many families develop a severe, if often concealed, crisis when they reach their limitations in providing care needed by the dependent relative (Hörl and Rosenmayr, 1992). There can be little doubt that the tolerable limits of intensity and time consumption in caregiving are frequently exceeded.

The Formal Structure of Care of the Elderly

The Social Security system in Austria has two major components: social insurance and social assistance. While social insurance is mainly financed by earnings-related contributions shared between the insured and employers and, to a smaller and varying degree, by central government subsidies, social assistance is financed by general taxation.

Social insurance is the most important program in the Austrian Social Security system, and 99% of the population is enrolled in one or more subsections of this system. It is responsible for 93% of total expenditure; the proportion that social assistance represents of total expenditures on Social Security has gone up in the last few years from 3% to the current 7%. One of the reasons for this is the increasing cost of care for very old and/or dependent persons (*Bericht*, 1991).

Under the Austrian constitution, both legislation for social insurance and its implementation are a federal responsibility. The social insurance institutions are formally autonomous, self-governing bodies, although their respective status is subject to control by the central government authorities. Influence of the "social partners" and of the political parties is considerable.

The various social insurance institutions follow, first, professional and occupational distinctions and, second, a territorial principle. They are linked together in the Federation of Austrian Social Insurance Institutes, established in 1955, which operates as a coordinating institution, representing its members in international matters and acting on their behalf in the negotiation of contracts with doctors, hospitals, and so on.

Civil servants fall into a separate category, and their pension payments are part of the work contract. They are included under personnel expenditure in the public budgets and therefore not integrated into the General Pension Insurance Act.

In 1990, total expenditure on social insurance amounted to 280 billion Austrian schillings (US$23 billion, about 15.6% of the gross domestic product or GDP). Of this sum, roughly two-thirds were spent on pension insurance, one-fourth on health insurance, and the rest on accident insurance and unemployment insurance (*Bericht,* 1991).

Social insurance, in general, has been compulsory since 1955, when the General Social Insurance Act was passed. A great number of amendments have been enacted to ensure that the law was continuously adapted to changing economic and sociocultural realities. It becomes automatically effective with employment or any other insurable activity. Coverage varies with professional and social status; for example, pensioners are only health-insured. Persons are insured either directly or indirectly as dependents.

The provinces are primarily responsible for providing social assistance. On one hand, the social assistance organizations of the provinces fulfill certain special tasks, such as the maintenance and running of various social services. On the other hand, they take over responsibility where the Social Security network leaves gaps. The costs of rehabilitation for older persons no longer gainfully employed are, for instance, borne by the local social assistance authorities.

All nine provinces have enacted their own Social Assistance Acts, passed between 1971 and 1978, which replaced older legislation (Weigel and Amann, 1987). The various bodies responsible for social assistance are the provincial authorities, the local authorities through the social assistance unions, and independent district-towns. These laws represent a modern understanding of social assistance and care but have also created considerable variations between the provinces.

A notable feature of social assistance activities at provincial and community levels is the close cooperation between the provincial and local institutions and nongovernmental organizations. These latter organizations have been entrusted through legal contracts with a number of tasks in the field of social services.

INCOME MAINTENANCE AND EMPLOYMENT

Principally, old-age pensions are calculated on the basis of the length of the insurance period and the average gross earnings over the last five years preceding retirement. There are certain ceilings with regard to earnings that serve as calculation bases for contributions. The theoretical maximum old-age pension amounts to 79.5% of the calculation base. Severely impaired elderly are entitled to special allowances in addition to their pension. They can also claim certain tax reductions (e.g., if a costly diet is necessary).

Due to the growing numbers of women who have become gainfully employed during the past decades, the number of women now drawing pensions under the pension schemes for workers and employees has increased, and the proportion of female pensioners now makes up two-thirds of the entire number of pensioners. The proportion of women drawing widow's pensions is stagnating (*Bericht,* 1991).

If the old-age pension is below a legally prescribed minimum, the difference is paid in the form of supplementary benefits, so-called compensation allowances financed from general revenues. This minimum is fixed annually. Generally, pensions are adjusted to the active salaries annually by the so-called pensions' dynamics on the basis of preceding wage developments. Inflation and unemployment rates are also taken into account. In addition, there are a number of other benefits available for older persons with low incomes, such as rent allowances from the federal authorities, exemption from payments for telephone and radio/television, reduced fares on public transport, and considerably reduced payments (or in some cases entire exemption from payment) for the costs of the various social services.

Entitlement to pension benefits is dependent upon preconditions of "waiting time" and "coverage of the third." Waiting time means that a person has to prove that contributions have been paid for a minimum of 180 months (or 60 months for survivors' and invalidity pensions). In addition, entitlement to benefits is conditional on payment of 12 monthly contributions within the last 36 months (i.e., coverage of the third). Persons satisfying these requirements are entitled to draw old age pensions from the age of 65 for men or 60 for women. Yet, unemployment pensions may be paid from the age of 60 for men or 55 for women, provided the person has drawn unemployment benefits for the preceding 52 weeks. Early retirement pensions are payable at 60 for men or 55 for women, if the person has been paying contributions for at least 420 months and has paid 24 monthly contributions within the last 36 months. Night-shift and heavy manual workers are allowed to retire after fulfillment of certain conditions at the age of 57 for men or 52 for women. There are no age limits for invalidity pensions.

The proportion of gainfully employed men between the ages of 60 and 65 has dropped drastically since the 1960s (from 65% in 1961 to 15% in 1990). Only 2% of men aged 65 and over participate in the labor force. Correspondingly, the occupation rate for women between the ages of 55 and 60 has been decreasing steadily (from 34% in 1981 to 26% in 1990), and 5% of women aged 60 and over are still gainfully employed (*Bericht,* 1991). Labor force participation rates in Austria for the elderly are among the lowest in the world. Changes in social legislation in the 1960s (such as the introduction of the early retirement scheme for employed persons and pension legislation for the self-employed), together with structural changes causing persons formerly employed in agriculture to move to other branches, were responsible for this reduction. In more recent times, the considerably increasing supply of labor force brought about a decrease in the supply of jobs for older persons. Job training programs for the elderly or reemployment schemes are practically nonexistent.

There are no general regulations requiring retirement at a fixed age for workers and employees of private firms, yet employers in general practice age discrimination. This is especially true with regard to hiring older unemployed persons.

Employed and self-employed persons pay regular, compulsory contributions into a pension fund; no exceptions are allowed. In addition, every employee can take out a voluntary insurance policy on a contractual basis.

HEALTH CARE SERVICES

Health insurance covers practically the entire population. A large proportion of public health expenditures is spent by the provinces and communities, especially on the construction of hospitals and operating costs not reimbursed by health insurance institutes. Apart from a small retention charge, hospital care is, in principle, free for all insured persons. Health insurance also covers treatment by doctors, medication, and medical aids. Rehabilitation and stays in health resorts and spas are granted to retired people only on a very limited basis. Treatment by a doctor is free if the patient is under contract to the health insurance institute. Otherwise the patient pays a fee and is partially reimbursed by the insurance institute. For needy persons (e.g., those receiving compensation allowances), there is an exemption from the prescription charges for (free) medications.

Since 1992, professional, qualified home nursing has been covered by the health insurance system in order to lessen the burden resting on hospitals and nursing homes (i.e., to postpone or shorten hospitalization periods).

Nevertheless, people who are chronically ill or bedfast often reach a stage where domiciliary services can no longer be effective. For these cases, requiring long-term care, provisions are made in institutions. About 20% of all Austrians aged 80 and over are accommodated in some sort of institution. It is estimated that in Austria there exist some 54,000 beds (22,000 in nursing homes and 32,000 in residential homes). This is a ratio of 55 beds for 1,000 Austrians above 65 years, a figure regarded as rather low by international standards. The distribution of homes for the elderly according to type of sponsor is as follows: municipalities run roughly half of all homes; districts and provinces run one-fifth; churches run one-fourth; and other private homes run one-tenth.

The regional distribution is very uneven; in Austria there are 2,317 communities but only 548 homes for the elderly. More than a third of those 65 and older live in cities over 100,000 inhabitants; yet, only a fifth of all homes exist in larger cities. Consequently, the mean size of the homes for the elderly in the larger cities is high; the largest single nursing home (in Vienna) accommodates more than 3,000 old people.

Differences in quality between institutions are quite pronounced. It is the exception to the rule that a home for the elderly has its own doctor, and only one-third of the total nursing staff has received full training as medical nurses (Badelt and Pazourek, 1991; Cserjan, Antalovsky, and Knoth, 1990; Winkler, 1989).

The case of nursing homes is most interesting with regard to the dual system of care in Austria. Perhaps Austria is the only European country that differentiates sharply between regular treatment of the elderly sick, on one hand, and long-term nursing care, on the other. If it is not to be expected that the medical treatment will succeed in rehabilitating the elderly, then medical treatment—as far as the health insurance system is concerned—comes to a stop. This is also true if the elderly person in need of long-term care is accommodated as a resident in a nursing home. The costs will have to be taken over by the patient and in some provinces family members and, if necessary, social assistance will contribute to costs. What is left over for the patient is a small amount of pocket money amounting to some 20% of one's pension (with a guaranteed minimum).

Familial care for frail relatives is barely compensated, neither in financial allowances nor in other benefits. Only one province, Vorarlberg, has developed such a scheme. However, a major federal reform act has proposed new ways to financially cover the risk of being in need of care. Every person in need of care will be entitled to receive cash payments at seven different rates up to a maximum of $2,000 per month. The actual sum is determined by the extent to which a person's capacity to live independently is reduced. Informal caregivers (primarily, but not necessarily, family members), as well as market-oriented social and health services, should benefit from this attendance allowance. Family caregivers will also be entitled to certain pension benefits.

HOUSING RESOURCES

The standard of housing of the elderly population is considerably worse than that of the population at large. For example, 18% of older people's dwellings (compared with only 6% of the younger population) are not equipped with bath or shower. More than half of the elderly do not have central heating (*Österr. Statistisches Zentralamt*, 1990).

There are historical, economic, and psychological reasons for this. Rents of substandard apartments (without running water and indoor toilet) still remain extraordinarily low. Housing standards for the elderly are not only inferior with regard to facilities, like baths and central heating, but these flats normally do not have elevators. This deficit may be decisive in case of impaired mobility. In Vienna, there is a program to establish elevators in old apartment buildings. There are also special improvement programs with interest-free public loans and easy terms of repayment for elderly apartment renters or owners. Improvements deal primarily with sanitation and heating. Household maintenance services (like home repair, laundry/ironing, and window cleaning) are available only in larger cities.

The question of special dwellings for the elderly, or residential homes for the elderly, is largely dependent on the area. In rural areas, one-family home ownership is very common. However, in the future the fast growing number of childless suburban and rural elderly will face severe difficulties since there are shortages of institutions and extramural services in both places (Fülöp, Schäfer, and Frisch, 1988).

In Vienna, after 1945, large complexes of public housing were erected, some including special self-contained apartments intended for elderly persons. However, these flats did not prove as popular as originally expected; there were no additional care services available, and it was felt that the local proximity between old and young did not lead to the expected reduction of the social distance between the age groups.

Since the 1960s, 30 so-called pensioners' homes were erected in Vienna. All told, 8,000 elderly men and women now live there. The average age of the residents is 82 years and getting older (Dinhof and Pilch, 1992). These old people, as a rule, are still able to manage their day-to-day activities on their own. The infrastructure in the homes offers many amenities that a citizen would not enjoy in a regular housing development. These homes for pensioners supply lodging and adequate food. In an effort to offer better medical treatment, the care wards have been systematically expanded in the 1990s. The key feature, however, is that the aged person can lead an independent life in a self-contained flat, with one's own furniture and an ability to move about freely and leave the home at all times. If necessary, tenants receive financial compensation from the social assistance authorities. The demand is very large, and long waiting lists of applicants for admission are reported.

By also opening these homes to aged people living in the neighborhood, several thousand Viennese a day are attracted to the clubs for pensioners set up in such housing. Furthermore, persons needing care as outpatients get it temporarily in the special stations of these houses.

There is a certain trend for private companies and even single individuals to set up residential homes and hostels for senior citizens on a commercial basis. Social assistance legislation prescribes that residential accommodations can be erected only with the permission of the authorities and that permission must be obtained to maintain and run such homes. This means that the social assistance authorities are faced with the obligation of supervising all these private installations. Thus, they bear legal responsibility not only for the establishment of such accommodations under the legal regulation but also for seeing that they are then run according to legal provisions. Due to understaffed authorities, supervision does not actually function so well.

SUPPORTIVE SERVICES

At least the following principles are common to all nine provincial social assistance laws (Amann, 1980):

- benefits to secure the vital needs are provided only if all other possibilities have been exhausted (no income from work, no coverage under the social insurance system);
- benefits are granted on the grounds of individual needs alone;
- benefits are intended to maintain existing family relationships and to strengthen the ability for self-help.

However, legal definitions for social services, retirement, and nursing homes, as well as the range of existing services, vary greatly between the provinces. To a certain extent this is justified since, apart from Vienna and a couple of other larger cities, Austria still is a country of small communities. Rural areas demand different kinds of social services. To give just two remarkable examples: in Burgenland, Austria's easternmost province, there is a service called "institutionalized neighborhood help." A volunteering neighbor takes on the responsibility for the care of an elderly person, is supervised by a social worker, and gets a symbolic payment by the provincial government.

In Vorarlberg, Austria's westernmost province, another unique and unconventional form of care can be found: mutual associations to provide home care for the sick and old on a purely private basis. Through this decentralized system about one-third of the province's population has an immediate right to be supported by a professional nurse in coordination with family care.

In all provinces, social services for the elderly are the major social assistance benefits. They cover all domestic health services, assistance in running the household, services for improving social contacts, recreation schemes, and homes for the aged. Unlike youth care, care for the elderly is not a separate section within the overall social welfare and assistance effort. The elderly, however, are an important group of clients cared for by the social welfare division for adults. Private and charitable services supplied by independent welfare organizations play an important role in the actual implementation of the services, cooperating with provinces and communities.

The city of Vienna, for example, is divided into ten small areas in which a coordinating center for all kinds of social and health services is set up and all types of independent providers are coordinated. This system also improves the information for the clients. Furthermore, all elderly are contacted by friendly visitors on a regular basis.

Among social services, meals-on-wheels is salient to provide adequate nutrition for the elderly. About 2% of all Austrians aged 65+ receive this service (Cserjan, Antalovsky, and Knoth, 1990). However, it is normally not offered in small municipalities and rural areas. Organized, "outdoors," congregate meal programs are practically nonexistent.

Both in terms of scope and organization, home help services are the most extensively developed services in the field of care of the elderly; 2–3% of all Austrians aged 65+ receive this service. In Vienna, home help is financed by the municipality and carried out through eight welfare agencies, having mostly partisan, but also religious and charitable (e.g., Red Cross), backgrounds. This service is usually granted for a maximum of two hours, five days a week. Since the early 1970s there has been an eightfold increase in home help caring hours. In Vienna (with a 1990 population aged 75 and over of 136,000), 12,200 clients (61% aged above 80 years, 83% living alone) were looked after in 1990. There were nearly 3,000 home helpers employed, principally fulfilling homemaker tasks but also providing certain health-related services and companionship (Cserjan, Antalovsky, and Knoth, 1990).

The importance of social services is especially marked for the very old; in Vienna, for instance, social services are the main source of support for a quarter of all persons in need over 70 years but only for less than 10% of the persons in need under 70 years (Hörl, Majce, and Rosenmayr, 1992). To repeat, the elderly are not entitled as a right to these benefits under social assistance legislation.

There are some efforts to establish linkages between health and social services (Rosenmayr, 1991). Geriatric day centers are only a recent development, and in Vienna two such settings provide various forms of therapy and combat loneliness. The centers are also concerned with rehabilitation, the assessment of medical conditions, and the maintenance of physical functioning. The centers make considerable use of transport; only 50 clients are allowed per day. In addition, a few dozen beds in short-stay care settings have been created to provide respite for caregivers or for coping with an emergency situation (Hilfs- und Pflegebedürftigkeit, 1991).

A special problem group are elderly people admitted to the hospital for treatment of a sudden illness or an accident. After successful medical rehabilitation there may be no further need for permanent surveillance, but some patients may not be able to live in their apartments completely on their own. So, in some hospitals, such elderly patients will be informed by social workers about available social services before discharge.

Ideally, upon arrival at one's flat, the discharged older person will find an already well-informed home helper who starts looking after the person's needs. There is empirical evidence that such a program yields a significant increase in use of social services by the ex-patients. There is also evidence that readmittances to hospitals—often primarily for social reasons—could be reduced through such a program.

Unfortunately, this positive example seems to be rather an exception, especially if the home-based elderly person requires both health and social supports. The ability to continue independent living arrangements relies, in the first place, on effective health care which is normally delivered by family doctors and specialists. Yet, doctors usually conceive of treatment of sickness in a rather narrow sense, and often enough they function in complete isolation from social services.

LEISURE-TIME RESOURCES

Analyzing leisure-time activities throughout the life span, one can observe a marked shift from outdoor leisure activities toward indoor activities. Elderly spend more time in activities like eating and resting and are (involuntarily) less engaged in family interactions. Watching television (76%), listening to the radio (53%), and reading newspapers (56%) are among the elderly's most popular daily leisure activities. However, mass media usage diminishes significantly beyond the age of 80 years, no doubt due to sensory impairments (Fessel, 1990).

The frequency of cultural behavior patterns among the elderly (reading books, visits to theaters, concerts, exhibitions, or museums) is rather low. Moreover, it depends largely on social class and educational level. Old age clubs run by many municipalities mainly provide opportunities for companionship and room for social activities like playing cards and chess.

Social outdoor activities that increase rather sharply with age are organized trips and excursions by bus. More than half of the elderly take part, at least now and then.

Approximately 45% of all Austrians aged 60 and over are members of pensioners' unions or senior citizen organizations (*National Report*, 1982). Nearly all these organizations for the elderly have close links with the political parties; some of them form subsections of parties while others developed as groups within trade unions. There are also senior citizen associations organized by religious denominations. From a legal standpoint these organizations usually constitute private associations, mainly financed by membership fees. Funds are also raised through certain commercial activities, like distributing travel arrangements, and through public subsidies for special purposes.

One of the major aims of these organizations is provision of opportunities for making and maintaining social contacts with peers, by arranging communal entertainments and meetings and organizing journeys and holidays. They also encourage attendance at cultural and educational meetings by providing the necessary transport and issuing tickets at special reduced prices. Usually, the programs consist of typical Austrian traditional folklore or light entertainment (circus, operetta, and so on.)

Regular lectures on subjects such as medicine and courses in arts and crafts are offered. Special advice and support are given to senior citizens wishing to attend university courses; these efforts are also supported by the Ministry of Science and Research and the official federation of universities. Senior sports (e.g., dance courses, swimming) are encouraged in a number of ways, and most senior citizen associations also arrange excursions and journeys, and their local groups run clubs.

ADVOCACY AND PROTECTION

Concerning advocacy groups, one has to bear in mind that the degree of affiliation to political parties and other organizations is traditionally high in Austria. After the end of World War II various societies and associations of older individuals were voluntarily set up. Apart from providing opportunities for leisure time, the aims of the pensioners' organizations concentrate on the provision of information for senior citizens in the form of printed matter, personal consultations, lectures, and advisory services; advice and practical support; and general public relations work with a view to fostering esteem for the elderly and recognition of their position in society.

In most cases, the pensioners' organizations hold seats and votes in the leading councils of the political parties to which they have close affiliations. They approach administrative authorities and members of both federal and provincial governments directly and also maintain contact with the elected members of local community councils and mayors. However, their actual lobbying power remains rather weak.

The officials of the branch organizations assist their members in asserting claims for benefits and in other ways. Experts can be consulted free of charge; where the assertion and recognition of Social Security claims are concerned, legal help by a lawyer is provided.

The pensioners' organizations publish periodicals for their members, carrying standing columns with the most recent information on Social Security, health insurance, special pension problems, and so on. The larger organizations have their own press departments. There are representatives of the elderly on the official board of radio and television consumers.

As far as the legal protection of the vulnerable elder is concerned, in 1983 new regulations on guardianship for disabled persons replaced the old law on deprivation of legal capacity (Ent and Hopf, 1983). As it was obvious that mostly older people were deprived of their legal capacity, the legislature sought a solution that should meet the needs of modern times. It was well known that deprivation of legal capacity of older (and disabled) people is not an adequate measure of social assistance and does not help the disabled. With the law on guardianship, rules were introduced according to which mentally disabled persons can be assisted by a guardian ("Sachwalter"), who will act for them according to the degree of their disablement. Therefore, the disabled will be deprived of legal capacity only as far as the person is actually disabled. The guardian can be appointed for certain acts, for certain kinds of acts, or for all matters concerning the disabled. The court will examine whether the person in question is mentally disabled and can or cannot look after (all or some of) his or her affairs without possible problems.

The choice of the guardian will depend on the nature and the degree of disablement and on the personal situation of the mentally disabled. Generally, the court will tend to appoint a person as guardian who is closely connected with the disabled. If, however, the nature of disablement demands special legal knowledge, a lawyer will be appointed as guardian. Specialized associations want to introduce vocational instruction and advanced training of professional guardians.

Instead of deprivation of legal capacity, compulsory detention can be imposed. The main consequence of this measure is the deprivation of personal liberty. In practice, mere dementia will suffice for such an order, although insanity is required by the law. Recent research proved that the probability of detention and long-term deprivation of liberty is directly linked with old age. Procedures take quite a long time until a formal decision is passed.

Questions on decision making for medical care and life-or-death choices are discussed within the frame of criminal law. Active, direct euthanasia—ending a person's life with his/her permission—is considered manslaughter. The reasons this kind of "support" was given to a victim can reduce the punishment. Active, indirect euthanasia—the patient voluntarily carries out his/her death with the indirect act (e.g., by making special medications available) of a physician, family member, etc.—will usually not be prosecuted. Passive euthanasia refers to allowing a person to die by not using available interventions. It is not a criminal act within the meaning of the penal code. Any duty of the medical doctor to assist the patient is of no significance if the latter determines otherwise. Moreover, such a duty does not exist in cases where the death of a patient would be prevented. Even if the old individual expressly wishes to continue life, medical doctors are not necessarily bound by that, because treatment should not become ruthless. In case of doubt, it is up to the doctor to decide what is right.

The penal code punishes homicide upon request; the person who kills another upon request is subject to a sentence of up to five years. The same holds true for aiding suicide.

In 1989, a horrifying crime shocked the Austrian public. Four women of the auxiliary nursing staff of a public Vienna hospital murdered some 40 bedridden, elderly patients. This crime lead to an intensive public discussion regarding lack of control and, in general, the problems of institutional care for the elderly. Recently, a kind of neutral "ombudsman" was installed to supervise Vienna hospitals and to secure patients' rights.

Among special legal protections against victimization of the elderly, the law on consumer protection should be mentioned. The law does not contain special rules concerning older consumers, but it is obvious that older individuals are more likely taken advantage of than other consumers. Thus, a consumer has a right to withdraw from a contract under certain conditions, especially when the contract was not concluded on the business premises. Further, certain components of a contract can be automatically null, and others be annulled if they were not expressly agreed upon.

FUTURE PROJECTIONS

As far as the public opinion in Austria is concerned, any far-reaching reduction of the welfare state (including its services for the elderly) is out of question. Despite this, the fiscal crisis of the welfare state and a certain conservative backlash in ideology have led some policymakers to recommend a strengthening of family solidarity and even a more or less pronounced "reprivatization" of support tasks. But there is no solution in a policy based on encouraging even more informal support by the kinship system, in the first place, because its full potential seems already being utilized and second, because irreversible social and demographic changes have already occurred.

To perceive phenomena, such as low fertility rates, increased divorce rates, or paid employment of women, as origins of social "problems" may be a biased view. Nevertheless, these phenomena cause problems for others, particularly for children and for the dependent elderly. Thus, we are forced to rate the future family's ability to manage support problems rather cautiously.

The rapid expansion of organized social services is symptomatic of these changes. This development toward increased utilization of formal sources of support does not mean that family and kinship are becoming unimportant or only suppliers of affection. But we should be warned not to overidealize and overburden family support networks with expectations that cannot be fulfilled.

Family interaction (including help) is more than ever determined by the wider scope and growing weight of self-definition of each individual family as a group. An individualistic mentality will impact more directly upon behavior patterns. This is particularly important in view of a self-conscious definition of familial obligation.

The point is that relations between the elderly and their families in the Austrian industrialized society of today can be understood and analyzed only when taking into consideration the intervention of the state, that is, the massive expansion of formal services.

Some kind of shared responsibility between family and state (represented in this case by social services) should be realized. They cannot live without each other, but their goals and communications may not concur. Knowledge learned by way of everyday socialization is the primary group's particular strength in the informal/formal complex. Formal organizations cannot emulate such an environment without any inconsistency. Frequently, organization members try to modify official rules, but the bureaucratic environment will allow the development of intimacy, love, and solidarity only within rather strictly defined limits.

It must be remembered that there are two target populations in caregiving policy: the elderly and their families. The elderly, due to their vulnerability to chronic disability, have one set of needs. Their families, engaged in the process of helping the older relative, have needs specific to the supportive role they have undertaken. The needs of each population may not always coincide; for example, personal sacrifices in the process of helping may eventually lead to the exhaustion of family support and demand the introduction of social services. Advice centers for caring families are still sparse. The linkage functions of the family to maintain communication lines to existing bureaucratic resources for the benefit of relatives in need of care should be much more promoted.

BIBLIOGRAPHY

Amann, A. Open Care for the Elderly—Austria. In A. Amann (ed.), *Open Care for the Elderly in Seven European Countries*. Oxford: Pergamon Press, 1980, pp. 31–59.
Badelt, Ch., and J. Pazourek. Care for the Elderly in Austria. In A. Evers and I. Svetlik (eds.), *New Welfare Mixes in Care for the Elderly*, vol. 2. Vienna: European Centre for Social Welfare Policy and Research, 1991, pp. 13–33.
Bericht über die soziale Lage 1990. Vienna: Bundesministerium für Arbeit und Soziales, 1991.
Cserjan, K., E. Antalovsky, and E. Knoth. *Altenhilfe in Österreich 1988–2011*. Vienna: Geschäftsstelle der Österr. Raumordnungskonferenz, 1990.
Dinhof, H., and Ch. Pilch. Darstellung der Altenversorgung aus der Praxis. *Aufbau-Perspektiven*, 1, 1992, p. 64.
Ent, H., and G. Hopf. *Das Sachwalterrecht für Behinderte*. Vienna: Manz, 1983.
Fessel + GFK Institut. Seniorenstudie—Allgemeiner Teil. Unpubl. research paper, Vienna, 1990.
Findl, P. Bevölkerungsentwicklung im Jahre 1991. *Statistische Nachrichten*, 47, 1992, pp. 524–539.
Fülöp, G., E. Schäfer, and R. Frisch. *Hauskrankenpflege in Österreich*. Vienna: Österr. Bundesinstitut für Gesundheitswesen, 1988.
Haller, M., and K. Holm (eds.). *Werthaltungen und Lebensformen in Österreich. Ergebnisse des Sozialen Survey 1986*. Munich: R. Oldenbourg Verlag, 1987.
Hilfs- und Pflegebedürftigkeit im Alter. *Lebensbedingungen, Versorgungsangebote, Zukunftserwartungen*. Vienna: Bundesministerium für Arbeit und Soziales, 1991.
Hörl, J. *Lebensführung im Alter. Zwischen Familie und sozialen Dienstleistungen*. Wiesbaden: Quelle and Meyer, 1992.
Hörl, J., G. Majce, and L. Rosenmayr, Familie und ältere Menschen. Unpubl. research report, Vienna, 1992.
Hörl, J., and L. Rosenmayr. Gesellschaft, Familie, Alternsprozeß. In H. Reimann and H. Reimann (eds.), *Das Alter*. Stuttgart: Enke, 1992, pp. 45–70.
Kytir, J., and R. Münz (eds.). *Alter und Pflege. Argumente für eine soziale Absicherung des Pflegerisikos*. Berlin: Blackwell, 1992.
Majce, G. Altersbild und Generationenverhältnis in Österreich. Unpubl. research report, Vienna, 1992.
National Report of Austria for the United Nations World Assembly on Aging. Vienna: Ministry for Science and Research, 1982.
Österr. Statistisches Zentralamt, *Mikrozensus Juni 1987. Ältere Menschen*. Vienna, 1989.
Report of the World Assembly on Aging, 26 July to 6 August 1982 (United Nations publication, Sales no. E.82.I.16), Vienna 1982.
Rosenmayr, L. Altenhilfe. *Ein soziales Anliegen der Jahrhundertwende*. Vienna: edition atelier, 1991.

Österr. Statistisches Zentralamt, Sozialstatistische Daten. Vienna: Österr. Statistisches Zentralamt, 1990.
Statistisches Handbuch für die Republik Österreich. Vienna: Österr. Statistisches Zentralamt, 1991.
Weigel, W., and A. Amann. Austria. In P. Flora (ed.), *Growth to Limits. The Western European Welfare States Since World War II.* Berlin: Walter de Gruyter, 1987, pp. 529–609.
Winkler, Th. Intra- und extramurale Leistungen der Altenhilfe in Österreich. Unpubl. master's thesis, Vienna, 1989.

4

BARBADOS

Farley S. Brathwaite

INTRODUCTION

Barbados is a small, middle-income, developing island state in the eastern Caribbean. It has a total area of 166 square miles and, at the 1990 census, had an estimated population of 247,282, of which an estimated 29,320 or 11.9% was elderly (aged 65 years and over). The size profile of the elderly population in Barbados (and in several other Caribbean islands) is therefore more like that of the urban industrial world than like that of countries in the lesser-developed regions of the world, a consequence of the intense modernization that Barbados has undergone over the past 30 years or so. Indeed, the elderly as a proportion of the total population has shown tremendous growth over the past 50 years, increasing from 8.8% in 1946, to 10.5% in 1980, to its present 11.9%. These trends have been explained in terms of declining fertility rates, declining death rates, increased life expectancy, and extensive outward migration of the younger population (especially during the 1950–70 period). Compared with the total population, the elderly population is growing at a much faster rate. Census data of 1990 show that the elderly are more likely to be female than male and married than single, with just over 25% widowed, with primary rather than secondary level education, and with nearly 30% living alone.

With respect to services for the elderly, there is a pluralistic or mixed approach, with provision being made by the state and by the voluntary, informal, and private sectors. There is no documented evidence of the extent of provision in the informal sector, but it is evident that the state is the main provider. In the voluntary sector, provisions are made in many instances with state assistance and/or facilitation by churches, service clubs, community groups, and other nongovernmental organizations.

Many social goods are obtained on the open market in the private sector;

prime among these is housing, followed by health care (even though the latter is available to the elderly free of cost in the state sector).

In the state sector, allocations take place, in some instances (pensions and health care), on a universalistic basis with entitlement based on age, while others (such as social assistance and personal social services) are provided on a means-tested selective basis.

In historical terms, social provisions for the elderly date back to the middle of the nineteenth century, when the state provided selective, residual relief in cash, shelter in the almshouses, medical help, food, and clothing—guided by a laissez-faire philosophy—for the needy and indigent. This was supplemented by a variety of charitable voluntary efforts by the churches and other voluntary bodies. There is also evidence of extremely limited provisions of occupational old age pensions for selected colonial public servants. However, the policy of the day was that the individual and families were solely responsible for meeting their own social needs "independently" of the state; hence, by the 1880s steps were taken in the poor relief regulations of the day to control and limit relief at all levels and to all groups. This philosophy and its related practices meant that individuals were generally expected to have their social needs met primarily in the arena of the private market dictated by the forces of demand and supply, with informal care in the networks of family also being widespread. The state and voluntary agencies played a residual role, providing for the poorest of the poor. This policy approach was dominant well into the 1960s, but during this 80-year period, 1880–1960, there was a gradual, ad hoc, incremental development of service provision for the elderly. For example, occupational pensions provided to public servants were gradually extended; by the mid-1930s a means-tested old-age pension was introduced, and by the mid-1960s a comprehensive national insurance and Social Security scheme was implemented. With respect to health, the poor relief arrangements (through the parish doctor scheme) remained in force, but the development of clinics extended these provisions, and in the early 1980s all persons aged 65 and over became entitled to free medical care and drugs. Housing provisions for the elderly have remained essentially a private market activity, but by the mid-1930s state provision of shelter for the indigent elderly in the almshouses was extended by housing welfare provisions. Finally, the period since the 1950s has seen a gradual increase in personal social services (especially in the state sector).

In summary, the development of service provisions for the elderly in Barbados has seen laissez-faire approaches giving way to increasing state involvement. Also, especially in the areas of Social Security pensions and health, development has moved from selective to universal provisions, and even in those areas of selectivity, for example, the personal social services, considerable expansion has taken place.

These developments can be explained in terms of a variety of social, economic, and political factors. Included among them are the working-class political upheavals of the 1930s; the coming of self-government in the 1950s and independence in the 1960s; the emergence in the aftermath of both these factors of a more explicit welfare state philosophy fostered not only by the emergence of similar trends in the overseas arena, such as International Labor Organization (ILO) and World Health Organization (WHO) conventions, but also by an emerging social democratic philosophy at home forged by a maturing and increasingly self-confident trade union movement. Also important was the fact that as competitive party politics became consolidated, the growth in the elderly population, with its greater probability of voting, was seen as an important political bloc. Of course, recent cutbacks in service have been influenced by international recession, the growth of supply-side economic policies, and consequential International Monetary Fund (IMF) and World Bank influenced programs and structural adjustment.

INCOME MAINTENANCE AND EMPLOYMENT

Income maintenance programs for the benefit of the elderly in Barbados include public income security programs, private retirement benefits, financial assistance for the impoverished aged and other economic benefits.

Public Income Security Programs

Public income security programs are provided through the state national insurance and Social Security schemes. There are two kinds of pensions: a contributory pension, which varies according to level of past earnings, and a noncontributory, non-means-tested flat rate pension for all those persons age 65 years and over who have not made contributions or adequate contributions and who are not in receipt of any other pension. This suggests that all persons aged 65 years and over in Barbados (except those residing in government health or social care institutions) are eligible for a National Insurance Scheme (NIS) pension, either contributory or noncontributory. Indeed, data from the 1991 returns of the NIS program show that 12,571 received contributory pensions and 15,744 noncontributory pensions, suggesting coverage of 28,321 (or 96.9%) retirement pensions among the elderly. The 3.1% not getting pensions may include those in state institutions and those not eligible for a contributory pension but getting other pensions and, therefore, not eligible for noncontributory pensions.

Private Retirement Benefits and/or Pensions

Private retirement pensions/benefits offer the best example of occupational pensions in Barbados. These are not as extensive as the public income security pensions but have shown tremendous growth in the past 30 years or so. The main occupational pension scheme in Barbados is provided by the state to public servants. In 1991–92 there were 5,742 retired public servants who received a total of BDS $63,414,920 (about $31,707,460 in U.S. dollars).

Private pension schemes for employees who are not public servants are generally of two types: employers' superannuation schemes, which are usually group schemes to which both employers and employees contribute, and annuity pensions, which are usually purchased by the self-employed. There is no exact count of the number of persons covered by such schemes, but a 1985 survey showed that there were 887 schemes, 250 of the superannuation type and 637 of the annuity type (personal communication, inspector of insurance, Inland Revenue Department, January 1993). Another such scheme is the sugar workers' Provident Fund, instituted in 1968, to cover sugar workers aged 65 years and over working on sugar estates of at least 25 acres for over 10 years. This is currently managed by the National Insurance Board.

Occupational pensions for those entitled to them may normally be drawn simultaneously with the contributory NIS pensions and are not presently taxable.

Financial Assistance Programs for the Unemployed Elderly

Financial assistance for the impoverished elderly is provided at two levels. First, the country's social assistance program, through the Welfare Department, provides, among other things, a system of cash payments to the nation's indigent. There are no age tabulations for applicants or beneficiaries of this program, but departmental reports (personal communications, Welfare Department, 1993) suggest that the elderly are a significant proportion of the beneficiaries. There are also reports (Best, 1992) about a number of voluntary, nongovernmental organizations, especially some churches, that provide cash benefits from specially established funds for some of the needy elderly in their congregations.

Second, there are also indications (Best, 1992) that some churches, from time to time, help to pay the bills—especially utility bills and land taxes—of their most indigent elderly. The extent of their voluntary input with cash grants to the elderly is not specifically known as yet, and it is clearly an area for further research.

Economic Benefit Policies

Economic benefit policies for the elderly are varied and diverse and include universally applied tax benefits: the nontaxing of pensions; special higher-than-normal personal income tax allowances for all persons aged 65 years and over; dependent relatives' allowance to young family members (which are intended to facilitate financial or other assistance by children or other relatives to their elders); and means-tested land tax exemptions for the indigent and needy elderly. Many of these benefits are now under severe threat from the effects of the IMF structural adjustment program now being implemented by the government.

In addition to these tax benefits, there are a number of other state and nonstate economic benefit policies for food, food stamps, housing assistance, subsidized transportation, and a host of other in-kind benefits. At the state level, benefits are provided mainly through the Welfare Department, and, except for the transportation assistance, are all means-tested. The in-kind benefits provided through the Welfare Department include such things as food vouchers, dentures, spectacles, and assistance with the payment of utility bills. Record keeping on these items is not done according to age, and therefore it is not possible to specify the number of elderly applicants or beneficiaries of many of these benefits. From unofficial reports in 1991, it is known that the elderly are disproportionate beneficiaries of most of these programs (personal communications, January 1993).

Assistance for transportation and utility bills is intended primarily for the elderly. In the former case, *all* elderly persons are entitled to travel free on state public transport (buses) on producing their national identification cards. The recent emergence of a larger private sector component in the public transport system has, however, created some difficulties. Assistance with the payment of utility bills, directed primarily at the elderly, is means-tested. In 1990–91, 2,976 individuals were receiving assistance with the payment of water bills, and 796 were receiving assistance with the payment of electricity bills.

At the nonstate level, assistance to the elderly with these in-kind benefits is ad hoc, varied, and apparently more widespread than anticipated. Best (1992) showed that there are a number of churches across the religious spectrum offering—admittedly on a small scale and piecemeal—in-kind benefits to small numbers of elderly persons in their congregations and/or communities.

There are also indications that other voluntary bodies offer help in similar ways. For example, the Salvation Army Meals Program is offered with the assistance of the state Welfare Department by providing meals at its headquarters and delivering meals to needy clients who cannot come to the center. Also, there is much informal individual assistance given to the elderly.

Employment Opportunities

The 1990 census indicated that 2,256 of the 29,322 elderly in Barbados were in the active labor force (employed or seeking work), and from a 1982 survey (Brathwaite, 1986) it was found that even larger proportions wanted to continue working. Nevertheless, there are no programs explicitly directed at job retention, redesign, or training in reemployment for the elderly. This absence can be viewed in the context of extremely high rates of unemployment in the national context. Indeed, it is not uncommon to hear various groups, including trade unions, express the view that the retirement age should be lowered as a means of providing greater employment and promoting opportunities for younger workers.

However, there are employment, placement, and training programs at the national level that elderly persons are entitled to use. Since data from these programs are not available according to age, the extent to which the elderly use these services is unknown. It should be emphasized, however, that there are a few small-scale initiatives in which day-care centers are providing opportunities for production of handicrafts, training in the same, and marketing of the products.

HEALTH CARE SERVICES

General Health Care System

Health care provisions for the elderly must be understood in the context of the general health care system. Officially the system is described as consisting of primary, secondary, and tertiary sectors, with services being provided in both the public and private sectors. These structural aspects and financial arrangements are presented in the following table.

Table 4.1
Health Care System Structure in Barbados

Type of Health Care	Public Sector	Private Sector
Primary	• Free walk-in service at all polyclinics • Emergency care at the general hospital	• Private general practice • Private clinics
Secondary	• Specialist consulting services at the general hospital	• Specialist consulting services in private hospitals/clinics • Private care in public hospital
Tertiary	• Free care within general and geriatric hospital system	• Care in private hospitals or private care in the public hospitals
Other	• National drug service providing drugs at subsidized rates for the general population, free to the elderly and specified vulnerable groups	• Private health insurance, which is still relatively underdeveloped, used by small proportions of the population

Health care in the public sector is provided free, financed out of general public revenue and with a specifically instituted health levy paid as part of one's national insurance contribution. It is expected that there will be changes under the current structural adjustment program.

In the private sector, health care is provided on a fee-for-service basis, and there are provisions for the private use of public sector health care facilities/ services at highly subsidized rates. Private health insurance, which is one method of meeting these costs, is a very recent development and is still very limited.

Acute care services for the elderly are provided in both the public and private sectors. Chronic care services for the elderly are also provided publicly and privately, and there are publicly funded provisions for those who may require medical care overseas. Facilities within the general health care system consist of two acute general hospitals in the public sector, one in the private sector, and a number of private clinics. There are also five geriatric hospitals and a number of private nursing homes. There are no specific provisions for hospice care, but the Cancer Society of Barbados is planning to build a hospice. In the meantime, hospice-type care takes place in the general hospital, the nursing homes, the geriatric hospitals, and the homes of patients.

Institutional Care of the Elderly

Institutional care is provided in both the state and private sectors. In the public sector five district hospitals (previously called almshouses, now sometimes referred to as geriatric hospitals) provide health care, some custodial care, and services in occupational therapy and social recreation. These resources cater to approximately 900 persons, the overwhelming majority of whom are elderly. There is also a leprosorium for eight persons. In addition, there is a senior citizens' home administered by the National Assistance Board and catering to about 30 elderly persons who pay (if possible) a nominal monthly fee. This home also provides ancillary services in social recreation and physical therapy and may be seen as offering minimum custodial services.

At the private sector level, about 14 nursing homes cater to just under 250 persons. These are essentially health care institutions, but they provide residual custodial care and cater primarily to the financially better-off elderly, as monthly rates may be as high as BDS $1,800 (US$900). In both state and private sector care, the demand for these services far outweighs their availability.

Health Care Services for Elderly Persons Living in the Community

Health care services for the elderly in the community are provided primarily in the state sector by the polyclinics as part of their general practice services and preventive services, both part of the outpatient services offered by the Ministry of Health. The Registered Nurses Association also provides a voluntary service with some state financial assistance. While there are no formal tabulations by age on these services, it is expected that the elderly are the prime beneficiaries. There are a few voluntary and informal sector initiatives, and, according to Best (1992), churches mobilize health care for some elderly persons.

HOUSING RESOURCES

The provision of, and access to, housing for the elderly must be seen within the framework of national housing policy. In this, housing needs are met primarily within the private sector, with the state being essentially a facilitator and regulator and making a small input as direct provider.

Data on selected housing indicators in relation to the elderly (Brathwaite, 1989) show that 82% live in owner-occupied housing, 9% in rental units, and 9% in institutions. Of the 2,346 elderly in rental accommodations, an estimated 400 get rental assistance from the state Welfare Department rental assistance program; of the 1,874 remaining elderly, 1,174 (or 5%) live in institutions providing care and custody, and 500 live in state-provided welfare houses.

Private Market Adjustments

The private housing market has not made any identifiable, specific adjustments to accommodate the elderly; hence the elderly—like all other groups—are expected to satisfy their housing demands in the open market. However, a large proportion of the elderly have used the system for purchase/credit of building materials to do piecemeal, incremental construction of their homes in the informal sector, as is the case with most other lower-income groups in the society.

Congregate Housing

Congregate housing is specifically designed for an elderly group, but communal services (such as a central kitchen, a dining room, housekeeping, social and health services) do not presently exist in Barbados. However, in a recent Inter-American Development Bank (IADB) feasibility study, proposals for halfway homes and group homes were put forward but have not yet been implemented (Brathwaite, 1989).

Retirement Housing Communities

Retirement housing communities do not presently exist for the elderly in Barbados. Such developments seem relatively distant, given the economic circumstances for the vast majority of the elderly.

Specific "Housing" Arrangements

A number of agencies provide housing, shelter, and/or related services to the elderly. The state geriatric hospitals, while having a specific health function, play a distinct housing and custodial function, in that many of the residents are there primarily because they are in need of housing and shelter. Homes for the elderly, like the geriatric hospitals, are really places of refuge for the abandoned and homeless elderly. One of these, a hostel, is run by the state under the National Assistance Board and provides accommodation for approximately 30 persons (the vast majority of whom are elderly). Other institutions serving similar functions are in the voluntary care sector and sometimes receive government financial assistance. They presently accommodate 39 persons. Private nursing homes, which were mentioned earlier, are officially deemed health institutions but also serve as a source of housing and shelter for *some* of the residents and are included in a housing strategy.

Housing Welfare Programs

There are three basic elements to housing welfare programs, provided mainly by the state. Programs organized by the National Assistance Board (NAB) are the largest ones and provide housing benefits for the needy, primarily elderly. Services include repairs to owner-occupied housing and the temporary *loan* of welfare houses to those in need, without homes, or whose houses are beyond repair. The specific benefits can include assistance with carpentry, masonry, electrical installations, well digging, painting, plumbing, and debris removal. The 1990–91 NAB report showed a stock of 514 welfare houses, 226 of which were repaired in 1990–91. During this same period, 25 houses were restored, 567 private houses were repaired, and 26 new welfare houses were built.

The record scheme is operated by the National Housing Corporation (NHC), and NHC tenants aged 65 years and over whose only source of household income is the minimum state noncontributory retirement pension are exempted from the payment of monthly rentals. An estimated 200 persons benefited from this scheme in 1988–89.

The third housing welfare scheme is operated by the state's Welfare Department, which offers rental assistance to persons renting housing in both the state and private sector who, through means-testing, are deemed in need. The majority of these are said to be elderly.

Community Services for the Elderly in Their Houses

Several community-based services permit the elderly to remain in their homes, rather than being institutionalized, and these are offered by the state, the voluntary, and (to a considerable, but not fully documented, degree) the informal sectors. The largest known of these is the Home Help Service provided at the state level by the NAB. The program, which is means-tested, provides domestic assistance with shopping, personal hygiene, housecleaning, visits to the doctor, the fetching of water, and laundry services for the indigent and needy elderly. It is national in distribution and serves approximately 750 to 800 clients, the majority of whom are female and live alone.

One Home Help agency in the private sector deals mainly with the identification and placement of home helpers for more affluent clientele who are able to pay for such a service. There are indications (Best, 1992) that such services are also provided on a limited scale by voluntary organizations such as the church.

Financial Assistance, Tax Benefits, and Other Economic Help

Other economic aid takes various forms and is provided in both the state and the voluntary sector. At the state level, the main assistance is in the area of waiving the annual land taxes for those deemed to be in need. Data from the land tax department do not specify age categories, but the elderly are believed to be disproportionate beneficiaries. Also in the state sector, the Welfare Department provides means-tested assistance with the payment of water and electricity bills to the needy elderly. In the voluntary sector, the Soroptomist of Barbados provides assistance with water connections to the homes of indigent elderly persons in the north of the island.

SUPPORTIVE SERVICES

Supportive services, directed at helping the elderly to maintain independent living, exist in both the state and voluntary sector and are provided by a diverse set of agencies.

Information and Referral Services

There is no centralized information and referral service for the elderly in Barbados, but these services are offered within most social work agencies, especially in relation to, or on behalf of, elderly persons who seek services that the agencies do not provide. To the extent that there is specialization in the provision of services for the elderly, the Welfare Department, the National Assistance Board, and the geriatric hospitals are the ones to which most elderly persons can be expected to turn for information and the ones most likely to provide information and referral services.

There is, however, a clear need for a specialized agency providing education about what services are available, since there are indications that some old people are not fully aware of, or knowledgeable about, services that are available. Such a service could, however, be set up as an arm of the NAB or the Welfare Department.

Nutrition Programs

There are a limited number of nutrition programs; however, they are not intended for the elderly exclusively (who are the major beneficiaries). A program provided jointly by the state and a voluntary sector organization (the Salvation Army Meals Program) has two elements: provision of hot daily meals (91 in 1991–92) to aged and indigent persons at the army's headquarters and a meals-on-wheels service for housebound, needy elderly persons in urban Barbados.

Programs to Care for the Elderly in Their Own Home

Besides the home help service and the district nursing service, respite care services exist and are provided on an ad hoc basis by the district (geriatric) hospitals, the NAB Senior Citizen Home, and some churches.

Program of Care for the Elderly outside Their Own Homes

There are no senior service centers or day hospitals, but there are day-care centers organized at both state and voluntary levels. These are a comparatively recent development. Most geriatric hospitals provide one of these centers, and the NAB, in conjunction with several churches and community centers, offers about three of these throughout the island. Furthermore, there is evidence (Best, 1992) that a few churches do offer day-care facilities, and the Soropotimist International Senior Citizens Village provides a facility as well. It is not certain how many persons are beneficiaries, but the numbers are growing rather rapidly. These day-care centers make provision for a number of activities where the elderly can use their skills, develop new ones, and engage in social recreation.

Mental Health Services for the Elderly

Mental health care of the elderly is provided within the framework of national mental health systems and consists of inpatient care at the psychiatric hospital and the geriatric hospitals and a district service operating out of the decentralized polyclinics' service, the general hospital, and the psychiatric hospitals.

Given the absence of comprehensive age tabulations, it is not known what proportion of those receiving care is elderly, but it is assumed that the elderly constitute a significant proportion of those in the psychiatric hospitals. For example, in a 1986 study (PAHO/IADB, 1986b), it was found that in 1984, 9.8% of all admissions to the psychiatric hospitals were persons over 60 years of age, compared with 14.0% in 1981. Some of the residents in the geriatric hospitals are there for mental health reasons, and it is reasonable to assume that some of those in the outpatient services are elderly, but in neither instance are there exact numbers or proportions.

Counseling and Social Work Services

Counseling and social work services are provided to the elderly in both the specialized elderly services and in the general social work services on the island, most notably by the Welfare Department, the NAB, and the medical and psychiatric social work services. In the voluntary sector, churches and other agencies provide "informal" counseling for the elderly (among other groups), and bereavement counseling groups are just beginning to be developed.

LEISURE-TIME RESOURCES

Most of the leisure-time activities of the elderly take place within the informal setting of networks of friends, family, and neighbors. Available research data (Brathwaite, 1986) suggest that the vast majority of old people engage in such leisure-time activities as watching television, listening to the radio, reading, shopping, visiting, and churchgoing and are not members of formal organizations.

Volunteerism and Voluntary Organizations in Relation to the Elderly

Volunteering cannot be described as a well-organized activity in Barbados, and therefore it is not possible to get an accurate picture of its extent. Yet, it is known that there are a large number of voluntary organizations in the country (suggesting that volunteering may be more widespread than is assumed). The role of the state in this is not very formalized, except that there are instances in which the state jointly provides services by making financial contributions. The role of the state is more facilitative, in that the Charities Act 1979 was implemented to facilitate the regulation, and perhaps the growth, of charitable voluntary organizations by enabling them, among other things, to claim tax deductions on their expenses. In addition, there are provisions within the income tax legislation for individuals to claim tax deductions for sums paid as covenants to voluntary organizations.

Voluntary activity is essentially carried out by nongovernmental organizations like churches, service clubs, youth and community groups, some private sector organizations, and individuals.

A number of voluntary organizations provide services for the elderly, churches and service clubs being the best known. Best (1992) identified a number of voluntary services provided for the elderly by churches: day care, literacy programs, arts and crafts, referrals, donations of cash, in-kind benefits, visits (especially to shut-ins), telephone ministry, companionship transport services, meals, feeding, and occupational therapy.

Social Recreation and Socialization

Provisions for social recreation and socialization are made largely through the voluntary sector, although the state also makes an input. The church can provide or organize concerts, parties, sightseeing tours, car rides, and other activities. A major input of these voluntary agencies into social recreation for the elderly comes at Independence Day and Christmastime, when widespread activities are organized for the elderly.

There is also evidence that day centers play a role in providing opportunities for acting groups. At the more formal state level, opportunities for social recreation and socialization exist at the geriatric hospitals, the NAB Senior Citizens Home, and the NAB Day Care centers, which has a social recreation program in which monthly sightseeing tours are organized for clients of the Home Help Program who live alone.

Educational Opportunities

The specific provision of educational opportunities for the elderly is almost nonexistent, but there are a large number of small-scale programs, especially in the day centers, where the elderly may develop skills in arts and crafts. The extent to which there are provisions in the informal sector is not clear. Of course, there is widespread provision for adult education at the national level from which the elderly may benefit.

ADVOCACY AND PROTECTION

There are few specially organized efforts for the advocacy, protection, and security of the elderly in Barbados. However, in recent times, the National Council on Aging (a voluntary nongovernmental organization) was formed with such objectives in mind. This body receives a small government grant and has been working very closely with Help Age International. At present, efforts seem essentially educational, with some effort directed at building community support and helping the elderly to mobilize their own protective efforts and resources.

In addition, two other groups—the Association of Retired Officers of the Services and Education (AROSE) and the Barbadian Organization of Retired Nurses (BORN)—also have advocacy and protection functions on behalf of the elderly. Much more research into their activities, their efforts, and their success is needed.

However, it would be misleading to suggest that these advocacy and protection functions may not reside elsewhere, and the Welfare Department (being the main national social work agency) points out that it performs such functions.

Legal Assistance

In Barbados, it is expected that an individual will look after his or her own legal needs in the private market, and the elderly are no exception. In the specific area of advice about wills, contracts, and policies, there is good reason to believe that this may be obtained in the private market. But it is also reasonable to assume that for those in special need, much of this takes place on an informal basis in the family or among close friends and through state agencies like the Welfare Department. There is a national legal aid scheme for which the elderly may, technically speaking, be eligible, but benefits seem more likely for defendants than victims.

Victim Assistance

There are no specifically organized victim assistance schemes for the elderly within the criminal justice system. One assumes that such assistance would take place only within the informal networks of family and friends or through the Welfare Department.

FUTURE PROJECTIONS

In looking toward the future, it is first necessary to examine the achievements in Barbados. As a middle-income developing country, Barbados has done remarkably well in providing services to meet the needs of the elderly in relation to income maintenance, housing, health, and the personal social services. That it has devised a pluralistic approach to the provision of these services is also an achievement. Free access to health care and a universal pension scheme are no small achievements for a developing society. Notwithstanding these achievements, however, there are significant difficulties in these services. Qualitative evaluations of the nonuniversalized services suggest that in most instances demand exceeds supply, and this is a real difficulty within the means-tested services. There is also evidence of pockets of poverty among the elderly.

In terms of needs, therefore, expanded provisions in those remaining areas of deficiency are necessary, but the specter of structural adjustment threatens such possibilities. There is also a need to address implementation issues. The most pressing needs, however, seem to be in the area of advocacy and protective services. Services to promote job retention, job training, and reemployment are also essential.

At an administrative level, statistical data in the official departmental reports must be upgraded to permit age tabulations, so that the elderly can be compared with the rest of the population. The voluntary services are much too diverse, and there is need for some coordination to prevent duplication and to facilitate referrals. There is also a dire need for an analysis of the informal system of care—its structure, provisions, and efficiency.

BIBLIOGRAPHY

Best, Carlyle. "Voluntary Social Policy in Action: The Church and the Care of the Elderly." Caribbean Studies Thesis, University of the West Indies, Barbados, 1992.

Brathwaite, Farley. *The Elderly in Barbados.* Bridgetown, Barbados: Carib Research and Publications, 1986.

———. "Social Problems of the Elderly in Barbados: Implications for Health Care." In H. Fraser and M. Hoyos (eds.), *Barbados Medical Update 1988.* Barbados: University of the West Indies, 1988.

———. "The Elderly in the Commonwealth Caribbean: A Review of Research Findings." *Ageing and Society* 9(3), 1989a.

———. "Housing Services for the Elderly in Barbados" (Mimeo). Paper presented at a Pre Congress of the Fourteenth Meeting of the International Association of Gerontology on "Coping with Social Change: Programs That Work." Acapulco, Mexico, June 1989b.

———. "The Elderly in Barbados: Problems and Policies." *Bulletin of the Pan American Health Organisation* 24 (3), 1990.

Chief Medical Officer (Barbados). Annual Reports of the Ministry of Health.

National Assistance Board (Barbados). Annual Reports.

National Housing Corporation (Barbados). Annual Reports.

National Insurance Board (Barbados). Annual Reports.

PAHO/IADB. Health Services for the Elderly in Barbados 1986a, ATC/SF-2521-BA.

———. Mental Health Services for the Elderly in Barbados 1986b, ATC/SF-2521-BA.

Welfare Department (Barbados). Annual Reports.

5

CANADA

*Victor W. Marshall and
Blossom T. Wigdor*

INTRODUCTION

Canada is a nation of about 27 million persons, of whom 10.9% are aged 65 or older. There are 10 provinces, and some northern territories also have a high degree of governmental independence from the central government in Ottawa. The country is vast, but much of its northern areas is largely uninhabited. The great bulk of the population lives close to the southern boundary of the country, and the population as a whole is highly urbanized. Forty percent of older Canadians live in urban places with populations of .5 million or more. In the rural areas, the concentration of elderly can be upward of 20% of the population in small towns but is very low otherwise. Older people tend to move off the farms into small towns, while young people tend to leave such towns and migrate to larger cities (see McDaniel, 1986, p. 41).

The population is culturally diverse, reflecting the presence of indigenous people at the time the Europeans arrived, the fact that these Europeans were initially from two "charter groups," the French and the British, and a continuing history of significant immigration. Immigrants currently constitute 16% of all Canadians, but over 35% of persons aged 75 and older and 22% of persons aged 65–74 (Gauthier, 1991).

There is a constitutional division of powers between the federal government and the provinces. Income security for the elderly is a federal concern, although some provinces have programs that supplement the national programs. Health care is in the provincial domain, although payment standards are enforced under the federal Canada Health Act. In this chapter, we describe the main lines of services for the elderly; space does not permit a detailed account that fully recognizes provincial differences.

The Role of the Elderly

In the international context, Canada has a relatively young population when compared with industrialized countries, with 10.9% of the population aged 65 or older. However, it is an aging population. Growth in the next two decades will be particularly strong among the oldest, aged 85 or older; but as the baby boomers become old, the ratio of very old to merely old people will decline. By 2031, almost 1 in 20 Canadians will be aged 85 or older, but almost 1 in 4 will be aged 65 or older (Stone and Fletcher, 1986). Canada's post–World War II baby boom was the largest in the world. Gender differences in life expectancy at birth and even at advanced ages result in a preponderance of women. In 1991, 58% of those aged 65 and older and 69.5% of those 85 and older were women. The median age of the population is now 33.5 years and will rise to about 42 by 2051 (Statistics Canada, 1992).

As of 1990, 76.6% of men aged 65 and older and 42.2% of women in this age group were married. Women were more likely (43%) than men (16%) to live alone. In terms of educational attainment, 7.5% had a university education, and another 23.3% had some form of postsecondary education (Lindsay and Devereaux, 1991).

In Canada, age 65 is generally taken as the dividing line demarcating old age for both men and women. This is based on the history of governmental income security provisions and legislative and legal provisions concerning retirement age. In 1991, 11.3% of males and 3.5% of females aged 65 or older were still in the labor force. In the age 55–64 bracket, the comparable figures are 62% and 35.7%. These reflect a strong decline over the 15 years since 1976 in male labor force participation after age 54 but a slight increase in participation rates for women (Gibson and Foot, in press).

In the political context, Canada has not been characterized by an active "gray power" movement (Gifford, 1990). Nonetheless, public opinion data have consistently shown that more than three-fourths of adult Canadians support the government's providing to the elderly more "social services and benefits from the government than they do now" (Cook et al., in press). An analysis of the stance toward the elderly and toward the young taken in newspaper and magazine stories shows a highly positive attitude toward the elderly and a virtual lack of stories reflecting intergenerational conflict (Marshall, Cook, and Marshall, in press; Cook et al., in press).

The Formal Structure of Care of the Elderly

When Canada was formed in 1867, responsibility for health services (with a few exceptions), social services, housing, recreational services, and education was assigned to the provinces (Schwenger, 1987). The British North American Act, which established the constitutional framework, made no mention at all of welfare services (Chappell, 1987, p. 489). Poor relief was administered, if at all, by local municipalities. In the ensuing 125 years, there was increasing encroachment of the federal jurisdiction on provincial territory (see Chappell, 1987; Guest, 1980; Le Clair, 1975; Schwenger, 1987).

The ground was laid for shifting control more toward the provinces when, in 1977, the federal government enacted the Established Programs Financing Act. This replaced a previous conditional matching grants program for hospital and medical services with a block grant fund. The funds transferred might have been spent on social programs in health; however, they produced little change because they provided no incentives to the provinces to redirect spending in this way (Mendelson and Sullivan, 1990).

Health and hospital care, in compliance with the Canada Health Act, are therefore provided without fee for service. Typically, care in nursing homes and homes for the aged is provided at government expense but with the resident billed for the "hotel" component. There is provincial variability in ownership of long-term care facilities, with extensive private sector ownership of nursing homes in some provinces and also active participation in the provision of extended care settings by municipalities and religious and charitable organizations. These, however, will be reimbursed by provincial ministries of health or community and social services. The billing to the client will always be such that a person relying on the public income security system will still have funds left over for some personal consumption or discretionary spending after the hotel component has been paid.

Provincial variability also characterizes home care services. Manitoba provides community-based care at no cost; Ontario generally charges a fee (often on a sliding scale); other provinces represent both alternatives.

In Canada, when fees are charged, there is typically an exemption or sliding scale based solely on income testing, often by simple declaration. Means testing, which includes an inventory of a person's assets, is not generally employed.

Canada is classified by political economists as a welfare state. Most benefits, including health services and, to a somewhat lesser extent, social services are provided as basic rights without means or income testing and regardless of ability to pay. Health care and most long-term care are provided on the basis of need rather than age (Marshall, Cook, and Marshall, in press). The regional diversity of Canada and the complex federal-provincial constitutional character of the society lead to a diversity of service provisions. Overall standards, though, are quite high by international standards.

INCOME MAINTENANCE AND EMPLOYMENT

Income Maintenance

Canada identifies seniors as those 65 and over, and most benefits are targeted to that group. Seniors in Canada receive their income primarily from government transfer payments. In 1988 seniors received only 16% of their retirement income from private pensions and about 21% from investments. Old Age Security (OAS) is the basic universal benefit to which all individuals over 65 who have been resident in Canada for 10 years are entitled. Full benefits are available only to those having lived in Canada 40 years after the age of 18. OAS is taxable income. This is supplemented by an additional allowance, the Guaranteed Income Supplement (GIS), to which individuals whose cash income is either only OAS or minimal from other sources are entitled, to the maximum GIS or a portion. GIS benefits are not taxable. Six out of 10 provinces, as well as two territories, provide income supplements to those senior citizens who have only OAS and GIS as sources of income. The federal GIS benefit tends to pay proportionately more to a senior living alone. Provincial "top-up" programs do not reduce support levels for persons who are married. The OAS (to June 1992) was indexed to the rate of inflation and was basically $374.44 (US$267), while at the same time, the federal GIS was $444.98 (US$318) for a single pensioner and $298.84 (US$213) if married to a pensioner, $444.98 (US$318) if married to a nonpensioner. The provincial and territorial top-ups varied from a low of $219 (US$156) a year in Nova Scotia to a high of $1,200 (US$857) a year in the Yukon and Northwest Territories (double these amounts for couples). About 15% of all seniors in Canada currently receive provincial and territorial supplements.

However, this does not reflect the true number of low-income pensioners, as some jurisdictions with large numbers of seniors (such as Quebec) do not provide the supplementary income for seniors. In Canada, 43% of seniors were receiving either full or partial GIS in 1990, 38% of males and 48% of females (National Advisory Council on Aging [NACA], 1991). For individuals with high incomes, the OAS benefit is taxed back on a graduated scale for those whose income is $50,000 (US$35,714) or more per annum.

As well as income supplementation programs, some provinces and territories provide shelter assistance for seniors and tax breaks (such as sales tax credits, property tax grants, relief from land taxes), and help with home heating. There have been recent changes in regulations to eliminate these benefits for higher-income seniors.

Canada has a second tier in the retirement income system, which is a compulsory, contributory pension plan known as the Canada/Quebec Pension Plan (CCP/QPP). All members of the paid work force must contribute to this plan. The two plans (Canada and Quebec) have essentially the same features. At retirement, workers receive a pension equivalent to 25% of their average annual lifetime earnings, up to a maximum, which is adjusted each year in line with increases in the Consumer Price Index. The maximum benefit for 1992 was $631.11 a month. Contributors to both plans have the option of retiring at any time between the ages of 60 and 70. If the contributor retires before 65 the benefit is reduced by .5% for each month before the person's 65th birthday. If the contributor retires between 65 and 70, it is increased by the same formula.

The third tier of the retirement income system is income received from private pension plans. Employees contribute during their working years to a plan, as does the employer. Vesting now takes place after two years and 25 years of age, but portability of private pensions is not yet part of the system. Only about half of all Canadians have access to pension coverage at work. The figures available (1986) show that 56% of men and 44% of women employed full-time were covered by occupational pension plans (NACA, 1991). In 1986, only 10.5% of the income of women and 20.1% of the income of men over the age of 65 came from private pension plans. Some plans, similar to CCP/QPP, also pay survivor's benefits and disability allowances.

Employment

Mandatory retirement still exists in Canada in 7 of its 10 provinces and territories. The mandatory age of retirement is, for the most part, 65 years of age. Quebec and Manitoba have abolished mandatory retirement, as has the public service of the federal government. New Brunswick has, for the most part, abolished mandatory retirement but allows variation in employee-employer agreements.

For those who do remain in the labor force, late-life employment is likely to be in part-time work and often at lower-paying service jobs, to supplement pension income or for personal satisfaction. Women may be working part-time in the 55-64 cohort because of heavy caregiving responsibilities. There has been little activity in redesigning jobs specifically for older workers, but flextime and part-time or shared work are available in a number of companies and industries (Tindale, 1991).

The federal government has in place a Program for Older Workers Adjustment (POWA). This program attempts to help older workers who are laid off and remain unemployed, until they can access pensions and after they have exhausted the unemployment insurance benefits.

There are limited training and retraining opportunities for older workers. In late 1985 the federal government did put in place an Innovations Program for Older Workers to offer wage subsidies and training opportunities to help older workers to rejoin the work force. This regionally limited project was successful, and in the 1990 budget, additional funds were targeted to train older workers. However, programs are evolving slowly and tend to be limited in scope and accessibility. There are significant regional variations. There are also scattered initiatives developed by volunteer organizations and Canada Manpower to offer reemployment services and opportunities.

HEALTH CARE SERVICES

A recent, comprehensive study of the Canadian health care system notes that it "is organized the same way as most health care systems in industrialized countries. It differs from most countries in its funding rather than in its medical care or its health promotion activities. Health services in Canada are funded predominantly through taxation, and it would appear that the national health insurance system has resulted, to some extent, in governments gaining more control over their health expenditures than some other nations'' (Crichton and Hsu, 1990, p. 3). Health care services in Canada are provided in a system that is heavily medicalized: physicians are the primary gatekeepers to health care, the hospital is the major budgetary component of health care, medical care is highly technological, and community-based services are a small component of the system.

About 85% of older Canadians see a physician at least once a year. Only .8% receive meals-on-wheels, 3.5% receive transportation services, 4.3% receive homemaker or home help services, 4.3% receive assistance with shopping or banking, and 2.7% receive nursing or other medical calls at home (Chappell, 1988, p. 75).

MacPherson (1990, p. 367) notes that "since the early days of gerontology there has been increasing ideological conflict between health ministries, which seek to care for the dependent elderly (often within institutions), and social service ministries, which seek to provide services that will keep the elderly in the community." Divided or unclear lines of authority lead to lack of coordination among agencies, rivalry over control of insufficient resources, and gaps in the continuum of care.

In all provinces, attempts are being made to shift from predominately medical care to a broader health care stance and to move care more extensively out of the institutional setting (hospital, nursing home, and so on) and into the community. This is thought to be particularly appropriate in the area of services for the aged. Whether community-based care should be run from the hospital or from the community, external to the hospital, is a matter of debate in some provinces (Marshall, 1989, ch. 2). Fried (in press) argues that the claim that community care reduces costs is unfounded since it only frees up beds for more expensive and acute patients. Hospital costs account for about half of Canadian medical care expenditures in general and are a large component of health care costs for the elderly.

Universal medical care is provided for all Canadians and is essentially an insurance system covering hospital and physician costs. The average value for seniors of these services is estimated at $2,000 (US$1,430) per year. Medicare is provincially funded but relies heavily on federal transfer payments to the provinces and meets standards agreed to in a federal-provincial accord.

Seniors in all provinces receive most prescription drugs free, through provincial drug benefits programs.

HOUSING RESOURCES

Elderly Canadians choose, for the most part, to remain in their own homes as long as possible. Home ownership is high among Canadians and particularly for those 65+. Approximately 68% of those 65+ are homeowners and most of these (72%) own their homes mortgage-free. A higher proportion of women are renters than men. There is significant variability by province. Home ownership ranges from about 80% in Nova Scotia and New Brunswick to about 53% in Quebec.

There are a number of housing options for seniors and the federal government, through Canada Mortgage and Housing Corporation (CMHC), the leader in social housing by providing low-rent mortgages for a variety of housing initiatives. The CMHC assists householders in need who cannot obtain affordable, suitable, and adequate shelter in the open market. It administers about 343,750 social housing units and beds targeted to families, older Canadians, and special needs groups (including 7,300 index-linked mortgage co-op units). It also provides national direction for the ongoing administration by the provinces of about 300,000 public housing units. In cooperation with the provinces, there are a number of federal-provincial programs of special interest to seniors, such as (1) a nonprofit housing program; (2) The Rent Supplement Program; (3) the Residential Rehabilitation Assistance Program (RRAP); (4) the Residential Rehabilitation Assistance Program for Disabled Persons; and (5) the Emergency Repair Program.

Housing Options

Provinces and municipalities, as well as charitable nonprofit organizations, have been active in providing a variety of housing options for seniors. These range from subsidized housing co-ops, housing with some services (e.g., meals or health unit on the premises) to homes for the aged, nursing homes, and chronic care hospitals.

The private sector has been involved in retirement homes, retirement complexes emphasizing complete life-style changes, condominiums, group homes, and flexible housing. The availability of any particular housing option varies considerably in terms of rural and urban settings and by region. The large urban centers are more likely to have a range of options.

Innovative arrangements are group homes, some Abbeyfield-like arrangements (a type of congregate living which emphasizes social interaction), and home sharing. Ethnic communities often provide retirement homes, housing with services, and nursing homes.

About 8% of seniors live in various types of institutions. However, there are policies in place to try to keep seniors in the community as long as possible, and there is a variety of community services available to assist Canadian seniors to remain in the community. These services vary in availability and quality from area to area and tend to be more plentiful in urban areas. Meals-on-wheels programs are well developed and are often provided by volunteer and nonprofit groups. Other services from homemaking, friendly visiting, shopping, and banking to yard maintenance and house repairs are also available. A number of seniors' groups have evolved that exchange services. Some municipalities will clear snow for seniors, if requested.

There are a number of tax benefits, such as a real estate tax rebate and financial assistance to rehabilitate or repair homes. These programs vary from province to province.

Canada has a fairly high institutionalization rate due to climate, transportation difficulties, and government payments for care in long-term care settings, as well as previous federal transfer payments, which paid for beds rather than services. However, the present policy is to shift more emphasis and services to maintain seniors in the community. Many communities, in addition to a variety of services, have special transportation for handicapped or disabled elderly.

SUPPORTIVE SERVICES

Canada has a history of providing a wide range of support services for seniors, and almost every type of program exists, at least in parts of the country. However, there is significant variability across the country, with rural-urban differences as well as regional and provincial differences. Most provinces have provincial government offices or secretariats that can be contacted for information and distribute print information. The federal government in Ottawa, through the Seniors' Secretariat, Health and Welfare Canada, is a source of information. Furthermore, there are municipal resources in most towns and cities for information and services, as well as nonprofit social service agencies.

Programs such as meals-on-wheels and wheels-to-meals (congregate dining), as well as a range of homemaking and home care programs, exist. Many of the home care and homemaker programs are either paid for under the health insurance plan under certain prescribed conditions or subsidized where necessary.

In terms of community-dwelling elderly, in addition to in-home services, a strong network of senior citizens' centers provides information, educational opportunities, and leisure activities. These have formed an Association of Senior Centers. There are day hospitals, day care, and respite care beds. There are also hospice (palliative care) units, and palliative care is also delivered in the home. Assessment units exist in some locations. However, not all services exist in all regions, nor are they necessarily organized into a well-integrated system to make them easily accessible.

Many self-help groups are also available, for example, for widows, for caregivers, particularly of Alzheimer victims, and for a range of other problems. Many communities have organized information and review programs related to medication use. A national organization, the Canadian Coalition on Medication Use and the Elderly, is composed of 18 organizations, including seniors, health care professionals, and the pharmaceutical industry, working together to provide information and more effective behavior in all three groups mentioned, in order to have more appropriate use of medication by seniors.

Mental health services exist, although they are not as likely to be found in rural and more remote areas. In urban areas, there are regular mental health services, most of which are covered by the universal health insurance plan. Geriatric psychiatrists are in short supply, but multidisciplinary teams exist in some areas. They are usually hospital- or clinic-based and provide assessment in the home as well as inpatient and outpatient services. Therapy is offered as well as assessment. All forms of social services and counseling to seniors and their families exist, although there is still a dearth of health care and social service professionals who have special expertise in counseling and treating seniors.

In urban areas at least, few seniors experience a lack of community-based services. Connidis (1985) assessed community service utilization and unmet needs as reported by a random sample of the elderly in London, Ontario, a typical medium-sized city. Only 7% of her sample used any social service, although some used more than one (the most frequently used were homemaker services and visiting nurse services, and the most frequent reason was posthospital care). When she asked, "Are there any services which you require but cannot find or cannot afford?" only 17 individuals of the 400 in the study replied affirmatively. Most "unmet needs" mentioned were in the area of cleaning, gardening, and home maintenance.

LEISURE TIME RESOURCES

There are a large number of programs for use of leisure time after retirement. Canadian seniors give a great deal of time to volunteering in a wide range of activities. In the 65–74 age group, 15% of the women reported volunteer work. There are no data on the actual number of hours worked, although for some it is reported to be high.

The federal government, through Health and Welfare Canada, has a New Horizons program, which funds groups (minimum 10) of seniors to initiate and carry out leisure activities and programs that improve independent living and support self-help community programs.

Educational opportunities are also popular leisure activities, with most universities offering free tuition for undergraduate courses to individuals 65+. Other initiatives by seniors are the Third Age Learning Association, Learning in Retirement, Elderhostel, and many lecture series. These are offered at all levels through school boards, community colleges, and universities. Some seniors take courses leading to degrees. For example, the oldest student to receive a degree at the University of Toronto through part-time studies was 100 years old! However, most educational programs are for the sake of enhancing one's own knowledge and tend to focus on current events like history, art, and music. Many include travel tours with a focus on a particular subject, for example, Renaissance art and opera.

Senior centers also provide opportunities for recreation, varying from card playing and dances to handicrafts, hobbies, woodworking, and educational opportunities. Some of these community activities and educational programs are sponsored by religious or ethnocultural groups. A mobile library service is also provided in some areas for shut-ins. Many cultural and entertainment events offer reduced rates for seniors. Public transit also offers seniors' rates in most cities. A wide range of opportunities for companionship is widely publicized. Nevertheless, there are still individuals who feel isolated and, for a variety of reasons, do not feel able to take advantage of the range of opportunities offered.

ADVOCACY AND PROTECTION

Elder abuse is an important issue for policymakers in the Canadian aging field. Statutes exist in several provinces but do not clearly define abuse in the legislation. No statutes explicitly refer to financial abuse (McDonald et al., 1991, p. 9). However, most forms of financial abuse of the elderly would be prohibited under the Criminal Code of Canada. McDonald et al. refer to three types of social protection. One form of protection for seniors is through adult protection programs. These vary provincially in Canada, and the legislative base generally lacks a compulsory reporting clause. Community-based agencies must balance the need to protect vulnerable seniors against the respect for privacy. As a second type of protection, some agencies dealing with domestic violence offer special programs targeted at seniors. One national survey of elder abuse found that 32% of elder abuse victims were "not very aware" or only "somewhat aware" of public legal services that might help them (Podnieks et al., 1989, cited in McDonald et al., 1991, p. 71). A third type of protection is through formal advocacy programs. The Advocacy Center for the Elderly (ACE) in Ontario is an example of an agency that provides legal advice and also serves as an intervenor in public policy discussions. In 1985–86, it provided advice to over 2,000 individuals and made about 1,500 referrals (McDonald et al., 1991, p. 73). Ontario has been judged a leader in Canada, but advocacy services are, nonetheless, viewed as "fragmentary" and "less than adequate" (McDonald et al., 1991, p. 75; Ontario Ministry of the Attorney General, 1987, p. 5).

Legal procedures governing power of attorney and related issues vary from province to province. In most provinces, power of attorney can be exercised only so long as the donor is mentally incompetent (Flett, 1988, p. 48). McDonald et al. (1991, p. 43) conclude that only three Canadian provinces have satisfactory legislation concerning guardianship (Ontario revised its legislation in 1992). The major weaknesses are a lack of clarity about criteria for appointment of a guardian and specification of powers and duties. A major flaw, addressed in the new Ontario legislation, is a failure to provide limited or sector-specific guardianship or substitute decision-making powers. Ontario now makes this provision. There is not as yet any legal recognition of documents, such as living wills, relating to "dying with dignity."

FUTURE PROJECTIONS

Canadian scholars have addressed the question of whether health and social services, including financial support, can continue to be provided for the aged in an aging society. Their general conclusion is that there will be no crisis in service provision but that population aging should cause policy concern. Evans (1985) has observed that the majority of Canadian demographic forecasts of health care costs predict a rise in per capita health care costs but that this rise will be slower than the general expansion of the economy. Denton, Li, and Spencer (1987), based on a range of possible population aging scenarios and assuming that the level of service intensity for health care remains constant within single-year age and sex categories, acknowledge a substantial impact on health care costs in the long term. However, they see any economic changes within the next decade or so as caused by changes in service intensity (see also Auer, 1987a, 1987b).

Examining a broader set of services, two economists from Health and Welfare Canada project that the "burden" of social expenditures will be relatively constant until 2011 and then rise sharply as the baby boomers enter old age. In addition, they forecast that the economy will grow rapidly enough to accommodate these expenditures so that "the burden of financing social spending falls well below today's levels" (Messinger and Powell, 1987, p. 570). However, their estimates may have to be revised in view of the slowing in economic growth in Canada in the 1990s.

Foot (1984) estimates that it costs about 2.5 times more to support an older person than a younger person, and he further points out that in Canada support of the young has been primarily a private sector responsibility while support of the old has been primarily a public sector responsibility, such that 72.3% of expenditures provided to the old come from the federal government.

The term *community* is often equated with *family* in policy usage. Aronson (1985) has suggested that women may be the hidden victims of our failure to adequately provide care for the elderly. She cites federal government policy documents that reflect an ambivalent position toward women as caregivers. She also notes that everyday practices of those who provide social and health services apply eligibility criteria and make discretionary decisions that are predicted on the assumption that women ought to provide care for the elderly.

It may be that the reason Connidis (1985) found so little utilization of formal services and even less unmet need is that the services are being assumed by family members, most often women. In any event, Canadian data (Marshall, Rosenthal, and Daciuk, 1987) do show that most older Canadians, as well as middle-aged Canadians, do not believe the family should be the major provider of care. They prefer family relationships free from dependency concerns.

Finally, the changing multicultural composition of Canadian society has implications for service delivery. Today fewer than 40% of immigrants to Canada come from Europe, which was formerly its major source (Ujimoto, 1987). Calls for ethnically specific services may actually be calls for community-based services, given the geographical concentration that characterizes many ethnic groups in Canada. Immigrant communities may contribute new models of services to the Canadian cultural mosaic. They may also contribute to a fragmentation of service delivery, further exacerbating the existing difficulties of coordination.

The future of services for Canada's aging population is difficult to predict. It will, however, be influenced greatly by some specific issues: the ongoing debate between medical and social models of care, and the growth of a health promotion approach; dynamics of institutional versus community care as these relate to Canadian values; the implication of the family in care for the elderly; and growing recognition that Canada is ethnically diverse (Marshall, in press).

Canada is a wealthy nation able to meet the services needs of its aging population. However, reallocation of wealth from one age group to another is no simple matter, given the jurisdictional differences in responsibility for services targeted to the different age groups. Demography, therefore, will not alone determine future services for the elderly in Canada. Large-scale economic changes and accompanying political pressures may act to lessen the public commitment to services for the elderly. For example, in the North American context, Canada allocates a relatively large proportion of public funds to social services in general, including those to the elderly. New economic alliances with the United States and Mexico, however, force Canada to compete with countries less willing to allocate public funds for social services.

Canada has developed an enviable network of health and social services. The challenge will be to improve the coordination and integration of these services and assure that they are equitably accessible across the nation. Furthermore, the current economic climate presents threats to maintaining the existing level of service. The choices that will be made will be greatly influenced by political forces.

BIBLIOGRAPHY

Aronson, Jane. (1985). Family care of the elderly: Underlying assumptions and their consequences. *Canadian Journal on Aging* 4 (3): 115–125.

Auer, Ludwig. (1987a). Canadian Hospital Costs and Productivity. Appendix A, *Aging with Limited Health Resources.* Proceedings of a Colloquium on Health Care. Ottawa: Economic Council of Canada, pp. 179–185.

———. (1987b). *Canadian Hospital Costs and Productivity.* A study prepared for the Economic Council of Canada. Ottawa: Minister of Supply and Services Canada.

Chappell, Neena L. (1987). Canadian income and health-care policy: Implications for the elderly. In V. W. Marshall (ed.), *Aging in Canada: Social Perspectives.* 2d ed. Markham: Fitzhenry and Whiteside, pp. 489–504.

———. (1988). Long term care in Canada. In Eloise Rathbone-McCuan and Betty Havens (eds.), *North American Elders. United States and Canadian Perspectives.* Westport, Conn.: Greenwood Press, pp. 73–88.

Connidis, Ingrid. (1985). The service needs of older people: Implications for public policy. *Canadian Journal on Aging* 4 (1): 3–10.

Cook, Fay Lomax, Victor W. Marshall, Joanne Gard Marshall, and Julie E. Kaufman. (in press). Intergenerational equity and the politics of income security for the old. In Ted Marmor (ed.), title not yet finalized. Washington, D.C.: Urban Institute Press.

Crichton, Anne, and David Hsu, with Stella Tsang. (1990). *Canada's Health Care System: Its Funding and Organization.* Ottawa: Canadian Hospital Association Press.

Denton, Frank T., S. Neno Li, and Byron G. Spencer. (1987). How will population aging affect the future costs of maintaining health-care standards? In V. W. Marshall (ed.), *Aging in Canada: Social Perspectives.* 2d ed. Markham: Fitzhenry and Whiteside, pp. 553–568.

Evans, Robert G. (1985). Illusions of necessity: Evading responsibility for choice in health care. *Journal of Health Politics, Policy and Law* 10 (3): 439–467.

Flett, D. (1988). *Review of Programs for Frail Elderly Persons, Persons with Dementia and Their Caregivers.* Prepared for Elderly Services Branch, Ontario Ministry of Community and Social Services by the DPA Group, Inc., Ottawa.

Foot, David K. (1984). The demographic future of fiscal federalism in Canada. *Canadian Public Policy* 10 (4): 406–314.

Fried, Bruce. (in press). Finding a course for Canada's health services system. In A. Kruger, D. Morley, and A. Schachar (eds.), *Public Services Under Declining Resources.* Jerusalem: Magnes Press of Hebrew University.

Gauthier, Pierre. (1991). Canada's seniors. *Canadian Social Trends* (Autumn): 16–20.

Gibson, Kevin, and David K Foot. (in press). Population aging in the Canadian labour force: Changes and challenges. *Journal of Canadian Studies.*

Gifford, C. (1990). *Canada's Fighting Seniors.* Toronto: James Lorimer.

Guest, Dennis. (1980). *The Emergence of Social Security in Canada.* Vancouver: University of British Columbia Press.

LeClair, Maurice. (1975). The Canadian health care system. In S. Andreopoulos (ed.), *National Health Insurance: Can We Learn from Canada?* New York: Wiley, pp. 1–96.

Lindsay, Colin, and Mary Sue Devereaux. (1991). *Canadians in the Preretirement years: A Profile of People Aged 55–64.* Ottawa: Statistics Canada, Housing, Family and Social Statistics Division, Ministry of Science and Technology.

McDaniel, Susan A. (1986). *Canada's Aging Population.* Toronto: Butterworths.

McDonald, P. Lynn, Joseph P. Hornick, Gerald B. Robertson, and Jean E. Wallace. (1991). *Elder Abuse and Neglect in Canada.* Toronto: Butterworths.

MacPherson, Barry. (1990). *Aging as a Social Process.* 2d ed. Toronto: Butterworths.

Marshall, Victor W. (in press). Services for the aged in Canada. In A. Kruger, D. Morley, and A. Schachar (eds.), *Public Services Under Declining Resources.* Jerusalem: Magnes Press of Hebrew University.

Marshall, Victor W., with the assistance of Susan Rappolt and Seanne Wilkins. (1989). *Models for Community-Based Long Term Care.* Report prepared for the Social Policy Directorate of the Policy, Communications and Information Branch, Health and Welfare Canada.

Marshall, Victor W., Fay Lomax Cook, and Joanne Gard Marshall. (in press). Conflict over generational equity: Rhetoric and reality in a comparative context. In V. L.

Bengtson and W. Andrew Achenbaum (eds.), *The New Contract Between the Generations*. New York: Aldine DeGruyter.

Marshall, Victor W., Carolyn J. Rosenthal, and Joanne Daciuk. (1987). Older parents' expectations for filial support. *Social Justice Research* 1: 405–424.

Mendelson, Michael, and Terry Sullivan. (1990). Impediments to reorienting health policy. Paper presented to the C.H.E.P.A. Health Policy Conference, Producing Health, Niagara on the Lake, Ontario.

Messinger, Hans, and Brian J. Powell. (1987). The implications of Canada's aging society on social expenditures. In Victor W. Marshall (ed.), *Aging in Canada: Social Perspectives*. 2d ed. Markham: Fitzhenry and Whiteside, pp. 569–585.

NACA (National Advisory Council on Aging). (1991). *Economic Situation of Canada's Seniors*. Report. Ottawa.

National Council of Welfare. (1990). *Pension Reform*. Ottawa: Minister of Supply and Services Canada, cat. H68-24/1990E.

Ontario Ministry of the Attorney General. (1987). *You've Got a Friend: A Review of Advocacy in Ontario*. Report of the Review of Advocacy for Vulnerable Adults. Toronto: Queen's Printer for Ontario.

Podnieks, E., K. Pillemer, J. Nicholson, J. Shillington, and A. Frizzel. (1989). *National Survey on Abuse of the Elderly in Canada: Preliminary Findings*. Toronto: Office of Research and Innovation, Ryerson Polytechnical Institute.

Schwenger, Cope W. (1987). Formal health care for the elderly in Canada. In V. W. Marshall (ed.), *Aging in Canada: Social Perspectives*. 2d ed. Markham: Fitzhenry and Whiteside, pp. 505–519.

Statistics Canada. (1992). *The Nation*. Ottawa: Statistics Canada, cat. 93–310.

Stone, Leroy O., and Susan Fletcher. (1986). *The Seniors Boom: Dramatic Increases in Longevity and Prospects for Better Health*. Statistics Canada Population Studies Division, Health and Welfare Canada Office on Aging and Secretary of State of Canada Social Trends Analysis Directorate. Ottawa: Supply and Services Canada, cat. 89–515.

Tindale, J. (1991). *Older Workers in an Aging Work Force*. Ottawa: National Advisory Council on Aging.

Ujimoto, K. Victor. (1987). The ethnic dimension of aging in Canada. In V. W. Marshall (ed.), *Aging in Canada: Social Perspectives*. 2d ed. Markham: Fitzhenry and Whiteside, pp. 111–137.

6

CHINA

Cai Wenmei, Song Yuhua, Luo Xiaoyui, and Jiang Leiwen

INTRODUCTION

The Role of the Elderly

The Definition of Old Age

What is considered old age varies between countries because of different social, economic, and historical situations and conditions. The Chinese State Council issued laws regarding the elderly in 1978. The first article of the Temporary Law of the Retirement and Resignation of Workers clearly stipulated that old people (males at age 60 and females at age 55) who took part in revolutionary work and had 10 or more years of continuous work experience be allowed to retire. This is still the standard of old age in China.

However, for the purpose of international comparisons, the First Chinese Gerontology and Geriatrics Seminar, held in 1964, determined that 60 would be the starting point of old age. In 1981, the Second Gerontology and Geriatrics Seminar proposed that the standard starting point of old age should be changed to the age of 65. In its policies and scientific research, China currently uses 60 years as the standard starting point of old age.

Perception of the Elderly

China is an old country, with several thousand years of historical civilization. Traditionally, Chinese people respect, support, and love the elderly. Respect is more important than support (which results from respect). The elderly who are living with the younger generation can enjoy family happiness. During the 40 years after the foundation of the People's Republic of China, this kind of traditional virtue has developed even further.

China's constitution stipulates that the elderly should enjoy the rights of being materially supported by the state and by society. Furthermore, the Criminal Law, the Civil Law, the Marriage Law, and the Inheritance Law also stipulate that the elderly are to be supported and protected. Thus, the legal rights of the elderly are defended by specific documents. As China is in the process of changing from a traditional agricultural society to a modern industrial society, the elderly are very eager to contribute something in their old age. They expect to continue contributing to society within the range of their capability. They want to demonstrate their social values by their behavior.

Demographic Characteristics

According to the data from the 1990 census, China has a total of 97,250,000 people over 60 years of age. This accounts for 8.6% of the total Chinese population. In 1990, Chinese life expectancy for females at birth was 72.3 years, and for males it was 68.6 years.

For those between 60 to 64 years of age, males number more than females. However, after 65, females number more than males, and the sex ratio between men and women steadily decreases with the increase of age. Among very old persons (over 85 years of age), two-thirds are females.

In 1990, the average education level of the Chinese elderly was fairly low. Among them, 70% were illiterate or semiliterate. Education at the junior-middle school level, and over, accounted for only 7.2%. The average education level of older males was higher than that of older females. The average education level of the elderly in the 60–64-year-old age group was higher than that of the elderly 65 years old and over. This shows that levels of literacy and education among the elderly are gradually increasing.

From the 1990 census, it was found that three-fifths of the elderly had spouses, less than two-fifths of the elderly were widowed, and the proportion of single and divorced people was very small. The proportion of widowed elderly females was 2.2 times higher than that for elderly males (51.5% versus 23.6%).

The employment rate of the Chinese elderly was 28.4% in 1990 (among this, the rate for the group 60–64 years old was 45.7%, and for the group 65 years and over, 19.1%). The main concentration of these people was in agriculture, forestry, fishery, and animal husbandry industries. The employment rate of the elderly male was 44.2% (among this, the rate for the group 60–64 was 63.3%, and for the group 65 and older, 32.6%). The employment rate for elderly females was 14.1% (among this, the rate for the group 60–64 years old was 27.2%, and for the group 65 and older, 7.9%). According to census data from 1982 and 1990, the distribution of the occupations of the elderly had changed and the proportion of workers in agriculture, forestry, animal husbandry, and fishery had increased. This trend reflects the fact that younger generations transferred from these occupations to become industrial and commercial workers. The trend is also consistent with the literacy levels and health conditions of the elderly.

Of all living arrangements for the elderly, 50% of the elderly reside within three generation households; 58% of such households are in rural areas, and

Table 6.1
Monthly Income of the Elderly (%)

Income (yuan)	City	Town	Rural
None	19.8	24.1	—
Under 15	3.2	5.8	9.5
16–25	4.3	8.4	26.7
26–45	8.7	11.3	44.6
46–70	15.8	14.5	14.9
71–100	20.9	16.2	3.3
101–150	16.7	14.2	.8
151–200	7.0	4.3	.2
200 and more	3.6	1.1	.1

Source: Population Science of China, 1988.

42% are in cities and towns. Two generations living together is the arrangement for 29.2% of all the elderly; 26.9% of such households are in rural areas, and 73.1% are in cities and towns. Old-age couples living together is the arrangement for 12.9% of the elderly and single-person households account for 3.4% of all living arrangements for the elderly.

In a 1987 survey of Chinese over 60 years of age, the elderly were questioned about their own health status. Three-fourths of the elderly thought that their own health status was fair or better, 17.6% indicated poor health, and 9.3% indicated very poor health. The city sample was similar to the rural sample (Population Science of China, 1988).

The 1987 sampling survey data showed that the economic resources of the Chinese elderly came mainly from pensions, children, and work income. In cities and towns, the main economic resources of the elderly were from pensions provided by the state and enterprises. Financial help from children and from work incomes were only supplementary forms. In rural areas, the elderly lived on their work incomes, but assistance given by children was also quite important.

Table 6.1 shows the monthly income status of the elderly. According to 1987 estimates on China's realistic life levels, below 45 yuan ($12 U.S. dollars in 1987) is low income, 46 to 100 yuan ($12–$27 U.S. dollars) is medium income, and 101 yuan ($27 U.S. dollars) and above is high income. Thus, the elderly in the city who have low incomes account for 36.0%, medium incomes account for 36.7%, and high incomes account for 27.3%. In towns, low incomes account for 49.7%, medium incomes account for 30.7%, and high incomes account for 19.6%. In rural areas, low incomes account for 80.9%, medium incomes account for 18.2%, and high incomes account for 1.1%. This shows that there is a considerable economic income gap between the elderly living in the city and those living in rural areas.

Table 6.2 shows the economic position of the elderly in their families. The economic position of the elderly in the family is connected with whether they

Table 6.2
Economic Position of the Elderly in the Family (%)

Category	City	Town	Rural
Dominance*	41.5	39.9	18.7
Partial Dominance	22.7	21.9	18.4
Dominating Oneself	13.3	14.2	13.2
Without Dominance	18.5	20.5	49.7

*Dominance refers to the rights a person enjoys, although the categories of dominance are (subjective) abstractions.

Source: Population Science of China, 1988.

have fixed economic resources. It was found that 41% of urban elderly had dominant economic positions in the family, compared with 18% of the elderly in rural areas. While 18.5% of urban elderly were without economic dominance in the family, this was true for 49.7% of rural elderly. Thus, the economic position in the family of the Chinese elderly living in the city or town is much higher than that for the elderly in rural areas.

The Formal Structure of Care to the Elderly

In Chinese cities, the source of care to the elderly is divided into two categories: support by the state and support by the family. With regard to such support, forms can be divided into concentrated support, separate support, and family support.

Concentrated Support

Concentrated support refers to the elderly who are relatively concentrated in support places of all kinds. They may spend the twilight of their lives in social welfare "Respect the Elderly Homes," in elderly apartments, and in other places. These support places are scattered within city, district, street, and neighborhood levels. According to statistical data from 1978 to 1986, social welfare homes in cities developed quite steadily (from 577 units in 1978 to 797 units in 1986) (Zhang, 1992).

The State Department of the Civil Administration held a Conference of the State Community Service in 1987 and in 1989 and promoted the development of services for the elderly. Up to 1987, there were 7,001 places caring for the elderly run by street committees throughout the country. In addition, 39 private "Respect the Elderly Homes" were developed (Xi, 1991). Up to 1989, the number of such homes found in cities or town collectives was 7,746. They were distributed in 5,986 towns and streets, had 137,681 beds, and supported 97,540 elderly people.

According to the different needs of the elderly, concentrated support can be divided into two forms: free support and support at one's own expense. Free support is provided for the elderly who have no fixed income and no child or spouse, and are generally placed into the "Respect of the Elderly Homes" sponsored by street or neighborhood committees. Those who are supported at their own expense are the elderly who are childless and have no spouse but have a fixed income and the elderly who have special difficulties. Some examples are the elderly who are childless or whose children live separately, who have bad relationships with children, or who have difficulties in living circumstances. The elderly can live in elderly apartments, if they apply and sign an agreement with a related agency. Most of the apartments for the elderly have good environments and good quality of service and are welcomed by the elderly. Presently, people from all walks of life are using such opportunities.

Separate Support

Separate support means that the state provides the fundamental expenditure for the elderly who have no income, are childless, have no one to depend on and no employment capability, and live in their own home. The main forms of support are the "service groups for fixed households" and the "life service stations." The service group for fixed households provides services through vertical and horizontal forms. The vertical forms are organized by neighborhood committees. Each group consists of three to five persons who are neighbors to the elderly. The horizontal forms are organized by members, cadres, staff, or students belonging to community enterprises or public unit organs of the communist Youth League, union, or militia. They are also called the "warmth sending group."

Up to 1988, 51,000 service groups for fixed households provided service to 88,000 old persons who had no income, were childless, and had no one upon whom to depend (Zhang, 1992). This is an efficient form of support, and the care of the elderly depends on the social forces about them. It is also presently the main means, in Chinese cities, for supporting such impoverished and dependent elderly.

Family Support

Family support is provided for the elderly who are retired or have no fixed income. It includes three forms: the elderly living with children, those living alone, and those living in day-care centers. The day-care center for the elderly is a new structure adapted to the process of family-size nuclearization and to the increasing number of two-career young couples (who have no time to care for elderly during the day). Such centers not only keep the traditional way of family support but can also solve problems for the younger generation. There are increasing needs for the development of such centers.

The rural citizens of the People's Republic of China enjoy the rights of being supported by the government (of the township and village collective) if they are old, ill, widowed, handicapped, or unable to work. These rights are called "five guarantees," which include food, clothing, fuel, free education, and burial expense. Such older persons can be cared for in households called "households of five guarantees," a kind of Social Security Chinese-style, whereby the people are supported by the state or the collective.

INCOME MAINTENANCE AND EMPLOYMENT

In 1988, there were over 21 million retired people in China. The Chinese government has devoted much attention to labor insurance and the social welfare of the aged. The Government Administration Council (State Council after 1954) released the Labor Protection Regulations of People's Republic of China in 1951, which provided old-age insurance for the workers and staff members of all the state-owned enterprises and collective enterprises in the urban areas. The regulations were adjusted and revised in 1953, 1958, 1978, and 1983. Apart from the retirement system, there is another system, "withdrawal system," which started in 1978 and provides the veteran cadres with full salary (and other welfare) when they withdraw from their work. The regulations and stipulations have played an important role in guaranteeing the basic life of aged workers and staff members.

Workers and staff members of state-owned units can get an average of 127.5 yuan (US $34.46) every month when they must leave their jobs to care for a seriously ill relative and 61.3 yuan (US $16.57) when retired. In 1989, an investigation showed that a person retired or "withdrawn" from a state-owned unit received an average of 119.4 yuan (US$32.24) per month, including life allowance, from the government (China National Committee on Aging, 1989b). Apart from superannuation, they also got other government allowances, such as for medical treatment and funeral expenses.

The Chinese government started considering setting up a Social Security system in early 1985, which has been included in the country's "Seventh Five-Year Plan" of economic and social development. Presently, the government is searching for a practical Social Security system which is economically bearable for the country. However, emphasis should be given to the role of the family and neighbors in providing for the aged in mutual aid in difficult times.

The employment of the aged includes mainly two forms. First, some specialists and high officials can work until 65–70 if they are needed to work continuously and also if they are in good health. Second, they can find new jobs after retirement or "withdrawal." By reemployment, on one hand, the aged can give full play to their knowledge and rich experience; on the other hand, they can get some payment to support their lives. Governments at all levels are always ready to help the elderly find chances to do something for society, such as organizing some of them to participate in writing the history of the Communist party or local chronicles. Many associations have been set up by the aged, such as the Association of Retired Engineers, the Association of Retired Teachers, and the Mobile Medical Team of Retired Doctors. Such organizations enable the aged to contribute to society. In addition, some of the aged are reemployed by units or organizations to set up consulting service offices, private clinics, and different kinds of schools. For example, in Beijing, 15 old people set up a center for exchange of personnel. In four years after its establishment, the center has helped 2,073 old people to find new jobs. In Shanghai, there have been more than 1,200 enterprises founded by old people, which produce more than 90 million yuan profit to subsidize the old people (China National Committee on Aging, 1991b).

There is still no retirement system in rural areas of China. Generally, farmers still participate in some physical work after they are 60. They mostly engage in agricultural activities, while a few are employed in industrial and commercial enterprises. The associations of the aged in rural areas have done some work in encouraging the aged to participate in social and productive activities.

Until the end of 1991, the country had more than 2,000 third-year schools purposely opened for the aged to renew their knowledge and learn new skills. But with the large aging population of China, with comparatively low education levels, these training services are really far from enough.

HEALTH CARE SERVICES

Health services for the elderly in China are provided by the nationwide medical and health network from the central government down to the grass-roots levels (which serves the entire population). It is a three-tiered medical service network embracing municipality, district, and neighborhood levels in the urban and county areas and township and village levels in rural areas. There were 132,000 outpatient departments and 60,000 hospitals with 2.6 million beds (averaging 2.3 per 1,000) in China in 1989 (China Research Center on Aging, 1992). The situation is better in urban than in rural areas. As the nationwide survey in 1987 showed, there were 4.32 hospital beds per 1,000 urban residents in total, but there was a demand for nine hospitals beds for every 1,000 urban aged residents (which accounted for 12.8% of the total urban population). Obviously then, the shortage of the hospital beds for the whole population (including the elderly) has been great (China Academy of Social Sciences, 1989).

In order to ameliorate such a shortage, especially of the chronic care facility beds, very good alternatives have been created by Chinese medical workers. These include running "home medical beds" by medical institutions at various levels and providing home-visit medical services to those residents who are chronically ill and have difficulty in mobility—mostly the elderly. There were 855,308 "home medical beds" in China in 1990.

Among the existing medical and health institutions in urban and rural areas, the majority of big and medium-sized ones (at and above county level) are under state ownership. Private practice is also allowed to serve as a supplement to the state and collective-run institutions. Only about 0.4% of the Chinese aged population received institutional care in 1990.

Medical expenses for the aged in China are covered in three ways. First, public health services provide free medical care, which is enjoyed by veteran servicemen and retirees from governmental departments and industrial enterprises. Second, medical services are received at the patient's own cost. The majority of the elderly in rural areas and those who do not have permanent employment in cities pay for their own medical services. Third, partial public medical services are provided to employees in small or collective-owned enterprises and to family members of those who enjoy public medical services.

According to a sampling survey of the aged in 1987, among the urban aged population, 51.2% enjoyed public health services, 22.1% enjoyed partial public health services, and only 26.7% had to pay for their medical services. Among the rural aged, 2.2% enjoyed public health services, 3.1% enjoyed partial public services, and 94.7% had to pay for health services on their own (Population Science of China, 1988).

A new system called fund-raised cooperative medical care seems quite hopeful. Early studies show the increasing rate of participation in the fund-raised cooperative medical care system. There has also been found to be a high degree of satisfaction among rural residents with the present system of medical care services in China.

HOUSING RESOURCES

Since 1978, the Chinese government has paid much attention to the people's housing problem, and the investment in housing increases every year. By 1988, the size of newly built housing—in only a decade—exceeded the total size of units in the 30 years after liberation. The average housing area per person increased from 5.3 square meters in 1981 to 9.0 square meters in 1987, and the housing conditions of the elderly have improved correspondingly. According to the Population Sampling Survey of Elderly (60 and over) in 1987, in cities there were 43.8% of the elderly families whose average housing area per person was under 8m and 27.3% whose average housing area per person was over 12m. The corresponding figures of the index in towns and in rural areas were 37.9% and 55.0%, respectively (Population Science of China, 1988).

The housing policies of urban areas and rural areas in China are quite different and are reflections of the housing problems of the elderly in these two geographic areas.

Most rural old people live in the house they built by themselves in an area that was allocated to them by the collective. The number of the rooms and the style of the house depend on their family's economic ability. The usual house is single-story with three to five rooms and is built with bricks and tiles. No rent is required. In some more affluent villages, clusters of residential buildings, designed and built by the collective, have already appeared. There are kitchens and bathrooms in each house. The rent is still free, but there are charges for water and electricity. About 2% of the elderly who do not have their own dwelling live in their children's home, supported by the children.

The houses in the city mostly belong to national enterprises and administrative organizations. Urban old people may still remain in their house, provided by the original unit, if they stay at the same place after retiring and pay rent every month. If a person after retirement is settled in another town, city, or province, then the authority of the new settlement area must solve the housing problem as best as possible. The houses of these retired cadres that need repairing or expanding will enjoy the priority to be listed in the local program (as self-raising funds permit construction and management by the new authority for the older person). The houses of other retired people will also be listed in the capital construction program and be solved in a united way. Those who have difficulties in their housing arrangements, after going back to rural areas, may get a certain sum of subsidy for housing from the original units.

The Department of City Construction has been planning to construct synthetic buildings for the elderly since the middle 1980s, in order to meet the changes of social structure, life-style, family forms, culture development, and population-age structure. Many facilities are set up on the first floor of buildings and include such things as snack counter, dining room, entertainment room, and medical and social services. These services are convenient and add to the quality of life for the elderly. Money is charged for services.

Consideration is given to the fact that housing should be convenient for married children to take care of elderly parents (i.e., a building will form a new pattern: two core families—when separated—and a vertical-relationship family—when necessary to merge). These efforts are in their exploratory stage for the coming aged problem in China.

While carrying on the tradition of the family's providing for the old people, departments (concerned with the development of community services) organize community service volunteer teams to serve incapable old people in their own dwellings. The elderly may pay a small amount of money or receive such assistance free. In some especially difficult situations, door-to-door services will be provided to widowed elderly persons, regardless of their ability to pay.

The scattered houses of widowed old people in urban areas can be repaired by a civil administration organization and residence committee. Such housing services for the widowed elderly in rural areas are provided by the village committee.

SUPPORTIVE SERVICES

Supportive services for the elderly mainly refer to the most basic social and medical services. It has become a rule in China that the family plays a main role in taking care of the elderly, along with efforts by the collective and the state.

In 1982, the State Council approved the foundation of the China National Committee on Aging, whose purpose was to safeguard old people's interests, give consideration to their lives, help them play their parts in life, and instruct the old to work concretely. So far, 27 provinces and municipalities, directly under the central government and autonomous regions, have set up Committees on Aging. Over 92% of prefectures (including cities therein) have established Old Age Societies. Thus, a national old-age network gradually has been formed to provide opportunities for the aged. Such committees, at all levels, propel old age welfare services by relying on the strength of society.

In 1986, the Old Foundation of China was established to raise and administer funds, promote research on aging problems, and initiate old age welfare work (for instance, to create special flats, recreation centers, hospitals, recovery centers, marriage introduction agencies, and special schools for the elderly). Also, efforts were made to offer living and tourist services to the elderly as well as legal advice. Branches were set up in several cities and towns in China.

Both national and local welfare organizations and old folks' homes provide full-time personnel for taking care of the elderly in daily life. With regard to those lonely old people scattered in cities, there are voluntary groups comprised of citizens working in various enterprises and institutions. Young Pioneers and members of the Communist Youth League tend specific old persons. They focus on the "three fixed"—personnel, home, and work—and the "five management"—food, clothing, shelter, transportation, and medical care. They help the elderly wash and sew clothes, buy and prepare food, maintain houses, go to hospitals, and so on. The childless and infirm old persons enjoy the "five guarantees"—food, clothing, medical care, housing, and burial expenses—provided by the government. Those living in rural areas are cared for by relatives or neighbors who are organized by village committees.

Many old people still live with their own families. In the face of the change of family structure and size, the issue of how society will provide services for the elderly living in families has been put on the national agenda. Some local groups have founded flats for the elderly. As long as they pay certain standard costs, they can move in and enjoy high-quality services in food, living, medical care, learning, and entertainment. Some locations have established age-care centers serving those elderly whose children work during the day and are not able to care for their parents at such times.

At present, China is still a developing country, and health care facilities cannot meet all the needs of the people. However, the central and local health departments have already taken a series of measures for the elderly to alleviate the difficulty of seeing a doctor. It is rather common for the elderly to take priority in registering for examinations and getting medicine. To ensure the old people's physical and mental health, some "Trust and Consolation Associations" have been set up. Experts are invited to form voluntary psychological advice groups to provide counseling for the aged. The "Old Age Health Association," the "Institute of Old Age Health Research," and the "Old Age Recovery Center" have emerged in some places. These organizations hold lectures on health longevity and resisting senility and ensure that the aged patients receive the best of care. In Shanghai, for example, a service network for elderly mental patients has been formed.

It has been found that 40% of Chinese old people have no spouse. In order to improve their living quality, matchmaker agencies for the aged were set up in the early 1980s in dozens of cities throughout China. Through 1987, Beijing (as one example) had 43 such organizations and had helped 254 elderly couples to marry.

In order to encourage the best supportive services and develop good habits of respect, esteem, and care for the aged, the Chinese mass media have made a significant contribution. More than 30 newspapers and magazines are specially for the aged. Among them, the *Chinese Newspaper for the Aged* distributes more than 350,000 copies per month. Central and local television stations and radio broadcasting stations have started special programs for the aged that provide them with information and advice. The government has set up the "Golden List Prize" for sons and daughters who best respect their elderly parents and gives a prize to an elderly person who is contributing to society. Such efforts have caused Chinese citizens to think positively about the elderly.

LEISURE-TIME RESOURCES

The Chinese elderly, generally speaking, have leisure time in their retirement years. They make use of leisure time in different ways, depending upon their social status, economic conditions, personal character, aim of life, health, and state and family responsibilities. Most elderly Chinese live with their children and grandchildren after retiring. They help with housework, take care of grandchildren, and enjoy family life.

Some retired people participate in social activities through mass organizations. Upper-class old people usually take part in the activities of consultative committees and participate in policymaking. The retired intelligentsia are involved in learned societies or associations and enjoy academic activities. The number of science and technology associations, which are sponsored and organized by retired people, had reached 120 in 1988, with over 50,000 members. For example, in the five years since it was founded in 1983, the Association of Retired Engineers, in Chong Qing, has provided technical consulting services to more than 600 agriculture units and middle-size and small-size enterprises; signed over 360 technology contracts; trained more than 3,000 professional members and employed young people; and translated many foreign materials. Other associations, such as medical personnel associations and educator associations, all adhere to the principle of voluntary participation and action according to one's capability and have developed many kinds of technical and knowledgeable services. Most of these technical consulting services are free, except that some charge low fees (as stipulated by the government).

Usually, retired people participate in public-interest activities through neighborhood committees at old people's activity centers. Such participation can include being a committee leader, maintaining public order and security, going on patrol, mediating civil dispute, helping young people who are released after serving a prison sentence, looking after children and old people in the neighborhood, assisting mental patients, and acting as price-examiner officers, traffic safety officers, or after-school activities counselors.

After the Civil Administration Department convened the nationwide community service symposium in 1987, city community services were developed in many cities. In old people's activity centers, old people's clubs, or old cadres' activity clubs—established by residential districts—there are usually reading rooms, activity rooms, and tearooms with a television set or video recorder, and chess, majong, and other activity equipment are provided. These clubs are open daily for old people, enabling them to take part in entertainment according to their own interests and hobbies.

In 1983, the Chinese Old People's Sport Association was established. It is a mass sports organization made up of representatives of government departments concerned with mass organizations, old sports workers, and sports activities. Until now, it has developed into 29 provincial associations, more than 300 urban associations, and 1,000 county associations. Some districts and towns also have established the Old People's Sport Association. The old people are organized to engage in such activities as Taiji, Qigong, gate ball, tennis, dancing, chess, and poker.

Education is one of the important ways to enrich the lives of the elderly. By the end of 1990, there were over 2,000 elderly colleges in China, with more than 200,000 students. A network of multidegree elderly education programs has gradually formed and continues to be a developing trend. The third-aged schools are usually run by the local people, and some are subsidized by the state. Only a few are run by the state. The aim of elderly education is to broaden their knowledge and enrich their lives so that they can achieve self-enhancement and meet personal goals. For this reason, course subjects are offered according to the needs of the elderly (literature, history, calligraphy, painting, gardening, nutrition, health care, family management). Some high-level courses are also offered, such as psychology, gerontology, and sociology. The length of schooling in most schools is one year but can range from several months to two years. Old people with secondary or higher educational levels, especially those retired cadres, enthusiastically attend the third-year school; those with low education levels have difficulty in receiving such education. Educational opportunities for the elderly exist only in urban areas.

ADVOCACY AND PROTECTION

According to a survey in Guizhou province, covering 2,310 people, adult children's attitudes toward the aged were quite positive. It was found that 97.26% of the elderly were supported and respected by their offspring. Only

1.85% of the elderly were coldly treated, .78% percent were abused, .16% were denied food and clothing, and no one was denied housing (China Academy of Social Sciences, 1989).

This indicates that, as a result of moral and ethical principles, the Chinese elderly are respected by the family and by society. After the foundation of the People's Republic of China, the state legislated these principles in the constitution, the Marriage Law, the Inheritance Law, and the Criminal Law, among others, and safeguarded the aged's legitimate interests with legally binding forces.

Some of the provisions that safeguard old people's legitimate interests are related to support of parents, maltreatment of the aged, and abandonment. Thus, the state safeguards the lives of retired persons. There is a series of regulations stipulating the retirement age, the standard of retirement pay, medical care, and so on.

There is no Old Age Law in China, at present. Under the circumstances of reform and opening to the outside world, the broad masses of those working with the aged are demanding the strengthening of safeguards for the elderly. In 1991, the judiciary issued a regulation for such safeguards. The action of signing a family supportive agreement has spread in China's rural areas, so that the old people's legitimate interests for support cannot be infringed upon and the social habit of respecting and taking care of the aged is promoted.

The Old Age Associations throughout the country take safeguarding old people's interests as their duty. They actively assist those departments concerned in mediating all kinds of supportive issues and help the aged to resolve the events that infringe upon their rights: inheritance, desertion, maltreatment, and remarriage.

In some places, there are efforts to protect the legitimate interests of the aged and disabled in the form of sanctuary (temporary protective places) for those whose personal basic living rights are infringed upon and for whom services are given. A sanctuary consists of a reception center and a shelter.

FUTURE PROJECTIONS

On the whole, China, as a developing nation, should formulate and adopt strategies to make full use of its relatively limited resources and improve productive forces. Especially, faced with the challenge of an aging population in the twenty-first century, China is far from ready for it—both economically and spiritually—due to its less-developed economy.

The government must define the guiding principles of those working with the elderly. In 1984, representatives from the Central Party Committee and the State Council indicated that "the problems of elderly are serious social problems of the modern world. It is also vital to social and economic development of our country that we should do it better and create gerontology with Chinese features and, therefore, put the work for elderly on a scientific basis" (China National Committee on Aging, 1991a).

The Seventh Five-Year Plan for Economic and Social Development of the People's Republic of China refers to Social Security affairs in the following: "We should try to establish an embryonic form of social security system with Chinese features, ... set up and amplify the social security system, further develop social welfare facilities ... and carry forward the tradition of our country that the family members, relatives, friends, and neighbors are always ready to help each other" (*People's Daily,* 1986). In 1987, the report of the 13th National Congress of the Chinese Communist Party pointed out that China should pay attention to the rapid aging population and take countermeasures to deal with the growth in time (Hu, 1987).

In the past several years, China has been guided by the principles of guaranteeing that the aged receive needed medical care, be active in society and properly provided for, and participate in leisure-time activities. China has begun to mobilize all forces of society to initiate and develop aged welfare facilities, through different channels and administrative levels, in line with local conditions and, in a planned way, to remove obstacles for ensuring the quality of the lives of the Chinese elderly.

Considering the special situations in the country, the Chinese population can depend only on government, collective and individual forces, and, eventually, developing productive forces. Some needed efforts include the following:

1. Government, at all levels, should consider the needs of the aged in plans of social, economic, and technical development.
2. There should be greater attention to, and fuller utilization of, the "golden period" of low dependency ratio, which has emerged and will last for about 30 years. China should try to improve productivity and quality of life, in terms of health and education, thereby laying a solid foundation to meet the needs of the increasing old-age dependency ratios.
3. The government should establish a "retirement foundation" to share pension payments, of various types of old age insurance systems, with all levels of government. Additionally, there is a need for a Social Security system in rural areas of the country.
4. Efforts are needed to initiate, and improve on, medical treatment systems and service networks for the homebound and to train medical personnel for the aged. Chinese traditional medicine sciences to serve the elderly should be encouraged.
5. There is a need to establish socialization services for the aged, thereby gradually lessening the burden on the family. Commercial departments should enlarge their services needed by the elderly and their families.
6. It is very necessary to set up guiding principles to professionals and to strengthen the training of adults at all levels of education.
7. Family's provision for the aged should be advocated. Emphasis on moral and ethical responsibilities should result in continued respect for, and care given to, the elderly family member.
8. Assistance should be given for setting up old-age administrative organizations at all levels and for giving full play to mass service associations for the aged.
9. The characteristics of old people's life should be taken into consideration in home

building, so as to provide housing suitable for old people and convenient for them and for their children.
10. The Chinese government should create a "law of the aged" as soon as possible.

BIBLIOGRAPHY

China Academy of Social Sciences. (1989). *Selected Works on China Aged Population in 1989.* Population Research Institute, Economical Administration Press.

China National Committee on Aging. (1989). *Collected Works of the Second National Conference on Aging.*

———. (1991b). *News in Brief on Aging.*

———. (1991a). *National Civil Administration Statistics in 1990 and Collected Works on Aging in 1981–1984 in China.*

China Research Center on Aging. (1992). *Survey Data on China Support Systems for the Elderly.*

Hualing Press. (1991). *Collection of the Aged Population Statistics in 1990.*

Hu Sheng. (1987). *The Road of the Seventy Years of the Chinese Communist Party.*

People's Daily (Ren Ming Daily). (15 April 1986).

Population Census of the People's Republic of China for 1990. (1991). Percent sampling tabulations.

United Nations' Economic and Social Commission for Asia and Pacific. (1989). *Population Aging in China: Report of a Study Undertaken in China Under the Project "Emerging Issues of the Aging Population."* Bangkok, Thailand.

Wu, Cangping. (1991). *The Aging of Population in China.*

Xi, Conggin. (1991). *Urban Community Services in 1989.* Jiang Press.

Zhang, Dejiang. (1992). *Collected Works of Community Services in 1991.* Chinese Society Press.

7

CZECH AND SLOVAK FEDERAL REPUBLIC (Former)

Ladislav G. Hegyi

INTRODUCTION

The Role of the Elderly

Official definitions of the elderly are based on statistical data that refer to people of postproductive age, that is, of retirement age, which is 55 years for women and 60 years for men. Experts, however, rely on the World Health Organization (WHO) classification where the elderly are defined as people aged 60–74, old age refers to 75–89 years, and the notion of longevity is reserved for those older than 90 years.

The past 40 years of communist rule in the Czech and Slovaks Republic (CSFR) have resulted in the decline of a three-generation family, people have been deprived of private property, and differences in society have leveled off. The family was no longer able to take care of its elderly members who were destitute and dependent on government pensions. Old-age care was formally taken over by the government, with a resulting decrease in the sense of family responsibility for the parents. Old people found themselves on the margin of society, and their role and status were evaluated with a view to their willingness and ability to aid the family financially, do household chores, or help bring up children. The only political party prevailing at the time heralded its humane nature and did not permit any criticism of the inferior position of the elderly in the country. The basic transformation of society that started after the 1989 revolution will bring about changes in the status of the elderly. However, it is unlikely that the outcome of this process can become visible before 10 years.

In the CSFR in 1990, there were 3,031,000 persons of postproductive age (1,056,000 men and 1,975,000 women). Over the past 70 years, the proportion of the 0–14 years age groups has declined by more than 5%, whereas the percentage of citizens of postproductive age has increased from 9.5% to 19.3%. During the same period, the population segment of those over 70 years of age rose from 3.36% to 7.15% and that of people over 80 went up from 0.65% to 2.22% (CSFR, 1991; Federal Statistical Office [FSO], 1990). It is projected that the elderly (those over 60) will account for 22% of the population by 2020 (*World Population Prospects,* 1988).

The quality of old-age care is influenced not only by the sheer numbers of the elderly but also by the rate of urbanization. Urbanization accelerates the disintegration of multigeneration families, with a more rapid increase in pensioners' households, especially of lonely pensioners.

The mean life expectancy in 1971 was 67.3 years for men and 73.6 years for women. The mean life expectancy for men in the Czech Republic was 68.1, and in the Slovak Republic, was 68.9; for women in both republics it was 75.4.

Between 1987 and 1990 a study on the health status and dependence on social structures in respect of 237,596 people aged over 60 years, was carried out in Western Slovakia. Taking part in the inquiry were general practitioners and geriatric nurses working in the region. The elderly persons included in the study were classified into four groups on the basis of their health and social status (Hegyi, 1992). The analysis of about one-third of Slovakia's elderly population makes it possible to project the findings to the entire elderly population of the CSFR.

Results showed that 38.1% of the surveyed elderly persons enjoyed good health and were self-sufficient and not dependent on any type of assistance. It was found that 32.0% were chronically ill with multiple risk factors but were either self-sufficient or had someone to take care of them. More than one-quarter of the elderly (28.3%) were chronically ill with multiple risk factors, aggravated by organic decompensation, with a present or impending psychosocial deficiency. The last group of the elderly, accounting for 9.1% of all surveyed, was made up of severely ill persons with recurrent organic decompensation, frequently—or to a large extent—immobile, lonely, and dependent on outside help.

Another survey of 6,511 elderly persons indicated that 30.5% of those aged over 80 enjoyed relatively good health and were self-sufficient (Hegyi, 1990).

The Formal Structure of Care of the Elderly

Care provision to the elderly in the CSFR is part of the government's social policy and is primarily confined to a pensions scheme, provision of health care to this population, and social care provided in households or social institutions.

Care is currently focused at two levels: social care and public health. Social care provision is supervised by the respective Ministries of Labor and Social Affairs in the Czech Republic as well as the Slovak Republic. Health care is provided under the supervision of the Czech and Slovak Republic Ministries of Health.

As of July 1, 1992, care could be provided through nongovernment health and social institutions. Since January 1993 in the Czech Republic, there is Health Insurance which enables the development of nongovernmental health services. At the beginning of 1994 in the Slovak Republic, there are health services paid for by the government and financial funds for health services for disabled from private sources. In Slovakia, most of the pharmacies are private, but there are only a few physicians in private practice.

It is envisaged that, in the future, health and social care institutional facilities will be largely community-owned. This is not feasible at present as communities cannot afford to fund these facilities. Social and health care services are provided, as required, with the exception of old-age pensions to which beneficiaries are entitled because of their age.

To sum up, social policy for the elderly has so far concentrated on three types of activity: institutionalized foster services, support to family care, and voluntary nonprofessional care.

INCOME MAINTENANCE AND EMPLOYMENT

In 1987, old-age pensions for men amounted to about 60% of mean gross wages in the national economy, which was at the time 2,941 Kčs (Czechoslovak crowns) (US $98) a month, while women received 44% of the same amount.

Mean nominal wages in 1990 were 3,887 Kčs (US $112.90) and the mean old-age pension was 2,024 Kčs (US $67.50) (or 52.07% of mean nominal wages). In 1990 the CSFR expenditure for all types of old-age pensions was 43,093,211,000 Kčs (US $1,436,440).

In 1989 there were in the CSFR 704,000 old-age pensioners in employment; working pensioners accounted for 31.6% of all old-age pensioners. By 31 December 1991 there were in the CSFR 638,117 pensioners in employment, accounting for 27.5% of all old-age pensioners.

It appears that the ratio of economically active pensioners will be diminishing, as their wage tax was recently increased by 100% and additional taxes were imposed on pensioners' employers. These measures were prompted by growing unemployment as well as by the efforts to create jobs at the expense of pensioners. A person of retirement age stands a better chance of keeping a job if he or she does not apply for an old-age pension. Transfers to alternative jobs or retraining programs for pensioners are rather an exception than the rule.

Incomes from private pension schemes are virtually nonexistent. Retired persons who receive their pensions from abroad are relatively well provided for, especially if the pensions are in hard currency. Government aid programs offer a variety of benefits, such as single and repeated allowances, regular financial aid for the disabled, which is graded into three categories, dietary compensatory allowance for diabetic patients, subsidized food prices in kitchens for pensioners, meals-on-wheels, reduced railway and public transport fares, and allowance repeatedly provided for meals taken in public catering facilities.

Pensions received by the elderly in the countryside are lower than in the cities, and old people on the lowest pensions largely live in multigeneration families. In-kind produce (like food originating from pensioners' own farming activity) constitutes an important part of livelihood in the countryside.

HEALTH CARE SERVICES

The Czechoslovak public health system had gone through a reform process between 1990 and 1993. In Czech Republic the rate of this reform process is high. This fact is demonstrated by the striking trend of privatization, mainly in outpatient health care services, and by the increasing initiatives in the care for the elderly.

Recently, there has been an explosive growth of health care expenditure. This growth was primarily influenced by the rising cost of medicines. In 1990 the drug bill was 7.7 thousand million Kčs. Over 70% of the total health care expenditure goes for outpatient and hospital services. Available data clearly indicate that the growth of health care expenditure is faster than the growth of the national economy, which is the source of funding for this sector.

Health services are provided by general hospitals catering to people living in a given area through their out- and inpatient departments. It is anticipated that outpatient services will be gradually privatized and that hospitals will be owned by respective communities. Health services, including medical drugs, have so far been provided free. General hospitals provide health care to acute and chronic cases through their facilities. Ambulance services, as well as intensive care units inside hospitals, are set up to handle emergency cases.

The Health and Social Network for the Elderly

Primary care for the noninstitutionalized elderly is provided by the general practitioner (GP), assisted by the geriatric nurse (GN). Patients are free to choose their own physician, whereas the GN has a fixed area to take care of and generally cooperates with several GPs. There are 744 GNs in Slovakia (an average of 1,200 persons of postproductive age per 1 GN). The author has not able to determine the number of GNs in the Czech Republic.

Specialized geriatric care is provided by geriatricians working in geriatric outpatient departments or in polyclinics. A diploma of specialization in geriatrics has so far been awarded to 79 physicians, 30 of whom are in the Czech Republic and 49 in Slovakia.

Social services are organized under the auspices of the Ministry of Labor and Social Affairs. Professional and voluntary nurses work in the field of primary care, providing a variety of services, such as food delivery, laundry, hygienic bathing, and pedicure. Charities, as well as private nursing agencies in the CSFR, are only in their inception phase.

The number of recipients of nursing care is 550.5 per 10,000 (5.55 per nurse) in the CSFR: 651 (8.33 per nurse) in the Czech Republic and 354.5 (2.52 per nurse) in the Slovak Republic. This difference is probably due to a different nursing structure in the two republics. The number of recipients of nursing care among citizens of postproductive age is 2,887.8 in the CSFR: 3,231.6 (3.2%) in the Czech Republic and 2,092.2 (2.1%) in the Slovak Republic. At a glance, the percentage of nursing care recipients does not correlate with the figure of 9.1% of elderly persons with major health problems. In reality, however, this difference relates to the number of elderly people who already are, or will be, in need of nursing services.

In the health sector, semi-institutional care implies senior citizens' day hospitals, of which there only a few throughout the CSFR. In the social sector, these include day-care facilities, pensioners' clubs, and foster homes.

Institutional care is provided in hospitals and long-term care facilities. In geriatrics, this encompasses geriatric departments, long-term care hospitals, and, in Slovakia, supplementary therapy departments, which can be regarded as facilities for chronically ill, largely elderly, patients.

The establishment in mid-1991 of geriatric inpatient departments in the Czech Republic can be regarded as confirming the trend nationally set by Slovakia's geriatric sector in 1979 (when it organized its own departments). Only a meager 476 beds have been set up in these departments in 12 years due to lack of funds and lack of cooperation from health administrators.

In the Czech Republic, additional therapy beds are mainly annexed to general clinical departments and primarily serve the purpose of supplementary or subsequent therapy following acute illness. In Slovakia, by contrast, chronically ill patients with frequent relapses are hospitalized at these departments. These patients are largely senior citizens. Until recently, beds at supplementary therapy departments were considered to be part of the bed stock of internal departments. The newest concept of internal medicine does not encompass supplementary therapy departments anymore.

Boarding houses, run by the social service sector, are designed essentially for senior mobile persons. Nursing homes for the elderly, on the contrary, feature a high percentage of immobile and chronically ill patients (Hegyi, 1992; Public Health, 1992).

HOUSING RESOURCES

The price liberalization of 1990 has resulted in dramatically increased living costs. Repeated rising food prices were followed by higher electricity, gas, and water prices and rents are expected to increase through 1994.

Elderly persons mainly live in very old houses with few amenities. Flats, especially in the towns and cities, are not sufficiently spacious.

Because of high living costs, lack of reserve funds, and low pensions, elderly persons can no longer afford to continue running their own households. Increasingly elderly persons, particularly in towns and cities, apply to be admitted to old people's homes where government grants help take care of the basic subsistence concerns.

Housing costs vary depending on family structure and may amount to different proportions of the family budget. For example, individual pensioners (in contrast to a full family of pensioners) pay a larger proportion of their income for municipal flats (39.9% versus 33.3%), cooperative flats (49.5% versus 39.2%), and detached housing (34.1% versus 25.2%).

Food expenses account for 54.4% of an individual pensioner's monthly net income, 56.7% in the case of a full family of pensioners. Percentages of living costs (food and housing) for individual pensioners versus a full family of pensioners in municipal flats are 94.3% versus 90%, in cooperative flats, 103.9% versus 95.9%, and in detached houses, 88.5% versus 81.9%.

Less than half of pensioners (43.68%) have basic amenities such as a washing machine, refrigerator, vacuum cleaner, radio, and television in their households.

Further, 4.40% pensioners own a country cottage, 6.27% a garage, 9.01% a motor car and 16.30% an automatic washing machine. It has been found that 13.32% of pensioners' households have no refrigerator, and 23.68% no washing machine.

The housing policy has so far been primarily focused on young people. In some housing estates elderly persons were allocated ground-floor flats. There is no sign yet of the development of special flats—so-called flats without barriers. Foster services have been an important resource, enabling persons dependent on outside aid to remain in their households. Such resources also include foster homes as well as centers of foster services.

The number of recipients of foster services increased from 4,959 in 1965 to 87,328 in 1988. It is forecast that by 2005 there will be 120,000 recipients of foster services in the CSFR. Foster homes are designed for largely self-sufficient elderly persons who occasionally require outside help. These homes offer differentiated nursing care and a variety of services. In 1988 there were 675 foster homes in the whole of the CSFR, with a total of 17,026 flats.

Centers of foster services offer short-term stays, for example, during the holidays of other family members or while regular housing is being refurbished.

Centers of personal hygiene offer basic hygienic care as part of their activity. In 1988 there were 490 such centers in the CSFR. Also in 1988, the foster service owned 417 cars and 456 laundries.

The Czecho-Slovak Red Cross, a voluntary organization, is also involved in foster care provision, especially in such simple activities as delivering food and maintaining households.

The development of modern housing estates specifically for senior citizens is not yet feasible because the elderly population is generally rather impoverished.

SUPPORTIVE SERVICES

Supportive services for the elderly are rather basic. The newly emerging Pensioners' Union is only beginning to create its own structure and services. Social workers and geriatric nurses do some counseling.

Meals are available virtually everywhere. In the countryside, catering is taken care of by kitchens of farming cooperatives, whereas special kitchens as well as meals-on-wheels are available in the towns and cities. Pensioners' clubs and similar organizations make it possible to have meals in groups.

Household jobs, shopping, cleaning, and other chores are dealt with by volunteers, mostly from the Red Cross. Some of these services and options have been previously mentioned.

Day health centers of the hospital type are still uncommon. Daytime stays for relatively healthy elderly persons are largely offered by centers of foster services.

Services offered to the elderly still have a very limited base since until recently they have been exclusively provided by the government. As nongovernment activities—as well as private and charitable initiatives—grow, they will apparently spread further.

LEISURE-TIME RESOURCES

The leisure time of elderly persons is to a large extent shaped by their family bonds and life-styles as well as by the differences between the urban and rural life patterns.

The broad family circle of an elderly person in the countryside typically differs from that of urban counterparts. Namely, there are more children, fewer childless elderly relatives, fewer of those who have survived their own children, richer structures of three- and four-generation families, fewer households of lonely persons, broader family milieu, fewer elderly persons without any relatives whatsoever, minimal dispersion in space of relatives, and greater emotional bonds with the family (which gives the elderly person a sense of certainty and security).

Elderly persons in the countryside are more dependent on family aid than in the city. Children in the countryside help their elderly parents one-third times more frequently than in the city. Elderly couples appear to be the most self-sufficient. Social services are most lacking in the countryside and are primarily focused on providing aid to lonely persons. Daily activities have a different structure, elderly persons spending less time on shopping and household chores but spending more time in their backyard gardens or working their allotments of land and being less involved in social life.

There are differences between the urban and rural patterns of leisure-time creativity. The countryside gives more opportunities for open-air activity, gardening, and household responsibilities whereas the city enables greater intellectual creativity.

Free recreational vouchers may be provided to nonworking pensioners if they are on the lowest pensions, whereas others are entitled to a 50% discount.

Universities and academies of the third age are very helpful in that they motivate elderly persons, help them find each other and meet regularly, expand their horizons, and are an important element of adult education. They emerged within university structures in Prague, Bratislava, and other centers of higher education and are held in high regard by senior citizens. At present, these institutions offer general education courses, and the completion of a course or term does not lead to a certificate or a job.

Voluntary organizations have no tradition in this country and are virtually nonexistent or at inception.

Pensioners' clubs are instrumental in helping fill leisure time with discussions, lectures, get-togethers, and social parties, and they enable and enhance personal contacts. The number of these clubs increased from 524 in 1965 to 1,523 in 1988. As an example of their increased popularity, the annual running costs for one such club were 5,099 Kčs (US$170) in 1965 and 42,851 Kčs (US$1,428) in 1988.

ADVOCACY AND PROTECTION

Legal and social counseling is available in major cities and is generally divided into several areas. Social counseling concerns itself with the issues of pension schemes, government benefits, and social care services.

General legal counseling primarily focuses on property law, restitution, rehabilitation, and privatization, as well as inheritance law.

There are no specialized advocacy organizations yet that would promote better quality of life and equality for elderly persons in society.

Talks began in 1992 with the President of the Police Force of Slovak Republic regarding the protection of life and property of senior citizens. In a period of rising crime, it is frequently old-age pensioners who become the victims of criminal assault and robbery. Efforts at safeguarding the elderly continue to be discussed.

FUTURE PROJECTIONS

Health is the major determinant of the elderly person's quality of life. The health status of the elderly population is directly related to the health of the population as a whole. Therefore, nationwide measures should be taken that are aimed at the entire population, in general, followed by specific provisions for the elderly and old population, in particular.

With a view to multiple diseases generally present in elderly people, it is necessary to adopt, as a basic principle, a comprehensive approach to the health and social aspect of old-age care. Such an approach should take into account the fact that health, social milieu, and the environment are closely interrelated.

In the health care area, the medical discipline of geriatrics will have to be further developed in order to build, by way of small area planning, an effective health and social care network.

The focus invariably will be on primary care, based on the assumption that the home environment of an elderly person is the most optimal one.

All private, charitable, and voluntary initiatives, self-help, and mutual help need to be promoted in order to establish the infrastructure of a social geriatric care system.

All measures should be taken in collaboration with elderly persons in an effort to motivate greater activity and involvement from them in organizing and providing care to the elderly generation. Similarly, the political involvement of elderly persons should be encouraged in a bid to improve their position.

In its social policy, the government will need to become significantly more committed to the improvement of the quality of life for the elderly and favor the formation of two-generation families willing and able to take care of their elders. The housing policy should take into consideration the specific needs of the elderly and should promote barrier-free zones, offices, and centers. Initiatives should be supported that are designed to accommodate concerns of the elderly, such as events of the "healthy towns" type, as well as integrated aid and service systems for the elderly.

Coordination of interregional and interstate approaches to old-age care may bring some very positive results, especially if it draws on the experience of WHO expert groups.

To improve the quality of life of the elderly, the government should increase their present living standards by means of social measures and better-quality health services, by encouraging sounder and better life-styles in society as a whole, by increasing the education standards of the elderly; and by providing incentives for greater activity of elderly persons themselves. The acceptance of the elderly person by modern society is just as important as the acceptance of modern society by the elderly person.

BIBLIOGRAPHY

Census of People, Houses and Flats. Preliminary Results. Federal Statistical Office. Prague, June 1991 (in Czech).
Czech and Slovak Republic. *CSFR Statistical Yearbook* (in Czech), 1993.
Hegyi, L. Experiences of differentiated care provision in the West Slovakia region. In L. Hegyi (ed.), *Topical Issues of Gerontology and Geriatrics* 4. Bratislava: West Slovakia Region Health Authority, 1990, pp. 59–63 (in Slovak).
———. Current aspects of old-age care in the Czech and Slovak Federal Republic. *Bold,* 2, 1992:2–5.
Public Health. Vol. 1 and 2. ÚZIS Bratislava, ÚZIS Prague, 1992.
World Population Prospects 1988. New York: UN Department of Internal Economic and Social Affairs (Population Studies No. 106).

8

FRANCE

Jean-Claude Henrard

INTRODUCTION

The Elderly

There are several definitions of old age in France. First, in a relative short space of time old age has come to be socially defined as beginning at standard retirement age. The age of 60 may be seen, in that case, as a convenient age limit for socially defining old age since the majority of salaried workers are entitled to draw an old-age pension at the age of 60 as of 1982 (it had been 65 before).

Second, in the early 1960s old age was replaced by the notion of *troisième âge* (third age)—a new definition stressing the possibility of pursuing social and leisure activities and greater independence. Old age itself was postponed to a later age and acquired a purely negative image, confused with the image of incurable illness.

This new culture of old age goes together with a depressed social status and a revalued life-style, on one hand, with great diversity and inequalities between generations and genders, on the other. Leaving the labor force excludes people of the most valued roles; we can deprive them of social utility, but we should not prevent them from having an extended life-style of leisure.

Old age may be seen as having both common features linked to a specific age group and various characteristics related to a generation, gender, and social environment. Old age is composed of several generations, each of them having its own history, different standards of living throughout the life course, and different values giving rise to various behaviors. Each generation differs in economic and social resources and health status. Planners and professionals may prefer to relate service needs to functional age. People aged 85 or over would then appear to represent the majority of elderly people, in the sense that they constitute the main age group among the physically or mentally frail. This partial view results in negative stereotypes of old age.

According to the definition of pensionable age, persons aged 60 and over constitute one-fifth of the 56.6 million French people (at the last general population census of 1990). Among them, 35% are aged 75 or over and 8% are aged 85 or over. The evolution of the age structure of the elderly population is shown in Table 8.1.

The increase in the proportion of the population aged 60 and over started earlier in France, at the beginning of the nineteenth century, than in the other European countries because of an earlier decrease in the birthrate. The death rate is also declining in a very significant way, especially since 1970, for the over 60 age groups, whence the tendency for an increase in numbers at the top of the age pyramid. Only in recent years have the numbers of people aged 75 or more and 85 or over been seen as a problem by decision makers and health and social service planners.

Because of the greater longevity of women than men, the number of women per hundred men rises with age. The gender ratio of people aged 60–64 is 113:100 (women to men), which rises to 328:100 for people aged 85 and over (INSEE, 1990). The imbalance in the numbers of elderly men and women has a number of obvious consequences. Women are more likely to be widowed and to live alone. Analysis of the distribution of elderly people according to marital status shows that elderly women are more often widowed than married whereas married men are six times more frequent than widowers.

Table 8.2 shows the household structure of elderly population by age and sex. Most (95%) elderly people live in private households. The majority of those live with a spouse or, after widowhood, alone (especially women aged 75 and over). An analysis of the different groups points out the move into households of younger generations, for widows of greater age (85 or over).

Throughout history a small proportion of elderly people has lived in an institution of some kind. At the 1982 census in France, 482,000 persons aged 60 and over were usually living in nonprivate households. Institutional living increases with age: 20.3% of people aged 85 or over were residents in an institution, according to the 1982 census (Robine et al., 1986). Because of gender differences, the institutions that cater predominantly to frail and lonely people are mainly occupied by very old women (52% of those institutionalized are women aged 75 and over whereas this group represents only 23% of the elderly people).

Data on the levels of education of the elderly have been obtained from a survey on the passage from active life to retirement. The authors (Paillat et al., 1989) found that 60% of their sample (salaried workers from the cohorts born in 1916 and 1922) had left school before the age of 15 (22% before the age of 13 for those born in 1916 versus 17% for those born in 1922). Only 12% had

Table 8.1
Evolution of the Age Structure of the Population of Elderly People in France, 1968–2010

| AGE GROUPS | CENSUS DATES |||||| PREDICTIONS ||
| | 1968 || 1982 || 1990 || 2010 ||
	%	N (millions)	%	N (millions)	%	N (millions)	%	N (millions)
60-64	6.1	6.8	4.7	6.5	5.6	7.3	6.0	8.5
65-74	7.6		7.2		7.2		8.2	
75-84	4.3	2.5	5.5	3.6	5.5	4.0	6.7	5.5
85 or over	0.8		1.1		1.6		2.5	
TOTAL POPULATION	100	49.7	100	54.3	100	56.6	100	59.7

Source: INSEE, 1984.

Table 8.2
Household Structure of Elderly People by Age and Sex

HOUSEHOLD STRUCTURE	60-74 MEN %	60-74 WOMEN %	75 OR OVER MEN %	75 OR OVER WOMEN %
LIVING ALONE	11.0	29.2	19.6	44.9
LIVING WITH SPOUSE ONLY	57.4	43.6	52.4	17.4
LIVING WITH SPOUSE AND OTHERS	23.8	12.3	10.8	3.2
LIVING WITH OTHERS	5.6	12.6	10.9	23.7
LIVING IN INSTITUTION	2.3	2.4	6.2	10.7

Source: INSEE, 1984.

completed their secondary school by obtaining the "baccalaureate" at the age of 18.

The economic situation of the elderly people has changed considerably in the last 30 years. First, withdrawal from the labor force has become generalized: in 1988, 25% of men between 60 and 64 years and 8% between 65 and 69 years were still working, against more than 70 and 40% of the same age groups in 1962. Second, on the whole, because of considerable increase in value of retirement pensions, the elderly population has passed from the position of poverty and social assistance in the 1960s to the position, in 1988, of having an average financial level equal to 80% of the last salary prior to retirement (for the large part of the elderly who had a salaried work life). Third, the standard of living has considerably improved (notably the housing conditions): elderly are more and more often owners of their homes (60% of households with a pensionable head in 1986), and the lack of amenities is decreasing. However, great inequalities persist between generations, by gender, and for socioeconomic groups. A large proportion of the older women who live alone still have low incomes and uncomfortable housing.

The life expectancy at 60 has increased by 20 to 30% for men and women between 1950 and 1987. The life expectancy at 80 has increased by 30 to 33% for men and women between 1960 and 1987. According to the Organization for Economic Cooperation and Development (OECD), in 1988, the life expectancy at 60 and 80, respectively, for men and women was 18.4 and 23.7 years and 6.6 and 8.4 years. Because these indicators do not reflect the quality of life, several authors have proposed (and calculated) the life expectancy without disability. Robine et al. (1986) has calculated this indicator for the year 1982 at ages 60 and 75. Table 8.3 shows that women at 60 have a life 5 years longer than men, but only 1.5 years more without disability. At 75 the life expectancy without a disability is the same for both sexes. Thus, the increase in longevity for older women is accompanied by increase in the period of disability.

Physical and mental disabilities are associated with increasing age. No national register of disabilities (or of disabled persons) exists in France. Several regional surveys have been conducted between 1978 and 1986. The synthesis of five disabilities has been undertaken by Gauthier and Colvez (1990). Within the ranges shown on Table 8.4, 2.2% of those aged 65 and over are confined to bed or armchair and 6.9% are housebound. Application of the figures to the national population gives about 320,000 elderly people in need of help for bathing and dressing and 1.7 million in need of help for usual domestic tasks. The prevalence of all disabilities increases perceptibly with age.

Some of the main characteristics of the elderly population are summarized in Table 8.5 in order to assess the proportion of elderly persons having social or health problems as compared with the general French population.

Before the 1960s, families were responsible for the care of their parents; those without a family were helped by social welfare, or a few nonprofit organizations that employed home helpers, or were institutionalized in almshouses. Since the

Table 8.3
Life Expectancy Without Disability (L.W.D.) in France in 1982 at Ages 60 and 75 According to Sex

AGE	L.E. (in years) Men	L.E. (in years) Women	L.E.W.D. (in years) Men	L.E.W.D. (in years) Women	L.E.W.D./L.E. % Men	L.E.W.D./L.E. % Women
60 ys	17.6	22.7	11.7	13.3	66.4	58.6
75 ys	8.5	10.9	4.4	4.3	51.8	39.4

Source: Robine et al., 1986.

Table 8.4
Percentages of People Aged 65 and over with Loss of Mobility and/or Unable to Perform Personal Tasks, Living in Private Households in 1982

MOBILITY OR TASK	PER CENT
Bed fast and confined to armchair	1.4 to 3
Not bed fast or confined to armchair but :	
-housebound	6.1 to 7.7
-unable to do without help or totally unable	
.bathe oneself or/and dress oneself	3.9 to 6.5
.usual domestic tasks*	23.7 to 28.1
.occasional domestic tasks**	32.3 to 41.3

*Cooking, shopping, washing clothes, and light domestic tasks.
**Heavy or painful tasks.
Source: Gauthier and Colvez, 1990.

1960s, families have been released from their obligations, and the state has laid down a living-at-home policy that claims to be universal. Service implementation has not followed the initial intention. In fact, the family has never ceased to play a major role in supporting and caring for older people. In the 1980s there was a rediscovery of the role of the family. Financial measures were taken to encourage and maintain the ability of families to provide care.

The Formal Structure of Care of the Elderly

Responsibility for the organization of care for the elderly is divided into different authorities, as much on the national level as on the local one. Various ministerial departments (social services, health, housing, welfare, budget, and so on) are involved at the national level in the implementation of measures for care and support of the elderly. The role of the national schemes (*caisses nationales*) for sickness, old age, and the family (within the general Social Security system) must be also considered. This system is based on a compulsory collective insurance mechanism. It includes several schemes connected with professional activities financed by employers' and employees' contributions. In the

Table 8.5
Main Characteristics of the Elderly Population in France

	AGE GROUPS 60-74	AGE GROUPS 75 AND OVER	TOTAL POPULATION
Numbers (millions)	7.3	4.0	56.6
Proportion of females (%)	55	64	51
Living in institution (%)	1.9	10.1	2.2
Living alone (%)	19.5	39	25
Uncomfortable housing (%)	32	43	21
Low income (%)[1]	6.2	21.5	–
Activity restriction (%)	18	34	10.6[2]
Dependency in A D L (%)[3]	7	24	–
Housebound (%)	1.3	5.4	0.7

[1] old age minimum recipients (1990)
[2] over 14 years of age
[3] ADL: activities of daily living
Source: Henrard, Casson, and Le Disert, 1990.

health sector, 99% of the total population are covered by sickness insurance. The contributors and their families are entitled to benefits in cash (a daily allowance in case of job relief) or in-kind (ambulatory and institutional health care, prescriptions). The health insurance schemes pay the main part of the care by means of reimbursement to consumers. The size of a consumer copayment depends on the kind of medical service. Some elderly people are exempted from copayment.

In the social sector consumers have to pay the service or can benefit from social welfare payments. Welfare assistance is a duty of solidarity toward the destitute members of society, but the conditions for obtaining it are related to a means test and a need recognition. It is financed by *departemental* welfare (France is divided into 100 *départements,* which have political and administrative roles) and provided by municipalities, since the introduction of decentralization laws in the mid-1980s. The *départements,* assisted by town councils, have the piloting role in social matters at the local level through their own services. The *départements,* which get their funds from local taxes, contribute through welfare programs with payments toward the cost of housing or full board in institutions or for certain domiciliary services. In respect of welfare expenditures, the departmental authority recovers cost from the family or from the heirs when inheritance is above a fixed ceiling.

Besides the compulsory assistance for the poor, municipalities and old-age pension schemes can develop optional measures or services intended for those having a social need (i.e., meals-on-wheels, home repair services for the disabled, including elderly people) or specifically for the elderly (i.e., home help services funded by old-age insurance schemes).

Responsibility for providing the care is shared among public, private, nonprofit, and commercial sectors for health, as well as social services.

INCOME MAINTENANCE AND EMPLOYMENT

The main source of elderly people's income is pension. To cover the risks of old age, France has a very complex system of pensions set up by the Social Security system under the guardianship of the state. The original purpose of a single fund was fragmented into a mosaic because of opposition from many sociooccupational groups. Organized on an occupational basis, the statutory pension system includes two levels. The first one, supplemented by Social Security pension, is based upon contributions generated during the active life of a worker. Its amount is connected to the length of the contribution period and to the contribution level proportional to the earnings level (up to a fixed ceiling; no contribution is made on the part above) attained during the working life. Since 1982, the claiming of full pension is contingent on 37.5 years of contribution and a fixed age of 60 years. Besides the basic pension, the second level is composed of a complementary occupational pension based on compulsory plans and constitutes a nationwide superstructure on top of Social Security pension schemes. These private schemes are initiated by a negotiated agreement between social partners. The state requires a firm to join an industry or a nationwide scheme once it has been set up. The income replacement through pensions is based upon monetary transfers from payroll taxes paid by employees and employers to pensioners—following the principle of sharing between generations.

The pension system is designed to meet, at best, the needs of those who have worked all their life without major interruptions and who have had a normal career. The system provides a kind of subsistence allowance for those formerly dependent on the income of pension fund members, such as widows. Traditionally, pension plans were geared to the concepts of lifelong marriage, with the husband earning an income and the wife maintaining the home, the pensions intending to replace salary and a survivor's pension referring to the widow as a dependent.

When pensions are too low or nonexistent, elderly people are entitled to the old-age minimum benefit (OAMB), which is determined by a means test. About half of the OAMB is paid by the Social Security in the form of a basic pension. The state budget provides the balance to the OAMB through a national solidarity fund. This second allocation allows the state to recover payment from heirs (when inheritance is in excess of a fixed amount).

For a pensioner, the full basic pension is 50% of the average wage of the 10 best yearly earnings. Because the amount of the basic pension is connected to the length of the contribution period and to the contribution level proportional to the earning level, the basic pension varies in one to two ratios (the lowest basic pension equals 66% of the guaranteed minimum salary). Knowing the pension amount paid by a scheme does not allow one to know the total amount collected by a pensioner because an average of 2.8 pensions is paid to pensioners.

Pension amounts vary according to one's former occupational status and career (reflecting the heterogeneity of the pensions system). The statutory old-age pension system is fragmented into a variety of special schemes (for public servants, special categories of salaried workers, independent workers, farmers) that preserve the status differences. Besides the complementary pension plans, composed of 400 superannuation funds, most plans are incorporated in manager, employee, or blue-collar schemes and follow social class differences.

A study of the type and amounts of benefits paid to a sample of four cohorts of pensioners (born in 1906, 1912, 1918, 1922) in 1988 shows (Table 8.6) the influence of occupational status, full career, gender, age, and marital status (the derived rights are for survivors) on the level of the pension. The gender differences are due to the unequal course of labor life: three men out of four have worked a full course; one woman out of three has worked a full course. Since a much higher proportion of women than men survive into advanced old age, age and gender combine their influence to determine inequalities. The differences between socioeconomic groups are due to differences in contributions.

The comparison of pensions and earnings for the older trade and industry workers having a full career shows that pensions equal 92% of the average earnings for men and 73% for women. For the generation born in 1922, the pension is 20% lower than the salary prior to retirement.

The dispersion, measured by the interdecile ratio (the ratio of the minimum collected by the pensioners in the top tenth of the pension distribution to the maximum collected by the pensioners in the bottom tenth), is 5.3 among all the men pensioners and 7.2 among the women. The pension dispersion shows the persistence of poverty among a part of the elderly in spite of the general improvement of the pensions.

The income of the elderly comes from different sources. Of the 6,481,000 families with a head aged 60 and over, there are .5 million with earned income. Earnings from employment are decreasing rapidly because older workers are excluded from the labor force by different schemes of early and anticipated retirement and by the lowering of the age for claiming full pension from 65 to 60. Property income counts for 13% of total income. Pensions and social welfare count for 73%.

Table 8.7 shows the changes in labor force participation of people aged 55

Table 8.6
Levels of Pensions According to Occupation, Gender, Socioeconomic Group, Age and Marital Status

PENSIONERS	AVERAGE MONTHLY PENSION ALL PENSIONERS	AVERAGE MONTHLY PENSION PENSIONERS WITH FULL CAREER
All	100*	127
Men	132	143
Women	70	90
Civil servants	/	200
Salaried workers (commerce and industry)	/	143
Independents (artisan, trader)	/	57
Farm owners	/	34
Born in 1906	86	94
Born in 1922	104	126
Direct right	104	/
Derived right	62	/

*reference index.
Source: Ministry of Solidarity, Health, and Social Welfare, 1988.

and over. Elderly men have been withdrawing from the labor force in increasing numbers and at an earlier age, with a steep fall since 1975. The trends among the women are more complex to assess; in particular, because of a substantial growth in the number of women employees, the decline appears only for women aged 60 and over. Property income is likely to be dominant for only a very small minority, but income from more modest savings (a savings bankbook is owned by more than 80% of people aged 70 and over) and from the imputed value of an owner-occupied house is significant for a large proportion of the pensioners.

Table 8.8 shows the fiscal income for elderly households. It may be seen that households of one person aged 70 and over, which represents more than 40% of the households, have the lowest income. Households of two persons or more have nearly twice the income of those households of one person.

The comparison of the average fiscal income of households with a head aged 60 and over and other households with younger household heads was assessed (INSEE, 1984). The average income by person of the elderly households is 20 to 30% higher than the income of all other households. The households of

Table 8.7
Labor Participation Rate of the Older Age Groups, 1962–88

AGE	MEN (%)				WOMEN (%)			
	1962	1975	1982	1988	1962	1975	1982	1988
55-59	85.3	81.8	76.9	67.3	42.8	41.9	45	45.3
60-64	71.1	54.3	39.1	25.4	34.2	27.8	22.3	17.9
65-69	42.4	19	9.4	8	19.8	10	5	4

Source: INSEE, 1990.

married couples with two children or more have lower incomes, when only one spouse is working, than the average income of elderly households.

Poverty rate, defined as households with disposable income below half of the median for all households in the population, is equal to 13.5% in households with a head aged 60 or over (against 11% in all households). The poor elderly households represent 26% of the total of poor households. Old-age minimum benefit is another way to define poverty, and 1,200,000 persons aged 65 and over (13%) are recipients of this benefit, which is half the figure of 30 years ago. Fifty percent of the beneficiaries are women aged 75 and over who are living alone. They are mainly widowed, without having worked a full course, and with a very low survival pension. They often live in rural areas.

Some French elderly can benefit from tax reduction or special allowance or are entitled to an exemption from Social Security contributions. Some can also benefit from social welfare payments, either those specifically intended for the elderly or those for the disabled (including elderly people). All are means-tested. Finally, all elderly people can benefit from reduced rates offered by commercial policies from many companies.

HEALTH CARE SERVICES

The general health care system in France can be described as pluralistic, based on the social principles of solidarity and equity embodied in national health insurance, on one hand, and the liberal principles of individual freedom embodied in free, independent medical practice, on the other. Ambulatory care is supplied mainly by independent practitioners on a fee-for-service basis, and hospital care is supplied by public and private nonprofit and private commercial hospitals. The Ministry of Health is heavily involved in regulating and organizing the system.

Table 8.8
Fiscal Income* of Household with a Head Aged 60 and over in 1984

AGE OF THE HEAD	1 PERSON FISCAL INCOME	% HOUSEHOLD	2 PERSONS FISCAL INCOME	% HOUSEHOLD	3 PERSONS + FISCAL INCOME	% HOUSEHOLD	ALL FISCAL INCOME
60-64	81	16.7	133	19.1	140	/	113
65-69	83		148				115
70-74	73	41.6	135	19.7	128	/	114
75-79	70		132				91
80 and over	70		132				81
TOTAL	74	58.3	136	38.8	136	2.8	100**

*fiscal income means income before income tax.
**reference index.
Source: INSEE, 1984.

Nearly everybody is covered by statutory sickness insurance funds administered by the compulsory national health insurance schemes. Care is mainly financed by social insurance, but there is often direct payment by patients. Some of the consumer copayment is covered by private, nonprofit supplementary sickness insurance (for about 80% of the population). Health insurance accounts for 71% of national health expenditures, supplementary insurance for about 6%, and public sector (state and local authorities fund public health services and public hospital investments) for about 4%, leaving about 18% for out-of-pocket payments by households (in 1989).

Health care services are not directed toward the elderly, but the elderly can benefit from them as well as anyone else. Thus, elderly seeking ambulatory care can choose to consult any medical practitioner or hospital outpatient department. If a prescription is required, the patient usually goes to a private pharmacist, an independent nurse, or physiotherapist. The patient will pay directly for the service and later can claim back a proportion from the health insurance funds. The cost sharing for consultations with a doctor is 25%, and patients with chronic disorders are often exempted.

In case of emergency, patients are referred to the emergency ward of public hospitals. If hospital care is required, the patient has the freedom to choose between public and private hospitals, both of which are covered by health insurance. About 80% of beds are in public or private nonprofit hospitals with salaried doctors. About 20% of beds are in profit hospitals with fee-for-service doctors. In practice there is much direct payment by the health insurance, leaving a fixed daily rate paid by the patient. About 25% of beds are medium-stay ones for rehabilitation and convalescence. They receive people whose treatment has to be prolonged for several weeks.

Long-stay hospitals (or wards) deserve special attention since they are the only hospitals specifically intended for elderly people who have lost their physical independence. These hospitals come under state control for health care management and are under departmental administration for accommodations. They are financed by two sources: health insurance and personal resources (supplemented by *departmental* welfare when required). A specific referral procedure exists to place elderly patients in institutions, beginning with short- and medium-stay hospitals and ending with long-stay hospitals and (sometimes) psychiatric hospitals.

There are various kinds of social institutions of different legal status, which vary because of either the date of their foundation or their management. Thus, a distinction can be made among almshouses, public or private nonprofit retirement homes, and private commercial residences. They are all run by municipalities (public sector) or by nonprofit or commercial organizations. They are financed by personal resources supplemented, if necessary, by housing allowances and, above all, by departmental welfare. As pensioners living in these residences have grown older, it has been necessary for them to have care staff available. It is possible to do this by establishing so-called medical care sections (they are, in fact, nursing care sections), which are thus eligible for reimbursement of costs from the sickness insurance funds. This solution avoids transferring to hospitals, but it entails also becoming officially recognized which, in turn, implies the provision of certain standards of service. The institutions can also use home nursing service. Admission into the residence depends on discretionary decisions, and admission to the medical care section depends on the degree of dependence in daily life, as decided by the medical adviser of the sickness assurance fund.

Table 8.9 shows the number of residences and long-stay hospitals. If we consider all the places, including the sheltered homes, we see that only one-third of them are giving care financed by health insurance. This shortage of financial contributions, added to a very low rate for care in medical care sections (in spite of the heavy burden of care), will be reflected in lodging costs. Thus, there is the contribution paid by personal resources, supplemented by welfare assistance. Otherwise there will be an overuse of independent nurses paid by health insurance on a fee-for-service basis.

HOUSING RESOURCES

The maintenance of disabled people in their own homes is made easier if the house is adapted to their needs. Thus, various measures have been taken in the French housing sector, including improvement of the existing housing

Table 8.9
Extent of Main Domiciliary Services and Places for People Aged 60 and over, 1970–90

SERVICE OR INSTITUTION	1970	1980	1990
. Home help (number of recipients)	70000	340000	500000
. Home nursing (number of recipients)	0	1800	42000
. Clubs for elderly (number)	1300	15000	/
. Luncheon clubs (number)	540	4000	/
. Sheltered homes (number of tenants)	33000	95000	133000
. Social institutions (number of beds) *with medical facilities*	263000 0	302000 7000	309000 96000
. Long stay hospital (number of beds)	0	43000	70000
. Total population aged 60 and over (millions)	9.4	10.0	11.3

Source: INSEE, 1981, 1982, 1991.

unit and building housing units distributed in either small or large housing blocks.

Programs for home renovation have been made possible by premiums or subsidies from the state (Ministry for Social Affairs and/or Housing Ministry) or by retirement funds to the elderly owner-occupier or by management (housing) associations, regrouped in the National Federation for the Protection, Improvement, Preservation and Transformation of the Home. In each case, the beneficiary must have resources below a certain ceiling. The grant is awarded to make the house conform to the minimal norms of habitation and to save energy or to install modern conveniences and adapt the home to the needs of those physically handicapped. About 45,000 houses benefit from this annual program.

In the 1970s, the concept grew of grouping elderly persons in dwellings served by a resident warden. This has become sheltered housing, providing a studio apartment for one or two elderly with bathroom and kitchen and minimum collective services (luncheon club and third-age club for leisure activities where the elderly's neighbors can come). These provisions have been progressively adapted to the increased aging of their occupants by installing new technical equipment and by providing some forms of medical care.

More recently, experiments in group housing have been put forward for more or less dependent elderly people. Such housing is managed by a resident housekeeper who is able to call on existing domiciliary care services in case of need. Lastly, housing within an existing family home is possible.

Altogether, in this whole sector, there is a wide range of innovative practices intended to maintain elderly people in their own homes as they grow increasingly older and have greater difficulties in meeting the demands of daily living. There is a housing allowance that is means-tested and can be allocated to elderly people or to a family with whom they live and is administered by the Family Allowance Office. The allowance permits the payment of a higher rent than personal resources would make possible. About 10% of those 65 and over are beneficiaries of such an allowance.

SUPPORTIVE SERVICES

Existing services intended for elderly people or used by them are numerous. The most typical ones, according to the types of activities for which elderly people receive help, include domestic tasks, personal care, technical care, surveillance, socialization, and housing improvements.

Two services are particularly relevant because they have been designed specifically for elderly people: home-help services and home nursing services. Home-help services have been in existence for nearly 35 years. Their purpose is to provide help with domestic chores for people who are unable to carry them out because of their state of health. The request is made by a doctor's prescription (or by a local social worker), establishing the number of hours needed weekly.

Two sectors are responsible for these services, each with its own type of clients and legal status. The first is the public sector. There is a statutory provision for people 65 or older who need help because they live alone or with a person unable to carry out the day-to-day maintenance of the house and whose income is less than a certain level. Services are financed by *departemental* social welfare and provided by municipalities. A total of 30 hours is the maximum help a person can receive a month.

The second sector is private, in which provisions are insured by associations financed by old-age insurances and complementary pension schemes (whose affiliated members have a higher level of resources than the social assistance ceiling). Each funding scheme freely determines its own social action, which results in great diversity in awarding home help. In the case of the general scheme for salaried trade and industry workers, the conditions regarding age and family commitments are identical to those for social assistance. They are more or less financed by users, depending on their resources.

Although foreseen in a law of 1975 relating to social and sociomedical institutions, regulations of home nursing services for the elderly were not specified until six years later. Home nursing services were recognized as one of the priorities of the minister responsible for the elderly. The service objectives are to prevent, postpone, or shorten stays in hospitals and in social institutions, and their principal function is to give nursing and personal care (by carrying out care that enables people to perform basic tasks of daily living). The care should be more continuous and better coordinated than that provided on a fee-for-service basis.

Home nursing service can be created and run by a public or private nonprofit body, for example, a social service center of a municipal authority or home help or home nursing care association. Home nursing is provided on medical prescription. Health insurance funds provide all the financing. Theoretically, home nursing functions 12 hours a day, 365 days a year. A salaried nurse coordinates and organizes the various interventions of nurses and auxiliary nurses. The functions most frequently carried out concern help with the activities of daily life and with mobility and the prevention of pressure sores. About 15% in need of home nursing care benefit from the service, which implies that independent nurses and the informal support of family and the neighborhood play a predominant role. Several recent studies confirm the importance of this support. For example, three regional studies (Gauthier and Colvez, 1990) show the importance of family help for elderly people confined to bed or armchair and for people with one or several disabilities. The help becomes more frequent as the dependence becomes more severe. Other domiciliary services are optional.

Other Domiciliary Services

Each social care area provides information and referral services for elderly people, which are spread out between different agencies, managed by municipalities, pension funds, and local elderly committees. Apart from home-help services, there are services for bringing meals to the home or ensuring more occasional help (e.g., helping out with small jobs). These services are provided by local authorities or by nonprofit organizations (in which case they are subsidized by the municipality). They are financed by the users, depending on their resources. Apart from help provided by the home nursing services, much technical help is given by medical auxiliaries working independently. The care from auxiliaries increases with age.

Day and night sitting services provide another form of specialist support to highly dependent elderly people and their caregivers at home. For mentally confused people, assistance may simply take the form of continuing surveillance and providing relief to the relatives. The sitting service is habitually provided by staff who are not usually well qualified and who are employed by associations or on their behalf. The bulk, if not all, of the cost rests on the elderly person or the family. Some retirement funds can be used to share the cost of night watch. When independent nurses offer this service, sickness insurance reimburses part of the expense on a contracted basis.

Telephone alarm systems have been organized in several *départements.* The scheme includes either a *départemental* telephone exchange linked to the public telephone network or local listening centers at emergency services. The telephone exchange or the listening centers, when called by the subscribing elderly person, mobilize volunteers in the neighborhood.

Socialization in the home is not well developed in France. Some organizations, often religious or friendly societies, send volunteers to visit isolated elderly people, but they vary in numbers.

Some social institutions in rural areas are experimenting with temporarily offering rooms to serve as a winter residence for rural elderly facing a harsh winter in isolated homes that have inadequate heating and sanitary facilities. These experiments are publicly subsidized.

Several measures have been taken to help caregivers. Respite care enables the elderly living at home with family to be periodically institutionalized and to allow a period of relief for spouses or relatives who normally care for the patient. They are presently offered by few long-stay or medium-stay hospitals.

Financial incentives for families, such as tax deduction, have been developed for taxpayers caring for a disabled (elderly) person living with them or taking in a person of 75 or over (the elderly person must not have resources above a certain ceiling).

Mental Health Services

Mental health care for the elderly is provided in different places, such as general hospitals, psychiatric hospitals, and long-stay hospitals, and in different ways at home, in day-care centers or in residential settings. Very few institutions are specifically oriented toward the elderly, with psychogeriatric or geriatric teams.

Mental health teams may ensure the link with other health care teams and family involved in the care of the disabled mentally ill elderly. Day hospital care, connected to geriatric or psychiatric hospitals, is sometimes designed for mentally ill elderly patients. Most of the elderly have to be provided with transport to be able to attend. These programs serve as a respite facility to support relatives by offering a hospital setting during the day.

LEISURE-TIME RESOURCES

In France, 15,000 clubs of the third age are spread out over the country. Some offer relatively simple recreational activities dictated completely by staff. Others are completely run by the elderly themselves, and have opened themselves up to the community by sponsoring joint activities with other groups. In rural areas some clubs use volunteer visitors.

Exercise and sports activities for the elderly have increased tremendously over the last 15 years. Many associations train people between 60 and 80 to participate in several sports. Training is often in groups, so that older people can draw confidence from each other.

Many municipal authorities provide vacation opportunities for low-income and disabled elderly by subsidizing vacation residence or travel in tourist areas or neighboring countries.

Many elderly remain active in the community, notably, by helping the younger generations, and some are involved in a wide variety of volunteer roles, such as working with children living in difficult circumstances or providing specific technical skills to developing countries.

Several *universités du troisième âge* provide an array of courses for pensioners. Courses can cover a great variety of subjects. A few offer courses to all age groups in order to encourage intergenerational contacts. Preretirement education is stimulated by several companies.

ADVOCACY AND PROTECTION

In 1981, the participation of retired and elderly persons in defining national policies was introduced with the creation of the Comité National des Retraités et Personnes Agées (National Committee of Pensioners and Elderly Persons). This committee is made up of representatives from labor union retired groups and pensioners' associations. Committee members are the most representative and qualified people for the job; yet their role is purely consultative. This consultation status depends on the goodwill of the secretary of state who assists the minister of social affairs and who is in charge of social services, including those for elderly.

The same type of committee exists at the *départemental* level, chaired by the *préfet du département* (the departmental government's representative). Large *départemental* elderly organizations federate nationally, in order to promote the interests of pensioners and the elderly. Residents' councils are required by legislation in almost every social institution. They are elected by the residents living in the institution and are, theoretically, advising their administrators. Some councils are very active in the daily life of their institution.

No protective services are specifically oriented toward the elderly. Legal protection may be given to mentally ill persons unable to protect themselves or make appropriate judgments about their safety or security. A family member may be entrusted with demented elderly guardianship or trusteeship, or another legal oversight may be established.

FUTURE PROJECTIONS

If the public authorities have laid down a medicosocial policy for the elderly that claims to be universal, they have not provided the means for its development. It has come up against, first, the impossible task of integrating policies from other sectors (owing to the weight of existing institutions and professional reasoning) and, more recently, an increasing scarcity of funds. The result today is that the system of care is fragmented and unbalanced, and it is the source of numerous dysfunctions and inadequate responses to the health and social problems of the elderly. The system of retirement pensions, on the other hand, appears to achieve efficiency, notably for those who have worked a full course.

The future imbalance in generations raises the problem of high-level maintenance of the pensions for the years 2004–5 (postwar cohort reaching pensionable age). The foreseeable rise in the number of people of very advanced age may increase the needs for care, if disability increases as average longevity increases. The reduction in family size and geographical mobility imply a change in the balance of social support and increases the importance of statutory services.

A flexible retirement policy coupled with an adequate level of pensions will need to be developed to allow elderly people both access to employment and a genuine choice about retirement. Development in intergenerational relations should be favored. A housing policy should separate housing needs from caring services. Flats suitably adapted by equipment designed for handicapped people should be available to elderly people.

Finally, domiciliary care services should be able to meet the needs of frail people in France. Their planning and catering should be entrusted to only one local authority. On the whole, the policy should aim at facilitating social integration of the very old.

BIBLIOGRAPHY

Gauthier, A., and Colvez, A. 1990. L'incapacité chez les personnes âgées en France et l'aide reçue. In A. Colvez and H. Gardent, *Les indicateurs d'incapacité fonctionnelle en Gérontologie—Information, validation, utilisation.* CTNERHI, diffusion P.U.F.-INSERM.

Henrard, J. C., Ankri, J., and Isnard, M. C. 1991. Home care services in France. In A. Jamieson, ed., *Home Care for Older People in Europe—A Comparison of Policies and Practices.* Oxford University Press, 99–117.

Henrard, J. C., Cassou, B., and Le Disert, D. 1990. The effects of system characteristics on policy implementation and functioning of care for the elderly in France. *International Journal of Health Services,* 60, 125–139.

Institut National de la Statistique et des Etudes Economiques (INSEE). 1981, 1982, 1991. INSEE Census of Population. Ministry of Social Affaires. Annuares Statistiques 1981, 1982, 1991.

———. 1984. *Recensement général de la population de 1982.* Paris, Collection INSEE.

———. 1990. *Les personnes âgées.* Paris, Collection INSEE.

Livre Blanc sur les retraites. 1991. *La Documentation Française, collection des rapports officiels.*

Organization for Economic Cooperation and Development. 1988. *Ageing Population, the Social Implications.*

Paillat, P., Attias-Donfut, C., Clement, F., Delbes, Co, Renaut, S., and Rozenkeier, A. 1989. *Passages de la vie active à la retraite.* Paris: P.U.F.

Robine, J. M., Colvez, A., Buquet, D., Hatton, F., Morel, L., and Lelaidier, S. 1986. L'espèrance de vie sans incapacité en France en 1982. *Population,* 6, 1025–1042.

9

GERMANY

Fred Karl

INTRODUCTION

The Role of the Elderly

In industrial countries the definition of elderly persons is closely related to their position in the labor market; thus, persons are regarded as elderly when they retire. According to this, many employees age 45 and more are already regarded as elderly workers. In addition to the extension of life expectancy, German gerontology speaks of the extension of the age phase. In the subjective view of persons growing old, most of them regard themselves as adult persons and not as "seniors." Twenty years ago, a majority of 70-year-old Germans regarded themselves as "old," but in 1989 only a quarter did so (Tews, 1994).

In spite of this structural change of the age phase in society, in the mass media and in educational institutions the negative stereotype of old age as a phase of deficit and illness still exists. The generalized perception of old age still has great influence on the individual view of aging.

In the academic scene there is a paradigm change from a view that regards old persons as incapacitated to a view that points out competences and the productivity of age in social and human matters. A new dogma of the "new age" is developing that may discriminate against all those persons who do not possess the resources and abilities to be "productive." Besides the external factors of social age values, the qualitative shape and self-consciousness of persons growing old will be determined by the cohorts of the growing old themselves. Contemporary old generations have survived two world wars in Europe and the Nazi era in Germany. Succeeding cohorts in the old age phase will bring with them other cultural values and attitudes.

In unified Germany in 1990, 11.8 million persons of the total population of

77.5 million were beyond the age of 64; this is a rate of 14.9%. It is expected that the population in Germany will decrease to 66 million in 2025, while the absolute number of elderly persons will increase, resulting in a rate of 22% of the people 65 years old in 2025 (see United Nations, 1991). In relation to persons 60 years and older, a rate of 34% in Germany, in contrast to 26% in the European Community, has been proclaimed.

Still existing is the discrepancy between the proportion of women to men (2:1) (due to war effects) in old age, which will decline to 1.4:1.

In other variables, the aged represent a very heterogeneous group in socioeconomic characteristics. Due to the level of education in their childhood, only 13% of men and 8% of women received a high school education. In the 1980s, 42% of the population 65 years and older (living at home) lived in a one-generation household, 39% lived alone, 16% lived in a household with younger and/or older generations, and 3% lived with other acquaintances. In the 1990s, the process of "singularization" goes on. Up to now, only 4% are residents of old people's homes (yet, in the age group over 80 years, the proportion increases to 25%).

Germany has the lowest fertility rate (1987: 0.64) of modern states, which is not expected to change, because of the life-styles of men and women (very small families, rising tendencies of divorce, elderly persons without children). Changes in the age proportion may occur with migration effects, if Germany continues to assimilate people from Eastern and Southern Europe and people searching for political asylum from Africa and Asia.

As far as life expectancy (at birth) is concerned, men now, on an average, will live 73 years old (in 2027, nearly 76 years), and women, 79 years (in 2025, 82 years). It is wondered if this increase will bring "quality years" or if the duration of illness in old age will be extended.

According to the negative stereotype of old age, economists use the quotient of "old age burden," which indicates the relation between the "unproductive" population older than 60 years, on one hand, and the potential of working people in age 20 to 60 years, on the other hand. This quotient will rise from 0.4 in 1990 to 0.7 in 2030 (see Barth and Hain, 1990).

As the proportion of very old persons increases above average (the number of people aged 95 plus was, in 1987, 20 times higher than it was in 1948 when the Federal Republic of Germany (FRG) was founded, and it will grow further) and the prevalence rates of diseases are age-related, we must expect a growing number of disabled elderly. Also, a significant increase in senile dementia is observed, resulting in a strong impact on the caretaking children (15–20%) and spouses (about 40%). More and more institutions are faced with an increase of dementia symptoms of the elderly patients.

Apprehensions are increasing that the capacities of families are overloaded: families provide more than 80% of the care for the elderly. In comparison with other countries up to the 1970s, Germany had a "caregiver pool" much higher than, for instance, the Nordic countries; therefore, a reduction in the formal help system occurred. As the caregiver pool rapidly shrinks (especially as female caregivers change their role into latent care receivers, without the same chance to receive help from subsequent generations), the existing formal help systems will become overburdened.

The Formal Structure of Care of the Elderly

As a welfare state, Germany provides protection against risks in life in the form of lawful insurance for pensions and health provision. The so-called contract between the generations consists mainly of financial transfers between the working populations and persons in education or retirement. This is regulated by the State and not by personal contracts. In regard to the immediate care of the elderly, the principle of "subsidiarity" reigns: only if family and self-help resources are exhausted may nongovernmental services by religious or nonreligious welfare organizations be called. In case offers from nonprofit organizations do not exist to the extent required, public institutions are obliged to provide services. The payments (benefits) of the Federal Social Welfare Act (Law of National Assistance, since 1961) have to be paid not by the federal government but, in first instance, by the cities. Yet, such financial resources are exhausted by the exploding payments for the unemployed and refugees and for long-term care.

Formal services for the aged are financed either by the statutory health insurance or by social welfare (national assistance), which is the last resort of social aid for everyone. The latter provides "assistance for the maintenance of life" and "aid in special circumstances of life" (unique benefits for special expenses, such as clothing, rent or heating subsidies, aids for care or nursing). It is granted and evaluated on the basis of need, not on the criterion of age.

INCOME MAINTENANCE AND EMPLOYMENT

In 1985, only 6% of persons age 65 and above were still employed (compared with 11% in 1975). Elderly employees in Germany are a risk group, because the employers are interested in getting young workers, who are considered to be more productive.

Currently, the pension system may be regarded as a reward for leaving the place of work. (This means that if workers are needed, the age limit for retirement will be extended again.) Historically, the pension system is an achievement of social progress. In Germany since 1889, there has been an Old Age and Survivors' Insurance for wage earners and, since 1911, there have also been benefits for salary earners. With the pension reform of 1957, pensions beyond the age of 65 years have been seen as a form of "wage compensation"; they are adjusted to gross wage increases (now set to net wage increases). The pension limit has been flexible since 1973, with the option for men to retire at age 63 and women at 60. Due to the situation in the labor market in the 1980s "early retirement programs" were established, resulting in an average retirement age of 58 years. Based upon future demographic projections, the pension reform of 1991 fixed an elevation of the pension age, step-by-step, beginning with the year 2001.

Besides the general compulsory pension insurance, other systems of insurance for civil servants, self-employed persons, free-lance professionals, farmers, and other professions have been developed. In public service and larger companies, additional retirement insurance schemes are available. Pension rights of the insured include pensions (because of reduced capacity to earn a livelihood), retirement income, pensions to surviving dependents, and pensions to widows and widowers.

The purpose of these insurances is to ensure a standard of living with an income of 60 to 90% of former wage earnings. A duration of 45 working years and average earnings are necessary to gain the highest possible benefits. The pensions are computed from the level of the insured earnings and the number of valid insurance years. Those with fewer years of work risk low pensions. This is true for working-class spouses (who have only the husband's pension at their disposal), widows of workers, and unmarried and divorced women. The pension payments are computed on the basis of former income. Therefore, differences in the earnings in middle life years will be prolonged and stabilized in old age. Poverty in old age is a real problem in an affluent country; therefore, systems of a minimum pension for all are being discussed as an alternative to supplementary national assistance (which may have a stigmatizing character for the recipients). Also, a harmonization of the different income security systems would be helpful for larger social balance.

Pensions are the main source of income for 80% of the elderly. Maintenance support by the spouse is the primary income for 13% (mostly women), and income by employment is the dominant resource for nearly 2%. Other sources come from personal property or national assistance.

Demographic changes influence the stability of the pension system and will become crucial after 2015. To keep up the pension system in the future depends on a productive economy and the full employment of contributors. A higher limit to retirement alone will not solve the financing problems, because it is uncertain if employers will be able and willing to create enough places for work. Apart from insurance and civil service provisions, the Federal Social Welfare Act of 1961 (which replaced the Social Welfare System of 1924) entitles those unable to help themselves or not receiving the necessary help from others (from relatives) to benefits. Social welfare is designed to enable the recipient to live a dignified life. It is intended primarily to be an aid to self-reliance; it aims at enabling the needy to live independently of welfare support. It is allocated according to the specific conditions of each case.

Help for life maintenance consists of reoccurring and onetime benefits. Reoccurring benefits are fixed by the state authorities, taking account of actual living costs. In addition, necessary benefits for clothing and household goods are paid.

Life maintenance support can also be paid to residents in a home, an institution, or a similiar facility. Support in special life situations for elderly people are preventive health care, nursing care, aid for the blind, housekeeping aid, and financial payments and support.

Social welfare has its origin in the poor laws from past centuries and in its association with charity, which the older cohorts have especially not forgotten. Therefore, not all old persons with a potential claim for social welfare use it. In 1979, of all those 65 years old (and above), 6.3% drew social welfare support (3.7% of the men 7.7% of the women); 3.5% of the total population depended on social welfare benefits.

A special paragraph (§75) in the Federal Welfare Act aims at special regulations to assist the elderly to prevent, overcome, and relieve difficulties peculiar to old age and to enable the elderly to continue to take part in communal life. Such aids include help in finding and maintaining a dwelling suited to the needs of the old person; help in all matters connected with admission to an institution taking care of old people, in particular, finding a suitable institution; help in all matters connected with claiming supportive services for the elderly; help to attend meetings organized by institutions that promote social activities, entertainment, education, or cultural activities for old people; help to enable old people to stay in contact with persons they are close to; and help to find an activity wanted by the old person. These aids can also be given to prepare for old age.

In reality, the regulations of §75 do not oblige the authorities to act. Indeed, it is hardly ever the fact that individuals or groups take it into account, because of insufficient senior citizens organizations, and seldom do individuals claim these unspecific regulations.

Tax privileges for old people depend on special circumstances (income and wage tax, property, and inheritance). Maintenance support, under the Burdens Sharing Act, is available to those from former German territories in East Europe and to other war victims. Rent subsidies are granted for more than 10% of all pensioners' households, and older persons include more than 50% of all recipients of rent subsidies. This shows the extent of insufficient income of elderly people and permanent rising costs of housing.

Special benefits for elderly people consist of low-price senior tickets on the railways, exemption from radio and television fees under certain circumstances, fare reductions in public transport, and free admission to zoos and museums. The types and scale of privileges for elderly people in Germany vary widely from area to area.

HEALTH CARE SERVICES

The statutory health insurance system (funded by contributions of employees and employers in equal amounts) protects 90% of the population as obligatory insured, voluntary insured, pensioners, and dependents from the financial risks of illness. It provides for medical care, sickness benefits, hospital treatment, home nursing, homemaker services, help for the family, and death benefits (according to the relevant legal provisions). The insurance protection also extends principally to measures of illness prevention and rehabilitation. Every dues-paying member has to pay a monetary contribution depending on income (those who have greater incomes must pay more). This is a form of solidarity with the poor in that the benefits are the same. Apart from the statutory health insurance, there are private health insurance schemes. The health insurance of pensioners (introduced in 1941) is financed by contributions of Social Security authorities, by contributions of the statutory health insurance system, and, since 1983, by the pensioners themselves.

Protection concentrates on acute sickness and not on long-term care (which still has to be financed by the families or, in the last instance, national assistance). Help for chronically ill persons and for caregiving relatives has been a main issue in political discussion for more than 10 years, and many proposals have been made by the political parties, welfare organizations, and other institutions—without any effect.

The Health Reform Law of 1989 brought with it some improvements in partial financing of ambulatory services for severe forms of incapacity. Up to now, the federal government and the political parties are still looking for a long-term care insurance, under the obligatory health insurance system, to be installed in 1996, offering financial support, ambulatory services, and four weeks of "vacation from nursing" for caregiving relatives.

Medical treatment of elderly patients is mainly provided by the general practitioner and the acute hospital. Though there has been an increase in the number of medical specialists (and a decline in the number of general practitioners), physicians are lacking geriatric education and further education. In the great majority of cases, they renounce possible rehabilitative and activating treatments and confine themselves to prescriptions for medicine or medication distribution. The objective must be joint treatment and therapy with other professional groups, not referral to a variety of specialists working parallel and consecutively. As far as the patients are concerned, it is generally known that visiting the doctor is often a welcome means of spending time. Cooperation of physicians and social professions might be an adequate approach to react to these needs.

Physicians' treatment of old people living in institutions is also a problem. The continuity and quality of treatment have been criticized, along with the nonavailability of doctors in emergency situations, unwillingness to make home visits, and inadequate supervision of nursing personnel.

In comparison to other countries, there is a reduction of acute hospitals in Germany. The diminution of the number of hospitals and the reduction of beds are a declared purpose of health politics. During the last decade, acute hospitals were inclined to withdraw from providing care to elderly patients in order to avoid misplacement of chronically ill elderly patients within acute care hospitals. More than one-third of the patients are 60 years and older. Establishment of geriatric hospitals, geriatric departments, and hospices is still exceptional, but some of the existing specialized geriatric and rehabilitative hospitals have a high standard. In general, the system of health provision in Germany is oriented toward the needs of the younger, employed population.

Ambulatory care is provided prior to hospital placement. Health insurance funds finance ambulatory services only in medical need, if the patients are ill, if their health is endangered, and if the ambulatory medical service can help to avoid hospitalization.

More attention must be paid to posttreatment training programs so that the rehabilitation gains in geriatric hospitals will not be lost again.

HOUSING RESOURCES

The federal minister for town and territory planning and housing market has announced accommodation improvements for elderly persons as a key topic for policy development. More than 1 million dwellings are substandard residences, in which mainly single old persons are living. However, other problems exist: an insufficient number of residences for all people and a great demand for renovation of houses (especially in Eastern Germany).

Special planning in urban and rural districts is influencing, in a direct manner, the living conditions of elderly people. Great attention has to be paid to the protection of elderly people in the Social Tenancy Law if they face the risk of being displaced because of modernization or privatization housing programs. Since 1965, rent rebates have been paid; two-thirds of the recipients are pensioners.

The proportion of residents living in substandard housing (without bathrooms in the accommodation, without central heating or lifts in multistored buildings) is estimated at 40% of the households headed by elderly persons. In the erection of new buildings, it is advisable to provide residences for elderly people on the ground floor.

Besides this quantitative demand for residences, attention has to be paid to qualitative issues, which are linked to the living experiences of elderly people. It is important to know what kind of environment they consider adequate to their needs. Many persons are living in great blocks of buildings and do not want to miss neighborhood relationships. Others have built self-contained houses with a garden; others want to move into rural areas. Considerable relocations are expected into suburban areas. For all these living conditions, various and differentiated supports exist and are needed.

The main issue of politics for the aged in Germany is the maintenance of independence and social networks. Therefore, the government focuses attention on the "living together of different generations." Policies of former years, to erect blocks for elderly persons (which can be more easily provided with support), will not be fostered in the future. The risks of segregation are generally recognized. Retirement communities will not be supported in Germany. In spite of this intention, we have the fact of aging concentrations due to the job mobility of the younger generation. Groups of higher-income persons are moving out of old residential areas in which older people live (in numbers above average). Other socially weak groups (e.g., foreigners) move in, with the effect of segregation. Typical for the old residential areas and the housing situation of the elderly in general is the continued lack of green areas and leisure facilities in the immediate surroundings, as well as high degrees of pollution. Shops and medical services are not always available near the home.

Great efforts by public and private institutions (e.g., the building and loan associations) are made to implement innovative housing arrangements. Residences for elderly persons will be integrated into usual buildings, with services provided by small district units. Such activities require case management and comprehensive support in cooperation of the variety of services. Some cities have implemented counseling teams for "the adaption of dwellings to old age" with a social worker and an architect. In most cases, only a few alterations in the dwelling equipment are necessary to better the living conditions of handicapped people and to avoid removal of persons into homes for the aged. Some of these age-adjusted dwellings are "looked-after"; that is, volunteer visitors and professionals periodically investigate the situation of the elderly person. Some technological instruments are available (e.g., portable emergency calls).

Independent, collective forms of living together still are exceptions. Those persons who want to live together with people of their own choice have to find one another in their middle age or in early retirement years.

SUPPORTIVE SERVICES

Types of social services are "open" or ambulatory, semi-institutional, and institutional facilities. The open area contains information and counseling, congregation points, and clubs. It is well known that information about services for elderly people is not very great because of the variety and fragmentation of such resources. Counseling services for the elderly are financed publicly, but they are installed in the central offices of authorities and do not reach the people in need of information. Investigations found out that the mobile and already informed part of the population is using these resources for their further advantage. Efforts have been made for counseling in the districts and in combination with home visits and group services.

Old people's day centers and meeting points are used by organized seniors and by persons who already know each other. Because of personnel limitations, this supportive opportunity is hardly able to do outreach visits to the lonely and poor elderly or to integrate them into a seniors' club.

Public and private firms provide meals-on-wheels in various locations. The distribution of the meals must be organized in an effective manner; thus, it is not always possible for the deliverer to add communication and counseling to the service.

Congregate dining services are offered within some old people's day centers or in canteens and messes of public institutions. The chance to develop friendships between the users is undertaken neither by the personnel nor by the elderly; individuals dine alone.

Various welfare organizations offer many homemaker services and home nursing, often in competition with each other. For the elderly it is a problem to overview all possibilities and opportunities. Further problems result from the division of labor between various groups of staff and between the different support activities. They are rarely done by one professional and/or volunteer person. Divisions in provision exist among basic nursing, qualified nursing, meals-on-wheels, and counseling. Various ambulatory services may attend to the same person. Support for the relatives is still minimal. Model counseling agencies give psychotherapeutic support to families with respect to the emotional problems linked with caregiving.

Attempts are made to combine these various support services in one organization: the social service centers (Sozialstationen). Since 1972, the governments of the different federal states (Länder) have given financial support to these institutions, organized by the welfare organizations. It is intended that social service centers will meet the requirements of 20,000 to 50,000 inhabitants in the cities and 15,000 to 25,000 inhabitants in rural districts. On the average, the centers provide assistance to nearly 3% of the population age 65 years and above.

Different professional staff (nurses, ergotherapists, social workers) may be integrated, if the finances are guaranteed. In reality, social service centers have to concentrate on ambulatory medical treatment, because the main financing fund is held by health insurances and restricted to activities avoiding hospital stay. They are restricted to "maintenance assistance" and are not for training on rehabilitation or for fostering potential self-help competences. Meanwhile, patients have to pay for rental of aids (wheelchairs, bed lifts) and for other services like foot care, hygiene, and housecleaning. Efforts are made to integrate ambulatory mental health services into the centers and to give further education in geropsychiatry to appropriate personnel. Day-care facilities still hardly exist (65 facilities in 1990), though efforts are made by the welfare organizations to establish them. Problems in financing such services are handicaps to stabilize such supportive semi-institutional services. The readiness of physicians and hospitals to transfer patients to day-care facilities has first to be instilled. At the same time, counseling relatives is necessary. A high organizational input also is required for vacation beds or short inpatient stays in hospitals. If health insurance is not ready to pay, users have to apply for social welfare benefits—and they often are not informed about how to do this or do not want to accept the welfare status.

If the requirements for care and nursing cannot be met by the families or by ambulatory services, elderly are dependent on homes or asylums. In West Germany, 500,000 people (or 4% of the elder population) live in 6,000 homes for the elderly. The former balance among boarding homes (for those living independently but wishing to get immediate help in case of need), homes or asylums for the old, and nursing homes is disappearing. The average entrance age for old-age homes has climbed from 70 years in 1970 to 82 years in the beginning of the 1990s. Elderly people are ready to move into institutional settings only when they are unable to live independently. Many homes have changed into nursing homes.

LEISURE-TIME RESOURCES

A developmental task for elderly people consists of the self-reliant formation of daily life after the phase of work and raising children. This has to happen in the context of coping with getting old and the consciousness of limited years.

Retirement is not to be equated with leisure time; many obligations in household, family, and organization of daily life remain. Empirical studies (see Tokarski and Schmitz-Scherzer, 1985) reveal a daily subjective leisure time of six to seven hours. In the foreground of activities are using mass media, staying at home in a "comfortable mood," and social contact with family members and relatives. Activities apart from family happen first in associations and clubs in which the person has been a member for many years. Increasing interest is paid to traveling comfortably and to seeing other countries. But, as a rule, retirement activities are rarely new; in most cases existing interests widen and continue.

Therefore, traditional formal services for elderly people should include opportunities for sociability (in clubs and seniors' day centers); for education and discussion groups (in the people's high schools or Volks-High-Schools, senior universities, and senior organizations); for workshops to practice hobbies and interests relating to handicrafts; and for recreation, gymnastics, and meditation. These opportunities reach 15% of the elderly persons in Germany. The great majority are not interested in solely "senior" services.

During the last few years, formal organizations have been applying for innovative programs for those cohorts growing old. In some cities, model programs like "exchange initiatives of interests and knowledge" have been established to bring elderly together on the basis of their competencies. Interactions with the younger generation are also included in these models. Other programs are "picking up the experiences of the elderly," intending to pass on the skills of retired persons to interested younger ones. In 1992, a federal program was established with the title Seniors' Bureau, which is a supported, self-help program in the 16 regional states to connect the existing volunteer activities and to encourage new solidarity activities. Another description for this effort is "to build up an infrastructure of communication and mutual help."

A new balance has to be found between the self-centered, leisure-time interests of the individual and contributions to the needs of others and the community. Such efforts are directed not only to seniors but to "people growing old" who look for new perspectives in their life course. Offers have to match the interests in life review, testing new areas of commitment, and getting further sources of challenges and appreciation.

Some universities have developed postprofessional senior curricula in the domains of social solidarity, networking, ecology, and town improvement. Up to now volunteers (1.5 million persons, mainly women between 40 and 60 years of age) found themselves organized by formal welfare organizations with no real chance of self-determination.

An educational model program for socially underprivileged older people was tested in five towns (see Knopf, 1987; Karl, 1990). It focused on the interests and needs of older people and aimed at the development of initiative, self-confidence, and the ability to act independently. Empowerment activities are effective when they are integrated in the immediate environment of the living areas of elderly persons. In an outreach approach, educational opportunities and home visits can complement each other when information, counseling, and group resources are integrated directly in the vicinity of elderly people and over a continuous period of time. Not public authorities, but churches, self-help initiatives, and associations have a good chance to be close to the interests and leisure structures of the local people. On the other hand, the private leisure industry is successful in offering opportunities for (individual) consumption of desired goods and services.

ADVOCACY AND PROTECTION

"The dignity of man shall be inviolable. To repect and protect it shall be the duty of all state authority" (Article 1 of the Constitution of the Federal Republic of Germany). A comprehensive judicial system for many dimensions of life has developed, which is affecting citizens of every age. Also, the risk of becoming handicapped is a common one and has to be generally solved by the public. Some rights (e.g., for rehabilitative measures) have to be realized also for elderly persons, not only for the persons who are capable of earning their living and are needed by employers. Preconditional for the use of rights is that citizens are informed and able to claim their rights. Empirical studies (see Federal Ministry of Youth, Family, and Health, 1982) in Germany have shown that, above all, elderly people (in the first instance, widows) know little about their social and financial rights and about the legal aspects of their householding (e.g., tenancy and eviction protection).

Public institutions are expected to give counseling services to elderly people so as to inform them about their social rights. Elderly people with low incomes can gain judicial advocacy (free of charge) and financial aid for lawsuits. With the beginning of the 1990s, the guardianship law has been improved.

No public institution, however, actively prosecutes violations of the interests of old people. Violence against handicapped elderly persons in institutions and families is a known reality. Often professionals have to be the agent for the elderly's rights.

Under the senior organizations of the FRG, the Grey Panthers see themselves explicitly as a "senior protection association." They claim, for example, a basic rent for all, financial nursing assistance by the state, and humane living conditions in homes for the aged and in psychiatric institutions.

With public protest actions, the elderly have sought attention and political influence. But to fill these interests into the form of a political party and to take part in elections have proven to be ineffective.

Not all human needs can be solved in judicial terms. Human rights, especially in old age, gain reality in the daily interaction of individuals on the basis of an ethnic of solidarity, which is part of the values of persons in every age.

FUTURE PROJECTIONS

It is expected that tomorrow's old will differ considerably from today's, that they will be more able to assert themselves, better educated, and less easily intimidated. Values and images of the elderly, especially of elderly women who are entering the labor market, will change. In 30 years, one-third of the total population and half of the population entitled to vote in political elections will be composed of elderly people. In the mass media, prognoses of a graying society and of "the coming war of the young against the old" are fashionable. Of greater importance is a cohort perspective: the old people of 2030 will be the members of the baby boom generation born in the 1960s. They are called an "ongoing problem group" because of their disadvantages in getting places in the kindergarten, school, companies, and employment.

The economic situation of the present population of old people might be the best one thus far because they have experienced manifold improvements in the standard of living under conditions of economic upswing. Following generations of elderly people might be confronted with decreasing living standards, due to changes in ecology and welfare. Inequalities between older persons may arise, considering the present work conditions (gainful employment on the one side, longtime unemployment and marginal employment for others on the other side). Distribution conflicts between the social groups and rivalry for a prior status in the welfare and social service system can arise if policies are not able to establish balances and mutual alliances between the generations and social classes.

Those within the welfare state are forced to adapt themselves to the changing economic conditions of the society. As far as the bureaucratic administration and the welfare organizations are concerned, resistance to innovation is to be observed. If the agencies and organizations themselves are threatened, they put the blame, in first instance, on their institutions, their personnel, and their share of the market. In spite of the growing numbers of very old people, it is assumed that social services for the old will be curtailed in the area of nursing rather than in other neglected areas (such as further education, counseling, preparation for old age). Models are looked for—such as referral and distribution centers for better coordination—to gain a higher efficiency.

Excellent gerontological knowledge and concepts are available but are not practiced if they are contrary to organization interests. It is assumed that financial restrictions and the changing demand and self-consciousness of service users will be the main factors of future innovation. An important intermediary group will be people willing to work in the social and health services. Much depends on their motivation and further education in gerontology and geriatrics to solve the problems of increasing numbers of physically and mentally handicapped old people.

BIBLIOGRAPHY

Akademie der Wissenschaften (ed.). *Zukunft des Alterns und gesellschaftliche Entwicklung.* Berlin, 1992.

Bäcker G., Bispinck, R., Hofemann, K., and Naegele, G. (eds.). *Sozialpolitik und soziale Lage in der Bundesrepublik Deutschland.* Vol. 2: *Gesundheit—Familie—Alter—Soziale Dienste.* Köln, 1990.

Barth, S., and Hain, W. Szenarien zur demographischen Entwicklung in einem vereinigten Deutschland—Perspektiven für die gesetzliche Rentenversicherung. In *Deutsche Rentenversicherung,* December 1990, 736–744.

Bundesministerium für Raumordnung, Bauwesen und Städtebau (ed.). *Ältere Menschen und ihr Wohnquartier.* Bonn, 1991.

———. *Wohnen alter und pflegebedürftiger Menschen.* Bonn, 1991.

Deutsches Zentrum für Altersfragen (ed.). *Die ergraute Gesellschaft.* Berlin, 1987.

Federal Ministry of Youth, Family, and Health. On the policy for the elderly and the system of their social security in the Federal Republic of Germany. In German Centre of Gerontology (ed.), *Report on the Situation of the Elderly in the Federal Republic of Germany.* Berlin, 1982.

Karl, F. *Neue Wege in der sozialen Alternarbeit.* Freiburg, 1990.

Karl, F., and Tokarski, W. (eds.). Die "neuen" Alten. 17th session, Deutsche Gesellschaft für Gerontologie. Kassel, 1989.

———. *Bildung und Freizeit im Alter.* Bern, 1992.

Knopf, D. *Verstehen, anknüpfen, entwickeln. Animatorische Bildungsarbeit mit sozial und bildungsbenachteiligten älteren Menschen.* Berlin, 1987.

Minister for Social Affairs (ed.). *Ältere Menschen in Nordrhein Westfalen.* Düsseldorf, 1990.

Robert Bosch Foundation (ed.). *Die demographische Herausforderung. Das Gesundheitssystem angesichts einer veränderten Bevölkerungsstruktur.* Gerlingen, 1989.

Schumann, J. Social services and social work practice with the elderly in FRG. In M. C. Hokenstad and K. A. Kendall (eds.), *Gerontological Social Work.* New York: International Perspectives, 1988, 61–76.

Schütz, R. M., Schmidt, R., and Tews, H. P. (eds.). Altern zwischen Hoffnung und Verzicht. 18th session, Deutsche Gesellschaft für Gerontologie, Lübeck, 1991.

Statistisches Bundesamt (ed.). *Statistisches Jahrbuch für das vereinte Deutschland.* Bonn, 1991.

Tews, H. P. *Soziologie des Alters.* Heidelberg, 1994.
Tokarski, W., and Schmitz-Scherzer, R. *Freizeit.* Stuttgart, 1985.
United Nations. *World Population Prospects—The 1990 Revision.* Population Studies 120-ST/ESA/SER.A/120. New York: Department of International Economic and Social Affairs, 1991.

10

GHANA

Charles K. Brown

INTRODUCTION

The Role of the Elderly

In both traditional and contemporary Ghanaian society, old age is regarded as a blessing and old people as sacred. Indeed, the long lives of old persons are regarded as proof of their righteousness (Sarpong, 1983).

To be old in Ghana is to be considered dignified and, therefore, deserving of honor, respect, and sympathy. It is believed that the respect that the young owe the aged compels the former to look after the latter tenderly. Therefore, to neglect one's father or mother is to commit an unpardonable act of ingratitude. Every parent looks forward to receiving the reciprocal treatment of love and affection from his or her children. In fact, a child cannot neglect this duty without considerably losing face (Brown, 1990).

Old age in Ghana also commands obedience. To fail, or refuse, to do what an old person tells you or orders you is to leave yourself open to trouble. This is because the words of an old person are believed to be prophetic, as well as maledictory. This gives the elderly an authority that is not imposed by brute force but enforced by the moral obedience expected of young people.

Ghanaians are also encouraged to be with the elderly as much as possible, especially since the elderly are attributed with wisdom and knowledge. An old person is regarded as the repository of the mores, folkways, and traditions of the society. The elderly have pragmatic and local knowledge, particularly about the flora and fauna of the society. Indeed, the number of years lived by a person is supposed to be commensurate with the store of wisdom. Hence the Akan proverb: "When your grandmother tells you something, you do not say you are

Table 10.1
Estimated and Projected Population Aged 60 and Over by Sex and Age Group in Ghana, 1960, 1980, 2000, 2020, 2025

(In Thousands)

Age Group	1960 Male	1960 Female	1980 Male	1980 Female	2000 Male	2000 Female	2020 Male	2020 Female	2025 Male	2025 Female
60 - 69	90	105	161	184	296	334	592	657	720	794
70 - 79	37	41	66	84	134	163	270	321	330	391
80+	7	8	11	16	27	38	65	88	81	109

Source: Derived from United Nations, 1982.

going to ask your mother whether it is true." In other words, if your grandmother does not know, your mother cannot know! (Brown, 1990).

However, with increasing social change, several of the traditional roles formerly performed by the elderly have been affected. These factors include formal education (with its inculcation of new values, an inquiring mind, and the projection of new models of social relations); industrialization and job opportunities (which tend to make the youth more independent and ignore—and sometimes even challenge—the authority of the elderly); rural-urban migration (which has resulted in the residential segregation of generations, with young people living in the urban sector, which emphasizes nuclear accommodation); the advent of Christianity and Islam (which has weakened the influence and authority of the elderly as the custodians of the traditional belief system and practices); and the decline of traditional technology (in which the youth served their apprenticeship under the aged).

Demographic Characteristics of the Elderly

The most outstanding feature of the age structure of Ghana's population is its youthfulness. The proportion of persons aged less than 15 years was 44.6% in 1960, and it is estimated that this figure will increase to 46.0% by the year 2000. In contrast, the proportion of persons aged 60 and over in 1960 was 4.2%, which will increase slightly to 4.5% by the year 2000.

The figures in Table 10.1 indicate that the total number of the elderly in Ghana will triple from 522,000 persons in 1980 to an estimated 1,933,000 in 2020 and then more than quadruple to 2,425,000 in the year 2025. However, the percentage share in the total population will remain low, representing 4.5% in 1980, 5.7% in 2020, and 6.4% in 2025.

The low proportion of the elderly in the Ghanaian population should not, however, obscure the increase in their absolute number or their importance, economically and demographically. Indeed, the Ghanaian population aged 60 and over is estimated to rise by a factor of 8.5 from 1960 to 2025, an increase larger than the factor of 5.6 projected for the total population. The main reason for the steady increase in the number of elderly persons in Ghana is that the cohorts of children who will become the elderly population over the next 40 years will be successively larger. This is attributable to the high fertility rates of recent decades, coupled with increased life expectancy, especially among the young (but affecting the older age groups as well).

With regard to the sex ratio, it is worth noting that, within the elderly population, females have consistently outnumbered males since the 1960s and will continue to do so even after 2025.

To summarize, we should note that the process of population aging will get under way in Ghana only after the turn of the century, in the sense that the population (as a whole) will become older. In the initial phase, the aging trend will be concentrated predominantly in the young and middle-aged adult group. Only after 2025 will the progressive aging of the population become manifest in the increasing relative proportion of the oldest segment of the population.

This account should not be misconstrued to mean that Ghana does not yet have a problem of the aging of its population. On the contrary, now should be seen as the right time to evolve a comprehensive program for the provision of an infrastructure of health and social services for the population aged 60 and over in Ghana (Brown, 1991, p. 15).

The Living Arrangements of the Elderly

The available data on household types and composition in Ghana do not specifically give the living patterns of the elderly. It is therefore difficult to describe in any detail the living arrangements of the elderly in Ghanaian society. However, a look at the household size and composition should throw some light on the residential pattern of Ghanaian elderly.

A Ghanaian household may contain both related and unrelated persons. The former group may also constitute one or more conjugal family nuclei consisting of married children and also the head's and/or spouse's sisters and brothers and their children, including grandchildren and in-laws.

The average household size ranges from 4.3 to 4.9 persons, with the rural average size exceeding that of the urban areas by 4% (Gaisie and De Graft-Johnson, 1976, p. 54). About 59% of the households contain four or more persons, and more than 20% of the population live in households with seven or more members. A conspicuous feature of the rural household structure is the predominance of large households, that is, households with four or more members.

With regard to the composition of the household, 44% consist of nuclear families (made up of husband, wife, and children), with an average family size of 4.6. The extended-family type make up about 40% of the total households, indicating the extent to which Ghanaian society is permeated by the extended-family system with its relatively large average family size of about 7.0 persons (Gaisie and De Graft-Johnson, 1976, p. 53). The same household patterns prevail in both the urban and rural areas except that nuclear and extended families are more commonly found in the villages than in the urban areas. On the other hand, one-person family households and one-parent family households are notable features of the urban household structure. Indeed, the loose kinship ties and social and economic constraints prevalent in the urban environment make people enter into certain living arrangements that would not be necessary under the traditional social system.

The sex differentials in respect of household patterns reveal some interesting features. One-spouse households contain proportionately more females than males, especially in the towns and cities, where 30% of the females (as against 22% of the males) live in one-spouse households, a phenomenon that is partly indicative of higher male mortality. Also, there is a higher proportion of males than females living alone (that is, in one-person households). This is suggestive of the tendency among unmarried, divorced, and widowed females to stay with relatives rather than to set up their own households. For example, while 60% of the male divorcés had established one-person households, only 20% of their female counterparts preferred that form of living arrangement, and the corresponding proportions for widowers and widows were 37% and 20% respectively.

This account on the size and composition of the Ghanaian household would seem to indicate that the elderly are more likely to stay with other family members than to stay alone. However, as has been indicated, there would be differentials in household patterns as to sex and urban-rural residence. While elderly males are likely to be more numerous than females in one-person households, one-spouse households are likely to contain more females than males. Furthermore, the one-person and one-parent households would tend to be a more common form of living arrangement for the elderly in the urban areas than in the rural areas. Gaisie et al. (1970) found that 1.7% and 18% of the rural female population lived in the one-person and one-spouse households, respectively. This is compared with 3% and 30% of the urban female population who lived in these types of households, respectively. The proportion of urban males living alone was nearly twice that of their rural counterparts, and for every rural male living in a nonrelated person's household, there were three male urbanites.

Education and Training

One of the peculiar circumstances of the current group of elderly in Ghana is that most of them grew up before the opportunities for formal education became available, except for those who availed themselves of the few educational centers with long Christian missionary contact in the South. Consequently, the educational status of the elderly is relatively low compared with the other age groups in the population. The available evidence indicates that the great majority of the elderly population (males, 84.3%; females, 95.0%) never went to school. However, higher rates of school attendance are found in the urban areas (which reflects the concentration of educational facilities in these areas).

Since the great majority of the elderly have not had any formal education and training, one would expect that any skills that they would acquire would naturally come from the nonformal type of education and training. A study by Brown (1984) showed that for most of the elderly males, their training had mostly been in handicraft, artisanship, driving, and farming; while for the elderly females, training had mainly been in trading, food processing, dressmaking, and farming. For the elderly males, their skills had been acquired mainly through formal and informal apprenticeship with established artisans, parents, or relatives; while elderly females had acquired their skills by working with their mothers or other female relatives.

Labor Force Participation

In Ghana, there is a surprisingly large number of persons in the labor force in the age group 60 and over, making up about 9% of the labor force. Data on age-specific activity rates for the population aged 60 years and over in 1970, male/female and urban/rural, generally indicate high activity rates for the age group 60–69. Indeed, in this age group, activity rates are generally higher than those for the total population aged 15 years and over. The main reason for the high participation rate is the need for persons in this age group to receive an income on which to live.

There is also a significant difference between the sexes. Male activity rates are consistently higher than those for females in all age groups (60–85 and over) and in both rural and urban areas. The difference in the ranking of males and females could perhaps be attributed mainly to the fact that men who survive to an old age usually retain their position as head of household and are, of necessity, forced to engage in some form of economic activity, even though their efforts and the returns from this activity may be minimum.

Rural activity rates of employment are consistently higher than urban rates for both males and females in all the age groups. The main explanation is that agriculture is the main occupation in the rural areas and allows individuals to carry on economic activities until they themselves decide to quit. Thus, the type of job not only permits flexibility in scheduling work but also ensures discretion in retirement decisions (Brown, 1987, p. 50).

The Formal Structure of Care of the Elderly

Both the colonial British administration and the postindependence regimes have apparently implicitly relied on the ability of the family network to cope with the problem of individual aging. Indeed, no concrete policies have evolved in anticipation of the problems of population aging in Ghana. The result is that in Ghana, at the moment, no law or comprehensive national policy caters specifically to the needs of, and welfare services for, the aged, although general laws on retirement and pension affect the aged. Not until 1982 was a National Commission on the Aged established by the government to advise on all matters related to the welfare of the aged.

While there are no specific policies for the welfare of the aged, some government departments (which deal with social welfare, community and rural development, public health, and adult education) cater, in some ways, to the needs of the elderly. For example, the problems of the needy, including the aged in urban areas, come under the schedule of the Department of Social Welfare, whereas the Department of Community Development caters to the elderly in rural areas. Similarly, the Social Security and pension schemes make some provisions for the elderly. Under the Social Security Act, 1965 (Act 279) and the Social Security Decree, 1972 (N.R.C.D. 127), all workers, whether in the public or private sector, should be covered by the Social Security fund. Workers are required to contribute 5% of their earnings to the fund, while their employers contribute 12.5%, thus making a total of 17.5% of the worker's wage. Under the pension scheme the worker has the following retirement benefits: a superannuation or old-age benefit, an invalidity benefit, and a survivor's benefit.

With these benefits retired workers are to take care of themselves and their family for the rest of their lives. However, since these benefits are not constantly adjusted to take care of inflation and changes in the cost of living, they do not provide the elderly with an adequate level of protection sufficient to maintain their financial independence. This is a far cry from the lofty and laudable ideals that the initiators of the Social Security Bill had in mind when it was introduced in 1965: "We require the assistance of our workers so that they continue to work till, and, if possible, after superannuation to ensure carefree, comfortable and happy old age, instead of living like parasites on the all too meagre income of some relations" (Republic of Ghana, 1965).

However, in 1991, a new pension scheme was introduced. The Social Security Law, PNDC Law 247, 1991, is now applicable to all workers of an establishment, and all self-employed persons may opt to join the scheme. Again, under the new Social Security Law, Section 39, pension payments will be reviewed when general salaries are reviewed. It might be said, however, that the scheme has just been introduced and would need to grow steadily if it is to be self-sustaining.

INCOME MAINTENANCE AND EMPLOYMENT

Until 1991, the existing income security schemes provided coverage to only a small minority of the elderly who had experienced paid employment in the public and private sectors. The schemes did not cover self-employed persons, agricultural workers, peasants, and farmers—who constitute the great majority of wage earners in Ghana. Thus, for this category of workers, there was no insurance against old age, except in the traditional family system.

The existing Social Security Law, PNDC Law 247, attempts to provide comprehensive coverage for all workers in the country. Under Section 34, the following benefits are payable: a superannuation pension (when a member of the scheme retires or is retired after attaining the pensionable age of 60); a lump sum equal to the member's contribution and interest equivalent to half the prevailing government treasury rate on it (where the contributor had 20 years minimum contribution prior to retirement); an invalidity pension for a member of the scheme who has contributed for not less than 12 months within the last 36 months and is certified by a medical board to be incapable of any normal gainful employment by virtue of a permanent physical or mental disability; and a survivor's lump sum benefit (on the member's death, to such members of the family who are dependents and in whose favor a valid nomination exists).

As comprehensive as the new pension scheme may seem, it still leaves out the elderly who have not had the opportunity to contribute to pension funds earlier in life. Also, to ask self-employed persons to contribute 17.5% of their monthly income may be too much for those who are in seasonal or irregular employment.

Income and Assets

Very few studies have provided actual estimates of levels of income and income distribution in Ghana. The major studies in this field include various household budget surveys conducted by the Central Bureau of Statistics (CBS), the Eastern Region Household Budget Survey conducted by Dutta-Roy (1969), a survey of farm incomes by Rourke (1971), and a study of the distribution of monetary incomes in Ghana. The available evidence from these surveys and other individual studies generally shows that incomes in rural Ghana are lower than incomes in the urban areas. However, in Ghana, the application of monetary income to determine the well-being of the elderly becomes difficult because none of the above-mentioned studies have examined the distribution of income by the various age groups. More important, for the majority of the aging in Ghana who are self-employed, a study to determine their well-being should focus on their real incomes, which include all the material services and favors that a person can receive.

Given the dearth of data on the economic status of the elderly, consider the data collected by Brown (1984) on a sample of elderly people in the Greater Accra Region of Ghana. The results of the study indicated that nearly half (48.9%) were living in their own houses. About 18% were living in family or ancestral homes, 12.1% in other relatives' houses, and 6.1% in their children's houses. Only 11.5% rented their houses.

The main sources of income from financial assets were salaries, pensions, Social Security, savings, and interest on money lent to others. For the sample the average annual income from these assets was 14,032.82 cedis (or US $35). In addition to income from these financial assets, the elderly had income from

Table 10.2
Some Socioeconomic Indicators Related to the Health Delivery System in Ghana

1.	Population per Physician	14,890	(1984)
2.	Population per Nurse	640	(1984)
3.	Nurses per Doctor	23.3	(1984)
4.	Life Expectancy at Birth	45.0	(1960)
		55.0	(1990)
5.	Population with Access to Health Services	61%	(1985–87)
6.	Population with Access to Safe Water	35%	(1975–80)
		57%	(1988)
7.	Population with Access to Sanitation	31%	(1985–88)
8.	Percentage of Total Central Government Expenditure for Health	6.3 5.8	(1972) (1983)
9.	Public Health Expenditure as Percentage of the GNP	1.1 1.2	(1960) (1986)

Sources: UNDP, 1991; World Bank, 1986.

rent from the land, farm, house, and other property; interests and dividends; and remittances from abroad and within the country. The total average amount received from other sources during the past 12 months was ¢28,930.00 (US $72). Thus, the total average annual income received was ¢42,962.82 (US $107). In contrast, the value of average annual consumption expenditure was ¢69,545.66 (US $174). Thus there was a deficit of 26,582.84 (US $66) between income and expenditures.

The enormity of the financial problem was echoed by 79.5% of the sample, who indicated that, in general, their income and assets were not adequate to meet their minimum requirements. Compared with their financial position five years earlier, the financial position of 77.8% was worse than before. Thus, the results of the study were in line with the a priori observation that, as a group, the aging constitute one of the poorest and most disadvantaged groups in Ghanaian society.

HEALTH CARE SERVICES

Existing Health Delivery Services

Table 10.2 gives some socioeconomic indicators related to the health delivery system in Ghana. From the table, it can be concluded that the health care system is characterized by a lack of medical and paramedical personnel; inadequate hospital and clinical facilities; insufficient equipment, supplies, and transportation; and a low per capita health expenditure.

Furthermore, not only is government expenditure comparatively low, but a large part of the money is spent on curative medicine and hospital maintenance, mostly in the urban areas. The result is that the majority of the population remains beyond the reach of modern health care. Indeed, until quite recently, preventive public health programs were neglected, resulting in the widespread incidence of many communicable and preventive diseases.

Health care services are mostly clinic-based and provided to those who seek them and can afford them; the current health delivery system in Ghana is also fragmented. The central government hospitals, mission hospitals, private medical practitioners, voluntary organizations, and mining and industrial hospitals provide useful services but rarely coordinate their activities at the local level. Even within the Ministry of Health (MOH) delivery system, the general hospitals are invariably controlled and supervised by MOH headquarters in Accra, the national capital. In short, the sectoral approach to health problems and needs, which largely characterizes the present health delivery system in Ghana, has failed to satisfy the needs of the majority of the people.

In connection with the elderly, the provision of health care services is usually targeted at the general population and not specifically at the older population or even the very old. Emphasis has been placed on community-based health services benefiting all the needy members of the community.

New Approaches to Health Care Delivery

With the introduction of the World Health Organization's (WHO) Health for All by the Year 2000, the government of Ghana has endorsed the principle of primary health care at the community level. In effect, the government is committed to implementing the recommendation of the Plan of Action of Aging, which states: "Health efforts, in particular primary health care as a strategy, should be directed at enabling the elderly to lead independent lives in their own family and community for as long as possible" (UN, 1983, p. 29).

The government has also recognized the particular circumstances of the elderly and has identified health issues concerning the elderly as being of special policy concern. In order to remove financial barriers to medical care, the Ministry of Health (in 1991) undertook to provide free health services to the elderly, without income restrictions. Currently, however, the modalities for implementing the decision have not been worked out.

Finally, in order to reinforce preventive strategies, health education campaigns are now being undertaken by primary health care personnel all over the country.

HOUSING RESOURCES

Suitable living accommodations are necessary for the well-being of people of all ages and stations in life. However, the suitability of living accommodations becomes even more crucial for older persons because of the proportionately greater amount of time they are likely to spend at home. Some older people spend almost every moment of their last years at home, and even when they do leave, they tend to limit their movements to their immediate environs.

As in many developing countries, inadequate housing—in both quantitative and qualitative terms—is a major problem in Ghana. Although the housing situation confronts the population as a whole, the elderly are particularly vulnerable to such deficiencies as inadequate water supply, poor sanitation, and overcrowding.

In many urban areas of the country, unplanned and uncontrolled settlements lack most of the basic amenities of daily living, such as proper sewerage systems, potable water supply, and hygienic conditions. Overshadowing the poor municipal service infrastructure is the problem of overcrowding, which creates physical and psychological strain and often hinders couples from providing shelter to older parents.

The vast majority of rural settlements also lack basic infrastructural facilities, such as good drinking water, electricity, modern sanitary facilities, effective communication, and a host of the social services that urban dwellers take for granted. For older persons whose children have migrated to urban areas, a major difficulty lies in having access to living amenities and keeping their shelter repaired and in good condition.

Even though the wish of most elderly in Ghana is to own their own houses, in a sample survey, Brown (1984) found that less than half (48.9%) of the respondents actually owned houses. With regard to the residential pattern, Brown (1984) found that 47.3% were living in their own houses, 18.2% in their family or ancestral homes, 12.1% in other relatives houses, and 6.1% in their children's houses. Only 11.5% had rented the houses in which they were living; the rent was paid by the children (45%), by themselves (40%), or by the spouse (15%).

SUPPORTIVE SERVICES

The Department of Social Welfare is the main government department charged with the ultimate responsibility of overseeing the affairs of the elderly and coordinating the activities of the various organizations and associations involved in the provision of voluntary social services and material help for the elderly. The department, however, does not have the resources to provide the services to the elderly. Instead, it encourages individual organizations to perform this function by coordinating their activities.

Voluntary associations have been generally more alert than the government in recognizing the needs of the elderly and providing the required help. Church organizations, such as Hope Society and St. Vincent of the Catholic Church of Ghana, Men's and Women's Fellowships of several Protestant and Spiritual churches, as well as other voluntary organizations such as Help Age Ghana, the Red Cross, Boy Scouts, Ghana National Association of Teachers (GNAT), and Women's World Banking (Ghana) Ltd., provide voluntary social services and material help for the elderly in Ghana. Help Age Ghana and Women's World Banking can be used to illustrate the point.

Help Age Ghana, a member of Help Age International, was set up in 1989 to improve the quality of life for elderly people, especially those experiencing poverty, loneliness, or isolation. Working in partnership with other agencies, Help Age Ghana implements a number of innovative and practical programs based at the community level. It also cooperates with governmental and other institutions that have similar programs in research and other activities with the aim of eventually developing policies and services for the welfare of the elderly. Currently, the association has the following programs: annually, a full week's program of activities to educate the general public and make aware the presence and problems of the elderly; a zonal program that enables member volunteers (with their leaders in the 11 zones) to undertake home visits; and an "Adopt-a-Granny" scheme by which any person can adopt a poor aged person to meet the basic necessities of life. The association also has the intention of opening a day-care center at Bubuashie, a suburb in Accra.

Women's World Banking Ghana Ltd. (WWBG), an affiliate of Women's World Banking International, was incorporated as a company in Ghana in 1983 and has been operational since 1988. Its main objective is to raise the living standards of Ghanaian women and their families by redirecting financial resources and by providing training in business management and technical skills to entrepreneurial women and representatives of women's groups.

Since 1991, WWBG has been operating an old-age project at Cape Coast, the capital of the Central Region. The aim of the project, which is the first of its kind in Ghana, is to provide a day center where the elderly people of Cape Coast can have some of their needs identified and met. The center provides facilities for the socially isolated to come and meet with their peers and buy a subsidized meal while attending day care. For the elderly who are more physically capable, the center provides some income-generating activities to enable them to earn income and be better able to support themselves. When the center is more established, WWBG intends to extend the level of care into the community and to those who are totally housebound. It also intends to replicate the experience in other parts of the country.

LEISURE-TIME RESOURCES

Unlike the elderly in developed countries, who gradually expand the time they spend in leisure roles as age increases (Riley and Foner, 1968), leisure roles cannot be said to be an integral part of life among the elderly in Ghana. In his study, Brown (1984) found that even though the old had enough rest periods to engage in various leisure activities, they did not do so. In effect, they were not able to fully utilize all the leisure time at their disposal, partly because of their reduced income and purchasing power and partly because leisure activities had not been properly planned for them.

Brown (1984) further found that leisure participation among the elderly was individual, in the sense that each person was free to choose the type of leisure activity. The various activities in which the majority of elderly engaged for relaxation were sleeping and resting (54.6%); conversing and playing with children and grandchildren (18.0%); and reading newspapers and magazines (15.5%). The elderly engaged in various activities of relaxation mostly by themselves (48.8%); with friends (13.8%); or with spouses (13.1%). Should their economic position improve, 61.4% would like to engage in more activities for relaxation. The kind of activities in which they would like to engage included watching videos and television; playing games such as chess, draft, and ludo; visiting age-mates and friends more frequently; receiving more visitors; reading magazines; and listening to music.

In a more recent study, Brown (1992) found that the main forms of leisure activities among a sample of widowed elderly persons included the following: playing with grandchildren (30.0%); spending time or conversing with age-mates (27.5%); reading (20.5%); attending fellowships and prayer meetings (7.5%); listening to radio (5.0%); or just sleeping and resting (5.0%).

With regard to their participation in organizations and associations, most of the elderly belonged to either religious types (such as the Choir, Singing Band, Women's Fellowship, Christ Little Band) or welfare types (such as Pensioners' Association, Veterans' Association of Ghana, the Lodge, or Old Girls/Boys associations). The main reasons given for joining these associations were spiritual fulfillment, companionship and emotional support, financial gain, and personal satisfaction.

ADVOCACY AND PROTECTION

Legal Assistance

The Social Security Law (PNDC Law 247) attempts to provide some form of protection and security on behalf of the elderly who have retired from active employment. Upon retirement at the age of 60, the elderly person continues to receive pension benefits until attaining age 72. If the elderly retiree dies before attaining age 72, a lump sum payment—based on the present value of the unused pension—will be made to beneficiaries.

Second, the Intestate Succession Law (PNDC Law III) of 1985 provides some protection to the bereaved spouse with regard to the disposition of the deceased spouse's estate. To reinforce the provisions of the law, the Intestate Succession (Amendment) Law of 1991, Section 16A, prohibits the ejection of a surviving spouse from the matrimonial home before the distribution of the estate of a deceased person. Any person who contravenes this law is liable, on summary conviction, to a minimum fine of ¢50,000 (US$125) and not exceeding ¢500,000 (US$1,250) or to a term of imprisonment not exceeding one year. In addition, the court provides for the reinstatement or reimbursement of funds to the person ejected or deprived.

Advocacy Organizations

In Ghana, several attempts have been made to form advocacy organizations to ensure a better quality of life and equity in opportunities for the elderly. Groups that have been formed by the elderly themselves include the Ghana National Council for the Aging, the Union of Retired Persons, the Senior Citizens' Club, the Veterans' Association of Ghana (VAG), and the Ghana Government Pensioners' Association. Currently, only the last two are operational.

VAG was established initially by law as the Ghana Legion. The main objectives were to cater to the welfare of all ex-servicemen, foster the spirit of comradeship among ex-servicemen, and provide free medical care to all ex-servicemen.

With branches in all the 10 regions of the country, the association has taken steps to ameliorate the hardships imposed upon the members by the high cost of living. For example, the minimum payment of ¢7,600 (US$19) a month to members of the association is higher than the minimum of ¢5,000 (US$12.50) paid to other pensioners in Ghana. To augment its income, the association also organizes a national weekly lotto—VAG West—which is open to the general public.

The Ghana Government Pensioners Association, which is open to all retired civil servants, also caters to personnel from the armed forces, police, prisons, fire service, and the Ghana Education Service. The association, which was formed in 1990, was to assist members financially or in-kind in case of bereavement, incapacity, or reasonable hardship; promote, aid, and encourage the establishment of cooperatives and other economic enterprises owned wholly or partially by the association and encourage the sale and use of the goods and services; and undertake, in conjunction with any other organizations with similar objectives, business ventures that will improve the living standards of its members.

As part of its educational program, the association organizes lectures and seminars aimed at increasing the knowledge and understanding of the members about national and international issues with a view to improving their chances for economic and social survival.

FUTURE PROJECTIONS

This discussion has revealed several distinguishing features of the service delivery system for the elderly in Ghana. First, the family and the general community have traditionally constituted (and continue to constitute) a strong social support network for the elderly. Second, the services provided are not specifically targeted at the elderly alone. Third, the services are provided in a fragmented manner without any appreciable system of service coordination. Fourth, the majority of the elderly in Ghanaian society do not benefit much from a state-run service delivery system. Finally, in recent years, voluntary associations and some associations formed by the elderly themselves have begun to recognize the need to provide social services and material help for the elderly.

With increasing social change, the interdependence that gave the family support system its strength has been eroded by a number of factors, including rural-urban migration, improved education, modernization, industrialization and the search for profit, competition, and salaried activity. The result is that the traditional social structures in Ghana are no longer able to adequately care for and support the elderly.

For the service delivery system to function effectively, the new emphasis is to devise a system that can coordinate the activities of the central government, regional and district councils, voluntary organizations, and private agencies in a pyramidal system of service delivery. In effect, it is envisaged that this arrangement will not only ensure that the service delivery system will be extended to the rural population but also attract adequate attention and the necessary funding.

Furthermore, given the fact that the state-based Social Security system is not developed enough to absorb the increasing demand for services and facilities to the elderly, it will be necessary to find a proper balance between family support and government assistance. In effect, the family should be helped to continue to be responsive to the needs of its elderly members and yet be provided with outside assistance when critically needed. Such a family-oriented policy may include the following measures: (1) the provision of community and home-based care for the elderly in health, housing, and social welfare; (2) the introduction of concrete measures in support of the family, such as income tax incentives, allowances, and housing subsidies; (3) the availability of professional assistance, financial aid, and counseling services to families caring for the disabled or chronically ill aging relatives; and (4) the development of new types of informal care networks, backed by a range of medical and social services (Brown, 1991).

Such a combination of services and financial resources will strengthen the capacities of the family. Thus, the family will be able to respond to the needs of its aging members and permit the continued integration of the elderly in family life.

BIBLIOGRAPHY

Brown, C. K. (1984). *Improving the Social Protection of the Aging Population in Ghana.* Legon: ISSER Technical Publication Series, University of Ghana.

———. (1987). *Social Structure and Aging: A Comparative Study of the Status of the Aging in the United States and Ghana.* Fulbright Report.

———. (1990). *Aging and Old Age in Ghana.* Tampa: International Exchange Center on Gerontology, University of South Florida.

———. (1991). Caring for the Elderly in Ghana: Present and Future Policy Challenges. *Bold* 1, No. 3, pp. 15–17.

———. (1992). *The Social Situation of Widowed Elderly Persons at Cape Coast.* Re-

search Report Series, No. 25, Centre for Development Studies, University of Cape Coast.
Dutta-Roy, D. K. (1969). *The Eastern Region Household Budget Survey*. Legon: ISSER Technical Publication, No. 6, University of Ghana.
Gaisie, S. K., N. O. Addo, and G. K. Kpedekpo. (1970). *The National Demographic Sample Survey: Demographic and Socio-Economic Statistics,* Vol. 2a. Legon: Demographic Unit, University of Ghana.
Gaisie, S. K., and K. T. De Graft-Johnson. (1976). *The Population of Ghana.* C.I.C.R.E.D. Series.
Republic of Ghana. (1965). *The Hansard* 38, p. 1083.
Riley, M. W., and A. Foner. (1968). *Aging and Society, Vol. 1, An Inventory of Research Findings.* New York: Russell Sage Foundation.
Rourke, B. E. (1971). *Wages and Incomes of Agricultural Workers in Ghana.* Legon: ISSER Technical Publication, No. 13, University of Ghana.
Sarpong, P. K. (1983). Aging and Tradition. In *Aging and Social Change,* Proceedings of the 34th Annual New Year School, University of Ghana, 29 December 1982–4 January 1983, pp. 13–20.
United Nations. (1982). World Population Prospects: Estimates and Projections as Assessed in 1982, UN Publication, Sales No. 83, XIII.5.
———. (1983). *Vienna International Plan of Action on Aging.* World Assembly on Aging, Vienna, Austria, 26 July–6 August 1982, New York.
United Nations Development Program. (1991). *Human Development Report, 1991.* Oxford University Press.
World Bank. (1986). *World Development Report, 1986.* Oxford University Press.

11

GREAT BRITAIN

Malcolm L. Johnson

INTRODUCTION

The Role of Older People

As one of the first countries in the world to experience the dramatic extension of largely healthy old age, Britain views its older population very differently from even two or three decades ago. Yet it continues to designate the "official" onset of later life at the state retirement pension-eligibility ages of 60 for women and 65 for men. These ages entitle people to the benefits of being "elderly" and act as the point at which special concessions (cheaper fares on public transport, reduced prices for certain services such as cinemas and other entertainments) are available. More specifically, they provide the thresholds for state benefits for income support, housing, and social services. Yet, most men and women now reach these retirement ages in sound health, with full independence and able to look forward to between 10 and 30 years of active life.

Perceptions of what constitutes being old are beginning to shift in much more noticeable ways than could be discerned even as recently as the late 1980s. Until the end of that decade, researchers reported media representations as highly stereotyped and reproducing images of older people as sick, poor, and incompetent (Midwinter, 1987; Johnson, 1988). In the 1990s there have been more positive accounts and a greater awareness of retired people as consumers of goods, services, and education as well as contributors to family and community life. Having marked up these less-negative developments, society is still somewhat ageist in attitude and orientation. It has a long way to go before those who are no longer in the work force due to age are accorded the same kind of citizen's rights and privileges that they enjoyed at earlier stages. But the empirical reality is that many more people are surviving into autonomous old age.

Since the turn of the century the demographic profile of the population in Great Britain has changed in unprecedentedly dramatic ways. In 1901 those over 65 years totaled 1.75 million and constituted only 4.7% of the whole population (of whom 50,000 were over 85). By 1991 the number aged 65 and older had multiplied fivefold to 9 million and 15.8% of the total, and those over 85 increased by 18 times to 900,000 (Central Statistical Office, 1989).

The British experience of the demographic explosion projects a rapid aging of the population during this century, when the total population is still increasing but at a much lower rate (Central Statistical Office, 1989). The principal causes of this societal aging are the same for all the countries of Western Europe—a marked reduction in mortality concurrently with reduced rates of fertility. In England and Wales the crude death rate in the mid-nineteenth century was 21.4 per 1,000 population. By the mid-1980s the figure produced by the Office of Population Censuses and Surveys (OPCS) was 11.8 per 1,000. The most dramatic fall in death rates has been in the first year of life, from 148 per 1,000 live births to 9 per 1,000. Thus, the driving force behind the inflated numbers of older people is the fact that so many of them survived the ravages of childhood, enabling them to live into adulthood and beyond. Contrary to popular belief, the demographic revolution is not essentially about people living much longer but about many more living a full life span. A healthier, better-housed, and better-fed population has seen mortality rates fall at all ages.

Fertility decline provides almost a mirror image. In 1900 the crude birthrate was 27 per 1,000 in the population. It had declined to 13.8 per 1,000 by 1988. The population used to be shaped like a pyramid: many young people forming a broad base, numbers declining (due to death) at all subsequent ages, and a tiny minority of very old people at the apex. Presently, it is shaped more like a barrel, with more equal groupings in each age band.

Women were always more likely than men to live into old age in Great Britain, but the gender differential has widened during this century. A man today can expect to survive 13 years after his 65th birthday, compared with 11 years at the turn of the century; but 65-year-old women in the 1990s can expect to live 17 more years, compared with 12 years at the earlier date. This process has been called "the feminization of later life" (Arber and Ginn, 1991). As they approach retirement, men and women appear in roughly equal numbers; but in each successive five-year period, many more women survive, and the male death rate increases sharply. As Victor (1991, p. 21) reports, "There is a marked gender inequality in the population aged 65 and older. Of the population aged 65 and over, 60% are females. This trend is at its most extreme among the very elderly (i.e., those over 85 years), with 250 females for every 100 males."

The prevailing predominance of women is not necessarily a permanent feature of the demographic structure. Those over 75 in the British population are part of a generation profoundly affected by World War II, when many young men were killed. As this group moved into later life, the earlier attrition of the male sector was amplified by the other predisposing factors that enable women to live longer. While successive cohorts will not exhibit loss of males due to wars, there may be other reasons for a modest shift toward male-female parity in life expectancy. The rapid reduction in hazardous occupations for men during the second half of the century will reduce premature deaths. Concurrently, women have increasingly adopted life-styles more like those of men, in terms of employment, smoking, and alcohol consumption, which may have the effect of increasing death rates at earlier ages.

Inevitably, the gender disparity has a marked effect on living arrangements. More than a third (36%) of people over 65 live alone, and this rises to over a half by age 85. By this stage, men alone number 37% (with 38% living independently with their spouse). For women, the proportion alone has risen to 61%, and only 8% still have a surviving husband with whom they live. As a consequence of increased frailty, those over 85 are more likely to move into the household of one of their children. This is the case for only 15% of men but for 23% of women. They will also contribute the largest numbers of the residents in long-term care facilities, which accommodate around 4% of the nation's total retired population.

Among those who are now old, employment was largely a male preserve. Many older women would have taken jobs at some time in their lives, but—for the majority—paid employment was either not part of their experience or a part-time activity without any career framework. Those women who did become part of the long-term work force were likely to be part of the larger-than-usual group who had never married.

Working beyond the retirement age of 65 became less common over the two decades after 1971. At that point, 19.2% of retirement-age men were still in employment, a figure that fell to 8.4% by 1991. This decline is more an artifact of the increased size of the retired population than any dramatic reduction in those working in the early years of retirement. In the age group 65–69, the employment rate actually rose from 13% in 1983 to 13.9% in 1991. However, these data need to be set in a context of overall decline in economic activities rates for men over 55, as a result of the extension of early retirement policies to cope with required work force reductions (Commission of the European Communities, 1993).

The great majority of older people have had little initial schooling and gained few qualifications later on. Roughly three out of four men aged 60–64 left school at 15 or earlier. The proportions for women are higher (as they are for both sexes for preceding age groups). Within this ill-educated retired group, the disadvantages were not corrected at later stages. Only 4% of men aged 65–69 hold university degrees; true for only 2% of women over 50. Indeed, 73% of people over 70 have no formal qualifications at all. Nearly 9 out of 10 unskilled and semiskilled workers have no qualifications at all.

Successive cohorts of the British population are significantly more educated. For example, the proportion of those with degrees rises from around 5% for those over 50 to over double that (11%) for people in their 30s, while the proportion of those with no qualifications declines from two in three for those over 60 to fewer than one in five for those aged 20–29 (Schuller and Bostyn, 1992).

The elderly population of Great Britain is generally more healthy than ever before yet contains larger numbers of people who are severely restricted by chronic illnesses and disabling conditions. The General Household Survey (GHS), conducted annually, produces data on the self-reported prevalence of acute illness in the previous 14 days. Recently (1988), it was recorded that 12% of people aged 15–44 experienced acute health problems; the corresponding figure for those over 75 was 21%.

Long-term illnesses of the more disabling sort are of greater concern to older people. Reliable statistics on disabilities are difficult to find, because definitions vary from study to study. Wicks and Henwood (1988) calculated that 1.1 million people over 65 are severely disabled and constitute one in eight of the total age group. A further 2 million were estimated by Walker and Phillipson (1986) to be moderately disabled. As the result of major surveys conducted by OPCS during the late 1980s, there are more reliable data sets (Martin, Meltzer, and Elliot, 1988); and it is claimed that of the 6.2 million disabled adults in Britain, 4.27 million (69%) are over the age of 60 (all but 7% of them living in private households). They also show a high level of association between age and severity of disability, the largest numbers being "younger" and mildly disabled alongside a much smaller group of profoundly restricted people, most of whom are aged 80 and older.

Although definitional problems beset information about mental illnesses, amplified by difficulty in clinical diagnosis, it is assumed that two-thirds of all mentally and physically handicapped people are over 65. Over a third of those 65 and older (rising to half of those over 80) are estimated to have hearing impairments, (Coni, Davison, and Webster, 1992). Again, there are no totally reliable figures for the numbers with significant visual handicaps, but it is known that three-quarters of the 100,000 people registered as blind are over 65. These conditions, along with other physical disabilities, mental frailty, incontinence, and the limitations of poor housing, represent the range of handicaps for older people in Britain.

Bond and Carstairs (1982), in their survey of elderly people in Scotland, identified heart conditions (15%), arthritis and related conditions affecting the back (10–15%) and joints (15–35%), and sight defects (2–21%) as the most widely reported illnesses that restrict functional capacity. These, in turn, have consequences for the performance of Activities of Daily Living (ADLs) involving bending and stooping. The ability to cope with everyday tasks of personal hygiene and domestic tasks in the home is critical to the maintenance of an independent existence. ADL studies provide a picture of about half of the older population coping without assistance. McGlone (1992) was able to conclude: "There is still only a minority of elderly people unable to cope. Only 16% unable to do their own shopping, 12% cannot sweep or clean floors and 10%

cannot open screw tops. A very small percentage have problems with self-care. Despite these small proportions, the numbers involved can be very large and an estimated 1.4 million are likely to be dependent on others for the performance of essential tasks."

Old age and poverty continue to be highly correlated in Britain. But this close association is changing, due to the growth of occupational pensions and housing ownership. Using official measures of poverty (140% of the minimum government support level), government statistics reveal that 55.4% of the pensionable population (5.2 million people) fall into this category.

The Formal Structure of Care Provision

History has shaped both the sense of social responsibility for older citizens and the nature and sources of assistance that are provided. From the time of Shakespeare, the local parish was responsible for the care of the poor, the sick, and the old. Under the Elizabethan Poor Law of 1601, which was refashioned during the Industrial Revolution in 1834, the local community was deemed responsible for maintaining those who had no viable means of support. But there were strict limits to these contributions to personal welfare. The motives behind the legislation were to control both the behavior of elderly paupers and the financial burden they put on the rest of the population. Thus, access to parish support—either in the workhouse or on the "out-relief" allowed by the 1834 act—was provided only at great cost to personal dignity and brought virtual loss of citizenship.

Because of the rapid urbanization occurring from the mid-eighteenth century onward, the twin forces of population growth and geographic mobility placed unmanageable strains on the parish system and its institutional provision. The able-bodied poor were increasingly allowed to remain outside the poorhouse, existing on the meager financial support provided under the act. Here were the origins of the British Social Security system. But for that seemingly irreducible small group of old with no means of support (remaining at around 4% for the over-65 population for as long as records exist), the institution was their fate. For a small minority, group living was provided by the church and, as the nineteenth century progressed, by a growing array of voluntary societies, which stemmed from Victorian middle-class benevolence. Small cottages, usually with one bedroom, were built in a terrace near a church or Christian community, which supplied simple but good housing for the infirm but "deserving" elderly, who received regular aid from clergy and parishioners. These cottages coexisted with another, longer-lived ecclesiastically provided institution: the almshouse.

In these early arrangements are the origins of state-provided long-term care and the voluntary (nonprofit) sector of residential and nursing homes and sheltered housing. From the same roots emerged two sorts of hospitals. One derived from the church's healing ministry (which goes back to medieval times), resulting in the voluntary hospitals that grew rapidly in the Victorian era. The better-known of these hospitals became leading medical schools, but all ultimately became part of the National Health Service (NHS) in 1946. The other grew out of the poor-law infirmaries, which provided free medical services to those in, or near, poverty. Inevitably, these hospitals had a clientele that presented more chronic illnesses, and they provided many beds for long-term care.

Hospital care of elderly people before World War II was to be found predominantly in these gloomy places. In the postwar period, the hospital-based speciality of geriatric medicine was established all over the United Kingdom (and most vigorously in Glasgow and London) in former poor-law hospitals, which—before their incorporation into the NHS—had been in the hands of local authorities.

The binary pattern of long-term care, where hospitals and nursing homes form one major service sector and the social care or residential home forms another, has clearly visible antecedents. When local authorities took over responsibility for elderly people by enacting the 1948 National Assistance Act, the Poor Law was terminated. In Part 3 of the act, local government was required to provide "old peoples' homes." Indeed, this is the origin of the colloquial term used by professionals in the United Kingdom when they refer to such an establishment as a "a Part 3 home." Again, the inherited stock was made up of large, overcrowded, badly maintained, dehumanizing institutions. Townsend (1962) described them with graphic precision and compounded the effect with data from a massive national survey of 800 homes. His work, which closely followed the work by Goffman (1961), set up a strong reaction against institutional care in all its forms. In Britain, the disaffection was further fueled by the publication of *Sans Everything* (Robb, 1967), in which a group of doctors and nurses wrote of their revulsion at the treatment meted out to elderly patients in long-stay care.

Anti-institutionalism in the 1960s eventually provided part of the basis for legitimating community-care policies. Yet, throughout the decade, most of the elderly residents of Part 3 homes lived in poor-law institutions. Even homes in the voluntary sector were large and forbidding places. The building of new, smaller homes (at first the desired norm was 60 beds, falling later to 30 beds) began slowly. Local authority homes continued to be for the poor—an inferior service for inferior people (Means and Smith, 1985).

In the immediate postwar period, a limited range of domiciliary services was introduced. Meals-on-wheels (mobile meals), luncheon clubs, day centers, an occasional home-visiting chiropodist, and a supply of canes, bathing aids, and so on constituted the assortment. Later, in the 1950s, geriatric day hospitals were experimented with and evaluated. A meager ration of home care, supplemented by in-home nursing from district nurses and by the attention of general medical practitioners, was all that existed until the mid-1970s. At that point, the demographic revolution began to make its first real impact as the over-75 age group started to swell. Policies that called for maintaining people in their own homes became central in the hope that the need for expensive long-term care could be minimized.

Out of these developments, Britain has created a nationally funded system of health care, free to those in need, alongside a social services system administered by local authorities. Throughout this century the voluntary (nonprofit) sector has remained part of the provision but not central to it. Similarly, there has always been a small commercial element. Since the election of Margaret Thatcher's Conservative administration in 1979, the private and voluntary agencies have become increasingly prominent. By the end of the 1980s, it was necessary to describe health and social care as a mixed economy. Since the set of NHS and community care reforms, introduced in 1992 and 1993, that description becomes even more apt.

INCOME MAINTENANCE AND EMPLOYMENT

The state retirement pension scheme, introduced in Britain in 1909, now forms the central core of income for the majority of people over the retirement ages of 60 for women and 65 for men. It was originally restricted to men in selected industries but was incrementally extended to encompass all occupations and, in the early postwar period, to women both on the basis of their own employment and through their spouses. While there is still a small minority of elderly persons who remain ineligible for the state pension, the system is essentially comprehensive. When there are pension levels below the national standard, due to incomplete employment careers or insufficient payments of "national insurance" (regular, compulsory deductions from earnings collected by employers and paid to the government), there is recourse to a range of means-tested Social Security payments.

In 1993, basic pension (taxable) weekly rates were as follows: £56.10 (US $86) for a single person, £33.70 (US $52) for a wife on her husband's contributions, £89.80 (US $138) for a married couple on the husband's contributions, and £112.20 (US $172) for a married couple if both paid full contributions. For those who do not meet the eligibility criteria for basic pension or whose income falls below a set minimum, recourse can be made to the income support provision. This is paid as a result of elaborate assessments of all income sources and is restricted, on a sliding scale, to those with savings (which exclude house ownership and other material capital assets) below £8,000 (US$12,307). Persons in receipt of income support, whether old or not, are recognized by the government to be in the nation's lowest income stratum and become eligible for other benefits, such as free dental treatment, exemption from medical prescription charges, access to the Social Fund, and a number of other benefits.

Retirement pensioners may also have access to a range of other payments and allowances on the basis of demonstrated need. All of these require authentication of personal and financial circumstances. On the basis of such assessments, older people may receive further regular or one-off amounts. For severely disabled people needing full-time care at home, payments of up to £44.90 (US$69) per week may be made to meet the costs of personal care. Those with less than total disability may receive more modest supplements, such as for special diets, fuel, house insulation and repairs, local taxes, transport, and special equipment.

In the event older persons with very low income need to enter a nursing home or residential home, their existing income may be supplemented by income support up to a maximum of £280 (US$431) a week to meet the fees in a nursing home and £185 (US$285) a week in a residential home. If new residents of one of these establishments moved from an accommodation that they owned (and that was not still occupied by a spouse), the property would have to be sold to meet the costs of their continuing care.

As in other countries there is considerable concern in government circles about the rising cost of state retirement pensions and associated benefits linked with them. Consequently, there have been sustained efforts to restrain rises in pension levels. In 1980 the Conservative government, in its first year of office, broke the existing link between annual rises in average earnings and pension increases. The pension is presently linked only with the retail price index, and it is calculated that as a result of this change United Kingdom (UK) pensioners are receiving about 20% less. This downward shift increased the number of old people in poverty. About one in five of the retired population now receives income support. If a more commonly accepted definition of poverty is used, that is, 140% of income support, the figure rises to 3 million people—a third of all pensioners. These circumstances render elderly people three times more likely than adults below pension age to be in poverty.

Despite the evident restraints on the level of pensions, government expenditure on them is vast and still rising. In 1990–91 about half of all Social Security expenditure went to elderly people, amounting to £28.6 billion (US$44 billion)—an increase of 30% over the 1980 figure.

While a third of the elderly population is demonstrably impoverished, the overall pattern shows a growth in the net income of pensioners. Between 1979 and 1987 it increased by nearly a third. The most significant contributions to this enhanced income come from occupational pensions and personal savings. Indeed, the long-established postwar pattern of predominant dependence on state pension income is shifting, as the increase in occupational pension schemes from the 1950s onward makes its impact.

Concurrently with a large group on severely restricted incomes, there is a growing group sometimes dubbed WOOPIEs—well-off older persons. This top fifth in the income distribution receive two-fifths of their income from occupational pensions and investments (McGlone, 1992). This group will inevitably grow as succeeding cohorts enter the pensionable age bands, bringing with them increased access to secondary pensions, a trend encouraged by government tax incentives.

Tax incentives have existed for many years to encourage life assurance and pension provision by individuals, but they are not a device greatly used for other purposes in Britain. Nor are economic benefits distributed on any meaningful scale by local government. The system is nationally run through the Department of Social Security, which, since 1993, has delegated some of these functions to local Social Services Departments.

As discussed, employment opportunities for older people have become more restricted in recent years. This has been an increasing trend over recent decades. In part, it reflects a wish by retired people to leave the world of work behind. However, those who need or wish to continue in employment still encounter great difficulties. Trade unions have not been supportive of postretirement ages. An endemic ageism, now showing the first signs of weakening, is the major independent influence. Rising levels of unemployment during the late 1980s and continuing into the 1990s are another obvious restriction on work opportunities.

HEALTH CARE SERVICES

Until the late 1980s it would have been possible to depict the British health care system as being the state-funded NHS, which provided almost all of the nation's health care needs, plus a small private sector. It delivered health care in hospitals to all citizens, regardless of age, income, or other status, free at the point of need. Primary health care was provided through teams led by primary care physicians (general practitioners), while local authorities had responsibility for environmental health. Hospital services were overseen at local levels by area health authorities, which, in turn, were accountable to regional health authorities and upward to the NHS Management Board, chaired by the secretary of state for health. General practitioners were "independent contractors" with local Family Health Services Authorities (FHSAs). All of these services were in a line-management relationship up to the secretary of state, who—through the treasury—provided all the funding for their work. Since the Department of Health publication *Working for Patients* (1989), the government has been systematically reshaping these services into a more entrepreneurial and mixed economy system. The macro structure just described remains largely in place, but the local organizational and financial systems are significantly different.

Throughout the changes, the services have remained essentially free to service users, but more charges have been added. Items for which payment is required have been extended from prescriptions for drugs and medications to now include dental care, optical services, and hearing services. However, people over retirement ages are exempt from almost all of them. The most notable exception is dental care, for which only the poorest (on income support) are relieved of the costs.

In 1990 the overall cost of the NHS exceeded £12 billion (US$18.5 billion) and amounted to 6% of the gross domestic product. Of that expenditure, 35% was spent on acute inpatient care, almost half of which was devoted to the treatment of people over 65. In excess of £1 billion (US$1.5 billion), 9% of the total, went to inpatient care in the geriatric departments of hospitals. Of a similar amount devoted to inpatients with a mental illness, 57% was taken up by people

65 and older, who were also the major consumers of other key services, for example, district nursing (75%) and chiropody (89%) (Victor, 1991).

It is very clear from these macro statistics that people over 65 are the largest users and the greatest single cost to UK health services. Bosanquet and Gray (1989) have estimated that of the total NHS expenditure, those aged 65–74 cost 17.0%, 75–84 cost 22.7%, and those 85 and over cost 8.6%. Their per capita estimates of expenditure show a linear rise with age: £16.5 (US$25) for 45–64-year-olds in 1986–87 and £145.2 (US$223) for a person 85 or older.

About 2% of elderly people are in hospitals at any given time, and they occupy approximately 50% of all beds and 40% of acute beds. In financial terms, this represents the greatest expenditure on the health of older people, but it does not account for the greatest amount of support activity, which takes place outside the institutions. A significant part of this care is provided by primary health care teams, which form the second most important part of the health service. Based on the service provided by general medical practitioners (GPs), operating mostly in small groups of three to eight, primary health care teams generally also include health visitors, home nurses, a psychiatric nurse, a part-time chiropodist, and (sometimes) a social worker.

Registration with a GP is expected of all members of the population, and more than 98% do so. The average patient population of a GP is 2,300, and he or she will serve that group of people within a prescribed local area, which enables regular house calls to the acutely sick or severely disabled who cannot attend the surgery/clinic. The doctor receives an annual capitation payment from the government, via the local Family Health Services Authority, as payment for medical care to patients. This payment is higher for people over 70 in recognition of their greater use of medical care. There is no charge to individuals for the professional services of the primary health care teams, though prescribed medicines are subject to a per item charge, which rose sharply between 1988 and 1993.

Older people, predictably, make more use of their GP than do younger citizens. Estimates indicate that 75% of those over 65 will visit their family doctor in the course of a year, with consultation rates slightly higher for women than for men. Moreover, their requirements are much more likely to involve a home visit, with the consequence that more than 27% of GP time is taken up in such visits. Under the new arrangements, whereby GPs will be allocated cash-limited budgets that they will use on behalf of patients to buy services they cannot provide, there is a marked disincentive to take on older patients, especially those with long-term and expensive care requirements. The consequences of such "fund-holding" are not yet established, but it is suspected that older people are likely to receive a lower quality of services.

In Britain the description "long term care" is usually reserved for a permanent or semipermanent alternative to home care. Outside the long-stay geriatric hospital provision, which is rapidly diminishing under government pressure to reduce hospitalization, older people are placed in nursing homes and residential homes. About 5% of those aged 65 and over live in some form of institutional care. These residents are, by definition, very old and dependent for their daily existence on the care of others. The average age of entry to a nursing or residential home rose from 70 to 80 over the decade 1975 to 1985. One in five people over 80 are in one of these forms of care.

Currently, there is considerable change in process, so the exact form of services to older people in the mid-1990s cannot be confidently predicted. Following the implementation of the National Health Service and Community Care Act on 1 April 1993, local social services departments became principally contractors or purchasers of services, rather than direct providers, as in the past. In their document *The Community Revolution: Personal Social Services and Community Care,* the Audit Commission (1992) wrote:

The delivery of care and support to adults in the community will undergo a fundamental change in the 1990s ... local social services authorities will move from being suppliers of a range of services to adopting the Lead Agency role. From April 1993 they will be required to assess the needs of individual people, arrange with them individually tailored services to meet these needs as appropriate ... secondly ... the core element of social security income support for nursing and residential home care, currently available to people through a means test, will be paid instead to local social service authorities. At present this form of income support is paid to some 200,000 people ... potential new claimants will need to approach social services for support. (p. 1)

It is anticipated that the balance of service provision will move significantly to a mixed economy of "independent" agencies and away from public bodies (local government and the NHS). Of particular relevance to elderly people will be the large-scale transfer of local authority (LA) old people's homes and homes for those with learning disabilities and mental health problems to either the private sector or independent (not-for-profit) trusts.

The changes will be an accelerated version of those that have taken place since 1975 in the long-term care sector. At that stage, there were 95,000 beds in LA old people's homes and only 18,750 in private homes. There was a small voluntary sector. At the same time, there were 25,000 beds in private nursing homes. In 1990 there were 328,00 beds in private long-term care (including nursing homes and other hospitals) and 140,000 in the public sector (Laing, 1991; Mitchell, 1993). There were about 69,000 beds in private nursing homes.

The expansion of long-term care beds between 1975 and 1990 has been driven largely by the dramatic growth in the numbers of very old dependent people (and in part by the failure of other support systems). Bond et al. (1989) indicate that the public provider has borne the major task of supporting the largest proportion of very confused residents. As the new policies and funding mechanisms come more fully into effect, the likely shape of long-term care is one dominated—for the first time—by commercial providers, alongside substantial but smaller charitable and not-for-profit sectors. LAs, historically the principal providers, are destined to become insignificant as direct service providers. Their role is prefigured to be that of purchaser and contractor on behalf of those occupants of long-term beds who are supported by the public purse.

HOUSING RESOURCES

Over 95% of people of pensionable age in Britain live in private households. Within this total, about 5% live in some form of sheltered accommodations with a warden to provide general support and emergency services. So the vast majority live alone or with their spouse in ordinary housing in the community. The common experience for an older person is to remain in the same accommodations as occupied prior to retirement. Some mobility from one type of housing to another in the same locality is recorded, but on a limited scale, usually the result of a marked change of circumstances, such as failing health or restricted mobility. Only about 10% of retired people (Law and Warnes, 1980) move more than 40 kilometers from their previous residence. The majority of these moves occur at or around retirement.

Government policy, now well established, has as its first priority the extension of private ownership, which has resulted in a massive reduction in public housing provision and a significant increase in owner-occupation. Alongside this privatization has come successive cutbacks in government expenditure on housing, promulgated on the premise that housing construction and management are best handled in the marketplace. A second stream of policy concerns the condition of the existing housing stock and is taking measures to deal with delapidation. Policies for older people are not well articulated but have two main aspects, which relate to the two streams just identified: specialist housing (particularly sheltered housing) and repair and upgrading of facilities.

People commonly associate old age and sheltered housing (a series of specially built accommodation units—houses, bungalows, or flats for the less dependent—in close proximity to each other, sometimes with common facilities for dining and recreation, served by a resident warden). It has become the standard format of special housing provision for those people who cannot sustain fully independent living and who require regular assistance with their ADL. The Department of the Environment estimated that there were 465,675 sheltered housing units in England in 1990. The majority, 303,061, were provided by LAs, 120,911 by housing associations (government-funded, not-for-profit agencies that exist to promote and manage special and low-cost housing), and 38,798 by the private sector.

In response to these new policies, the private sector embarked in the 1980s on a major program of building sheltered housing units for sale. Most had one bedroom, but some had two. They were attractive to existing homeowners, who were often able to "trade-down," yielding a capital sum to invest. As Warnes (1992) points out, these developments were initially concentrated in the more prosperous southeast of England and in the coastal retirement areas. The majority of purchasers were over 75 years, widowed or single. Activity rates slowed as the recession of the late 1980s continued and deepened in the early 1990s, causing depression in the housing market. As a result, many elderly homeowners who wished to move to more appropriate housing were unable to make the transition.

Just as the private sector of sheltered housing is almost exclusively the preserve of former homeowners, local authority provision is predominantly the preserve of previous renters, and patterns of tenure during earlier life become formative features of postretirement. Homeownership has grown progressively since the 1950s, but at an accelerated rate in the period since 1980, when the Conservative policy of selling off local authority houses at below-market rates to sitting tenants began. In the ensuing decade, 1.5 million properties were sold. These two phases of extension to private tenure have resulted in much higher rates of ownership among retired people. The most recent national figures are from 1987, when 49% of people over 65 owned their homes outright, and 7% were still completing mortgage payments. Of the remaining group, 35% lived in rented local authority housing, 4% in rented housing association properties, and 6% in privately rented accommodations. This distribution is roughly in line with the population at large in terms of the public/private split.

The most common type of dwelling for older people is a house rather than a flat (apartment). More than four out of five live in houses, mostly of the semidetached type (one half of a pair of houses sharing a common dividing wall). Flats are much less common in Britain than in other parts of Europe and the United States and preferred by younger people.

A predominant feature of the houses older people live in is that they tend to be old: 26% constructed before 1919, 33% between 1919 and 1944, 17% between 1945 and 1964, and 14% in 1965 or later. There is also an association between social class and age of dwelling, with the professional and managerial groups most likely to live in the newest accommodations.

Recent decades have seen a marked improvement in the existence of basic amenities in the whole housing stock in Britain, and older people have also been beneficiaries. Thus, by 1987, 99% of all age groups lived in households with exclusive use of a toilet and a bath or shower. However, heating and insulation are not well provided; only 68% have central heating, and many older people have insufficient heating for their winter needs. The English House Condition Survey (Department of Environment, 1988) indicated that 4% of all households lived in "unfit" dwellings and that 13.1% were in "dwellings requiring repairs costing at least £7,000 [US$10,700]"—prominently represented in such dwellings were the old and those from minority ethnic groups.

Apart from the tax relief available to all mortgage holders buying their own houses, there are no tax concessions for householders. Indeed, it is an issue of political contention that those who rent are denied assistance when the better-off half of the population is advantaged. Benefits derive from demonstrations of low income and severe disability. In particular, housing benefit is available for those on income support. This will meet the cost of rent payments for people in houses, flats, and boardinghouses and may cover certain service charges. Council tax (local property tax) is also paid. In appropriate circumstances, special payments are made to contribute to fuel costs. In 1993, the maximum weekly amounts are heating, £8.60 (US$13), hot water, £1.05 (US$1.62), cooking, £1.05 (US$1.62), lighting, £0.70 (US$1.08), and fuel costs, £11.40 (US$17.54).

It is established public policy to help elderly people remain in their own homes for as long as possible. The new community care provisions have this as an objective. So, the whole range of community support services described in this chapter, both statutory and voluntary, direct their attention to preventing institutionalization and sustaining independence.

Congregate housing of the style common in North America is not common in Britain. Sheltered housing is the British idiom. Similarly, there are very few retirement communities of the kind seen in the United States. Those that do exist are of three types. The first is provided for the frail elderly members of particular occupations and associations (such as the clergy, officers in the military, members of the licensed victuallers trade—that is, proprietors of pubs—and teachers). The second is provided by charities that have built up a preference for independent community living. The third is a new wave of exclusive retirement villages created by private companies (modeled on facilities in California, Florida, and other American retirement locations). As yet they are few but are likely to grow as the wealthier section of the British elderly gets larger.

SUPPORTIVE SERVICES

The overwhelming proportion of support to older people comes from family, neighbors, and friends. The General Household Survey report on informal caregivers (1988) reports there are over 6 million caregivers in Britain, with 1.7 million caring for someone in their own home. Of these, 3.5 million are women and 2.5 million are men. While there is no doubt that women are the principal caregivers—numerically and in contribution—it is worth noting that so many men are involved. Indeed, over 65, men caregivers outnumber women by 7 to 6.

For those older people who are sick at home or discharged from a hospital, a variety of domiciliary services are supplied by the NHS and by local authority social services departments. Supplemented by home-based voluntary services, these inputs build upon family and other informal care. Linkages between hospital and community services have been notoriously poor, and the system's ability to coordinate services so that an elderly person returning home from hospital care gets home help, home nursing, or meals-on-wheels at the point of discharge is very limited. The Continuing Care Project's survey (Amos, 1980) showed that 14 days after discharge, about half of all elderly patients could not cope with domestic tasks or personal care, and more than a quarter of these people had no one to help

Table 11.1
Domiciliary Services for Elderly People

Service	Provider	Service	Provider
Primary health care teams	NHS	Night sitting	Local authority/voluntary/private
Clubs	Local authority/voluntary	Sheltered housing	Local authority/voluntary/private/trusts
Day centers	Local authority/voluntary	Incontinence laundry	Local authority/NHS/trusts
Meals-on-wheels	Local authority/voluntary	Community psychiatric nurse	NHS
Luncheon clubs	Local authority/voluntary	Social worker	Local authority/voluntary/private
Health visitors	NHS	Respite care	Local authority/NHS/trusts
Domiciliary physiotherapy	NHS	Geriatric day hospital	NHS/private
District nursing	NHS	Good Neighbor scheme	Voluntary
Nursing auxiliaries	NHS	Community rehabilitation	NHS/trusts
Aids for daily living/house adaptation	Local authority	Care managers	Local authority/NHS
Nail-cutting services	Voluntary	Community physiotherapists	Local authority/NHS
Library service for housebound	Local authority/voluntary	Home care organizers	Local authority/private

Source: Johnson, 1990, 1993.

them. Of these two categories together, 84% either had a caring person who could not cope or had no caring person at all. By 28 days after discharge, 39% of the principal caring persons were themselves found to be frail and at risk. Home visits from GPs are also delayed. The same survey showed that 63% of patients had not received a GP's call 14 days after discharge.

An increasingly impressive range of services exists for elderly people at home: Table 11.1 summarizes the domiciliary services available for elderly people in the United Kingdom. However, there are considerable variations in the extent and availability, and in the quantity and quality, of these services across the country.

From 1993 onward, almost any of these services could be supplied by the different trusts that have taken over NHS or local authority responsibilities. But the identification of what an individual client will need is determined by care managers (social workers, nurses, health visitors, or other categories of staff). They will arrange "packages" of care from different suppliers and will be responsible for coordinating and monitoring those services.

Current and reliable data on the delivery of these services are difficult to find, but the Department of Health figures for 1988 serve to indicate the relative weighting of the most important services. Of the £1.167 billion (US$1.8 billion) spent on the local authority domiciliary care approach, half (£535 million) (US$823 million), was spent on home helps (who provide domestic cleaning, shopping, and sometimes cooking services), and £59 million (US$91 million) went for meals-on-wheels, £49 million (US$75 million) for equipment and adaptations, £155 million (US$238 million) for day-care facilities (mostly day centers), and £202 million (US$310 million) for social work.

To translate these expenditures into service delivery terms: about 7% of those over 65 received home help services (36% of those over 85), 3% received meals-on-wheels, and 3% attended a day-care center (with the proportion rising to 37% for those over 85). Over the 10-year period from 1979 to 1989, services failed to keep pace with the increasing number of very old people. Social services have continued to rise. Unofficial estimates suggest that total expenditure rose by 22%, in real terms, during the decade, but this represents only an average rise in gross spending of 2.3%. As a consequence, demand has greatly outstripped supply and ensures that the young old will have a much lower likelihood of receiving active support.

Mental health services to elderly people at home are supplied by primary health care teams, with GPs taking the lead and community psychiatric nurses (CPNs) providing the continuing care in the more severe cases. Information about the levels of service delivery is not readily available, which signifies the low status of such services (despite evidence that 10% of the elderly population suffer mental health problems, which increase in incidence and severity at older ages).

Counseling and social work services for elderly people are very restricted. Statutory obligations on social services departments to provide social work for children and young people command the vast majority of the qualified work force. Only a small minority of retired people receive more than a single visit from a social worker, though there is now an emergent group of social workers specializing in old age care. Counseling is even rarer and is likely to be provided by a voluntary agency (such as one that specializes in bereavement counseling and group work).

In general, community social services are seldom provided, apart from home helps and meals, and when they do exist are routinely charged at close to, or at, the economic rate. Other services are greatly restricted, leaving many to turn to the growing private sector of chiropody, incontinence services, and physiotherapy. Under the new regime of care management, these commercial providers will become a much more prominent feature of national provision for the old in Britain.

LEISURE-TIME RESOURCES

Leisure is a defining characteristic of retirement, yet it is not a prominent feature of the life-style of Britain's elderly population. For a select minority with enough income, there is evidence of a much fuller and more interesting leisure experience. But for the majority, the barriers to participation seem daunting, and their home remains the focus of living, for both work and play.

In his comprehensive review of leisure among older people, Midwinter (1992) reveals that participation levels "at best sustain or just surpass average levels," despite the abundance of leisure time available. Some activities stand up well to retirement (gardening, use of the library), others (like attending the cinema) fade, even though concessionary prices are often available. Indeed, there is a decline in both outdoor and indoor activities. Among all people over 60, the decline in activity prevails, with the exception of gardening and country outings among women and book reading among men. Even the pastimes popularly associated with retirement (such as going out for a drink, decorating, and house repairs) show a marked fall.

A study of leisure activities in the General Household Survey (1988) showed that the most popular pursuits were watching television, visiting friends and relatives, and listening to the radio and recorded music, followed by reading books, gardening, do-it-yourself (DIY) activities, dressmaking, and walking. Attending the theater, ballet, art galleries, museums, and stately homes, dancing, and watching sports all received mention, but none were engaged in "at least once in four weeks" by more than 8% of the respondents.

As a rough approximation, half of Britain's older people make, and about two-thirds receive, a visit each week. More optimistically, 47% take a holiday (compared with 58% of the general population), but there is a class gradient here, with those in the higher social and economic groupings taking more holidays and more likely to do so abroad.

From Midwinter's examination (1992), leisure behavior is far from the popular image of an active, hobbying old age, and he speculates that current cohorts of old people may not have developed leisure habits in earlier life and that younger generations will be more engaged when they enter this stage. He also considers the proposition that British older people and the society at large hold negative attitudes toward leisure seen as time-wasting and inconsequential.

If activity levels are low, opportunities have nonetheless multiplied in the past decade. Specialist holiday companies, organized theater outings, visits to cultural events, and so on are more in evidence and tailored to the circumstances of the older consumer. However, Britain still lacks the infrastructure of facilities and organizations seen in some parts of North America and Scandinavia.

Somewhat at odds with this picture of apathy is the participation of third-age people in volunteering. A detailed study by the Volunteer Centre (1991) showed that almost 60% of people below retirement age were involved as volunteers, but only one-third over the age of retirement; participation rates fell steeply after age 75. However, the retired volunteers contributed more time, giving on average five hours a week, compared with three hours for younger people.

Older women are slightly more likely to volunteer than men. The most common activities for volunteers of all ages were raising or handling money. Other common activities were helping to organize or run events, serving on committees, and visiting. Their work is more likely to be directed toward other older people in need and less likely to be linked with sports, children, education, or the environment. Their main motivations included the desire to contribute to achieving something worthwhile and to meet other people. The survey found that 9 out of 10 older people subscribed to the view that "a society with volunteers is a caring society."

Participation in formal learning is low (less than 5% of retired people). This no doubt reflects the educational disadvantage characteristic of this group, many of whom will have been put off education by poor-quality schooling. Those who do take part are almost all pursuing leisure interests and taking courses that do not lead to qualifications. Such courses are offered in local continuing education colleges, which devote small and declining proportions of their resources to these classes. Much to the distress of the older students, the range of classes is narrowing and the fees are rising in response to greater financial pressures placed on the colleges.

ADVOCACY AND PROTECTION

There is yet to arise in Great Britain any national body of older people to represent the views of the older population. No organization exists of equivalent scale or importance to the American Association of Retired Persons (AARP) or the Gray Panthers. Some groupings aspire to be large and significant, such as the National Pensioners' Convention and the Association of Retired Persons. The former grew out of the retirement groups of a number of trade unions and is actively led by Jack Jones, who was a very prominent trade union leader. The latter aspires to match its American counterpart, AARP, and was founded in 1988. It developed within four years into an organization with 120,000 members. Both groups focus on political lobbying but are not—as yet—considered to carry great weight.

Since 1970 the Age Concern movement (previously known as the National Old People's Welfare Council) has been the most effective political advocate body for elderly people. It has developed an impressive range of research, advice, and publication sections that ensure it is well equipped to comment on public policy. A similar role is played by the other major national charities in the field (e.g., Help the Aged and the Centre for Policy on Ageing).

In the absence of any mass pensioner organizations, postwar governments have tended not to take policies for older people very seriously. Perhaps as a consequence, few formal agencies can provide support and expertise. There are no special legal aid systems for older people nor any formal recognition of the particular needs of older citizens in dealing with the criminal justice system—either as victims or perpetrators.

In circumstances where individuals lose the capacity (e.g., through stroke, dementia, or brain damage) to conduct their own affairs, their interest may be taken over by the Court of Protection. This is a national governmental agency legally authorized to act in the best interests of those who are formally deemed incompetent. It takes over the control of money, assets, wills, and other statements of intent until they regain their capacity (or until death).

FUTURE PROJECTIONS

Despite all of the changes and deficiencies highlighted in this account, Britain still has a good health care system. Current older people are much healthier, better-off financially, and better housed than at any previous time. But there is genuine and evidenced concern that these great advances will be eroded as numbers grow and resources are further curtailed.

As the demographic revolution works its way through to an equilibrium in the second decade of the next century, there will be a massive increase in dementia and confusional states, to which there will be a need to develop more skillful and appropriate responses. Similarly, as death becomes the almost exclusive province of old age, sensitive and culturally meaningful ways must be found for handling the dying process and the ritual aspects of death. As the caring requirement increases, it will be essential to provide better support to informal caregivers if they are to continue as the principal support workers. Alongside them, there needs to be a better-trained work force skilled in dealing with older people, including better provision for long-term care.

For older people themselves, British society should be addressing ways of providing more access to the central arena of citizenship. This will mean more adequate pensions, a cheaper and more effective public transport system, and the creation of a housing stock in all localities that will enable people in later life to live more appropriately in familiar surroundings.

In short, Britain must take old age far more seriously by recognizing that its postretirement population has more to contribute to its corporate life. At the same time, it must provide more forms of support when the fourth age of dependency becomes a reality.

BIBLIOGRAPHY

Amos, G. (ed.). (1980). *Home from Hospital—to What?* Community Care Project, Birmingham.
Arber, Sara, and Ginn, Jay. (1991). *Gender and Later Life*. London: Sage.

Audit Commission. (1992). *The Community Revolution: Personal Social Services and Community Care.* London: HMSO.
Bond, John; Atkinson, A.: Gregson, B.; Hughes, P.; and Jeffries, L. (1989). "Evaluation of an Innovation in Community Care for Very Frail Elderly People," *Age and Ageing* 18, pp. 96–102.
Bond, John, and Carstairs, Vera. (1982). *The Elderly in Clackmannen.* Edinburgh: Scottish Home and Health Department.
Bosanquet, Nicholas, and Gray, Andrew. (1989). "Will You Still Love Me? New Opportunities for Health Services for Elderly People in the 1990s and Beyond." NAHA Research Paper No. 2, Birmingham.
Central Statistical Office. (1989). *Social Trends,* 19. London: HMSO.
Commission of the European Communities. (1993). *Older People in Europe: Social Policies and Economic Policies.* Third Report of the European Observatory, Directorate General V. Brussels.
Coni, N., Davison, W., and Webster, S. (1992). *Ageing: The Facts.* 2d ed. Oxford: Oxford University Press.
Department of the Environment. (1988). *English House Condition Survey.* London: HMSO.
Department of Health. (1989). *Working for Patients.* London: HMSO.
General Household Survey. (1988). *Informal Carers.* London: HMSO.
Goffman, Erving. (1961). *Asylums.* New York: Anchor, Doubleday.
Johnson, Malcolm L. (1988). "Never Say Die." *Listener,* 23 June, pp. 21–22.
———. (1990, 1993). "Dependency and Interdependency." In John Bond, Peter Coleman, and Sheila Peace (eds.), *Ageing in Society.* 1st and 2d eds. London: Sage.
Laing, William. (1991). *Laing's Review of Private Health Care 1991/92.* London: Laing and Buisson.
Law, C. M., and Warnes, A. M. (1980). "The characteristics of retired immigrants." In D. T. Herbert and R. J. Johnston, eds., *Geography and the Urban Environment: Progress in Research and Applications,* vol. 3. London: Wiley, pp. 175–222.
McGlone, Francis. (1992). *Disability and Dependency in Old Age: A Demographic Audit.* London: Family Policy Studies Centre.
Martin, J., Meltzer, H., and Elliot, D. (1988). *The Prevalence of Disability Among Adults.* London: HMSO.
Means, Robin, and Smith, Randall. (1985). *The Development of Welfare Services for Elderly People.* London: Croom Helm.
Midwinter, Eric. (1987). *Redefining Old Age.* London: Centre for Policy on Ageing.
———. (1992). *Leisure: New Opportunities in the Third Age.* Carnegie Enquiry into the Third Age, Research Paper No. 4, London.
Mitchell, A. (1993). "Community Care Act: Implementation," *This Caring Business,* 18 February.
Robb, Barbara (ed.). (1967). *Sans Everything.* London: Nelson.
Schuller, Tom, and Bostyn, Anne Marie. (1992). *Learning: Education, Training and Information in the Third Age.* Carnegie Enquiry into the Third Age, Research Paper No. 3, London.
Townsend, Peter. (1962). *The Last Refuge.* London: Routledge and Kegan Paul.
Victor, Christina R. (1991). *Health and Health Care in Later Life.* Milton Keynes: Open University Press.

Volunteer Centre. (1991). *Voluntary Activity: A Survey of Public Attitudes.* Berkhamsted: Volunteer Centre.

Walker, Alan, and Phillipson, Chris. (1986). *Ageing and Social Policy.* Aldershot: Gower.

Warnes, Anthony (ed.). (1992). *Homes and Travel: Local Life in the Third Age.* Carnegie Enquiry into the Third Age, Research Paper No. 5, London.

Warnes, Anthony, and Law, C. (1985). "Elderly Population Distributions and Housing Prospects in Britain." *Town Planning Review,* 3, No. 56, pp. 292–314.

Wicks, Malcolm, and Henwood, Melanie. (1988). "The Social and Demographic Circumstances of Elderly People." In Brian Gearing, Malcolm Johnson, and Tom Heller (eds.), *Mental Health Problems in Old Age.* Chichester: Wiley.

12

HONG KONG

Nelson W. S. Chow

INTRODUCTION

Hong Kong is a British colony and will remain so until 1997, when it will be returned to China to become a special administrative region. As over 98% of the population in Hong Kong are ethnic Chinese, the place has been dominated by the Chinese culture, though Western practices have also been prevalent, especially among the young and the educated. Hong Kong is, no doubt, a typical example of where the East meets the West. This encounter of different cultures is most apparent among the elderly, as most of them have come from an agrarian social and economic background and are now the first generation to grow old in a highly industrialized city. It is therefore not surprising to find that the majority of the elderly in Hong Kong are unprepared for the kind of retirement life that they are now experiencing.

According to the Chinese tradition, a person is considered old when he reaches the age of 60, and this is also the age commonly perceived to be elderly in Hong Kong. The planning of both welfare and housing services for the elderly uses the age of 60 as the cutoff point, but 65 has been employed for the planning of medical and health services. In March 1991, when the last census was conducted in Hong Kong, 13.5% of the total population (or 772,400 out of 5,674,114 persons) were found to be aged 60 and over, and 8.7% of the total were aged 65 and over. It is projected that by the year 2000, more than 15% of the population in Hong Kong will be aged 60 and over and the actual number will approach 1 million. In terms of the sex ratio, as in other industrialized countries, the proportion of male elderly population in Hong Kong to female is around 2 to 3. Life expectancy in Hong Kong is still rising and stood at 75 years for males and 81 for females in 1991. The majority of the elderly now living in Hong Kong came from China and had received little formal education while they were young, as it was then the period of World War II. As to their marital status, the 1991 census findings revealed that nearly 40% of the elderly population were widowed, while about 5% had never married, and very few had actually been divorced or separated.

Economically, the elderly in Hong Kong are probably among the poorest in the population. Since most of them are not receiving any retirement pensions, their only way to maintain a living is to rely on their own savings or the support of their children, if they have any. For those who can find a job, they can go on working for as long as their health permits. In 1991 about a quarter of the elderly population in Hong Kong were classified as "economically active," implying that they were still being employed. Judging from the meager incomes that most received, it is obvious that the elderly have worked mainly to earn a living.

The relatively inferior economic position of the elderly has produced an adverse effect in eroding the traditionally prestigious social status held by the elderly. Though the elderly in Hong Kong are still described as "liken unto a treasure at home," recent studies (Chow, 1990) indicate that their social image has dropped so low that it is indirectly contributing not only to an increasing number of suicides by the elderly but also to the emerging problem of elder abuse. Indeed, evidence suggests that the younger generations, once married, are increasingly unwilling to live with their parents. The 1991 census found that "one vertically extended nuclear family," more commonly known as a "three-generation family," represented only 10.7% of all households, a decrease from 13.6% in 1981. Other current data sets on the elderly (Census and Statistics Department, 1991) reveal that about 4% of the elderly in Hong Kong are living in various types of institutions and 24% live either alone or with another elderly person, thus leaving about 70% living with other members in a family. Compared with other industrialized countries, the percentage of the elderly in Hong Kong who are still residing with their children is still very high, but the decreasing trend suggests that many of the three-generation households are maintained only grudgingly. Some recent studies (Chi and Lee, 1989) found that an increasing number of the elderly are expressing a wish to live on their own, suggesting that the social value of residing with one's children may no longer be as sacrosanct as before.

The social and economic status of the elderly in Hong Kong is obviously changing rapidly under the pressure of modernization and urbanization. For a society and culture that have for centuries held dear the value of filial piety, the eroding status of the elderly has naturally been viewed with misgiving, and attempts to revive this traditional value are not unheard of. While much can be said about the importance of preserving filial piety, circumstances have changed so much that a new strategy of approaching the aging problem would probably bring about a better support system for the elderly and at the same time promote among the elderly themselves a more positive outlook toward life.

The Formal Structure of Care of the Elderly

Since the need of the elderly for care and support outside their families has been recognized only recently, a formal system to provide care to the elderly was not in existence before 1977, when the government issued a policy paper on developing services for the elderly. Instead of committing the government to meeting every need of the elderly, the policy paper pronounced a "care in the community" approach, in which the responsibility of taking care of the elderly would be shared between the government and the "community," including the family in which the elderly lived. The adoption of the "care in the community" approach was based upon the premise that the elderly would be most satisfied when they were residing with their families; institutional care was only a second best and should be provided only when the elderly were too frail to take care of themselves or when their families were unable to do the job. In terms of provision, the policy paper held the view that, as far as possible, the government should refrain from directly operating the community support and residential services; they should best be taken up by nongovernment organizations (NGOs), as they would cost less and probably be more effective in enlisting voluntary support.

Except for the old age allowance, which is regarded as an entitlement of the elderly, all the other public services for the elderly are provided on the basis of need and, for some, a test of means is also required. The definition of need varies from service to service. In general, the need of the elderly is measured by their degree of urgency to receive support and the extent to which it can be met either by the elderly themselves or by their families, if available. Although most community support and residential services are operated by different NGOs, similar criteria have been employed in assessing needs as the services are uniformly funded by the government. The provision of housing and hospital services, on the other hand, is administered by two quasi-government organizations, the Housing Authority and the Hospital Authority, and each has its own criteria in determining the needs of the elderly.

The formulation of service policies for the elderly lies with the Secretary for Health and Welfare, and two committees, namely, the Social Welfare Advisory Committee and the Medical and Health Development Advisory Committee, have been set up to advise the government. In 1987 a Central Committee on Services for the Elderly, comprising representatives from both government and nongovernmental organizations, was established to review the various public services provided to the elderly, and a number of improvements were subsequently made. In addition, the Hong Kong Council of Social Service, a coordinator of NGOs in Hong Kong, established in 1972 a division to monitor the work of the NGOs in the area of services for the elderly and to draw up the relevant service standards.

In summary, services for the elderly have developed in Hong Kong largely as a result of the efforts of the NGOs, with resources first coming from local and overseas donations and now from government subsidies. Although fees are charged for using the various public services, they are either just nominal or set at a level the majority of the elderly can afford to pay; the general principle governing their provision is that they should be offered to the elderly with the greatest demonstrable need. Since public services provided for the elderly are generally insufficient, elderly persons who are prepared to pay more may be impatient with the long waiting lists and turn to the private market to purchase the relevant services. Private nursing homes and other profit-making, home-based services are becoming a permanent feature of the support system to the elderly. Hence, together with the effort of the government in recent years to expand its social services to the elderly, there is also room for the existence of a private sector to cater to the needs of those who can afford to pay a higher fee.

INCOME MAINTENANCE AND EMPLOYMENT

The provision of income maintenance for the elderly is relatively simple and, in a way, underdeveloped in Hong Kong. The issue of income security in old age was discussed in Hong Kong in 1967, when a government working party was set up to examine the need for it. Although the working party was in favor of the introduction of a contributory retirement pensions scheme, the government had not deemed it necessary, arguing on the ground that the capitalist system of Hong Kong would best be served when income security matters were left to the private arrangement between the employers and the employees, with little interference from the government. As a result, retirement pensions remain only the entitlement of the government servants and a small number of the fortunate ones employed in large enterprises. As to the rest, at retirement they must depend either on their own savings or on the support of their children. The absence of such an important social measure is obviously unacceptable and after incessant demands from the public for the introduction of an old age income security scheme, the government issued a paper on a community-wide retirement protection system in October 1992 for public consultation. A decision was still pending at the end of 1993.

As it now stands, what the elderly in Hong Kong are entitled to are the old-age allowance and the support from public assistance (if they are also poor). A Hong Kong resident who has not been away from the territory for substantial periods in the five years before reaching the age 65 can apply for the old-age allowance. Those aged between 65 and 69 have to declare that they have neither an income nor assets above certain prescribed levels to be eligible. In 1992, the limits were set at monthly incomes of HK$ 2,600 (US $333) for a single person and HK$ 3,900 (US $500) for a married couple; assets were set at HK$ 100,000 (US $12,820) for a single person and HK$ 150,000 (US $19,230) for a married couple. For applicants reaching the age of 70, no income declaration is required.

The old-age allowance that those aged 70 and over can receive is higher than that given to those aged below 70; in 1992, the amounts were, respectively, HK$ 470 (US $60) and HK$ 413 (US $53) a month. As the old-age allowance is non-means-tested, noncontributory, and regarded as the right of every elderly person residing in Hong Kong, the amount given has to be kept small in order not to financially overburden the government. The old-age allowance should therefore in no way be compared with retirement pensions provided in other countries. The purpose of the old-age allowance when it was first introduced in 1973 was seen as an incentive to encourage families to take care of their elderly members; it has never been meant to be enough for the support of a basic living. In March 1992, over 400,000 elderly persons were receiving the old-age allowance and costing the government an annual outlay of over HK$ 2 billion (Social Welfare Department, 1992).

The other Social Security measure that the elderly can avail themselves of is the public assistance scheme. As the majority of the retirees in Hong Kong are deprived of a steady income from retirement pensions, some of them have found it necessary to apply for public assistance when they have exhausted other means to maintain a living. To be eligible for public assistance, a person has to be almost penniless, and it is not surprising that often only the lonely elderly are eligible. In March 1992, about 60,000 elderly persons in Hong Kong were receiving public assistance, with the basic rate for a single person set at HK$ 825 (US $106) a month. Those aged between 60 and 69 can also receive an old age supplement at HK$ 413 (US $53) a month, increased to HK$ 470 (US $60) a month for those aged 70 and over. In addition, public assistance recipients are eligible for a subsidy to cover rent. Admittedly, the total amount provided under the public assistance scheme is only sufficient for a living above the subsistence level, hardly enough to provide the elderly with anything more than the bare necessities.

Very little attention has so far been paid to the employment needs of the elderly, though about a quarter of them are still participating in the labor force. As no compulsory retirement pensions exist, many of the elderly have continued to work out of necessity rather than choice. At present, elderly persons who require employment assistance can approach the Job Placement Unit of the Labor Department or the Employment Assistance Service of the Hong Kong Council of Social Service. As the unemployment rate in Hong Kong has been kept very low, jobs are available to the elderly who want to work, but they are not necessarily suitable for their abilities and past experiences.

HEALTH CARE SERVICES

The medical and health care system in Hong Kong is made up of two parts: an extensive public sector meeting the needs of the general public and a vigorous private sector catering to those who can afford to pay. In general, about 80% of the patients requiring hospital treatment make use of the services provided in public hospitals managed by the Hospital Authority, while the majority of those requiring only consultative services turn to the private practitioners. Since very few of the elderly are protected by private medical insurance and most are limited in means, they tend to make greater use of the services provided in public hospitals and outpatient clinics.

Public medical and health services currently available to the elderly consist of preventive health care, community nursing service, community psychiatric nursing service, priority medical consultation for the elderly, infirmaries for the elderly, psychogeriatric services, and hospice care. The purpose of preventive health care is to impart to the elderly knowledge of a healthy life-style and the importance of the prevention of disease. Presently, health promotion work is carried out by the Central Health Education Unit of the Department of Health and consists mainly of publicity campaigns and other community programs aimed at educating the elderly about disease prevention.

The community nursing service was formally established in 1977. It is operated on a referral basis and accepts only patients discharged from hospitals. In 1991 there were over 50 such community nursing "stations" to which patients can be referred in accordance with their place of residence. Services rendered by the community nurses include a wide range of skilled nursing care, such as injection, ostomy care, removal of stitches, catheter care, wound dressing, and irrigation. Rehabilitation exercises, blood pressure measurement, urine testing, diet instruction, and general health education can also be performed. Although the community nursing service is available to all patients who have such needs, nearly half of those benefiting from it are the elderly. Similarly, most of those using the community psychiatric nursing service belong to the elderly group. The community psychiatric nursing service is also operated on a referral basis with the purpose of ensuring continuity in care and prevention of relapses. The above two community services have reported success in preventing unnecessary hospital admissions, thus enabling many elderly patients to continue remaining in the community.

The elderly are especially making use of the public outpatient clinic services. Because of the heavy demand, patients using the public outpatient clinic services often have to wait for several hours for their turn for consultation. The purpose of the priority medical consultation scheme for the elderly is to shorten the waiting time of the elderly by offering them priority to consult the doctor. The actual operation of the scheme varies from clinic to clinic, but, on the whole, it has provided elderly patients with much convenience.

Elderly suffering from chronic physical and mental illnesses and in need of constant nursing care and some medical supervision are provided with infirmary care. The existing planning ratio of infirmary care is 5 infirmary beds for 1,000 elderly persons aged 65 and over (Social Welfare Department, 1992). At the end of 1990, the provision of infirmary beds stood at around 2,000 while the demand as expressed by those on the waiting list was about 3,500, with a shortfall of more than 1,500 beds. The severe shortage of infirmary beds has caused not only much suffering among the elderly waiting for admission but also tremendous stress upon their families shouldering the burden of care.

A substantial number of elderly persons suffer from both physical and mental problems and are in need of psychogeriatric services. Depending on the nature of their needs, the elderly suffering from such problems may receive treatment at psychiatric outpatient clinics, day hospitals, or geriatric wards of general hospitals or receive visits by community psychiatric nurses. Like infirmary care, services provided to meet the needs of the elderly with both physical and mental problems are in severe short supply. Terminally ill elderly patients can now receive hospice care, introduced in the mid-1980s in a few public hospitals.

In summary, as very few of the elderly in Hong Kong are covered by private medical insurance, the majority have to turn to the public sector for the satisfaction of their medical and health care needs. Over the last 20 years, the government has developed a wide range of domiciliary and institutional services, as part of the larger network for the general population, to meet the medical and health care needs of the elderly. The quality of the services is generally acceptable but they are often so short in supply that they can be available only to those in urgent need.

HOUSING RESOURCES

With a population of nearly 6 million people and a hilly geography, housing naturally is the most difficult problem for most people living in the congested city. The public housing program in Hong Kong was started as early as in 1953, when a fire on Christmas Eve made more than 50,000 people homeless. At the end of 1991, 40.5% of the population were living in public and aided housing, with another 7.5% in Home Ownership estates built by the Housing Authority (Phillips, 1992). The need of the elderly for housing has long been attended to, with the first hostel for the elderly set up in the late 1960s; since then, a great variety of housing resources has been developed for them.

Prior to 1985, hostels formed the major form of housing resource for the elderly, and most who were thus accommodated were lonely and without a family. In March 1991, 2,120 elderly persons were staying in these hostels, which were run by the NGOs with subsidies from the government (Social Welfare Department, 1992). Since 1985, there has been a change in policy and instead of building more hostels for the elderly, those requiring accommodation were housed in "sheltered housing" managed by either the Housing Department or the NGOs. In March 1993, about 15,000 elderly persons were staying in these hostels. Besides the provision of hostels and "sheltered housing," elderly persons can apply for accommodation in public housing estates through either the Elderly Persons Priority Scheme or the Compassionate Rehousing Scheme. Under the Elderly Persons Priority Scheme, two or more unrelated persons reaching the age of 58 or over who agree to live together can apply for rehousing. They can normally be rehoused within a reasonable period of one to two years. From its implementation in 1979 up to the end of 1991, about 17,000 elderly persons have thus been rehoused. For elderly persons who want to live by themselves, they can opt for the Single Persons Allocation Scheme, but the waiting time, due to the limited supply of single-person units in public housing estates, is admittedly much longer. Other than the above arrangements, elderly persons who are faced with social and medical problems can apply for the 1,100 public housing units allocated each year under the Compassionate Rehousing Scheme, which aims at catering to the housing needs of families and individuals encountering social difficulties.

The above-mentioned schemes are intended mainly for the elderly who are capable of self-care or in need of only minimum assistance. Two other types of residential care are provided for those who cannot manage on their own. The first one is homes for the aged, which, by March 1991, housed a total of 6,993 elderly persons. The planning ratio of the homes for the aged is 10 places for every 1,000 elderly population. Nearly all homes for the aged are run by NGOs, with financial support from the government. The other type is care and attention homes, more commonly known as nursing homes in other countries, which are intended for elderly persons requiring not more than 2.5 hours of nursing care per week. In March 1991, 3,232 elderly persons were staying in these homes (Social Welfare Department, 1992). In recent years, there has been an upsurge in demand for nursing care places, and the number of the elderly waiting for admission is often larger than those taken into care. As a result, this has turned many who can afford to pay a much higher fee to seek help in the private sector. At the end of 1991, more than 9,000 elderly persons were known to be staying in private nursing homes, three times the number of those in the subsidized sector. Recognizing the increasing demand for nursing care places, the planning ratio of such services in the subsidized sector has been increased from 8 to 11 for every 1,000 elderly population.

In addition to these housing arrangements, families applying for public housing can have their waiting period shortened by two years if they have elderly members included in their households. If these families are prepared to move to the new towns, where public housing units are more readily available, they can even apply for two units in the same block so as to facilitate mutual support between the married children and their elderly parents. Since various measures have already been introduced to meet the housing needs of the elderly, no additional financial assistance or tax relief measures are deemed necessary to help those living in private housing.

Despite the efforts of the government to provide housing for the elderly, there are still several thousand of them who, for various reasons, like wanting to be near their place of work or unwillingness to move to another district, are occupying just a bed space in some of the dilapidated private tenement blocks. These elderly persons, often male, are termed the "caged men," as they often surround their bed space with fences in order to protect their own belongings. It is also known that there are about 1,000 homeless elderly persons sleeping in the streets, and there are plans to house them in a few specially designed hostels located in the urban areas.

Thus, the existing housing policy for the elderly is to accommodate the elderly in various types of public housing or residential arrangements. Though the preference of the younger generations of today is to set up their own families, coresidence of elderly persons with their married children remains the dominant practice, and measures are taken to encourage its continuance.

SUPPORTIVE SERVICES

Less than 4% of the elderly in Hong Kong are living in institutions; the great majority are staying in the community either by themselves or with their families. Community support services, comprising home help service, social center, multiservice center, and day-care center, constitute an important part of the social support network. Home help service renders to the elderly such help as the preparation of meals, personal care, escort, laundry, and home management. Around 3,000 elderly persons were being served by home helpers in March 1991. Social centers for the elderly provide a meeting point for them to meet their social and recreational needs. The planning ratio of such centers is 1 per 3,000 elderly persons and, in March 1991, 155 centers were in existence. One multiservice center is planned for 25,000 elderly population, and services provided in these centers, as of March 1991, include home help, counseling, social activities, laundry, bathing, and canteen facilities, as well as the organization of community education programs. Day-care centers, wherever possible, are attached to a multiservice center and provide such services as personal care, nursing care, and rehabilitative services.

Supportive medical and health services have already been discussed, and the other services, which have the same purpose of assisting the elderly to remain in the community, include respite service and various kinds of community programs. After a trial period of two years, respite service was formally introduced in 1991 to help relieve the burden of families with frail elderly members to look after. An outreach service for the "elderly at risk" was also started in 1991 for an experimental period of 2.5 years to reach out to the elderly who are in need of support but who would never come out for the services. In addition, mass programs, such as health education and festivals for the elderly, have been organized on a regular basis to encourage the active participation of the elderly in community activities. Lastly, a great variety of indigenous organizations, such as the mutual help associations and the religious bodies, also play an important role in enabling the elderly to live in the community by providing them with channels to associate themselves with other members of the community.

LEISURE-TIME RESOURCES

As the majority of the elderly in Hong Kong are still living with their families, most of their leisure time is involved in family-related activities. Studies on the leisure activities of the elderly in Hong Kong (Kwan, 1990) found that the most common activity engaged in by the elderly, whether living alone or with other family members, is watching television programs. A very high percentage of the elderly who are living with their married children revealed that they are so busily occupied by household chores and in looking after their grandchildren that they have little time left for themselves. Culturally there is also a resistance among the Chinese elderly to engage in activities outside the home environment and with persons other than their own family members.

For the elderly who want to spend their leisure time outside their homes, social centers for the elderly provide the most convenience. In March 1991, about 70,000 elderly persons were members of 155 social centers, which, other than providing the elderly with various kinds of social and recreational activities, also encourage the elderly to serve as volunteers for other frail elderly and the handicapped. In addition, an increasing number of the elderly are now becoming followers of various religious beliefs, and it is not uncommon for them to regard religious activities as their major pursuit in life.

Besides these more formal activities, as people in Hong Kong are geographically living close to one another, elderly people who are residing in the same housing block or nearby often come together for such activities as playing mahjongg or doing t'ai-chi exercises. In fact, chatting with neighbors is commonly regarded by the elderly as the most convenient way to spend their leisure time, and this form of informal companionship may even be more valuable than the formal ones. Lastly, despite the efforts made by some of the NGOs to organize educational programs for the elderly, they have never been found to be popular, as it is still believed by the Chinese elderly in Hong Kong that to be wise is not necessarily to be learned.

ADVOCACY AND PROTECTION

No laws in Hong Kong specifically protect the welfare of the elderly, since they enjoy the same rights as other residents. The only benefit exclusively available to the elderly is the old-age allowance, which is given on a universal basis to nearly all the elderly aged 65 and over, subject to an income declaration for those aged between 65 and 69. Concessionary fares are offered to the elderly for limited community facilities and public transport services to encourage the elderly to participate in community activities. Another measure, which is seen as an incentive to encourage children to support their elderly parents, is the dependent parents' tax allowance, which is increased in amount if the children are not only supporting their elderly parents but also living with them. Applicants for public housing can have their waiting period shortened by two years if they have elderly members included in their households.

Since the development of formal support services for the elderly has a history of less than 20 years in Hong Kong, most advocacy organizations that set their goals at seeking a better quality of life and equity in opportunities for the elderly have been established only recently. The Hong Kong Council of Social Service set up a division in 1972 to coordinate the work of the NGOs providing services for the elderly; since then the division has acted as the main body to work hand in hand with the government in developing various social services to meet the needs of the elderly. Another organization, known as the Association for the Rights of the Elderly, was formed by a group of social workers in the late 1970s to fight for the rights of the elderly. This group has not achieved very much, as their actions have been rather sporadic. In the mid-1980s, a group of professionals working in the field of gerontology came together and formed the Hong Kong Association of Gerontology. At present, the activities of the association include the publication of journals, the organization of seminars, and the promotion of research into the aging problem. Other than these services, the care of the elderly has been the focus of many debates in the Legislative Council, which is the law-making body in Hong Kong. No doubt, as the population in Hong Kong matures, people will show a greater interest in the welfare of their elderly members.

FUTURE PROJECTIONS

The future development of welfare services for the elderly in Hong Kong is determined, on one hand, by the rate of increase of demand for such services and, on the other, by the priority given to them in terms of the allocation of public resources. The Hong Kong government published a policy paper on the future development of welfare services in 1991 in which it stated that "a rising population of elderly persons will result in a corresponding increase in the demand for services for the elderly in quantity, variety and duration" (Hong Kong Government, 1991, p. 6). Furthermore, "Increasing life expectancy will result in a consistent increase in the age group 75 and above, which is a group likely to have a greater need for services such as long-term health and residential care" (Hong Kong Government, 1991, p. 31). As a result, a rapid expansion of both community support and residential services for the elderly was projected in the policy paper over the next 10 years, with a greater proportion of public resources devoted to such purposes.

The government, nevertheless, maintained in the policy paper that the "care in the community" approach, adopted in 1979 as the guiding principle for the development of services for the elderly, was the most appropriate one, though it recognized that "while it will remain the policy to encourage the care of the elderly by family members within a family context and to strengthen support for their carers, it should also be recognized that the needs of the elderly vary and that residential care for some may be the most appropriate service" (Hong Kong Government, 1991, p. 30). It was proposed that instead of merely putting the thrust on the provision of community support services as in the 1980s and neglecting the needs for residential care, a more balanced approach would be adopted with the broad objective of promoting "the well-being of the elderly in all aspects of their life."

Furthermore, since there is still a severe shortage of community support services and in order that the "care in the community" approach may truly become a reality, not merely a slogan, the policy paper proposed a strengthening of the social networks in Hong Kong. "Social networks are part of Chinese culture and tradition and . . . [are] most clearly demonstrated in the role of the family as the primary providers of care and welfare and by the contributions of clansmen associations, neighborhood organizations and volunteers" (Hong Kong Government, 1991, p. 18). It has, however, yet to be seen how social networks could be strengthened to achieve the purpose of enabling the elderly to live in the community. In the meantime, it appears that other than increasing the supply of community support services, including public medical and housing services, the following measures are also necessary.

First, families in Hong Kong need to be helped to provide support for the elderly. Although the trend toward nuclear families is clear and there is little likelihood that it will be reversed, greater incentives can be given to individuals who are prepared to live with their elderly parents. The recent changes in public housing policies regarding the elderly are an example toward such a goal. Second, evidence in Hong Kong shows that children are more prepared to live with elderly parents who are economically independent. The introduction of income security measures that ensure the economic independence of the elderly is therefore urgently called for. Third, evidence also shows that most of the elderly in Hong Kong are still contributing to their families by assisting in caring for the young and preserving the stability of the family, and it is therefore a matter of paramount importance to maximize the roles of the elderly in their families and to enhance their contributions.

Hence, the question now facing Hong Kong, as its population matures, is not simply the increasing necessity of caring for the elderly but also the form of care that should be adopted and the ways in which the community, including the family, can continue to be a source of support. An approach that integrates the efforts of the government and the community would be the most viable solution.

BIBLIOGRAPHY

Census and Statistics Department. (1991). *Hong Kong 1991 Population Census, Summary Results.* Hong Kong: Hong Kong Government Printer.

Central Committee on Services for the Elderly. (1988). *Report of the Central Committee on Services for the Elderly.* Hong Kong: Health and Welfare Branch, Hong Kong Government.

Chi, I., and Lee, J. J. (1989). *Hong Kong Elderly Health Survey.* Hong Kong: Department of Social Work and Social Administration, University of Hong Kong.

Chow, N. W. S. (1990). Aging in Hong Kong. In B. K. P. Leung (Ed.), *Social Issues in Hong Kong* (pp. 164–78). Hong Kong: Oxford University Press.

———. (1992). Hong Kong: Community Care for Elderly People. In D. R. Phillips (Ed.), *Aging in East and Southeast Asia* (pp. 65–76). London: Edward Arnold.

Hong Kong Government. (1965). *The Aims and Policy for Social Welfare in Hong Kong.* Hong Kong: Hong Kong Government Printer.

———. (1977). *Services for the Elderly, a Green Paper.* Hong Kong: Hong Kong Government Printer.

———. (1991). *Social Welfare into the 1990s and Beyond.* Hong Kong: Hong Kong Government Printer.

Kwan, Y. H. (1990). "A review of the recreation and leisure activities patterns of older people in Hong Kong." *Hong Kong Journal of Gerontology* 4 (2):28–34.

Phillips, D. R. (1992). Hong Kong: Demographic and Epidemiological Change and Social Care for Elderly People. In D. R. Phillips (Ed.), *Aging in East and Southeast Asia* (pp. 45–64). London: Edward Arnold.

Social Welfare Department. (1991). *Study of Public Assistance Recipients 1989.* Hong Kong: Social Welfare Department.

———. (1992). *The Five-Year Plan for Social Welfare Development in Hong Kong: Review 1991.* Hong Kong: Hong Kong Government Printer.

Working Party on Housing for the Elderly. (1989). *Report of the Working Party on Housing for the Elderly.* Hong Kong: Hong Kong Government Printer.

Working Party on the Future Needs of the Elderly. (1973). *Services for the Elderly.* Hong Kong: Hong Kong Government Printer.

13

INDIA

S. D. Gokhale and Chandra Dave

INTRODUCTION

Defining Old Age

There is no one definition of aging in India. In the case of working people, aging is widely considered synonymous with retirement. In government jobs, 58 years has been set as the retiring age; in universities and in banks, which are governed by special acts of government, the mandatory retiring age has been fixed at 60 years; for the judiciary, there is yet another set of rules: judges of the High Court retire at 63 years, whereas those at the Supreme Court level retire at 65 years.

Among Hindus, who form 83% of the Indian population, religious tenets dictate that when a man passes the Rubicon of 60 years, he is considered old. He is then enjoined to refrain from participating in worldly activities and to worship and perform acts of service.

The 1982 World Assembly on Ageing, sponsored by the United Nations, in which India officially participated, decided upon 60 years as the onset of aging. However, different states in India have adopted different age demarcations for allotting old-age pensions and other benefits related to the aging years. For such requirements, the age span swings between 55 to 74 years for men and 55 to 75 years for women.

The Indian social system, with its network of caste and gender demarcations, has been age-integrated socially, psychologically, and vocationally. Traditionally, the bulk of the elderly in India have occupied a generally enviable place in society; however, some social historians believe that the respect for the elderly by their families in the past was a bit exaggerated. But while there is no animosity between the generations, there is no great interaction either, and the majority of the elderly remain rather an ignored lot.

The Characteristics of the Elderly

The Indian population is mostly rural. Only a little over 25% live in the urban areas (217 million out of a total of 844 million people, as counted in the 1991 census). The census also revealed that the total population of the 60 and older population was 55 million or 6.5% of the total population.

In 1947, the year of Indian independence, the average age of an Indian was about 32 years (*India Today,* 30 September 1991). It is hard to believe that, in the last decade of the twentieth century, Indian life expectancy at birth has reached 62 years (*India Today,* 30 September 1991), despite malnutrition, insufficient potable water, pollution, and a plethora of ills that adversely affect the health of the people.

The maximum longevity potential of human life has not shown any increase (Pathak, 1987). What distinguishes the 1991 demographic position of the elderly from that of earlier cohorts of the elderly is their increasing number, longevity, and proportion to the total population.

The 60-plus age group increased from 12 million in 1901 to 20 million in 1951 (a 61% increase) and from 32.7 million in 1971 to 43.2 million in 1981 (Registrar General, 1981). In the 1991 census, the number reached 55 million (representing a 175% increase since 1951), and by 2000 it is projected that there may be about 76 million people 60 years of age and older (or nearly four times the number in 1951) who will constitute 7.6% of the total population. The increase in the population between 1951 and 1991 is greater for the elderly (38%) than for that of the general population (18.9%).

More than four times as many older people live in the rural areas of India than in urban areas. The sex discrepancey between elderly women and elderly men is higher in urban than rural areas. In the later 1980s, in rural areas, about 74% of elderly men were "currently married," as opposed to 34% of the elderly women; in urban areas the corresponding figures were 78% for men and 30% for women. Literacy in the population 60 and over, for both men and women, is much lower than in the general population. Mandatory retirement is applicable only to the organized section of the employed, constituting less than one-tenth of the total.

In rural India, despite the expectation to join the family system, 12.4% of the elderly men and 1.43% of the elderly women live alone. The corresponding figures for urban elderly men and women are 9.52% and 0.80%. The proportion of physically impaired elderly men and women in rural areas was 44% and 66%, respectively, and in rural areas the proportion was 47% and 67%, respectively. In a study of old-age homes (Dave, 1989), it was discovered that an old person waited 9.8 years before being admitted into an institutional setting.

INCOME MAINTENANCE AND EMPLOYMENT

Retired employees of the government and organized sectors of industry are comparatively better off with regard to old-age benefits. In government service, retired employees are eligible for pension, gratuity, leave encashment, and provident fund programs.

The system of payment of pensions to government employees dates back more than 100 years—ever since the enactment of Pension Act of 1871. According to revised rules of 1972, in order for the retiree to receive a pension immediately after retirement, the work for the calculation of the pension amount and so on is supposed to mandatorily begin two years prior to superannuation of the concerned employee. In 1991, the Union government initiated the move to introduce a pension scheme for employees covered by the Provident Fund Act. In 1991, the Union Government's pension bill had increased to Rs. 31,000 million (US $100 million), with defense, railways, and telecommunications sectors taking the lion's share.

Retirement benefits are sometimes liberalized, including payment of pension to family in the event of an employee's death in service and relief to neutralize price increases. Some of the measures introduced recently reflect the government's concern toward the well-being of its retired employees. Two other measures for the benefit of Central Government employees are an insurance scheme that assures payments at retirement or death at a per prescribed schedule, and the general provident fund, deposit-linked insurance payment. The government is contemplating introduction of a medical insurance scheme for Central Government employees, who are presently required to make a compulsory contribution to the general provident fund, which is returned with interest on retirement. Income tax rebates are allowed on such contributions. Retired government employees are permitted to take up employment after superannuation, but if any person intends to take employment within two years of retirement, permission is required from the government.

In the organized sectors of industry, retirement benefits are available to employees. Under the Employees' Provident Fund and Miscellaneous Provisions Act, 1952, three schemes have been framed: Employees' Provident Fund Scheme, Employees' Family Pension Scheme, and Employees' Deposit-Linked Insurance Scheme. Under the Employees' Provident Fund Scheme, which covers employees drawing less than Rs. 1,600 (US $52) per month in establishments employing 20 or more persons, contributions are made to the provident fund by the employees, with a matching contribution by the employer. After attaining the age of 55, a person is entitled to a full refund of contributions by him or her and by the employer to the fund, along with interest. More than 10,000 establishments have adopted this scheme, covering 11.31 million employees.

The Employees' Family Pension Scheme provides benefits to the members of the family of a deceased employee. Under the Employees' Deposit-Linked

Insurance Scheme, in the event of death of a provident fund member while in service, the person receiving the provident fund is paid, in addition, an insurance benefit.

The Gratuity Act, 1972 (as upgraded in 1987) is applicable to factories, mines, plantations, and so on, and covers employees earning less than Rs. 2,500 (US $81) per month. The benefit available under the scheme is a lump sum amount equal to 15 days' wages for each year of continuous service (not less than 5 years). A maximum amount of Rs. 50,000 (US $1,613) is paid on termination of employment, superannuation, retirement, resignation, or death.

For workers in coal mines, similar benefits are available under the Coal Mines Provident Fund Miscellaneous Provisions Act, 1948, under which three schemes have been framed: the Coal Mines Provident Fund Scheme, which covers about 1,000 coal mines; the Coal Mines Family Pension Scheme; and the Coal Mines Deposit-Linked Insurance Scheme, which provides insurance coverage to members of the Coal Mines Provident Fund. The Provident Fund and related benefits are also available under the relevant legislation to workers in plantations, seamen, and so on.

Old-age pensions, in the nature of public assistance, have been introduced by the state governments in keeping with the goal of a welfare state. Pensions to the destitute old are now in operation in most parts of the country. The eligibility criteria vary from state to state. Most of the states have laid down 65 years as the minimum age of eligibility, while in a few states the age limit is 60 plus. Some states prescribe a lower age limit for females, widows, or persons suffering from physical or mental handicap and require a period of continuous residence in the state, in some cases, 10 years or more. Old-age pensions are given to a person with no source of income or with nominal income that is inadequate for survival and with no one to support the person.

In some states, the period of entitlement for certain categories is for a limited time, and in others it is on a continuous basis with a provision for review of individual cases. This assistance is discontinued when the beneficiary migrates to another state. In 1980–81, about 3 million people benefited under this scheme in different parts of the country.

Several voluntary pension plans are operated by the government, statutory bodies, and nationalized banks. Many of the facilities fall within the tax rebate schemes of the government. In fact, for many subscribers the attraction is the tax rebate rather than provision for old age. Life Insurance Corporation, Unit Trust of India, and National Small Savings are some of the noteworthy organizations that have come out with schemes for people to ensure a steady income in old age.

Several insurance organizations offer some tax rebate in one form or the other. No doubt they are altruistically motivated, but they are financial institutions nonetheless and hence are interested in keeping the invested amount with them as long as possible. Efforts need to be made to formulate plans that do not stress terminal payments but ensure steady and optimum flow of income to the concerned party. Naturally, the invested amount may keep on decreasing but should never reach rock bottom.

In government services, employees get pensions, gratuity, Provident Fund, payment for leave not taken, and so on. The retirement benefits are liberalized, usually after negotiations. Presently, there are pensions for the family in the event of the death of the employee which are adjusted for price increases. Recent measures, like the Government Employees' Compulsory Insurance Scheme, assure payment on retirement or death, and also General Provident Fund Deposit-Linked Insurance payments have been introduced. The latter benefits the organized sector of industry, which includes over 40 million workers.

The government of India urged states to grant a uniform dole of Rs. 150 (US $5) per month to a destitute elderly person. The states were encouraged to cover at least 30% of their qualifying old population. In 1969, the Central Government announced a pension for the freedom fighters who had fought the British rule in India, mostly old men and women. Additionally, most state governments grant a freedom fighters' pension, and in 1990, the Indian Railways granted them a free air-conditioned travel pass. All in all, they are well looked after, albeit the main consideration is the sacrifices made by the group and not old age per se.

HEALTH CARE SERVICES

Under the "Health for All by 2000" program of the World Health Organization, India is committed to providing at least a package of health care services to all segments of the population, giving priority, however, to the underprivileged sections of society. Health care of the old is integrated into the overall health care system in the country, the basic unit of which is the prime health center in rural areas and municipal clinics in urban areas.

Elderly people make use of free medical services provided at government hospitals and dispensaries, and they also use privately run medical services, for which payments have to be made. For retired workers in the organized sector, certain facilities for health care are extended so that they continue to have benefits (with nominal payment) even after retirement. Under the Central Government Health Services Scheme, employees and their families receive health care provided at a nominal cost.

In some of the large establishments (like the post and telegraph, railways, defense services), outpatient medical services, domiciliary visits by doctors, laboratory tests, and supply of medicines are available to retired employees. Most of the state governments also provide health facilities to their retired employees and their families. Help-Age India and Age Care India, two well-known national organizations, operate mobile health care units in some metropolitan areas.

The national program for control of blindness, launched by the government of India in the late 1970s, has a large component of old people suffering from cataract-induced blindness. In over a decade, 9.5 million cataract operations have been performed in India. However, as the number of the old increases, so does cataract blindness.

HOUSING RESOURCES

Common residence, especially with adult sons, is the general living arrangement for the elderly, except where circumstances render this difficult, such as the shortage of housing accommodations in the cities and high price rentals, reluctance of the son's family to accommodate the old, and the unwillingness of the older people to be uprooted from their community to stay with their migrant sons. There are no separate housing schemes for the elderly; they are expected to derive benefits from the general housing schemes that cater to the requirements of different categories of the population.

The National Housing Policy of 1988 has recognized the aged as an especially disadvantaged group for whom housing schemes should incorporate dwelling units of appropriate designs, formulated to meet their specialized requirements. However, a few social organizations are providing shelter to old people on a nonprofit, no-loss basis. A few state governments are also doing their part, but all the efforts are rather meager.

Recently, the Central Government set up the innovative Central Government Employees' Welfare Housing Organization. Central Government retirees can join this organization within five years of their retirement. Under this scheme this organization proposes to acquire land, in the first instance, in all important cities and build self-financed units. Employees and eligible pensioners will have to contribute to the construction of buildings and the organization will help pensioners get bank loans for this purpose.

State Housing and Area Development Boards (undertakings of state governments) usually reserve a few blocks in their housing schemes for their retirees. The government has recently announced a housing scheme for retired government servants residing in government quarters. According to the scheme, the state government allots land for building houses for such pensioners; the scheme is confined to urban areas only.

SUPPORTIVE SERVICES

Governments of each state, under the departments of social welfare, have lists of organizations working in the field of aging. Also, there is a list of old-age organizations put out by a national organization working in the field of aging. Other social welfare lists may have a section devoted to the list of old-age organizations. Seminar and conference reports on old age may add lists of such organizations at the end of the report. But these lists are of little use to illiterate persons, and therefore many needy elderly may be in the dark with regard to the services available to them.

Congregate meals programs have been initiated by a national organization (working in the field of poor aboriginal old folks). Some rich and philanthropically oriented people and organizations, working for causes other than deprived old age, are known to invite the inmates of old-age homes for a meal to commemorate an occasion dear to them or during a holiday period (like Christmas).

No formal homemaker services or chore and shopping assistance is available in India. But family visitor service is operated by some old-age organizations. The government offers nominal payment to persons who look after an old person not belonging to their own family.

While there are no day hospitals for the old, the concept of day-care service is slowly catching on in major cities and towns. There are a few day-care centers, which are used by the able-bodied old. A typical day center has a place for reading, where newspapers, books, and magazines are provided. Periodical medical checkups are arranged. Picnics and excursions are organized.

Geropsychiatry is a very new concept in India, and no mental health services for the old are documented. However, many psychiatrists have conducted research in the field of mental health in the community and have found a significant number of age-related psychiatric disorders. Many authorities, including the medical fraternity, have been educated on the preventive aspect of geriatrics. Seminar papers have warned about the prevalent confusion among medical practitioners regarding curable disorders, like depression, which may occur in the aging years, and presently incurable mental disorders, like dementia, occurring in old age.

A beginning has been made in the field of group therapy. Forum-oriented exercises have been conducted with regard to the worth of counseling both for the elderly and for the family. Perhaps there is no need for separate counseling centers for the old, and such a service may not be economical to run. Also, integrative policy demands that the old should be a part of services for all age groups.

In India, "adoptions" are well-received programs. In 1987 a progressive old-age home in Bombay started a "grandparent adoption" scheme whereby the students of a nearby school adopted institutionalized elderly persons, fostering a one-to-one relationship. Some voluntary organizations invite members of the public to sponsor a destitute old person for a sponsorship fee. The government of India gives partial compensation to a family that "adopts" an old person.

LEISURE-TIME RESOURCES

Volunteerism

Some NGOs have experimented with organizing elder volunteers to work in welfare institutions by matching the needs of an institution with the capabilities of an older person. It has been reported that to maintain the interest of the old, as a group, there must be a continued boosting of their morale. Where safeguarding one's own interest is pursued, the old (indeed, every age group) work better. Thus, most organizations working for the old are manned by the old themselves. Under such organizations, some leisure-time activities are conducted, some of which are religious in orientation. For example, one organization in Bombay (India's second largest city, with a population of about 10 million) arranges city tours of temples for the old. Many organizations arrange programs of devotional music.

Recreation

Old-age homes, as well as day-care centers, have facilities for many indoor (and a few outdoor) games. As emphasis always is on custodial care, not much encouragement is given to assist the old to go out and participate in activities outside the home. Periodically, however, athletics for the old are arranged by some organizations. A few organizations encourage daily walks by the elderly. In Bombay, there is a park exclusively for the old.

Through old-age homes and other multipurpose organizations for the old, socialization of the old is attempted. The number of efforts for the elderly increases very quickly. In Bombay alone, 37 organizations are working for the old.

A beginning has been made to provide educational opportunities for the old by at least one university in India.

ADVOCACY AND PROTECTION

The Indian constitution (under the Directive, Principles of State Policy) outlines its recommendation for the welfare of the old "to make effective provision for securing the right to work, to education and to public assistance in cases of unemployment, old age, sickness and disablement and in other cases of underserved want within its limits of economic capacity and development." This provision is strengthened by section 125 of the 1973 Code of Criminal Procedure, which enjoins every person, having sufficient means, to maintain parents unable to maintain themselves (up to Rs. 500 [US $16] per month). The provision is in addition to a section of the Hindu Adoptions and Maintenance Act in 1956, making it obligatory for a person to maintain aged/infirm parents.

The Study Group on Income and Wages, appointed by the government in 1978, recommended standardization of criteria for awarding old-age pensions by the states to the destitute old and government pensioners. The Finance Commission, in the same year, stressed the desirability of uniformity in the award of the public assistance schemes. A National Development Five-Year Plan (1980–85) recognized the vulnerability of sections of the population, including the aged. An Inter-Ministerial Committee on Ageing has also been created as a working group for the eighth Five-Year Plan. Acting along the above guidelines, the Ministry of Social Welfare has stressed pensions and welfare of retirees, and efforts have led to the creation of a separate department in the Government

Center in 1985. The Congress party election manifesto, in the 1989 elections, declared its desire to strive for a better deal for the old.

Through seminars on planning for retirement, advocacy has been attempted through newspaper articles and in the electronic media, in the form of plays and dramas. A consciousness has certainly dawned upon educated Indians to take stock of legal matters in the aging years, rather than leave them to the unreliable munificence of young family members.

In India, many crimes victimize the lonely, helpless old, many times by those whom the elderly trusted. However, not many formal provisions exist for protecting them. Vulnerability of the old is sought to be reduced through advice for them not to indulge in activities that may invite harm (like staying alone, going out at night, and so on).

Advocacy organizations for equal opportunities for the old still have not been well developed in India. A semblance of equality is, however, in evidence through the power of vote, and (during the 1989 and 1991 general elections) the elderly have made their presence felt. By and large, the old are apologetic about their age. Thus, after retirement, one learns to introduce oneself as a retired person. The pension schemes, based on the salary pattern of the working people, account for *half* of the *dearness* allowance for working people (monetary allowance added to one's salary to keep up with inflation). Similarly, life insurance schemes (while providing for monthly income to the old) retain a major portion of the money deposited with them after payment to the heirs of the old after their demise. Innovative advocacy in these matters is lacking and, thus, is needed.

FUTURE PROJECTIONS

The unique features of Indian society, in the last decade of the twentieth century are first, still a largely unresolved population problem and second (a consequence of the first), widespread poverty. Only 6.5% of the poor and the disadvantaged are old. Fortunately, respect for age does not let matters reach extreme neglect. Most of the elderly continue to be a part of the family. Interestingly, the electronic media have begun taking a good deal of interest in the positive aspects of aging. Similarly, hotel rates are offered to the elderly at tourist spots, thereby taking cognizance of the sound financial capacity of many of the "young old."

The emerging needs of the elderly, as their numbers increase, may put a severe strain on the family. A small family may further limit the choices for the old. While poverty may be the main reason for entry in an old-age home, it was discovered in the city of Bombay that loneliness, coupled with the death of the spouse, surpassed the poverty factor (Dave, 1989). Customary stigmatization pertaining to remarriage of the old (especially those with adult children) may have to be reconsidered to fight loneliness and avail some of the elderly of the care that can be given by a spouse. Similarly, the right to live and die with dignity is being advocated to build up enlightened public opinion. Two bills were introduced, though they failed in recent legislatures. Indian law does not accept suicide; however, renunciation of life sustenance (food and water) is not new to the Indian psyche. Jainism, an offshoot of Hinduism, in fact, openly accepts it. It is argued that while life is precious, its termination in old age can itself be a challenge of the highest order.

Thus, an important aspect of the aging situation in India is its widely prevalent philosophical base, which recognizes the inevitability of old age and death. The acceptance of aging as a part of human destiny provides consolation and contentment to the aging population without inciting much psychosocial disturbance (which seems to be more common in the countries of the West). On the face of it, few Indians suffer from typical old-age anxieties, though fears and uncertainties may underly the surface.

BIBLIOGRAPHY

Ambannavar, A. P. *Second India Studies-Population,* p. 61, Table 2.15, Registrar of Census, New Delhi.

Berghern, Forrest J., et al. "The Urban Elderly: A Study of Life Satisfaction, Allanheld, Osmum, p. 183, 1978.

Bose, A. B. *Ageing in India, Societal Responses and Future Perspectives,* Planning Commission, New Delhi.

Dave, Chandra. "Psycho-Socio Aspects of Ageing: A Study of the Old Age Homes in Maharashtra with Special Reference to Instutionalized Old Men in the City of Bombay." Doctoral thesis, University of Bombay, 1989.

Fischer, David Hackett. *Growing Old in America.* New York: Oxford University Press, p. 30, 1977.

Gokhale, S. D. *Towards Productive and Participatory Ageing in India.* International Federation on Ageing, 1990.

India Today. 30 September 1991.

Mandelbaum, Seymour J. *Community and Communications.* New York: Norton, 1972.

Pathak, J. D. *Ageing: A New Human Challenge.* Bombay Hospital Medical Research Center, Bombay, 1987.

Registrar General of India. "Population-Projections for India Medium Projection—1981– 2001, Census of India 1981, Series 1, Paper 1 of 1984," 1981.

Soodan Kripal, S. *Ageing in India.* Calcutta: Minerva Publications, 1978.

Verma, S. S. "Services for the Aged," paper presented at National Symposium on Aging, Bombay, 1987.

Yajur Veda. Third of the four Vedas. Vedas are the most ancient of the Hindu scriptures.

14

ISRAEL

Howard Litwin

INTRODUCTION

The character of the state of Israel has been determined, more than anything else, by large-scale immigration at several points in the country's relatively short history. The fact of massive immigration in an emerging nation has also impacted in several ways upon the age structure of the country and upon the development of social services for its elderly population. Other influential factors shaping Israel's national response to the challenges of aging include the moral dictates of Jewish ethics, which prescribe respect of elders, the socialist tradition of the country's founders, and the exigencies of a strongly centralized governmental structure in a single constituency electoral system. The portrait of the Israeli aged and the inventory of services outlined in this chapter draw their roots from these major themes.

Aging in Israel

Israel is a comparatively young country, experiencing rapid aging of its older population. This seeming contradiction, a result of uneven immigration patterns and high fertility rates, underlies the dual approach to older persons in Israeli society. Accounting for less than 4% of the national census at the founding of the state in 1948, persons aged 65 and over made up almost 10% of the population in 1991, for a total elderly population of over 410,000 people, and are projected to constitute 13% by 2015. Seen for many years as a marginal part of the population, albeit deserving compassionate care, the elderly are now seen to constitute a group requiring greater societal attention.

This changing perspective of the elderly has been particularly spurred by the changing age structure within the elderly cohort. Persons aged 75 and over, who constituted only 32% of all elderly in 1980, accounted for 42% of the aged population in 1991 and are expected to constitute 50% by 2020. The increasing relative prominence of the "old-old" within the elderly population has contributed, of late, to making aging a more central concern in Israeli society.

The elderly population in Israel is also overwhelmingly Jewish. While Jews constitute about 82% of the total population, 94% of the elderly cohort is Jewish. Non-Jews (Muslim Arabs, Christian Arabs, Druze, and others) make up only 6% of persons aged 65 and over in Israel. However, while the Jewish elderly are expected to have an annual rate of increase of 1.1% by the year 2000, the corresponding rate of increase among non-Jewish elderly is projected to be 3.8% annually (Be'er and Factor, 1989a).

Old age is defined by the age of eligibility for retirement pension, which may begin within certain income limitations at age 65 for men and 60 for women (although women may elect to defer pension until age 65, as of 1987). Unconditional retirement eligibility occurs at age 70 for men and 65 for women. Nevertheless, 40% of men and 10% of women aged 65–74 remain gainfully employed to some degree. Among persons aged 75 and over, the number of gainfully employed falls to 15% among men but remains at about 10% among women (Habib, 1986). Many additional older persons are actively engaged in nonremunerative undertakings, however, such as volunteering and social activity. The notion of old age in Israel, narrowly defined as commencement of payment of retirement pensions, is not yet fully commensurate with the emerging notion of the third age in the life cycle.

Persons in Israel enjoyed a life expectancy in 1987 similar to the rates prevailing in Western Europe: 72.5 years for men and 76.2 years for women. Unlike other countries, however, the ratio of men to women in the current old age cohort is almost equal. This situation is likely to change in the 1990s, with projections predicting the elderly population in the year 2000 to be 58% women and 42% men.

While the rate of widowhood among the elderly has increased slightly, from 38% in 1980 to 42% in 1990, the number of older persons residing in joint households with their children has declined over the years. In 1961 almost half the elderly lived with their children. In 1980 only about a quarter of the elderly resided jointly with adult children, while 29% lived entirely alone. In general, 81% of men aged 65 and over are married and reside with their spouse, but only 41% of women in the same age cohort have a living spouse. Among women aged 75 and over, less than 24% are married.

On the whole, persons aged 65 and over in Israel are overly represented in the lower-income brackets. Close to half of all elderly have incomes in the lowest three brackets. A third of all married elderly Israelis and two-thirds of the unmarried have incomes only from public Social Security sources.

In regard to health status, in 1988 the number of elderly persons disabled in activities of daily living (ADL) and still residing in the community was estimated to be 36,600, or 9.6% of the elderly population. Relative ADL disability rates varied significantly across groups, however, with 8.7% of Jewish elderly in the community and 22.6% of non-Jewish elderly reported to be disabled. Disability in instrumental activities of daily living (IADL—assistance with shopping, cleaning, etc.) showed less variance across these same groups. Jewish elderly were estimated to have an IADL disability rate of 39.7%, and non-Jewish elderly, 43.1% (Factor and Primak, 1991). However, disability rates are likely to rise among the Jewish elderly when the effects of mass immigration begun in late 1989, 15% of whom were elderly, are taken into account.

The Formal Structure of Care of the Elderly

The strains of new nationhood and the meager resources available to the fledgling Israeli government in 1948 limited the state's initial capacity to respond to the needs of its elderly immigrants. As such, governmental responsibility for needy elders was first assumed through the activities of MALBEN, a voluntary organization funded by the American Jewish Joint Distribution Committee (AJJDC), the international framework of Jewish philanthropy. Established in 1949–50, MALBEN provided services primarily to aged and handicapped immigrants and particularly stressed institutional care as the solution of choice (Bergman and Lowenstein, 1988).

As the state matured, however, the public sector took over as provider of most services for older adults. Three governmental bodies now provide the bulk of services to the aged: the Ministry of Labor and Social Affairs (formerly the Ministry of Welfare), the Ministry of Health, and the National Insurance Institute. Other governmental agencies provide selected services for specific subgroups within the elderly population, such as the Ministry of Education and Culture, the Ministry of Immigration and Absorption, and the Ministry of Construction and Housing. Characterized by a strongly centralized administration, each governmental agency sets policy guidelines for its own areas of responsibility and carries them out through regional offices or through service units within the local municipal authorities.

Local social services for the elderly are funded almost entirely by their corresponding national government agencies, with allocation levels being determined by a range of social and economic indicators. Thus, for example, municipal departments of family and community services are funded at about 75% by the Ministry of Labor and Social Affairs, with the remainder allocated by means of local tax rates. However, financially well-endowed localities may elect to individually augment the basic service packages provided or may choose to enter into cooperative arrangements with local voluntary agencies for enhanced service development and provision.

The multiplicity of governmental bodies serving the elderly underscores the lack of a coordinated and categorical approach to meeting the needs of older adults in Israel. In order to offset service fragmentation and to prevent gaps in service delivery, a national planning and coordinating body was established in

1969. The Association for the Planning and Development of Services for the Aged (ESHEL), funded on a matching basis by the AJJDC and the ministries of labor and social affairs, health, and finance, works to encourage partnership between the public and voluntary sectors, particularly at the local level. Ninety local associations for the aged, many initiated by ESHEL, also function as facilitators and operators of local services for the elderly and as advocates for service development, maintenance, and quality.

Alongside the prevailing public service system, there exists a network of voluntary service organizations that provide selected services for the elderly, including institutional and residential care services, day care, and social activity centers. Most such organizations, like MISHAN—the network of services for members of the Workers' Federation—the HISTADRUT, immigrant associations and communal religious organizations, provide services on a particularistic basis for members only. Other voluntary, charitable associations, like YAD SARAH, which provides life-support equipment to the chronically ill at no charge, serve all applicants regardless of ethnic and religious affiliation. The national network of community centers, located in some 135 neighborhoods and towns, is a quasi-governmental service system that provides social and recreational services on the basis of locality or catchment area to all residents of the area.

A late entry to the service system is the proprietary sector, which offers a limited range of services on a fee-for-service basis, particularly in the areas of enriched residential facilities and domiciliary-based personal care. The growth of proprietary home care agencies has been particularly spurred by the implementation in 1988 of the national nursing care insurance law, through which the National Insurance Institute contracts for the purchase of personal care services for severely disabled elderly insurees. Exclusively private service delivery, on the other hand, is a relatively infrequent phenomenon.

INCOME MAINTENANCE AND EMPLOYMENT

Income security for the elderly in Israel is provided through two major sources; a universal Social Security program operated by the National Insurance Institute (NII) and a system of occupational, wage-related pensions. For those with low incomes, due to lack of occupational pensions or other reasons, a supplemental benefit is made available from the NII. The dominant trend in third-age income maintenance among the general population as of 1992 was the decreasing relative necessity for supplemental benefits and increasing reliance upon occupational pensions.

The National Insurance Law, which established the NII, was enacted in 1953, 5 years after the founding of the state, and was implemented a year later. Old-age and survivors insurance was one of three initial categories of coverage. The legislation introduced a flat rate benefit for all insured retirees, conditional upon having paid into the program during at least 5 of the 10 years preceding qualifying age or during 144 noncontinuous months. The benefit was paid to all men at age 70 and all women at age 65, or at age 65 and 60, respectively, for those with incomes not exceeding a certain level defined by law (Achdut and Habib, 1991).

Benefit levels are linked to average wage rates and are subject to adjustment methods according to the cost-of-living index. An unmarried individual receives 16% of the average wage, and a married couple, 24%. There is also an increment of 2% of the basic pension for each year over 10 years of paid insurance, to a maximum of 50%, and a deferred retirement addition of 5% of the basic pension for each year of deferment, to an upper limit of 25%. Old-age benefits are financed by contributions paid by insurees and their employers and by a small subsidy from general revenues. As of this writing, the NII old-age pension is still tax-exempt, although there are periodic proposals by treasury officials to make the benefit income-tested.

A unique problem exists in Israel as a young country subject to continuous immigration: the large number of persons who immigrated at pension age or shortly before and who had insufficient time to accumulate new occupational pension rights. Many of these individuals also forfeited previous pension rights that had been accumulated in their country of origin. A government-financed pension benefit is partially available for this portion of the elderly population.

Occupational pensions are primarily rooted in two different sources: government-financed pensions for civil servants and contributory programs organized through the workplace and affiliated with pension schemes of the Workers' Federation—the HISTADRUT. A range of smaller schemes also exists. However, self-employed persons, constituting some 20% of the work force, are often uninsured.

Occupational pensions are wage-related and can reach up to 70% of preretirement salary levels (60% for widows). While about 40% of the elderly population actually receive an occupational pension benefit, only a small proportion has reached the maximum benefit, due to insufficient time to have accumulated full rights. The average pension level in the late 1980s was almost 50% of preretirement wages. This is likely to change as future pension recipients reach retirement age having had longer periods of covered employment. One-third of the occupational pension is tax-exempt.

Since occupational pensions are still somewhat limited and the flat-rate NII old-age insurance is insufficient to provide a decent standard of living, a supplementary Social Security benefit was introduced in 1965. Eligibility for this benefit corresponds to general standards for guaranteed minimum income in Israel, 40% of the median family income. The benefit ranges from 25% of the average wage for unmarried individuals to 37.5% for married couples. In 1975, the proportion of elderly persons receiving the supplementary benefit was almost 50% of all NII old-age pension recipients. This fell to 35% in 1988, a trend that is expected to continue (Achdut and Habib, 1991).

Older Israelis are eligible for a limited number of discounts and other economic benefits on the basis of their age. Some discounts, like reduced rates on public transportation, are available to all men aged 65 and women aged 60. Other benefits, like special allowances for purchase of heating fuel in cold areas, granted to 17,000 elderly households in 1990, are available within income-tested limits. A senior citizen card, issued in 1992 according to a recent law of the legislature, is meant to identify and spur various discounted goods and services for all elderly persons. As of yet, however, the scope of age-related benefits is lower than that found in many Western countries.

Programs for job retention, retraining, and employment among the elderly hardly exist at all in Israel. There is compulsory retirement for civil servants, while retirement age for others is regulated by collective bargaining agreements, a fact that counters the probability of electing deferred retirement. High unemployment rates in the general population as of 1992 and an expected increase in unemployment due to continued immigration render a low likelihood that this situation will change in the near future.

A significant exception to this last point is the work arrangements for elderly members of Israel's collective settlements, the kibbutzim. Rooted in the work ethic, these small and very close-knit societies have successfully instituted job rotation, flextime in the workplace, and phased retirement. However, the kibbutz elderly comprise only about 2% of the total elderly population in the country.

HEALTH CARE SERVICES

Health care in Israel is primarily provided by two major sources: the Ministry of Health and the sick fund of the Workers' Federation—the HISTADRUT—known as the General Sick Fund (GSF). The Ministry of Health is dominant in the provision of preventive care and is also the main supplier of acute-care hospital beds. The General Sick Fund, on the other hand, is the leading provider of primary care in the community and the largest insurer of acute hospital care, accounting for 80% of all insurees and over 90% of elderly insurees in the country. Although essentially a voluntary organization, the history, scope, and funding of the GSF have resulted in its serving as a parallel quasi-public health care system, even prior to establishment of the state.

Preventive care is delivered through a network of community-based mother-and-child health stations, operated directly by the Ministry of Health, or through local municipalities. Some of these units offer specific preventive services for the elderly population, such as vision and hearing examinations, dietary counseling, and diabetes screening. Health screening in other settings is partially available through combined efforts of the Ministry of Health, the Ministry of Labor and Social Affairs, and the sick funds, serving about 20,000 persons annually, 5% of the population aged 65 and over, and through programs of geriatric assessment developed by ESHEL in various hospital and community settings.

Primary care is delivered mostly through GSF local clinics at some 1,300 different sites. This fund also operates eight general, acute-care hospitals. Health care and hospitalization coverage is funded through a contribution tax linked to income level rather than to health risk, which is paid to the sick fund by workers and their employers according to legal statute. Subsidized for many years from general tax revenues as well, the GSF network has, until recently, resembled a public service more than a private, voluntary health care scheme.

Three additional sick funds, LEUMIT, MACCABEE, and MEUCHEDET, serve individuals who have elected to forgo association with the GSF. Each has its own package of services, including local clinics or reimbursement arrangements for participating doctors, hospitalization insurance, and other selected benefits. Moreover, about 10% of the general population maintains supplemental commercial health insurance to cover care not insured by sick funds. These insurees are primarily middle-aged persons with higher than average incomes (Cohen and Barnea, 1991). A very small portion of the population manages its health care exclusively through private insurance arrangements, such as executive health insurance packages.

In the case of chronic care coverage, the service delivery system is more complex, involving funding and provision by both governmental bodies and the sick funds. The source of funding is related to the functional level of the care recipient: (1) semi-independent, (2) frail, (3) mentally frail, (4) nursing-dependent, or (5) complex nursing-dependent. The Ministry of Labor and Social Affairs provides or funds institutional care for the first two levels, which require IADL assistance and some ADL support. The Ministry of Health provides or funds IADL assistance and extensive ADL support for the third and fourth levels of impairment. The fifth level, which requires skilled medical services alongside IADL and ADL supports, is funded by the sick funds (although it is frequently difficult to distinguish this group from the nursing-dependent level of impairment).

In regard to bed availability in long-term care facilities, about 40% of the total 18,000 beds are geared to semi-independent adults. Almost 20% are targeted for frail elderly. The remaining 40% serve older adults with higher levels of disability.

The public sector operates about a sixth of all institutional beds; proprietary interests provide almost a third. The remainder, close to half of all institutional beds, are supplied by a variety of nonprofit associations. The rate of institutionalization in Israel is currently 45 per 1,000 among all persons aged 65 and over and about 200 per 1,000 among persons aged 85 and over (Be'er and Factor, 1989b). However, a major expansion of long-term care facilities planned for 1991–95 is expected to add some 5,000 beds, 60% of which will be public.

The sick funds also provide some home-based medical-nursing services for insured members who are homebound (particularly by the GSF's department of continuing care). Rehabilitative-medical day care, on the other hand, is provided by consortiums of sick funds and the Ministry of Health.

Israel's most notable innovation in the field of long-term health care was the implementation in 1988 of the Nursing Insurance Law. This provision establishes the right of all insurees of the National Insurance Institute to in-home personal care services, subject to a disability level and income test. Funded by employee/employer contributions to Social Security (NII), the program employs multidisciplinary teams composed of Ministry of Health-based public health nurses, municipal-level social workers, and NII clerks, who assess applicants' eligibility and construct care plans on their behalf.

Through the Nursing Insurance Law, home care services purchased from private service agencies approved by the NII are provided directly to applicants as an in-kind benefit. This arrangement has spurred the rapid development and expansion of private home care agencies in Israel. In unique cases where services are unavailable for purchase, due primarily to geographic isolation, a financial benefit may be given directly to the applicant. In late 1991, over 31,000 persons were recorded as users of the program. Eligible recipients received, on average, 11 weekly hours of personal care distributed over three or four days each week.

In sum, the socialist roots of Israeli society are still evident in several aspects of the structure and delivery of health care to its citizens, as exemplified by the role of the General Sick Fund. However, a growing movement can be recognized toward markedly declining governmental participation in the financing of these services. Also evident are a greater independence on the part of physicians and an increase in the role of private for-profit health care (Rosen and Ellencweig, 1988).

HOUSING RESOURCES

A central characteristic of the Israeli housing system is the predominance of owner-occupied units in the general population, some 70% of the overall housing stock. A significant part of the remainder of the population dwell in subsidized public rental apartments, and only a small proportion live in private market rental units. Hence, most Israelis reside in permanent housing when they reach old age. In certain cases, elderly public housing tenants may be required to move to smaller quarters to adjust for smaller family size. In other cases, dwellings of the elderly may require serious repair. Lack of housing among older adults, however, is rare.

Various programs of sheltered housing exist for elderly persons who require some degree of assistance. The rate of sheltered living units was 17 units per 1,000 elderly in the population in 1989 and has increased since. Such units, arranged most often in congregate facilities, offer a variety of services, including safety features and design, household help, communal meals options, health care on call, and social club activities. They are provided primarily through three different bodies: voluntary organizations, the public sector, and the private market (Shtarkshall, 1987).

The voluntary sector was the first to develop special housing for the elderly, particularly social organizations like the Women's League for Israel and the Central European Immigrants Association. The largest of the programs is by

MISHAN, an affiliate of the Workers' Federation—the HISTADRUT, which sponsors 1,800 apartment units in five cities. These apartments are geared for functionally independent elderly who are members of the Workers' Federation and their parents. The projects are often built nearby the federation's old-age institutions and outpatient health clinics. A down payment is required for entry to the facility.

Public sector housing consists mostly of projects executed by the Ministry of Housing in conjunction with local public housing corporations, such as AMIDAR and PRAZOT, and with the support of ESHEL. One direction is the renovation of public housing units in the first two floors of buildings in areas with high concentrations of elderly residents. Ten such projects are in existence. Another direction is construction of new units designed to compensate for partial disability among residents: widened doorways, elevators, and so on. A particularly successful project, which combines both approaches, is the GILO housing project in Jerusalem, in which 51 apartments out of 150 were designed for elderly people. The arrangement offers elderly residents both an assortment of formal support services and informal support from younger project neighbors. In total, the public sector in Israel offers about 2,000 units of sheltered or enriched housing for the elderly.

The most recent addition to the senior housing field and its fastest growing member is the private market, which is focusing on construction of retirement congregate housing. Organized in large, multistory complexes, these mostly for-profit projects are geared to the financially secure and well elderly. This type of housing provides high-quality facilities along with the option of utilizing support services as they become needed, including skilled nursing care units. Residents either purchase a share in the congregate facility as an investment that may be resold or pay a nonrefundable entrance fee. In both cases, a high monthly maintenance fee is also required. About 2,000 rental units of this type are estimated to be in operation or under construction.

Evidently, most elderly persons elect to remain in their own apartments and homes. Retirement status of a resident constitutes grounds in some localities for a discount in the municipal tax rates, which are computed on the basis of dwelling size and location. In other places, impoverished elderly may be granted an income-tested discount. Aid in home repairs for those residing in their own dwellings is available as a volunteer community service in several localities from the community centers' "repair patrol" program.

SUPPORTIVE SERVICES

Many agencies at the community level in Israel work together to assist elderly persons to retain acceptable levels of personal and social functioning while remaining in their homes. Municipal social service bureaus, governmental ministries, voluntary organizations, and others provide selected in-home and community-based services for older persons and their informal caregivers. Services are targeted to older persons with one or more of the following problems: functional disability, ill health, cognitive disorientation, low income, interpersonal difficulties, loneliness, and malnutrition. While the joint aim of such efforts is to create a caring community for frail elders, the limited scope of such services often falls short of this worthy goal.

Nutritional assistance is provided by means of daily delivery of hot meals-on-wheels or weekly supply of frozen dinners. Some 3,500 homebound or needy elderly received this aid at home or in the framework of day centers in 1990. The target population of this service was estimated to be 15,000 persons.

Other home-based aid includes personal care and household management assistance, provided to about 8,000 persons. Transportation to medical services, medical equipment, and basic home furnishings are given to another 2,000 elderly, for a total of about 10,000 persons receiving such instrumental aid in 1990. Respite care available in Israel allows elderly care recipients and their families a short break at times of crisis. This arrangement allows a stay of up to a few weeks in special units in five old-age institutions and encompasses some 100 persons at a given time.

Socially supportive day care for frail elders is also available within the facilities of old-age homes. This service, sponsored by local social service bureaus in conjunction with the Ministry of Labor and Social Affairs and ESHEL, was provided in 1990 to 500 elderly persons in 10 such settings across the country. Day centers in the community, on the other hand, may offer a more comprehensive menu of support services for disabled elderly. This includes personal care, laundry, and meals for as many as 10,000 persons in 50 facilities. Community-based day centers are variously sponsored by the previously named agencies, together with the sick funds, voluntary organizations, and, to a lesser degree, the Ministry of Health.

Psychogeriatric community services are provided in a range of settings. In 1988, 24 community mental health centers, sponsored either by the Ministry of Health or the General Sick Fund, served the mental health needs of adults of all ages. Only in some clinics, however, were specific days designated for psychogeriatric care. Similarly, outpatient clinics in 14 psychiatric hospitals and 11 general hospitals served psychogeriatric patients as part of their overall service. Only 1 psychiatric hospital offered a categorical psychogeriatric service in 1988, although others may have set a specific day for the elderly. Accurate figures concerning utilization rates by psychogeriatric elderly are not available, as most of these facilities served wider populations.

Psychogeriatric day centers accept elderly persons in various stages of mental or cognitive incapacity. Activities include therapy, exercise, and personal care. Four hundred mentally impaired elderly were reported to have been served in these centers in 1990.

There are also six psychogeriatric day hospitals operating in Israel. Three are in government-operated geriatric-rehabilitation hospitals and function with a focus on diagnostic and medical aspects of care. The other three are in psychiatric hospitals and primarily serve mentally ill persons who have grown old or elderly individuals who developed functional psychiatric problems in later life. The scope of this service is limited, however, with all six day hospitals serving only from 10 to 30 patients each in 1988 (Bergman and Levy, 1988).

The last community support service to be discussed is sheltered workshops, which provide employment to a limited number of older persons able to work. This activity assists up to 3,500 persons to augment their income, to increase their social contacts, and to manage their use of unobligated time. Several agencies, including TELEM, the Ministry of Immigration and Absorption, voluntary organizations, and local social service bureaus, share responsibility for this undertaking.

LEISURE-TIME RESOURCES

As a traditional immigrant society, Israeli culture maintains a strong family orientation. As such, much of the leisure activity of its elderly population is carried out within the context of the family in informal settings. There are, nevertheless, several formally organized opportunities for recreation and activity for older adults. These include volunteer programs, voluntary organizations, community centers, and third-age programs for higher education.

Volunteering is an important national value in Israel and finds expression among all age groups, including the elderly. The National Insurance Institute, for example, offers the opportunity for newly retired persons to engage in volunteer helping in a program called "Oldster to Oldster." In this nationwide effort, recent retirees serve as friendly visitors to homebound elderly. While the immediate beneficiary is the homebound elder, the volunteer is also assumed to gain satisfaction from both the productive use of unobligated time and the social interaction that ensues. Volunteers are generally well-off, both in terms of socioeconomic status and functioning. The focus of volunteer service is mixed, with both problem solving and quality of life benefits available to helper and helpee.

Voluntary organizations provide the bulk of opportunities for social activity among third-age adults in Israel. Retiree clubs associated with the Workers' Federation—the HISTADRUT, immigrant associations, and other interest groups provide frameworks for a variety of leisure-time activities. Fifty old-age clubs operate in Tel Aviv and 30 in Haifa. Their participants constitute 17% of the elderly population in each city. A very popular source of social association among many elderly men, moreover, is the local synagogue, where prayer, continuing religious study, and social interchange occur on a daily basis.

Social recreation activities are also widely available in some 135 facilities associated with the Israel Association of Community Centers. Most of these centers include services geared specially for older adults, ranging from social gatherings in lounge-type activities to full-fledged occupational, social, and preventive services. Elderly persons may participate in the general age-integrated activities of the center as well, like public lectures and holiday celebrations. Activities for the elderly per se, however, are most often concentrated in a special branch of the center, often physically separated from the main activity areas, and offered in hours when other age groups are not present.

The socioeconomic status of elderly community center participants varies according to community but, in general, tends to be lower than the national average, as these centers are located primarily in areas of social distress. Elderly participants in the age-integrated mass activities of the center tend to have higher incomes than those engaging in the age-homogeneous activities. The latter are also more likely to be relatively less mobile.

A growing addition to the range of social activities available to older adults in Israel is the field of continuing education. Most universities now operate special programs for the elderly population, offering individual participation in regular university classes as well as courses organized specifically for the old-age cohort. Educational outreach to organizational settings of elderly persons is also available through such means as the Mobile Audio-Visual Center, which provides videotapes and discussion leaders for consideration of gerontological topics.

In sum, a fair number of formal arrangements for meeting recreational needs of older adults exist in Israel, organized principally through the voluntary sector. There is, as yet, little private sector activity in this field. As the aging cohort changes and grows in relative importance to other age groups in society, however, expansion of activity in this area is to be expected.

ADVOCACY AND PROTECTION

Advocacy and protection arrangements for the elderly population in Israel have been formally constituted only since the 1980s, coming much later than similar arrangements for other dependent populations. These include, to varying degrees, statutory protective services, voluntary legal assistance programs, and advocacy organizations.

In 1986, the Department for the Elderly in the Ministry of Labor and Social Affairs took upon itself to apply a 1966 governmental statute regarding the right of protective intervention on behalf of vulnerable individuals to the population of older adults. Sixty area social workers around the country were trained to serve as welfare officers empowered to initiate legal action. They may intervene on behalf of institutionalized elderly who are mentally incompetent or otherwise deemed to be in danger due to lack of appropriate care. As of 1990, one such case was brought before the courts each month.

Legal assistance is also a recent addition to the repertoire of services available to older adults in Israel. Legal aid had been available for some time to a selected group of impoverished persons of all ages, according to criteria of the Ministry of Justice. Two new organizations, YAD RIVA in Jerusalem and KESHET in Tel Aviv, on the other hand, have initiated legal advice and services targeted specifically to needy elders. At YAD RIVA, elderly residents are entitled to free consultation, checking of documents, and problem-solving advice. For a minimal fee, low-income pensioners may also receive legal assistance in matters of wills and inheritance, tenant conflicts, financial claims, and bureaucratic injustice. This service is funded by the municipality, the Ministry of Justice and Labor, the Ministry of Social Affairs, and voluntary organizations and is staffed partly by volunteers.

Unlike several Western countries, there is not yet a strong aging lobby in the state of Israel. In a highly politicized single constituency governance system, in which party politics touch upon most aspects of daily life, the issues of aging have not gained priority among most parties. There are many elderly politicians in Israel, but very little politics of aging. A small number of legislators function sporadically to safeguard against cuts in social benefits to older adults, but this arrangement is informal and temporary.

Where advocacy organizations exist on behalf of the elderly population, they do so on a very limited basis. Groups like Sixty Plus in Jerusalem have attempted to organize around issues of interest to the elderly population but have not been singularly successful in mounting major campaigns. The most successful organizational advocacy efforts on behalf of the elderly, on the other hand, are those carried out by the country's major interest group organizations, like the Workers' Federation—the HISTADRUT, which represent a range of age groups in the society.

FUTURE PROJECTIONS

As currently constituted, the system of social services for the elderly of Israel provides a basic safety net of support for those in need but falls short of offering an opportunity structure for the general welfare of all members of the third age. Elementary needs in a wide range of functional areas can be met through a mixture of public and voluntary auspices and through some involvement of the private sector. However, public income security arrangements remain inadequate, and inequalities continue in benefit levels between men and women. Moreover, the fragmentation of service delivery and its resultant obstacles to continuity of care compromise the effectiveness of the varied programs and benefits available to older adults.

Israel's service delivery system has made an important shift to increased development of community and in-home services, as opposed to stressing institutional solutions to problems of the elderly. The nursing care insurance law, moreover, established certain basic home care provisions as an elementary right of all eligible citizens. Many benefits, however, are still granted by power of administrative arrangements and not by legislative statute. As such, several social services for the elderly remain vulnerable to the exigencies of budgetary politics, a situation that limits long-term planning and the integration of service responsibility.

Three emerging needs of the elderly in Israel will have important implications for service delivery in the future. These include the increasing numbers of persons over 80, the high relative proportion of pre-elderly persons among the immigrants of the 1990s, and the growing percentage of well elderly whose needs are not currently met by public authorities.

The increase of the old-old cohort, particularly persons over the age of 80, will require expansion of home-delivered and community-based services if the current goal of community service alternatives is to be maximized. The influx of pre-elderly immigrants who may remain unemployed, and hence are at risk of premature social marginalization, will require a major increase in programs of social prevention developed especially for this group. Finally, the special needs of the well elderly will have to be addressed more creatively. An effort to provide more adequately for needs that emerge at the outset of the aging experience will likely have implications for the scope of services required by older adults at subsequent stages of the aging spectrum.

NOTE

The author would like to express his appreciation to Johnny Lemberger of ESHEL (the Association for the Planning and Development of Services for the Aged in Israel) and to Dr. Gail K. Auslander and Professor Abraham Doron, both of the Hebrew University, for their helpful comments on previous drafts of this chapter.

BIBLIOGRAPHY

Achdut, L., and Habib, J. (1991). "The System of Retirement Benefits for the Elderly in Israel." In M. Tracy and F. Pampel (eds.), *The International Handbook on Old-Age Insurance.* Westport, CT: Greenwood Press, pp. 121–132.

Be'er, S., and Factor, H. (1989a). *Demographic Developments of the Elderly in Israel in the Years 1988–2000.* Jerusalem: JDC-Brookdale Institute of Gerontology and Adult Human Development in Israel (in Hebrew).

———. (1989b). *Long-Term Care Institutions and Sheltered Housing: The Situation in 1987 and Changes Over Time.* Jerusalem: JDC-Brookdale Institute of Gerontology and Adult Human Development in Israel.

Bergman S., and Levy, E. (1988). *Mapping of Psychogeriatric Services in Israel.* Jerusalem: JDC-Brookdale Institute of Gerontology and Adult Human Development in Israel.

Bergman, S., and Lowenstein, A. (1988). "Care of the Aging in Israel: Social Service Delivery." *Journal of Gerontological Social Work,* 12, 97–116.

Cohen, M., and Barnea, T. (1991). *The Rise of Supplemental Commercial Health and Long-Term Care Insurance in Israel: Market Description and Implications for the Health Care System and Government Policy.* Jerusalem: JDC-Brookdale Institute of Gerontology and Adult Human Development in Israel.

Factor, H., and Primak, H. (1991). "Disability Among the Elderly in Israel and Projections to the Year 2000." *Gerontologia,* 53, 28–38 (in Hebrew).

Habib, J. (1986). *Population Aging and Israeli Society.* Jerusalem: JDC-Brookdale Institute of Gerontology and Adult Human Development in Israel.
Rosen, B., and Ellencweig A. (1988). *A Mapping of Health Care Reimbursement in Israel.* Jerusalem: JDC-Brookdale Institute of Gerontology and Adult Human Development in Israel.
Shtarkshall, M. (1987). *Sheltered Housing for the Elderly in Israel: Developments Over the Past Five Years and Present Status.* Jerusalem: JDC-Brookdale Institute of Gerontology and Adult Human Development in Israel.

15

ITALY

Massimo Mengani, Cristina Gagliardi, Micaela Tonucci, and Giovanni Lamura

INTRODUCTION

In Italy, there is no precise definition of the term *elderly*, not even from the point of view of age. There are, however, some norms that specifically refer to age, such as the right to retire from work at the age of 65. There also exists a great deal of legislation on retirement, in which the pensionable age varies between 55 and 65. Social pensions for the needy are payable at the age of 65.

Interest in the problems of the elderly population has greatly increased in Italy over the last few years. In the past, measures were directed toward the elderly in general, specifically, in favor of those in financial difficulty, and individual demands were met through subsidies or institutionalization.

Later on, these measures—whether public, private, or voluntary—were directed to the elderly with social and psychological problems, because the often uncontrolled economic development of the country found the weaker part of society unprepared, and intervention was necessary to avoid its isolation. Typical services included the organization of summer holidays, bus tours, and third-age "universities."

Present problems involve all categories of people, but the elderly are particularly sensitive to them. Modifications of the family structure, low birthrate, high percentage of female employment, great difference in the mean age of the sexes, and increase in the life span have all contributed to amplify the problem of the elderly who live alone in precarious self-sufficiency.

The great drop in the birthrate and the considerable increase in the average life span have strongly influenced the Italian demographic structure since World War II. The consequences of this evolution have not always been adequately assessed, probably because they did not affect very much of the total population, but they have rather altered its age structure. In the 15 years from 1973 to 1988, the total population has increased by 5%, whereas the under-20s decreased by 14%, the over-60s increased by 21%, and the over-80s increased by 57% (CNR, IRP, 1988).

The trend toward falling birth and death rates is confirmed by more recent data (Melograni, 1989). In 1987 the mean number of children per woman was 1.31, the lowest value ever reached in Italy and certainly one of the lowest in the world. The average life span reached, meanwhile, 72.7 years for men and 79.2 for women, which places Italy among the top countries in the world in terms of population longevity.

These tendencies are accompanied by other important factors, such as the large increase in the number of families and the radical transformation of their structure. The number of households composed of elderly people living alone has rapidly increased; while in 1983 one person out of four aged over 75 lived alone, by 1987 this ratio reached one out of three. Rarely has a similar intense sociodemographic change occurred in such a short time. An inversion of this trend is certainly not to be expected in the future if, as is forecast, the number of those over 65 years old, who were 13.4% of the total population in 1987, reaches 18.6% in 2007 and 28.8% in 2037 (CNR, IRP, 1988).

To quantify, evaluate, and analyze the state of health of a population, it is necessary to identify its illnesses and symptoms and divide them according to the nature of the disease and the involved organs. According to a study carried out in Turin (northern Italy), 57.5% of the elderly men and women interviewed declared themselves to be in a condition of well-being (Borzaga, 1988). This condition changes obviously as age increases, but not so significantly, dropping from 59% of the 65–70-year-olds to about 35% of the 80-year-olds. Similar results have been found for the rate of dementia, which in the over-65-year-olds varies between 1.3% and 18.5%, increasing with age. All epidemiological studies show that women suffer most from this disease, in particular, from Alzheimer's disease and vascular dementia.

Some Italian local studies have tried to quantify the degree of disability of the elderly who live at home (Mengani, 1987b, 1989). The results showed completely different levels of unfitness for different sociobiological activities; for example, the activity with the highest disability degree was "having a bath," involving 18% of the total sample (equal to 3,624 elderly), while "eating unaided" concerned only 1.8% of them. The biomechanical action that most needed the help of another person was "carrying a bucket of water for 10 metres" (22.7% of the interviewed), followed by "cutting the toenails" (21.5%) (Mengani, 1986a).

Legal Provisions

The basis of the present sociohealth legislation is formed by articles 32 and 38 of the Italian constitution. Article 32 declares that the state "considers health as a fundamental right of each person and an interest of the community." Article 38 promotes the concept of assistance as a "subjective public right," replacing the view of assistance as a charitable institution for the needy. This article also confirms that "suitable means must be assured and provided for the necessities of life in case of invalidity and old age."

Several health laws have subsequently provided for specific measures in favor of the elderly population. Law n. 132 of 1968 established that hospital beds are to be provided for bedridden individuals, and this has contributed since then to the problem of an excessive, not always necessary, hospitalization of the elderly. In 1978 law n. 180 abolished mental hospitals and called public attention to the problems of the mentally ill elderly.

A meaningful step was undertaken in 1978, when the National Health Service was founded by law n. 833. This law has been of great importance not only for the health sector for which it was specifically created but also for the social one, since it establishes a correlation between the two, which are no longer to be considered separate entities when programming. The most prominent aims of this law concern assistance for the elderly, defining them in terms of prevention, treatment, and rehabilitation of invalidity, as well as health care of the elderly through specific projects, diagnosis, and therapies.

After law n. 833, legislative activity concerning the social sector came to a standstill. This is particularly significant if we consider the nonimprovement of the whole sector, which finds itself today governed by an old, outdated law. However, to solve the needs of integrating both social and health aspects, obtaining effective services, and drawing greater attention to the growing problem of the non-self-sufficient elderly, further measures were taken in the last few years.

In 1983, law n. 730 stated that local and regional councils can use the "local health units" to provide social care services, bearing the financial costs themselves, while the National Fund pays the expenses of all health services connected to the social care. This measure allowed a further concretization of the regional system founded in 1970, according to which each one of the 20 Italian regions has to guarantee the programming of both social and health services and has the further responsibility for their territorial organization and administration.

Laws n. 595 in 1983 and n. 67 in 1988 have recognized the need to increase the number of beds for the non-self-sufficient persons. The first one, better known as "health program law," regulated long-term assistance/hospitalization, setting the standard number of hospital beds as 6.5 per 1,000 inhabitants, of which one bed per 1,000 inhabitants is for rehabilitation. The same law established further that hospital space left free, following a reduction of beds, must be used for the rehabilitation of long-term and high-risk patients. Since health service beds in private hospitals were half of those in public institutes, an indirect consequence of this provision was that in order to double the number of available beds, some local health units sent chronic patients to private hospitals. The second law proposed a ministerial program, which provided 140,000 beds in residential structures for elderly people who could not be assisted either at home or in a hospital.

Another important document is the ministerial decree of 13 September 1988 on hospital standards, which makes a distinction between rehabilitation and long-term hospitalization, separating beds for acute patients from those for long-term ones. The latter can be placed in normal operative units, like medicine or geriatric wards, which usually provide 32 beds. The same decree also establishes that home and semi-institutional assistance should be provided by day hospitals, not by hospital centers. This norm, however, does not specify the kind of public it is intended for, nor does it take into account the lack of alternative health structures. In any case, it has not yet been fully applied by the regions.

The present legislation is still incomplete and undefined, above all, with regard to two types of services, the sociohealth ones and the social care, and the local sociohealth units still lack effective coordinating power.

INCOME MAINTENANCE AND EMPLOYMENT

In Italy it is possible to apply for a pension after 35 years of social insurance. The sum of pension and salary can be paid, legally speaking, only once retirement age has been reached, after which one cannot be employed by a third party.

An old-age pension can be obtained after 15 years of seniority insurance and at least 15 years of overall contribution. Proposals have been made to raise the minimum contribution period for old-age pension to 20 years for men, while it should remain at 15 years for women. This measure should reduce the need of an "integration of the minimum," which was introduced into the social insurance system with law n. 218 in 1952, whose aim was to guarantee a basic life standard for the working person. This meant (in absence of fixed salaries) that all pensions were reduced to a minimum level. At present, minimum integration of the old-age pension and of the reversionary annuity is allowed if all other income sources are less than twice the minimum pension.

No existing norm prevents a person from having more than one pension; it is, in fact, possible to receive several pensions if, during one's life, one has regularly paid the necessary contributions to various pension schemes.

Pensions are the most important source of income of the elderly, most of whom reached a medium-low income by the end of 1990. Nearly 70% of them have post office savings, and 16% have state bonds, but owning a house is their most important patrimonial asset. Today, in fact, 65% of the heads of the family over 65 years of age own the house in which they live, 7.4% own other houses, and 13% own both houses and land. About 30% of the elderly who live in large towns have no patrimonial estate whatsoever (LABOS, 1988).

On the whole, Italian elderly have a moderately good economic condition, even though the average pension level is rather low and does not guarantee the subsistence of more than one person. Because pensions are so low, most elderly people supplement them with savings or continue to work without Social Security. However, nearly 30% of the elderly have no other economic activity and live in rented accommodations.

In 1970 a special report issued by ISTAT (the Italian National Institute of Statistics) showed that 4,298,000 individuals between the ages of 60 and 70 (equal to 82% of the age class, of whom 61% were women) did not belong to the work force (Italian National Institute of Statistics [ISTAT], 1988). Of these, a group of 229,000 subjects (5.3%) were willing to work for a salary. The percentage was higher for men (8.8%). In 1971 ISTAT gave a figure of 385,000 subjects over 65 years of age working at one or more jobs; three years later the figure rose to 885,000. In 1982 a local survey revealed that in the Como district (northern Italy), 12% of those over 65 still worked (even if on an irregular basis), and 6.7% declared a "definite" willingness to work.

Although elderly employment represents only a limited financial burden for local administrations and at the same time could easily let elderly people feel psychosocially integrated, this form of public intervention has been developed only recently. Pioneers in this field have been the communal districts of Emilia-Romagna, a region in central Italy, setting an example that has been gradually followed by the other central and northern regions. Currently, 245 communes have already organized such a service, for a total of 6,123 elderly. Generally, the elderly who collaborate in these public services are mostly former employees of the local council or civil servants. They usually work from one to four hours per day (a maximum limit of hours per week is always set) and belong to the younger group between 55 and 65 years old, while the maximum age is around 75, over which the elderly cannot work. Those who do work must, in any case, present a medical certificate of their physical-mental state.

HEALTH CARE SERVICES

Institutional care was the first and most important service for the elderly in Italy. It is interesting to analyze its evolution, in order to understand its importance.

In spite of the changes made in 1971 by ISTAT in the standards of classifying institutional admissions, the number of the elderly admitted in institutions has not greatly changed over the years, going from 108,872 in 1962 to 120,866 five years later, to reach 131,366 admissions in 1972. In those 10 years there was, therefore, an increase of about 20%, lower than the one registered in the same period for the elderly population, which increased by 27.7% between 1961 and 1971. This was especially due to decreased admissions of people 60–64 and 65–69 years old, while an increase took place for those over 70 years old.

If one looks at the geographic distribution, one observes a greater admittance of old people in the north and in the north-central regions. Moreover, distinguishing between the two sexes, one notices a larger number of women among institutionalized elderly, who also show a higher mean age, reflecting the general situation to be found in Italian society.

Following 1972, there has been a diminished interest in the problems of the elderly. The only new survey was done by the Administration for Italian and International Assistance Activities in 1973, according to which, in the various

Italian regions, were to be found 172,216 beds in 2,422 old people's homes. In 1985, ISTAT counted 1,974 specialized institutions plus 120 other institutions. Compared with the previous year (1984), there was a reduction of two institutions with a loss of 3,068 beds. This reduction involved mainly Public Institutes for Assistance and Charity (IPAB) (with a loss of 33 institutions and 3,253 beds) and Public Boards (a loss of 9 institutions and 639 admissions), while the number of private institutions increased (by 44 institutions and 826 beds).

HOUSING RESOURCES

The Italian sociohealth policies, in general, and those aimed at the elderly, in particular, have been theoretically well formulated but not put into practice. Although both national and regional legislations aim at keeping the elderly in their home environment, it is difficult to dismantle structures that provide services for the elderly, mostly through hospitals.

Regional legislation provides the following measures:

- privileged assignation of accommodation for the elderly (11 regions out of 20);
- assignation of suitable public housing (6 regions);
- concessions of grants to support rental expenses (5 regions);
- accommodation maintenance and improvement (sanitary and heating systems, bathrooms, and so on) (5 regions).

Regional legislation also provides various solutions regarding nontraditional accommodations, such as polyfunctional flats (in 11 regions), housing communities (11 regions), and accommodation houses (7 regions).

On a national level, in 1988 the Parliamentary Commission investigating the condition of the elderly stated the need to build experimental lodgings made up of small flats without architectural barriers and with joint services for the whole building (laundry room, refectory, television room, and so on), in order to reduce domestic work to a minimum.

The possibility for the elderly to keep on living within their original home environment is connected with economic resources, as well as with the benefits provided by the pension system. Most of the elderly living in towns live alone or with their spouse, while families in the country tend to be large and multigenerational. The urban elderly have a much higher level of education in comparison to those living in rural areas. The latter have a greater degree of dependence and are less likely to use a family doctor and a hospital, perhaps because of the wider family structure and for cultural reasons. Even non-self-sufficient rural elderly continue to live with their family.

There has been some experience of giving the elderly the opportunity of staying at home with complete health assistance (i.e., experimental projects of hospital assistance at home). One such project started in Turin (northern Italy) in October 1985, when some professional nurses, who were not involved in basic health assistance, organized themselves as a team for home intervention, together with some doctors from the local University Geriatric Division.

In order to adapt the home environment to the needs of the patient, this project tried to ensure availability of walking aids, fulfillment of psychological needs, and control of hygienic and environmental conditions, as well as the willingness of the family. Moreover, the home hospitalization service was undertaken by doctors and nurses belonging to the hospital the patient was last in and included not only chronic patients coming from the wards but also those sent directly by their family doctor.

Another important aspect of the project was the health education of the family. Families were given the possibility of continuing therapy during the day, which (for some patients) visibly contributed to the achievement of a favorable outcome.

During the first year of this experience, 7,138 days of home hospitalization were insured, with 4,479 visits by nurses and 2,072 visits by doctors. Much time was dedicated to each single patient, usually over an hour per day by the nurse and/or doctor. The second year was characterized by fewer calls: 4,362 nurse calls and 930 medical ones.

SUPPORTIVE SERVICES

In 1969 law n. 743 extended the economic benefits already granted in 1966 (by law n. 625) to the totally (100%) disabled, maimed, and invalid civilians and to the partially maimed and invalid with an acknowledged permanent invalidity of over two-thirds. In 1980 law n. 18 increased further the benefits of the totally disabled, maimed, and invalid civilians "unable to walk without the constant help of an attendant, or unable to perform daily life actions" by granting them a "companion allowance." This contribution, which is paid independently of the individual's financial situation, is aimed at permitting the elderly to remain in their own home environment through the cooperation of family members. In only six years, the number of Italian civilians acknowledged as invalid has more than doubled, while the number of the non-self-sufficient invalid civilians has grown 252%.

The data relative to the new service of Home Assistance have been made available by a research program promoted by the Ministry of the Interior in 1982–83 (Ministero dell'Interno, 1984). Out of the 187 questionnaires sent throughout the country, replies were received from 88 local councils, which granted a service of home help to 7,735 elderly. This figure is equal to 0.2% of the total concerned population.

This service of home help, which has been active only for a few years, is still not well defined. It began in the communes of northern Italy in 1972, followed by the central region (1978), and then the south (1979). The research showed that the main services offered to the 7,735 assisted elderly included sorting out paperwork, help in house chores, help in looking after the elderly person, settlement of administrative papers, and washing clothes and linen.

In order to have an idea of how quickly the supply of home help services has been spreading in Italy, in 1986, four years after the survey carried out by the Ministry of the Interior, the region of Emilia Romagna alone organized home assistance for 8,364 old people (equal to 1.3% of the elderly resident population over 65 years). The services offered in this region consisted mainly of nursing care for the middle-old group, 15% of whom were under 65 years, 26% between 66 and 75, 43% between 76 and 85, and the remaining 16% over 85.

Service centers, together with home assistance services, constitute one of the necessary premises for carrying out territorial services to maintain persons in their normal environments. Also, in this case, data were taken from a survey by the Ministry of the Interior carried out in 1986, through which 607 centers for the aged were censused (Ministero dell'Interno, 1987). This kind of service originated mainly in northern Italy toward the end of the 1970s and has been organized almost exclusively by the communes or communal districts.

Two-thirds of these centers (66.4%) took in only self-sufficient elderly, and nearly one-third (31.5%) took both self-sufficient and non-self-sufficient ones, while only three centers specifically accept non-self-sufficient old people. According to their size, only 16% of the centers usually take in more than 100 elderly per day, 21% take between 50 and 100, 36% take between 21 and 50, and 27.4% take fewer than 20 people per day. Recreational-cultural activities take place in 30% of the centers, and among them "refreshment bars" show the highest frequency (21% of the cases).

Since 1985 the region of Veneto has been trying out a Tele-Aid service, which is very much in demand because most old people wish to live alone even when over 70–80 years and often live in isolated areas. Tele-Aid is an organization which contacts elderly persons (usually living alone) by telephone. The elderly can ask for an alarm instrument to use in case of emergency. The call reaches the operators who then contact that person. If necessary, a doctor or other professional can come to help the elderly person in difficulty. After the necessary trial period, the service was extended over all the regional territory to about 8,000 elderly persons, with a budget of 10 billion lire (US $5.9 million) (of which half was paid by the state). First results show that the old people who use this service live alone (80.4% of the users in Veneto), are women (80.7%), and are at an advanced age (56% over 75).

LEISURE-TIME RESOURCES

Summer holiday services for the elderly have mostly developed over the last few years and include all communes in the country. In 1986 in the region of Emilia Romagna, for example, 284 communes organized holidays for 27,100 elderly participants, equal to 4.2% of the over-65-year-old resident population. This service, which finds an increasing demand by the elderly, was initially offered free of charge by the local councils. However, over the years, in order to cover the greater costs involved, there has been a partial charge for certain groups of elderly with higher incomes.

In 1985 there were 106 third-age universities in Italy. This phenomenon is recent and reached a development peak in 1982, mainly in the medium-sized to large cities of the north. In the last few years, however, there has also been a diffusion in the smaller towns and in areas farther south. The teaching activity offered by these initiatives is generally concentrated on traditional scholastic culture and only secondarily on new subjects. Most courses deal with health and food education, as well as with local sociocultural traditions. Out of the 20,000 enrolled participants in the more than 50 centers, 58% are between 60 and 80 years old, with unusually high academic qualifications (50% finished secondary education).

One of the first Italian studies on voluntary service was conducted in 1983 by the Ministry of Work and Social Security and revealed 7,024 voluntary groups, of which only 50 (equal to 0.7% of all examined groups) expressly dealt with the elderly. In fact, social care associations came into being only between 1984 and 1986. It should be clear that when we talk about Italian voluntary groups, we mean voluntary organizations with paid staff members (IREF, 1990).

Successive studies have shown that 15.4% of the Italian population between 18 and 74 years old work on a voluntary basis, while 7.2% work voluntarily in the fields of social care and health. These operations are more numerous in the north and center of Italy, especially in larger towns, and show a much larger participation of women than of men. The participation rate is inversely proportional to degree of education, maximum frequency being among those with primary school education. On the other hand, a much higher number of social care volunteers is to be found among the higher social classes, the young (25–35 years), and the old (55–74 years).

ADVOCACY AND PROTECTION

The Italian legal system does not automatically take into consideration elderly persons, who are protected only when they find themselves in particularly precarious conditions (e.g., unable to provide for themselves or with no means of subsistence). This, however, does not apply to old people only, since such a policy aims at not separating the elderly from all other individuals, unless they find themselves in dangerous and risky conditions.

Civil law in Italy recognizes a few regulations that regard the elderly person as the principal (not exclusive) receiver, granting protection of basic rights, particularly concerning the personality and the dignity of the individual. These rights are often violated, when, for instance, in some nursing homes the elderly are not spoken to by name, their habits are not always respected, they cannot make requests, or there is little respect for individual privacy. These violations of a person's fundamental rights are normally fought by the judicial authorities, but it is not always easy to find someone who defends and represents elderly persons to ensure that their rights are protected.

The civil law provides the institutes of "protection" and "trusteeship," which tend to apply more to the patrimonial aspect rather than to the protection of the individual. The institute of "protection" operates in the case of mental illness and incapacity to provide for oneself. The protector thus represents the legal subject in all the proceedings, both ordinary and extraordinary.

"Trusteeship" presupposes minor mental illness, where the individual can perform ordinary administrative duties but not extraordinary ones, which may radically affect one's property. While this type of protection aims at the conservation and increase of a person's estate, there is no provision for any form of psychological support for the mentally ill subject, which could be a useful means to make advantageous choices for the person (e.g., through investments to assure the future). In nursing homes, the nongrowth of an elderly person's property because the holders do not worry about using it advantageously is an increasing phenomenon.

The civil law protects incapable subjects who lack sufficient means of subsistence, providing them with an allowance in addition to their (limited) social pension. The assigned amount is calculated according to the need and to the economic condition of the person administering the sum (spouse; legitimate, natural, or adopted children; other heirs). The provisions about financial assistance and about the subjects (mostly relatives) entitled to act as administrators of the incapable person imply, however, a model of society based on a patriarchal family, willing family helpers, and nearly no public assistance (i.e., a social structure very different from the present one).

The existing Italian legislation provides different private and voluntary initiatives that aim to protect the population in case of illness. Among these we find, for example, the several "courts for the rights of the ill person," the 1983 regional law of Tuscany n. 36 ("norms to safeguard the rights of the health service users"), and the 1985 regional law of Ligury n. 27 ("protection of the rights of the health services users").

These activities often make reference to the "charter of the rights of the elderly person," particularly, Article 30, which deals with disabled and non-self-sufficient persons. Among the "rights of the elderly" provided by the charter are the following:

1. not to be hospitalized unnecessarily;
2. to make use of appropriate alternative structures of assistance that aim to keep the elderly person within his or her own social context as well as to maintain and recover self-sufficiency;
3. not to be considered chronically ill and incurable;
4. to enjoy equality of treatment without discrimination;
5. to be looked after by the family without unnecessary time restrictions;

6. to receive help from medical staff in case of reduced self-sufficiency, above all, when no family assistance is provided, to perform basic tasks such as feeding, washing, and moving;
7. not to be sent to hospitals that are very far away from other family members;
8. to maintain legal and social rights in case of mental regression, unless the individual has been deprived of civil rights or regarded as an incapable person; and
9. to receive, in case of disability or non-self-sufficiency, all the necessary assistance in washing, feeding, moving, socioassistance problems, and similar activities.

FUTURE PROJECTIONS

In a society heading toward maximum economic development, persons have often become objects because those who are unable to contribute to the development are put aside or discriminated against—the old person is one of these. If the elderly individual (or whoever does not contribute to development) creates problems, then the society tries to find some place to put that person (i.e., an old people's home).

Up to the present time, measures regarding the elderly population in Italy have often resulted in the institutionalization of the self-sufficient old person to "face" social-economic problems. Living alone with a low pension meant, until a short while ago, ending up in a geriatric home. Currently, the problem of the care of non-self-sufficient elderly involves so many families that it makes one doubt that an increased life span should be considered a successful result of the improved social and economical conditions. An aging relative often becomes cause for worry, expecially when the person cannot look after personal needs.

In Italy there are only few concrete measures for the non-self-sufficient elderly. Explanations include the following:

- A "culture of the elderly," whether self-sufficient or not, is still far from being socially promoted;
- The elderly, like any other persons in difficulty (e.g., the physical handicapped or mentally ill), often get "hidden";
- There is little voluntary tradition in Italy, at least compared with other North European and North American countries;
- Economic development has contributed to family disintegration;
- Socioeconomic inequalities within the country have sometimes increased, instead of decreased, thus maintaining a certain instability.

The solution to the problems of the non-self-sufficient elderly started off on the wrong foot. Law n. 67 of 1988, for instance, allocated 8,500 billion liras (US $5 million) for the following nine years in order to create and restructure buildings as assisted health residences (AHR). This was done without taking any concrete measures for the families who bear the greatest burden for the care of the elderly. Moreover, few regional laws promote home help measures with financial coverage, and their formulation still remains at a theoretical level, so that we find nurses assisting at home only in very few areas.

Measures can no longer be delayed to face the problems of the elderly:

- The elderly person should have medical coverage like the rest of the population and enjoy the same rights to hospitalization;
- The elderly should have access to complete medical facilities even in their own home, especially when becoming non-self-sufficient;
- All social-medical projects for the non-self-sufficient elderly should be supported, especially for those who live alone, with an elderly spouse, or with few financial means or in any case of failing help from family or friends;
- Institutes for the non-self-sufficient elderly should be small structures and more numerous in the countryside, rather than large buildings in town centers;
- Families willing to keep at home elderly people in difficulty must have access to facilities to help them, even when the old persons are totally dependent and medical care is no longer of help;
- When evaluating proposals in favor of the elderly, it is necessary to look not only at the financial side but also at the efficiency of the offered services, including qualitative aspects that cannot always be easily quantified;
- The recomposition of the family units (brothers and sisters, widowed or unmarried) living separately should be, if wished, encouraged by granting assistance to the newly formed nucleus;
- Housing structures must be better planned, keeping in mind the possibility that the elderly may live in them and paying greater attention to the chance of installing equipment and aids for the non-self-sufficient elderly;
- Greater economic security (and therefore greater economic possibilities) makes the old person feel safer in a daily living context;
- Proposals should be forwarded so that in compulsory service (alternative to military service) a young person could be asked to help elderly persons at home;
- The possibility of constituting service cooperatives of young people who offer home help, especially to the old (but also to anyone living alone and in difficulty), should be developed;
- Family members who assist a non-self-sufficient old person should be allowed to leave work to stay at home (or wherever required) for the time necessary to assist that person. The period of absence should be considered as leave;
- Overlapping public, voluntary, and private services for the elderly should be avoided, if possible, by paying attention to the division of duties among the intervening operators;
- The creation of new services and structures in favor of the elderly population should be accompanied by an analysis of the costs and efficiency of the planned initiatives.

Services for the elderly, like those for any other group, should answer a specific demand, solve a real problem, satisfy an actual need, and not offer something that already exists. This is even more evident when we are faced with demands coming from "new" elderly, who have "new" requirements and demands. Old-fashioned services that have never been updated cannot meet the needs of the "new population" of older persons in Italy.

BIBLIOGRAPHY

Associazione Aiuti Internazionali (A.A.I.). *Le case di riposo per anziani in Italia.* Rome, 1975.

Associazione Nazionale Enti Assistenziali (ANEA). *Libro Bianco sull'assistenza in Italia.* Rome, 1976.

Borzaga, C. La cooperazione di solidarieta' sociale: Prime riflessioni su un settore emergente. In *I nuovi scenari della cooperazione in Italia.* Milan: Franco Angeli Editore, 1988.

Centro Studi Investimenti Sociali (CENSIS). *La situazione sociale del Paese.* Rome, 1987.

Consiglio Nazionale delle Ricerche, Instituto per le Ricerche Sulla Popolazione (CNR, IRP). *Rapporto sulla situazione demografica italiana.* Rome, 1988.

Council of Europe. *The Social Protection of the Very Old.* Strasbourg, 1984.

———. *Actes du Colloque sur la protection sociale des personnes tres agees: Alternatives a l'hospitalisation.* Strasbourg, 1986.

Fabris, F., and Pernigotti, L. *Ospedalizzazione a domicilio.* Torino: Rosemberg and Sellier, 1988.

Hanau C., Tragnone, G., Lanfranchi, G. A., Labo, G. Gli anziani in Medicina Generale: Valutazione dell'urgenza e della conformita' dei ricoveri. *Giornale di Gerontologia,* 32, 621, 1985.

Hanau, C. (a cura di). *I nuovi vecchi: Un confronto internazionale.* Rimini: Maggioli Editore, 1987.

Instituto ricerche economico-finanziarie (IREF). *Rapporto sull'associazionismo sociale.* Naples: Tecnodid Editore, 1990.

ISFOL. *Le universita' della terza eta'.* Rome: Edizioni Lavoro, 1987.

Italian National Institute of Statistics (ISTAT). *Statistiche della previdenza, della Sanita' e dell' assistenza sociale,* Vol. 26. Rome, 1988.

Laboratorio per le politiche Sociali (LABOS). *Quarta eta' e non autosufficienza.* Rome: Edizioni T.E.R., 1988.

Melograni, P. (a cura di). *La famiglia italiana dall'ottocento ad oggi.* Bari: Laterza editori, 1989.

Mengani M. Disability: Metodo di rilevazione del fabbisogno riabilitativo nella popolazione anziana. In Audiovisivi, Bioingegneria ed Informatica. Naples: Idelson, 1986a.

———. La protezione sociale delle persone molto anziane. *La Rivista di servizio sociale,* 2, 102, 1986b.

———. Diverse esigenze degli anziani in diversi contesti ambientali. *Difesa Sociale,* 5, 31, 1987a.

———. *Le esigenze degli anziani.* Iesi: Associazione Intercomunale Aesina, 1987b.

———. *I nuovi anziani.* Vol. 13. Ancona: Regione Marche, 1989.
Mengani, M., and Gagliardi, C. *Interventi assistenziali familiari nei confronti della popolazione molto anziana.* European Foundation, 1991.
Ministero dell'Interno. *I servizi di assistenza domiciliare.* Rome, 1984.
———. *I Centri di servizi "aperti."* Rome, 1987.
———. *Provvidenze legislative a favore dei mutilati ed invalidi civili, ciechi civili e sordomuti.* Rome, 1988.
Ministero della Sanita', Comitato Operativo Anziani. *Rapporto conclusivo.* Rome, 1989.
Santanera, F., and Hanau, C. Per non morire d'abbandono: anziani cronici non autosufficienti. *Il Regno,* 18, 573, 1990.
Santanera, F., and Breda, M. G. *Vecchi da morire.* Torino: Rosemberg and Sellier, 1988.
Systed, Third International Conference on Systems Science in Health-Social Services for the Elderly and the Disabled. Bologna, 1990.

16

JAPAN

Yutaka Shimizu and Junko Wake

INTRODUCTION

Demographic Characteristics

Population aging in Japan is characterized by three aspects. The first is the high proportion of elderly people (Ministry of Health and Welfare [MHW], 1992a). People aged 65 and over constituted 13.0% of the total population (approximately 16.2 million) in 1992, which is one of the lowest percentages among the industrialized countries. It is predicted, however, that the proportion will be 21.3% in 2010 and 25.8% in 2025, both of which will be the highest in the world. The second aspect is the rapidity of this growth. The number of years required for the proportion to shift from 7 to 14% is expected to be only 25 in Japan, while it took 45 years in Great Britain and Germany, the shortest among Western countries (United Nations, 1956, 1991). The third aspect is a sharp increase in the number of the very old. The number of people aged 80 years and over will reach nearly 10 million in 2025, 3.3 times as many as in 1990, in contrast to 1.8 times for those aged 65 to 79 (MHW, 1986).

Population aging in this country is a result of the decline of the fertility rate and the extension of the life expectancy. This has been observed concurrently during the post–World War II period and can be clearly exemplified by the fact that the birthrate of Japan is the second lowest (10.2 per 1,000 people in 1989) and the average life expectancy of the Japanese is the highest (male = 76.1 years, female = 82.1 years in 1991) in the world (MHW, 1989, 1991a; United Nations, 1988, 1989). These drastic demographic changes will unavoidably expand the needs to be met by a variety of health and social programs.

Socioeconomic Status

The labor force participation rate of men aged 60 to 64 in 1989 was 71.4%, in contrast to 54.2% in the United States, 53.5% in the United Kingdom, and 24.1% in France (Organization for Economic Cooperation and Development [OECD], 1989). This higher rate is primarily due to the "immaturity" of public pensions as well as the fixed mandatory retirement at an early age. Almost all private enterprises still adopt a fixed mandatory retirement age at 60 or under (Ministry of Labor, 1991). Besides, although the average amount of the benefit of the Employees' Pension Insurance is by no means inferior to amounts in Western industrial countries (MHW, 1992b), a considerable number of retirees can receive the pension benefits only under the minimum standard of living. Above all, the benefit of the National Pension Insurance for the self-employed is still very low due to the late start of the scheme. Many elderly persons are thus forced to continue working.

In addition, the higher labor force participation rate of the Japanese elderly can be partly explained by their relatively strong desire to continue working. According to an international comparative survey, for instance, 31% of Japanese people aged 60 and over report that the proper age of retirement from paid jobs is around 70 years of age, whereas the proportion is 26% in Korea, 13% in the United States, 5% in the United Kingdom, and 3% in Germany (General Management and Coordination Agency of the Government [GMCA], 1992a). In Japan, therefore, employment policies that match the motivation of the elderly are vital to enhance their social participation and economic productivity.

Another conspicuous difference in the socioeconomic status between the elderly in Japan and those in most Western industrialized countries is observed in their living arrangements.

It has been found that a little more than 40% of people aged 60 and over live with their married children in Japan and only 5.6% have been found to live alone (GMCA, 1992a). Thus, a large proportion of the Japanese elderly still live with their married children and children-in-law and are cared for by them when they become frail.

It should be noted, however, that such traditional living arrangements have been steadily declining in recent years. According to the national census, the proportion of people aged 65 and over living with their adult children has substantially decreased from 86.8% in 1960 to 60.6% in 1990. Therefore, one of the essential goals of social policy for the elderly in this country is to provide a variety of measures to support and supplement family care.

Perception of Care of the Elderly

The traditional respect for the elderly is expressly stipulated as a basic philosophy in the Law for the Welfare of the Aged, enacted in 1963: "Article 2. Senior citizens shall be treated with dignity and respect as individuals who have

Table 16.1
Plan of Middle-Aged Persons Aged 30–49 Years for Care of Parents When They Become Bedridden

Year	Should be cared for mainly by family	Family care supplemented by formal community care	Should be cared for mainly by formal care including institutional care	Don't know
1981	72.6	24.1	1.9	1.4
1987	62.2	32.2	3.7	1.9
1992	55.7	37.5	5.1	1.7

Source: GMCA, 1992b.

contributed to the progress of our society for many years, and who possess a wealth of knowledge and experience. With this in mind, they shall be guaranteed a high quality of life that is sound and secure."

The root of the respect for the elderly goes back to both filial piety as one of the Confucian precepts and to the even more ancient ancestor worship (Palmore and Maeda, 1985). However, as a result of the Westernization of lifestyles and social attitudes due to the rapid industrialization and urbanization after World War II, this traditional respect has been substantially declining, especially in urban areas and among younger generations.

Table 16.1 shows the plan of middle-aged persons for the care of their parents when they get bedridden over three time periods. In the 1992 survey, 55.7% answered "should be cared for mainly by family." On the other hand, 37.5% selected "family care supplemented by formal community care services." Only 5.1% answered "should be cared mainly by formal care services including institutional care." These survey results suggest that the majority of middle-aged people in Japan still believe that the care of bedridden elderly parents is the responsibility of family. As the table indicates, however, it is certain that the consciousness of family responsibility has weakened and that expectations for formal services have risen during the past 10 years. Thus, though the Civil Code stipulates the responsibility of children toward care of their aging parents, the stipulation is very leniently applied at present with respect to the enforcement of the responsibility of financial support and actual caregiving.

The Formal Structure of Care of the Elderly

The Japanese Social Security system after World War II is based in principle on Article 25 of the constitution of Japan: "All people shall have the right to maintain minimum standards of wholesome and cultural living." This article also stipulates in its later portion that it is the nation's responsibility to promote and expand Social Security and related measures to cover every aspect of the lives of the people. The Social Security benefits amounted to approximately 45 trillion yen (US$307 billion) in 1989, which is nearly 14% of Japan's national income. The proportion was 40% in Sweden, 36% in France, 25% in the United Kingdom, and 15% in the United States in 1986 (MHW, 1992b). This relatively smaller size of Social Security benefits of Japan compared with the Western industrial countries results mainly from the lower level of the present population aging.

Under such a Social Security system, social policy for the elderly has been steadily taking comprehensive shape. The first stage of its development was marked by the establishment of public pensions. Although the public pension for employees of private enterprises was inaugurated in 1941 (designated as Employees' Pension Insurance in 1944), it never performed its original function due to the financial disruption caused by World War II. Therefore, the real start of public pensions was not made until the reconstruction of the Employees' Pension Insurance in 1954. This was more than 60 years after the inauguration of the world's first public pension in Germany. Still later, in 1959, the pension for the self-employed (called National Pension Insurance) was established. The late start of public pensions primarily accounts for the low levels in the average amount of benefits at present.

In 1963 the Law for the Welfare of the Aged was enacted, which marked the second stage of policy development. It stipulates basic principles for a wide range of policies for the elderly as well as social welfare services, including institutional and community care services for the aged. In 1982 the Law for the Health of the Aged was enacted, which implied the third stage of policy development. The medical financing program and a variety of health care services are covered by the law.

In comparison to the previously mentioned measures, namely, pensions, social welfare programs, and health care programs, such measures as employment, housing, and education are relatively underdeveloped and must be enhanced to achieve a comprehensive policy for the elderly. In order to promote comprehensive and coordinated policies among the multiple departments of the government, the cabinet decided on the "General Policies for a Long-Life Society" in 1986.

In 1990 a consumption tax was introduced in Japan for the first time so as to secure a new source of revenue necessary for the coming aged society. In 1989 the national government promulgated the "Ten-Year Strategy to Promote Health and Welfare Services for the Elderly" (the so-called Gold Plan), which can be described as an epoch-making social plan, with quantified goals, toward the substantial expansion of formal services for the elderly. It is composed of an expansion of major community care services and long-term care facilities, a campaign for the reduction of bedridden elderly, promotion of measures for productive aging, a 10-year project for the promotion of research on aging, and so on. The total amount of governmental expenditure for this plan from 1990 to 1999 is estimated to be over 6 trillion yen (US $41 billion).

So that the Gold Plan can be successfully carried out, the Law for the Welfare of the Aged and other related laws were amended in 1990. The major items of amendment are (1) to coordinate the health and welfare services, as well as community and institutional care services, by the municipal government, (2) to expressly specify major community care services in the laws, and (3) for both the municipal and prefectural governments to formulate a 10-year plan with a quantified goal for the development of health and welfare services based on the characteristics of demands and service supply in each local community.

Furthermore, so as to secure and train the manpower necessary for realizing the substantial expansion of services, the following measures have been recently taken: (1) the establishment of the national license scheme for care workers and social workers in 1985, (2) the setting up of the Task Force on Securing Manpower for the Health and Welfare Services in the Ministry of Health and Welfare in 1990, and (3) the amendments of related legislations in 1992.

INCOME MAINTENANCE AND EMPLOYMENT

Income Maintenance

Japan's income maintenance programs for elderly people basically comprise public pension insurance and public assistance. With the reform in 1985, the public pension scheme changed to a so-called two-tiered structure. The National Pension, which had covered only the self-employed, became a "basic benefit" covering both the self-employed and the employed. The Employees' Pension and other employees' pensions individually provide their own benefits in addition to the basic benefit. The basic benefit is aimed at universally guaranteeing a minimum income for all elderly people regardless of the amount of income earned before old age. The additional benefits, on the other hand, are provided in the amount proportionate to the remuneration of individuals before retirement. No additional benefits are provided for the self-employed under the compulsory application except for the National Pension Fund of voluntary application. Employees' spouses with no job who did not have their own pension right under the old pension scheme are entitled to a basic benefit under the reformed scheme.

Table 16.2 shows the eligibility requirements and benefits of major public pensions. It is quite obvious that despite the introduction of the basic benefit, there still exist substantial disparities in both requirements and benefits among different pension schemes. There is an urgent need to lessen these disparities as much as possible so as to enhance the equity in economic lives of elderly people, as well as to financially stabilize the total public pension scheme. In addition, another unavoidable task (for the sake of balance and stability of pensions and their financing) is to extend the pensionable age of employees to 65 years of age, as in most Western countries. To do so, however, the extension of the mandatory retirement age up to the same level is required.

Furthermore, what should not be overlooked is that Japan's public pension includes a noncontributory pension (financed by the National Treasury), Old Age Welfare Pension, besides the previously-mentioned contributory pensions. It was established for those who were too old to participate in the National Pension

Table 16.2
Eligibility Requirements and Benefits of Major Public Pensions (as of 31 March, 1991)

	No. of persons eligible for old age pensions (thousand)	Pensionable age (years)	Contribution [1] (yen/%)	Average monthly amount of old age pension
National Pension	(Total 11,990) Self-emp.7,730	65	9,700 yen (US$ 72.4)	32,000 yen (US$ 239)
Employees Pension	4,760	male 60 female 57 [2]	male 14.5% female 14.3%	146,000 yen (US$ 1,090)
Mutual Aid Association of National Govern't Employees	500	59 [3]	15.2%	189,000 yen (US$ 1,410)

[1] The contribution is indicated as a flat amount or the proportion to the remuneration.
[2] 60 years of age from 1999 on.
[3] 60 years of age from 1995 on.
Source: MHW 1992b.

when it started in 1961. Recipients of this pension are required to be 70 years and over and to have a low income under some amount. The fixed amount of its monthly benefit was nearly 31,000 yen (US$231) in 1991. The number of recipients is steadily decreasing and numbered approximately 960,000 in 1991.

Finally, the public assistance program has served, and will continue to serve, an indispensable role in income maintenance for the Japanese elderly. Although public pensions are presently still "immature," even though they become mature, there will inevitably appear a significant number of old people whose contributions are too small, for various reasons, to receive even a moderate amount of pension benefits. Thus, although public assistance is the last public relief measure for all people, elderly people are more likely to depend upon it. In fact, 15.8 per 1,000 people aged 60 years and over were on relief, in contrast to 7.5 per 1,000 people of all ages in 1991, though both ratios are extremely low compared with those of Western industrial countries. The minimum standard of living in large cities in 1991 amounted to nearly 137,000 yen (US$1,022) a month for elderly couples.

Employment

The employment situation for elderly people is much less favorable than for the younger generation. For instance, the unemployment rate in 1990 was 5.1%

for males aged 60–64 in contrast to 2.1% for the total labor force population (GMCA, 1990).

The primary cause of such relatively unfavorable situations is the early fixed mandatory retirement age. More precisely, almost 9 out of 10 private enterprises with more than 30 employees adopt a fixed mandatory retirement age. Regarding their retirement age, 67% have a fixed retirement age at 60, and 29% do so under 60, while only 4% have a fixed retirement age over 60 (Ministry of Labor, 1991).

The Law for Stabilized Employment of the Elderly, enforced in 1986, stipulates that all employers must make every possible effort to extend the retirement age to 60 or over. Based on this law, the following major employment policies for the elderly are carried out: (1) to secure the continuous employment of those aged over 60 (e.g., to provide governmental subsidies to employers who continue to employ or reemploy their elderly persons after retirement), (2) to newly employ those who have retired from other enterprises, (e.g., to provide governmental subsidies to employers who hire the unemployed elderly), and (3) to provide temporary and short-term jobs for the retirees through the "Silver Human Resource Centers," which are organized by senior citizens themselves in each municipality (495 centers, with nearly 225,000 members, are subsidized by the national government throughout the country).

HEALTH CARE SERVICES

Background of Health and Medical Care for the Elderly

A "Patients Survey" (MHW, 1991b) illustrates the health status of the Japanese elderly across the country: 1 out of 5 elderly persons aged 70 and over, in contrast to 1 out of 15 persons of all ages, received some medical care on a certain day in 1990, and 38% of the total number of inpatients were aged 70 and over in 1990. Thus, the elderly tend to need medical care more frequently than other age groups, though their ability to pay for necessary medical care is generally restricted.

All Japanese, in principle, can receive medical care under a certain kind of public medical insurance program. In addition to these public insurance programs, a special medical care financing program for the elderly is based on the Law for the Health of the Aged. The law also stipulates the provision of comprehensive health and medical care services appropriate for old people, such as disease prevention, treatment, functional training, and home nursing care.

Medical Care Financing Program

The medical care financing program for the elderly, originally started in 1973 as a free medical program for those under a set income based on the Law for the Welfare of the Aged, became a universal provision with a moderate fee charged under the Law for the Health of the Aged in 1982. Under this program, people aged 70 and over and the bedridden aged 65 to 69 can receive almost all medical care with a moderate fee. Of the remaining expenses, 70% are covered by the fund composed of all public medical insurance programs and 30% by public expenditure.

For those retired under 70, there is the Medical Care Financing Program for the Retired. Under this program, 80% of medical care expenses of the retired is paid by the fund financed by both the retired and their former employers. The remaining 20% is paid by the retirees who received medical care.

In addition, for needy elderly persons who are not entitled to any public medical insurance benefits, the public assistance program provides medical care that is almost identical to that under special medical care financing programs for the elderly.

Community Health Care Programs

Community health care programs under the Law for the Health of the Aged provide those aged 40 and over with health passbooks, health education, health consultation, health checkups, functional training, and home nursing guidance. These services are implemented by municipalities, based on the successive five-year national plans, while their expenses are shared equally by the national, prefectural, and municipal governments. As a rule, fees are not charged.

In addition, a home nursing service has just started under the amended Law for the Health of the Aged of 1991. It provides the bedridden and those with similar disabilities aged 70 and over with nursing care at their homes through "home nursing stations" set up by various service providers in the community. The service provision is subject to the instruction of the recipients' home doctors. Moderate fees are charged to recipients of this service, and the remaining expenses are shared evenly between public expenditure and the fund of public medical insurance programs.

HOUSING RESOURCES

Historical Development of Institutional Care for the Elderly

Welfare provisions for the elderly were part of the public assistance program until the Law for the Welfare of the Aged was enacted in 1963. In particular, the "poorhouse" for the aged and hospitals had been major institutional arrangements for the elderly.

The Law for the Welfare of the Aged originally defined three types of institutional facilities: nursing homes for the elderly, homes for the aged, and homes for the aged with moderate fees. In regard to the nursing homes for the elderly and the homes for the aged, admission can occur only after an authoritative decision is made by the local public welfare office and, in general, the facility is not allowed to reject an applicant. In 1992, the residents were charged up to 220,000 yen (US$1,833) per month for nursing homes and 130,000 yen (US$1,083) per month for the homes for the aged. The remaining costs are paid by municipalities (half subsidized by the national government; one-fourth can be subsidized by the prefectural government). These monthly payment levels are based on the resident's ability to pay, and the difference must be supplemented by the resident's legally designated family members on a sliding scale. On the other hand, the homes for the aged with moderate fees can be rented by a free contract between the resident and the facility. The moderate fee, set by the national and local governments, is paid directly to the facility by the resident.

Outline of Facilities for the Elderly

Based on the Law for the Welfare of the Aged, the national government determines eligibility guidelines and standards, including equipment and staffing of each facility, and administratively oversees its operation. The nursing homes for the elderly provide nursing and personal care for the aged 65 and over who need constant care due to physical and/or mental functional limitations and who are without adequate family care. There is no income eligibility requirement. In 1991, there were 2,403 facilities accommodating 171,267 residents.

The homes for the aged, on the other hand, provide daily life assistance for the low-income frail elderly. The resident is usually entitled to the national public assistance program or falls into the low-income category that is exempted from the municipality tax. In 1991, there were 947 homes and 65,043 residents. The homes for the aged with moderate fees are an income-tested housing scheme for the functionally independent aged 60 and over who lack adequate housing for financial and environmental reasons. Type A homes serve meals, while Type B homes require residents to cook for themselves. In 1991, there were 254 Type A homes with 14,761 residents and 38 Type B homes with 1,541 residents.

The Diversification of Institutional Care Needs of the Elderly

The majority of housing arrangements have so far focused on institutional care for the limited number of low-income elderly persons with no adequate family support. Along with the growing aging population with a relatively affluent economic status, however, the economic eligibility requirement and older structures (with less privacy) have become increasingly out-of-date. Instead, the need of frail elderly persons who desire to stay in the community and lead independent lives is considerably increasing.

The "care house" facility, inaugurated as an alternative housing arrangement in 1989, is especially designed so that even elderly residents in wheelchairs can live independently, with consultation services available regarding daily living, meals, and related social services. Although there were only 14 facilities serving 541 persons in 1991, substantially more are expected in the future.

Growing Needs for Long-Term Care

The traditional institutional scheme can no longer correspond to the drastic expansion of care needs of the elderly. It was estimated that in 1990 there were 265,000 bedridden and 739,000 demented persons aged 65 and over in the home environment (MHW, 1990). Furthermore, the number is expected to increase not only due to the growth of the aging population but also due to the sharp increase of the very old, who tend to be more frail and disabled. In particular, a lack of beds available in nursing homes for the elderly has become evident, and the term *social hospitalization* was created to describe the situation where elderly patients must be hospitalized not due to medical problems but due to social necessities, when adequate family care cannot be provided. The increase of frail or disabled elderly persons who are in need of rehabilitation and recuperation after discharge from the acute care hospitals led to the establishment of a new type of health care facility in 1988. These so-called health care facilities for the aged operate under the Law for the Health of the Aged. The main objective of the facility is to promote the recovery of elderly patients in order for them to return home. The patient pays approximately 50,000 yen (US$416) per month, and the rest of the costs are subsidized by public health insurance funds as well as national and local governments. In principle, the patient is expected to be discharged within three months. However, a 1991 government survey of 522 existing facilities across the nation has found that the average length of stay was 141 days and only 57% of the patients could return home (MHW, 1992c). Others moved to either the medical facilities, such as hospitals, or welfare institutions. This implies a lack of variety of formal supports available in the home environment.

In order to avoid unnecessary hospitalization and to meet the nursing care needs of chronically disabled elderly persons, the Ministry of Health and Welfare put forward a plan for the urgent development of institutions in the "Ten-Year Strategy to Promote Health and Welfare Services for the Elderly" (the so-called Gold Plan). The types of facilities for the elderly are to be substantially expanded by fiscal year 1999.

New Housing Initiatives for the Elderly

Although other housing options exist, they still do not meet the growing needs of the elderly. For instance, the Ministry of Health and Welfare offers loans to families living with those aged 60 and over when they adapt their houses for the elderly. The Ministry of Construction also provides public housing specifically designed for the elderly and families living with the elderly. Furthermore, in cooperation with the Ministry of Health and Welfare, housing for senior citizens has been built since 1986 as a "silver housing" model project. This is congregate housing for either the elderly living alone or elderly couples. The facility is equipped with an emergency alarm system, and assistant workers are assigned to every 10 to 30 households in order to coordinate necessary health and social services.

Finally, the development of the private housing industry should be noted. These private elderly people's homes usually provide meals and other daily services in a relatively luxurious environment. There were 228 facilities in 1991, accommodating 21,825 residents. The Law for the Welfare of the Aged requires each facility to submit a proposal prior to its opening for business. There is an increasing interest in these initiatives; however, they usually require considerable amount of property, and the majority of them are targeted for the upper-class, healthy elderly.

SUPPORTIVE SERVICES

The Shift from Institutional Care to Community Care

As in any other country, the elderly in Japan desire to continue living at home as long as possible. Enhancing supportive measures to help these elderly maintain an independent life in their own community is one of the central issues to be tackled in Japan.

Currently the municipal government is administratively responsible for delivering all the community care services. In terms of financing, the national, prefectural, and municipal governments share the cost evenly, whereas half of the cost for "the three major supportive services" (to be described) is subsidized by the national government.

Major Community Care Services

Four major community care services are defined in the amended law so that these services can be provided with less diversity across the nation. These services include home help services, day-care services, short-term stay services (respite care), and services providing special appliances to the disabled. Among these services, the first three services are designated as "the major supportive services" and are planned to be substantially expanded under the "Gold Plan."

Home Help Services

The home help service is the oldest one articulated in the original Law for the Welfare of the Aged and helps keep families intact and enables an older person to remain at home. The service may be provided up to four hours per day, six days a week, totaling 18 hours per week to those approximately 65 and over and their families in need of personal care and homemaking services. The home help services encompass homemaking activities such as laundering, shopping, and preparing meals and some personal care, including giving baths.

The home help service can be contracted out to other nonprofit and profit-making organizations that meet the national guidelines defined by the Ministry of Health and Welfare. In 1992, these services were offered in almost all municipalities. A moderate fee may be charged if the household income exceeds a certain limit.

A nationwide survey showed that 66% of the recipients were the elderly living alone, and 93% were receiving services free of charge. Furthermore, 79% were neither bedridden nor demented (Foundation of Social Development for Senior Citizens, 1991). This implies that the services are largely given to the frail and low-income elderly persons who are living alone and in need of assistance with homemaking. However, it is argued that the increasing number of the disabled elderly and the lack of family care will inevitably demand more flexibility and a wider range of availability of these services. In addition, a multidisciplinary team approach and more effective coordination with other relevant services, such as home nursing services, will be increasingly essential.

One of the major impediments in supplying 100,000 home helpers by 1999 (promulgated in the Gold Plan) is securing manpower. Both professionalization, based on the consolidated wage structure, and flexible employment, to meet the varying and changing needs of the service users, should be concurrently achieved. Since 1991, the training program for the home helper has been revised so that 360-hour, 90-hour, and 40-hour curriculas are required in accordance with the nature of work to be performed.

Day-Care Services

The day-care service provides care programs to residents of the community aged 65 and over who are either frail or disabled. The service may maintain and promote their physical functioning, help to relieve their sense of isolation, and minimize the burden of family caregivers.

The day-care center, which was legally articulated in the amended Law for the Welfare of the Aged of 1990, provides the following services: (1) core provision, including information and advice, rehabilitative activities for daily living, custodial care, education for family caregivers, health checkups, and transportation; (2) optional provision at the center, including bathing and meal services; (3) optional home-delivery provision, including bathing, meals, and laundry services; and (4) sending of care workers to housing for the senior citizen (Silver Housing). By fiscal year 1999, 10,000 centers are expected to be built.

Short-Term Stay Services (Respite Care)

Short-term stay services were established in 1978 as respite care for family caregivers in case they could not provide care at home due to social matters, including the caregiver's illness and attendance at public occasions. The services are offered at accredited facilities, such as nursing homes and homes for the aged. Service utilization has been conspicuously increasing, especially since its eligibility requirement was moderated in 1986. The principal length of stay is seven days, but exceptional extensions have been admitted since 1990. In 1988 a so-called community care promotion program was introduced in which frail or bedridden elderly and their families stay together at nursing homes for a certain period to learn caregiving skills. Furthermore, a night care service has been implemented since 1989 for the severely demented elderly who require constant care during the night.

Programs Providing Special Appliances for the Elderly

This program provides or rents special appliances for the disabled and their families to ease their caregiving and to improve their quality of life. These appliances include wheelchairs, special beds, special bath tubs, and so on. In 1989 the income eligibility restriction was repealed, and the program can now be utilized by any individual on a sliding-scale payment basis. In order to make effective use of the appliances, corresponding to functional abilities, the rental provision instituted in 1986 has been promoted.

Other Community Care Services

Besides nationally defined community care services, municipal governments provide their own supportive services with a grant from prefectural governments or with their own budget. These services range from supplying diapers and other necessary daily goods and services for the bedridden elderly to subsidizing activity programs and transportation for senior citizens. These services can be flexibly arranged, responding to the local needs. However, great disparities exist between municipalities.

Establishing a Regional Aging Network

In order to institute a comprehensive community care system, the following goals were proposed: (1) to establish an accessible service base in each community so that necessary services can be obtained in a coordinated manner, (2) to provide services on a 24-hour basis, (3) to improve the quality of care, and (4) to coordinate health, medical, and social welfare services.

Toward these goals, the In-Home Care Support Center was inaugurated in 1990. These centers provide overall information and advice on a 24-hour basis regarding care for the elderly and coordinate various services on behalf of the individual client. Under the "Gold Plan," 10,000 centers are planned to open by fiscal year 1999. Thus, the case management function may be applied as an effective method to achieve coordination of various services for each client.

Furthermore, the Program to Promote Coordination of Services for the Elderly has been implemented since 1987. The program consists of the Council for Promotion of Coordination of Services for the Elderly and the Service Coordination Team for the Elderly. The former is set up at the prefectural level, in which administrative personnel in related fields participate to exchange information for coordinating and planning services. The latter is organized at the municipal level and assesses and coordinates the individual needs.

LEISURE-TIME RESOURCES

Promoting a Meaningful Life for the Elderly

Another important issue concerning the elderly is the promotion of their meaningful lives. Indeed, the early retirement age and the world's greatest longevity have significantly changed the life-style of retirees in Japan.

According to an international comparative survey, 15% of Japanese aged 60 and over report that they often or usually join social gatherings, whereas the proportion is 63% in Germany, 60% in the United States, 53% in the United Kingdom, and 30% in South Korea (GMCA, 1992a). Similarly, the participation rates of the Japanese elderly in other social activities, including religious, volunteer, and group activities, are generally low compared with other countries. These figures illustrate the inactive social involvement of the Japanese elderly and imply a considerable need to create opportunities for their social participation.

The Ministry of Health and Welfare enforces several measures to promote a healthy and vigorous life of the elderly, although most have been implemented recently. One of the traditional measures is the provision of senior centers where various services are offered to the elderly in the community. These services encompass information and advice, health checkups, and rehabilitation programs. The center also serves as a meeting place for social and educational activities. Another measure is subsidizing senior citizens' clubs. The clubs in which the elderly participate voluntarily were established in the hope that the elderly could enjoy various social and meaningful activities within the community. There were 35,873 clubs throughout the nation when the program was initiated in 1963 and 131,653 in 1991.

A recent initiative called for the establishment of the Foundation of Social Development for Senior Citizens at the national level and the Promotive Organization for Active Long-life at the prefectural level. These organizations promote productive and healthy aging through public education, organizations of various social and leisure-time activities and research, and education of senior volunteer leaders.

The Ministry of Education also offers provisions targeted to the elderly, with an emphasis on the promotion of lifelong education. The provisions include offering educational courses for the elderly, subsidizing programs to promote the meaningful lives of the elderly, coordinating educational courses for volunteers, establishing the Long-Life College for the Elderly, implementing the program to promote intergenerational exchange, and organizing programs to recruit the elderly so that they can reuse their knowledge and skills.

ADVOCACY AND PROTECTION

Although there has been an increasing awareness with regard to the vulnerability of elderly persons due to their physical and mental disabilities, no national protective legislative scheme exists that is specifically geared toward the elderly. However, some local governments have recently started to offer their own protective service provisions for disabled residents, including the elderly. For instance, in 1991 the Tokyo metropolitan government initiated counseling and legal services to mentally retarded and senile residents, including the demented elderly. An ombudsman program is another measure that has been introduced recently by a few municipalities to protect the rights of the elderly. However, these services are on an experimental basis and are concentrated in large cities.

FUTURE PROJECTIONS

The population aging in Japan is expected to continue to proceed at an unprecedented rate until the early twenty-first century. Until then, Japan faces the monumental goal of building a productive as well as secure, aged society. The major tasks for that purpose are summarized in the following.

Securing Employment as Well as Stable and Adequate Income

The existing public pension schemes need to be reformed, primarily to improve low benefits. Thus, it is essential to establish a stable financial basis by unifying the current divided schemes, as well as raising the pensionable age of the Employees' Pension to 65.

This will unavoidably call for the extension of the fixed mandatory retirement age to 65. It is imperative for businesses to improve work conditions, redesign jobs, and arrange retraining programs for the elder employees. Moreover, considering the strong desire for work among Japanese elders, a variety of part-time jobs are required for their social participation and health maintenance.

Expanding Further Health and Social Care Services Along with Improvement of Systems and Quality of Care

The "Gold Plan" certainly aims to build a secure aged society. However, many Japanese social gerontologists believe that the goals of the plan mark a merely initial, though important, stage for the further development of service provisions in the future. A secondary plan must be formulated in order to meet the expanded needs brought about by further population aging during the first few decades of the next century.

Along with service expansion in terms of quantity, the systematization of various service programs and improvement of quality of services are indispensable. The service systematization should result in the integration and coordination of health and social services and the continuum of care among sheltered housing, long-term care facilities, and hospitals, as well as between community and institutional care services. The improvement of quality of services should be aimed at so-called normalization in both hardware (physical environments) and software (direct helping practices) included in any service programs.

Securing Financial and Human Resources

It is essential to secure necessary financial resources to expand and improve a wide range of formal programs for the elderly. In 1989 the proportion of the nation's total burden, composed of tax and Social Security contributions to the national income, was nearly 40% (which is 10 to 30% lower than those of major European countries) (MHW, 1992b). However, the rise of the proportion is unavoidable, as a result of further population aging in the future, and what is important is to avoid a rapid and unjust increase of this burden. In addition, the development of a variety of quality programs in voluntary and private sectors should be encouraged so as to avert an excessive burden on the public sector.

Another essential requirement for the development of health and social services is to secure the proper number of qualified personnel. Though the national licenses for social workers and care workers instituted in 1987 are worth noting, difficult problems (such as securing a large number of nurses and care workers, along with improvement of their salaries and work conditions) remain to be solved.

Rearing and Educating Young Generations as Sound Supporters of the Future Aged Society

The rapid decline of the birthrate in recent years has turned attention to the problems of children. The establishment of the One-Year Child Care Leave in 1991 is one of the products of this change. A secure and productive aged society in the future will not be realized without the sound support of young people. There is no doubt that they are needed as valuable labor force participants and contributors to Social Security. What is more important, however, is to raise and educate children and youth so that they can hold positive attitudes toward aging and an aged society. A wide range of educational efforts and programs by schools, families, and communities are required for that purpose.

Cooperating with Other Asian Countries Coping with Their Aging Problems

Japan is currently one of the most advanced aging societies in Asia. The experiences it has had, and will have, must be a model for many countries with a similar culture in this region that will have to cope with their aging problems. Therefore, Japan can help these countries by sharing scientific, technological, and educational knowledge.

BIBLIOGRAPHY

Foundation of Social Development for Senior Citizens. (1991). *Haken-jigyou Jittai Chousa Kekka Houkokusho* (The report of the survey results on the actual conditions of home-help services). Tokyo.

General Management and Coordination Agency of the Government (GMCA), Bureau of Statistics. (1990). *Roudouryoku Chousa* (Survey on labor force). Tokyo.

———. Section on Policy for the Elderly. (1992a). *Rojinno Seikatsuto Ishikini-kansuru Dai-san-kai Kokusai Hikaku Chousa* (The third international comparative survey on the life and opinion of the elderly). Tokyo.

———. (1992b). *Rougono Seikatsuto Kaigo-nikansuru Chousa* (Survey on the life and care in old age). Tokyo.

Ministry of Health and Welfare (MHW). (1992b). *Kousei Hakusho* (Annual report on health and welfare). 1991. Tokyo.

———. National Institute of Population Problems. (1986, 1992a). *Nipponno Shourai Suikei Jinkou* (Estimation of Japan's population in the future). Tokyo.

———. Statistics and Information Department. (1989). *Jinkou Doutai Chousa* (Vital statistics). Tokyo.

———. (1990). *Kokumin Seikatsu Kiso Chousa* (Fundamental survey on the life of people). Tokyo.

———. (1991a). *Kan-i Seimei Hyou* (Abridged life tables). Tokyo.

———. (1991b). *Kanja Chousa* (Patients survey). Tokyo.

———. (1992). *Roujin Hoken-shisetsu Chousa* (Survey on health care facility for the aged). 1991. Tokyo.

Ministry of Labor. (1991). *Koyou Kanri Chousa* (Survey on the employment and administration of enterprises). Tokyo.

Organization for Economic Cooperation and Development (OECD). (1989). *Labour Force Statistics*. Paris.

Palmore, E., and Maeda, D. (1985). *The Honorable Elders Revisited: A Revised Cross-Cultural Analysis of Aging in Japan*. Durham, NC: Duke University Press.

United Nations. (1956). *The Aging of Population and Its Economic and Social Implications*. Population Studies, No. 26. New York.

———. (1988, 1989). *Demographic Yearbook*. New York.

———. (1991). *World Population Prospects 1990*. Population Studies, No. 120. New York.

17

JORDAN

*Amal H. El-Farhan and
Muhsen A. Makhamreh*

INTRODUCTION

The aging generation in Jordan is similar to that in most Arab and developing countries, as far as its increasing proportion of the population. The elderly in Jordan have been classified to include that portion of the population 60 years old and above. The Department of Statistics and the Social Security Act use this classification for statistical purposes and for Social Security benefits to the elderly. However, lately there has been a move to consider only those over 65 years as the elderly population. This is in accordance with international definitions of the elderly.

The elderly population in Jordan constitutes a small percentage. The statistics of 1990 show that the elderly constitute 4% of the total population (National Population Commission, 1991). Projections for 2005 show that the elderly percentage of the total population will reach 5%. Table 17.1 shows the statistical characteristics of the elderly in Jordan.

Statistics on elderly levels of education, marital status, labor force participation, and so on are not available. However, life expectancy in Jordan was estimated at 67 years for males and 71 years for females in 1988. Currently it is expected to be more because the trend in life expectancy has shown a consistent increase since the 1950s.

Economic Characteristics

Most of the elderly in Jordan are living below the poverty line (Ministry of Social Development, 1990). Seventy-two percent of them earn less than 100 Jordanian dinar per month (US $142) as shown in Table 17.2.

On the other hand, most of the elderly are economically supported by their

Table 17.1
Statistics for the Elderly in Jordan in 1990

Age Category	Males	Females	Total Elderly	Total Population
60–69	48,500	41,900	90,400	
70–79	19,600	21,800	41,400	
80+	11,000	11,700	22,700	
Total	79,100	75,400	154,500	3,453,000

families and relatives, specifically the elder sons and daughters, as shown in Table 17.3.

The needy elderly are usually the recipients of *zakkat,* a religious tax of 2.5% on capital assets and 10% of annual income, based on one of the five main doctrines of Islamic religion. As a religious doctrine, it is left to the individual to implement and is considered a social practice whereby the rich contribute to the well-being of society.

History of Care for the Elderly

The extended family and the tribal system of the Jordanian society, with its Islamic institutional principles of family solidarity, are still the main caretakers of the elderly. The Islamic culture gives special respect to the elderly as parents and as relatives with high status, whom the nation owes gratitude, not as a philanthropic attitude but rather as a duty for their previous roles.

However, in recent years a few forms of caretaking have slowly emerged alongside traditional forms of care by the extended family. A small number of independent institutions have been established to take care of the elderly in both the public and private sectors. The public sector role is confined to the Ministry of Social Development and its related agencies, while the charitable and voluntary organizations are the source of caretaking for the elderly in the private sector. Elderly are provided services on a nonprofit basis and often free of charge, based on their needs. However, in 1992, one profit organization had been established to care for the elderly as a business venture.

The Formal Structure of Care of the Elderly

Jordan has a mixed economy, in which both the public and private sectors work together to promote the economic well-being of the country. Both sectors of the economy provide caretaking services to the elderly.

The role of the public sector is managed by the Ministry of Social Development, which provides the following services:

Table 17.2
Monthly Income for the Elderly in Jordan (in JD)

Income Category	Percentage of the Elderly
No Income	15.90
Less than 50 (US $71)	31.50
50-100 (US $71-142)	25.00
101-140 (US $144-200)	12.00
151-200 (US $216-286)	6.60
201-250 (US 287-357)	7.10
251-300 (US $358-429)	1.90
Total	100.00

- *Shelter:* The ministry provides shelter by contracting with charitable and voluntary organizations to make available shelter for the needy, and the ministry pays the dues for these organizations.
- *Financial Aid:* This takes two forms: monthly salaries for certain periods of time or emergency assistance for one time. These forms of aid are very small and very limited in size.
- *Training and Occupational Rehabilitation:* The ministry provides training for the needy elderly to establish small-scale business so as to make a suitable living. In addition, the ministry provides financial assistance to help start such businesses.
- *Health Insurance:* The elderly are given access to public hospitals and are treated free of charge.

The Private Sector Role

Mostly, services to the elderly are provided by private Christian or Islamic organizations. Table 17.4 classifies the sponsors of elderly caretaking organizations and the associated charges. Services for the elderly are not free, and charges depend on the sponsor of the organization and the degree of need of the elderly.

INCOME MAINTENANCE AND EMPLOYMENT

Several public income security programs assist the elderly.

1. Retirement income exists for governmental retirees in both civil and military sectors. Retirees in both sectors are entitled to retirement income if they serve a minimum number of years (more than 20 years) and are retired according to normal and legal procedures. Income from this source is not high but does cover the basic needs of the retirees. Those benefiting from civil and military retirement, as of December 1991, totaled 118,000 persons (civil, 15,830; military, 76,525). These numbers include both

Table 17.3
Sources of Income for the Elderly

Income Category	Percentage of the Elderly
Family and relatives (sons, daughters, spouse, others)	61.80
Job	12.60
Retirement Income	11.00
Savings and Investment	8.70
Other	5.90
Total	100.00

the living and beneficiaries. The actual numbers of those who receive assistance are civil, 14,722; military, 71,167; and beneficiaries, 32,111.

2. Social Security benefits are available for government and private sector employees who are not covered under the first program. Males are eligible at the age of 60, and females are eligible at the age of 55, if they served 15 years or more in their organization and paid dues to the Social Security Department. Social Security benefits are financed by a joint contribution from the work organization and the worker (prior to retirement). As of March 1992, the Department of Social Security paid 4,747 elderly benefits from the retirement fund.

3. The National Aid Fund (NAF) provides income for the needy who have no other source of income. The income from the NAF is very low and ranges from $30 to $60 per month. The needy person should prove that there are no other sources of income. In addition to this monthly income, the NAF provides emergency funds for onetime assistance (equal to $150).

    Data from the NAF indicate that 66.1% of all recipients of monthly cash assistance are women. This is rather a high proportion, not only corroborating the saying that women are the poorest of the poor but also giving some indication of the importance of addressing the issue of women-headed households, since the assistance in NAF is given to the head of household.

    However, the other programs administered by NAF—vocational rehabilitation (income-generating projects), emergency aid, and physical rehabilitation—show a very small proportion of women beneficiaries. It can be deduced either that women have not acquired any skills to enable them to start income-generating projects or that women do not find willing granters for their loans for income generation.

    The NAF also provides training for the elderly to start their own business under the following conditions: (1) the beneficiary should be unemployed; (2) the family income should be less than $150 per month; and (3) dependents' ages should be less than 18 years. In addition to training, NAF provides a loan that does not exceed $4,500. The loan is paid back in installments over a very long period of time.

No other sources of income are available for the elderly (i.e., food stamps, tax benefits).

Table 17.4
Sponsors of Elderly Caretaking Organizations

Sponsor	Number	%	Charge
Religious	6	67	Variable according to need but relatively low
Nonreligious, voluntary	2	22	Moderate fees
Private: Profit org.	1	11	High fees
Total	9	100	

HEALTH CARE SERVICES

The health care system in Jordan depends on the joint efforts of the public and private sectors. The government provides health care services to all of its employees and their dependents at a very low cost. It also provides health care services to military personnel and their dependents at a low cost. Given the fact the government is the largest employer in the country, a large portion of the population is covered for health service. Moreover, any citizen can visit public care centers and hospitals and be treated at nominal cost.

The government health services are highly subsidized and almost free to Jordanian citizens. Thus, the elderly can use these services at low cost. For those seeking better health care, services can be utilized that are provided by the private sector. Medical checkups and hospital treatment of all kinds are available in Jordan, but more expensive services, of a better quality, are provided by private sector medical centers.

The Ministry of Health is responsible for general health conditions in the country, and its objective is to maintain and improve these conditions over time. Acute and chronic services are provided by the Ministry of Health.

Health care facilities are available to most citizens in the various parts of the country; however, health care services are more available and of better quality in urban areas. Remote areas in the desert lack these facilities.

The elderly per se have no special provisions that allow them to use the health care facilities, but they use these services if they are retirees of the civil service or the military, or they are given direct by the Ministry of Social Development. Otherwise, they use the health services in both sectors, on the condition that they pay for their health care.

There is no specialized health care system in Jordan for the elderly, as is the case for infants, gynecology, or specialized surgery. Nor are there specialized departments for the elderly in hospitals and health care centers. The elderly are treated according to their required service and type of sickness.

The trend nowadays is to emphasize the importance of treatment in the community rather than in hospitals. Community centers of the voluntary sector can play a major role. This is a threefold system. First, hospital-based services could be given in hospital sections to diagnose and evaluate the sick elderly and do the follow-up. Treating the elderly in one department or hospital would not be feasible, for it would impose an economic strain (in the light of Jordan's economic situation). Furthermore, such an approach would affect the morale of the elderly and increase their sense of alienation. Second, day hospitals can provide medical and social services for those elderly who do not have social supports during the day. This requires transportation services, as well. Third, community-based services are the most comprehensive in the sense that they include health visits to those elderly who are kept at home or who live in old-age homes.

HOUSING RESOURCES

The government in Jordan has no special policy or provisions to provide housing facilities for the elderly. Private housing is open to the elderly on a competitive basis in the market, and they are given no special treatment. The reason for the absence of public housing policy for the elderly is related to the social system of the extended family in the country. The elderly in Jordan normally live with their sons and daughters or immediate members of the family. Only in cases where there is no immediate family member who is capable of supporting the elderly does the need arise for public housing. In those cases, the elderly are housed in those facilities with religious, voluntary, and private sponsorship.

SUPPORTIVE SERVICES

The nature of the social system of the extended family provides all supporting services for the elderly; there are no public programs or policies to provide these services.

LEISURE-TIME RESOURCES

The elderly in Jordan spend all their time with their families. Thus, all their leisure time is spent in family affairs and associated social activities. In case of picnics, weddings, and celebrations of various kinds, the participation of the elderly is tied to the participation of the family. No special events are singled out for the participation of only the elderly, and their leisure time is spent in social occasions like weddings, child rearing, and religious activities. Sporting events or voluntary organizations are not for the elderly in Jordan, as they are in the West, but for middle-aged individuals. This is why there are no public programs for the elderly.

Visiting by females, especially in mornings, is an important and widespread practice in both urban and rural areas and represents the close-knit nature of community life.

Leisure time for men is slightly different. Mosque attendance is a common practice. Men usually go to the mosque for their dawn prayers, and the elderly usually stay longer. Men go to the mosque for the Asser prayers (which occur about 4 P.M.) and then stay until the evening. Historically, the mosque has offered a setting for religious discussion and has been (in Jordanian and Islamic culture) a place to learn religion and exchange opinions about community issues. This is still commonplace in both urban and rural areas, where the elderly spend time and remain members of the community.

In rural areas, the rich men of the tribe or family own a Madafah, which is an open guesthouse offering comfortable seating and free Arabian coffee, usually open afternoons and evenings, and free for all to enjoy. Elderly men, in particular, join the gatherings for easy talk and discuss community affairs, and many engage in storytelling.

In the cities, where the Madafah is not as widespread, men go to street coffee shops, which are common meeting places. They often play cards and backgammon (which is a widespread game in the Middle East) and smoke tobacco.

However, one leisure-time hobby quite important for the elderly is television. Almost in every home, television is both a pastime and educational means, particularly to noneducated persons.

ADVOCACY AND PROTECTION

The safety and protection of the elderly are a family responsibility. They are not left alone, and they are rarely subject to victimization in society. Family ties and the culture in general advocate the care and protection of parents and grandparents (and all those who are the elderly). Given the large size of the extended family in Jordan, there is always someone who takes the responsibility to care for and protect the elderly.

FUTURE PROJECTIONS

The elderly population—due to the higher life expectancy—has increased and will continue to increase, but services for them are still limited in Jordan due to the small percentage of the elderly in the total population in the country and the role of the extended family in the social system. However, with increasing urbanization and development and the declining role of the extended family, public services for the elderly have begun to emerge and will increase. Apart from charitable and nonprofit organizations for caretaking, profit organizations for the aged emerged in 1992. This is a trend that has to be taken into consideration for future planning.

In spite of the Jordanian society, which has special values for respecting the elderly built in the network of its traditions and value systems, economic and social changes—due to modernization of society—require preplanning to meet the needs of its elderly population (such as Social Security, health services, and the social, physical, and psychological protection of the elderly).

These goals require both formal and informal efforts for the establishment of a council or a national committee for the elderly. Such a council or committee could be established under the umbrella of the Ministry of Social Development and could have several duties. It could educate the public about gerontology and maintain the family unit as the basic caretaker of the elderly. It could give basic services to the elderly and maintain self-dependency in order to sustain social integration, and it could change the present outlook of the Ministry of Social Development (which assists the elderly on the basis of being homeless) to consider that the elderly have special needs and demands that could affect the process of social development of the nation. The council could aid policymakers in planning a strategy for the requirements and needs of the elderly. This could follow the council's research and survey of the needs and services required for the elderly.

BIBLIOGRAPHY

Ministry of Social Development. *Annual Report, 1990.* Amman, Jordan, 1990.

National Population Commission. *Population Projections for Jordan for the Period 1990–2005.* UNFPA, 1991.

Papers presented to a seminar, entitled "Toward a Better Future for the Elderly," Amman, 18–20 February 1989.

18

MALAYSIA

Cho Kah Sin and Abdullah Malim Baginda

INTRODUCTION

The Role and Status of Elderly Persons

There is no standard or consistent definition of old age in Malaysia. The retirement age for government civil servants is still fixed at 55, while an increasingly larger number of private sector employers allow their workers to retire at 60. The government retirement age has, in turn, reinforced the popularly accepted notion today that anyone who is 55 and above is "old."

In all the major cultural traditions in Malaysia (Malay, Chinese, and Indian), the elderly are accorded great respect, particularly in the rural communities, where elderly parents hold title to land and make decisions regarding inheritance. Contemporary conceptions of filial piety continue to be linked to the notion that parents must be provided shelter and other basic needs and that, ideally, they should live with their sons and/or daughters.

What is often forgotten is that many elderly today are better educated and financially independent and prefer to live independently. The decline of coresidency has often been taken to mean that filial piety has declined with modernization. Even without coresidence, most elderly maintain close contact with their adult children (Chan and DaVanzo, 1991). Although official policy places the burden of caring for the elderly on the family, there is little in the way of supportive services in the community to prevent premature institutionalization.

Demography of Aging

The 1991 national census estimated the population of Malaysia at 18.2 million people. Actual age breakdowns from the census are still unavailable, but United Nations (UN) projections (1991) indicate a steady growth rate of persons 55 and above: 8.23% in 1990, 9.40% in 2000, 12.25% in 2010, and 16.23% of the total population by 2020. The absolute numbers of people 55 and over are projected to increase from 1.47 million in 1990 to about 4.63 million by the year 2020. In all age groups of the elderly, women constitute a larger proportion.

While total population in 2020 will be 2.07 times that of 1980, the population of elderly persons 55+ in 2020 will be 4.13 times the 1980 total (UN, 1991). Elderly women will be the fastest growing group; their numbers will be 4.37 times larger by 2020, in contrast to the males, who will be 3.89 times larger (UN, 1991). The greater increase in elderly women is partly reflected by their increased life expectancies (UN, 1991).

Among the three major communities in Malaysia, a higher proportion of the Chinese are 60 and over (6.9% in 1986) than the Malays (5.3%) and the Indians (5.4%) (UN, 1991).

Social and Economic Life

A study in 1986 (Chen et al., 1986) revealed that about 64% of the elderly sampled owned their own homes and the majority lived with adult children. The elderly tended to coreside with an adult child if they were widowed, if housing costs were high, if they had little education, and if they were in poor health (Chan and DaVanzo, 1991). Of the three races, the Indians and Chinese were more likely than the Malays to live with their children. Wealthier and more educated elderly preferred to live on their own—a trend that is likely to increase as fertility declines (hence, fewer children), education levels rise, and incomes and home ownership increase.

According to the 1980 census statistics, the literacy rate for males above age 55 was 39.6%, but only 12.6% of women in the same age group were literate (Hamid et al., 1989, p. 18). Literacy rates were higher in urban areas, particularly for younger groups of the elderly. For example, while only 39.1% of men 65 and above in 1979 were literate, 58.5% of those 55–59 were literate. Another survey (Chen et al., 1986, p. 16) showed that 56% of the elderly had not attended school, the majority being female and from the rural areas.

Most elderly Malaysians are, or have been, married. In 1980, 83.4% of elderly men 55 and above were "currently married" (compared with only 44.3% for women), with only 11.0% widowed (47.3% for women), 3.3% "never married" (1.8% for women), and 2.3% "divorced" (6.6% for women) (Hamid et al., 1989, p. 17).

Despite the official retirement age of 55, 58% of elderly persons, in a 1986 study (Chen et al. 1986), thought they should be allowed to work beyond age 55. The same study noted that most elderly persons (62%) relied on the family as their main source of income, 19% relied on work, 12% received a pension, and 2% received welfare benefits. Overall, the 1980 census showed that 62.8% of those men 55 and over worked in the labor force, compared with only 25% for the women.

Health Status

According to a survey conducted in 1988-89, about 38% of a random sample of 50+ elderly reported frailty (defined as a condition of poor health affecting daily functioning for more than a year) (Haaga et al., 1990). Not surprisingly, the study observed that frailty increased with age. An Association of Southeast Asian Nations (ASEAN) Population Program survey in 1986 (Masitah and Nazileh, 1988) reported on the major causes of hospitalization among its respondents: heart problems (19.8%), diabetes (12.9%), hypertension (12.9%), operations (10.9%), and accidents (5.9%). In yet another study, 68% of a sample of elderly persons indicated problems with sight (due to cataracts); 37% needed dentures, and 16% needed hearing aids (Chen et al., 1986).

The Formal Structure of Care of the Elderly

Government-sponsored social services are provided through the Ministry of National Unity and Social Development, which, before 1990, was known as the Ministry of Welfare Services. The change in name reflects an emerging priority to strengthen the "developmental" aspects of social welfare, that is, to evolve a capacity for anticipating social problems and to promote community and family participation, as spelled out in the 1990 National Social Welfare Policy. The policy proposes to strengthen family and community support for the elderly and states that "institutionalized help will be the last resort for the care and protection of the elderly" (Kandiah, 1992). The emphasis on community and family is consistent with the government's privatization policy, first announced in 1983, which aims to "decrease the level and scope of public spending and to allow market forces to govern economic activities" (Economic Planning Unit, 1991). How this priority will affect social welfare provision is still unclear.

The Malaysian constitution considers the provision of welfare services the joint responsibility of the state and federal governments. The federal government wholly finances services for children and families, juvenile delinquents, women and girls, the physically handicapped, and the elderly. State governments pay for public assistance (poor relief), school aid, and disaster relief.

The government also provides annual grants to selected private charities and voluntary organizations, some of which work with the elderly. These grants are often insufficient but the nongovernment organizations (NGOs) raise their own funds with varying degrees of success.

Access to government services for the elderly is given without charge, but eligibility is determined by a means test: one has to prove insolvency and/or the lack of family ties.

INCOME MAINTENANCE AND EMPLOYMENT

A number of formal and informal arrangements exist to provide elderly persons with income. This section first discusses the various forms of public and private old-age pensions.

Public Sector Employees

Only permanent employees in the public sector who have served for 25 years and more are entitled to monthly pensions upon retirement at age 55. The full pension is calculated at 50% of the last-drawn basic salary and is payable until the pensioner's death. When a pensioner dies, the surviving spouse is entitled to the full pension for a period of 150 months (12.5 years) provided the survivor does not remarry. Elderly parents of the pensioners who had been supported by them are also eligible for this pension. After the 150-month period, spouses are entitled to 70% of the pension for the rest of their lives. If the spouse of a pensioner dies, the surviving children of minority age will receive the pension. The disabled children of pensioners are also eligible for a proportion of the pension for life. In 1992, pensioners numbered about 210,000.

Private Sector Employees

Private sector employees do not come under any pension schemes when they retire. However, they can withdraw their cumulated savings from the Employees' Provident Fund (EPF), a forced savings scheme, upon reaching age 55. Under the Employees' Provident Fund Ordinance of 1951, every employer with more than one worker must register with the fund, and each employee is required to contribute 9% of his or her monthly salary to the EPF while the employer must contribute 11% of the worker's salary. The combined contributions total 20% of the wage earner's salary.

Employees may withdraw all their accumulated contributions, plus interest, once they are 55. Contributions are optional after age 55 if one continues to work. The EPF is considering alternatives to the lump-sum withdrawals at age 55 to ensure that funds are not squandered. One suggestion is that money should be paid out in installments.

In addition to the EPF, a number of large corporations operate private pension schemes modeled after government pensions and meant exclusively for their employees. Some corporations also offer large gratuities to employees, based on the number of years served. Many private sector employees from large corporations can afford to retire comfortably without the need to continue working.

Many people who work in the informal sector—self-employed farmers, fishermen, or street vendors—are not covered by the EPF or similar schemes. Proposals have been made for the EPF to include such people.

Social Security Organization

The Social Security Organization (SOCSO), established by the Employees Social Security Act of 1969, is not specifically meant for the elderly but provides some forms of income security should an individual be disabled in the course of employment. In 1990, 4.6 million workers were registered with SOCSO.

Workers who earn RM$2,000 (US $800) per month or less, along with employers, are required to make a compulsory contribution to SOCSO.

SOCSO provides many benefits, but the one most related to old-age security is a pension scheme to cover work-related injuries and death. To qualify for the scheme, a person must first be an "invalid" (inability to earn one-third of former wages because of a disability) and must also have contributed to SOCSO for at least 36 out of 60 months prior to the occurrence of disability. A pension of 50% to 65% of monthly wages, subject to a minimum of RM$171.43 (US $69) per month, is paid to those who qualify. In 1992, about 20,000 persons were served under this scheme.

Welfare Assistance

The government has a program to assist the indigent elderly, particularly those without family or kin. Eligible persons are given RM$50 (US $20) a month for the rest of their lives or until their circumstances change. The monthly stipend has been acknowledged as inadequate, and attempts have been made to advocate for a larger sum.

Special Benefits

The elderly in Malaysia enjoy a number of indirect benefits in the form of tax exemptions. For example, income from pensions is exempted from taxation. Since 1991, taxpayers who pay for their parents' medical expenses are given tax deductions of up to RM$1,000 (US $400) per year. Beginning in 1992, taxpayers who purchase supporting equipment for disabled parents are also eligible for a RM$3,000 (US $1,200) tax exemption. Estate duties were abolished in 1992. Many charitable organizations, including those catering to the elderly, continue to enjoy tax-exempt status.

Housing subsidies and food stamp programs for elderly persons do not exist, but discounts for air (50%) and rail (40%) travel are available for people aged 55 and over.

Employment Opportunities

Although the retirement age is 55, exceptions are made. The vast majority of retirees will be unemployed at 55, even if they prefer to continue working. Retraining to help them find other kinds of work does not exist, but very limited placement services (through a public employment exchange or the Expertise Resource Association) are available.

A number of private sector corporations have begun retirement preparation courses for their employees. Some of these courses include a segment on future employment opportunities and point out the various options available for work.

Most self-employed workers in the informal sector continue working for as long as it is necessary and they are capable of working. They stop only if their children are able to work and support them. This group is most in need of some form of old-age security (presently received only through the family).

Informal Social Security

The family and community remain the bedrock of Social Security for most elderly persons who have not worked in the formal sector. One study (Chen et al., 1986) noted that almost two-thirds of respondents had worked as unskilled laborers, thus suggesting that they were outside the formal sector. Predictably, about 62% said that family members were the main source of income (14% indicated pensions and/or EPF; 20% had continued working). These findings suggest that old-age security is intimately linked to family resources, especially for those who have not worked in the formal sector. As more people enter the formal sector to take up wage employment, we may expect increasing proportions of future cohorts of elderly persons to be protected by the formal Social Security system.

HEALTH CARE SERVICES

Overview

The Ministry of Health is the primary provider of health services in Malaysia. In 1986, it owned 86% of all hospital beds in the country and operated a network of outpatient facilities that extended even into remote rural areas. Medical services are almost completely subsidized; users pay only a token fee. On the whole, it is reasonable to say that "the government health care delivery system ... is still relatively egalitarian and accessible to the poor and disadvantaged" (Chee, 1990, p. 87). Geriatric medical facilities do not presently exist, although the Ministry of Health plans to train geriatric specialists. A number of other government agencies also provide medical services, most notably, the Ministry of Education, which operates two teaching hospitals.

The privately run, for-profit health care sector has seen tremendous growth since the the 1950s. The percentage of doctors practicing in the private sector increased from 53.6% in 1984 to 58.4% in 1986. In 1980, 4.7% of all hospital beds were in the private sector; by 1986 it was 13.6% (Chee, 1990). Largely available in the cities, fee-for-service medical care is often preferred by the relatively wealthier urban dwellers.

An informal sector in medical care comprises practitioners of traditional medicine like the Malay *bomohs,* Chinese *sinsehs,* and Indian Ayurvedic doctors. Though private, the fees are inexpensive and are particularly affordable for the poor and the rural dwellers. Quality control is a major concern, however, because the sector is completely unregulated.

An emerging trend in national policy is to "privatize" publicly sponsored services, resulting in the concern that health services may be privatized and allowed to operate unsubsidized, on a fee-for-service basis. Although 12 hospitals were proposed for privatization in 1991, it is not expected to happen until after 1996 (Economic Planning Unit, 1991).

In 1991, the government, acting to promote a "caring society," allowed a tax deduction of RM$1,000 (US $400) for medical expenses provided to an elderly person by the taxpayer.

Acute Care Services

Government acute care services are provided mostly through a network of hospitals, specialist centers, polyclinics, health centers, and airborne medical services. Hospitals take up the largest proportion of the Health Ministry's budget. There are four types of hospitals: (1) district hospitals (found in small towns); (2) general hospitals (located in the state capitals), which render comprehensive specialist care; (3) specialist care hospitals (e.g., the National Heart Treatment Center); and (4) teaching hospital complexes (administered by the Education Ministry). Private hospitals account for only about 14% of the 30,000 hospital beds available in 1986.

Chronic Care Facilities

People with chronic medical conditions (including elderly persons) requiring regular follow-up, monitoring, and treatment can go to government outpatient clinics or private clinics. More expensive, private clinics are often preferred, especially in the urban areas, because the wait is shorter. The government's outpatient facilities include a network of health centers, midwife clinics, and traveling dispensaries.

Nursing Homes

Most nursing homes are for-profit enterprises that register as businesses and are regulated by neither the Department of Health nor the Department of Welfare. Generally set up by doctors or nurses and staffed with trained or untrained nursing aides, they provide nursing care for chronically ill or disabled persons, the majority of whom are elderly. The fees range from RM$500–RM$1,500 (US $200–600), which is beyond the reach of most except the middle class. The Department of Welfare is drafting legislation to regulate these homes.

Home Nursing Services

Three types of home nursing services now exist: publicly funded, volunteer, and private for-profit services. A government-sponsored home nursing program already exists to promote maternal and child health in remote areas. Although it does not presently serve elderly persons, the program is being adapted to reach the frail elderly.

Home nursing care is also available from two volunteer organizations without charge (or only at nominal charge for those who can afford). The Rotary Club, a service organization, started the Kuala Lumpur Home Nursing Service Association in 1970 and funded its activities for about four years. The association is now independent of the Rotary Club and raises its own funds. The service is available only in the Kuala Lumpur metropolitan area, and referrals mostly come from nearby hospitals. More recently (in 1992), the St. John's Ambulance initiated a home nursing service to provide nursing care to the disabled and persons who are chronically ill in their homes (many of whom are elderly) and to teach basic nursing skills to caregivers.

Several private nursing agencies in the major urban areas serve the sick and disabled in their own homes. The charges are expensive, and few can afford these services. Likewise, some physiotherapists provide their services in the home but charge expensive hourly fees.

Hospice Services

Government-sponsored hospice services for the terminally ill do not now exist. However, the government has allocated funds in the current five-year development plan (the Sixth Malaysia Plan, 1991–95) to renovate an existing welfare home into a hospice for the terminally ill.

An innovative NGO effort to provide community-based hospice services was launched in October 1992. Staffed mostly by volunteer doctors, nurses, and social workers, this service is intended to provide basic nursing care and counseling to dying persons and their caregivers without charge. It receives referrals from hospitals in the Kuala Lumpur area.

Chinese clan houses formerly provided shelter to those who were dying, usually elderly members who were without family or kin. A modern variant of these "death houses" provides shelter for a fee to those who are dying, and several can be found in Kuala Lumpur.

Health services in Malaysia are comprehensive and generally accessible but tend to be concentrated in hospitals. Supportive services to assist those with chronic conditions or disability are underdeveloped and will be in greater demand as the population age 65 and above increases. NGOs have begun to fill the need for community support services, but such efforts can have only limited impact without the systematic commitment of government resources.

HOUSING RESOURCES

A national housing policy does not yet exist in Malaysia in 1992, much less one for elderly persons. Elderly persons do not receive special preference for the purchase of homes, whether built by the private or public sectors. Despite the lack of a special policy to promote home ownership among the elderly, the proportion of elderly persons who own homes is high. One survey found that as many as 64% of elderly persons owned the homes in which they lived (Chen et al., 1986). Home ownership will increase for future cohorts of the elderly, largely as a consequence of the greater availability of housing stock and government policy to promote low-cost housing.

Elderly with Shelter Needs

About 72% of all Malaysians live in a family; the majority (57%) of elderly persons live in households of four or more people (Andrews et al., 1986 p. 55), and the more children they have, the more likely that they will live with their children. The Chinese elderly are most likely to live with their children, while rural Malays are least likely to do so (Chen et al., 1986). If access to shelter depends on one's ties to family, then those in need of institutional shelter are likely to be single, widowed, or childless. One study showed that almost 77% of inmates in these government welfare homes were single or widowed (Normah et al., 1986, p. 32).

Many of the homes for the elderly, popularly known as "old folks' homes," had their origins during the colonial period (before 1957) and primarily served Chinese and Indian immigrants who did not have family or kin upon whom to depend. Although the largest homes are government-run, others have been established by charitable, nonprofit agencies and, more recently, by private, for-profit companies.

Government Homes

The government provides shelter for indigent elderly persons through two of its agencies: the Department of Welfare and the Ministry of Rural Development. The Department of Welfare runs nine homes around the country, which accommodate up to 2,550 persons. Admission is on a means-tested basis: applicants must prove that they are insolvent and have no family or kin. Applicants must be at least 60 to qualify and be able-bodied and capable of self-care. Residents are given meals, clothing, counseling, medical care, and access to religious and recreational facilities and are expected to perform housekeeping chores. All expenses are fully borne by the federal government.

Since 1980, the Ministry of Rural Development has provided rudimentary homes for some rural elderly. Each home (or *pondok*) accommodates about 5–20 persons. The need for a *pondok* is established by the village head, who submits an application to the ministry. If approved, a grant is provided for construction costs. Volunteers from the village help construct the *pondok* and later donate food or clothing to the residents. The Ministry of Rural Development generally provides only the initial construction grant; maintenance costs are borne by the local community with assistance from the Department of Welfare. In 1991, a total of 300 persons lived in 30 of these *pondoks* all over the country.

Charity Homes (Volunteer Organizations)

Sponsored by religious charities and the Central Welfare Council, charity homes provide shelter, clothing, and food without charge and accept only indigent elderly persons who have no one to care for them. Waiting lists for these homes are very long. About 71 homes (housing 2,368 persons) receive yearly grants from the Department of Welfare. Such grants are insufficient, and most must raise funds through public appeals or receive funding from a parent church organization (like the Catholic church).

Congregate and Retirement Housing

Congregate housing and retirement communities do not seem commercially viable, and a specialized housing market to cater to the housing needs of the elderly has not emerged. The government has no special programs to promote such forms of housing.

Community Services

Formalized friendly visitor service, shopping service, and maintenance and home repair service do not exist for elderly persons. The elderly, of course, benefit from such services informally provided by friends, relatives, or members from their place of worship. Some shops deliver to the home, a service available to everyone and not just the elderly.

Financial and Tax Benefits

Economic incentives (like tax benefits) to help elderly persons maintain independent living in the community do not exist.

Shelter in Old Age

Access to housing in Malaysia depends on one's ties to family and earning capacity during one's working life. A person who has not worked or married will be least able to find shelter security in old age. With a bouyant national economy, low unemployment rates, and an even greater government sponsorship of low-cost housing for the general population, most cohorts maturing into old age in the next several decades will enjoy unprecedented levels of home ownership.

SUPPORTIVE SERVICES

Information and Referral Services

Four government organizations can perform the referral function most effectively in the Malaysian context: (1) the Department of Social Welfare; (2) the social work departments of major hospitals; (3) the Village Development and Security Committees; and (4) the neighborhood associations (Rukun Tetangga).

The Department of Social Welfare, with its staff of social workers and branch offices throughout the country, is the natural referral point. It is widely perceived as the main resource for welfare matters in the country, has extensive contacts with volunteer welfare groups, and is also the main vehicle for dispensing government welfare assistance. Hospital social work departments are another reliable and professional referral source, although such a service is now limited to the two or three largest hospitals in the country. Clearly there is great potential for further developing referral services in this setting.

At the village level, the Village Development and Security Committees, led by the village headman, have extensive connections with government agencies and programs and, thus, are best able to offer information on services available. People who live in urban areas can obtain information from the committees of the neigborhood associations, known as Rukun Tetangga.

Many of the NGOs concerned with elderly affairs have the information and contacts to make referrals, but few people besides their own membership think of asking them. Some of these organizations are the Malaysian Government Pensioners' Association and its state branches, the Expertise Resource Association, the Senior Citizens' Clubs, USIAMAS (Golden Age), Gerontological Association of Malaysia, and the Home Nursing Association.

Nutrition

Meals-on-wheels services or congregate meal services do not exist. Having cooked meals delivered daily to the home for a fee is a common practice for many families, and elderly persons can avail themselves of such a service if the need arises. However, most elderly persons live with family members and have their meals, along with other needs, provided for by the family. In most cases, the need for cooked meals does not arise.

Respite Care and Homemaker Services

Homemaker services, assistance with shopping and chores, friendly visitors, and respite care programs are available informally from family members, relatives, neighbors, and friends. Formal provision of such services by paid or volunteer workers does not exist. A recent study of disabled elderly persons

(Abdullah and Cho, 1991) suggests that most caregivers are not interested in respite care, friendly visitor programs, or help with chores since most live in large households where labor for the caring chores is widely available and rotated.

Day-Care Services

A day-care center for stroke rehabilitation now operates in Kuala Lumpur, the capital city. Funded originally by the Rotary Club, it is now operated by PERKIM, a Muslim welfare organization. Some services provided include physiotherapy, nursing care, and congregate meals. Transportation to and from the elderly person's home is also provided. Charges vary with ability to pay.

The USIAMAS (or Golden Age) organization, a local affiliate of HelpAge International, plans to start a day-care center in Kuala Lumpur. The new center, which is cosponsored by the Kuala Lumpur City Hall, is expected to become operational in early 1993. Drawing on volunteers who are retirees, it plans to provide physiotherapy, recreational activities, and a home nursing service.

Mental Health Services

On the whole, mental health services are poorly developed and inadequate. The number of trained psychologists, psychiatrists, social workers, and counselors in the country is very inadequate, even if inpatient and outpatient psychiatric care is available in all general hospitals. No geriatric mental health service exists. It is likely that the appearance of mental illness in an elderly person will be dismissed by family members as senility, and thus medical help will not be sought.

LEISURE-TIME RESOURCES

Volunteers

A study from 1984–85 (Chen et al., 1986) reports that only a quarter of its sample of elderly persons were members of social organizations. Of these, the majority (89%) said they rarely participated in the activities of the social organizations. Only 4% of the total sample were members of a group or association for elderly persons. This profile suggests minimal involvement in formal organizations and volunteer work.

There is a tendency for lifelong involvement in volunteer work to ebb after retirement, and many stop altogether upon reaching 60. Nonetheless, the opportunities for voluntary work abound, with some specifically meant for the elderly.

There is a great variety of registered voluntary organizations in Malaysia, and there are no age limits imposed on membership. People normally get involved in their prime and continue to be active as they grow older. Such persons eventually take on leadership positions in the organization after they retire. There is a tendency, out of deference, to offer such positions to elderly persons.

Voluntary Organizations

Several organizations cater to the elderly, and the elderly are especially encouraged to join them. The Senior Citizens' Clubs are found in most states and largely cater to the recreational needs of middle-class urban retirees and their spouses. Members organize popular activities such as dancing, outings, cooking lessons, aerobics, t'ai chi, and group tours. The nine member clubs also organize charity drives to secure donations for other welfare organizations.

The Expertise Resource Association of Kuala Lumpur offers technical and professional expertise on a voluntary basis and also serves as an employment referral service for retired professionals. Most of its members, though elderly, are still very active in their respective professions.

USIAMAS (or Golden Age), the local affiliate of HelpAge International, is in the process of establishing a day-care center, which is expected to open early in 1994. It plans to recruit retired persons as volunteers for its many service projects.

Other forms of community involvement, though not especially meant for the elderly, are open to them. The study cited earlier (Chen et al., 1986) also indicated that the majority of Malays who participate in social organizations are members of UMNO (United Malays National Organization), the national Malay political party in Malaysia, which also serves as a convenient vehicle for social activities, particularly in the rural areas, where such opportunities are few. The mosque also serves as a social gathering place for Muslim males, besides being a place for prayer and study. The majority of Chinese who are members of a social organization hold membership in a clan or dialect association.

All these activities serve an important socialization function, particularly those sponsored by the Senior Citizens Clubs, the national Malay party, and the mosques. These social activities give participants opportunities to interact among peers from similar religious and ethnic backgrounds, to form and strengthen friendships, and to share common concerns.

Recreation

Traditional forms of recreation are still found in many rural areas, including kite flying, top spinning, and the martial arts. The practice of martial arts (like *silat* among the Malays and t'ai chi or kung fu among the Chinese), the art of shadow play (*wayang kulit*), and the Chinese operas are often passed on from the older generation to the young, thus strengthening the ties between them. The importance of such a process for fostering respect for the elderly cannot be overemphasized. Unfortunately, such opportunities for collaboration and learning between the generations have diminished, particularly in urban areas, where passive forms of modern entertainment (like television and videocassettes) now dominate.

Religious Activities

Many elderly persons seem more inclined toward religion once they retire, and they flock to the many study courses and discussion groups in mosques, temples, and churches or in their own homes. In many instances the elderly are seen to take natural leadership roles in such classes or other activities. The places of worship also double as important places for social interaction and provide important opportunities for companionship and the forming of friendships for all races.

Education

Education opportunities in the form of adult or continuing education courses generally do not exist in Malaysia. None of the universities in the country conduct special programs for the elderly, whether in the form of degree or nondegree programs. Efforts to promote educational opportunities for the elderly have been made by some concerned individuals and organizations, but so far without success.

Informal, Family-Based Social Activities

Although formal activities outside the family are beginning to develop in the country, the majority of the elderly spend their leisure hours in family activities—domestic chores, child care, social visits among relatives, and family functions. In the World Health Organization (WHO) study mentioned earlier (Chen et al., 1986), up to 54% of the respondents—especially the women—said they provide care to their grandchildren. Only 17% of the elderly respondents complained that they did not see enough of family members and friends; a mere 7% said they did not know people well enough to visit them. Overall, a pattern emerges to suggest that much of their leisure time is overwhelmingly spent with family activities, even if involvement in formal social activities seems minimal.

ADVOCACY AND PROTECTION

Advocacy Services

Legal Aid

The Ministry of Justice, through its network of Legal Aid Bureaus established in all 13 state capitals, provides free legal advice and legal representation to the poor. The service is established by the Legal Aid Act of 1971. Rural inhabitants are served by the Legal Aid Rural Counseling Service, which sends its staff into rural areas to dispense advice. The Malaysian Bar Council, a lawyers' association, also provides a similar service. Eligibility in both cases is solely determined by a means test and is open to any person, including elderly persons, who qualify. Legal aid services that specifically target elderly persons do not exist.

Advocacy Organizations

USIAMAS (Golden Age), established in 1991, is a direct service and advocacy organization dedicated to improving and providing care for elderly persons. Apart from day-care services, the organization also conducts numerous training courses for institutional care providers (private and public) to upgrade the standard of nursing and medical care in the country. Another important activity of USIAMAS is its course on preparation for retirement. The service provides counseling to elderly persons and helps them cope with retirement (usually at age 55), particularly with specific concerns like managing money, time, health, family, and relationships.

The Malaysian Pensioners' Association had about 10,000 members in 1992, all of whom were former civil servants who retired at age 55. The association represents the interests of about 210,000 persons receiving pensions. Apart from being concerned about the timely arrival of pension checks, in 1991 the association started an employment service to help its members find part-time work, and it has attempted to get discounts (particularly for travel and the purchase of medicines) for members.

The Gerontological Association of Malaysia was set up in 1991 to promote research and to raise awareness about the problems of elderly persons. It is still very new, but it is quite likely to be an important forum for advocating policy changes that will affect elderly persons, particularly through its roles as a sponsor of policy-relevant research and also as a catalyst for mobilizing public opinion.

The Expertise Resource Association (ERA), established in 1987, had about 200 members in 1992, most of whom were professionals but not all of whom were elderly. Its stated objectives are to promote adult education opportunities for elderly persons, as well as employment among retired professionals. The association has also made attempts to obtain special concessions for rail and air travel.

All nine chapters of the Senior Citizens' Associations have been amalgamated into the National Council of Senior Citizens' Organizations, Malaysia, which is headed by a president. Apart from social and recreational activities, the National Council attempts to advocate for issues concerning the elderly and liaises with the government.

The Ministry of National Unity and Social Development is responsible for running all government-sponsored homes for the elderly in Malaysia. It is required to appoint a "board of visitors," constituted of prominent members of the community—usually government servants and business leaders—to ensure that the homes meet the standards prescribed by law. The boards are empowered to make surprise visits and to bring deficiencies to the attention of the minister and the director-general. In theory at least, the boards can be a very potent instrument to ensure quality care.

Until 1992, for-profit nursing homes and those run by voluntary organizations—except for those that receive some government funding—were not subject to the laws or government supervision. A much-needed Care Center Act, drafted by the Ministry of National Unity and Social Development, was passed by Parliament in 1993 but has not yet been implemented. The act will provide for the registration, control, and inspection of all residential care centers, including those for the elderly, and govern such aspects as staffing, diets, opportunities for recreation, safety, and sanitation. In the meantime, nursing homes can operate as long as they satisfy minimum safety regulations required by the local or municipal authorities.

Protective Services

Special services to safeguard the interests of severely frail and/or mentally incompetent elderly persons do not exist, but it is conceivable that the existing legal aid services could take up such cases in the course of their work.

Elderly persons who are destitute and without family members are especially eligible for admission to government and volunteer welfare homes. Homeless persons who are elderly are given priority in admission to the government homes.

On the whole, although special, formalized advocacy and protection services are lacking, many organizations working with the elderly, from the grass-roots level to government boards, have the potential to take up a larger advocacy role for vulnerable elderly persons. The constraint may be that such organizations tend to have specific interests and constituencies that will likely limit the kinds of issues they decide to take up.

FUTURE PROJECTIONS

Formally organized services for elderly persons are still underdeveloped and inadequate in Malaysia, in part because the family continues to meet most of the needs of elderly persons. Official policy continues to emphasize the importance of the family's taking up the burden of providing for dependents, whether young or old, and an expansion of institutional facilities is unlikely in the foreseeable future. In all likelihood, the family will be made to bear an even greater burden in caring for the elderly, especially without a highly developed formal sector of care. Can the family cope?

There are already signs that the family institution may not be suited for the caring role. The increasing numbers of women entering the work force, declining household size, and increase in the proportion of nuclear families contribute to undermine the family's capacity to care for the elderly. As longevity increases, the older elderly (the majority of whom will be widowed women) will also develop disabilities and other chronic health conditions that will demand intensive and skilled care. Unless family care is supplemented with a range of formal services, it is unlikely that it will be able to meet the challenge.

To view future developments more optimistically, later cohorts of elderly will be more educated, and greater numbers will be covered by pensions and other retirement schemes. They will have less need for housing and income security—two main foundations of old-age security—but the need for community-based health services will probably be greatest. The family can provide housing, companionship, food, and income security, but even the most dedicated families cannot provide medical care without proper training.

The development of formal services must be specifically planned to strengthen the family role and to anticipate some of the needs for chronic care that many elderly will increasingly need. The first priority must be to provide more comprehensive, health-related, community-based services like day care, respite care, home nursing services, and day hospitals. A fledgling network of day-care services already exists but needs more extensive development. The frail elderly should have more than a "choice" between the family or institutionalization; with a range of intermediate care services, the family role will be very much strengthened, and the frail elderly will be better able to remain independent in the community.

BIBLIOGRAPHY

Abdullah, Baginda, and Cho, K. 1991. "Family care of the frail elderly in urban Malaysia." Paper presented at the International Conference on the Care of the Elderly, Hong Kong.
Andrews, Gary R., Esterman, Adrian J., Braunack-Mayer, Annette J., and Rungie, Cam M. 1986. *Aging in the Western Pacific.* Manila: World Health Organization.
Chan, A., and DaVanzo, J. 1991. "Living arrangements of older Malaysians." Paper presented at the 1991 annual meeting of the Population Association of America, Washington, D.C.
Chan, K. E. 1991. "Population aging and the aged in Malaysia: Patterns, prospects and problems." Paper presented at the Seminar Series on Aging and Public Policy, Kuala Lumpur: Institute of Strategic and International Studies.
Chee, H. L. 1990. *Health and Health Care in Malaysia.* Kuala Lumpur: Institute for Advanced Studies, University of Malaya.
Chen, A. J., and Jones, G. 1989. *Aging in ASEAN: Its Socioeconomic Consequences.* Singapore: Institute of Southeast Asian Studies.
Chen, Paul, Andrews, G. R., Josef, R., Chan, K. E., and Arokiasamy, J. T. 1986. *Health and Aging in Malaysia.* Kuala Lumpur: n.p.
Economic Planning Unit. 1991. *Privatization Masterplan.* Kuala Lumpur: Prime Minister's Department.

Haaga, John, Peterson, Christine, DaVanzo, Julie, Mengchee Lee, Sharon. 1990. "Health status and family support of older Malaysians." Paper presented at the annual meeting of the Population Association of America, Toronto.

Kamid, Arshat, Tan, P. C., and Tey, N. P. 1989. *The Aging of Population in Malaysia.* Asian Population Studies Series. No. 96. Bangkok: Economic and Social Commission for Asia and the Pacific.

Kandiah, M. 1992. "The national social welfare policy." In K. Cho, and S. Ismail (eds.), *Caring Society: Emerging Issues and Future Directions.* Kuala Lumpur: Institute of Strategic and International Studies.

Masitah, M. Y., and Nazileh, R. 1988. *Malaysia Country Report on Socioeconomic Consequences of the Aging of Population Survey, 1986.* Kuala Lumpur: National Population and Family Development Board.

Normah, Mohd Dali, Lau, T. K., and Wahid, Abu Bakar. 1986. *A Study on the Welfare And Recipients in Malaysia.* Kuala Lumpur: n.p.

Sushama, P. C. 1985. "Malaysia." In J. Dixon and S. K. Hyung (eds.), *Social Welfare in Asia.* Beckenham, UK: Croom Helm.

United Nations. 1991. *Sex and Age Distributions of Population.* New York: United Nations.

19

MALTA

Marisa Scerri and Mario D. Garrett

INTRODUCTION

The Role of the Elderly

The island of Malta and its sister island of Gozo are cradled between North Africa and Southern Europe in the center of the Mediterranean. From the dawn of civilization in Malta around 4,000 B.C., this geography has had a direct influence on the cultural heritage of the Maltese archipelago. With a combined landmass of 316 square kilometers and a population of just over 358,000, Malta has become known as an island with more history than land. With a juxtaposition of Arabic architecture and language, Roman Catholic religion, and European bureaucracy, various cultural strands are woven together on this crossroads of the Mediterranean to produce a unique blend of social life (Laspina, 1966).

The influence of this geographic setting, together with its miniature size and population, has resulted in a social and cultural cohesiveness among its inhabitants, which is not so apparent to the near-million tourists who visit this limestone-colored land. Such uniqueness within a micro state is not easily understood or explained, especially when we attempt to focus on the role of elderly people, since this role traverses sociocultural, historic, and economic boundaries.

If we look at the overall dynamics, however, we find that the main factors that influence the role of the elderly in Malta are the widespread following of the Roman Catholic religion and the paternal system of administration inherited from the Knights of Saint John (1530–1798) and further developed under British colonial rule (1800–1964). This influence has permeated the social fabric of Malta and has had a direct bearing on the role of, and services for, the elderly (Pirotta, 1991).

Definition of Old Age

In step with the British system of bureaucracy, the definition of old age in Malta is primarily an administrative one, based on the arbitrary retirement age of 60 years for females and 61 for males. Although there is a certain latitude to this retirement ceiling, the large majority of workers are obliged to retire at this age.

There is a growing acceptance, however, that this obligation will become less strictly enforced. In 1992, an amendment to the Social Security Act was introduced that made it less difficult for people to work after retirement by giving pensioners the right to indulge in economically gainful activity without forfeiting the right to their contributory pensions (White Paper, 1992). Nevertheless, for the majority of workers, this arbitrary age for retirement still dictates the definition of elderly to mean those who are over 60 years of age for both males and females.

Perception of the Elderly

With a consistently low unemployment level and with workers' maintaining multiple jobs, paid employment in Malta not only is a fiscal activity but also determines social status. It is of very little surprise, therefore, that the loss of such activity has complex personal repercussions. Nonetheless, very little empirical data exist on the experiences and conditions of retirees who, together with elderly women, seem to occupy a low priority in empirical research concerns in Malta.

From anecdotal sources, the commonly held assumption is that elderly people are respected and valued by the family and within society. Nevertheless, this does not explain the mushrooming demand for community homes and long-term nursing homes for the elderly.

In a small-sample (n = 932) survey on institutionalized elderly conducted in 1988 by Caritas Malta, it was reported that as high as 24% of the elderly entered an institution because their children could not look after them. A small but significant proportion (2%) reported that it was because their children abandoned them, while 5% indicated that it was because their children needed their house. Only 18% reported entering the institution because of an illness. Such indications from this survey make grim reading, especially in a society dominated by a long Catholic tradition (*Il-Gens,* 1988). The reality unfolds as being unarguably more complex and less easily explained.

Demographic Characteristics of the Elderly

The most recent census in Malta was held in 1985 (Central Office of Statistics, 1986). A secondary analysis study was performed in 1987 that focused specifically on the elderly population (Ministry of Social Policy, 1989). This special study adjusted the census data for the year 1987, using linear projections on the basis of the population growth rate. Specific information in this section is ob-

Table 19.1
General Demographic Statistics in Malta

	1950	1990	2025
Total Population	312,000	353,000	389,000
Elderly Population (60+)	29,000	52,000	95,000
Proportion (%) elderly population (60+)	9.2	14.7	24.4
Young population (under 15)	109,000	82,000	70,000
Proportion (%) young population (under 15)	34.9	23.2	17.9
Urban population	191,000	307,000	361,000
Population density (per sq. km.)	987	1,117	1,230
Median age of the population (in years)	23.7	33.0	41.2
Average annual rate of population growth (%)	0.1	0.4	0.0
Crude birthrate (per 1,000 persons)	29.3	13.4	11.3
Crude death rate (per 1,000 persons)	10.1	9.3	11.1
Total fertility rate (per woman)	4.1	1.8	1.9
Infant mortality rate (per 100 live births)	75	9	5
Life expectancy at birth for males (in years)	64.2	72.0	76.2
Life expentancy at birth for females (in years)	67.7	75.7	80.6
Life expectancy at birth for both sexes (in years)	65.9	73.8	78.3
Life expectancy for males at 60 (in years)*	16.0	17.3	17.5
Life expectancy for females at 60 (in years)*	16.1	22.6	24.7
Life expectancy for males at 65 (in years)*	14.5	14.9	14.5
Life expectancy for females at 65 (in years)*	14.0	20.5	22.2
Life expectancy for males at 70 (in years)*	13.6	12.5	13.6
Life expectancy for females at 70 (in years)*	12.0	18.6	19.8
Life expectancy for males at 75 (in years)*	14.5	14.5	14.5
Life expectancy for females at 75 (in years)*	10.3	17.0	20.7

*M. Garrett using UN Population Estimates, 1988 Revision (Garrett, 1990).
Source: UN Demographic Projection and Estimates, 1950–2025 1989.

tained from this secondary analysis of 1987. However, for general demographic indicators, the figures reported here refer to the United Nations (UN) population statistics, since this source might provide a more reliable comparative base (United Nations [UN], 1989).

Of interest in Table 19.1 is the shift of the Maltese population from a young population to an old population. This can be seen very clearly when we look at the changing proportion of the population of those over 60 years of age and of those under 15, from 1990 to 2025. This demographic change will radically influence the method of financing services for elderly people since the potential work force will diminish in size, with contributions similarly diminishing.

Level of Education

From the 1987 secondary census analysis, 58.3% of the elderly population left school at the primary stage, while 23.8% never attended school. With only 13.4% having gone to secondary school and 1.2% being graduates, it is not surprising that the illiteracy level is high, with 30% of elderly males and 33% of elderly females reported as illiterate in the census of 1985. As expected, regional variations exist, with agricultural areas reporting a higher coefficient value for illiteracy (Ministry of Social Policy, 1989).

Since age is positively correlated with less formal education, it is likely that this relates to a historic artifact whereby older people were less likely to be formally educated during their youth than the more recently old. Through the provision of state-funded compulsory education in 1947 and the provision of free university education in 1972, the emerging elderly population is expected to be much better educated by the year 2010.

Living Arrangements

The 1987 secondary census analysis indicated that 54.1% of elderly people live in terraced houses (the most prevalent general habitat), with 20.2% in maisonette accommodations. Within these structures, 17.9% of the elderly live on their own, while 36.7% and 22%, respectively, live in two- and three-person households. Out of these, 54.2% live in owner-occupied accommodations while 42.9% live in rented accommodations.

From this study, out of 2,109 households with one or more elderly persons, 4% have no stove, refrigerator, washing machine, telephone, television, or car. This figure rises to 11.1% for single-person households, while 19.1% have a stove, refrigerator, washing machine, telephone, television, or car (Ministry of Social Policy, 1989).

Marital Status

From the 1987 secondary census analysis, the majority of elderly people are married (55%), with 25% widowed, 19% single, and 1% separated or divorced. As expected, widowhood increases with age group.

Labor Force Participation

The average age for the population in 1990 was 33 years, with a life expectancy at birth of 73.8 years for both sexes. However, this figure hides the dynamic changes in the population structure, in particular, the effect of the baby boomers (1945–65), which climaxed in 1965. We expect, therefore, that this average age, together with the number and proportion of elderly people, will climax in 2025. In the interim period, the potential labor force population has reached an apex, and has contributed to the sustained economic growth of the Maltese economy, which has shown an average annual gross national product growth rate from 1965 to 1988 of 7.4%. After Botswana, this is the highest recorded rate of growth for all countries in the world (World Bank, 1990). More recent, unpublished figures indicate that this rate of growth is on the increase.

Services for the elderly are directly influenced by the labor participation rate of women. With easier accessibility to education and more opportunities for employment, Malta is witnessing an increased participation of females in the labor market (Central Office of Statistics, 1986).

Health Status

In keeping with results from international surveys, elderly people in Malta are, in general, in good health and live independent lives. In a recent unpublished survey, 72% of respondents reported feeling healthy (Delia, 1992), a proportion similar to another survey in 1980, when 79% reported feeling healthy (Delia, 1982). Nevertheless, 83% reported suffering from nondebilitating illnesses, with only 17% reporting that they did not suffer from any illness (Delia, 1992). In a small-sample study (n = 148), Camilleri reported that half the sample were on some medication, while a third took vitamin supplements (Camilleri, 1990).

Economic Characteristics

The primary source of income for the elderly is their state pension allowance, which covers all retirees in Malta. The results from an unpublished report, however, indicate that 46% of respondents reported additionally benefiting from a British Service pension, while 3.9% reported being in employment, with 3% receiving benefits from rents and 11% earning interest from their capital. In comparison with these additional sources of income, only 0.3% reported having a separate private pension (Delia, 1992).

Interesting results emerge when we compare similar surveys carried out at two different time periods. In a 1980 survey (Delia, 1982), 77% of respondents reported that their income was sufficient to cover their needs, whereas only 19% reported that they required additional assistance. In contrast, in the 1990 survey, only 21% of the respondents reported that their income was sufficient, with 79% reporting that their income was inadequate to satisfy their needs and 14% reporting that they received financial help from their family to make ends meet (Delia, 1992).

The mean weekly income in 1980 was $68, ranging from $60 to $121, depending on the marital status and educational attainment of the beneficiary. Expenditure patterns, as would be expected, also varied. Preliminary analysis from the 1990 survey shows that for private car owners, the average weekly expenditure for the elderly was $114, compared with $94 for non-car owners. Out of this income, 49% or 51%, respectively, is spent on food; 24% or 27% on clothing, leisure, drinking, and smoking; 13% or 16% on housing; 5% on health for both categories; and 5% on car maintenance and 1% on public transport (for non-car owners).

The Formal Structure of Care of the Elderly

Under the Knights of Saint John (1530–1798), Malta developed an extensive system of administration and an established practice of paternalism in which the

Knights were seen, and acted, as the "fathers" of the people, controlling not only the economic and military concerns but also the social welfare of the people.

Recent governments have not only inherited this need and demand by the people but also have learned to make full use of such expectations in their electioneering and style of government. (Two thousand voters can elect a politician in parliament; such personal contact and paternalism are not only feasible but necessary.)

As a result, most of the services currently available for elderly citizens are provided by the government and, to a lesser but significant extent, by religious and voluntary organizations. Nevertheless, the development of private services for the elderly requires further evaluation in future research.

The government provides Social Security provisions, free health schemes, home care/help service, Telecare service, community homes, social groups, and day excursions for the elderly, while charitable, nonprofit, and religious institutions run services such as meals-on-wheels, community and nursing homes, community nursing, good neighbor schemes, and social clubs.

Hospitals and Specialized Geriatric Residences

The largest institution run by the government is Saint Vincent de Paule Residence (SVPR), with an average of 1,121 beds (which went down to 1,007 functional beds in 1992, due to structural work in some special wards and to an implicit policy to minimize the number of residents at this institution). This complex, which was originally built in 1892 (Cassar, 1956), saw a radical refurbishment program in the late 1980s, with Victorian wards being partitioned into smaller units to cater for more specialized treatment according to the functional level of the patients. An admission and assessment unit and physiotherapy and occupational therapy units were also developed in 1989. With an approximate annual intake of 308 elderly (for 1990), of whom 60% were females, this complex remains the main institution for elderly Maltese. A day clinic service provides care for around 422 patients annually.

Zammit Clapp Hospital opened in 1991 as an acute and rehabilitation geriatric hospital, housing a day hospital and physiotherapy and occupational therapy departments. Zammit Clapp Hospital is spatially and administratively separate from St. Lukes General Hospital, and promises a new philosophy of geriatric care. With a capital expenditure in excess of $4.5 million, over 200 casual and full-time staff, and 35 functional beds, this hospital is spearheading geriatric medicine in Malta.

A small nursing unit is the Tal-Ferha Estate at Gharghur, which caters to surviving elderly victims of leprosy. This unit, which is totally funded by the government, serves the five elderly survivors of this condition, now totally eradicated in Malta.

Other general hospital services include Saint Lukes General Hospital, Boffa Hospital, Gozo General Hospital, and Mount Carmel Psychiatric Hospital. Although these are general hospitals, we find that a significant proportion of their clientele is elderly. Zammit Clapp Hospital could have relieved St. Lukes General Hospital of the burden of long-term-stay elderly patients and provided specialized care and rehabilitation to a larger elderly population, but it was designed for a different function.

In addition, a hospice at St. Michael in Hamrun does not specifically cater to elderly patients, but of its total of 21 patients, 15 are elderly.

Community Homes for the Elderly

A growing demand for specialized housing facilities for the elderly has been mirrored by a similar burgeoning provision of such community homes by government and religious institutions.

Each application to government homes is evaluated by a panel under the auspices of the Parliamentary Secretariat for the Care of the Elderly. The main criteria is that potential applicants must be independent (but not wheelchair-bound) and that they do not require regular nursing care. Once the resident is in a community home, if a disability develops, the elderly resident is transferred, but no rigidly implemented policy exists. At these community homes there is, as a matter of policy, no resident physician or nurse, although medical help is available through government-financed and run health clinics that are spatially close to all government homes.

Religious homes tend to be run efficiently by nuns, who have taken this task as their vocation. Although the running of these homes is highly subsidized, the varying rates of charge for religious homes make some homes too expensive for those under the National Minimum Pension. However, exceptions are made for deserving cases. Since the church owns approximately a third of all property in Malta, with bequeathing of land in wills still prevalent, more accountability is required without damaging the autonomous role enjoyed by the church.

As an indication of their popularity, there exist quite long waiting lists for both the religious and the government homes, although admittance is not necessarily sequential, nor is each application exclusive to each home. Overall, institutional care is seen as a plausible and sometimes attractive alternative, both by the elderly and by their relatives and/or caregivers. In general, however, despite inaccurate indications suggesting otherwise, the proportion of institutionalized elderly (5.1%) is similar to the European and American experience.

Community Services

The Home Care/Help Service is a community help provision that benefited over 2,066 elderly people who are residents in their own homes (in March 1992). This service, which is provided by 429 casual social assistants, not only provides social support but also assists with shopping, errands, bed making, laundry, ironing and housecleaning, dressing, and the preparation and cooking of meals. This service is provided mainly by females between the ages of 25 and 55, who attend a seven-day course prior to enrollment as casual social assistants. Care assistants are the frontliners in the care provision to the elderly and provide an excellent and as yet unexploited network to develop an accident prevention service for the frail or vulnerable elderly.

The Telecare service, which was initiated in 1991, was introduced by the Parliamentary Secretariat for the Care of the Elderly. Telecare is a telephone life-line system providing 24-hour, daily link-up to a central office via a portable emergency button which can initiate services. Since its introduction this service has had a very positive response. Home help care and Telecare are provided on the basis of need and are not exclusively reserved for the elderly, although they are the main benefactors of these provisions.

Fees for these services seem reasonable. Home help is provided according to need, from a minimum of 3 hours to a maximum of 24 hours per week. Such service is charged at a flat rate of $3 per week for one elderly and $4.50 if the person requires the preparation of a daily meal, rising to $4.50 and $6.75 for a married couple, respectively. With community homes, the government employs a system whereby it charges 60% of all income (from pension and other income) up to a maximum of $84 weekly, whereas religious homes charge approximately the value of the minimum wage ($110). Residents at Saint Vincent de Paule have 40% of their Social Security contributory pension withheld. These and other charges for services provided by government are transferred to a Welfare Committee; which, in turn, utilizes these funds for the well-being of the elderly in such institutions. In effect, the government does not receive any compensation from the beneficiaries. It is of no surprise, therefore, that we find that these services are highly subsidized from both government and religious sources. Eligibility is purely on the basis of age.

INCOME MAINTENANCE AND EMPLOYMENT

Public Income Security Programs and Policies

Malta has a broad system for Social Security provision. Every citizen is entitled to a pension, either contributory (having contributed while in paid employment) or noncontributory (means-tested). Formal Social Security began in the late 1920s. With the Workmen's Compensation Act (1929) and the Widows and Orphans Act (1927), contributions were paid equally by the employer and employee. These schemes had very limited coverage, with the Widows and Orphans Act being limited to civil servants. The Old Age Act of 1948 provided a means-tested pension to those over 60 years of age who, for the preceding 10 years, were British subjects. The enactment of the National Assistance Act of 1956, which provided for the payment of noncontributory social and medical benefits, together with the National Insurance Act of 1956, which provided for contributory benefits and pensions, introduced Social Security on a quasi-national scale. In 1965, when the self-employed were included, a fully comprehensive system became operative.

The present system came into fruition through the Social Security Act of 1987, which, besides consolidating previous acts, also provides for a generous contributory retirement pension scheme equivalent to two-thirds of the insured person's income. Moreover, annual preassessments ensure that pensions become virtually inflation-proof. A recent addition has been the introduction of a Carers Pension, payable to the caregiver of an elderly parent.

Contributory Pensions

Retirement pensions may be divided into flat-rate and earnings-related categories. In 1978 the flat-rate retirement pension was split into two basic schemes. In those cases where no service pension is paid, the National Minimum Pension applies. This is the lowest benefit that is paid by any pension and is approximately $90 (or four-fifths of the minimum wage). Where an employment-related pension is being received in addition, the basic rate of retirement pension is still paid to make up two-thirds of the declared income prior to retirement. This adjustment is referred to as the Increased Retirement Pension.

The second category, which is based on earnings-related rates, is referred to as the Two-Thirds Pension (1979), whereby the beneficiary, upon retirement, becomes entitled to a pension equivalent to two-thirds of the average of the best three years of salary of the last 10 years or in the case of self-employed, the average of the last 10 years. These retirement pensions are payable upon reaching 60 years for females and 61 for males. However, if a pensioner is still gainfully employed, and the earnings from this activity do not exceed the minimum wage (approximately $110 per week), then they still reserve the right to receive a pension. After 65 years of age, any income is allowed and does not in any way affect pension entitlement. Once in receipt of a pension, even though still employed in gainful activity, a pensioner is not liable to pay Social Security contributions.

In both types of pensions, full entitlement is linked to a full Social Security contributions record. When the record is incomplete, as a result of unpaid contributions, this is reflected accordingly in the pension rate.

Other types of benefits are provided by the government. For widows who are not receiving a pension from another source, there is a flat-rate pension referred to as the Social Security Widows Pension. Upon the death of her husband, the widow is entitled either to a pension equivalent to five-ninths of her husband's former income or to a flat-rate pension, whichever is the highest. Similarly, Invalidity Pensions are not paid exclusively on the basis of age, yet these invariably affect the elderly population. A person who has been certified by a medical board to be incapable of work will still, upon retirement, apply for the Two-Thirds Retirement Pension. Even though applicants might not have paid Social Security contributions (since they were in receipt of an Invalidity Pension), the deficit is credited by central government funds for the period when the invalidity pension was paid, so as to complete the full contributions record. By law, on reaching retirement age, the invalidity pensioner will receive the higher of the two benefits. All retirement, widows, and invalidity pensions are regularly revised to reflect salary and cost-of-living increases.

Noncontributory

Noncontributory pensions are a means-tested benefit, and, in the case of the Medical Assistance benefit, the health condition is also taken into consideration.

Age Pension is the benefit paid to those who have reached retirement age but who have not paid Social Security contributions (either because they were never gainfully employed in Malta or because their income was so minimal as to have excluded their obligation for payment of such contributions). Entitlement is on the basis of a means test, and this benefit is related in scale to the National Minimum Pension under the contributory scheme. Both types of age pensions are paid four weeks in advance. In the case of Sickness Assistance, the beneficiary is periodically required to reappear before the medical board for reassessment. In addition, all benefits are augmented with an annual bonus of around $350 (1992 rates), which is also provided to those in gainful employment.

As a result of the full coverage of the public Social Security system, together with the belief and acceptance that the government acts as the paternal provider, a role further augmented through repeated election manifestos, there is little desire for employees to take up additional private insurance for their retirement (0.3% of retirees have a private pension). Moreover, since a pension paid by an employer positively affects the rate of the pension payable, private pension schemes might negatively affect this rate.

Additional policies that benefit the elderly are small but important, such as a $300 bonus tax free for persons suffering from chronic diseases, a sliding-scale rent charge in government-owned flats and houses, and a sliding-scale charge for government-provided services. The ferry service to Gozo is also reduced by 70% for those over 61 years of age.

Local, Regional, State, or District Supplemental Economic Assistance

The introduction of government-sponsored community services for the elderly burgeoned as a result of the establishment of the Parliamentary Secretariat for the Care of the Elderly. However, since their trial introduction in 1987–88, there has not been an equal regional uptake of these services. The south of Malta, which constitutes the poorest but most industrialized region, still has a lower uptake of, and application for, such services as home help/care, community homes, Telecare, and meals-on-wheels.

HEALTH CARE SERVICES

In Malta there is no coordinated health policy specifically developed for the elderly, but existing strategies provide for the population at large. Hospitalization and treatment are free to Maltese citizens. A number of general hospitals, complemented by health clinics in various localities around the islands, are for limited emergency treatment, consultations, checkups, prescriptions, and outpatient facilities. What is unique is that health centers provide the services of a medical doctor to visit the patient at the community home, as well as the attendance of a community nurse to administer injections and pre- or postoperative treatment.

In the case of chronic diseases, legislation provides for free medicines. In other cases, medicines and prosthetics are provided without charge, subject to a means test. Supplementing this service are a number of small government clinics whose primary activity is to dispense medicines. All these services are provided by the government.

The general financing arrangements of such services are from central funds, what is locally known as the Consolidated Fund. This fund incorporates all taxes, Social Security contributions, customs, and other additional income that the government might procure through the selling of assets or services.

Various acute care services are provided by the government. Specialized units at St. Lukes General Hospital provide services for burn injuries and intensive, psychiatric, and specialized cardiac care. Boffa Hospital, a smaller establishment, provides radiotherapy and chemotherapy services. Chronic care services are offered by most hospitals; however, for the elderly, Saint Vincent de Paule Residence remains the main provider, although St. Lukes General Hospital does provide for a considerable number of chronically ill elderly patients.

Private involvement in health care also comes from the Malta Memorial District Nursing Association (MMDNA). MMDNA is a privately run nursing association that was initially aided by the government to become established but is now an independent, nonprofit organization. This association caters to all the population in Malta and provides routine nursing care to people in their home. Around 60% of all recipients of this service are elderly people.

HOUSING RESOURCES

The social settings available for the elderly in Malta and assistance for maintaining the elderly in the dwellings of their choice deserve special emphasis. Any development in this area will come from facilities that already exist for the handicapped, in particular, from housing provisions for paraplegics and for the blind (there is no working definition of *handicapped* used by civil servants). Although the director of social housing, in consultation with a medical panel, has discretion to provide structurally and economically appropriate housing to other cases that fall outside this criterion, entitlement on the basis of age has not been the established exception. There are, however, some minor provisions for financial assistance in the form of a means-tested, flat-rate rent allowance payable to heads of households who are beneficiaries of noncontributory pensions and assistance.

The development of congregate housing, retirement housing or communities, and innovative housing arrangements is not being proposed, but their existence is perhaps more apparent in holiday homes for foreign-born nationals who retire to Malta. These types of private complexes are not uncommon, but their advertising is not on the basis of elderly housing provisions, for obvious commercial reasons. The government, on the other hand, sees its provisions of community homes and home help/care service as primary fulfillment of its obligations toward housing needs of the elderly, but innovative ideas are not lacking. Although individual requests for specific housing requirements are sometimes granted, such exceptions are not ensured through law or established policy.

As with most gerontological issues that cross disciplinary boundaries, within central government planning, the boundaries are mapped by different government departments. The Parliamentary Secretariat for Social Housing adheres to a policy of providing affordable housing to all the population. The numerous provisions and subsidies make it relatively easy for people to purchase property, since prices are quite diverse at both extremes. With over 70% of the general population having home ownership, including 54% of elderly people, such a general policy seems to be very effective. Together with protected rents, social housing in Malta remains the main basis for ensured political stability and, for the elderly, provides the most potential benefit, since this can ensure that elderly citizens are provided with the opportunity to have control over their immediate environment. The allocation of government-built apartments at ground-floor level to the elderly or disabled is one such development, which involves very little financial outlay. Alternatively, external services can be channeled into providing adjustments to make for a safer living environment.

This complementary service will become a reality once the consideration of a Handyman Service is put into force. This provision will involve a team of general laborers, employed by the government, to carry out minor maintenance to adapt certain features of an elderly person's home to make it safer or more habitable. This will help the government to pursue a policy of helping the elderly to remain in their preferred habitat by providing concrete and practical help.

SUPPORTIVE SERVICES

Each village in Malta is served by a local Social Security district office with an attendant welfare officer who deals mainly with matters relating to financial benefit entitlement. The main beneficiaries of this service are the elderly, since they have the most consistent contact with the benefit office. This service might be further developed by the introduction of an advisory service dealing with social issues. This can be effected through a network of social workers employed within these offices.

In 1991 a meals-on-wheels service was initiated by the Parliamentary Secretariat for the Care of the Elderly and is now run together by the Maltese Cross Corps, Social Assistance Secretariat, and Catholic Action. There is a low use of this service, with just under 100 highly subsidized meals provided a week, and the charge is minimal (weekly cost of one-sixth of the minimum wage). In conjunction with this service, there is also an outpatient service provided by the resident nutritionist at St. Lukes General Hospital. This service is open to all ages but seems to be very little utilized by the elderly or by those providing catering provisions for elderly people.

Financial assistance under a noncontributory scheme is payable to persons who are suffering from a chronic ailment. This Sickness or Medical Assistance Scheme is means-tested and evaluated by a medical board set up by the Department of Social Security.

Another scheme, which is referred to as the Social Assistance Female, provides spinsters with a monetary benefit if they cannot go out to work because of caretaking obligations to an elderly relative. Again, this scheme is paid on the evaluation of a medical board set up by the Department of Social Security. In 1992, a Carer's Pension was introduced for offspring who look after their elderly parents. This differs in three aspects from the Social Assistance Female in that the recipient can be male, the recipient of care must be the parents of the caregiver, and the elderly person must be bedridden or wheelchair-bound.

Together with these supportive services, St. Lukes General Hospital, Saint Vincent de Paule Residence, Mount Carmel Hospital, and Zammit Clapp Hospital all provide outpatient services.

Inpatient services for the elderly are numerous. Half of the elderly people enter an institution after first going for treatment as inpatients at the general hospital; their relatives then become reluctant or unable to resume responsibility for their elderly relative. The general hospital considers such cases "bed-blockers" and applies to Saint Vincent de Paule Residence for continued care. Half of the residents of SVPR come directly from St. Lukes General Hospital. However, it is likely that a large proportion of the remainder have also experienced in-patient treatment at St. Lukes but were discharged to their homes before their admission to SVPR could be processed.

LEISURE-TIME RESOURCES

Formal leisure-time resources for the elderly are organized by both government and religious organizations. Apart from the transient and philanthropic Christmas and Easter activities, arranged by a variety of clubs and organizations, the main motivator in this area is religious organizations. However, some cultural practices are still common in Malta.

Culturally, church, band, and political clubs remain the center of village activity. Although social tastes are changing, these foci are still significantly important to the understanding of Maltese social life. The church feast provides some structure to village life, but elderly people tend to congregate in the band clubs. These clubs, normally two in each village, are nearly exclusively dominated by elderly men and are used both as a place to drink and also as a meeting place to discuss politics, football, and other issues of current concern. Since these clubs are adjacent to a village square, the cultural topography consistently finds elderly men sitting on square benches, whereas elderly women are generally seen sitting on chairs on the pavement outside their home. This is a Mediterranean scene that is still a cultural reality.

Most local villages also contain a small playing field with a pitch especially reserved for what is known as bocci. A game very similar to the French boules, this game seems to be primarily dominated by elderly men. Contests are held in each village, and national competitions prove to be proudly challenged. This activity seemingly facilitates some form of socialization, although it is exclusively restricted—by etiquette, rather than by any established regulations—to males. However, Tombola (or bingo), a national pastime, especially at seaside resorts, seems to be the exclusive domain of women. It is not by coincidence that most Tombolas are to be found adjacent to bocci clubs.

Offering socialization activities that facilitate a more pronounced female participation are the Social Clubs which are initiated, developed, and coordinated by Caritas Malta. Caritas Malta is a religious nonprofit organization which organizes social and religious activities for underprivileged segments of the population, especially the elderly. Caritas runs over 40 social clubs for the elderly within most localities in Malta, and approximately 2,000 elderly attend such clubs, with 250 volunteers who help out with their organization and day-to-day running. Caritas also organizes a Good Neighbor Scheme. This scheme focuses around village churches. Volunteers who organize and oversee these activities provide support to elderly people living alone and perform some personal assistance tasks such as letter writing and transporting elderly to the hospital. In total, 16 parish-based Good Neighbor Schemes with 104 active members and 159 volunteers provide a service to 660 elderly or ill people (whom 260 are frail elderly living on their own).

No specific educational programs for the elderly exist, apart from substantial ad hoc seminars and speeches within specific clubs and organizations. Most trade union organizations, pensioners' associations, and political organizations tend to focus on issues that concern elderly people, mainly reflecting the general age structure of their members or clientele. There has been considerable interest in establishing a third-age university, but so far no concrete action.

Educational programs that are not directed at the elderly but might have direct bearing on them are run by Caritas Malta. One of the priorities of Caritas Malta is the training of volunteers, to equip members with knowledge and skills to enable them to provide a much more efficient and appropriate service to the elderly. Another activity is the "School's Program on the Elderly," which was initiated in 1987 to enable schoolchildren to become aware of their responsibility in helping elderly people. This program has been successful in annually motivating over 5,000 students from 22 local private schools.

ADVOCACY AND PROTECTION

It is of particular importance for the government to establish some standard of care in institutions so as to ensure that private enterprises are not purely profit-orientated, at the expense of service, and also to provide residents in institutions the right to complain without punitive results. In a small-sample survey, Cutajar (1992) found that the regime of some institutions obscures the rights of the elderly to complain.

Although no specific legal assistance is provided for the elderly, there is, on paper, the provision for legal aid for the poor (L-Avukat tal-Fqar). From a group of lawyers who are appointed and paid by the government, a lawyer is present twice a week at the law courts to provide this service. Eligibility for this service is assessed on the basis of a means test and the provision of a statement of assets from the commissioner of inland revenue. The complexity of the Maltese legal system, with its bureaucratic labyrinth, somehow ensures that this resource is minimally utilized. Fortunately, most inquiries that relate to income/pensions can be dealt with effectively by local Social Security offices.

As such, no specific provisions are available to help and represent elderly victims in the criminal justice system. In Malta, neglect and abuse of elderly persons have not, so far, been addressed by any legal hearing.

With the establishment of the Parliamentary Secretariat for the Elderly in 1987, elderly persons in Malta acquired a focal point for their demands. Once the Parliamentary Secretary started to initiate concrete programs, after the initial delayed demands by the elderly, there was a more developed formal presentation by local, newly defined representatives of elderly groups.

Various associations represent some of the elderly. Invariably, the most prominent associations are run for civil servants. The National Association of Pensioners, with up to 4,000 paying members, is perhaps the largest of such organizations. The trade unions also have associations for their retired members; both the General Workers' Unions and the Confederation of Malta Trade Unions represent their retired members on a national level. Together with these associations, the two main political parties provide their own pensioners' association with the Assocazzjoni Pensjonanti Nazzjonalisti and the Ghaqda Veterani tal Malta Labour Party. Other, more localized associations exist, especially the Floriana Senior Citizens' Association, with a membership of 150.

The important role of advocacy is slowly being realized in Malta. In 1988, Caritas Malta HelpAge initiated an Independent Living Advice Center (ILAC) to promote the use of aids for daily living among frail and disabled elderly people. ILAC, which is run by volunteers, publishes a variety of self-help booklets.

FUTURE PROJECTIONS

Given the general economic independence of elderly people in Malta, together with the high proportion of home ownership and a free (or heavily subsidized) health provision, elderly Maltese have a well-developed supporting infrastructure. However, by 2025, Malta will witness the apex of the aging of its population, with 24% of its population living up to and beyond 60 years of age. With this growing proportion, it is also expected that there will be an increase in the number of the old-old and their higher level of formal education.

The cultural and geographic inheritance of the Maltese and, in particular, the causal implications for the Maltese elderly should be placed in the context of methods to improve the quality of life for elderly persons in Malta. With the established system of formal provisions for the elderly, it would be shortsighted to expect this burgeoning future demand to be reflected by a similar economic growth. With a gross national product growth rate comparable with that of the "dragon" countries of the East, the development of services for the elderly has been conceived in an economic climate of prosperity. The stability of such services depends on this economic optimism.

The trend for the government to provide community homes and specialized geriatric services for elderly people cannot be maintained in proportional growth to the growth of the elderly population. However, it is realistic to assume that, because of the small size of the island, there will still be a demand by potential caregivers to be spatially separated from their dependent elderly parents (or vice versa). The current subsidy by the government cannot be proportionally maintained. Although private enterprise—in providing community or sheltered housing—is developing in Malta, it would seem that the government cannot depend, or be seen to depend, on such developments to lead it from this imminent quandary.

As a portend, the "welfare gap," which is the discrepancy between the amount of benefits paid out by the government and the amount of contributions received, has been increasing exponentially. As it is not feasible for any government to finance social services, pensions, and health services totally from contributions, there will always be this kind of deficit. The particular concern in the context of Malta is that the economy is highly dependent on tourism, and fluctuations in this volatile market will directly affect the capacity for the government to continue to provide such services.

In conclusion, with the expected increase in both the real number and the proportion of elderly people, we can expect that two main developments will emerge that will exacerbate the demand placed on the government. Socially, the future elderly population will be better educated, will be more aware of the services being provided, and, together with the established National Council for the Elderly, will have a more easily accessible platform from which to voice their demands publicly and directly to the government and civil servants. Second, with the increase in longevity, we will see an increase in the proportion of the old-old population (75+). This group will have different needs and make more intense use of the services provided. These two issues, together with the realization that the indigenous working population will be declining in size, will determine the response by the government.

The aging of the Maltese population will have to be dealt with appropriately, taking into consideration the good of the general population rather than that of the selected few. The end result relies heavily on the ability of the government to slow the present rate of institutionalization and centralized facilities, in preference to developing services based within, and run by, the community. By transferring funds from a centralized and technologically intensive service to one which is based on social-care assistance, domiciliary nursing and rehabilitation services, and accident-prevention programs, not only will the majority of the elderly receive timely treatment but future generations will have better coverage of services than has been the case.

NOTE

Grateful acknowledgment is made for comments by Carmen Delia, who performed special economic analysis on her M.A. thesis for this chapter; Eddie Gatt for clarifying the Social Security benefits system; Doreen Agius Cutajar for sharing her unique nursing experience; Salvina Bezzina for providing most of the information on Caritas and religious homes; Anthony Fiorini for sharing some policy issues on the care of the elderly; Marika Borg for providing overall knowledge about community services; Vince Tonna and Victor Xerri for contributing their experience at the grass-roots level; and John Xiberras for selecting pertinent economic data. The spirit of this paper is attributable to them, but mistakes and omissions are purely the responsibility of the authors.

BIBLIOGRAPHY

Busuttil, S. (1971). "The Aged in Urbanizing Societies: Malta." Mimeograph, Foundation of International Studies, Malta.

Camilleri, K. (1990). "The Elderly and Their Nutritional Habits." B.Ed. thesis, University of Malta.

Cassar, P. (1956). *The Medical History of Malta.* Malta-Aquilina.

Central Office of Statistics. (1986). *A Demographic Profile of Malta and Gozo* (Vol. 1). Malta: Government Press.

Cutajar, D. A. (1992). "Residents' Expectations and Need Fulfillment on Admission to St. Vincent de Paule Residence and Perceived/Actual Changes After Residence." B.Sc. thesis, University of Malta.

Delia, C. (1992). "A Survey on the Aged in Malta." Unpublished M.A. research, University of Malta.

Delia, E. P. (1982). *The Characteristics and Life-Style of the Aged in the Maltese Islands.* Malta: Center for Social Research, Social Action Movement.

Garrett, M. (1990). "Life Expectancy Indicators for the Elderly: A Global Analysis and Critique." *Bold* 1 (2).

Il-Gens. (22 July 1988). Nidhol Jew ma Hidholx ("To Go In or Not" [to a residential home]). Caritas, Malta.

Jefferys, M. (1973). "The Elderly in Society." In *Textbook of Geriatric Medicine and Gerontology,* ed. J. C. Brocklehurst and Churchill Livingstone. China.

Laspina, S. (1966). *Outline of Maltese History.* Malta: A. C. Aquilina.

Lopata, H. Z. (1979). *Women as Widows: Support Systems.* New York: Elsevier.

Ministry of Social Policy. (1989). *The Elderly Population in Malta.* Office of the Parliamentary Secretary for the Care of the Elderly, Malta.

National Center for Health Statistics. (1979). *The National Nursing Home Survey: 1977 Summary for the United States.* Vital and Health Statistics, Ser. 13, No. 43. Washington, D.C.: U.S. Government Printing Office.

Office of the Parliamentary Secretary for the Care of the Elderly, Ministry for Social Policy. (1989). *The Elderly Population in Malta.* University of Malta Press.

Pirotta, G. A. (1991). "The Administrative Politics of a Micro State: The Maltese Public Service 1860–1940." Ph.D. diss., Bath University, Great Britain.

United Nations Demographic Projection and Estimates, 1950–2025 (1988 Revisions). (1989). Department of International Economic and Social Affairs, ST/ESA/SER.R/79. New York.

White Paper. (1992). *Amendment to the Social Security Act.* Parliamentary Papers, Government of Malta.

World Bank. (1990). *World Development Report 1990.* Oxford, England: Oxford University Press.

NETHERLANDS

*Theo N. M. Schuyt and
Gerard H. van der Zanden*

INTRODUCTION

The specific situation of the elderly and of services for the elderly in the Netherlands is determined in part by five cultural, historic factors: (1) the high birthrate following World War II, (2) the particular relationship between public and private services and facilities in the care sector, (3) the high percentage of older persons living in homes for the elderly, (4) the broad scope of the public pension system, and (5) the low level of participation by the elderly in the labor market (Baars, Knipscheer, and Breebaart, 1992).

The high birthrate following World War II continued in the Netherlands longer than in other Western countries. From 1945 to 1965, this stood at 2.6. After 1965, the rate decreased sharply, to 1.4 by 1974. This demographic change has had considerable repercussions for all areas of Dutch social life. For example, between 1980 and 1990, a very large group of young people entered the labor market, with the consequence that a large group of older workers—in part influenced by the general economic stagnation beginning in the late 1970s—left the workplace early, whether forced to do so or not. Another consequence is that the percentage of persons aged 65 or older is currently low but will increase to 14.7% in 2010 and will thereafter grow markedly to a probable 21.3% in the year 2030. "During recent years these demographic prospects have invited intensive discussions on the financial consequences, especially upon the cost of the public pensions and of the social and health services for the elderly (Baars, Knipscheer, and Breebaart, 1992, p. 1).

The specific relationship between public and private resources in the area of care for the elderly involves the financing of care by private institutions with federal (public) funds. This unique situation has a direct relationship to the historically developed religious compartmentalization within society, which has led to a compartmentalized structure of care services by Protestant, Catholic, and nonreligious institutions (polarization). While the majority of services for the elderly are financed by the government, their implementation is in private hands (boards of directors and professionals). The policy regarding services is determined by the government, in consultation with private institutions. This leads to the need for increasing coordination and cooperation among the separate institutions at the local level.

The high percentage of the elderly residing in homes for the elderly is a specific characteristic of the services for the elderly in the Netherlands. In 1975, 9.3% of all persons over 65 lived in a home for the elderly, and about 2.2% of those over 65 lived in a nursing home. Government authorities drastically changed the policy, with the result that by 1988, 7% of those over 65 lived in a home for the elderly and 2.5% in a nursing home. In comparison with other countries, these figures are still high.

The expanded public pension system was founded in 1957. In 1972 the amount of these benefits was set at a level equal to that of the minimum income. The broad scope of the public pension system has, perhaps, led to the fact that private pension systems are less developed in the Netherlands.

The limited participation of the elderly in the labor market is due to the pressure of young people entering the labor market and the existence of a good Social Security system for older employees. Many employer and employee organizations (labor unions) have been able to resolve their reorganization and redundancy problems by providing a large number of older employees with early retirement at the expense of the government and the taxpayer. Traditionally, Holland is also faced with a very low level of labor market participation by women.

The Role of the Elderly

Status in Society

There is no easy answer to the question of the social status of the elderly in Dutch society. On one hand, the system of Social Security, especially the public pension system, is an expression of intergenerational solidarity. In the first half of this century, an important goal of the workers' movement was to secure the financial position of elderly workers. Many of them were below the poverty line and were totally dependent on their families. After World War II, with the development of the public pension system, elderly persons could live their own lives, independent of financial help from their children. According to some, the public pension system suddenly emancipated the aged from unwanted familial ties. However, others argue that the Social Security system and other services can be classified as "passionate ageism." Based on the age criterion, the elderly may benefit from systems and services, but the costs are loss of power and less integration in the mainstream of society. The fact that the majority of Dutch elderly workers stop working before the official retirement age of 65 is, to a certain extent, an expression of this paradox.

The position of aging individuals in the labor market is weak. Age is used as a criterion for worker selection, and institutions like labor offices do not invest much activity on behalf of aging workers. Many workers leave the labor market by means of special early retirement schemes. Social Security systems that provide workers with an income when they are not capable of working anymore have been applied to elderly persons with little difficulty. As a result of both practices, the older working person considers himself or herself an exception to the rule. As a social phenomenon, the free choice to retire early therefore becomes mandatory early retirement.

There is a growing political movement on the part of the elderly in the Netherlands. Their priorities relate to securing good public pensions and care systems. On the other hand, for being able to live a decent life, they do not want to pay the price of a loss of societal power, loss of power to make decisions about their own lives, and reduced societal integration. In recent years their strategy has been to abandon rules and practices that prevent persons above a certain age from having a role in decision-making processes or that result in their being excluded from activities.

Aging is much more of a topic in the popular press than it used to be. There is growing attention for the challenges of "the financial burden of an aging population." There is also increasing attention for the new stereotype of the "wealthy, healthy, and active" senior citizen and for questions about the place of old age in modern society. Of course, growing attention is stimulated by the awareness of the aged as a growing consumer group.

In social policy there is a certain trend to minimize upper-age boundaries, to redefine the position of the elderly in the labor market, and to withdraw governmental influences from economic life. This last trend may have negative consequences for Social Security and the social and health services for the elderly, especially for the category of persons without a supplementary private pension and for those with chronic health conditions. There is evidence, however, based on survey research (Moors, Leusden, and Hogen Esch, 1989) that in the general population the foundations for the concept of intergenerational solidarity are still very strong. Nearly 70% of the Dutch population hold the opinion that the state has the main responsibility for the care of the elderly and that the population as a whole should be obliged to support the costs. In the field of care, two-thirds of the population are negative about a family duty to provide care, although only one-third holds the opinion that there are no tasks for the family in the care for the elderly. The attitude of the population about aging and the aged cannot be considered negative. It is a mix of positive, negative, realistic, and sometimes unrealistic beliefs and opinions.

Demographic Characteristics

In the Netherlands in 1990, 1,910,000 persons were 65 years or older—almost 13% of the population. In 1980 this proportion was 11.5%. The number of old

old in the 65 plus population—those persons 80 years and over—is also increasing, from 19.3% in 1980 to 22.6% in 1990. This demographic development will continue until the middle of the next century. According to realistic forecasts, the percentage of elderly people in the total population will be above 20% in 2025. The aging of the population is a consequence of the decreasing number of births and the increasing life expectancy. The trend in increasing life expectancy continues (Stuurgroep, 1992). In 1989, a newborn boy in the Netherlands could expect to live 73.7 years, and a newborn girl, 79.9 years. In that year, at the age of 65 a man could expect to live for another 13.9 years, and a woman for 18.5 years. The life expectancy of the old old is also still increasing: an 80-year-old man has a life expectancy of 6.9 years, and a woman, 8.6 years.

The number of women 65 and over is greater than the number of elderly men. The sex differences are related to differences in civil status: 75% of men 65 and older are married, but only 39% of women; 48% of women 65 and older are widows, but only 16% of the men are widowers. The level of education will increase in the future. In 1990, 36% of the men and 56% of the women had the lowest education level. In 2010 these proportions will be 20% and 31%. Especially in the 75 and older category, the number and proportion of persons living alone will increase. In the population 55 years and over, the proportion of men living alone will increase from 14.9% in 1990 to 20.1% in 2005, and the proportion of women 55 and older living alone will increase from 35.5% to 38.6%. In 2005 in the population 75 and older, the proportion of persons living alone will be 26% for men and 63% for women.

The Formal Structure of Care of the Elderly

In the Netherlands, the government plays a predominant role in care for the elderly. Incomes for the elderly are guaranteed at a given minimum level. All elderly persons have obligatory insurance for health care, and the Dutch authorities have, moreover, seen to a very thorough package for intramural (homes for the elderly and nursing homes) and extramural (home care services, including home help and home nursing) care. Care for the elderly is, in short, guaranteed by the government and is virtually completely financed by the public sector (the AWBZ). Management of care is, for the most part, in the hands of private organizations. This special relationship between public funding, guarantees, and policymaking, on one hand, and implementation by private institutions, on the other, is an example of the particular manner in which the Dutch welfare state is organized.

Because of the compartmentalization of the sociopolitical structure, the Netherlands is subject to a strongly centralized administration. Taxes are collected nationally and divided among provincial and local authorities by the federal government according to legally binding regulations. The Netherlands has three levels of administration: national, provincial, and town or city. Under the national regulations, city or town authorities carry out policy with regard to homes for the elderly, and the provincial governments manage the nursing homes and general hospitals. Local governments are the administrators for income maintenance and health insurance, and most of the social services for the elderly (including home help, senior citizen centers, and the like) are also organized at the municipal level. In recent years, a political course of decentralization has been put into effect, leading to broader financial and policy-making freedom at the provincial and local levels.

Since World War II, the Netherlands has developed a disproportionately high level of institutionalized care for the elderly. This development reached a peak around 1975, when about 9.3% of all persons over 65 lived in a home for the aged and about 2.2% in a nursing home. The majority of homes for the elderly and nursing homes are administered by private organizations. About 90% of their finances are from public resources. Following 1975, the government policy toward homes for the elderly was changed; no new homes were allowed to be built.

The welfare package is increasingly taking on the characteristics of an insurance model in which individual elderly persons take out additional insurance for specific services alongside the minimum package already provided. The welfare state in the Netherlands provides a standard package of services to which all individuals over 65 years of age have a right. The use of special services for the elderly, intramural and extramural, is on the basis of need, determined through intake procedures and committee recommendations.

INCOME MAINTENANCE AND EMPLOYMENT

Income Maintenance

The most notable characteristic of income for the elderly is the existence of a basic public pension. For over 30 years, every person over 65 has had the right to a pension, regardless of whether or not the individual had taken part in the labor process prior to that age. The two other sources of income for the elderly are the supplemental pensions from the workplace and personal capital. In the Netherlands, income from employment does not play a role. In 1990 there were over 2 million persons entitled to a public pension. The total amount of funds distributed in that year was Hfl. (guilders) 280 million (US $154 million).

The public pension (AOW) is financed through the social securities taxation system, with the work force providing the annual pension benefits. When the system came into being, the relationship between employed personnel and those on pensions was 1:4. It is now 1:2 and is tending toward 1:1.7. In 1988 there were 228,100 elderly persons whose incomes consisted only of the basic public pension; 950,000 had a supplemental pension in addition to the public pension. Single women are noticeably overrepresented in the category of those with only the basic state pension.

Along with the public pension, a number of additional financial resources are provided that are dependent on the amount of one's income. The most prevalent are the rental subsidies for housing. Ten percent of persons aged 50–56, 21% of those aged 65–74, and 20% of those aged over 75 make use of such subsidies. Besides resources dependent on one's income, there are discounts dependent on age, including discounts on travel and on cultural and recreational facilities such as theaters and museums.

Supplemental pensions are accrued by individuals during their working life. These came into being immediately after World War II and were, in most cases, obligatory pension arrangements. There is very wide variation in the pension plans for each respective branch of industry. In most cases, the pension to be received is dependent on the amount of salary earned during the last period of one's working life. It is estimated that about one out of five employed persons has no pension arrangement, primarily women who are working part-time. The portion of supplemental pensions in the average income for the elderly is increasing slightly, but the basic state pension remains the stable source of income. In 1970 the average income for elderly persons consisted of 20% supplemental pension, 32% personal capital, and 47% public pension. In 1988 these proportions were 25%, 18%, and 55%, respectively.

The general principle behind the public pension is income security. Every person in old age has the right to a basic living standard. Although the level of the basic pension is, in general, considered a minimum, it is reasonable to state that old age in the Netherlands is not the equivalent of living in impoverishment or below the poverty line. Income from the public pension in 1992 was equal to that (minimum) of single persons in general. In 1988 the average income before taxes was Hfl. 30,100 (US $16,538). The 20% of the elderly who had no supplemental pension received an average of Hfl. 23,900 (US $13,132). The 80% with a supplemental pension received an average of Hfl. 32,000 (US $17,582). Buying power on a public pension has decreased in the last decade. Since 1990 the interrelationship with welfare developments has been reestablished. Not a great deal is known about how the elderly spend their money. Housing takes the biggest share, on average, about 35% of the spending income; other expenses include groceries (20%), clothing (6%), and miscellaneous (23%).

Employment

Only 4% of persons over 65 years of age have an income from employment. More important, the labor market position of aging workers has declined dramatically in the last decade. Only one out of five who had been part of the labor force at a younger age is still employed between the ages of 60 and 65. In 1960 that figure was 85%. Not working at that age has recently become an accepted phenomenon. It can be traced back to a silent agreement between employers' and employees' organizations and the government, by which the pressure on the labor market could be somewhat reduced by allowing older employees to take part in redundancy and early retirement schemes by means of various arrangements. The most exceptional route out of the labor market was a provision based on the consequences of disability. According to the general disability law (WAO), disability insurance will provide the ex-worker (if 50 or older) with up to 70% of prior income in case of disability. The enormous increase in the number of older former employees who are entitled to the WAO is the consequence of the employers' policy, sanctioned by labor unions and the government, of dismissing older workers for medical reasons.

Another arrangement, alongside Social Security provisions for unemployment, is early retirement. As a result of an accord reached between employers' organizations and labor unions, elderly workers can retire early (most frequently, at age 60) with benefits of about 80% of their previous income. These early retirement schemes are of a voluntary nature. In practice, however, it has grown to be the exception in some sectors of the labor market when someone fails to take advantage of early retirement. Colleagues would consider it improper, saying that it contributed to the continuing high unemployment among young people. Presently, unions still consider it correct to defend these schemes.

Only since the beginning of the 1990s has there been any large-scale concern about this development. Various initiatives are now being undertaken to stop this tendency and to strengthen the position of older workers in the labor market. It may also be expected that, in the next few years, these initiatives will be of influence for the "younger" individuals among older employees.

HEALTH CARE SERVICES

Development

The Dutch welfare state system was developed after World War II. At that time the Netherlands changed from an agrarian society to one that was highly industrialized and urbanized. Until well into the 1980s, there was a centralized political approach toward care services. Only in the last decade has a policy of decentralization been put into effect, by which responsibility at the national level is being moved to provincial and municipal levels.

An extensive and complex professional care system has been developed in recent decades. This system still reflects its historic origins. One characteristic is found in the balance of power between services financed by the government and services administrated privately. Another characteristic is that most services are meant for the population as a whole. There are hardly any specific services for the elderly as such, although some services have almost exclusively an older clientele. A third characteristic is the divided development of three subsystems in the care for the elderly: Social Security for financial support, social care in the form of nonmedical community care, and health care, including home help.

A specific national policy for care for the elderly came into being in the 1960s. The emphasis lay with the acute problem of long-term care and residential services, in particular, nursing homes and residential homes. In 1963, a legal basis for homes for the aged was created, the first legal act of this nature in Europe.

As part of the Exceptional Medical Expenses Act (AWBZ) in 1968, the financing of care for chronic illness was made possible, leading to the rapid development of nursing homes. Intramural care was, and is, a characteristic of the Dutch care system for the elderly. About 10% of the elderly live in an institutional setting, one-fifth of whom are in nursing homes.

Important changes have been proposed in the organization and especially the financing of the health care system. Generally speaking, 90% of the Hfl. 53 billion (US $30 billion) currently spent annually on health and social services come from employee premiums, and only 10% come directly from the government. If one's income falls below a given level, the person is required to be insured against illness via national or regional insurance funds. This involves nearly 70% of the population. Those (30%) in higher-income categories hold health insurance with private insurance companies. There is also a Social Security system for exceptional expenses, especially care for chronic illness. The nursing homes and home nursing services are paid for through AWBZ, often with direct contributions from the user.

Excluding residential care in homes for the elderly, the proportion of elderly people (65 and older) in the total costs of health care was 36% in 1988. The elderly are predominant in nursing homes (95% of total costs going to the elderly), district nursing (about 75%), and home help (about 65%). For most age groups, the average cost per person for health care is about Hfl. 2,000 (US $1,100) per year. However, this figure increases for persons 55 years and older. For the group 75 years and older, the costs are over Hfl. 8,000 (US $4,400) a year.

Primary Health Care

The general practitioner (GP) is seen as the "backbone" of medical care, and is important for the referral of patients to other specialized services and serves as the mediator for other medical or social workers. The GP is increasingly confronted with the aging of society, for instance, in the amount of time required for consults or house visits and in the nature of the ailment. In 1987–88, about 70% of elderly men under age 70 had contact with their GP, about 10% higher for men older than 70. For women aged 65 to 70, the figure was about 78%; for women over 70 it was well over 80%. The frequency of contact with the GP varies: 5.1 visits per man and 5.8 visits per woman in the 55–59 year category and 6.7 visits per man and 7.4 visits per woman in the 75 and over category. There has been a stabilization over the last 10 years in both the percentage of people who have contact with their GP and the frequency of contact.

Home nursing care in the Netherlands is provided by organizations that have evolved out of volunteer charity organizations. The work of these organizations is more and more geared toward the activities of the home help organizations. The policy is to integrate both forms of home care. The number of clients per 100 in home nursing in 1988 was 1.3 for the age group 40–59, 5.5 for those

60–69, 16.9 for those 70–79, and 46.4 for persons over 80. Although home nursing is not a service specifically intended for the elderly, most clients are elderly people. In 1988, 82% of all such contacts were for the aged, especially in very advanced age. New forms of home care have been developed in recent years. For example, nearly all home nursing organizations can now be reached 24 hours a day, and all provide nursing care during the night.

Hospital and Chronic Care

The number of admissions to hospitals per year increases proportionate to age. In 1988 the proportion of hospital admissions was 204.9 per 1,000 in the 65–74 category and 269.5 per 1,000 for the category 75 and older. For all ages combined, the proportion was 103 per 1,000 residents. The frequency of admissions to hospitals of the population under 65 has been lower over the last 10 years, but that of the older population has risen markedly. The average number of days of inpatient care has dropped for the elderly, as it has for the population at large. This is at an average of 15 days for the 65–74 category and 19.2 days for persons over 75. Though the total number of days of hospitalization dropped for the elderly, that for younger persons did so more appreciably and resulted in an overall increase in the average age of hospital patients. There is a slow tendency toward the establishment of geriatric wards in general and academic hospitals. There were six in 1986, and there are plans to increase the number.

A nursing home in the Netherlands is a professional residential facility for patients who need extensive nursing care without extensive specialist treatment. Although nursing homes are not exclusively intended for the aged, over 95% of the beds are used by the elderly. Specific hospice care is not known in the Netherlands, and nursing homes are used for terminal care.

There are major problems relating to waiting lists, especially for dementia patients. In 1989 there were 112 nursing homes for somatic patients, 77 for psychogeriatric patients, and 135 combining both patient groups. The total number of beds was 50,571 (26,616 of which were for somatic patients). There has been an annual increase in recent years of 1.2% in the number of beds, with a higher increase in psychogeriatric beds (over 3.4%). New forms of chronic care have been developed recently. The number of places for day treatment in nursing homes increased to about 3,000 in 1988. Other developments include chronic nursing care of patients in residential homes and patients who live in their own homes to delay admission to a nursing home. Projections do, however, suggest a sharp increase in nursing home beds in the future. In 1988 there were 50,571 beds, but it is predicted that the population 65 and over will require 72,600 beds in nursing homes by the year 2003.

Traditionally, the Netherlands has had a high percentage (about 8%) of older people in residential homes (or housing for the elderly). However, current policy is directed toward lowering this percentage. In 1988 there were nearly 145,000 beds in about 1,600 homes. In these facilities, residents live in small apartments. Meals, housekeeping, and activities are provided. In recent years these homes have also provided services for elderly people in the neighborhood, and sheltered housing has been built for these activities. The expense of living in a residential home is paid by the resident. In cases where the resident is not able to cover the costs (actually, almost always the case), the social welfare system at the local level does so.

The policy for building residential homes is very restrictive. In the middle of the 1970s an assessment procedure was put in place to determine the degree of an applicant's need for a residential home. The lower number of places available has resulted in a sharpening of the criteria for admission into a residential home. That, in turn, has resulted in a rise in the average age, and the average ability (ADL) has decreased. In 1992 there were policy proposals to abandon residential homes in the care spectrum and to replace them with new, less-institutionalized forms of living arrangements with care facilities.

HOUSING RESOURCES

General Overview

The Netherlands experienced a long period of housing shortages after World War II. Currently there is only some question of local shortages. The number of houses between 1945 and 1988 grew from 2 million to 5.6 million. Although the rapid population growth has decreased, the number of households will continue to expand over the next 40 years. The individualization, increased welfare, and increasing average age in recent years have brought about an increase in the number of households, with generally fewer people per household. In 1950 the average household still consisted of 4.6 persons but by 1990 decreased to 2.5 persons. Although attention will be paid to quantity in the coming century (one can assume 7.3 million homes for the year 2025), more concern is being given to quality standards.

In 1990, 2.6 million homes (45%) were privately owned. In the social rental sector there were 2.4 million homes. The remaining were rented out by private owners. An average of 18% of annual income was spent on rental homes, and 11% was spent on privately owned homes. In the home rental sector, the elderly spent more than the average, about one-fifth of their incomes, on rents. Expenses for older homeowners are, indeed, lower. The mean rent for existing housing stock is Hfl. 452.00 (US $248) per month, and initial rent for new housing in the social sector is Hfl. 567.00 (US $312) per month.

The federal government—in this case the Ministry of Housing, Physical Planning, and the Environment—has a legally binding responsibility in the area of housing. Emphasis lies primarily in the formulation of quality standards and in financial support. Housing corporations, or building societies, play an important role in the Netherlands. These are nonprofit foundations that build and distribute housing in the social sector for those not able to do so themselves. About 80% of housing stock is in the hands of about 800 corporations. Towns and cities manage 7% of the housing stock.

National politics will, in the future, concentrate on special groups, namely, persons below a certain income level. One of these groups is the elderly. Currently the most important instrument in realizing affordable housing for low-income groups is the individual rent subsidy. In 1989–90 there were 950,000 recipients, with an average subsidy of Hfl. 1,800 (US $989). About 35% of the recipients are pensioners.

Housing and the Aged

The composition of the household alters with increasing age, as does the proportion of the elderly living alone. Among the group above 80 years of age, 30% live alone, 25% live independently with a partner, and 10% live within another context (e.g., with children). In total, 33% live in a home for the elderly or a nursing home, (Social Cultured Planbureau [SCP], 1990).

Most elderly in the Netherlands are living independently in ordinary housing, that is, in family housing that is not especially meant for elderly people and/or has been technically adapted for elderly. Of all persons 55 years and over, 65% live in a house with four or more rooms; 20% live in a three-room house, 13% have two rooms, and only 2% have one room.

On the basis of 1990 national survey data, nearly 60% of the elderly of 75 years and over are living in normal private housing. In recent years there were some successful initiatives to adapt the normal housing stock for a graying population. A goal of one of the programs, for example, was to build elevators in existing housing blocks. On a small scale, forms of group living of independent young elderly were initiated.

About 20% of those 75 years and over are living in some form of adapted housing. *Adapted housing* can mean different things. About 4% of the aged 75 years and over are living in "service apartments." In most cases the apartment is owned by the elderly person who has to pay for extra services, for example, a meal or cleaning services. These apartments are mainly owned by elderly with higher incomes. Although meant for aged persons, there is often an upper age limit for buying an apartment. The buyer is probably not meant to be an old-old person.

About 10% of the 75 and older population is living in "special housing for the elderly"; in most cases this is an apartment or a small house with a tiny garden with some technical and safety provisions. In this special housing, one lives independently. All rooms are located on one floor, and most houses are grouped in blocks in normal neighborhoods. Until recently this type of special housing was sometimes characterized as small.

Housing and Care

In the mid-1970s, 10% of the elderly lived in a home for the elderly. Around 1975 a break in this trend could be discerned, and the official policy of the national government then restricted the number of people admitted to an old people's home. In the first years this resulted in an increase of the average age of admission to a residential home. Also, one could argue that the growth of home care was, in part, a result of this policy. The policy toward restricting institutional care did not directly result in the development of alternative forms of sheltered housing. In the last decade, however, these housing alternatives have captured increasing attention.

The "sheltered housing" option in the Netherlands combines adapted housing with some forms of extra services, especially services of a ward or caretaker with a 24-hour alarm system. A special form of sheltered housing is apartment blocks directly situated near an old people's home, with the possibility of using facilities of the home. Special housing and sheltered housing are mainly available in the rent sector; however, the average rent is high, especially for sheltered housing. Many persons need the supplementary governmental rent subsidy to pay the rent. About half of all elderly households 75 and older living in noninstitutional but adapted houses need individual rent subsidy.

A recent development in the "gray area" between nursing home and independent living is the *woonzorg* (living-care) projects. Through cooperation of local governments, care services, and housing corporations, a special form of sheltered housing was initiated, using several mixed forms of finances from the traditionally separated sectors of welfare and/or health and housing. Independent living in all situations, including when an aged person is disabled, is the major goal of this form of housing. Instead of asking a person to move to a form of housing that is suitable for one's health and need of care, the living-care housing is flexible in providing different and individual packages of care. This is possible through strong cooperation with the care services. A new trend makes it possible for the aged who meet the criteria for admission to such a home to live in such a housing project, consisting of some 75 to 150 apartments, each with two or three rooms. There are severe difficulties in governmental rules for the mixed financing of living in these projects; however, they are considered very promising in replacing an institutional form of living with an independent, sheltered form of living.

SUPPORTIVE SERVICES

The standard of care in the Netherlands is high. This is also the case for facilities that support elderly persons living on their own. Included are such resources as centers for advice and information, service centers, coordinated work for the elderly, family services, district nursing, services for the elderly by regional institutes for mental welfare (RIAGG), day centers, social work, and neighborhood work for the elderly.

Within this broad spectrum of facilities, the political system has made two structural changes: a shift in emphasis from intramural to extramural care and closer coordination with, and greater involvement from, informal support. Here, government policy is responding to the growing desire on the part of the elderly to continue to live at home for as long as possible. Both changes mean that the role of the supportive services in the community is increasing in significance.

Older persons can receive advice and information from various subsidized facilities in their own neighborhoods. The most prevalent are the service centers for the elderly, where social workers are available, as well as coordinated work for senior citizens. The availability of this service appears to be adequate. For the provision of meals at home for the elderly, the Netherlands has a meals-on-wheels (*tafeltjedekje*) program and other initiatives run by volunteers and nursing homes in the neighborhoods.

Home help is a large-scale service in the Netherlands. It is an important service for elderly people living independently at home; about 12% of persons over 65 use such assistance, and 64% of the Dutch home help service is used by the elderly (Kastelein, Dijkstra, and Schouten, 1989). When the elderly are in need of household or medical help, they receive assistance primarily from professional helpers, through subsidized home help and district nursing, and second, friends and relations (SCP, 1990). The use made of service centers is not very extensive (SCP, 1990).

The number of day-care centers for early dementia and for other problems of a psychic and psychogeriatric nature is increasing. There are also the RIAGGs as a main service for community mental health care. The elderly make very little use of individual therapy and counseling services; younger age groups have priority. Within the RIAGGs, separate departments for older adults are increasing in number. There is growing attention to health promotion and health education of the elderly and their caregivers. Most prominent are the initiatives in the departments of prevention and older adult departments of the RIAGGs. Important themes are dementia, depression, loneliness, and grief.

The elderly make little use of general social work. Where social work is concerned, the Netherlands has for many years had coordinated services for the elderly, as well as service centers employing qualified social workers. These professional personnel do not have specific gerontology training. In recent years, schools of higher training in social work and departments of social gerontology at the universities have incorporated training specifically oriented toward the elderly.

A very important development in the organization of care for the elderly is case management. Because of the excessive scope of professional intramural care facilities in the Netherlands, two changes have been put into effect within the policy concepts of "substitution" and "case management." First is a shift from professional intramural to professional extramural care, involving the general practitioner, district nursing, and home help. The second is a move from professional care to informal care.

These developments are stimulated by proposed changes in the Dutch insurance system. It will, in the future, be to the advantage of the more commercially oriented health insurers that the elderly are in a better position to live independently. The task of the case manager will be carried out by neighborhood social workers and nurses. Most certainly, community centers will also be increasingly involved in this effort.

LEISURE-TIME RESOURCES

Activities for the elderly are organized through ideological organizations (church and humanistic groups). Volunteers visit the aged at home, in hospitals, or in nursing homes. It is noteworthy that many younger elderly do voluntary work for the benefit of those older than themselves. Two interesting initiatives can be reported in this context. First, "guilds" or organizations of elderly persons arrange tourist trips through Amsterdam and offer their services and knowledge (e.g., odd jobs at home or piano lessons). Second, organizations of ex-managers, for reimbursement of expenses only, provide on-location advice to firms in Eastern Europe. Both initiatives offer the elderly the possibility of placing their knowledge at the disposal of others.

An active institutional framework is provided by senior citizen associations or "unions," which primarily organize elderly people at the local level. Most of these activities take place in the recreational sphere. Recreation for the elderly is financially stimulated by the Dutch government by means of the Senior Citizens' Pass, which provides discounts on entry fees for virtually all recreational facilities, as well as an over-65 pass for train travel. This discount travel must take place outside rush hours. Presently, a travel agency specializes in trips for the elderly.

Where the social integration of the elderly in the community is concerned, the way has primarily been paved by coordinated community work for the elderly, service centers, and the general welfare facilities in the community. Clubhouses organize recreational and cultural activities during the day.

With the growth of the young-old in Dutch society, there is increasing attention to educational resources for the elderly. Although stimulation of senior education is a governmental priority on the national level, the actual development is rather limited. For example, new forms of higher education for aged persons, comparable with the university of the third-age in other countries, do not receive much grant money; confronted with other financial problems, the Ministry of Education is still hesitant to invest in old age.

Besides organized educational forms, elderly are engaged in "self-directed learning"; it is estimated that in old age, the major individual learning projects are self-directed. Other traditional educational resources are courses in preparation for retirement; basic education for older individuals; media education;

creative, political, and intellectual courses in special centers; and "built-in" education in unions and advocacy groups. New educational resources are senior study circles, memory courses, and higher education for seniors (universities of the third-age). Compared with investments in career and professional education for younger persons, investments in these kinds of educational resources for senior workers are not great. It is estimated that per year there are 200,000 to 400,000 aged persons involved in organized education and that about 20% of all participants in adult education are the elderly.

ADVOCACY AND PROTECTION

Protection is not a topic of much concern, although there is an increased concern regarding advocacy. For instance, protests have taken place against age limits in cases involving medical action, and senior citizen associations are developing more political activities on both national and local levels. The question of mental incompetence is still being resolved within the existing legal framework.

The elderly feel quite unsafe compared with younger people (Timmermans, 1992): 18% of the people age 15–54 are afraid to go out in the dark alone, compared with 51% of those age 65–74 and 59% of those age 75 and older. But in fact, they are less likely to be victims of a crime (25% of the men age 15–54 are victims of theft compared with 9% of the men 65 and older). But everyone who is a victim of a crime can obtain help from a special office (*buro slachtoffer-hulp*).

Euthanasia is a topic of greater public concern. It is forbidden by law. However, a protocol exists concerning how physicians are to conduct themselves in order to avoid legal action in the case of intentionally ending life. Along with this, the senior citizens' organizations, supported by Christian political parties, have been undertaking action to achieve maximum protection in the position of aged persons under psychiatric care. In homes for the elderly and in nursing homes, both the number of patient associations and the extent of regulations concerning complaints are increasing. These provide evidence of improved empowerment for the elderly. More generally speaking, it can be said that the role of clients and patients in supervising the quality of care services is receiving more attention than ever, and binding legislation in this area is presently pending.

FUTURE PROJECTIONS

The extent to which care services are institutionalized is specific to the situation in the Netherlands. Because of exceptional (historic) roots, a system has developed that interweaves privately run, compartmentalized organizations with government financing. This results in a certain amount of inflexibility.

Social developments of both a demographic and an economic nature will put this system under pressure. This will likely result in decreased use of services, a longer working life, a stronger inclination toward insurance for old age (more private pensions and more insurance for care in case of vulnerability in later life), and the institutionalization of informal care. Where this last is concerned, one thinks of the creation of legal conditions for exemptions for employees involved in informal care. This could entail a form of "parent care leave," alongside the existing nine-week maternity leave that is already in place. (In future hiring procedures, information will be required not only concerning the number of children but also whether or not one has parents.) Moreover, because of the pressure on general services due to the increase in the numbers of elderly persons in both the absolute and the relative sense, the problems of age discrimination may come more sharply to the fore.

Between 1990 and 2005, the total population of the Netherlands will grow by 8.7%. Especially the age category of 40–64 years (30% increase) and the 80 and older category (36% increase) will grow very fast. There will be growing demands by the year 2005 for residential institutions (33% increase) and for nursing homes (30% increase). In the community services, home help care will be a growing need, with a 23% increase. The total costs of care (exclusive of old people's homes) will increase by 15% to 46,5 milliard (billion) per year. It is concluded that present social and health policies will not meet this growing demand (Van den Berg Jeths, Poos, Hulshof, and Jager, 1992).

BIBLIOGRAPHY

Alber, J., Guillemard, A., and Walker, A. *The Impact of Social and Economic Policies on Older People in the European Community; EEC Observatory on Older People, First Report.* Brussels: Commission of the European Communities, 1991.

Baars, J., Knipscheer, K., and Breebaart, E. *The Impact of Social and Economic Policies on Older People in the Netherlands.* Amsterdam: Vrije Universiteit, 1992.

Berg Jeths, A. van den, Poos, M., Hulshof, J., and Jager, J. *The Influence of Population Developments on the Burden of Disease and Care Services: Projections till 2005* (in Dutch). Utrecht: Uitgeverij Jan van Arkel, 1992.

Kastelein, M., Dijkstra, A., and Schouten, C. G. *Care of the Elderly in the Netherlands: A Review of Policies and Services 1950–1990.* Leiden: Institute of Preventive Health Care, 1989.

Koedoot, N., and Hommel, A. Case management and incentives for the elderly: Findings from the Rotterdam experiment. In Coolen, J.A.I (ed.), *Changing Care for the Elderly in the Netherlands.* Assen/Maastricht: van Gorcum, 1993.

Ministry of Social Welfare, Health, and Cultural Affairs. *Ageing Matters: Portrait and Policy: Focus on the Elderly 1990–1994.* The Hague: SDU, 1991.

Moors, H., Leusden, H. van, and Hogen Esch, J. *Opinions About the Population—Question and the Acceptance of Policy.* The Hague: Netherlands Interdisciplinary Demographic Institute (NIDI), 1989.

Rijsselt, R. van. *Dutch Report on Social Integration.* Amsterdam: Vrije Universiteit, in press.

―――. Ouderen en maatschappelijke verandering. Diss., Rijksuniversiteit Utrecht, 1991.

Sociaal Cultureel Planbureau (SCP). *Social and Cultural Report, 1990.* Netherlands: The Hague, Staatsuitgeverij, 1990.

Stuurgroep Toekomstscenario's Gezondheidszorg. *Ouderen in het jaar 2005: Gezondheid en zorg. Geactualiseerde scenario's over gezondheid en vergrijzing 1990–2005. Scenariorapport 1992.* Houten/Zaventem: Bohn Stafleu van Loghum, 1992.

Timmermans, J. *Report on the Elderly.* The Hague: Social Cultural Planning Office, 1992.

NEW ZEALAND

Peggy G. Koopman-Boyden

INTRODUCTION

New Zealand has seen enormous changes in its economic and social policies during the 1980s and early 1990s, brought about by an economic recession and a move from welfare policies to policies of the free market. With respect to the elderly, policies have also been influenced by the increasing numbers of older people and the consequent increase in pension and health costs.

The Role of the Elderly

Old age has traditionally been defined as the age at which one is eligible for the government pension, but as this age has changed (in 1976 to the universal age of 60 and in 1992 to 61), there has been some confusion as to the "age of old age." For most policy purposes, however, it is between 60 and 65 years, although many of the elderly do not consider themselves "older people" until their late 70s, and others never consider themselves old.

A considerable degree of ambiguity exists as to the status and power of the elderly in New Zealand. While age discrimination before the age of eligibility for the old-age pension (61 years in 1992) is illegal, retirement is compulsory after this age, and job opportunities for those over 50 years are often limited. With their increasing numbers, the older population is becoming politicized and more likely to question discriminatory practices. Many people over 60 years hold important public positions in parliament and local bodies, especially in the private sector. Few of these people, however, identify with the problems of their age group.

As of 1991 New Zealand has a population of 3.3 million people, with half a million people (527,400) over 60 years (15.43%) and 384,800 over 65 (11.26%).

Of those over 60 years, 55.6% are female. Feminization is particularly noticeable over the age of 80 years, of which age group 67% are female. Almost half of these women are widows (42%), while only 12% of the men are widowers. Most older people live either with their spouse or alone, with relatively few living with their children or other relatives.

The life expectancy of New Zealanders is one of the highest in the world, but within the population there is considerable variation. Life expectancy at birth for the total population is 71.6 years for males and 77.6 years for females, with life expectancy at 60 years being 17.2 years for males and 21.4 years for females. For the Maori population (who make up about 15% of the population), life expectancy at birth is 67.4 years for males and 72.3 years for females. Maori life expectancy at 60 years is 13.4 years for males and 16.4 years for females. Because of the shorter life expectancy, older Maori account for only 3% of the Maori population (Department of Statistics, 1991).

The economic circumstances of the elderly population are largely prescribed by the level of the government pension, for about a third of them rely solely on the government-provided pension for financial support. Other sources of income include interest payments (a source of income for 68%), occupational superannuation (43%), dividends (22%), wages/salaries (9%), and so on (Age Concern, 1991, p. 69). After the age of 60, there is a marked drop in labor force participation. Whereas 65.6% of the 55–59 year-olds are in full- or part-time paid employment, only 28.9% of the 60–64 year-olds are employed. For those over 65 years, the labor force participation rate is 7% (1986 figures). It is not surprising, therefore, to find that those over the age of 60 fall largely into the fourth and fifth deciles of income distribution (Social Monitoring Group, 1989, p. 112).

Indirect indicators of the health status of the elderly population in New Zealand need to be used in the absence of direct indicators. Two-thirds of the young old (60–80 years old) and over half of the old old (80+ years) have no disability. In the 60–64-year age group, the mortality rate (per 10,000 estimated mean population in each age group, in 1988–90) for men is 186 (105.7 for women), and in the 80–84-year age group it is 1,175 for men (766.5 for women). Heart disease is responsible for 52% of the deaths of those over 60, particularly men, with 22% due to neoplasms and 13% respiratory illness in 1985–86.

The old-age pension has existed in New Zealand for almost 100 years and has been available universally or to a large proportion of the elderly after an income test. Because of this, there has been a widespread perception that financial support in old age is the government's responsibility. Only in the late 1980s and 1990s has this perception been challenged by successive governments anxious to cut welfare expenditure by limiting access to the pension and the amount of pensions.

Similarly, public perception of the care of the elderly has often seen the provision of institutional care as the financial responsibility of government or charitable and religious groups. While such institutional care has involved about 6% of the elderly in the 1970s and 1980s, most of the care is undertaken by the family and community organizations. The amount and burden of such unpaid care were little recognized or documented until the late 1980s, when the increasing costs of institutionalization forced the government to encourage greater family and community care.

The Formal Structure of Care of the Elderly

New Zealand has always had a system of "welfare pluralism" for the care of the elderly, incorporating the public, private (commercial or voluntary and religious), and informal (family) sectors. Since 1938 a range of welfare policies has supported the elderly (and other age groups), including subsidized primary care, free prescriptions, and free hospitalization, along with subsidized housing and telephone rentals. Changes in social policy since the late 1980s have, however, seen the introduction of user-pays and the privatization of some social services for the elderly, along with other population groups. In the area of health and social services, those solely dependent on the government pension still receive subsidized primary care, free secondary care in public hospitals, and subsidized care in the private sector. For the first time, however, financial stratification of the elderly population has occurred, so that those with higher incomes are required to pay for part or all of their health and social services. Entitlement to such services has thereby moved from being based on age and health needs to being based on family income and health needs.

INCOME MAINTENANCE AND EMPLOYMENT

In 1898 New Zealand was one of the first countries in the world to establish an old-age pension. Since 1938 the pension has been universally available to everyone over 65, and since 1976, to everyone over 60. With recent fiscal constraints and the increasing size of the population eligible for the pension, the government has found it necessary to impose a tax surcharge, raise the age of eligibility, cut the amount paid, and raise people's awareness of the need for private superannuation schemes (although tax incentives for payments into such schemes have been disallowed). Such policies have also been implemented in response to the perception of government policymakers that the amount of economic assistance to elderly people is disproportionate to total government expenditure.

A tax surcharge was introduced in 1985 to withdraw a proportion of the old-age pension from recipients with high additional income. Between 1992 and 2001 the age of eligibility is to be progressively raised to 65, while the rate is no longer as generous as in the 1980s. In April 1992 the rate of the pension was $187.27 (net) per week for a single person living alone and $144.05 (net) for a person who is married. Based on the February 1992 Labor Force Survey, the net pension for a single person represents 45% of the average after-tax ordinary time wage and 34.6% for a married person (Department of Statistics,

1992). The gross ordinary time wage (males/females) was $548.83. While everyone over a certain age (61 years in 1992) receives this pension, those on higher incomes have a higher tax imposed, so that eventually all of the pension is taxed away (for a single person living alone this occurs at an income of $35,802; for a married couple where each partner earns half their total income it is $54,846 per annum). Nevertheless, in 1990, 19% of net government expenditure was spent on the old-age pension (called National Superannuation).

About a third of the population over 15 years contribute to an occupational pension scheme (30% males and 24% of females), with the most significant contributors being over 40 years and the biggest contributors being in the 40–49-year age group. Given the differential in male/female wages and the different expectations held for male/female occupational and financial security, the weekly contribution of males is higher in amount than that for females—four times higher (St. John and Ashton, 1990).

The most generous occupational pension scheme is provided for members of parliament, judges, and government employees. The latter pay 6.5% of their income into the Government Superannuation Fund and are subsidized an equal amount by their employer. In 1992 there were 45,000 pensioners under the Government Superannuation Fund and approximately 55,000 contributors. The scheme has been deemed too generous, so since July 1992 new contributors are no longer admitted, and existing contributors have had their anticipated superannuation benefit lowered.

The government has concentrated its financial assistance on the provision of a reasonably generous tax-based pension (50% of social welfare expenditure was spent on the pension in 1990) and provides few other direct forms of financial assistance apart from supplementary financial assistance for those with special financial needs. Similarly, local and regional governments do not give any direct financial assistance to the elderly. Some private sector organizations provide regular or occasional subsidies, discounts, and off-peak prices on transport, movies and theater performances, holiday accommodations, insurance, new car maintenance, and so on.

Many older people, once retired, endeavor to find a part-time job to supplement their financial resources. In a country with an unemployment rate of over 11% of the labor force (1992), this is not easy, especially when opportunities for job retraining and job redesign are practically nonexistent for older people. Self-employment is increasingly likely to be the solution. Of those people over 65 in the labor force, approximately half are self-employed and are most likely to be in the agricultural, horticultural, and professional sectors.

HEALTH CARE SERVICES

Since 1938, health care services in New Zealand have operated on a dual public/private system, with secondary care being largely publicly funded and provided and with primary care involving user-part charges. In the 1990s, however, the system is changing to a more user-pays system.

Hospital and related services are publicly funded through the distribution of tax funding to 14 area health boards. The boards are responsible for all of the public hospital and related services in their geographical area. User-part charges, based on family income, were introduced for hospital and related services on 1 February 1992. In 1990-91, area health boards were funded $345 million to cover long-stay public hospital continuing care, area health board rest home care, respite care, home-based services, assessment and rehabilitation services, and some equipment (Department of Health, 1992).

In contrast to the secondary care system, the primary care system is based on private providers, with the government contributing at a much lower level through subsidies on a fee-for-service or, in some cases, on a capitation basis. On 1 February 1992, the basis on which subsidies are paid changed from age and health needs to family income and health needs (Department of Health, 1992).

Hospital and residential continuing care services for older people are provided through public and private hospitals and rest homes, the majority of which are privately operated. Services are free through the public system, while care in the private sector is financed by subsidies and a higher level of user-contribution. Major private sector organizations include Presbyterian Support Services, providing residential homes and hospitals, cottages and flats, day relief, and temporary care.

Community care services are provided publicly through the area health boards and the Department of Social Welfare and by private, nonprofit voluntary or religious organizations. Major private providers include Age Concern and Presbyterian Support Services (Aged People's Care).

In 1991 the total health expenditure (nominal) in New Zealand as a proportion of gross domestic product (GDP) was 7.36%, with 81.7% of that expenditure being publicly funded and 18.3% from the private sector. Financial support of the public health system comes from general taxation.

Health services have recently undergone major restructuring. From 1 July 1993, the funding function of the 14 area health boards was taken over by four regional health authorities, which are responsible for purchasing both primary and secondary health services from competing public, private, and nonprofit providers. The future funding and responsibility for a range of long-term care services have yet to be decided. At present the health sector has responsibility for hospital, domiciliary, and community-based health professional services, while the Department of Social Welfare has responsibility for funding other home and community-based services. The split in funding and responsibility has created a number of problems, but in future services will be bulk-funded through a single agency, the Ministry of Health, as announced in late 1992.

Institutional acute and chronic care for older people is provided in long-term public and private hospitals or wards and in rest homes (sometimes called residential or nursing homes). There is a noticeable increase in dependency and frailty in the upper age range, which is indicated by the increased number of the old old living in residential care. About 6% of the elderly live in institutions (hospitals and rest homes), while of those over 85 years, 36% live in residential care. The average age of admission to residential care has been steadily rising in recent years and is about 85–86 years (Department of Health, 1992). A needs assessment is generally undertaken by a geriatrician or a multidisciplinary assessment and rehabilitation team. The 1986 Department of Health guideline recommends that five assessment and rehabilitation beds per 1,000 people over 65 years should be provided, but few area health boards have attained this level of provision. Public hospital geriatric services are free regardless of the older person's ability to pay. However, after 13 weeks in a public hospital, a patient's old-age pension paid by the Department of Social Welfare is reduced to a weekly living allowance of $24.00. There were 2,180 designated long-stay public beds and 1,788 long-stay patients in public beds in December 1991 (Department of Health, 1992).

At the same time, there were 5,521 private long-stay hospital beds. The Geriatric Hospital Daily Patient Benefit is paid by the Department of Health for every long-stay geriatric patient in a private hospital. Where there is no public bed available within the guideline figures, a subsidy for private care is available under the Geriatric Hospital Special Assistance Scheme (after appropriate assessment of the person's needs). This subsidy meets any shortfall between the patient's contribution from income, the Geriatric Hospital Daily Patient Benefit, and the private hospital fee (the patient is means-tested). There were 4,313 patients receiving the Geriatric Hospital Special Assistance Scheme in December 1991. On the basis of an occupancy rate of about 95% for private long-stay hospital beds, it is estimated that a further 932 private long-stay patients were paying the full costs of their care at that time (Department of Health, 1992).

With the introduction of the Geriatric Hospital Special Assistance Scheme in 1977, there was a major increase in funding for private hospital care. Thus, more than two-thirds of private hospital continuing care beds are occupied by older people on the Geriatric Hospital Special Assistance Scheme. Area health boards have now been limited in the total number of long-stay geriatric patients (in both public and private care) placed under the Geriatric Hospital Special Assistance Scheme to the departmental guideline of 18 beds per 1,000 people over 65 years.

There has been a similar increase in the number of rest home beds, due to the possibility of assessed residents occupying such beds being eligible for a Department of Social Welfare subsidy. Between July 1989 and July 1991, expenditure on the subsidy doubled (from $51.7 million to $109 million), with the number of licensed rest home beds increasing from 17,638 to 19,635. While a planning guideline has been set at 30 rest home beds per 1,000 people aged over 65 years, the ratio in 1991 was at a level of 51 beds (Department of Health, 1992).

The Rest Home Subsidy is a demand-driven individual entitlement available to everyone 65 and over who meets specified income, assets, and needs criteria as determined by an assessment and rehabilitation team. The subsidy makes up the difference between the recipient's contribution and the total fee for rest home care. Of the 19,635 licensed rest home beds in July 1991, approximately 17,000 were occupied; 7,500 of these residents received the subsidy (Department of Health, 1992). Few of these rest home beds are owned by the government or area health boards. Instead they are owned by the private (commercial) sector or the private (voluntary and religious) sector.

People seeking admission to a rest home are usually assessed as to their need by an assessment and rehabilitation team. Rest homes are graded according to the level of services provided, and a higher level of rest home subsidy is paid to homes able to care for more dependent persons. The rest home subsidy also makes up the difference between the client's contribution (after an income and assets assessment) and a nationally negotiated fee level.

The provision of multidisciplinary assessment and rehabilitation units is seen as a priority of public sector provision, with services being provided in every area health board. Elderly people must be assessed by the service before qualifying for a hospital or rest home subsidy and graded according to the Composite Dependency Scale.

In June 1982, the Department of Health established a new category of home care, "Stage III Rest Home," and offered a subsidy to 750 places for highly dependent, mentally infirm elderly people, including those with Alzheimer's and related dementias. It is recognized that the service needs of these people are distinctive and labor-intensive and, as a result, more costly. On the dependency scale, such home care is between that provided in Stage II rest homes and that provided in geriatric hospitals.

While most of the public funding for continuing care services is directed toward such institutional care, the Department of Social Welfare also provides financial assistance to means-tested older people for home help care, on the recommendation of a general practitioner. Similarly, area health boards provide a range of home care services. Community organizations, such as the Nurse Maude District Nursing Association and the Women's Division of Federated Farmers, provide a variety of domestic assistance to older people. In the past they have been partially funded by government grants, but in recent years such organizations have been contracted for their services. From 1 July 1993, as a means of encouraging the provision of a diverse range of community-based services, all noninstitutional services compete for contracts from regional health authorities to provide services.

Coordination between the sectors at the provider level has been a long-standing problem in the area of long-term care, with split-funding responsibilities between the area health boards and the Department of Social Welfare encouraging cost-shifting. In addition, institutional care was often more accessible than community care. From 1 July 1993, the funding and provider functions of health services are separated, with a single agency having responsibility for purchasing support services for all people with disabilities. It is hoped that the integration of funding under one agency will improve coordination between service providers and encourage the provision of a wider range of services to allow more people to remain in their own homes.

HOUSING RESOURCES

Most people over 60 years in New Zealand live in a private house (92.4%), which is likely to be single storied and have two or three bedrooms and a garden. Most older people own their home (85%), usually without a mortgage (72%). The commonest form of living arrangement among elderly people is that of couples living on their own, without any children or other family members (59% of elderly males, 40% of elderly females). Only 13% of the elderly men and 7% of the elderly women live in "couples with children" households. The proportion of couples living together, either with or without children, declines significantly with advancing age. On the other hand, the proportion of elderly people living in one-person households rises dramatically with increasing age: one-sixth of those aged 60–64 live on their own, compared with almost half of those aged 85 years and over (Department of Statistics, 1990, p.17, 1986 figures).

Government assistance with housing for older people has taken a variety of forms: special lending loans to house older people (assisting 351 households in 1990–91) or to assist them to shift into more suitable housing (226 people in 1990–91); the provision of subsidized housing (25% of the Housing Corporation tenants in 1990–91 were over 60); and the provision of relocatable cottages (229 households in 1990–91).

Beginning in July 1993, however, the government no longer provides subsidized housing or loans for elderly people. Instead the private sector is expected to meet the housing needs of the elderly, but, where necessary, elderly people are eligible for the special Accommodation Supplement to help pay for rent or mortgage repayments.

Over the years, local government has also subsidized housing, so that low-rental local government housing is available in most cities and large towns for elderly people in need (e.g., in Christchurch, with a population of 57,453 over 60 years, 2,100 twin/single units at 102 locations are available). Such housing is usually in clusters, single-story, and with a small garden. Each house usually has a single bedroom for the sole occupant or a married couple, a living room, kitchen/dining room, and bathroom facilities. Between 5 and 100 people often live in such housing complexes. Few of these complexes have a supervising warden. Over the whole country, 10,722 people over 60 years live in local authority houses, compared with 17,161 living in government-provided, or Housing Corporation, accommodations.

Recent innovations in housing policies include the 1990–91 trial of a "Helping Hands" project, by which elderly homeowners can convert the funds tied up in their homes into cash to help with housing expenses. The loan does not have to be repaid in the homeowner's lifetime. Instead, the money borrowed and the interest charges are paid back from the homeowner's estate. However, interest in this scheme has been very low (although higher than in other countries at a similar stage of development) and suggesting that older people in New Zealand are cautious about capitalizing housing wealth (to them it equates with borrowing money) and prefer to bequeath assets to their children at the highest possible value.

With the increasing awareness of ethnic diversity in New Zealand, another new development has been the provision of residential care for those who prefer to observe their own customs and language. For example, there are Jewish residential homes in Wellington and Auckland, and a Dutch residential home, "Ons Dorp," in Auckland.

Since the mid-1980s the establishment of many retirement villages has also been a major innovation in housing for older people. Such communities usually have a minimum entry age of 55 years. Many include recreational facilities, such as billiard and craft rooms, a bowls lawn, and a swimming pool. Entry criteria to retirement villages involve income rather than need. Residents pay a market rate for their unit, which is repurchased by the village trust when the owner leaves or dies. Thus, residential villages operate as a capital resource scheme, as well as providing for social and physical security.

Currently, those living in the retirement villages are mainly active older people who require little medical or other outside assistance. Many older people living in other private housing, however, require the support of community services to remain in their own homes. As well as the health care services provided largely by the state, organizations such as Age Concern (Canterbury) provide transport for shopping expeditions and a list of reasonably priced maintenance and home repair services. The government has contracted Age Concern (New Zealand) to provide a visitor service for people in rest homes who have no family or friends but who would like a regular visitor (the Accredited Visitor Scheme).

There are no financial incentives for the elderly to remain in their own home. Instead the system encourages the use of institutional care, through the provision of institutional subsidies. However, financial assistance can be given to caregivers through the Domestic Purposes Benefit. Respite care is also available.

SUPPORTIVE SERVICES

There is a wide variety of supportive services provided by both the public and the private sectors. Generally, however, there has been little recognition of those who care for the elderly at home. Funding and coordination of services for older people (and for people with psychiatric, intellectual and physical disabilities) and their need for long-term care services are currently under extensive review. The debate centers on which agency (the Department of Social Welfare or Regional Health Authorities) should be responsible for the purchase of the whole spectrum of services after 1 July 1993.

In the meantime, the number of private, nonprofit organizations that provide home-based support services is growing, for example, Presbyterian Support Services, which has taken a major initiative in developing home support services. These services include a wide range of domiciliary services, integrated with the health care services provided in residential care. Such a service allows the older person to vary the form and extent of care and to move from home-based care to residential care with minimum disruption.

Another innovative program is provided by the area health boards to allow the caregiver to take a break. Each board has facilities for respite care, and, after consideration by the assessment and rehabilitation services, an elderly person can be admitted for up to 28 days annually. Many families prefer to admit their relative for shorter periods at a time or to use the entitlement for day-care services. A benefit from the Department of Social Welfare meets some, but often not all, of the costs, which depend on the service used. It is estimated that 80% of the 2,000–3,000 people who are using this service are looking after dependent older people (Department of Health, 1992).

Government programs maintaining the elderly within their own homes also include the provision of the Domestic Purposes Benefit to a person who gives up work to look after a sick or frail elderly person and who is not the wife, husband, or partner. During 1991, 780 people caring for the sick and infirm received this assistance. The number caring for older people is not separately recorded. In special circumstances, a relative caring for an older person may be eligible for an Emergency Unemployment Benefit.

Up to 15 hours per week of home help assistance can also be provided as an individual entitlement by the Department of Social Welfare's Home Help Scheme. On 30 June 1991, 3,000 elderly people had received this type of assistance (Department of Health, 1992). Area health boards also provide a limited linen service to clients, home help, meals-on-wheels, social work, podiatry, home nursing, counseling services, and occupational and physiotherapy. Often such assistance is provided by voluntary organizations, which are increasingly operating on contract to the government, for example, meals-on-wheels is provided by the Red Cross in conjunction with area health boards.

A Homecare 60's Plus scheme was introduced in 1988 to promote and develop home-based services for the elderly as an alternative to institutional care. The service operates seven days a week, providing housework, meals, shopping, bathing, and so on, up to a maximum of 14 hours per week for an individual user. The service providers are contracted to the area health board. Access to the scheme is by social work assessment. Most of the clients are in the "low dependency" category, but a few are of "moderate" or "appreciable" dependency. A part-charge is levied, but a means-test subsidy is available. Eventually it is hoped to integrate the service with other domiciliary services, using a "key worker" approach.

An important form of support for the elderly outside their homes is through the day-care centers and day hospitals operated by the area health boards and by the private/voluntary sector. The major sources of funding are user payments through the Aid to Families Scheme (maximum 56 days of day care each year) and Disability Allowance (maximum $38.50 a week). Other, more specialized organizations offering support include the Stroke Clubs, Alzheimer's Disease and Related Disorders Society (ADARDS), the Hearing Association, and the Arthritis Foundation of New Zealand.

A traditional source of information for New Zealanders has been the Citizens' Advice Bureau, a nationwide telephone network, but expansion of Age Concern in the 1980s provided a more personal basis for information sharing, along with more specialist information. In 1991 Age Concern (Canterbury) established a computer-based telephone information service for older people, which is planned to go nationwide by the mid-1990s.

Counseling and social work services are provided by a number of agencies, including, for example, Age Concern and Presbyterian Support Services (Aged Peoples Care).

It is not possible to include the number of older people who use mental health services, for statistics are not kept according to age group. There are, however, several psychogeriatric services throughout the country, and the Department of Health has recommended the guideline that 3–5 beds per 1,000 people over the age of 65 should be allocated to psychogeriatric patients. There is concern, however, over the lack of facilities and support for psychogeriatric patients and the large number of older people with an age-related dementia who are cared for at home, without adequate caregiver support. ADARDS has approximately 60 support groups throughout the country that provide support to families of people with such diseases and help to raise the public's awareness of the needs of sufferers and their relatives.

LEISURE-TIME RESOURCES

In a major survey of the sport and recreation pursuits of New Zealanders in 1989, the Hillary Commission of Sport and Recreation established that the older that New Zealanders get—especially those over 65 years—the more likely they are to be involved in home-related activities. For both men and women, such activities are likely to be watching television, reading, talking with family, and listening to music (Hillary Commission, 1990).

The same survey established that of those over 65 years, 28% of the men and 21% of the women worked as a volunteer for at least one hour per week. Both men and women were more likely to volunteer for welfare work, women (51%)

to a greater extent than men (37%). Such voluntary work often serves as a social contact for the older person with their own age group. For example, the voluntary work undertaken through the Returned Services Association usually involves older members (usually men) assisting other older members and their wives.

One of New Zealand's major voluntary organizations, Age Concern, involves many older people as volunteers and also acts as an umbrella group to facilitate the coordination of services for older people. Its 35 branches provide home-based support services (housework, home maintenance, befriending, gardening, transport), information and advisory services (financial and management advice, personal counseling, education seminars, newsletters, and newspapers), meals, and social activities (bus trips and recreational classes) to over 8,000 older people each week throughout the country. An estimated 27,000 clients used Age Concern's services in the year ending February 1992. Volunteers are the major providers of the services, with over 1,640 volunteers being coordinated on a regular weekly basis.

In the last five years there has been an increasing awareness of the recreational needs of older people. Initiation of the annual Veterans' Games is a good example, along with "masters" or "veterans" events in swimming and triathlon meetings. In 1991, the Hillary Commission for Sport and Recreation began a nationwide program, "Active in Age," to show older New Zealanders the benefits of a healthy life-style. Included are such strategies as New Start Exercise Clinics for those 50+, a television exercise program, assistance to sports clubs to encourage older adults to participate, and Fun Festivals to encourage older adults to "have a go" at a range of physical activities.

There are a number of age-segregated organizations for older people, including a well-established Craft and Care Centers network throughout the country. These centers provide for a range of interests through handicrafts and other social activities for adult disabled, elderly, and housebound people, called "guests." Voluntary helpers are an essential part of a center's providing care and assistance. For the more active who seek age-segregated organizations, such groups as the Returned Servicemen's Association, Age Concern, and Probus Clubs provide a variety of social and recreational activities, while also being concerned with their members' welfare.

Older people are, however, more likely to be involved in organizations that span various ages, such as church-affiliated groups, sports clubs (bowls, golf), and hobby groups (bridge and garden clubs, playing *housie,* china painting). For those with a sight disability, the provision of large-print or "talking books" by libraries or voluntary organizations allows them to continue their hobby of reading.

Few older people are involved in formal educational activities, but in the 1990s greater opportunities for less-traditional forms of education are being established. The New Zealand College for Seniors, offering live-in learning holidays for the over-50s, has been established in conjunction with several universities and polytechnics. The college is associated with an international network, especially Australia. The internationally known concept of the university of the third-age has also been successfully established in Wellington. Other local examples providing educational opportunities for older people include the publication of a regular newspaper (*Age Concern*), radio/television programs (e.g., "Life Span," with an emphasis on empowering older people), and various media presentations by the Hillary Commission endeavoring to break down ageist stereotypes.

ADVOCACY AND PROTECTION

With the huge economic and social changes occurring in New Zealand since the mid-1980s, older people have seen the old-age pension come under threat with respect to the age of eligibility and its amount. Concerned about such cuts in the old-age pension, older people have become more politically active. Groups such as Grey Power and Superants, composed largely of older people, have sought media attention when pension cuts have occurred or been threatened. Less radical groups, such as Age Concern (New Zealand), ADARDS, and the Gerontological Association have also adopted an advocacy role for older people on such issues as elder abuse and ageist discrimination.

While no special programs advise the elderly of their rights relating to the law or to victim assistance, elderly people on low incomes have access to the Legal Aid program, providing free legal advice. The larger offices of Age Concern also offer free legal and financial assistance.

Elderly people who are unable to manage their finances or general affairs adequately are protected by the Protection of Personal and Property Rights Act of 1986, which enables the court to appoint a guardian who acts to safeguard the dignity of the older person while promoting and protecting that person's personal rights, welfare, and property.

However, cases of abuse, neglect, and self-neglect occur. Appropriate legislation has yet to be introduced that would make notification of such behaviors mandatory. In the meantime, Age Concern (New Zealand) is seeking to raise public awareness of the problem through research and the distribution of a resource kit on elder abuse, neglect, and self-neglect.

The personal security and peace of mind of older people living alone are often ensured by the use of a personal alarm system worn around the person's neck, as a wristwatch, or strategically placed around the house. The Department of Social Welfare will pay rental costs for an elderly person who has a medical condition and is below a certain income. Advocacy organizations, such as Age Concern, assist older people in the use of protective devices and in strategies for general personal security.

Advocacy organizations such as Age Concern, ADARDS, and the Gerontological Association are also strongly supportive of health promotion campaigns for the elderly. Most of these campaigns have been undertaken by organizations catering to all age groups but now beginning to realize the special needs of older people. In 1991–92, for example, the Family Planning Association undertook workshops on menopause and osteoporosis, the Department of Health specifically targeted older women (over 50) to have a cervical cancer smear, and the Hillary Commission for Sport and Recreation initiated a number of sports-related programs for older people. Several statutory agencies have also initiated and resourced promotional/preventive health strategies specifically for the elderly, for example, the publication *Empowerment of Older People* (Board of Health Standing Committee on the Elderly), the "Older and Bolder" promotional campaign (Department of Health), and the "Take Five" radio program (Radio New Zealand).

FUTURE PROJECTIONS

General Conclusions

New Zealand has over half a million people over 60 years, 15% of its population. Most of these people live in their own homes, are supported by a state-provided pension, and are not disabled in any way.

New Zealand is a small society and has one of the fastest aging societies in the world. By international standards it has a high standard of living, but in the last two decades this has fallen noticeably. The current cohort of older people grew older knowing that they would have a pension to rely on in their old age. While this has eventuated, the changing economic situation in the country has meant that for many of them the amount of the pension and the cost of living make the pension much more difficult to live on than they had anticipated. They do, however, still have access to free or relatively inexpensive medical care.

The country's services for the elderly are marked by cooperation—but not integration—among government, private sector, and voluntary services, with a strong emphasis on public funding and provision of institutional care rather than community care. This has meant that flexibility and choice in service provision have not been possible, and much of the value of informal care has been overlooked.

Emerging Needs of the Elderly

Future cohorts of the elderly are likely to be more heterogeneous than previous cohorts. The aging of ethnic groups (Maori, Pacific Island Polynesian, and migrants from Asia) is likely to bring a demand for a wider diversity of services, such as housing and personal services. With smaller families and an increasing incidence of divorce, all ethnic groups will have fewer children available to care for their aging parents (or step-parents). The increasing numbers of people who live to old age, particularly to over 80 years, will mean an increasing level of dependency and need for service provision. On the other hand, the larger number of fit, active people in the 60–80-year age group will seek recreational and educational opportunities.

Methods to Improve the Quality of Life for Elderly Persons

New Zealand's health services in 1992–93 are undergoing major restructuring, with a greater emphasis on user-pays, separation of funder and provider, and encouragement of diversity in provision and thus greater competition among providers. The main policy issue is the need to develop an integrated, coordinated system of cost-effective services, for the lack of flexibility in present funding arrangements has meant a favoring of institutional care over home-based services. One of the goals of the new restructured health system is to allow public, private, and voluntary services to compete for funding on an equal footing and thus allow for greater consumer choice.

At the same time there is a need to recognize more appropriately the provision of care by informal caregivers and, in various ways, provide respite care for them, along with a wider range of home care services. In general, older people prefer to live in their own homes, but it has often been easier to have them cared for in an institution in the absence of home-based support services.

The future of New Zealand's older people lies not only in the regular assessment of its health services but also in the provision of promotional programs to ensure that older people themselves can maintain their own mental and physical health. It is to be hoped that the initiatives in this area, begun in the early 1990s, will continue.

NOTE

The contributions of the following are gratefully acknowledged: Members of the Health of Older People Policy, Department of Health; Odette Waanders (Age Concern—New Zealand); Ken Irwin and Anne Ny (Presbyterian Support Services); Gaynor Duff (ADARDS); and Kay Dobson-Hill.

BIBLIOGRAPHY

Age Concern/National Mutual. *The Lifestyle and Well-being of New Zealand's Over 60s.* Wellington: Age Concern, 1991.
Department of Health. *Care of the Frail Elderly in New Zealand—Report to the OECD.* Department of Health, March 1992.
Department of Statistics. *Elderly Population of New Zealand.* Wellington: Department of Statistics, 1990.
———. *Demographic Trends 1991.* Wellington: Department of Statistics, 1991.
Hillary Commission for Recreation and Sport. *Life in New Zealand: Summary Report,* prepared by N. C. Wilson, Hillary Commission, 1990.
———. *Life in New Zealand: Commission Report,* prepared by University of Otago for the Hillary Commission, 1991.

Koopman-Boyden, P. G. *New Zealand's Ageing Society: The Implications.* Wellington: Daphne Brasell Associates Press, 1993.

Muthumala, D., and Mckendry, C. G. *Health Expenditure Trends in New Zealand, 1980–1991.* Department of Health, 1992.

St. John, S., and Ashton, T. *Private Pensions in New Zealand—Country Report for the OECD.* 1990.

Social Monitoring Group. *From Birth to Death II—The Second Overview Report.* Wellington: New Zealand Planning Council, 1989.

22

NORWAY

Eva Beverfelt

INTRODUCTION

Norway is a welfare state with an advanced Social Security system and highly developed social and medical services. In principle, it is generally accepted as the responsibility of society to organize the measures needed to prevent disease and social misery and to treat those suffering from poor health or personal adjustment problems.

These positive aspects of the welfare state are also reflected in the situation of elderly people. Anyone above 67 years of age is entitled to an old-age pension through the national insurance scheme. Substantial sums are appropriated over the state budget for various schemes of importance to the elderly.

Since 1973 the lowest retirement age has been 67, and the compulsory retirement age is 70. The term *gammel* (old) is often associated with negative traits, so old people describe themselves as *eldre* (elderly), which is also used in public documents and mass media. In statistics and the context of service and care, the elderly are those 67 years of age and more. An elderly worker is defined as a person between 45 and 70 years of age.

Status and Roles of the Aged

Despite the positive aspects of the welfare state, its development has not been entirely in favor of the elderly. The disintegration of the multigenerational families and increased geographical and social mobility, to some extent, have separated younger and elder family members. The younger generation is leaving the farmland and the fishing villages in order to obtain education and jobs, while the elderly remain in the remote areas. Some coastal districts of the country, therefore, have a predominantly elderly population, and in some places only the elderly remain. Poor communications and long distances to neighbors and to shops are creating needs for specific health and welfare measures.

Along with the increasing geographical distance between younger and older family members, there is a growing psychological gap. This is mainly due to a more hectic and stressful life of the middle-aged generation, leaving less time available for being together with the elderly. Moreover, because of rapid technological development, the knowledge of the older generation is often outdated and without interest for the younger ones. The elderly no longer hold a significant role as teachers for their children and grandchildren.

These circumstances have inspired laymen and researchers to dwell on nostalgic descriptions of the past, although there is certainly no evidence about the full truth about old people in the old days. We do have knowledge about different groups of elderly in those days, such as the privileged and the underprivileged. The privileged elderly enjoyed life in supportive environments, and the underprivileged elderly passed their later years under most unfavorable and humiliating conditions (Liaboe, 1980). The latter group, which disturbs the image of the "good old days," is somehow forgotten in spite of available information about poverty and social misery among old people.

Elderly people have been looked upon as more homogeneous than younger groups. Stereotyped thinking about aging and the aged is reflected when people talk about what the elderly want, wish, or need. This judgment, wrong and unfair as it is, has hampered the planning and provision of adequate work and leisure-time activities. To soften these attitudes, great efforts have been made in recent years by gerontologists, social workers, and, somewhat later, politicians and civil servants. Some progress has been made, but much still remains to be done in order to raise the awareness of individual differences in old age.

The increase of the elderly in numbers and as part of the population has made them more visible and significant for the different political parties. In fact, pensioners constitute a massive element of voters that no political party can ignore. Some of the elderly have answered this challenge by becoming more active in calling for their rights and, thus, have managed to strengthen their influence on matters concerning elderly citizens. Their demands to public committees and other policy-making bodies have been clearer and stronger over the last decade. Since 1979 an agreement with the Ministry of Health and Social Affairs (MHSA) has guaranteed Norsk Pensjonistforbund (the national association of pensioners) the right to be informed and consulted concerning regulation of pensions and other issues of significance for the quality of life of the aged. Another achievement by the pensioners is a bill of Councils of Elderly People, passed by the parliament in 1991. This act requires every municipality and county to appoint a council in which pensioners should be in majority of the members. Those elderly who are active in pressure group movements have attained a growing influence, despite the fact that they constitute a relatively small part of the aged population. Norsk Pensjonistforbund, the main organizer of the elderly's actions, has about 120,000 members (or one-fifth of the elderly).

The remaining pensioners are not necessarily more passive. Some are gainfully employed. Hundreds of the young old participate as volunteers in social services, mainly for the elderly (i.e., at senior citizens' centers). Other pensioners have maintained their identity and prestige through various kinds of substitutes for paid work. Some people extend their social contacts and activities after they retire. More and more of the aged enjoy traveling both in Norway and abroad. Visiting relatives in the United States is no longer a privilege for the very few. A better economy and numerous guided tours enable the aged to undertake travels that their parents would not have been able to consider.

On the other hand, unforeseen negative consequences of the welfare state policies, in general, also have their impact on the well-being of the elderly. Along with improved material conditions, there is a growing concern about the content and quality of life. Another problem is the failing ability of the welfare state to obtain a fair distribution of public resources for all its members. Among elderly people this is demonstrated by growing inequality in living conditions. An increasing number of people over 80 will be in need of care and support to an extent that may sometimes be difficult to meet. Loneliness, isolation, and the feeling of being useless, a burden, even unwanted by family and society are serious problems. Loneliness also occurs in younger age groups, even at nearly the same rate as among the elderly (Thorsen, 1990). But this fact does not diminish the problems for the old person suffering from lack of social contact and support. The lonely elderly person is often difficult to identify, both for the researcher and for the social worker. Especially when it comes to the more severe cases of isolation, an older person may be ashamed of deterioration in appearance or a neglected home and may therefore refuse to participate in a research project or to accept any social contact.

Demographic Characteristics

In 1990, every seventh Norwegian was above 67 years of age. After a decrease of the 67 and older population projected from 1995 (14.3%) and during the first decade of the next century (12.8%), the projections indicate a marked increase both in numbers and proportion, lasting beyond the year 2030 (17.3%).

When planning services for the aged, one has to bear in mind the proportions of the age groups involved, because the need for assistance and care will increase with advancing age. Especially important is the number of those 80 years and over, which will continue to increase up to the year 2030. From constituting slightly over one-fourth of the elderly in 1990, the group of the very old in 2010 will account for more than one-third of the aged population.

In Norway, as in most industrial societies, women outlive men and their proportion of the old population increases with advancing age. During the last 40 years the difference in life expectancy between men and women has almost doubled. This difference has, however, increased at a slower rate during recent years. The relative number of men and women in the future is, therefore, more complicated to predict than the development of the total number of elderly (Noack and Texmon, 1991).

In 1991 the life expectancy at birth was 79.8 years for women and 73.4 for men. The elderly population consists of 60% women and 40% men. Among those over 80 years, the figures are 67% women and 33% men. While 69% of men over 67 are married, only 36% of women over 67 are married.

A higher proportion of elderly are living in remote areas and in some areas of the cities. In Oslo, the share of persons 80 years and over is five percent (as against two percent in the surrounding municipalities).

Health Conditions of the Elderly

The proportion of different age groups applying for disability benefits indicates a marked health decline with advancing years. The incidence of chronic disease, which is 30% in the age group 35 to 44 years of age, increases to 64% and 74% of the 75 to 84-year-old men and women, respectively (Helset, 1991).

Based on different studies, it is estimated that 5% of the over-60 population and 15% of those over 75 years of age suffer from Alzheimer's disease or other types of dementia. Physical and mental health decline have a more or less negative impact on the individual's ability to cope with the matters of everyday life and to maintain social contact. About one-third of the elderly population is in need of help with household chores and/or personal care. Due to illness, 4 out of 10 elderly have difficulties with taking part in leisure-time activities and social gatherings. The corresponding share of the 45–66-year olds is less than 2 out of 10 (18%) (Statistik sentralbyrå [SSB], 1989). The age distribution of the population in long-stay institutions also demonstrates increasing dependence with advancing years. Three of four patients are over 80 years, 23% are from 67 to 79 years, and only 4% are under 67 years of age. Among the young old (67–79 years of age), nearly all are living in private households, while this is the case for only half of those who are 90 years and over (Søbye, 1990).

Although women outlive men, elderly women and the young old have poorer health than men, whether measured by diagnoses or self-evaluated state of health. The proportion evaluating their health as "good," for example, includes 53% of the elderly women as against 61% of the elderly men (SSB, 1987).

The Formal Structure of Care of the Elderly

Policies guidelines, and broad principles for the aging are established by the government and the Storting (parliament). Government programs for the elderly are provided by various ministries. Most involved is the Ministry of Health and Social Affairs. Old-age pensions and administration, planning, and legislation in the field of health and welfare services are the responsibility of this ministry. In close cooperation with the ministry, three other units also operate on the national level. The National Council for the Aged, appointed by royal decree, has an advisory function and is a common denominator for the interests concerning service and care to elderly in the community. The council coordinates state authorities, municipalities, and voluntary associations. The Norwegian Institute of Gerontology (NIG) was established by a private organization and is a typical example of pioneer activity and significant contribution by a voluntary agency. Turning the institute into a state institution shows the readiness by the government to assume responsibility for gerontological research and dissemination of information. The primary task of the institute is research and education, but it also participates in planning, guidance, and advisory services. The third central unit in this field, the Joint Committee on Preparation for Retirement, was founded in 1969 on the initiative of the Ministry of Health and Social Affairs, NIG, and other public and private bodies. The aim of the committee is to stimulate the individual, as well as society, to engage in issues concerning the transition to retirement. The joint committee produces films, slides, and brochures, gives lectures, and conducts courses. Its administrative expenses are covered by the ministry. A number of nationwide organizations and institutions are affiliated with the committee, among them the Norwegian Federation of Trade Unions and the Confederation of Business and Industry (Employers' Federation). According to the bylaws, the NIG shall be represented on the board of the committee.

According to the Social Care Act (1991) and the Municipal Health Service Act (1982), social care and health service for the aged are the responsibility of the municipalities. Fields of emphasis include preventive and curative measures, cultural and social programs, various in-home services, and housing and institutional care. Expenses are covered partly by a municipality's own budget and partly through a block grant from the government.

INCOME MAINTENANCE AND EMPLOYMENT

The postwar years have witnessed a tremendous rise in the level of education of the population. This trend has been especially pronounced since 1960, implying a generation gap in education between young and old. Less than 10% of the over 60 group have university training. The corresponding proportion of the 30–39-year-olds is approximately three times higher (SSB, 1989). The length of education also has a clear impact on how long the employees remain active in the work force. In the age group 50–59 years, 9 of 10 with academic education are gainfully employed, as against 7 of 10 among those with lowest education. Corresponding proportions for the 67–69 group are 33% and 11%.

In general, however, the development of the labor market is inclined to disfavor elderly citizens. An increasing unemployment rate, first appearing in Norway in the 1980s, causes problems, especially for elderly who want to remain active in the work force. Efficiency, competition, and demand for new methods and new knowledge are necessary for mass production. The oil industry and related fields of work require high technical skills. Faced with these aspects, the elderly are often at a loss, and persons over 50 years of age have difficulties in getting new jobs. Yet, approximately 6 of 10 persons in the age group 55–66 years are active in the work force. As of 1991, among those 67–74 years of age, 14% of the men and 9% of the women are gainfully employed (SU, 31–32, 1991).

The proportion of persons receiving disability benefits increases markedly from the age of 55, including 23% in the age group 55–59 years and 44% of the 65–66-years-olds. These disability rates indicate an age-related health decline but may also partly be due to lack of job opportunities. Thus, an extensive part of the working population has left the labor force before they reach retirement age.

The general old-age pension is based on the national insurance scheme. Compulsory insured, under this scheme, are all residents or those working in Norway. Also certain categories of Norwegian citizens working abroad have compulsory insurance. The national insurance scheme is financed by contributions from the insured person, employers, the state, counties, and municipalities. Contribution rates and state grants are decided by parliament.

Arrangements implying possibilities for gradual retirement are introduced in the national insurance scheme. There is a legal right to continue to work between 67 and 70 years of age. Persons in this age group may choose to take out a full or partial pension. The option to draw part of the pension is used by a small minority of those eligible. This may partly be due to a significant restriction of the right to gradual retirement, namely, that this right is not valid if a lower retirement age than 70 is decided by a formal agreement between the employer and the employee.

Old-age pension consists of a basic pension and supplementary pension or a special supplement. The basic pension is independent of previous income or contributions paid. A full basic pension requires, however, an insurance period of 40 years, and the pension is reduced proportionally in the case of a shorter period. The minimum old-age pension consists of the basic pension and a supplement.

The supplementary pension scheme was introduced in 1967. The aim of the scheme is to prevent a marked decline in the standard of living upon retirement. The supplementary pension is salary-related, and the amount of the pension also depends on the number of pension-earning years, which must be 40 for a full pension.

In 1990, approximately 50% of old-age pensioners enjoyed supplementary pensions. The remaining benefited from the minimum pension, which in May 1992 amounted to NOK 58.580 (US $7,959) per year for a single person and NOK 94.760 (US $12,875) for married couples.

Some retired persons also draw pension from special occupational pension schemes, annuities, capital interest, or other income from self-owned trade or business. Civil servants are, for example, entitled to pensions according to a special scheme. Full pension is obtained after 30 years of service and amounts to 66% of the salary at the time of retirement. Old-age pensioners are entitled to tax limitation provisions and to a special deduction from their income, thus making the minimum pension from the national insurance scheme, together with additional income, tax-free.

Elderly living in the bigger cities—or other densely populated areas under rapid industrial development—may have a strained budget if they draw only the minimum pension. This is particularly apparent in urbanized areas with high expenses, as far as dwelling and heating are concerned. But even if a person draws a minimum pension, there may also be additional income. Among all retirees under the national insurance scheme, the proportion who enjoyed interest income from savings increased from 40% to 60% during the period 1982–88 (NOU, 1992, p.1).

HEALTH CARE SERVICES

Hospital Treatment and Technical Equipment

General and special hospitals are the responsibility of the counties and regions, while primary health services are the legal obligations of the municipalities. For all Norwegian citizens, regardless of age, the national insurance scheme covers most hospital treatment and two-thirds of the doctor's fee for surgery or home calls. The rest is paid by the patient. Medicines are partly paid by the insurance scheme when they are of vital necessity for the patient. Health control of elderly people has been discussed, and pilot schemes have been tried out; the conclusion is that the most adequate system for the elderly would be a regular yearly medical examination by their own doctors.

The first geriatric ward was established at the Municipal Hospital of Oslo in 1952, but very few such wards have been built since then. A high proportion of elderly in hospitals is partly due to the fact that their stay is unnecessarily prolonged because of a shortage of in-home service and nursing home accommodations. Therefore, some hospitals are reluctant to admit elderly patients, who may find themselves displaced by younger and more resourceful persons on the hospitals' waiting lists. Technical equipment (including hearing aids and spectacles) needed by handicapped retirees can be borrowed locally. If they have to be bought, the expenses will be paid entirely or partly through public schemes.

Home Nursing

Provision of home nursing is an obligation for the municipalities, according to the Municipal Health Service Act. Since 1984, when this act was put into force, home nursing schemes have been introduced in all municipalities in Norway. The aim of home nursing is to render sick care in the home when it is deemed medically acceptable to give the patient treatment outside ordinary health institutions. The service is not limited to elderly people, but in practice the great majority (about 75%) are more than 67 years old. A large proportion of the elderly benefit from home nursing: 10% of the young old and 30% of those 80 years and over. During the 1980s there has been a larger increase in number of visits than in number of patients. This trend, especially prevailing from 1985, implies that home nursing is caring for more seriously ill persons. The service had been free of charge for patients, but since 1991 the municipalities are permitted to cover some of their home nursing expenditures through payment from the patients. The government has, however, decided a maximum level of the patient's yearly payment. The maximum amount is income-related and includes the total expenditures for nursing and care (i.e., home help, day care, and temporary stay in institutions).

Residential Homes, Nursing Homes, and Psychiatric Care

Residential homes are designated for the elderly who can cope with their personal care but who need congregational living. To a great extent, this group of elderly is now being cared for in service flats, and the number of ordinary residential home accommodations actually diminished in the late 1980s. Slightly less than 3% of the elderly are residents in these homes (SSB, 1990).

The provision of residential care is left to each municipality, and when the municipalities offer such care, they are free to choose whatever solution they prefer. The homes, in most cases, are municipal, but there are also private residential homes. Public health and welfare authorities, however, are responsible for inspection of all homes, irrespective of ownership.

Nursing home care, like home nursing, is a legal obligation of the municipalities. Nursing home patients constitute 5% of the elderly population in Norway. However, a number of homes, especially in the larger cities, have long waiting lists. The waiting period is a great problem for the elderly, as well as for the relatives. Among those living in institutions, 7 of 10 are women, and their proportion of the institutional population is increasing by age.

Policymakers and health planners emphasize the rehabilitation function of nursing homes. The idea is that, as far as possible, the health condition of patients should be improved so that they can go back to their own homes or to residential care. A growing number of nursing homes (6 of 10 in 1990) provide temporary rehabilitation stay. For many elderly, however, the nursing home becomes a permanent place to stay. Therefore, it is important to have single-bed rooms in these institutions. In the last years, conditions have improved in this respect: single-bed rooms now constitute between 60% and 70% of the total number of rooms. The corresponding share of single-bed rooms in residential homes is 80% (Søbye, 1990).

In residential homes, as in nursing homes, residents and patients cover part of the expenses through their old-age pension, but they are entitled to keep a minimum share of their income for personal use.

In Norway, like in other developed countries, the treatment and care of psychogeriatric patients are a serious problem. Some of these patients are admitted to mental hospitals, others to psychiatric nursing homes, and quite a number to residential homes or somatic nursing homes. In many of the two latter institutions, care of patients suffering from mental disease is a main concern, and nearly one of five institutions operates special units for the senile demented patients.

HOUSING RESOURCES

The great majority of the aged, about 85%, are living in their own homes or flats; a small minority are living with relatives. Improvement of the general standard of housing in Norway has also benefited the elderly. Yet, their housing conditions are poorer than those of younger age groups. The elderly more often live in houses built before 1945, more often have an outdoor toilet, and more frequently lack bath facilities (Lyng and Mikaelsson, 1986). About 20% of all private households in Norway include houses or flats with low standards. The corresponding proportion of the over-80 group is 44% in cities and 32% rural areas.

In order to improve housing conditions and thereby enhance the possibility of the elderly remaining in their own homes, a housing policy for the elderly has become an important link in the planning of services outside institutions. An important preventive measure is that of the State Housing Bank, which encourages those building a house to apply a *livsløpsstandard* (a life span standard) to meet certain qualifications, so that conditions of the house will be adequate also for a person in wheelchair. Such projects are promoted by considerably higher loans than the ordinary ones from the State Housing Bank. This bank also grants favorable loans to private borrowers, as well as to municipalities, for the purpose of modernizing and repairing flats and houses. Improvement loans from the State Housing Bank can be granted to persons 7 to 10 years before their retirement (while they still have work income). Experience has shown that some elderly people are reluctant to raise loans on their property, even if they have to pay only the interest. The reason most frequently given is that they do not want to leave any debt to their heirs, who would be responsible for the payment after their death.

Housing grants, another governmental scheme, aim to compensate for high rent and heating costs of households with low income. Some municipalities also have their own projects for housing grants, which are subject to a means test and vary in size.

Flats for the elderly are built in separate houses or as parts of buildings with family flats. Some of the housing projects, especially in the rural areas, are linked to institutions. These housing projects are partly built and owned by the municipalities, partly by private organizations or professional associations. In the public schemes, the elderly usually rent their flats; more rarely they pay a lump sum and become owners of the flats. A club for saving for retirement housing is a private enterprise operated by the elderly themselves in cooperation with a bank. The housing projects developed by these clubs have become very popular and successful. After some years of saving, the members are entitled to a retirement flat of which they become the owner. A trend during the 1980s in the field of housing and service provision is the establishment of "service housing" or "assisted living." This form of group housing arrangements is also offered to the frail elderly in other European countries and in North America. In the continuum of care, it falls between nursing and congregate housing and consists of independent housing units with supportive services for personal care and housework (Regnier, 1990).

A countrywide survey (Lauvli, 1991) suggests that assisted-living facilities have met the intention of reducing the need for residential care. It remains to be seen whether these group housing arrangements will also diminish the need for care in nursing homes. Furthermore, due to the short time of experience, we do not know if there will be special problems related to such service housing. Residents of service housing constitute about 1% of the old population. The total share of elderly living in purpose-built flats of any kind has increased from 4% to 5% during the last decade.

SUPPORTIVE SERVICES

Within the broad frame of policies set by the government, the development of services and care varies from one municipality to the other, according to local demography, financial capacity, and political priority setting.

Home Help and other In-Home Services

Home-help service, introduced in all municipalities, is the most significant supportive service and is usually at a low cost for clients with a minimum pension. Otherwise, the payment is income-related. The payment, as well as the criteria of eligibility, for home help varies from municipality to municipality. The gross expenditures of the home-help service in 1990 amounted to NOK 2.243 billion, of which 10% was covered by payments by clients (SSB, 1992).

One-fourth of the elderly benefit from home-help service; three of four clients are living alone. Waiting lists indicate an unmet need. The main obstacle for a further development of home-help schemes is financial problems of the municipalities. Lack of home helpers may also be a problem, but to a less extent than a few years ago, because of the prevailing unemployment.

The number of households receiving home-help service has increased slightly over the last decade. Simultaneously the share of home helpers employed fulltime has increased, and part-time helpers have more hours of work than 10 years ago. Hence, the number of home helpers decreased from 44,800 in 1981 to 30,000 persons in 1988 (Beverfelt and Mordal, 1990).

The job as home helper is not professional in the sense that particular training is required, and the majority of the present home helpers have only a brief course or no relevant training at all. In some cases home help is the formalizing of previous family and neighbor help. The only difference is that the helpers are now paid. The proportion of home helpers working only for their family, however, decreased from 30% to 20% during the 1980s.

In order to improve the quality of home help, the personnel and those who intend to enter the service are offered a variety of training programs. Training is provided on local and regional levels and varies from a few weeks to two years. On request of the Ministry of Health and Social Affairs, the NIG has prepared a videoprogram that includes an extensive textbook and instruction material. The project, including distribution of the teaching material to all municipalities, was financed by the ministry.

A number of other kinds of measures and services have been introduced to meet needs for safety and independence. These services are financed partly by the state and partly by local authorities and/or voluntary associations. The state, for example, finances a subsidy arrangement for telephone installment and subscription expenses. These grants are subject to a means test, giving priority to frail elderly and those living alone. The organization Telefonkontakt (Telephone Contact), partly financed by the state, has calling services for elderly in several municipalities. Volunteers, known as telephone friends, call the elderly as often as the client decides. If there is no answer, the telephone friend finds out whether there is a problem. Another state-subsidized measure entitles everybody who has reached the age of 67 to obtain travel tickets at half-price when traveling by most of the country's means of transportation.

Counseling Work and Service Centers

Social and legal counseling is provided by social workers and lawyers. A fairly new trend is guidance centers administered by local groups of the pensioners' association. Counseling is provided by retired experts from various fields; thus, the centers represent an important resource for the aged. The operating cost of office, telephone, and so on is usually paid by the municipality, but the advisers are volunteers, and the service is free for the client. Yet, the need for this service remains great, partly due to a paucity of guidance centers and partly because social workers in the public service do not consider work with the elderly an attractive field.

Meals-on-wheels services are operated by public or voluntary agencies or through cooperation between these agencies. The food is usually prepared by industrial enterprises. In some municipalities, mobile domestic cleaning service is organized, and a number of municipalities offer transport service at a low cost.

The idea of the service center for health and welfare is to assemble a wide range of measures under the same roof and thereby meet, as far as possible, the service needs of elderly people living in their own homes. The center is also intended to serve as a point of safety. The services are available to all elderly people living within the geographical district of the center, and there is no means test for attendance. Between 250 and 300 centers are now in operation, mainly located in the most densely populated areas of the country. Half of them are operated on a voluntary basis, but in nearly all cases the municipalities grant subsidies, covering 25–100% of the operating cost. The centers have been in existence for 40 years, yet there are no general standards for services and personnel.

To meet the service needs of elderly who live at home and are too frail to use a health and welfare center, some municipalities offer care in day nursing homes. These institutions, in most cases, are affiliated with ordinary nursing homes, but some are independent. Day nursing homes are considered an important link in domiciliary services. Yet, their appearance has been slow. In Oslo, the most developed municipality in this respect, there are about 800 day nursing home accommodations available for a population of 79,000 elderly.

LEISURE-TIME RESOURCES

Voluntary Agencies

With a few exceptions, measures in favor of the aging were originally started by voluntary associations, but gradually, when it was proved that these activities had a broad community value, many of them have fully or partly been taken over by public authorities. Nevertheless, the contribution by humanitarian, religious, and other voluntary associations is still important. To some extent, the recession has actually brought the significance of nongovernmental organizations into the foreground. Pilot studies have been financed by the MHSA in order to gain knowledge about models of cooperation between statutory and voluntary agencies. In 1991 the Storting provided a substantial grant for innovation projects concerning centers of voluntary work. The ministry has underlined the need for voluntary associations, and their efforts have found new ways of service delivery and have incorporated otherwise inactive personnel resources. Despite the positive attitude of the authorities, some of the associations have difficulties (Lorentzen, 1988): they need paid staff to organize the volunteer activities, and with the wage increase in Norway, some of the associations have financial problems. Besides, more and more women have paid jobs, so the group of women who formerly constituted the basis of voluntary manpower is diminishing. Also lacking is community work in the field of mental hygiene, where professional skill is necessary (Beverfelt, 1991).

Voluntary agencies are making a significant contribution when it comes to providing recreational and leisure-time activities. Visiting schemes, physical exercise programs, hobby clubs, adult education courses, and library service are found in most of the local communities.

Educational Opportunities

Since the late 1970s, voluntary associations, as well as the elderly themselves, have developed educational activities on various levels through Senior Schools and open universities for retired people. The two Senior Schools are operated as boarding schools with one-or two-week courses, thus offering good opportunities for recreation and social contact as well as education.

The most-developed university of the third age (U3A) is in Oslo, but similar educational opportunities are available in a few other cities and villages. Although the education leads to no diploma, the organizers stress the aim of keeping education on a high intellectual level. A growing number of participants apparently justify the U3A movement. But most of the aged seeking education are participating in general adult education programs and in study groups organized by the Retired Peoples' Association or by service centers for health and welfare.

Leisure-Time Activities and Contribution by the Aged

Among the recreational activities offered by service centers are physical exercise (walking and skiing), hobby groups, dancing, and participation in choirs and orchestras. From 60% to 70% of the elderly in districts with service centers are registered as users of the services and activities. It should be stressed that 8 of 10 among the volunteers working at the centers are elderly themselves. This emphazises the value of the centers as an arena where elderly people can use their experiences and skills and where they can act as givers (not only receivers) of services and care.

ADVOCACY AND PROTECTION

Protection

In old Norse law, elderly and frail people were regarded as legally incapable. According to a law from the twelfth century, a man could dispose of his property as long as he was "able to ride his horse and drink his ale" (Kjønstad, 1988). If he became weaker, his heirs could divide his property (i.e., they could behave as if he was dead).

According to present law, advanced age is no special cause for a declaration of legal incapacity. From a legal point of view, the main principle is that the same rules apply to all members (15 years and more) of society. In some instances, however, this does not secure elderly people the same degree of protection and rights as younger persons. An example is compensation for personal injury. The method of calculating such compensation often entails that people tend to get less with age. On the other hand, old age may also be an extenuating circumstance, for example, in relation to punishment of an elderly wrongdoer. It will then be taken into consideration that the offense committed may be due to mental decline and that imprisonment implies considerable mental and physical strain for an elderly person (Kjønstad, 1988).

Anxiety about crime and violence increases with advancing age, in spite of the fact that elderly are actually more rarely becoming victims of crimes or threats of crimes than younger age groups (SSB, 1987b). But in the Norwegian society of today, where there is a general concern about increasing crime, it is expected that vulnerable groups—less able to defend themselves—will be those who are most worried. Whether the anxiety is strongly justified or not, there are bag-snatchings from older women, and elderly people are robbed and sometimes are victims of violent burglars. To strengthen self-protection, police and voluntary agencies disseminate information among elderly (e.g., concerning security locks and keeping cash on hand).

Elderly crime victims by strangers do not always make reports to the police. Such cases are, however, easier to reveal than crimes committed against elderly persons by their own family. Elder abuse was a practically unknown problem in Norway until the early 1980s. Interest first emerged among researchers, but public authorities were slow in starting to pay attention to the problem. But now the MHSA and local authorities are supporting research and information activities provided to health and welfare personnel. Moreover, a guidance center is established as an experiment to help victims and extend insight into this problem. A study among home nursing patients in Oslo showed that about 1% of the patients during a four-month period had been victims of abuse by their families. Estimates so far suggest that 20,000 to 30,000 elderly persons in Norway are maltreated (in one way or another) by family members. The main problem is that—even if revealed—the cases are most complicated to treat, because the elderly person may resist any change of the family situation leading to the trouble.

Elder abuse should not be overlooked, but it must be kept in mind that only a small proportion of family caregivers is involved. Extensive help and support by the family are often the condition enabling old people to avoid institutionalization. According to the Social Welfare Act and the Municipal Health Service Act, everyone is entitled to health and welfare services; municipalities are legally obliged to provide a number of these services. Yet, with the maximum of public, home-based services, very frail elderly persons cannot remain in their own homes without additional help by family.

Love, affection, tradition, and moral obligation may be among the motives for family care. Certainly there are also more selfish motives (among potential heirs). Legally, however, children are not obliged to take care of their parents. This duty was abolished in Norway by the introduction of the Act on Social Welfare of 1964. In the current welfare state, the responsibility for maintenance and care has been turned over to society (Kjønstad, 1988).

No one can be forced to go into a nursing home or residential home. However, compulsory commitment may occur under the Act on Mental Health Care if an elderly person is seriously mentally impaired. In practice, it is also a matter of definition as to whether a person is forced or talked into moving to an institution. But, at present, this question is only of theoretical interest. The availability of accommodations is sufficient to meet the needs of those on the waiting lists who clearly express the wish to move into an institution.

Centers for health and welfare offer guidance by lawyers. Moreover, legal aid (for all age groups) is provided free of charge according to a means test.

Advocacy

In addition to the Norst Pensjonistforbund and the National Council for the Aged, elderly groups and individuals make themselves spokespersons for the sake of the aged. Most active, in this respect, are middle-aged family caregivers. In Norway, like in other developed countries, persons caring for demented elderly have formed an organization to improve conditions for caregivers and the quality of life for care recipients. Elderly caregivers, often caring for their spouse, more rarely take an active part in advocacy organizations, maybe because most of their strength and capacity is used on the caring tasks. In 1990, however, a man of 80 took the lead in a campaign for better public old age care. Frustrated by the burden of care for his senile demented wife, he proclaimed his thoughts through writings and interviews in mass media. A performance on television brought him strong public support, which could not be neglected by the government. The result was a government grant of 1 billion NOK, earmarked for elderly care and transferred to the municipalities for each of the years 1990 and 1991.

FUTURE PROJECTIONS

The majority of elderly persons in this country experience old age in a positive way. Their adaptation patterns and coping styles are characterized by great individual variability, yet most often they succeed in coping with the stress of daily life, loss, and health impairment. Clearly, however, a minor group suffers from an accumulation of disadvantages that may occur in old age, single elderly women constitute the greater part of this group.

Setting Priorities

In general, the conditions of the aged in Norway's welfare state (their status, roles, and the services offered) are related to the priority given to this part of the population. The financial position of the nation, dependent on the oil and gas industry, is vulnerable, and the deficit of the state budget is increasing year by year. Any decision about giving priority—to build a new national airport or to arrange the international Olympic winter games (in 1994)—restricts the resources available for obligations on other sectors (e.g., health services and social care). The way of setting priorities, supported by a majority, cannot be changed unless the voices raised against it become more powerful. Yet, politicians and the public express doubt about the ability of the welfare state to fulfill the ambitious goals set during the prosperous 1960s and 1970s.

Introduction of the national insurance scheme in 1967 was the final achievement in efforts to develop Norway as a welfare state and is fundamental in the realization of this idea. With a few exceptions, it applies to all persons domiciled in the country, and it offers law-based benefits in case of sickness, physical or mental defect, loss of supporter, unemployment, and old age. After 25 years of experience, there is, however, a growing concern about the marked increase of the social budget, the future financing of the national insurance, and the very model of the welfare state. There is no doubt about the positive elements of the system. The question is to what extent the state, that is, the productive part of the population, should accept the financial responsibility for the nonproductive part. The latter group, consisting of children, retired persons, disability pensioners, unemployed, and other groups, constitutes a considerable part of the total population.

The national insurance budget will be strongly influenced by the gradual application of the system of supplementary pension. Another financial problem is caused by the number of disability pensioners, which has been increasing at an unforeseen rate: from 98,600 in 1967 to 238,520 in 1991 (Rikstrygdeverket [RTV], 1992), and the estimate for the year 2020 is 357,300 persons. The budget of the national insurance, amounting to NOK 23.8 billion (US $3.2 billion) when the law became effective, is supposed to be NOK 175 billion (US $23.8 billion) in 2020. In order to cope with the problem thus far, the government has decided to lower the basis of the maximum pension and to introduce a means test, implying that additional pension to elderly supporting a spouse is no longer automatically provided but is subject to an evaluation of economy.

Cash Benefits or Services to Improve Quality of Life?

A general policy problem is whether the standard of living of the elderly should be raised by increasing cash benefits or by subsidizing services. The considerable growth of expenditures for pensions has led to a stage where this problem must be continuously discussed. There is a cross-political agreement as to the decisive importance of retirement income for individuals' freedom of choice. On the other hand, it seems obvious that even with a higher income, not all retired persons will be able to satisfy their needs if they have to buy services on the open market in competition with younger age groups. The problem is not a matter of one procedure or another, but rather a question of priority. In 1988 the expenditure for old-age pensions was approximately twice the amount used for institutional and home-based care (home help and home nursing). During the second part of the 1970s, the increase of expenditure for care and services was relatively higher than the one for old-age pension. From 1985 to 1988 there was an opposite trend; a committee, appointed by royal decree, recommended giving a higher priority to services than to pensions in future years (NOU, 1992, p. 1). This may, however, threaten the solidarity between the young old, who would appreciate money more than service, and the old old, more often in need of care. My suggestion, therefore, is that we should aim at maintaining the 1988 balance in transfer of resources through services and cash benefits.

Should the Elderly Pay for Services in a Welfare State?

Provided there is no considerable cut in the old-age pension, a growing number of elderly people can enjoy an improved economy, since a larger proportion will be entitled to full supplementary pensions and more women will retire from paid work. This should also have an impact on their contribution to cover service expenses. Payment from the elderly in 1988 constituted 12% of the total cost of care and services. This share should not be enlarged to any great extent. It is claimed, however, that many elderly in 1992 can afford to pay more for some of the services from which they benefit. In the near future, especially starting in the second decade of the next century, it will be even more important to charge consumers according to their income.

Can Home-Based Services Replace Institutional Care?

Enabling the aged to remain in their own homes as long as possible was stated in a policy document submitted in 1955. Since then it has been repeated ever so often in Norway, like as in other countries. This idea was also the rationale for the emphasis on home-based services during the 1980s. Advocates for this policy also stressed that institutional care is expensive and that, by providing care for old people in their own homes, more people could be supported at less cost. Suggestions were made in 1991 that institutions should be replaced by independent dwellings, grouped together and offering 24 hours of service. In a 1992 newspaper article, the Norwegian prime minister (who is also a physician) supported the emphasis put on home-based care. She did, however, add: "But in the years to come there will be more people in need of institutional care. Therefore we need more nursing home accommodations or sheltered housing offering 24 hours' care" (Brundtland, 1992).

The problem would have been solved if both home-based and institutional care could be expanded at the rate necessary to meet the need, but the present recession prevents the local authorities from doing so. Clearly, it is not a question of one approach or the other. The point is, however, that the extensive expansion of home-based services has led to a growing gap between supply and demand, as far as institutional care is concerned. Some elderly people reach a stage where they cannot, or do not want to, remain in their own home. The reasoning is simply that our need for independence and safety often change by aging; thus, for frail and helpless persons, the safety of an institution may be more important than independence in their own home.

Care for the Caregivers

When ill elderly persons can avoid institutionalization, it is generally thanks to care provided by the family. Some of these elderly also receive help and support from formal care services, while others have the family as their only resource of help. Exclusively public care, on the other hand, would not be sufficient to enable totally dependent elderly persons to remain at home. Due to shortage of financial resources, services, and personnel, the public authorities, when allocating services, are inclined to give priority to the single aged who have minimal or no access to family care. This means that families caring for their elderly have an unfortunate position when needing (formal) in-home services. Some of the caregivers feel bitter, frustrated, and somehow punished, in the sense that they receive little support and recognition from a society which is saving money through the free work of the caregiver (Nygård, 1982). In addition to an unmet need for practical help, there is also a lack of emotional support, information, and guidance, especially among those caring for senile demented patients. The challenge for public authorities is to provide adequate support for families who, in spite of problems, want to do whatever they can to enable their elderly to remain in their own homes. Key words for a support system are flexibility, reliability, continuity, help in line with individual needs, and awareness that caring involves both instrumental and emotional obligations.

But lack of institutional care facilities should not be an acceptable reason for being cared for at home. When conflicts in a caring situation have become so serious that they represent a threat to the quality of life of the elderly person, the caregiver, or both parties, there should be the possibility for the elderly person to move to an institution.

Quality of Life in Later Years: Also an Individual Responsibility

Dissatisfaction among elderly people can be justified. Negative stereotypes hamper intergenerational contact. Social conditions should be improved to enhance opportunities for an active participation in local communities and society at large. Services and care are still insufficient, in quantity as well as in quality.

Underlined is the duty of the individual to assume responsibility for his or her own quality of life—maybe a self-evident fact, but nevertheless, a necessary reminder for elderly in a welfare state. How they themselves can influence policymakers and programs is important, as are efforts on the personal level to keep fit, maintain social contacts, use the leisure-time resources available, and seek information on relevant services.

But the risk of becoming dependent increases with age and the associated decline of physical and psychical strength. Accordingly, some elderly people are left with few options to influence living conditions and life-style. Therefore, the obligation of society is above all to provide supportive environments in order to enhance the quality of life for those who are dependent on services and care, in their own homes or in institutions.

BIBLIOGRAPHY

Beverfelt, E. *Elderly Women in the Nordic Countries Today and Tomorrow.* In Altern-Ein lebenslanger Prosess der sozialen Interaktion. Darmstadt, 1990.

———. *Morgendagens frivillige hjelpere.* GerArt 6-1991. Norsk gerontologisk institutt, Oslo.

Beverfelt, E., and Mordal, T. *Hjemmehjelper-en nøkkelperson i eldreom-sorgen.* Håndbook for hjemmehjelpere, 2. Utgave. NGI rapport 1-1990. Oslo: Norsk gerontologisk institutt.

Brundtland, Gro Harlem (Prime Minister) i Arbeiderbladet, May 1992.

Helset, A. (ed.). Gamle kvinner i Norden-deres liv i tekst og tall. NGI rapport 6-1991. Norsk gerontologisk institutt, Oslo.

Kjønstad, A. *The Legal Situation of Elderly People.* Manus 1988. University of Oslo.

Lauvli, M. Utbygging av serviceboliger i Norge. Delrapport. NGI-rapport 2-1991. Norsk gerontologisk institutt, Oslo.

Liaboe, I. J. *Gammel i "gamle dager."* NGI rapport nr. 7-1980. Norsk gerontologisk institutt, Oslo.

Lorentzen, H. *Mellom byråkrati og bevegelse.* De frivillige organisasjonenes rolle i sosialsektoren. INAS rapport 3/88. Oslo.

Lyng, K., and Mikaelsson, M. *Eldres boforhold.* NGI rapport 5-1986. Norsk gerontologist institutt, Oslo.

Noack, T., and Texmon, I. Dagens og morgendagens gamle kvinner-en demografisk beskrivelse. In NGI-rapport 6-1991. Norst gerontologisk institutt, Oslo.

Norges offentligeutredninger. NOU 1992:1 Ministry of Health and Social Affairs.

Nygård, L. Omsorgsressursar hos nære pårørande. NIS, SINTEF Rapport 2/82. Trondheim.

Rikstrygdeverket (RTV). Kvartalsoppgave, Sosiale trygder 1992.

Søbye, E. *Institusjoner for eldre 1989.* Statistisk sentralbyrånr. 90/22. Oslo 1990.

Statistisk sentralbyrå (SSB). Helseundersøkelse 1985. Norges offisielle statistikk B 692. Oslo 1987a.

———. Levekårsundersøkelsen 1987b.

———. Statistisk ukehefte (SU) 31–32/91.

———. Social Survey 1989. Oslo.

———. Statistisk årbok 1990.

———. Statistisk årbok 1992.

Statistik ukehefte (SU). Weekly issue, 31–32, 1991.

Thorsen, K. *Alene og ensom, sammen og lykkelig?* NGI rapport 2-1990. Norsk gerontologisk institutt, Oslo.

23

POLAND

Brunon Synak

INTRODUCTION

The Role of the Elderly

When we speak about the definition of old age or the social status of the elderly, we must relate the issues to the family, as well as the society on a wider scale. Polish society can be identified as a traditional one. Before World War II, almost three-quarters of the population lived in rural areas, whereas in 1991 the figure was almost 40%, with about 25% being employed in agriculture. The role of the Roman Catholic church and religious values was very important, informal ties and relationships in primary groups were very strong, and in these groups the family played a basic role. This situation began to change noticeably during the last decade of socialism in Poland and became even more visible during the transitional period both at the family level and at the national level[1] (Frackiewicz, 1991).

It is suggested that at the end of the former system, family integration and intergenerational solidarity even increased due to mistrust of extrafamilial and formal structures and institutions. The initial period of political changes in Poland (1989–91) did not cause any worsening of the economic and protective function of the family. There was a slight downward tendency in the help children afforded their elders, but there was a simultaneous increase in the role of the elderly as a source of assistance (this concerning mainly financial support).

On the national level, at that time, characteristic of the position of the elderly in Poland were fewer rights and fewer responsibilities. Their low status also had an influence on the institutions and organizations involved in assisting them. The following description, referring to the communist period, emphasizes the source of the issue: "The problems of the elderly are dealt with in a publicly ostentatious manner, and they themselves are treated rather like objects to serve an ulterior motive. ... The elderly and their unresolved problems do not exert any pressure—neither in a moral nor in a direct sense—upon social policy in Poland'' (Hrynkiewicz, Starega-Piasek, and Supinska, 1991, p. 66). The beginning of the "Solidarity" government did not see any improvement in the situation of the elderly in the country. Privatization, market economy, changes in values, total criticism of the postwar period, the emergence of new competitors, and hazy aging policy resulted in society's being less favorable and friendly to the elderly. Such phenomena gave rise to severe material and psychosocial deprivation among the older generation.

Generally speaking, the definition of old age is evidently connected with retirement age. On retiring, persons are mainly considered old, which immediately changes their social role and behavior. In rural areas, however, old age is identified rather as a period of life when people become dependent on others, due to both age and poor health. In the case of farmers, the fact of handing over property to others is crucial and means that the person in question has already crossed the threshold of old age.

In demographic terms, Poland belongs to those countries with a fairly high share of children and adults and a relatively low percentage of elderly people. The process of aging of the population, however, is developing at a fairly high rate, as in other European countries. During the postwar period, the number of people aged 65 and older has tripled, and the overall percentage was almost twice as high in 1990 as 40 years ago (Table 23.1).

Surprisingly, however, during the last decade only a very slight increase in the proportion of old people has been noted. This unexpected phenomenon is common to almost all the European countries and reflects the results of the two world wars. It is expected that in the immediate future there will be a substantial increase in the percentage of elderly in the population, when those born between the wars, during the demographic explosion, attain old age.

There are sharp differences between urban and rural areas, both in the proportion of the aged and in rate of the aging process. This process is much more advanced in the rural areas, particularly as regards women. The more intensive aging process of the rural population in Poland results mainly from heavy migration of young people from village to town.

In Poland the gender breakdown of the elderly population is similar to that in other countries, where older women prevail considerably over men (in 1991, 40% were men and 60% women among those aged 65 and over), and this disproportion increases with the passage of time and age.

Most elderly people in Poland are married: of those aged 60 and over, about 62% are married, 34% widowed, 3% never married, and only 1% divorced. Among women, widows predominate; among men, the married prevail.

One of the factors very closely connected with the process of aging is the life expectancy of the population. During the postwar years, the life expectancy increased considerably for all ages in Poland. This resulted predominantly from

Table 23.1
Percentage of the Elderly (65+) in Poland by Gender and Place of Residence, 1950–90

Years	Total	Gender		Place of residence	
		Men	Women	Towns	Countryside
1950	5.2	4.5	6.1	4.8	5.5
1960	5.9	4.6	7.1	5.5	6.3
1970	8.3	6.7	10.2	7.7	9.1
1980	10.0	7.9	12.1	8.9	11.7
1990	10.2	7.8	12.5	9.0	12.1

a lower death rate and drop in fertility (rather than from lengthening of life span). Most significant, however, is the fact that during the last decade the average life expectancy, in the case of males, has dropped and as a result the difference between genders is greater by nine years.

The health status of the elderly is usually described by functional ability and self-evaluation of health. In both respects, the health of elderly people in Poland can be considered poor, with a downward trend. It is estimated that about 10% of these people are confined to their homes due to locomotive disability and 55% always or often suffer from some ailments. As regards self-evaluation, only 15% of males and 9% of females do not complain, estimating their health positively. This low health status of the older generation in Poland corresponds directly with the high rate of mortality (in 1990 in the 65–69 age group it was almost 30%) and the trend in average life expectancy (Frackiewicz, 1991).

The elderly in Poland are rather poorly educated. Only 3% of people aged 60 and older have attained university level, and almost 75% have no more than an elementary education. The majority of these people grew up at a time when there was a high rate of illiteracy in the country and the education of many of them was interrupted by World War I or II.

The Formal Structure of Care of the Elderly

The perception of responsibility for care of the elderly is very strongly influenced by the culture and history of the country. Traditionally, particularly in rural areas, the family was the very institution expected to care for all its dependent members. This conviction has not changed completely in the case of the elderly. It is enough to say that the first national act on public care was established in 1923 and replaced by a new one only in 1990. During the communist period in Poland, public assistance was seen as failing family solidarity and increasing dependency. Social care for the elderly has also something of a stigmatizing effect. It seems that the perception of responsibility was changed much more by the post-totalitarian transformation of the country than it was by the communist "welfare state." At the beginning of the 1990s, more and more people accepted help for the elderly from the state. This concerns mainly financial support, but other forms of care were still perceived as the obvious responsibility of the family.[2]

According to the Polish constitution, citizens have the right to health care and help in case of illness, old age, and inability to work, guaranteed by various forms of social welfare. Thus, care for the elderly covers all situations where individuals are unable to cope with their own means and resources. Assistance may be requested, but the granting and extent of such depend on assessment. A wide range of free social services are available for the elderly whose monthly per capita income is less than the lowest retirement pension. In practice, only the needs of such persons are covered by the public welfare system, priority being given to the childless and those living alone.

The new law on social welfare in Poland, introduced at the end of 1990, emphasizes the necessity for those receiving help to play an active role in solving their problems. In the new political reality, it has been realized that the state was responsible for too much of the former welfare policy, thus making those in need "passive receivers" and depriving them of the opportunity to become actively involved. The suggestion was also that more freedom should be afforded in the choice of options in the process of caring. There is great encouragement to develop free enterprise that would support services for the elderly, but the commercial sector delivering goods and services to the elderly was practically nonexistent at the beginning of the 1990s, mainly due to the fact that the buying power of older clients was limited and they were not used to paying for such things, which were formerly free.

This law has totally changed the formal structure of care for the elderly, as an integrated part of the entire social welfare system. First, the responsibility of the government has been divided between two ministries: Ministry of Health and Ministry of Labor and Social Policy (in the past there was a Ministry of Health and Social Affairs). Second, responsibility for social care at the vertical level has been divided into tasks for the state administration and those for the local authorities. In fact, however, all forms of services are organized and provided by local government. "State administration responsibility" means that the money for these tasks comes from the state budget, not from the local authority. As regards the elderly, the local government is obliged to run old people's homes and care centers and provide meals, clothing, and home care for solitary persons from its own financial resources. The state administration obliges the local government and guarantees financial resources, mainly for such tasks as family care, granting allowances, and supporting charity organizations.

Home help for the elderly is organized by Social Welfare Units and mainly provided by a network of helpers from the Polish Social Welfare Committee (PKPS) and the Polish Red Cross (PCK). Both are basically social organizations and are considerably subsidized by the government.

It should be emphasized that at the beginning of the new political order in the 1990s, services for the elderly were still almost exclusively sponsored by the state. Many private and religious groups and initiatives have emerged, but they suffer from lack of money, which they mainly expect from the state. In the rural areas there is a very small middle class, which is usually the main supporter of charitable activities.

INCOME MAINTENANCE AND EMPLOYMENT

A statutory retirement scheme has existed for many years, and retirement benefits are a common source of maintenance for the elderly, embracing the whole of the population. There are three principal forms of pensions for older persons: old-age pension, disability pension, and family pension (granted to a spouse and children after the death of an employee). The old-age pension is a long-term cash benefit paid from the Social Security fund (there are no private retirement benefits or pensions in Poland). It is granted on the basis of age (65 years for men and 60 for women) and service. Apart from the general system, there are some specific retirement regulations that encompass, among others, war invalids, teachers, miners, policemen, armed forces members, and farmers.

The country's financial situation and apparent disruption in the obtaining of money for insurance during the economic transformation (the collapsing state firms are unable to pay insurance contributions) resulted in the modification of the retirement law at the end of 1991. On the positive side, the changed regulations equalized the level of pensions conferred in different years and resulted in an increase in the amount of the lowest pensions. However, they introduced severe disadvantages for the elderly, including restriction of the possibilities of pensioners' undertaking paid employment, new rules for calculating the amount of pensions (some have decreased substantially), and war invalids losing their supplementary pensions.

The changed law, along with the high rate of unemployment and closing of many places of employment, has resulted in older employees taking early retirement. The number of pensioners increased from 4.5 million in 1980 to 7.3 million at the beginning of 1992. Obviously, there are almost no opportunities for retaining employment or reemployment for elderly persons. Moreover, there have never been any job training programs or reemployment services. Thus, during the high inflation period, when the elderly experience particularly painful material deprivation, they do not even have opportunities to earn extra money.

The Social Security system in Poland includes a financial assistance program for the impoverished aged. According to this, there are three types of financial allowances: permanent, temporary, and single. A permanent allowance is granted to an old person unable to work, without means of subsistence, or with a very low income. A temporary allowance can be granted for a few months (at least two) to persons who have temporarily found themselves in difficult circumstances (e.g., during long-term illness, to cover the cost of medicines, convalescence, and so on). All the types of allowances constitute 90% of the lowest retirement income.

Single allowances have the widest range, the number of these having increased in the 1990s when every fifth person received such material assistance. It is mainly awarded in the form of coupons for the purchase of warm clothing, underwear, or fuel (in 1991 over 10% of the elderly received all types of allowances).

Poland has a limited number of economic policies for the elderly. Financial assistance for housing is the most important benefit and has the widest range. According to the social welfare law introduced in 1990, those whose income is less than 150% of the lowest retirement pension receive financial support to cover the rent expenses if constituting more than 10% of an old person's monthly income (this absorbs a quarter of the budget for social services). Other economic benefits include reduced fares on local transport for all pensioners (free for those aged 75 and over), as well as special benefits for war veterans (who do not pay radio-television licenses and have reduced telephone charges).

These forms of economic assistance are the same throughout the country. There are no local or regional forms of economic support or supplementary benefits for the elderly.

HEALTH CARE SERVICES

The Polish constitution guarantees everyone the right to health care, free for all employed persons and their families. Expenditures for medical treatment by the national health service are not charged to the social insurance funds but constitute an integral element of national expenditures on health and social assistance, covered directly by the state budget. The beginning of the 1990s saw the commencement of discussions on changes in the principles of free medical care. In view of the difficult financial situation of hospitals and other medical centers, some have begun to introduce voluntary reimbursement. For example, previously free sanatoriums have been abolished and the extent of reimbursement for medicines has been increased (pensioners previously received all medications free). Changes in the constitution and the law on medical care can be expected in the near future, the latter most probably directed toward increased privatization and payment for medical care.

The Ministry of Health is responsible for matters concerning medical care in Poland. This is conducted mainly by Health Care Authorities (ZOZ), covering one or several villages and towns, and providing both basic and specialized medical services. These authorities embrace hospitals, specialized centers (surgical, dermatological and venereal diseases, and so on.) ambulance centers, medical care for students and university staff, and workers' health centers. At the *voivodship* (or regional) level, apart from the ZOZ centers, there are also *voivodship* hospital complexes, *voivodship* specialist consulting centers, and *voivodship* emergency care centers. In larger towns there are also teaching hospitals and medical research centers. The state health service also embraces sanatoriums, health resort hospitals, homes for the chronically ill, and pharmacies.

Apart from the state-controlled network of medical care establishments in Poland, there are medical cooperatives and private medical practices. These resources offer services on the basis of full reimbursement of costs.

Despite the principle of the universal availability of medical care, the practical availability of hospitals is often hindered or restricted, primarily due to the lack of doctors and hospital beds. In 1990 there was a total of 250,000 beds in all the types of hospitals, which means that there were barely 68 beds per 10,000 persons (these beds constitute only one-third of the number recommended by the World Health Organization [WHO]) (Rocznik Statystyczny, 1991). The availability of medical care is particularly difficult in rural regions. (As of 1972, farmers have been covered by the state-controlled medical care system, with free access to doctors and subsidized medication and care.)

Under control of the national health service infrastructure, medical personnel to the elderly are often said to "block" hospital beds. Too few doctors are trained in the care of this age group, and not all of them are ready to acknowledge the specific traits of aged persons. In "competition" with younger patients, the elderly usually lose and are treated as "second-class patients." There cannot be any other explanation for the fact that beds standing in the corridors of overcrowded hospitals are often occupied by elderly persons, so-called social patients. Moreover, lack of geriatric wards in Polish hospitals and the shortage of special institutions for elderly people result in the "geriatricization" of hospitals (patients over 60 constitute 50% of the patients on medical wards and over 25% on surgical wards).

Apart from hospitals, there are special homes for the chronically ill, for those adults who have chronic somatic diseases or other serious handicaps and who require not only treatment but also constant attention. These homes take people who are at least 18, but 80% of the patients have reached retirement age. The homes for the chronically ill cover about 60% of the demand. There are also homes for the chronically ill with nervous diseases, as well as some homes for the blind run by the state or "Caritas"—one of the main and oldest nongovernmental organizations in Poland.

Terminal care is provided in hospices and hospitals. Those engaged in work in hospices include doctors, nurses, medical students, priests, nuns, volunteers from other professions, and also the sick and their families. The Polish model of a hospice is based on the assumption that incurable patients should remain at home until the very end (unless hospital intervention is necessary), as they feel best among their family and friends. Members of the hospice do not take the place of the family, affording only succor. Hospices are potentially the most important social initiative in helping the elderly in Poland, although much of their attention is devoted to patients of all ages suffering from cancer.

The basic assumption of care of the elderly in Poland is to help ensure suitable conditions at home, treating institutionalization as a last resort. Medical care in the homes of the elderly is organized by regional consulting units in towns and health centers in villages. Those responsible for organizing such care are doctors, nurses, and social workers. House calls by medical personnel are mainly supported by Polish Red Cross nurses. Only a relatively small proportion (7%) of elderly persons are afforded such care.

Private agencies offering services of "family doctors" (both general practitioners and specialists) and nurses began to appear in Poland in the 1990s. It can be expected that with the development of a market economy in Poland, the private sector of medical care will become more widespread and a "public-private" medical care service will appear.

HOUSING RESOURCES

It is difficult to refer to the existence of a well-defined national housing policy for the elderly in a country in which there has never been a rational housing policy and where the housing shortage has always been tremendous. One must wait between 15 and 20 years for a cooperative or council flat (only very few can afford to buy their own, very expensive flat), and the average living space is only about half that in Denmark or Sweden.

The housing situation of the elderly in Poland is much worse than the average. The problem is not only the size of flats (about 15 square meters per person) and overcrowding (1.2 persons per room) but also the poor standard and state of repair of flats occupied by the elderly. Most flats occupied by them are in old buildings, without basic facilities: 23% have no running water, 55% have no central heating, 35% have no toilet, and 40% have no bathroom (in rural areas the situation is even worse). In such conditions it is difficult to ensure functional independence for an elderly person and also to secure nursing help for the disabled or sick.

Housing programs for the elderly in Poland mainly concern people who are alone, have no family, are of low economic status, and find living alone very difficult. One of the forms of help for such persons is congregate housing. The most common type of such housing is pensioners' homes, to which pensioners can be sent who are physically independent and do not require special nursing care. In fact, a considerable proportion of the inmates are physically handicapped and require constant care. There are very limited possibilities of transferring the disabled and sick from pensioners' homes to those for the chronically ill, due to an acute shortage of such accommodations. As a consequence, residential homes become nursing homes, and the difference between the two types of institutions is, in practice, nonexistent.

A program for the building of homes for the elderly, so-called departmental homes (sometimes called "Golden Autumn Homes") was introduced in the mid-1970s. These homes are erected on the lines of cooperative buildings, and obtaining such accommodations necessitates paying a substantial sum of money for membership. Hence, they are available only for rich people. They are buildings situated mainly on housing estates and consist of over 100 one- and two-roomed flats and a social services section (refectory or dining room, community room, reading room). These homes have a duty nurse (usually living in); there also can be a doctor on duty at certain times. Some of these homes are available only for specific groups of elderly persons (e.g., miners, teachers, veterans). Altogether, there are not much more than 100 such residential homes for the elderly in Poland, accommodating about 10,000 residents. They are usually located in cities, only a few being in small towns or rural areas.

At the end of the 1970s, "Old Farmers' Homes" began to be established in some villages, mainly designed for those who had handed over their farms to the state (due to lack of successors) or who had very bad living conditions. Such homes are in small buildings (10–15 persons) and are usually of poor standard, poorly equipped, and devoid of nursing services.

Innovative housing facilities for the elderly began to appear at the beginning of the 1990s. The most significant initiative is the "Gniazdo Rodzinne" (Family Nest) foundation established by the church, which builds and organizes small homes (for about 15 persons) occupied by three groups: the old and single, students, and nursing staff or wardens. The main aim of such a center is the accommodation and care of the elderly on the basis of reciprocity by the whole community.

Generally speaking, only a very small percentage of the elderly are accommodated in homes or institutions especially designed for them—barely 1.3% of the older generation (including those in homes for the chronically ill). This is due not only to the lack of places in such institutions but also to the reluctance of the majority of elderly persons to accept such assistance.

Thus, community assistance for maintaining the elderly in the dwelling of their choice assumes specific importance. In Poland, this form of assistance is also restricted. Those aided by the social assistance agencies are almost exclusively childless persons and those in a difficult economic situation. The forms of assistance afforded by home helpers (omitting nursing care) include cleaning, shopping, and helping to prepare meals. Depending on the situation, such help is rendered daily or several times a week. The poorest persons also receive assistance in the form of free fuel. It is possible to obtain subsidized help from social assistance for the repair of domestic appliances and housing. In actual fact, however, due to limited financial means, the latter form of help is rare, although the demand is great.

As mentioned, due to the substantial increase in the cost of electricity, gas, and rents in the 1990s, financial assistance for the poorest persons was introduced (90% of those receiving such help are elderly persons). Despite such help, increasing numbers of elderly persons are interested in changing accommodations to smaller and cheaper ones, as it is becoming increasingly difficult to manage.

SUPPORTIVE SERVICES

One of the main aims of aging policy in Poland is to leave elderly persons in their initial environment as long as possible. Such a policy requires the development of supportive services in order to guarantee the elderly independence and suitable living conditions.

One form of such services is the nutrition program, which provides meals for the elderly. The basis for granting such help is difficult living conditions. Poor people, those who are alone, and those who have difficulty in preparing meals can take advantage of having food brought home from nearby canteens, hospitals, or bars (there is no meals-on-wheels in Poland). This usually covers one meal (lunch). In certain cases, the home help prepares meals in the home of the elderly person.

Of a much wider range are nutrition programs providing meals outside elderly persons' homes. Persons with very low incomes receive coupons entitling them to receive free dinners in canteens or cheap restaurants. Such programs developed rapidly after the fall of communism in Poland. The number of persons taking advantage of the nutrition programs in 1991 was 10 times higher than in 1980 (almost 4% of the elderly presently receive such help). Free dinners for the elderly or dinners at low prices are also provided by some churches and charities.

Social assistance by home help is afforded primarily by nurses from the Polish Red Cross and home helpers from the Polish Social Welfare Committee. The PCK nurses take care of the sick at home (washing and bathing, dressing, administering medicine, preparing meals, shopping, cleaning and tidying). In addition, home helpers from the PKWS offer their services free to the physically disabled, those living alone, and those living with families, if they are unable to ensure necessary care or if the per capita income does not exceed 100% of the smallest pension. The PKWS provides services in the home (cleaning, cooking, shopping, providing meals, gardening, bringing up coal from the cellar, lighting the stove, laundry service, bathing, sewing), transport to the doctor, and other everyday needs. Generally speaking, however, ho me service programs for the elderly in Poland embrace a relatively small section of the older generation (about 2–3%) and should be expanded in the future.

The range of programs of care for the elderly outside their homes is also not very extensive. The only help of this kind is day-care centers, a kind of transitional form between institutional and home care. The task of such a center is to provide for the everyday needs of the elderly and invalids, those who are unable to attend to their own needs (those living alone and receiving financial allowances have priority). A center provides four main types of services: meals throughout the day, hygiene (e.g., bathing, small washing), cultural activities (library, films, meetings, excursions), and occupational therapy and rehabilitation (handicrafts, physical exercises). Nurses and, several times a week, doctors are available for those attending the centers. Day-care centers are often located in old people's homes. The first such center in Poland was established in 1976, and by 1992 there were already about 200 centers (mainly located in larger towns).

There are no special mental health services, counseling services, group therapy, and so on for the elderly. There is a great shortage of information and referral services. Persons seeking information concerning services for the elderly must contact the Social Welfare Center in the community. At the beginning of the 1990s, local papers connected with social assistance and containing extensive information on the subject began to appear.

LEISURE-TIME RESOURCES

The model of the way the elderly spend free time in Poland could be called "traditional," embracing primarily religion, family-related activities, and solitary pursuits. The most frequent forms include watching television, religious practices, gardening (men), and care of grandchildren (women).

The part played by the elderly in social organizations has diminished, particularly as the result of political changes. During the communist period, a considerable percentage of the older generation constituted party members, members of the trade unions, or various other societies. It was, however, mainly formal membership, without any other activity. During the period of transformation of the system, most of the former parties and organizations ceased to exist, others took on a new shape, and many new ones arose. Most common is the membership of the Polish Pensioners' and Disabled Association and the Association of Fighters' for Freedom and Democracy. Among the new organizations are the Solidarność Labour Veterans' Association, the Siberian Deportees' Union, and the Union of the Victims of Stalinism.

Toward the end of the 1980s, various charity groups began to take shape, mainly to provide material help to the elderly. Some were self-help groups, in fact, as the majority of members were elderly persons. These groups mainly arose around the churches and the Citizens' Committees (which were established to help carry out the first free elections in Poland in 1989), as well as the housing cooperatives. There are also groups of a purely religious character in the churches (e.g., the Rosary Society), and the members are almost solely elderly persons.

The most general organized leisure for the elderly is available in the Seniors' Clubs (or Golden Autumn Clubs). In 1990, there were about 1,700 such clubs in Poland, where the elderly can meet to talk, organize entertainment, and enjoy lectures, advice groups, excursions, gymnastics, music and dance groups, and embroidery, as well as other kinds of hobbies and recreational activities. Seniors' Clubs are organized and conducted by the Polish Social Welfare Committee with the help of a social worker; some are organized at work and are usually called Pensioners' Circles. Similar forms of activities are conducted by cultural centers and, in villages, there are Village Housewives' Circles. These forms of activities lost some of their popularity at the beginning of the 1990s due to financial difficulties (the state cut their subsidies and there are only a few other sources of support).

Third age universities (TAUs), operating according to the French patterns, play a very important role in the leisure activities and educational opportunities for the elderly. In 1992, there were 16 TAUs in Poland, each with 50–300 elderly students. These institutions are mainly organized with the help of the community, backed by universities, Estate Clubs, and others. Lectures and workshops take place 1–3 times a week, each for 2–3 hours, and consist of lectures in various fields (mainly medical sciences and the humanities), as well as workshops in literary, artistic, and theatrical areas. Very popular subjects are foreign languages and recreational activities. The TAUs are free, open forms of studying irrespective of age. This form of activity primarily attracts those reasonably physically fit, of relatively high social status, and living alone.

ADVOCACY AND PROTECTION

There are almost no organizational efforts for advocacy, protection, and security on behalf of the elderly, as they are rather dispersed and not very noticeable. They have no allies to effectively defend their interests.

Legal assistance for the elderly is provided mainly by social welfare (some pensioners' associations also offer such advice). Advice is organized by social workers, with the aid of legal advisers employed in Social Welfare Centers, and mainly concerns family conflicts connected with alimony or allowances, division of estate, and questions of living accommodations.

The questions and problems of the elderly have been taken up by other social groups during important political periods (e.g., during the August strike of 1980, one of the demands concerned higher pensions), but very little has been done about them. In the 1980s, certain organizations were introduced into the political system of the time and were to fulfill protective and supportive functions. They were, in fact, artificial and "decorative" annexes to the government functions.

With greater freedom and as the result of the drop in the standard of living at the beginning of the 1990s, various pensioners' societies came into being (e.g., the Polish Pensioners' and Disabled Association and the Association of Labor Veterans). These societies organize protests and demonstrations objecting to the low pensions.

The only advocacy organization regularly acting on behalf of the standard of living and the appropriate place of the elderly in society is the Polish Gerontology Association. Apart from research, the association submits expert opinions, suggestions for solutions of problems, and appeals to the authorities in defense of the elderly. The mass media play an increasing role in this respect, calling attention to the symptoms of growing victimization of elderly persons under conditions of an economic crisis.

FUTURE PROJECTIONS

An analysis of services for the elderly in Poland proved them to be poorly adapted to the factual needs of the elderly in the conditions of the post-communist transformation of the country. The centralistic-state system of services became inefficient and, at the beginning of the 1990s, no new solutions have emerged. The services presented are directed more toward satisfying the particular needs of the individual than toward comprehensive, complex solutions of the problems of elderly people. Services are mainly of an extemporaneous, dispersed, and uncoordinated character. The constant lack of financial means impedes the setting up of rational, long-term programs to help ward off the negative effects of the physical aging process and psychosocial deprivation. It is, thus, paradoxical that as the need to help the elderly is growing, there is a simultaneous diminishing of resources to meet this need as well as inadequate protective mechanisms.

An essential feature of services for the elderly is that, as in the past, they are designed almost exclusively for those who are alone and for the poorest. There are, thus, many elderly persons whose families do not afford them any care, whose relationships with their families are bad, and who are exposed to considerable deprivation of their needs. The problem is similar in the case of elderly persons whose financial situation is reasonably good but who require help as regards services or psychological support. The poorly developed network of services and lack of agencies rendering services for remuneration constitute serious obstacles in the elderly's retaining their independence.

Another negative feature of the welfare services for the elderly is their being restricted to "traditional" forms of help (particularly material assistance). Those in need play a very small part in solving their own problems. Recreational activity is also poor, formally organized leisure-time resources are not very extensive, and referral and advocate services are almost nonexistent.

The needs of the elderly for services in the near future will depend primarily on economic and demographic factors. Financial assistance and material safeguarding of the standard of living will continue to be important, as the elderly will be subjected to powerful competition from the unemployed and those threatened with poverty. The number and percentage of persons in the oldest age groups will increase substantially in several years, which will increase the demand for health care, home services, and old people's institutions. It will be necessary to expand the network of health visitors, home helpers, social workers, and specialized centers and clinics. The need will also arise to establish institutions that are intermediate between old people's homes and hospitals (and the growing need for more geriatric wards).

Indispensable for the improvement of the existence of elderly people during the transitional period in Poland is that the state should remain the main guarantor for the provision of their needs. The development of paid services and other sources of assistance is imperative, but these should be of a supplementary, not substitutional, character in relation to public care. To enable more efficient use, access, and functioning of the resources of the elderly, it is necessary to ensure close relationships between informal groups (family, nongovernmental organizations) and social welfare. Permanent interaction, negotiations, and cooperation between the partners would better protect the elderly against further deterioration of their living conditions. The state can gradually withdraw from the scene of social services only with increasing efficiency of the three-link chain between the state, the informal sector, and voluntary organizations.

Given limited financial means on the part of the state and the strong position of the family in Polish society, help for the elderly should primarily be directed toward facilitating the family in fulfilling its function as guardian. For example, unemployed persons who take care of the elderly in need of help could be awarded a certain income from social welfare. Neighborly ties—still fairly strong in Poland—could be utilized on a similar basis.

Multirole centers, embracing health care, social help, and recreational facilities, should be established for the elderly. These would enable more extensive provision for the needs of the elderly (they could be established on the basis of existing Seniors' Clubs or day-care centers). The forms of help should extend beyond care services and in-kind services. Preventive and physiotherapy programs related to "normal" aging, as well as special programs for different kinds and degrees of disabilities and diseases of old age, should be created. Help should be organized before there is a loss of independence, and the elderly should be recruited to actively participate in such efforts.

In order to introduce such solutions, it is necessary that the approach of society and the elderly themselves should change; the older generation should play a greater role as a pressure group. There exists a fear that on Poland's list of priorities over the next few years, the question of elderly people will come after the needs of the unemployed, young people, and large families.

NOTES

1. Until the end of the 1980s, Poland was a country organized along socialist lines, grappling with political disturbances and severe economic problems. Since then, after the collapse of communism and the coming into power of Solidarity, almost everything has begun to change: the economy, the political system, social policy. This chapter concerns mainly the transitional period in Poland, particularly the very end of the 1980s and the very beginning of the 1990s.

2. It is difficult to say what proportion of the elderly population are recipients of social care. Statistical data available do not discern the elderly as a separate group. One may estimate that 8–10% of the elderly in rural areas and 12–14% in towns receive some form of social care.

BIBLIOGRAPHY

Frackiewicz, L. (1991). *Polityka ochrony zdrowia.* Katowice, Akademia Ekonomiczna.
Hrynkiewicz, J., Starega-Piasek, J., and Supińska, J. (1991). "The elderly and social policy in Poland." In *New Welfare Mixes in Care for the Elderly,* Vol. 1, No 40/1. Vienna: European Centre, pp. 59–72.
Kolankiewicz, G., and Lewis, P. G. (1988). *Poland: Politics, Economics and Society.* London: Pinter.
Les, E. (1992). "Poland." In J. Dixon and D. Macarov (eds.), *Social Welfare in Socialist Countries.* London: Routledge, pp. 156–183.
Łopato, J. (1991). *Pomoc społeczna wobec ludzi starych na wsi.* Warszawa: Uniwersytet Warszawski.
Midré, G., and Synak, B. (1989). "Between family and state: Ageing in Poland and Norway." *Ageing and Society,* No. 9, pp. 241–259.
Pedich, W. (ed.) (1991). *Trends and Problems in the Care for the Elderly in Poland.* Białystok: Polish Society of Gerontology.
Rocznik Statystyczny. (1991). Warszawa, Gowny Urzad Statystyczny.
Rysz-Kowalczyk, B. (ed.) (1991). *Społeczne kwestie starości.* Uniwersytet Warszawski.

Synak, B. (1987). "The elderly in Poland: An overview of selected problems and changes." *Ageing and Society,* No. 7, pp. 19–35.

———. (1989). "Formal care for elderly people in Poland." *Journal of Cross-Cultural Gerontology,* No. 4, pp. 107–127.

———. (1990). "The Polish family: Stability, change and conflict." *Journal of Aging Studies* 4, No. 4, pp. 333–344.

Worach-Kardas, H. (1989). "Retirement in Poland." In K. S. Markides and C. L. Cooper (eds.), *Retirement in Industrial Societies.* New York: Wiley, pp. 271–286.

SOUTH KOREA

Kyu-taik Sung

INTRODUCTION

The concept of social welfare for elderly people is relatively new in Korea, where care for the elderly from family and kin has been accepted as a customary and normative duty and obligation. However, as Korea underwent dynamic social changes in the process of rapid industrialization and urbanization during the 1970s and 1980s, the care for the elderly has gained increased attention from policymakers and human service professionals. Concerned Koreans now question the willingness of families to care for their elders, a basic moral issue that until recently has not been doubted. Thus, the decline of parent care has become a serious issue in Korea.

Certain social trends in Korea have, in fact, given rise to this concern (Yoon, 1985; Kong et al., 1990; Lee et al., 1990). The average size of Korean families has been getting smaller (5.7 persons in 1955; 3.8 persons in 1990), and the number of females participating in the labor market has increased (married 44.3%, unmarried 36.9% in 1970; married 46.4%, unmarried 47.2% in 1990) (Kong et al., 1990). A large number of young people have moved into cities, leaving their aging parents behind. Added to these changes is a prominent increase in the sheer size and proportion of the aged population. Korea has completed the demographic transition from high birth and death rates to low birth and death rates during the last 30 years. The proportion of the population aged 65 and over, which was 5% of the total population in 1990, is expected to increase to 6% by 2000 and 11% by 2020 (Economic Planning Board [EPB], 1986, 1987, 1989). With this demographic background, Korea will very soon face an aging society; life expectancy at birth for both sexes, which was 55.3 in 1960, reached 71.3 in 1990 and is expected to be 74.3 in 2000 (EPB, 1970, 1980, 1985, 1988, 1990a, 1990b).

A major consequence of such social change has been the emergence of massive and multifaceted problems for the elderly, notably diminishing status in the family and society, loss of income and economic dependence on children, role loss and feelings of alienation, health care problems, and the need for new services to resolve these and other such problems (Yoon, 1989; Kim and Han, 1990; Kong et al., 1990; Lee et al., 1990). Koreans were virtually unprepared technically, as well as financially, to meet this new, immense challenge.

In the 1970s and 1980s, seminars and conferences on aging were held by academic, cultural, and social organizations. These activities helped to clarify elderly people's needs and related policy issues.

Recognizing rising public concerns over, and growing needs for, social welfare of the elderly, the government promulgated the Senior Citizens' Welfare Act (Noin-Bokji Bub) in 1981. The act emphasizes opportunities for support services to enable the elderly to maintain the social status of respected persons, satisfactory levels of activity, and physical, psychological, and social well-being. These objectives are consistent with Koreans' traditional ideal of filial piety and they emphasize the moral responsibility of children and families to care for aged persons.

The Formal Structure of Care of the Elderly

Several new programs were developed under the law by the Department of Aging, the Bureau of Family Welfare of the Ministry of Health and Social Affairs, which administers policies and programs for the aged. A range of services is being provided. In 1992, the government budget for social welfare for old persons amounted to 30% of the total budget for social welfare of the nation.

The task of bringing uninformed and isolated elderly clients into the service delivery system has been a major problem for program planners in Korea. Transportation, along with income assistance, has been the highest-ranked need of elderly people (Sung and Kim, 1988).

Currently, in all areas of the country, thanks to the rapid expansion of mass transit systems and an enormous increase in the number of cars owned by relatives and friends, the elderly have much greater access to transportation. Thus, most elderly have access to transportation to doctors, senior citizens' centers, and other such places, since they live with their families, who usually provide such support. For a large number of the elderly, however, transportation is still a major problem. Since almost all elderly persons in Korea do not drive a car, many of them depend on public transport—either bus, subway, taxi, or train.

The campaign for transportation for the elderly started in the 1960s. Various approaches have been used to increase transportation availability, in compliance with Article 10 (Preferential Treatment for Elderly Persons) of the Senior Citizens' Welfare Act. A number of innovations have been introduced such as reduced fares, public subsidies for transportation, use of church buses, and use of volunteers driving their own car. For instance, under a program jointly sponsored by the government and by bus companies, elderly persons aged 65 and over are provided with free bus rides. Every Korean bus has front seats specifically assigned to elderly riders. Design aspects that facilitate access by the elderly have been included in some new public transit systems. Korean streets are virtually crime-free, and someone in the family or a friend usually escorts a very old relative when he or she uses public transportation.

Thus, informal systems of family, neighbors, relatives, and church members provide frail and socially and psychologically insecure elderly persons and those with ambulatory impairments with escort services. Outreach service to those elderly persons who are uninformed, isolated, and unwilling to have outside help is provided by an increasing number of senior citizens' welfare agencies, though mostly in urban areas. Most of these programs, however, fall short of meeting the needs of the elderly, particularly those in rural areas.

INCOME MAINTENANCE AND EMPLOYMENT

According to a recent Korea-Gallup report (1990), 65% of the surveyed elderly persons aged 65 and above expressed needs for financial assistance. About 21% of them were below the poverty line (Ministry of Health and Social Affairs [MOHSA], 1989). Of those elderly living alone or with a spouse, only 29% received financial support from their adult children, and 45% depended on their own savings and/or spouse's income. Some adult children may be unable to provide support and some may be reluctant to do so. These data indicate that aged persons living separately from their children or without adult children would face financial difficulties.

Major income maintenance programs for aged persons are (1) public pensions, (2) public assistance, (3) retirement benefits, (4) discount services and tax exemption, and (5) job placement (Chung, 1992).

The National Pension program started in 1988 (and is based upon the National Welfare Pension Act, 1973 and the National Pension Act, 1986). The coverage of the program has been extended to a number of previously ineligible groups, including self-employed and farm and domestic workers, while the number of memberships has been steadily increasing. This national program is expected to cover all workers aged 18–60 who are not covered by special pension programs for three occupation groups (government employees, military personnel, and private school and university teachers). Currently, employees of workplaces with five or more full-time workers are eligible to participate in this program. The program provides old-age pensions, invalidity pensions, and survivor pensions. One must have had a membership for 20 years or longer to be eligible for an old-age pension, the major benefit under the program. Those who do not meet this condition are given a lump-sum refund. Contribution to the program is made from the employee's wages and the employer's liability.

The retirement program provides some supplementary income for the elderly (Labor Standard Act, 1953). This program has been the only income maintenance measure for workers in preparation for their retirement. Those in a workplace with 10 or more full-time workers are eligible for this retirement benefit. The benefit is paid in a lump sum when the worker retires or leaves the workplace. By 2003, 70% of all aged persons 65 and above (and by 2008, all of them) will be covered by the pension program.

Three public pension programs for retired government employees, military personnel, and teachers have been in operation since the 1960s. Benefits of these programs include payments for old age and work-related injuries, disability, and survivors' pensions. About 7% of all employed persons are covered by the programs.

For low-income persons, the government is planning to develop the so-called noncontributory pension system, whereby low-income persons can receive pensions as one form of public assistance without having contributed to the system.

Public assistance programs for old persons started in 1961, when the Livelihood Protection Act (Saenghwal-Boho Bub) was promulgated. Aged persons 65 and above who are poor (as judged by the means test) and do not have a legally responsible supporter are entitled to this public assistance (cash allowance, medical aids, relief aids, funeral assistance, public nursing home care, tuition for children in school, and so on). In 1991, 328,000 elderly persons received this assistance (14.8% of all persons aged 65 and above; 15.4% of all recipients of public assistance) (MOHSA, 1991; Bureau of Statistics [BOS], 1991). The types and amount of benefits vary by specific subprogram: at-home protection, institutional protection, and self-reliance protection. It is a restricted public provision for which eligibility requirements are strictly enforced. The central government contributes 80% of the program budget and local government contributes the rest. Despite the fairly rapid expansion of the program, the support level is still very low.

Allowance for seniors is provided from January 1991, in compliance with the Senior Citizens' Welfare Act (Article 13: Allowance for the Aged). Beneficiaries are those aged 70 and above who maintain an independent household separately from adult children, who are financially disadvantaged and without a legal or obligatory supporter, and who are in an institution. In 1991 there were 76,000 aged persons who received this allowance, mostly those who could not benefit from the new National Pension program (Chung, 1992, p. 19). From 1992 the allowance will be provided to 8.4% of all aged persons aged 65 and over, and from 1997 it will be provided to those who belong to a general low-income category. Some 25% of all aged persons will receive the income supplement by 2001.

Discount services are one of the special treatment programs for the elderly, as stipulated in the Senior Citizens' Welfare Act (Article 10: Preferential Treatment for Aged Persons). These services, started in 1980, provide persons aged 65 and over with free fares for subway and ferryboat rides and free admissions to public parks, gardens, temples, public theaters, and museums. The railroad system provides only a 50% discount. For bus rides, persons aged 65 and over receive 12 free bus tokens monthly from private bus companies. Services provided by private sources—hair services, public baths, movie houses, and so on—are not fully covered at this time. In 1992, about 2.3 million elderly persons had benefited from the discount services.

In order to reward and encourage adult children to care for their parents aged 65 or over (for mothers, 55 or over), the government has instituted partial exemption of inheritance tax and a tax exemption for the amount of $6,000 under Income Tax Law (Article 66). Additionally, government employees who are living with their parents aged 60 and over (mothers 55 and over) receive a monthly allowance of $200. For those who have been living with their parents or spouse's parents for more than two years, several large banks provide low-interest loans for construction, purchase, and repair of their own houses.

The proportion of employed persons aged 55 and over in the total population has been increasing. In 1990 the proportion was 13.7% (Lee, 1992). Employed elderly persons are engaged in various industries, for example, farming and fishing (60.4%), wholesale and retail restaurants and hotels (13.7%), manufacturing (9.1%), private business (8.3%), construction (3.9%), financial, insurance, and real estate (3.2%), transportation, storage, and communication (1.2%), and utilities (0.1%) (EPB, 1990a).

Of all employed aged persons, 77% wish to continue being employed, and of all those currently not employed, 41% would like to find work (Lee, 1992). Both the public and private sectors have developed programs for job training and placement of elderly persons who are willing to work.

In 1991 the Senior Citizen Employment Promotion Act was promulgated. The principal requirement of the legislation was that the Ministry of Labor establish a community employment program for low-income elderly persons who wanted to work. In order to encourage industry to hire older workers, the ministry stipulated Standard Employment Regulations under the Employment Promotion Act. Under these laws and regulations, an employer is advised to hire a certain ratio of older workers. An employer who has hired older workers above the recommended ratio is entitled to receive tax exemptions or a tax reduction, according to the Tax Exemption Law.

The Ministry of Labor has issued the following types of jobs suitable to older workers and advised government agencies and private industries to fill these positions with older workers: parking lot attendants, ticket agents, ticket collectors, information desk attendants, receptionists, janitors/guards, parks, maintenance persons, railroad-crossing guards, traffic controllers, fee-fare collectors, utility meter checkers, restaurant workers, salespersons, air-conditioning inspectors, librarians, bookbinders, forestry conservation agents, plant growers, environment beautifiers, car drivers, advisers, consultants, building managers, dormitory superintendents, child-care workers, sorters, storeroom clerks, label stickers, guides, car dispatchers, recreation facility maintenance persons, packers, product inspectors, and delivery persons.

Under the Senior Citizens' Employment Promotion Act, job placement programs are administered by the Senior Citizens' Human Resources Bank and the Senior Citizens' Employment Information Center, both of which are supported by the government. The resource banks have been in operation in major cities and industrial regions since 1981 to provide employment counseling and locate employment for elderly persons. In 1991, the banks found short-term employment for 59,445 persons and long-term employment for 25,837 persons. Between 1984 and 1990, 521,145 elderly persons found jobs through 264 of these banks (Lee, 1992, pp. 1–37).

To help the elderly earn extra money, cooperative workshops and stalls are set up in parks and public places. There are about 300 workshops where mainly light manufacturing work takes place, and hundreds of such stalls are managed by elderly persons. Employers of elderly workers are generally pleased with the efficiency and reliability with which the older workers perform. Community welfare service centers and voluntary organizations also run job banks and placement services.

There has been a shortage of labor in major industry. In 1991, manufacturing industry, for instance, was short of about 10% of its normally required work force. As the labor shortage increases, the prospect for hiring older workers increases. The private sector of industry will assume a greater initiative in tapping the potential resources of older workers. Although many old persons in need of work benefit from the services, the proportion of eligible old persons who are helped remains small.

HEALTH CARE SERVICES

Due to marked increases in the number of aged persons, the number of chronic diseases, and the increase in medical care costs, health care has become a major social issue. Major types of diseases affecting the aged in Korea are respiratory, digestive, and neurological disorders of a degenerative and chronic nature. Thus, in 1990 the leading causes of death for people aged 60–69 were cancer, cerebral vascular disease, hypertensive disease, and heart disease (Song, 1992, p. 54).

Since 1989 all Koreans are covered by the National Medical Insurance, which is financed by monthly premiums paid equally by employees and employers. For farmers, fishermen, and self-employed workers, the government and the insuree pay equal amounts. The insurance covers the cost of hospital and related services. To be eligible for this insurance, one has to be the insuree or a dependent of the insuree. The policy pays for diagnosis, inpatient and outpatient treatment, operations, nursing, prescription drugs, and ambulance services. Currently, 97% of all aged persons are covered by this insurance. However, medical care services covered by the insurance are restricted; preventive and long-term supportive care is specifically excluded from coverage. Before the inception of this national insurance program, there was a separate medical insurance program solely for government employees, military personnel, and teachers and professors. This special program has merged into the national program. Medical insurance is administered by the Federation of Korean Medical Insurance Societies under the supervision of the Ministry of Health and Social Affairs.

Since 1983, for the purpose of detecting possible abnormalities, free health examinations for the aged have been provided annually by the government with priority given to low-income persons, in compliance with the Senior Citizens' Welfare Act (Article 9).

For low-income persons, medical assistance is provided under the Livelihood Protection Act. It also provides medical care services to veterans, nationally valued artists, and disaster-stricken persons. Under this program the government share ranges from 50% to 80% of health care payments. The program, financed by the government, pays for prescription drugs, supportive services, and long-term nursing home care, in addition to the basic medical care services covered by the National Health Insurance. But the payment level varies, depending on the need for primary or secondary care and the status of the recipient. This is a welfare program and is based on restrictive limitations of income and assets. However, it is a major source of payment for long-term care for disadvantaged elderly persons. One out of five elderly persons aged 65 and over is covered by this program.

The number of the elderly utilizing health care services has increased, as the following statistics for 1987 (compared with 1981) show: medical care satisfaction rate of 78% (15-day study) (51%, 1981); physician visits per person per annum of 8.77 times (4.01 times, 1981); hospitalization rate per annum of 71% (31%, 1981); and 15-day medical care institution visit rate of 11.4% (6.6%, 1981) (Song, 1992).

Under the Health Center Act, health centers based in townships and districts provide medical checkups, detection of disease, treatment services, physical therapy, and home-visit physician and nurse services (Lee and Park, 1990). Mobile clinics are in use in remote areas. It will be increasingly difficult to care for disabled and bedridden elderly persons at home. Hence, construction of nursing homes is urgently needed. However, social preference of cohabitation and prevailing pressure to enforce this value in Korean society have been delaying the full-scale development of homes for the aged and nursing homes.

Medical care for the elderly has focused on cure and rehabilitation and needs to be reoriented toward prevention. In particular, geriatric medicine needs to be more professionalized, and its manpower needs to be developed. Only two geriatric hospitals specialize in medical care services for aged persons. Health care centers providing specialized treatment for persons with paralysis and cerebral diseases are under construction. Currently, university hospitals and general hospitals are serving these types of patients.

Government health policy has the following objectives: (1) management of chronic degenerative diseases by constructing small clinics, opening education classes, expanding early diagnosis and treatment centers, and supporting rehabilitation programs for heart and blood vessel diseases; (2) extension of health insurance coverage to include chronic diseases; (3) establishment of public health administration units in local governments; and (4) modernization of facilities for physical therapy and rehabilitation.

Thanks to the relatively small size of the aged population, Korea is not experiencing the problem that exists in industrialized nations of the heavy financial burden for the payment of large medical care expenses. However, medical care expenses of Korean elderly are estimated to increase to 9% of the nation's total medical care expenses by 1995 and 17% by 2020 (Song, 1992, p. 65).

HOUSING RESOURCES

Housing for the aged is emerging as a major social concern. In 1991 Korea built some 120,000 apartment units. Such massive construction indicates the effort of the government to meet the growing needs of people in general and low-income families in particular. The types of housing programs include guaranteed and direct government loans for construction, congregate and shared housing, and provision of small, low-rent apartment units.

One way for the elderly to cope with the high cost of housing, to reduce their loneliness, and to gain a source of assistance and security is sharing a house with their children and relatives. Currently, around 75% of persons aged 60 and over live with their married or unmarried children, while one in four lives only with their spouse (Lee et al., 1989). Although a number of elderly Koreans tend to place a high value on the privacy of their own homes, the majority of them still find both financial and sociopsychological rewards in shared housing with children.

The Ministry of Construction and the Korea Housing Corporation have been jointly developing three-generation (shared) housing projects (Korea Housing Corporation [KHC], 1987). Several types of apartments, including apartments designed to accommodate three-generation families, have been built (about 400 units in 1987), and more are under construction. The projects include apartments with a partition between the room for the adult child and spouse and the room for the parents, separate apartments for the two parties to live apart from each other in the same building, and arrangements to live separately in different buildings while in the same apartment complex.

Special priority is offered by the government to purchase these and other types of apartments for adult children who live with, and support, their parents. In a country where it is highly competitive to purchase an apartment, such an offer is a privilege. To those who live with an aged parent, the Bank of Housing provides low-interest loans up to $40,000 and additional loans up to $6,500, if requested. Also, those elderly who maintain a separate household are provided a similar offer. The Korea Housing Corporation is planning to undertake senior citizens' (congregate) welfare housing projects for low-income elderly persons. However, such conveniences will not be available to needy persons in all locations.

The number of aged persons who own their own houses is high—89% of all aged persons living at home or 79% of all households headed by aged persons (Lee et al., 1989). A reason so many old persons own their own houses seems to be that they live with their adult children, who probably own a good number of the houses. The elderly persons themselves must own houses since they are the heads of households. But, in cities where many new small houses—such as apartments—are built recently, owners most often are young people or adult children. In the Korean family system, traditionally "a parent's house is a child's house"; since they live together there is not much distinction of who owns the dwelling.

The Senior Citizens' Welfare Act (Article 18) stipulates that "the government and the local administrative authorities shall provide nursing homes and shelters needed by the elderly in due consideration of appropriateness of facilities for the elderly." As of September 1991, 102 institutions for the aged (80% of which were built in the 1980s) accommodated 6,700 elderly clients. This indicates the increasing needs of old persons for such services. All but 11 of these homes are free homes for the aged and free nursing homes supported by the government for disadvantaged aged persons. High fees, a lack of information, and complicated procedures for admission are creating barriers to elderly persons seeking admission to these homes. Thus, some homes for paying clients have the chronic problem of empty beds. Adult day-care centers, which opened recently, offer a variety of support services, including day care, social activities, meals, health and rehabilitation services, personal care, and other social services.

In view of the changing trends of Korean society, the need for homes for the aged will increase. Therefore, the traditional negative attitudes toward nursing homes as a "dumping ground" for miserable old persons must be changed. Retirement homes may inevitably be the pattern of the future in Korea as well as for many other countries. In fact, the government of Korea has finally decided to permit the private sector to undertake enterprises for the elderly, whereby care and services of nursing homes, day care centers, etc. (operated by private enterprises) can be purchased by those elderly persons and their families who can afford such resources.

SUPPORTIVE SERVICES

The Senior Citizens' Welfare Act stipulates several types of social services supporting elderly persons and their families, such as counseling, home help services, services by welfare centers, senior citizens' clubhouses, senior citizens' schools, and senior citizens' rest facilities.

Voluntary agencies specializing in services for elderly persons, funded by the government under the Senior Citizens' Welfare Act, provide a range of supportive services to elderly persons in need (Choi, 1991; Lee, 1992). In 1991, there were 10 agencies of this type in urban areas; this number is expected to increase. Their services are designed to support efforts by older persons to maintain optimal levels of activity, social involvement, and independence. Included in the services are meals, nutrition education, home help, counseling, protective services, friendly visiting and telephone reassurance, day care, and job placement. Meals-on-wheels are provided to elderly persons confined to their homes. Home help is provided to those without a caregiver; currently 720 home helpers, who are paid by the government, provide such services. Home help focuses on personal services, household management, housekeeping, preparation of meals, and related activities. Home helpers work under the guidance of a social worker or nurse. Congregate meal services and nutritional education are sponsored by church groups, voluntary agencies, and neighborhood social welfare centers. Presently, some of these services are also provided by the Community Social Welfare Centers operating throughout the country.

In recent years, campaigns for welfare rights of senior citizens (and other issues affecting them) have taken place, conducted largely by old persons themselves. Some coalition groups participated in these campaigns to support their causes.

Informal networks of neighbors and friends provide support through personal visits and telephone visits. Volunteers often perform these functions for agencies, with guidelines and coordination provided by professional staff members. Telephone reassurance programs are directed toward high-risk older persons who live alone.

However, at this stage, some of these efforts are limited and inconsistent. A lack of understanding about home visits, unwillingness to receive outside help, and feelings of guilt on the part of children of old persons are some of the problems to be resolved.

LEISURE-TIME RESOURCES

Programs for leisure time are in an early stage of development. According to a Korea-Gallup survey (1990), Korean elderly people spend their leisure time watching television (73.7%), listening to radio (32.4%), playing games (cards, chess, and so on) (20.1%), reading (16.7%), not doing anything in particular (14.7%), walking (13.2%), traveling (11.5%), fishing/exercise (6%), gardening (5.5%), and knitting/sewing (5%), among others. Thus, the majority of the elderly spend their leisure time watching television. Knitting/sewing and cooking are most popular leisure-time activities for female elderly, and gardening was most popular for male persons. These figures reflect a rather dismal picture of Korean elderly people's leisure-time activities. A lack of organized leisure services, of acculturation to leisure activities, and of financial resources would seem to be major reasons the elderly spend their times in this way.

In recent years organized leisure programs have been developed, while others are under experimentation (Kwon, 1991). Senior Citizens' Welfare Centers (Noin-Bokji Hoekwan), as stipulated by the Senior Citizens' Welfare Act, are multipurpose agencies for senior citizens. At present, only five such centers are in operation. The basic package provided by a center includes recreation, education, nutritional education, preventive health services, counseling, information, referrals, and outreach services. Some centers incorporate adult day care and rehabilitation therapies as supplements to the basic package. Currently, some of the functions of these centers are being assumed by an increasing number of community social welfare centers operating throughout the country, which numbered some 200 in 1992.

Senior citizens' clubhouses (Noin-Jung) are the most widely used and most common facilities for elderly people in Korea (Kim, 1989). They are located within both urban and rural residential areas throughout the country, where elderly persons spend their daytime and participate in leisure-time and social activities. Some 20,000 senior citizens' clubhouses are used by 1 million elderly people aged 60 and over—about one-third of all elderly people in the country. Every township has between one and three such clubhouses. The government provides limited financial support to the clubhouses, and local groups provide additional resources. Each year, 50 senior citizens' centers are selected for their successful operation and are awarded a prize by the Ministry of Health and Social Affairs. Small space, lack of quality programs, and limited maintenance funds are problems for these facilities.

The Recreation Center for Senior Citizens, which will provide a comprehensive package of services to elderly persons, is under construction in Chungmoo, a medium-sized city situated on a southernmost island of Korea that is endowed with warm weather and scenic surroundings. If this project is successful, more recreation centers will be constructed.

The desire of Koreans for a high level of education is held by aged persons as well. Elderly people in retirement enjoy educational opportunities at senior citizens' schools (Noin-Hakkyo) or the so-called senior citizens' colleges (Noin-Daehak) (Korean Continuing Education Organization [KCEO], 1991).

Continued education for elderly people takes place at senior centers, social service agencies, housing projects, public meeting facilities, or churches founded by voluntary organizations and well-wishers. Nationwide, there are about 1,000 such "voluntary" senior citizens' schools, which are attended by some 60,000 old persons.

Senior citizens' schools are also set up in public schools (Senior Citizens' Education Act, 1991). The schools are open one day a month to offer classes in community activity participation, knowledge in daily living, occupational education, and so on. In 1991 there were 7,000 senior citizens' schools in public schools throughout the country.

Education programs for senior citizens vary in duration, level, and purpose (Sung, 1991a). The programs help older persons cope with social and technological change, personal and health problems, and needs for self-fulfillment. (Senior citizens' schools are stipulated as leisure facilities for elderly people by the Senior Citizens Welfare Act.)

Courses most popular among the elderly are (in ranked order) (1) crafts, (2) business administration and real estate, (3) arts (dancing and painting), (4) health care, and (5) home economics. Almost all of the courses taken by the elderly are noncredit. Very few older persons are enrolled in the formal university system (KCEO, 1991).

The level of participation of the elderly in such programs has been steadily increasing. Participation rates are higher for females than for males. Participants are more likely to have relatively high incomes and higher educational levels than nonparticipants.

Major barriers to increased participation by older persons include lack of appropriate counseling, poor transportation, high tuition costs, low-quality programs, and shortage of teachers specialized in senior citizen education (Sung, 1991a). Despite these barriers, senior citizens' schools are almost everywhere, and well-wishers would like to set up senior citizens' schools in their communities. Several voluntary organizations, including the Korea Continuing Education Organization (Hankook Pyungsaeng Kyoyook Kiku) and the Korea Senior Citizens' Association (Daehan-Noin-Hoe), have become involved in lifetime learning projects for elderly people.

ADVOCACY AND PROTECTION

In recent years, national efforts to preserve the traditional values associated with the care of the elderly have been made under joint public and private auspices in Korea. The Campaign for Respect for Elders, the enactment of the Senior Citizens' Welfare Law, the provision of various social and health services for elders, and the establishment of Respect for the Elderly Day, Parents' Day, and the Filial Piety Prize System are all examples of such efforts.

The moral ideal underlying the motive to establish such social institutions is that the elderly should be respected and cared for as they are the ones who suffered to raise a new generation and who contributed for years to their family and society. It is thus felt that when parents are at the age when they can no longer take care of themselves, it is only right that they should be cared for by those whom they themselves raised.

Filial piety is the keystone of social efforts in Korea (Sung, 1990, 1992). Korea, as is true of other Far Eastern nations, has shared the ideals of filial piety for many generations (Palmore and Maeda, 1986; Dixon, 1981). Values associated with filial piety are reflected in the ritual and propriety of the Koreans (Park, 1989). The traditional basis of such values is the teachings of filial piety that have long dominated the culture of the nation. Throughout Korea's history, elderly persons have been seen as socially important, revered, and treated with dignity and respect.

A movement of senior citizens to advocate for their rights has been taking place in Korea. However, any movement that is iconoclastic would be avoided by senior citizens, who are not socialized to taking their demands to the street and are overly concerned with saving face (*ch'e-myun*). Talks of the gray panther movement have been around for some time. But, for the time being, it seems unlikely for Korean elderly to actually stage such a movement.

The main rallying ground for elderly people is the Korean Senior Citizens' Association, a national institution with local agencies. Major goals of this association are to protect the rights of senior citizens, to improve their living conditions, and to restore their dignity and social status. To promote these causes, it has organized pressure groups that lobby in the National Assembly for the legislation affecting senior citizens' well-being. So far, the main target of these groups has been the provision of various forms of public services for indigent elderly persons. As the number of the aged continues to increase, the power of the association becomes ever stronger. Politicians can no longer make light of its demands, and its lobbying more often yields good results.

In the last presidential election, the association requested all presidential candidates to appear before the assembly of its national representatives and present their platforms specifically aimed for the improvement of senior citizens' rights for decent social treatment. All of the candidates obligingly appeared before the assembly and presented their promises for various types of services—comparable to those provided in advanced welfare states.

Some social organizations advocate the causes of senior citizens as well. For instance, an agency held a mock national assembly where legislative activities took place involving debates over critically needed public assistance for the elderly. Another agency conducted an annual seminar designed to promote filial piety; several notable personalities made presentations, and television transmitted the event nationwide. Korea Housing Corporation has been constructing apartments for three-generation families designed to protect privacy of both elderly parents and their children. Samsung and Hyundai, the largest business concerns, as well as the Ministry of Health and Social Affairs, annually award filial piety prizes to those who have cared for and respected their elderly parents in an exceptional manner and distribute stories of prizewinners to schools and communities.

Legal rights of the elderly have been stipulated in the Senior Citizens' Welfare Law; these written rights need to be translated into quantitative and qualitative services. The institution of this law, the filial piety prize, and provision of health and social services are efforts taken by the government.

FUTURE PROJECTIONS

During the past three decades, Korea has become an industrialized nation and is now facing the serious problems of aging. Such problems have literally exploded in this hitherto stable society in terms of the traditional life-style of elderly people in the extended family. Koreans were virtually unprepared to meet this immense challenge.

Recognizing the urgent needs for social welfare of elderly people, organized public efforts have been undertaken. Laws have been enacted, policy issues clarified, Social Security measures put into effect, new types of public services delivered, and more public funds provided to maintain these societywide efforts.

However, the formal system will be unlikely to keep pace with the growing needs of small families in the industrialized and urbanized society of Korea. The importance of informal support systems needs to be stressed, and the ability of the family as an informal caregiving institution has to be enhanced (Sung, 1991b).

We must recognize the substitution potential of the informal support network for the public support system. However, we should not underscore the importance of examining family resources of the elderly which are at risk. In fact, there are increasing needs for Korean society to develop ways of replacing some of the support roles of informal networks by publicly supported services. A major issue involved in the Korean family support network is how to alleviate the burdens and strains on family members giving care to the elderly living with them and highly dependent on them.

Thus, there is an increasing need to develop ways of resolving the problems inherent in informal networks and to supplement some of the support roles of these networks, particularly the family network. Currently, many elderly Korean people living with their children need public services, such as counseling for supporters, training for caregivers, adult day care, social services, financial aid, home help, home health care, health education, and other services performed by professionals and agencies. In order to maintain the caregiving function of the family for longer periods, many families need such services to facilitate care of their parents. A service delivered to the parents can be seen as service to the whole family.

Therefore, emphasis should be on integration of at-home elder care by the family and institutional care by the state. That is, a dual approach would have to be adopted to balance both types of efforts—expansion of institutional care and expansion of at-home care of elderly persons. How the state and the family can balance or share the two responsibilities is a task that needs to be resolved with creativity and patience. The debate on balancing the two responsibilities is expected to continue.

Meanwhile, the problems of elderly people are multiple and complex. Practitioners and researchers should continue to exchange information as to what organizational and intervention approaches work best with elderly clients and their families. Koreans must study the serious approaches being taken by other nations in order to prevent and alleviate the problems of elderly people.

In this relatively early stage of development, some of the programs are largely exploratory; every so often, some new programs emerge and go into trial. Periodic review of the development of such new efforts is needed. As experience is gained in service delivery, the programs will have to be constantly reviewed and modified.

So far, public social welfare programs have focused on very disadvantaged groups of elderly persons, based on the residual perspective of social welfare.

Korea has attained success in economic development, and its accumulated wealth can now be used to expand social welfare. Hence, such programs will have to be gradually expanded to cover all elderly persons in need, so that these people can ideally consume the services as public utilities.

Therefore, agencies providing services to old persons need to be diversified in terms of being able to provide more specialized services and widen choices of selection for elderly people by setting up more voluntary and even proprietary agencies. Thus, by opening up a wider free market where more consumer-oriented services are available, both public and private resources can be mobilized to provide more acceptable and efficient services to the elderly. Fortunately, Korea is moving in this direction: eldercare institutions built and operated by the private sector will start to provide care and services for fees from 1994 on. A large number of elderly persons are expected to be able to purchase such services.

However, the pace of the development of public services is likely to lag behind that of economic growth, due to two major, interrelated factors: the traditional cultural influences that emphasize the moral responsibility of children and families to care for aged parents and the guiding principle of the government, which is directed toward the restoration of the family's parent-care function.

Korea embodies the relative commitment to two divergent values, the traditional values associated with family-centered, informal parent-care and the new values of public commitment to the provision of efficient services for the elderly. Thus, Korea needs to continue to expand public services for the elderly while retaining the cultural tradition that has had valuable results in the integration of the elderly with the family and society.

BIBLIOGRAPHY

Bureau of Statistics (BOS), Economic Planning Board. 1991. *Future Population Estimates (1990–2021)* (in Korean).

Choi, S. J. 1992. "Welfare Policy for Social Services for the Elderly" (in Korean). *Senior Citizens' Welfare Policy for Year 2000.* Korean Institute of Health and Social Affairs.

Chung, K. B. 1992. "Improvement of Living Conditions of Low-Income Families and Social Welfare Policies for the Elderly" (in Korean). Policy discussion paper, Democratic Liberal Party Policy Committee.

Dixon, J. 1981. *The Chinese Welfare System: 1949–1979.* New York: Praeger.

Economic Planning Board (EPB). 1970, 1975, 1980, 1985. *Census Report on Population and Housing* (in Korean).

———. 1986. *Population Estimates: Long-Term Estimates of Population Based on the Results of Population and Housing Census of 1985* (in Korean).

———. 1987. *Population Statistics and Future Population Estimates* (in Korean).

———. 1988. *Recent Conditions of Population Mobility and New Population Estimate Outcomes* (in Korean).

———. 1989. *Social Indicators of Korea* (in Korean).
———. 1990a. *Annual Report on Economically Active Population* (in Korean).
———. 1990b. *Standardized Life Tables of Koreans* (in Korean).
———. 1991. *The 7th Five-Year Planning Committee: Social Welfare Section (Draft)* (in Korean).
Korea-Gallup Institute (KGI). 1990. *The Life Style and Consciousness of Korean Elderly* (in Korean).
Korean Housing Corporation (KHC). 1987. *Study on the Development of Public Housing for Three-Generation Families* (in Korean). Seoul: Korea Housing Corporation.
Korean Continuing Education Organization (KCEO). 1991. *Continuing Education and Education for Senior Citizens* (in Korean). Seoul: Ewha-Munwha-Sa.
Kim, D. B. 1989. "Study of Participation of Elderly People in Senior Citizens' Clubhouses (Noin-Jung)" (in Korean). *Journal of Korean Academy of Social Welfare*, 12.
Kim, T. H. 1991. "Study of Conflicts between Mothers-in-Law and Daughters-in-Law" (in Korean). *Journal of Korea Gerontological Society*, 11(2).
Kim, T. H., and Han, H. S. 1990. "The Study of Conflict Between Mother-in-Law and Daughter-in-Law." *Journal of Korea Gerontology Society*, 10.
Kong, S. K., Cho, A. J., Kim, J. S., and Suh, M. K. 1990. *The Function and Role Change of Korean Family* (in Korean). Korean Institute of Health and Social Affairs.
Kwon, D. S. 1991. *Senior Citizens and Education in Leisure Activities, Continuing Education and Education for Senior Citizens* (in Korean). Seoul: Ewha-Munwha-Sa.
Lee, K. O. 1992. "Income Maintenance Policy for Elderly People" (in Korean). *Senior Citizens Welfare Policy for Year 2,000*. Korean Institute of Health and Social Affairs.
Lee, K. O., Kwon, S. J., Kwon, J. D., and Lee, W. S. 1990. *Study on the Support for the Elderly* (in Korean). Korean Institute of Health and Social Affairs.
Lee, K. O., et al. 1989. *Study of Actual Conditions of Independent Households of Old Persons* (in Korean). Korean Institute of Health and Social Affairs.
Lee, S. H., and Kwon, J. D. 1993. *Living Conditions and Welfare Service Needs of Elderly Persons with Dementia and Their Families*. Northern Areas Comprehensive Welfare Center of Seoul City. Research Report 93-1.
Lee, S. J., and Park, H. S. 1990. "Assessment of the Needs of Elderly Persons for Home Visit Nurse Services Through Health Care Agencies" (in Korean). *Journal of Korea Gerontological Society*, 10.
Ministry of Health and Social Affairs (MOHSA), the Republic of Korea. 1989, 1991. *The Current Conditions of Recipients of Livelihood Protection Services* (in Korean).
Palmore, E., and Maeda, D. 1986. *The Honorable Elders Revisited*. Durham, N.C.: Duke University Press.
Park, J. K. 1989. "Traditional Ideals of Filial Piety and Its Contemporary Meanings" (in Korean). *Modern Illumination of Traditional Ethics*. Center for Korean Studies, Korea.
Park, J. K., and Kim, T. H. 1986. "Study of Leisure-Time Life of Elderly People in Modern Days" (in Korean). *Journal of Korea Gerontological Society* 6.
Song, K. Y. 1992. "Policy Direction for Public Health and Medical Care for Old Per-

sons" (in Korean). *Senior Citizens' Welfare Policy for Year 2,000.* Korean Institute of Population and Social Affairs.

Sung, K. 1990. "Study of Filial Piety: Ideals and Practices of Family-Centered Parent Care." *Gerontologist,* 30(5).

———. 1991a. "Problems of the Elderly in Modern Times and Continuing Education" (in Korean). *Continuing Education and Education for Senior Citizens.* Seoul: Ehwa-Munwha-Sa.

———. 1991b. "Family-Centered Informal Support Networks of Korean Elderly: The Resistance of Cultural Traditions." *Journal of Cross-Cultural Gerontology* 6(4).

———. 1992. "Motivations for Parent Care: The Case of Filial Children in Korea." *International Journal of Aging and Human Development,* 34(2).

Sung, K., and Kim, K. S. 1988. "Study of the Well-being of the Elderly" (in Korean). *Journal of Korea Gerontological Society,* 8.

Yoon, G. 1989. "Current Status of Research on Korean Elderly: Psychological Aspects" (in Korean). *Journal of Korea Gerontological Society,* 9.

Yoon, J. 1985. "Current Researches on Elderly Persons in Korea: Psychological Area" (in Korean). *Journal of Korea Gerontological Society,* 5.

25

SPAIN

Ricardo Moragas Moragas

INTRODUCTION

The Role of the Elderly

Spain is an old country in history, and old age has been traditionally valued in the past, as many elderly had positions of ascribed status and power in society. The Industrial Revolution developed in Spain later than in most Western countries, as well as the accompanying criteria of acquired status due to merit rather than inheritance. The nineteenth and twentieth centuries were periods of turmoil and change for Spanish society, which was trying to find its political climate from among monarchy, republic, and authoritarian regimes for the final objective of any true modern society: the well-being of the majority of its citizens through a democratic system. Spain had to endure, since the 1930s, a civil war and world isolation (after World War II) due to its autocratic regime before becoming a Western democracy. It was not until 1978 that the Spanish people voted for a democratic constitution with similar objectives as other European countries. In 1986 Spain became a member of the European Economic Community (EEC), thus ending what was an unusually fast process of modernization, progressing in 11 years from an authoritarian regime to a modern democracy. This fast process has also changed many of the political, social, and economic values of society and influenced the status and power of the elderly (which had been based on the ascribed status of being old).

The aged are defined in Spain, as of 1992, by being retired from work due to age. Legal retirement age for public administration and business is 65, but many people retire earlier in the private sector due to redundancy. It is estimated that people in metropolitan areas retire at an average age of 62, but in the armed forces and in mature industrial sectors (metal, textile, and so on) people retire earlier.

This description covers large number of "young aged" who are not going to work again and hence are defined as nonproductive. The elderly are very heterogeneous and include, besides the new elderly, the traditional retired, mature old and very old, all sharing the same economic condition of drawing a pension (instead of a salary), but very different in personal, social, and economic conditions.

An important element in the identification of being old is physical appearance. People are defined as old if they look old: white hair, wrinkled skin, bent position, and so on—traits common to Western cultures, which identify social roles with physical appearance. Finally, a criterion of functional ability is used, based on the activities of daily living. Those who cannot perform one or a few of them enter the class of the old. The collective definition of the elderly is based on these three criteria: retired from work and drawing a pension, looking old, and having some limitation in activities of daily living.

In 1986, the proportion of those who were 65 years of age and older was 12.2% of the Spanish population (Instituto Nacional de Estadistica [INE], 1986, 1991). About 60% of these older persons were females. It is projected that by the year 2000, the proportion of those 65 years of age and older will increase to 15.1%. Only 37% of those individuals who are 65 to 74 years of age have a handicapping condition, which is true for 66% of those older than 75. About 10% of those who are 65 years of age and older are illiterate, almost half can read and write; over one-quarter have primary education, and 13% have middle-level or university education (Sociedad Española de Geriatría y Gerontología [SEGG], 1986).

The Formal Structure of Care of The Elderly

Article 50 of the Spanish constitution establishes that public authorities will guarantee adequate pensions for old citizens and shall promote services for their health, housing, and leisure. These rights can be claimed in court, if there is a specific law covering them. The law regarding the National Health Service (Servicio Nacional de Salud), approved in 1986, provides universal coverage for all citizens, but no such universal statute exists for social services, which are developed by regional and local government. Therefore, the entitlement of citizens to social services is less definite than for health care. The Ministry of Social Affairs was established in 1987 and is still in the process of developing the basic rights of citizens for social services and the authority of national, regional, and local government to carry them out. National laws in health and social services define the standards and objectives to attain equality of treatment for all citizens, but each region manages the organization and delivery of services. Therefore, there are differences in the levels of social services offered in the regions according to their economic and social development.

Traditionally, elderly people in need were cared for by a variety of private, religious organizations, some of which still exist, although their objectives have changed with the new needs of the population at risk. The Spanish system of protection for the elderly combines public Social Security with private initiative. In spite of universal coverage for health, many citizens (who can afford it) choose to buy their own services, as public resources are limited and health and social services have long waiting lists. The quality of services varies across the country in relation to the economic and social development of the regions, but the general quality of public hospitals is good. As the number of elderly increases and limits are imposed on available public resources, the government is establishing schemes with nongovernment organizations (NGOs) to provide services financed through the public budget. A new philosophy has begun to develop that public services can be performed more efficiently, with better quality, and at a lower cost by private organizations than by public administration. Accordingly, government should restrict itself to establishing standards of care and financing and controlling the quality of service given to the public. This concept is starting to be applied not only to health but also to social services for the aged (like management of nursing homes, home-delivered meals, and home help).

A National Gerontological Plan has been in the making since 1989, but its approval is pending. Different regions have approved plans for their own territories before the national plan. Eligibility for public services is based on need, being older than 65 years, and a minimum residence period. Public services are free, but in retirement homes the elderly can contribute up to 85% of their pension, the rest being paid by regional or local authorities.

When people are not able to remain at home, due to health or social reasons, nursing homes (skilled or with minimal care) are possible next steps for the elderly. However, a shortage of 40,000 beds in Spain is estimated by the Ministry of Social Affairs in 1994. There are some initiatives by regional authorities to develop chronic care facilities of different levels, freeing beds in acute care hospitals for their proper use. The autonomous region of Catalonia approved, in 1991, an Integrated Plan for the Elderly, based on extensive research and a general survey among the elderly. It is considered a progressive tool to integrate health and social services for the elderly, its implementation has started, and it will be developed through the year 2000.

INCOME MAINTENANCE AND EMPLOYMENT

Income maintenance for the elderly has experienced great improvements in the 1980s, both in quantity and in category of people covered. This has been possible as a result of rapid economic development, but economic growth has produced two-digit inflation and only in the late 1980s has it been reduced to around 6%. The elderly have suffered economically, as social policy can never keep up with rapid economic development and still, today, the average pension is below the minimum wage.

The majority of Spanish elderly draw a pension from Social Security, which is universal and covers most everyone: the self-employed, domestic workers, artists, writers, and even bullfighters. Excluded from Social Security are civil servants (who have their own public system, MUFACE, with lower pensions) and some professions considered independent (lawyers and physicians in private practice) who have no public coverage. The system has evolved from a social insurance scheme covering wage earners in private business to a universal system of Social Security covering all people (wage earners, managers, self-employed, and so on). The main difference in pensions is between contributory and noncontributory pensions; the first are for people who have contributed during their working life through payroll deductions (3% of their total income in 1992). The noncontributory pensions are a form of social welfare for people without, or with partial, contributions to Social Security who do not qualify for a contributory pension.

Requirements for contributory pensions are to have contributed to Social Security for 15 years and be 65 years or older. The average pension for the contributory pensions in 1992 was $450 per month, and the highest was $3,000 per month. To qualify for the noncontributory or social welfare pension, one has to be excluded from the contributory ones, be below the poverty level, and be without relatives who have an obligation to contribute to the individual's survival. The amount of the noncontributory pensions in 1992 was $250 per month. Both types of pensions are revised every year according to the government's estimated increase in the cost of living. Upper limits are also revised, but the percentage of increase is greater for the lower pensions. The lowest pensions are for widows who have not worked under Social Security and amount to 45% of the husband's pension.

The social policy of government is to progressively increase pensions, but as there are budgetary limits, an alternate policy has developed, offering social services with some benefits in-kind. Medicine, for instance, is dispensed free to the retired, while regular workers pay 40% of the cost. Utilities have reduced rates for retired people whose total income is below $10,000 a year. Some municipalities exempt the retired from sanitation and other local taxes. Discounts vary around the country; national railroads and airlines offer discounts to the over 60 or 65 who fly on days with less passenger load. Most cities issue golden cards to the elderly below a certain income for transportation on municipal lines (with a varied scale of discounts). Regional governments responsible for the development of services for the elderly vary in their approaches because the needs of the elderly also are different around the country. Private businesses offer different discounts to the retired, the most prevalent being in entertainment, at times and hours with less demand.

The private protection of income of the elderly involves a variety of schemes, but it has not been, in general, very developed by the general population. Due to the recent economic growth in the last 30 years, the rate of inflation has been very high, and people with unsatisfied consumer needs prefer to use their increased incomes to consume rather than save, given the low value of money over time. This collective attitude does not help the government in controlling inflation, while, at the same time, Social Security costs kept increasing. Due to the reduction in receipts by Social Security, because of unemployment and the increase in expenses resulting from the aging population, in 1985 a law approved a reduction in Social Security pensions and a private pension law was approved to induce people to save and take care of part of their future pensions. The public pension should be, in the future, only one portion of the income of the elderly but not their only source, as it was until 1985 for the majority of the people. Response to the new laws has been uneven, but younger cohorts have started to realize the importance of planning and saving for their future economic needs.

Private pension plans are of two kinds: collective, in which the employer and employee contribute to the fund, and individual, where the person contributes to a fund controlled by a financial institution, usually a bank or savings institution. There are important tax advantages for contributions to the plan, but also limitations on the use of the accumulated capital. Pension plans usually include life and disability insurance.

Another form of fighting inflation for the middle and higher urban classes has been investment in real estate, as the needs for housing have been great for decades and the increase in property prices have been well ahead of inflation.

Work as a source of income for the elderly is very limited for two reasons. First, labor and Social Security laws forbid the work of the retired who draw a pension. Although this law has been frequently criticized, it is still in existence. In the past, the retired could work illegally due to the high labor demand. Present rates of unemployment (around 15% during the last decade) make it very difficult for the retired to find a job. Membership of Spain in the EEC has motivated the restructuring of many older industries with massive early retirement. Second, unemployment among the young is reaching 50%. All these factors make it very difficult for the retired to legally work. Among areas where the elderly keep working are in family business, independent professional activities, self-employed farmers, and so on. In these activities the self-employed formally retire and transfer the property to family members but keep working as before. No job training for the elderly exists, as the legal or real possibility of finding a job is not there.

HEALTH CARE SERVICES

The National Health Service covers, according to the 1986 law, all the health needs of Spanish citizens and foreign residents free of charge in primary and hospital care. The national government regulates the basic rights and economic aspects of health. The National Health Service is financed through general taxes of 66% and contributions of employers and workers (30% and 4%, respectively). Social Security had been managed from a centralized organization; after the constitution of 1978, a regional structure was established transferring authority to 17 regional governments to organize health and social services. Six regions are already managing health facilities (as of 1992), and the rest will in the future. All health services are free for the population; the patient pays 40% of the cost of medicine, but the elderly get all prescribed medicines free. The quality of clinical services is good, but waiting lists force many people to seek private health insurance to obtain services when desired. Thus they pay twice for their health care: first, to the public system through Social Security and second, to the private insurer.

Geriatric health services for the elderly are not very developed at the primary level. Surveys (SEGG, 1986) show that people over 65 can amount to 50% of the primary care patients in a health facility or in house calls. In some areas the elderly go to the Primary Care Health Center to spend their free time meeting other retired people and eventually having a contact with the nurse or physician to get their free prescription. Around 3-5% of the elderly receive help at home from different professionals: general practitioner, geriatrician, nurse, social worker, home aide, and so on. There are efforts to develop primary care for the elderly within geriatric interdisciplinary units to help the general practitioner assist the elderly at home to avoid unnecessary admissions to hospitals.

Hospitals having a geriatric department are few, but old people use 53% of hospital beds, with a mean length of stay of 22.9 days (as compared with 13.7 days for younger hospital patients) (SEGG, 1986). A common problem for many Spanish hospitals is the occupation of acute care beds by chronically ill elderly. The use of high-cost hospital beds by the elderly reflects one of the structural problems of the Spanish health system, which solves social problems through health resources. Another common problem in the health care of the elderly is the admission through emergency departments to general hospitals of old people with minor conditions (explained by the greater prestige of hospitals as health facilities and the limitations in community facilities).

Day hospitals or day centers are facilities for patients who can live at home but have to finish a functional rehabilitation process and need some health and social supervision. They are being promoted as a way to bring back the elderly to the community, free acute hospital beds, and avoid unnecesary institutionalization. These facilities can be located in primary care facilities, hospitals, or even senior centers and provide an adequate environment for dealing with health and social problems of the elderly in the community. Day hospitals provide global treatment for the problems of the elderly, avoid unnecesary admissions, facilitate discharge from hospitals, assist the general practitioner in the community, and help the family.

Training in geriatrics is increasing, but fully trained geriatricians number only about 100 in 1992. To satisfy the demand for geriatric care, there are general practitioners with some training and professional orientation toward geriatrics. They number, according to the Geriatric Section of the Spanish Medical Association, more than 600 and are growing in number. Geographical distribution of geriatricians follows the general rule of medical specialties, with a high concentration in metropolitan areas and few professionals in rural areas. The practice of geriatrics requires an interdisciplinary approach, and the need to work with other professionals (nurses, physical therapists, social workers, and occupational therapists) is recognized by geriatricians as being very important (90% positive answers in surveys). There is especially a need for occupational therapy training because only two schools exist in Spain.

Care for the terminally ill is carried out by units of palliative medicine in some hospitals and by ambulatory teams and is developing very rapidly through a national association started in 1992. Hospices do not exist as independent units, but only as units in general hospitals where palliative medicine is practiced. Geriatric teams to assist the terminally ill aged at home are developing in many communities.

HOUSING RESOURCES

In Spain, as in many countries, elderly people do not like to change their residence and prefer to stay in it as long as possible. One basic feature of Spanish real estate is the rigidity of laws regulating tenancy in old dwellings, mostly occupied by elderly people. One-quarter of the homes of the elderly are older than 75 years. Spain is one of the European countries with a high percentage of home ownership. Survey results indicate that 64% of the people older than 60 years own their homes (similar to population of all ages), 15% live in a facility owned by the family, and 21% rent their residence. Rented homes with old leases have very low rents due to public control, but they are poorly maintained and equipped, as owners do not make necessary repairs because of the low profitability of their investment. Regarding home equipment, all homes have electricity, piped water, and bathroom facilities; 75% had hot water; 37% had heating; 70% had a telephone; and 80% had a washing machine. However, great differences exist among regions because of variations in climate and economic development. Equipment is, in general, better in cities and metropolitan areas than in rural environments (Instituto Nacional de Servicios Sociales [INSERSO], 1991).

Both factors, the subjective attitude of the elderly and the legal rigidities, reinforce each other and result in a high stability of old people in their usual premises, unless changes appear in their marital status or ability to live independently. More than half of the elderly living at home (53%) do so with family members, spouses, or young children; 16% live with adult children, and 10% live with a brother or relative. When age and incapacities increase and it is not possible to live at home, moving to the homes of sons or daughters is the first alternative as a place of residence.

Institutional living for the elderly in Spain is defined as a place of permanent and collective residence with total assistance. Total assistance means that the institution should provide not only food and lodging but health and psychosocial development through different services. Public residential facilities have to promote, by law, the participation of residents in activities, which is sometimes difficult to accomplish because they belong to cohorts with little experience or desire to assume social responsibilities. The growing life expectancy of the elderly has produced a transformation in residential facilities from institutions for independant people to skilled nursing facilities (with corresponding consequences in staffing and cost).

Private initiative has opened many residential facilities in cities to meet the large demand not being filled by public facilities for people needing medical supervision and living alone or with a disabled spouse. The demand is especially strong in metropolitan areas where it is more difficult to house elderly parents due to the work of husband and wife and limited space in the homes. Legislation and control of private facilities have been developed by regional authorities to avoid abuses by operators. The variety of facilities—their services and prices—is as wide as the diversity of the demand. Some private facilities can have beds contracted by regional or local government and others may be owned by public bodies (but management can be contracted with NGOs). There is little demand for congregate housing by the elderly because people prefer to remain in their homes. However, a few projects, built by local authorities or by private initiative in large cities, have been well received by people living alone or disabled.

On the Mediterranean coast, large communities of foreign residents from Western countries and some from the Middle East have developed since the 1970 to take advantage of the mild climate. The number of retired foreign residents in Spain can be estimated at around 200,000; most of them are now in good health and can manage their lives. When disability or ill health strikes one spouse, the foreign residents in Spain start the second migration and return to their home countries to receive health and social care, and they eventually die at home.

The responsibility for the care of the elderly has always been a family duty and there has been a strong social stigma for not taking care of elderly family members. Now, multiple factors (e.g., increased female participation in the labor force, migration from rural to urban areas, longer life expectancy of the elderly, small size of new homes) make it difficult for the family to take care of their elderly, but the ethos of being responsible is always there. One way to maintain the filial responsibility, if it is not possible to have the parent at home, is to cover part of the cost of an institutional facility among family members. As indicated before, 16% of all elderly live with adult children; 29% of those older than 80 do so (INSERSO, 1991).

The institutional alternative is the last one to be considered, after all other possibilities have been discarded. In Spain people more than 65 years old living in institutions are 2.8% of the total over 65, although differences are great among regions. In the last decade an effort has been made by the national and regional governments and by religious orders and foundations to remodel old and large residential facilities and build new ones. The Gerontological Plan sets the objective of providing institutional beds for 3.8% of people older than 65 by the year 2000.

The Spanish constitution establishes in Article 50 that public authorities will promote the welfare of the elderly through housing services. Development of this objective has not taken place, except by some regional and local authorities who have established priorities in the occupation of public housing by the elderly. The Gerontological Plan establishes a quota of 3% reserved units (without barriers) for the elderly in public housing projects. An important element in the quality of living for old people is removing architectural barriers, reforming unsuitable homes, installing elevators and so on. This is promoted by central, regional, and local governments and by private initiatives.

As in other Western countries, the "empty nest" home is characteristic of the desire for autonomy by sons and daughters and economic opportunities for the young. Nevertheless, in the last years, with an increase in real estate prices in large cities and high unemployment among the young (50% for 16–25-year-olds), many young people delay their marriages and remain in the parental home or, in some cases, marry and bring the wife to the nuclear home. Whether this is to become a revival of the three-generation family cannot be assessed at present. In any case, the parental home, even when descendants live independently, is a commonly used facility for intergenerational relations and services. Older parents in good health mainly take care of their grandchildren. Sons and daughters often care for their parents in case of poor health. Many young people, when marrying and selecting a home, consider the proximity to their parents as a positive factor, because of the frequent relationships, mutual help, and services received and given by each generation.

Innovative housing arrangements are starting to appear, as public and private initiatives cannot answer the variety of demands of the elderly. Examples are as follows:

1. *Good Neighbors.* In a specifically interesting arrangement in rural areas, neighbors agree to supervise elderly people and even render them minor services if needed. There are a variety of possibilities and arrangements, with or without compensation, and all are based on the need of solidarity and reciprocity to fullfill needs that the formal system cannot satisfy.
2. *House Sharing.* Old people living alone move into the home of a friend to have company and share the costs.
3. *Family Homes.* Owner-managers of regular homes take care of 5–10 people trying to have the advantages of family living and avoid the shortcomings of institutionalization. They are not considered institutions and therefore are not controlled by Social Services.
4. *Intergenerational Homes.* Old people provide lodging in their homes for young workers or students in cities and receive in exchange services like shopping, night attention, housecleaning, and cooking. The interchange is beneficial to both parties, and no cash transactions are involved.
5. *Family Placement.* Old people living alone can be placed by Departments of Social Services in selected families to live as another member and get help when needed.

This is similar to the scheme of placements of children who are without regular families. The family obtains compensation for the expenses and agrees to provide a home environment. This is a pilot project and not yet evaluated.

SUPPORTIVE SERVICES

From the previous section on housing it should be clear that the will of the Spanish aged is to remain in their home for as long as possible, unless disability or loneliness makes it impossible. To remain at home is defined by the elderly as a subjective definition of quality of life. Therefore, supportive services are a logical instrument to attain this objective. Most of the support old people receive from outside their home is informal, given mainly by family, neighbors, and friends. When informal support cannot cope with the needs of the elderly, the formal support services appear. The needs of the elderly at home are more difficult to solve, because of higher cost in large cities and isolated rural areas due to transportation expenses. The small community is the best environment to receive and give support services to neighbors.

In Spain, as in all Western countries, reduction or containment of budgets in social services and the increasing needs of the elderly have directed governments to search for alternatives to avoid or delay expensive institutionalization. One alternative is to increase support services in the home by the family, the community, or social services. Actually, all alternatives operate and are complementary, as the welfare state cannot cope with the increased demand for services.

Information services are the first level of support, and surveys show that many old people in Spain do not receive services because they ignore their existence and entitlement. Present cohorts do not expect much from public information, as they have experienced the lack of solutions to their problems. Information and referral for the elderly come through the network of health and social primary care. Private information services constitute an important tradition for some organizations, like parishes, Caritas, Red Cross, or foundations. Such associations were, in the past, the only places to learn about needed resources or to receive the services from them. This tradition is still alive today, but a public network of information for health and social services has been deployed through the country, and new generations of the elderly use it regularly (as with any public service).

Services provided in the home are important for the elderly and were valued as the preferred help (98% of responses) desired by the residents of Catalonia in an extensive survey that led to the drawing of its integral plan (Generalitat de Catalunya, 1991).

Services given to the elderly at home are performed in cities by 248 different organizations: Social Security, regional governments, local authorities, and religious and private associations. Services can be provided directly or contracted with cooperatives, NGO's, foundations, and so on. The array of services includes home help; taking care of activities of daily living like shopping, cleaning, laundry; and meals-on-wheels. Users of formal services were estimated in 1989 to be 24,000 (Nijkamp, 1991), but it is impossible to evaluate many services performed by small organizations at the community level. The best solution for the needs of the elderly at home is the integration of health and social services in a single unit at the primary care level, where a global evaluation can be developed and adequate professional help can be provided. This is being started by some regional authorities through the introduction in health teams of a social worker, psychologist, and so on.

Nutritional programs are important for people living alone. Meals are delivered at home (once a day) in most cities, through contracted services administered by the municipalities. Congregate meals served at a day center or a senior center (once or twice a day) provide a nutritional, as well as a social, opportunity for solitary people. Such programs are usually subsidized or given at a reduced price.

Senior centers in Spain started in 1972 as public facilities where retired workers could assemble and have social activities and games. Some of them provide dining facilities, laundry, library, entertainment, regular medical or nursing care, podiatry, physiotherapy, and occupational therapy. The number of senior centers in 1992 was estimated to be around 2,000, with varying numbers of members in each (from a few to several hundred), reflecting the variety of the elderly, regional distribution, and diverse initiatives. There is no uniform classification of the facilities, but those only recreational are called clubs. When more health services are offered, they become day centers, and if they offer the full range of health services, including rehabilitation, they are called day hospitals. Community facilities, as support services for the elderly, avoid the institutionalization of many people living alone at home and offer them an improvement in their quality of life.

Respite care is not very well developed in Spain, except for vacation time, when there is a great demand for beds in private residential facilities; some of them are offering this possibility for weekends or short stays.

Mental health care for the elderly is delivered through regular health services including community mental health centers at the primary care level, but no specific programs exist for the elderly. Counseling for families of Alzheimer's disease patients is promoted by different associations as a way to ease the burden of home care.

Technical aids are developing quickly to improve the home environment of disabled people and avoid institutionalization. Removal of architectural barriers in the home, installing elevators, widening corridors and doors, and adapting bathrooms and kitchens are all means to maintain people longer at home. Financing is provided by both public and private funds, but the needs are great due to the old age of buildings. Telephone alarm systems are being installed by different municipalities for people living alone, at no cost to them. The elderly receive a collar, bracelet, or some other device that can be easily activated in case of need through the telephone line. The call is received by a central switchboard operator who talks to the person and decides if the person needs help and if so, sends somebody to the home, usually a neighbor, to check the situation (or, in case of emergency, the appropriate help goes to the home).

LEISURE-TIME RESOURCES

Establishment of leisure-time resources for the elderly in Spain started in 1972, when restructuring of older industries created an excess of workers in the industrial sector. A Gerontological Plan established a network of Homes for the Retired (Hogares del Pensionista), or senior centers, financed by Social Security. Centers were established through the country where people could assemble and occupy their free time. Senior centers could vary in their equipment and facilities but basically had a meeting room, a television room, a catering service, and varied services like library, restaurant, hairdressing, podiatry, activities room for handicrafts, gymnasium, and so on. They were especially successful in cities, where the environment for the elderly is not favorable, and provided physical space where the retired could fill their free time and engage in social activities.

As demand for gerontological services increased, the initial senior center has diversified, and some of them are offering more health and social services. Thus, day centers with a full range of services are increasing in number. In some residential facilities, senior centers have been established where both residents and nonresidents meet for leisure. The typical public senior center is managed by an administrator and usually has a social worker, clerk, and janitors, plus outsiders who come to deliver specific services like meals, podiatry, arts and crafts, and sports. Participation of members is fostered through an elective board, which decides on activities and appoints committees as needed. The degree of participation and the range of activities vary among centers, geographical locations, and type of institution sponsoring the center. Fees are low, not exceeding $30 a year, except in a few high-class private centers where fees can be as high as for any private club. Some criticism is directed at the senior centers because of the age segregation they impose and their limited services. But in many localities they have been a useful resource to occupy the free time of the retired; as new cohorts of retired appear with more complex demands, senior centers are starting to offer more services and opening themselves more to the community.

Public senior centers started being national Social Security facilities and, since 1980, have been transferred to regional authorities. Some municipalities also operate facilities. Private senior centers have developed basically through cooperative savings banks (Cajas de Ahorro). These institutions are well appreciated by working people for placement of their savings and have tax-exempt status. Some of their profit has to be spent in social activities, one of which is senior centers. These banks usually provide physical facilities and some supervision, but the range of activities is left to the members, and policies vary among the different savings banks. Other private senior centers are run by parishes, associations, pensioners in a certain sector, public administration, utilities, large firms, and so on. Leisure for the elderly is associated now with senior centers by both politicians and the general public, as they are a strategic place where leisure takes place (or is organized and carried out somewhere else). One-fourth of all people more than 65 years old attend senior centers, and when they are asked about the most important social institution in Spain, 53% choose senior centers (Centro de Investigaciones Sobre la Realidad Social [CIRES], 1992). One activity frequently selected by people attending senior centers is ballroom dancing, which takes place once or twice a week.

Activities preferred by the elderly differ according to sex and reflect the varied roles performed by present cohorts. Men with low education who are retired from manual work interpret retirement as a period of rest after exhausting physical demands. Therefore, they prefer social activities that involve little or no effort, such as socializing with friends, card games, or passive entertainment. Males with higher levels of education who are retired from clerical or professional jobs prefer leisure with a cultural, educational context. For all ages the activities most often practiced are physical—walking for men and housework for women. Socializing is the preferred activity for both sexes in their free time, followed by watching television. No specific television programs exist for the elderly, but some advertising has started to include seniors as models.

Educational and cultural activities are preferred by a quarter of the elderly population, with reading being the most preferred activity for males slightly more than for females (Master en Gerontología Social [MGS], 1990). Learning is practiced by people of middle to high educational levels in a variety of settings, like at senior centers, lectures, visits to museums, and so on. The content of education encompasses the humanities, art, culture, history, languages, and so on. The university of the third age encompasses a variety of programs and activities in many sites all across the country, even where there are no university facilities. These programs follow the French model started in Toulouse and are federated in a national association as well as regional ones and have international exchanges with many countries of the EEC and with the United States. Few seniors attend formal programs for a degree. Many regional organizations belong to the Association International of Universities of the Third Age (AIUTA) and maintain exchange programs with foreign regions.

Adult education is being pushed by the national and regional governments to combat illiteracy in the older cohorts who are mainly from rural areas and now live in the cities. Preparation for retirement is very scanty in Spain, as business and public administration do not consider it an employer's responsibility and only a few companies have it as a regular benefit to employees. Survey results (MGS, 1990) indicate that the majority of retired people would have appreciated preparation for retirement; some groups at senior centers have organized pre-retirement preparation.

Active sports are not important, in general, except for people in cities who have practiced them up to retirement. There are special categories in competitions for seniors in sports events: running, tennis, skiing, and so on, as well as sections in regular sports clubs. Some local sports, such as open-air bowling without pins (*boccia*), are practiced in parks and squares with wide community acceptance and often with intergenerational involvement. Seniors may rediscover some regional sports forgotten for decades and teach them to the young, who show interest in finding their cultural identities around them. Walking and gymnastics are the preferred physical activities for elderly people. Entertainment among the elderly is concentrated on television; the next alternative is being a spectator in sports, movies, and theater. There are differences between rural and urban areas, as the types of entertainment vary.

Spiritual needs of the elderly are taken care of by religious organizations. The position of chaplain as a regular employee in public hospitals for more than 250 beds was established in 1984 and provides professional help for the institutionalized elderly. Priests take care of the elderly with regular home visits for those too infirm to go to church; volunteers offer visiting services, comforting the sick and their families through different organizations staffed by laypeople.

Tourism and travel are now important activities for the elderly of Spain. Among the present cohorts of retirees, there has been a great desire to travel, as most of them have not traveled during their active lives except for work-related reasons. The National Institute of Social Services (INSERSO) has capitalized on this demand by establishing a nationwide program of subsidized tourism. The program objective is twofold: enabling people to travel to other parts of the country through group travel at a discounted price and, with Spain being a tourist country that receives its visitors mainly in the summer, offsetting the seasonal unbalance and keeping hotel and other tourist facilities open in winter through the influx of the retired. The program started with the name of Social Tourism. In 1986, 16,000 persons participated; in 1991, more than 300,000, with the subsidy for that year paid by the Ministry of Social Affairs amounting to $50 million. There are creative aspects to the program that explain its rapid development: the retired can be accompanied in their trip of 15 days by a family member of any age (also at the subsidized price), and the discounted rate is 20–30% below the regular offer of any travel agency. Hotel owners are happy with a program that keeps facilities open for periods when they had to close, and the retired experience an activity outside their usual reach. The program seems to have attained its social, economic, and political goals. Besides the long, subsidized stays, short trips by bus for one or two days have developed very strongly in many regions, so as to use the vacant capacity of hotels, restaurants, and tourist facilities during weekdays and off-season periods.

Another creative program for the elderly of Spain (combining social, health, and economic objectives) started in 1989 and is called Thermalism or Hot Springs for the elderly. It enables elderly people to spend 10 to 15 days at a hot spring at a discounted price, provided it is recommended by their attending physician. The difference in price compared with regular rate is assumed by

Social Security. It is estimated that most of the cost of the program will be saved through the reduction of costs in medical care for the years to come (and is in line with a preventive approach to health care).

Volunteerism has two different meanings in Spain. On one side, there is the traditional approach by the upper classes, who consider it a part of their obligation as members of the Catholic church to take care of the poor and destitute. The help may be through financial contribution, personal involvement, or both. The church, for centuries, has provided assistance for basic needs such as food, clothing, and care of the sick. In the same tradition but based on the relationship to work, fraternal organizations (such as guilds or workers' cooperatives) existed for centuries before the start of Social Security, protecting their members against misfortune and based on the solidarity of its members. The contribution was also personal and financial, often covering other family members besides the worker. This traditional approach still survives in certain instances but has lost its main significance, as the whole population is covered by National Health and Social Services, although there is always room for charitable efforts as needs are permanent and ever-changing.

The modern concept of volunteerism, based on the free contribution of individuals to cooperate in activities not covered by the public system, is also starting to develop in Spain. The basic spirit is the same, solidarity toward fellow human beings in need, in organizations open to all classes and ideological options, guided only by the humanitarian objective. Most organizations of volunteers are associations and foundations regulated by regional governments that maintain a registry and supervise their operations. The modern concept of the volunteer effort is developing very fast in Spain, especially in the more-developed regions, but the importance of church-related organizations is still paramount. The number of associations concerned with the elderly is growing. There are regional federations of volunteers' associations and a national federation belonging to the international bodies of volunteers of Europe.

The main volunteer organization for the elderly in Spain is Caritas, the social services arm of the Catholic church. Caritas offers services in practically all parishes around the country, mostly staffed by volunteers but also with professionals in large cities running a variety of services. Health, physical, economic, and social needs are all satisfied through Caritas, directly or through contracted services, such as meals-on-wheels, help in-kind, day centers, home-delivered services, and social relations. Caritas also has schools for volunteers to train members in the principles and complexities of modern social action. The variety of services is very wide across the country, as each location has a particular demand due to the availability of public services, but the emphasis of Caritas is to concentrate on the most destitute and needy cases not cared for by the public system.

The next volunteer organization in importance is the Red Cross, which has a long tradition in Spain of working in health services. The start of the National

Health Service has changed the objective of the Red Cross to social needs, including programs for the elderly. Some of them, such as home visiting, bring volunteers of all ages to work with the elderly.

Different private associations work for the elderly, mainly in large cities, but there is no national study to identify all of them.

ADVOCACY AND PROTECTION

The concept of advocacy and protection for the elderly is not socially important in Spain. There have been some cases of abuse or ill treatment in nursing homes in 1989, when the media started to debate the topic. This prompted an inquiry by the national Senate and a report. Afterward, the national ombudsman (Defensor del Pueblo) conducted an investigation in 18 public nursing homes, two in each region of Spain, and requested information on rules and regulations from the regional governments with authority over private nursing homes. A report from both studies has been published; its recommendations emphasize the need for regional regulations and inspection, training of personnel, and user participation (Defensor del Pueblo, 1990).

Legal assistance to the elderly does not differ from assistance to the rest of the population. Public information and referral are performed by each department of public administration, whether national, regional, or local, for all citizens (except in large municipalities, where there is some type of specialization in social services according to age). Civil servants and social workers are the professionals more in contact with the elderly in public administration. Private organizations, like Caritas, devoted to the elderly, often have a legal service where the elderly can receive consultation at no cost about their problems. Private consulting is performed by lawyers and paralegal professionals, specializing in health, Social Security, social services, and so on.

Consumer organizations have not started specific services for the elderly but, in cases of nursing home abuse, have been instrumental in bringing cases to the attention of authorities. Senior associations have voiced their views in the media when some abuses appeared in the marketplace. At present the "gray market" is not recognized, in general, by merchandisers or manufacturers.

Crime against the elderly is not different from crime against other ages, except in thefts or aggression in which the criminal takes advantage of the physical impairments of the older person. No special services of victim assistance exist. Old age is considered an extenuating circumstance by the penal code.

Civil law provides for the declaration of incapacity, which used to be a lengthy process ending with a formal sentence by the judge. A new law was passed in 1988 that has taken into consideration the new social realities, such as the increase in the number of people becoming unable to take care of themselves, and the process of incapacitation has been eased. Guardianship of the incapable, because of infirmity, can now be awarded to individuals or institutions, helping to solve the problem of incapable institutionalized people without families.

FUTURE PROJECTIONS

The future of the Spanish elderly is linked to the politics and economy of the country, still in the process of accelerated change. Income per capita and social spending are still below the average of the EEC. After the Maastricht agreements of 1991, it is not clear—for EEC members—if there is going to be more uniform or diverse social policy. The Maastricht agreements result from the original European Community Treaty which calls for political, economic, and social integration. Due to economic problems in many countries they cannot attain such objectives. It is still unknown if there is going to be only one social policy, including the aged, among other topics, to be attained sometime in the future by all countries or whether there are going to be two social policies, one for the rich Northern and Central European countries and another for the less-developed southern Mediterranean countries, of which Spain is a part.

What will determine the future policies for the aged of Europe and Spain are the definitions of subsidiarity and solidarity. Subsidiarity refers to the absence of government services, if there are private organizations willing to perform them, with or without public money. Government activities are justified only if civil society is not providing the services. It is obvious that, according to the definition and willingness to finance private initiatives, subsidiarity will have different consequences. Solidarity, as a show of humanity for fellow human beings, should specify the expected roles of the informal system of care for the aged (private parties, family, neighbors, friends, and voluntary organizations) and if they should be compensated and in what form. Meanings of subsidiarity and solidarity vary greatly around Europe, and if there is going to be a common policy it should recognize these differences. The EEC must also recognize the importance of thousands of foreign retirees in the Spanish Mediterranean and request, from governments involved, solutions to solve their health and social demands, which are growing.

Unique features of aging in Spain are the rapidity of its demographic changes in the last decade, an increase in the percentage of older people in the population, and a decrease in fertility. Projections show a profile similar to that of the rest of the developed countries of Europe. Public response to the problems of the elderly has been uneven; sometimes it has been positive, like the universality of the National Health Service. However, some indefiniteness continues, such as the provision and entitlement to social services and the fragmentation of responsibilities among central, regional, and local government. All the questions should have an answer in the National Gerontological Plan, which has been awaiting legislative approval for two years and may be never be approved due to budgetary limitations. Nevertheless, some of its objectives are being incorporated in the new laws passed, and the value of the plan is partly put to practical use.

The coordination of health and social services is one of the main priorities to offer a better quality of life to the elderly and control the increase in the cost of services. The most important needs are now the care of the disabled, poor, and dependent, and the lack of facilities to take care of them. Some of these people are experiencing conditions new to them and do not know about their rights or the availability of social services.

After the service users, the most important needs are for education and the professions. There is no recognition of the importance of knowledge about aging, and the realities of biological and psychosocial aging appear in few school curricula. Training in geriatrics and gerontology is scarce at all levels and should be developed at both the generalist and specialist level. There are, at present, only four postgraduate programs in social gerontology at the universities of Alicante, Barcelona, Autonoma de Madrid, and Salamanca, and they should be enlarged. The future cohorts of more educated, more independent, and more capable retirees will demand more services, and professionals should be trained to dispense them. Research about aging is well developed in medicine, but it should increase in all the social sciences with creative schemes as the conditions of the Spanish elderly of the future will have no precedent from the past. The common culture and language shared with Latin American countries could be useful for them, as they will experience social conditions similar to the ones in Spain. In this respect, innovative initiatives can help the future of Latin American gerontology, like the master of social gerontology program at the University of Barcelona, where nationals from Latin America are trained and research is carried out for these countries.

Income for the elderly is always a basic issue, but the retirement of couples with two pensions is starting to be a new event, as most couples have benefits from only one pension. To maintain the purchasing power of the elderly, government at national, regional, and local levels will offer alternatives in services, discounts, and free services, so as to combat the demands for direct increases in pensions, which will not be able to keep pace with the increase in the cost of living. Private pensions will develop swiftly from low to middle levels of income in both business and government.

The most important need in health is education, especially in preventive medicine, nutrition, exercise, and avoidance of drugs, tobacco, and alcohol. Palliative medicine and rehabilitation services should be extended to the whole country in all levels of care—home, clinic, and hospital. The needs of training for health professionals are universal in all aspects of geriatrics and gerontology, and, besides the technical knowledge, there is a need for training in teamwork because, traditionally, medicine has been an individualistic profession.

In housing, new laws have to address the diverse needs of the elderly, including the change from present inadequate facilities to environments better suited to their needs. Public housing will have to take into consideration the needs of the elderly, and private initiatives will offer a variety of housing alternatives not available at present.

Support services will experience great development, given the preferences of the elderly to remain at home and the cost of institutionalization. These services will be delivered at the home or at neighborhood facilities. Some of these services will be provided by nonprofessional help, neighbors, and volunteers (under new schemes) to avoid the high cost of external services and recognize the variety of needs of the elderly. Intergenerational relations will offer a service to each generation on an interchange basis.

Legal regulations for the elderly will experience profound changes, as protection for the disabled and demented and their families will be needed. Living wills and durable powers of attorney will be more common, establishing clearly the preferences of the sick person, avoiding uncertainties, and facilitating decisions by professionals.

The needs of the elderly are perceived vaguely by society, but little effort is devoted to research on them, analysis of the problems, and arrival at logical conclusions. Some professionals are educating themselves and trying innovative programs, but frequently the problems of the aged are reduced to their health or economic component, ignoring the psychosocial realities that so often define quality of life. The same definition of quality of life in Spain that has been praised by foreigners is redefined by nationals as their living habits, especially in cities, change and become equal to other developed cities around the world. The extended family (at least those with two generations) has been a reference and framework for social relations, self-realization, and protection in the event of need. There are many external pressures in the present organization of work that make difficult, if not impossible, the maintenance of loyalties and responsibilities in the family. Government is discovering the importance of the family as a resource but this should not be a substitute for the rights to which elderly citizens are entitled. There is a need in Spain for a social policy for the aged that takes into consideration the rights of the elderly and also the realities and value of the family.

BIBLIOGRAPHY

Altarriba, F. X. *Gerontología*. Barcelona: Boixareu, 1992.
Centro de Investigaciones sobre la Realidad Social (CIRES). *La realidad social en España*. Madrid: Publicaciones CIRES, 1992.
Commission of the European Communities. *Social and Economic Policies and Older People*. EC Observatory, 1991.
Defensor del Pueblo. *Residencias públicas y privadas de la Tercera Edad*. Madrid: Publicaciones Defensor del Pueblo, 1990.
Fernandez-Ballesteros, R, and Jiménez-Herrero, F. *Evaluación e intervención psicológica en la vejez*. Barcelona: Martínez Roca, 1992.
Generalitat de Catalunya Department de Benestar Social. *Plan integral de la gent gran*.

Approved by the *Consell Executiu de la Generalitat de Catalunya* in Barcelona, November 1991.
Generalitat valenciana. *Plan Integral de Atención Socio-sanitaria a la Tercera Edad.* Valencia: Area de Planificació. Direcció General d'Afers Socials, 1991.
Instituto Nacional de Estadistica (INE). Madrid, 1986 and 1991.
Instituto Nacional de Servicios Sociales (INSERSO). *La Tercera Edad en España necesidades y demandas.* Madrid: Ministerio de Asuntos Sociales, 1990.
———. *La Tercera Edad en España aspectos cuantitativos.* Madrid: Ministerio de Asuntos Sociales, 1991.
———. *La Tercera Edad en Europa necesidades y demandas.* 2d ed. Madrid: Ministerio de Asuntos Sociales, 1991.
———. *Plan Gerontológico.* (unpublished) Madrid: Ministerio de Asuntos Sociales, 1991.
Jiménez-Herrero, F., and Fernandez-Ballesteros, R. *Gerontología,* 1992. Madrid: CEA, 1991.
Master en Gerontología Social (MGS). *Occasional Reports.* Universidad de Barcelona, 1987 to present.
Moragas, R. *Gerontología Social.* Barcelona: Herder, 1991.
———. *La Jubilación. Un enfoque positivo.* 2d ed. Barcelona: Grijalbo, 1991.
Nijkamp, P. *Services for the Elderly in Europe* Leuven: Kathlieke Universiteit, 1991.
Sociedad Española de Geriatría y Gerontología (SEGG). *El Médico y la Tercera Edad.* Madrid: Lab. Beecham, 1986.
———. "El Médico y la Tercera Edad: Libro Blanco." Madrid: Lab. Beecham, 1987.

26
SUDAN

Niemat A. Latiff Mursi

INTRODUCTION

The Role of the Elderly

Sudanese society was, and still is, committed to the family and its members. This is particularly true for the elderly, who are seen as highly valued and given due respect and reverence in keeping with religious values and Sudanese traditional ideals. The elderly are in all spheres of the Sudanese community. No daily event passes in Sudan without the constant remembrance of the elderly by younger persons. In the Sudan, the child respects youth, who in turn respect adults and parents, all of whom respect the elderly. Religions, particularly Islam, have guaranteed the continuation of such respect for older generations. Islam and Sonna texts mandate the respect of one's elders.

The Sudanese community has been imbued with these high ideals, which have been inculcated in tribal and clan structure in different parts of Sudan. This structure is socially and culturally based on a distinctive place for the elderly, where they enjoy prominent influence and respect.

Those who reach the age of 60 find their positions consolidated and elevated and become—between the ages of 60 and 80—a source of knowledge and wisdom used to solve many problems. Within the family, older persons become counselors and provide advice for others. Thus, each elderly person, whether male or female, has a role to play in society regardless of physical capability.

Islamic Law, based upon the Koran and Sonna, orders respect of the parents and considers the family a nucleus of Islamic society. The Koran says:

Your lord has ordered that you worship none but Him and show kindness to your parents, whether either of them or both of them attain old age in your life, never say to them

Table 26.1
Distribution of the Sudanese Population According to Age and Sex, 1985 (in percentages)

Age Group	Male and Female	Male	Female
Less than 15	44.6	44.9	44.3
15 to 59	50.6	50.6	50.6
60 and older	4.8	4.5	5.1

Note: The age group 60 and older represents about 1.8% of the total population of the Sudan.

"ough" [an angry outburst] nor be harsh to them, but speak to them kindly. And serve them with tenderness and humility and say: "My lord, have mercy on them, just as they cared for me as a little child." The Prophet says, "Those who do not love our youngsters and respect our elderly are not part of us."

Elderly women have been a source of knowledge in such areas as maternity, child-rearing, household tasks, and relationships within families (including marriage). These women relay the culture's folklore through stories conveyed to youngsters. The process of social adaptation of the members of society is a result of such transmissions of knowledge, tradition, and wisdom, thus ensuring the continuation of the Sudanese way of life.

The aged Sudanese nomads have particular importance and their opinions are very influential among such rural people. They are sought out to provide information on a variety of topics (such as health, illnesses, and domestic relationships). And as is true for all Sudanese elderly, the nomadic aged are given a prominent place in all social celebrations.

In 1985, the age distribution by sex in Sudan was undertaken by the Department of Statistics of the National Population Commission (Saghairon and Amin, 1989).

Table 26.1 shows that the percentage of the elderly is quite small in the Sudan. In addition, elderly men and women appear in very similar proportions.

Women live longer than men (Saghairon and Amin, 1989). The population of Sudan is distinguished by rapid population growth, due to the decrease in child mortality and the increase in the rate of fertility. Thus, the structure of the age pyramid has a broad base of younger persons. The rate of dependence of children less than 15 years of age is quite high. This dependency includes those 60 to 64 years of age who are still a part of the labor force.

The legal age for retirement is 60 years; yet, there are many who continue to be employed and do not seek to retire. There is a need for the community to provide suitable programs so that older persons may have their needs met in their old age and not have to continue employment. The majority of farmers and laborers, who compose the bulk of the work force in Sudan, are between the ages of 15 and 64; yet many individuals continue in these occupations well into advanced age.

Population projections (Department of Statistics, 1987) indicate a drop in the proportion of the elderly and Sudan is continuing to rejuvenate itself up to the year 2038. It is expected, according to the Department of Statistics, that fertility will remain high, although it is not clear whether the rate of elderly women will increase in a comparable way. The projections regarding Sudan's future demographic trends are governed by economic and social factors and the population movement in Sudan. Migration in Sudan varies between states and involves individuals of all age groups (the highest proportion of migration is for those between the ages of 15 and 44).

Natural catastrophes that have taken place have obstructed family care and led to population movements in search of employment. The search for education also has led to internal migration from rural to urban areas (Research Department, 1987a).

INCOME MAINTENANCE AND EMPLOYMENT

The Sudanese law on pensions indicates that any employee in an occupation may retire at any time after reaching 50 years of age and having completed 25 years of pensioned service. A person must retire at the age of 60. The pension is counted by the number of years on the job. The higher the status of the job, and the longer the period of service, the greater the amount of the pension.

The social insurance law determines an individual has the right to old age pension if he or she satisfies the following conditions: an insured man must reach 60 years of age; an insured woman must reach 55 years of age; and the duration of the paid subscription must not be less than 15 years.

Labor force statistics in Sudan (Mudawi, Suliman, and Ahmed, 1987) indicate that there are fewer working women than men, with regard to all ages. The active labor force increases in the 20s and peaks in the 40s, and then declines with the advance of age. This general decrease of working women, compared to men, is due to traditions in wide areas of the country where the appropriate work of women is supposed to be at home.

It is important to note that older landowners and workers in agriculture and pasturing were not included in the statistics. Thus, one must be cautious in viewing the extent to which elderly men and women are working in Sudan, for their activities may not be accurately known. In fact, many of the elderly have creative talents, particularly those working in government who have retired after their record of service is complete. As has been noted, the aged are closely involved with the rearing of the young. Unemployment is great among immigrant groups (especially in urban areas), because their education and training are not suitable to the jobs in towns and competition is great among the unskilled. This situation makes it difficult to find suitable work for the elderly who suffer from poor health and illiteracy. With transportation difficulties as well, employment opportunities are often very difficult to find.

This does not necessarily mean a bleak picture for all elderly; if they can find suitable training, it is expected that the rates of their employment participation will increase in both rural and urban areas. There are occupations for both elderly men and women which permit them to continue their independence through various forms of employment (e.g., selling wares in markets, watchmen, selling food, and in light textile manufacturing).

HEALTH CARE SERVICES

Many studies have tackled the general health situation in Sudan and its effect upon all the population, including the elderly (El Amman, 1988). Malaria and dysentery are among the prevalent health problems in Sudan.

Health care resources for all Sudanese in general, but for the elderly in particular, are located in urban areas of the country. For example, the number of physicians and specialists in the Southern State does not surpass 100, and only 85 physicians provide services for more than 5 million people. The number of physicians in Kordofan State is 140 for a similar number of the population (El Amman, 1988). In the Eastern State, physicians number 245 for a population of 2 million. In the Northern State, there are 1,520 for a similar number of people and in the Middle State, with a population of more than 4 million, the number of physicians is 449.

The report by El Amman (1988) clearly suggests that the extension of the agricultural schemes, without extending the relevant medical services, is a sign of the deterioration of the environmental health services. The past years of drought that has struck parts of the country have caused many diseases of malnutrition, and complications have affected the children and aged in particular. Women are exposed to the dangers of illness and death during pregnancy, especially in those states that have no maternity and family planning hospitals for women above the age of 40 (the ages when women are more susceptible to the dangers of pregnancy and childbirth).

Aging brings a steady decrease of medical treatment. Women are suffering more than men, resulting from the consequences of malnutrition and environmental health. Demographic statistics show that the number of elderly males is similar to the number of elderly females, contrary to industrial societies where older females are more numerous.

Among social problems in Sudan (such as vagrancy, crime, and unemployment) is that of begging by elderly women (Research Department, 1987b). This unfortunate situation occurs because often disabled older women are dependent on such activities to provide them with financial resources to pay for their daily needs of food and shelter. Furthermore, the income derived from begging often goes to support the older woman's family members as well.

Some of the begging elders show a desire to join lodging institutions. They have sufficient justification for such a decision. There is also a group who stipulate that when they accept housing within such facilities, they be allowed to have their families with them.

HOUSING RESOURCES

Based upon its beliefs and traditions, the Sudanese family has a duty to care for its sick and dependent members (including children, the handicapped, and the elderly). Despite the fact that lodging for the elderly is not provided by the Sudanese community, social welfare has paid some attention to the establishment of homes for the aged after the natural catastrophes of drought and desertification. Although there are limited funds, such housing facilities are believed to be necessary to provide for the housing needs of elderly persons whose family members are unable to provide such care.

The Sudan is divided into a number of states each with different government services provided to the elderly and their families. In all states, housing is used only to supplement the family or when there is no family.

The Northern State has a population of 1,083,476 and the elderly number 73,624 (or 6.7%). The family provides care and protection to the elderly. However, in this state, drought, desertification, and floods have affected public revenues from agriculture which, in turn, have affected the ability of families to care for their elderly relatives. Families have sought assistance from social welfare. Such aid has provided families with monthly allowances or, on occasion, a lumpsum amount. However, such aid has been generally inadequate to satisfy the needs of the elderly who live with their relatives. For those elderly without families, the state maintains homes for the aged. These facilities provide for rehabilitation and personal care needs, as well as rest and security.

The Kordofan State has a population of 3,090,815 and the total number of aged is 175,450 (or 6%). The elderly here include those who live with families and are employed and self-reliant (many are involved in such rural activities as farming and tending livestock). Some of these elderly persons apply to social welfare for financial assistance or for tools to continue in their occupations. In this state, elderly persons without families live in homes for the aged which provide free food, clothing, and medical care (in cooperation with health care assistance from a medical center). The home may also provide transportation for the elderly residents.

Darfur State includes elderly who have come mainly as migrants from abroad many years ago. The authorities assist them within their families (sending beggars back to their families) and give them financial assistance for continuing their occupations.

Central State has a social welfare directorate which provides the elderly with assistance through their families. A number of elderly persons in this state enjoy pensions and social insurance services (for former employees in the private and public sectors). There are also some medical services provided to the elderly (for example, a specialized medical center for diabetes that provides curative medical treatment to the elderly).

SUPPORTIVE SERVICES

One organization offers service programs for the aged: the British Help the Aged. The organization works in cooperation with other organizations to ameliorate the problems of the elderly through such assistance as mobile clinics, rehabilitation of existing homes, and furnishment of equipment, furniture, and medication. The organization also funds some private projects to improve the earnings of families caring for elderly relatives.

In spite of the efforts of the country to establish independence for the aged (through, among other resources, provision of homes), some problems hinder the continuity and effectiveness of national efforts, including limited public financial resources, lack of supportive services within the homes of the aged, absence of skill training to the elderly, and lack of specialized health care resources.

Sudan also is committed to the establishment of facilities for disabled persons (including the elderly). These resources are the responsibility of local social welfare councils.

The is no system of special services relevant to the elderly in Sudan, but they use services within the public health sector, which are provided to all citizens.

Economically, socially, and psychologically, the Sudanese family is responsible for the welfare of the elderly, giving them emotional peace. The problem of the elderly is not only a problem of housing and daily living; it also has social and psychological dimensions.

LEISURE-TIME RESOURCES

There are no specialized clubs in Sudan for the elderly to spend their leisure time; instead, in the house or living quarter, they meet their colleagues and spend the evening in pleasant conversation while drinking coffee. Aged women spend most of their leisure time taking care of the young or weaving, and sometimes they do light traditional work suitable to their physical activity. Aged men spend their leisure time taking care of their crops or cattle; sometimes they do light work in their neighborhoods suitable to their physical conditions.

There are two kinds of citizens in Sudan: those whose family position and environmental conditions provide opportunities for education, and those who do not have such opportunities due to their circumstances. For the latter group of persons, the state has established a special branch at the Ministry of Education, called Adult Education, to provide educational opportunities for all those—including the elderly—who have not received formal education.

ADVOCACY AND PROTECTION

Sudan is one of the countries that accepted the Universal Declaration of Human Rights which acknowledges that each individual doing any job has the right to a just and satisfactory salary that guarantees the worker and the worker's family dignity and security. Each person in Sudan has the right to a standard of living sufficient for the maintenance of health and welfare, and necessary social services, and the right to guaranteed assistance in cases of unemployment, illness and disability, widowhood, and old age.

FUTURE PROJECTIONS

The proportion of the elderly population is small due to the predominance of children; 46% of the population is less than 15 years old (Saphairon, 1983), and the population census has not projected an increase in the proportion of the elderly Sudanese through 2038. But there is a need to emphasize the growth of problems relevant to the number of elderly in Sudan and their economic difficulties (along with any social, medical, and psychological difficulties). The small number of the elderly does not justify ignoring their problems, regardless of the deteriorating economic conditions in the country.

Poor living conditions are suffered mainly by children and disabled elderly. The poor economy has adverse ramifications for health, education, and training. Such problems are the result of deepening poverty and misery in life and must result in changes within the extended family. The need for policies and programs for the elderly is indisputable and is in keeping with the history and tradition in Sudanese culture. The family has had a central role in society but may be unable to improve the conditions which affect the elderly. There is a strong need to formulate clear directives for relief and to consolidate official and popular efforts for making the life of the aged productive and rewarding.

Toward such an end, the following social welfare formulations to benefit the Sudanese elderly are suggested:

1. The establishment of rehabilitation institutes for the elderly throughout the country (in rural as well as urban areas) is necessary to assist them in maintaining their independence and in permitting them to continue contributing to their family and society. Currently, physicians, allied health care cadres, and health care resources are all concentrated in the national capital, in particular, and in the capitals of the states, in general. Such medical services and personnel are lacking in the rural areas.

2. Education and training of specialized cadre for working with and for the elderly is needed so that those involved with the elderly will have proper motivations, skills, and knowledge.

3. Formulation of suitable projects is needed to enable the elderly to participate in activities that will maintain their psychological health and help them feel they are still productive.

4. Economic support of the elderly and their families is needed to increase their incomes and to avoid their feeling needy and dependent (eliminating their need to beg on the streets).
5. Establishment of old-age clubs, where the elderly may discuss their problems with others and socialize in a healthy and supportive environment, is needed.
6. Creation of special hospitals and medical centers for the elderly, education of physicians and assistant cadres in the field of geriatrics and mental health problems, and provision of sufficient medications, nursing, and nutrition services, would be beneficial.
7. Establishment of pension funds is needed.
8. Delivery of pensions to homes for the aged (for those who cannot go to the office of the cashier to pick up their pensions) is needed.
9. Special cards for the aged to permit them to use public facilities and services at no charge or at reduced rates would be beneficial.

BIBLIOGRAPHY

Department of Statistics. 1983, 1987. Sudan National Population Commission Reports.
El Amman, Mohamed Ibrahim. 1988. "The Medical Situation and Its Effect upon the Population." Presented at the National Conference on Maternity Safety, Khartoum, Sudan.
Mudawi, Abdel Wahab, Suliman, Naem, and Ahmed, Irbrahim. 1987. "Population and Labour and Balancing Programmes." Presented at the Third Annual National Conference on Population, Khartoum, Sudan.
Research Department, Ministry of Social Welfare. 1987a. "Internal Migration."
———. 1987b. "Study of Begging Phenomena at the National Capital."
Saphairon, Atif, and Amin, Samira. 1989. "Research About Women Demographic Characteristics." Presented at the Seminar of Women in Sudan, Khartoum, Sudan.
Saphairon, Atif. 1983. "Values and Cost of Children in Rural Sudan." *Sudan Population Studies* 1:34.

27

SWEDEN

Gerdt Sundström and Mats Thorslund

INTRODUCTION

The Role of the Elderly

Old age in Sweden is commonly perceived as age 65 or more, maybe for the historical reason that Sweden was the first country to introduce universal old-age pensions (in 1914). Originally these pensions were for persons 67 and above, lowered to 65 in 1976. Significantly, it is now being discussed to raise the retirement age again. This is partly a response to recurrent reports in mass media about the healthy and well-to-do elderly—a paradoxical success of gerontology! Partly it is also felt that public finances can no longer afford this "generosity."

Another reason to see age 65 as a decisive cutoff point may be the unusually abrupt retirement pattern in Sweden. In a number of countries, larger fractions than in Sweden have retired well before 65, but more people may also continue in some paid job after 65. That is relatively uncommon in Sweden.

The way the elderly are perceived can be characterized as ambivalent. The consensus seems to be that being young is more "valuable," but, at the same time, all political parties and other interest groups support pensions, programs for health care for the elderly, and so on. Opinion polls tell the same story of unanimous support of the aged by those at least from age 30. We would even suggest that the image of aging has *improved* over the years, in pace with the strengthening of the resources of old people. It is easy to find examples from previous times of seeing old people as "drains" on the resources that should rightly go to younger people.

This was the tone of the time, but it is difficult to find anything similar from the postwar years. Rather, all public commissions appointed from 1952 and later have taken pains to point out that the *total* "burden" of the "productive" generations is not changing noticeably. Up until recently, there has been a general agreement that we can well afford the welfare programs and pension systems that have been established.

Sweden has, and will have for some years to come, the world's oldest population: the 1.5 million elderly make up 19% of its population, and—as elsewhere—the aged themselves are, on average, becoming even older.

The general idea about care for the aged, in Sweden as elsewhere, is certainly that this was provided by the family in the "past" but that care has been lately transferred to the state. This contrasts with empirical facts: substantial proportions of the elderly lived in institutions (also in the not-so-recent past), and there may be a continuity rather than a dramatic change when it comes to responsibility for the sick and frail elderly. The only new and unique features are the availability of an acceptable income guarantee (pensions) and the provision of public Home-Help/Home Health Care to everyone in need.

In 1989, 43% of the Swedish elderly were men; 57% were women. In 1988, of all the elderly, 11% were single, 5% were married, 31% were widowed, and 7% were divorced. In 1980–81, 36% of the elderly lived alone, 54% lived with a spouse (or coresident), 3% lived with offspring, and 7% lived with others. Of all the elderly in 1980–81, 87% had no more than elementary school education, and 50% indicated "good general health" (Statistics Sweden, 1991a, b).

The Formal Structure of Care of the Elderly

Overall responsibility for the care of the elderly in Sweden rests with the state. Government and parliament legislate and formulate guidelines for how the elderly shall be cared for and who shall bear responsibility for the various services. Virtually all medical and social care services in Sweden are publicly run and financed. Sweden has a very large public sector, which is supported by high taxation. The welfare state is characterized by the general nature of its benefits, based primarily on need. Only a few benefits require means tests. Health care and social services are heavily subsidized, with the recipient usually paying only a fraction of the actual cost.

Sweden's smallest units of local government, the 286 municipalities, administer social services. Responsibility for the running and shaping of health and medical care rests mainly with the regional units of local government, the 23 county councils, and the three metropolitan municipalities of Malmö, Gotland, and Göteborg.

The work of both the municipalities and the county councils is regulated by legislation. In 1982, the new Social Services Act came into effect. This is a framework legislation that emphasizes the right of the individual to receive municipal services at all stages of life. Everyone who requires help in day-to-day existence has the right to claim assistance, if these needs "cannot be met in any other way."

In 1983 a new Health and Medical Services Act came into effect. According to this act, health care and medical services shall be available to all members of society, with the goal of ensuring a high standard of general health and care for all on equal terms.

Compared with most other countries, Swedish municipalities and county councils enjoy an unusually autonomous position vis-à-vis the state. Local politicians are directly elected at general elections, and both municipalities and county councils levy taxes. The legislation on social services and on health and medical care allows the municipalities and the county councils great freedom to plan and organize their own services and levy taxes in order to finance them.

The autonomy of these two levels of local government also means that services for the care of the elderly have, to a certain extent, come to be organized differently in different parts of the country. Thus, for example, the number of institutional beds in relation to the size of the local population and the scope of the home help and the home nursing services vary considerably, especially between urban and rural areas (to the advantage of the latter). On the other hand, the general principles of the Swedish welfare state regarding the care of the elderly are the same nationwide, namely, that social services and health care for the elderly are primary public sector responsibilities and that care shall be given by trained and qualified staff.

Several voluntary organizations offer support and help to the elderly, such as the Salvation Army and the Red Cross. It is not known how much help is given by such organizations, but it is reasonable to assume that such activities are less extensive in Sweden than in most other countries, since the tradition of the public sector's assuming principal responsibility in this area is so firmly established. Swedish trade unions have also been opposed to greater emphasis on informal care by volunteers.

INCOME MAINTENANCE AND EMPLOYMENT

The universal flat-rate pension introduced in 1914 was ambitious for its time but provided poor coverage. Contemporary studies found that at least a third of the aged also had to rely on poor relief and/or their family (Sundström, 1983). Old people were the largest single client group in the poor relief up to the late 1940s (Sundström, 1983). Then pensions were raised substantially, and municipalities began to pay housing allowances to elderly in need. The latter still show large local variations. In a 1954 survey, 20% thought their economic situation unsatisfactory; 31% said that it had "improved" (SOU, 1956). In recent surveys, very few elderly (about 2%) complain that they have trouble making "both ends meet" or that they have recently worried about money.

These subjective appraisals of the elderly themselves do *not* indicate that nearly all old persons are well-off. Incomes for the aged are very unevenly distributed, partly because the pension system perpetuates income inequalities in the labor market and partly because some of the aged have substantial income besides pensions. Some of the elderly are "squeezed" against rising costs, especially of their dwellings. On average, nearly 90% of the incomes of the aged derive from pensions of various kinds. The flat-rate system is, for most of the aged, supplemented by superannuation plans (graded according to number of years employed and income during those years) that cover most of the income lost when retiring. For persons with good salaries this means that retirement reduction in income is quite modest, and for others, pension incomes can be low. The latter holds true especially for women and for the oldest among them. Even among women currently retiring, nearly one in five gets only the flat-rate pension, and most of the others get small superannuation pensions, due to having held low-paid jobs, often part-time and not for a long enough time. Yet, the pensions and housing allowances are so constructed that no elderly person should have to rely upon social welfare (nor are they eligible, being above the subsistence level). But a sizable fraction is not far above that level of living.

In addition to public Social Security pensions, there are also negotiated plans of the private sector (included in the discussion of pension income). There is, further, an expanding market for individual (so-called) pension insurances, which also provide tax benefits. In the age group 50–64, about a fifth are covered with schemes of that kind, and the proportion will probably grow in the future.

A minor tax benefit has been applied to older persons, but their general rate of taxation (pensions constitute taxable income) is the same as for others. About a third of the elderly benefit from housing allowances, graded according to income and cost of housing (homeowners are also entitled to this). There are no special food stamp programs for the aged (or for other age groups), nor any general reduction of transportation fares. Yet, Sweden may boast of having the world's most extensive system of transportation services. This applies not only for the elderly but for handicapped persons of any age.

Although pensions should be enough for subsistence, about 4% of the aged use social welfare. These persons often are single, not-so-old men (sometimes alcoholics) or recent immigrants who have not, as yet, been granted a pension. Social welfare is a local, means-tested program.

Most of the aged stop working at 65 (or shortly before then). In fact, one can make no legal claim to keep the job after 65, even though there are extensive job security laws for younger persons. About 8% of elderly persons (65–74) are employed (11% of those 65–69, 5% of those 70–79), usually as farmers or workers in small enterprises (Statistics Sweden, 1992b). Partial pension programs, unique for Sweden, operate for those who want to step down gradually before 65, but there is little in the way of job redesign or other attempts to utilize the work potentials of the elderly. In opinion polls, elderly persons generally seem delighted with the timing of, and experience with, their retirement. Few would like to continue working or to take up a (another) job, contrasting with popular stereotypes of the "trauma" of retiring (Sjöberg, 1985). Younger groups generally do not want old people to pull out to ease the entrance of the young; the only group consistently affirming propositions of that kind are the aged themselves and those nearing retirement age.

HEALTH CARE SERVICES

Health and medical care are regarded as an important part of the Swedish welfare system. Its fundamental principle is that all citizens are entitled to good health and equal access to health and medical care, regardless of where they live and their economic circumstances. In line with this principle, health and medical care is seen as a public sector responsibility supported by a national health insurance system and other social welfare services.

Health and medical care are financed primarily by income taxes levied by the county councils. These taxes are proportional; that is, they represent a given percentage of a person's taxable income, regardless of its size. Between 1960 and 1990 the average county council tax increased from about 4.5% to 13.5%. The county council taxes in 1990 covered around 60% of the cost of health and medical care. General state subsidies, to level out differences in income between the county councils, add approximately a further 15%. The remainder comes from state funds for education, research, and psychiatry (12%), reimbursements from the national health insurance system (8%), and patients' fees (4%).

In 1989 the number of hospital beds in Sweden was relatively high, some 11.9 per 1,000 inhabitants (4.0 in general, 1.8 in psychiatric, and 6.1 in long-term facilities). However, during the 1980s the total number of beds and the number of days of somatic short-term care decreased, the number of beds being around 36,000 in 1989. On the other hand, the proportion of days of care consumed by the elderly has risen continuously. In 1988, 59.2% of all days of somatic, short-term hospital care were accounted for by persons in the 75+ age group (7.9% of the total population). There are many factors behind this trend, like the rise in the number of elderly and the advances made in the field of geriatric medicine, with larger numbers of old people being able to benefit from new forms of treatment. Furthermore, it is often difficult to discharge elderly patients whose medical treatment has been completed if they cannot be cared for at home and if there is a shortage of beds in long-term institutions to which they should otherwise be transferred for more appropriate care. Such patients, consequently, remain in ordinary somatic, short-term wards.

Many elderly patients need more care and rehabilitation than can be given by home-based nursing. In 1990 there were almost 46,000 beds for somatic, long-term care (geriatric departments and nursing homes). Geriatric departments (*långvårdskliniker*) are often linked to general hospitals, and the aim is to rehabilitate and allow the elderly patient to return home as soon as possible. Such departments offer so-called relief care, whereby the patient is admitted for a certain time to allow the family (taking care of the elderly person at home) to have some relief. The departments also provide respite care, when patients spend certain regular, fixed periods in the department.

Nursing homes (*sjukhem*) provide care for longer periods under more home-like conditions. Local nursing homes are usually independent of hospitals and, since 1992, they come under the organizational auspices of the respective municipality. In 1992 the number of beds in such local nursing homes has increased. Almost one-tenth of the long-term care beds are found in private nursing homes.

The first Swedish institution for hospice care was established 1991. There are more to come, but the emphasis will still be to help elderly patients in terminal stages to remain in their own homes until the end.

Home nursing services (*hemsjukvården*) were expanded during the 1970s and 1980s. In 1991 there were almost 6,000 district nurses (calculated as number of full-time posts), a threefold increase since the mid-1970s. The number of assistant nurses and district physicians has also increased significantly in recent years.

The number of outpatient visits to physicians is comparatively low in the general population—about 2.5 visits per inhabitant per year. The most recent comparable statistic about the elderly (1988–89) indicates that 51% of the 65–84-year-olds have seen a doctor in the last three months (personal communication, C. Skjöld, Statistics Sweden). Most elderly people living at home see the district nurse or doctor at a clinic. Home visits to those who have difficulty in getting to their local clinic are paid mainly by district nurses and assistant nurses. The former divide their time between clinic-based care and home visits, while the latter spend most of their time out on home calls.

HOUSING RESOURCES

At the level of national policy for housing of the elderly, the general objective—set forth in the Social Services Act—states that old people should, if possible, remain in their own homes. This official policy of "staying put" has been under debate. The municipalities are mandated by law to supply sheltered living for needy elderly, but it is often felt that this is insufficient. The elderly can exercise freedom of choice, but only after being assessed as in need.

Except for the types of residential living that are institutional in character, no segment of the housing market is reserved or designed for the elderly. Postwar "pensioner flats" were, in no way, adapted for handicapped or frail persons but only meant to relieve the housing shortage of the time. These apartments are usually no longer reserved for the aged.

The general tendency is for the residents in special housing for the frail elderly to become ever older and frailer. It is becoming more and more difficult to find residence in such housing, as the number of old-old persons rises and the number of rooms/apartments for them does not expand. Over the last 5–10 years, cooperative and private organizations and companies have constructed several units that can be *bought* by anyone who is (usually) 55 or above (and who has the money). Currently, they number nearly 10,000 apartments and are to be found in at least a fifth of all the municipalities (Malmberg and Sundström, 1992). This is a type of housing obviously attractive to many elders, and "privatization" is partly made possible by the welfare state itself. By providing well for some segments of the elderly, an increasing number can afford private alternatives. Sometimes this housing is being marketed as "service housing," though most (so far) provide only little or no service. Nevertheless, this is an interesting development that will—in the future—provide competition to public residences. At present, the latter outnumber the former by about 10–15 to 1. An innovative public development is the special group-living units for demented elderly unable to live in ordinary housing. These units, which numbered 5,000 in 1991, are small (6–10 residents) and provide homelike living and 24-hour personnel. The unit will typically have rooms for each resident and a large kitchen-dining area, where most of the awake time will be spent. The unit is physically not unlike a small old-age home, but with a different philosophy and higher staff-patient ratios. The residents officially hold contracts on their rooms ("apartments"). The same holds true for the 40,000 public "service apartments," usually located together in service houses. Many municipalities still do not have any of these or have very few facilities.

In 1991 there were some 800 municipal old-age homes (ålderdomshem), with around 35,000 places for elderly people unable to cope at home, even with the aid of the home help and the home nursing services. With increasing numbers of people remaining in their own homes, the construction of old-age homes started to decline during the 1970s and almost completely ceased during the following decade. In 1991 the number of places decreased by some 5,000 (Statistics Sweden, 1992a).

Most residents of old-age homes live in small, single rooms with their own toilets. Residents may bring their own furniture with them. Communal meals are served at set times, and various types of services and activities are available. Care is provided around the clock by regular staff. Monthly fees are income-related.

Very little in the way of special community services for the elderly exist; help with shopping and so on is mainly provided by the Home Help Service. Surveys show that help with home maintenance and social activities is mainly provided by the family (Sundström, 1983; Johansson and Thorslund, 1992).

Housing allowances, which benefit about a third of the elderly, provide the financial means for spacious and modern living for elderly persons of limited means. These allowances are in no way restricted to the aged but apply to all on the basis of need.

SUPPORTIVE SERVICES

The municipality is responsible for Home Help Services (hemtjänsten), which provide help with shopping, cleaning, cooking, washing, and personal hygiene to elderly and disabled persons living at home. In November 1991 about 13% in the age group 75–79 years received home help. In the age group 80–84 years, the corresponding figure was 25%; in the age group 85–89 years it was 39%; and in the group 90 years and older it was 44% (Statistics Sweden, 1992b). Most help is given during normal working hours, but help is also available on weekends and at night. Most municipalities provide night patrols, which include both nursing and home help staff. Each municipality sets fees for these services, based on income. The fees vary among municipalities but usually cover about 5% of the real costs.

Other forms of service, such as meals-on-wheels, podiatry, hair care, and help with bathing and snow clearing, are often given in combination with home help. A number of these services are provided at day centers, which are either freestanding units in the community or incorporated in sheltered accommodations or residential homes. Day centers function as meeting places where the elderly can get together for meals and activities. The number of these centers is increasing. All were originally run by the municipalities, but it has become increasingly common for the elderly themselves to take over the running of such centers.

Currently, there is a rapid expansion of day-care units *(dagvård)* for elderly people with senile dementia. Many demented individuals continue to live at home with spouses or other relatives. These units offer supervision and care during the day for the demented, and provide relief for the caregiving relatives.

Municipalities provide transport services *(färdtjänst)* to and from day centers, doctor appointments, and so on. This is available to elderly or disabled persons who cannot use the public transit system. It can consist of regular taxis that provide door-to-door service or specially constructed vans that can take wheelchairs. Eligibility is based on need; the charges for the user vary among municipalities. In 1991 there were 439,000 persons (of all ages) who were assessed and given the right to transport services. More than half of the elderly in the oldest age groups (80+) were entitled to transport services.

In rural areas it can be difficult for some elderly people to do errands or go to the post office. After consultation with the municipal Home Help Service, rural postmen can provide postal and banking services to elderly people who live alone and far from neighbors.

In spite of the scope of the formal services for the elderly, the informal care given by families and other volunteers is of great significance. There are no reliable nationwide figures for the amount of such help given, although several local studies have demonstrated that it is extensive—so extensive, that if Home Help Services were to take over this informal, voluntary work, they would have to more than double their staff (Johansston and Thorslund, 1992). With increasing numbers of elderly people remaining in their own homes, it seems likely that families will have to take greater responsibility for their elderly relatives in the future. An extension of the availability of relief and respite care within the long-term care system is an important prerequisite for the functioning of informal family care. The extension of day centers and day-care units should also, to some extent, be seen as support for informal care.

Relatives who take care of their elderly family members can receive payment from the municipality and county council. It is also possible for relatives to take time off from work, for up to a total of 30 days per relative, to care for an

Sweden

elderly family member and receive compensation from the social insurance system. Allowances are available from municipalities if the family can provide care. They are given when the need has been assessed. When persons of working age (less than 65) give up normal employment to care for elderly relatives, they can be employed by the municipality as caregivers. They receive a salary equivalent to that received by home helpers (usually a certain number of hours a week). There are no accurate statistics regarding how many people receive these benefits. In 1992 it was estimated that about 20,000 families receive cash allowances and that there are about 10,000 paid caregivers.

LEISURE-TIME RESOURCES

A number of nationwide surveys have uncovered how elderly (and nonelderly) persons use their time. For the elderly (65–79 years of age), about 40% of their time is spent on "basic" activities: sleeping, personal grooming, and eating. Some 15–20% of their time is used for "work activities" (very few elderly have paid jobs): shopping, household work, transportation. The remaining time is "leisure," a large part of which is spent on media (about a third), on socializing (about a fifth), and on "fun" (11–18%). "Pastime" activities are also extensive (daydreaming, looking at old photos, and so on) (Sjöberg, 1985).

Other studies (see Sjöberg, 1985) indicate that socializing is a highly significant ingredient in the lives of the elderly and that the family absorbs most of such time. "Organized" activities seem to dwindle in comparison—quantitatively, at least. Most of the elderly have access to a car, and many to second homes and even boats. Many activities decline in frequency with age (such as sports, promenades, fishing, moviegoing, and bingo and related games). Of those elderly who are homeowners, about half spend time with garden work.

The use of "organized" activities is hard to document and measure. The active elderly tend to be those who are generally active; persons in great need of "being activated" are often hard to reach. However, it is known that participation in a typical Swedish phenomenon—the "study circle"—declines from age 50. Of the aged, some 10–20% engage in courses on languages and so on (Sjöberg, 1985). There are also special courses for old persons and for family caregivers. In some places, Home Help Services has initiated groups of elders who cook together. The elderly who visit day centers, financed by (and sometimes run by) municipalities or else run by organizations of pensioners, tend to be "active" persons, with few opportunities for the frailer ones. These day centers are very unevenly spread through the country.

There is, so far, very little organized volunteerism in Sweden. Interest seems to be increasing, and lately friendly visiting and similar programs run by the Red Cross and others have been expanding. The national church and other religious denominations also do extensive visiting with the elderly. A number of self-help groups (elders who help other elders) exist as well. Indeed, the most important group is no doubt the large national organizations of retired people themselves, who arrange a vast array of recreational activities, dances, travel, and so on.

ADVOCACY AND PROTECTION

Since the 1960s, the Swedish elderly have been well organized in two big interest groups, which together include about 33% of the elderly and are sometimes called upon to react to government plans at national or local levels. They also take action on various issues and typically watch out for economic support for the elderly. There are local organizations in all municipalities, and they are on the lookout for declining provisions of homemaking services and institutional care. These organizations also arrange leisure-time activities for the aged.

In spite of the fact that *ombudsman* is a Swedish word, an innovation to assist and protect citizens against misconduct and negligence on the part of public institutions, it has not been instituted for the aged in Sweden. There is no special legal assistance for elderly persons, but those in need may apply for assistance (as may other age groups). The assistance is granted as an economic subsidy to the lawyer dealing with a case, provided the case is deemed important and the client's income is not too high. Some general counseling may also be granted. However, seldom would there be help with testaments and similar legal matters, nor would assistance be relevant for elderly persons dealing with public bureaucracies. The Law of Public Administration (Förvaltningslagen) states that authorities should assist those citizens with whom they deal, and there are explicit procedures built into the legislation. Those dissatisfied with a decision on Home Help Services, institutional care, and so on, may appeal to the administrative courts (from a regional court up to the national court). Very few elderly use the option of appealing; many fewer than would have good reason to do so. Generally, Swedes embrace the idea of "good government," even if there are some suspicions as to whether the representatives of that government always act in one's best interest.

Historically, the state has acted to protect (but also to control) young and old citizens, especially poor citizens (and the elderly were, as a rule, poor). It should be noted that big regional inequities in health care and social services are not open to appeals or legal complaints, which lie in the jurisdiction of the authority itself. It is thus a political issue, not a legal one.

Furthermore, there are no specific bodies in Sweden to help elderly victims of crime. With the exception of dementia sufferers, there are no special groups to represent any subgroup of frail elderly. Victims of dementia—and their families—have established a network to promote care for this syndrome. However, such opportunities are still inadequate, relative to the needs.

FUTURE PROJECTIONS

In international comparison, Sweden has a highly comprehensive system of care for the elderly. The development in Sweden from post–World War II until the 1980s has resulted in one of the most extensive systems of publicly financed and managed medical care and social services. This development was feasible because of a favorable economic situation and led to shifting responsibility for the care of the elderly from the individual and the family to the public sector. There is legislation to back up demands on the different services and to provide equally well to everyone according to their needs.

In quantitative terms, during the 1960s and 1970s the care of the elderly in Sweden developed in pace with the increasing needs for services and care. The number of elderly increased rapidly and so did the number of institutional beds, as well as the number of elderly persons receiving home help services and home nursing.

The number of elderly persons increased continually during the 1980s. However, the number of institutional beds, as well as the number of persons receiving home help, has been about the same (or even lower) during this period. Therefore, there has been a *relative* decrease in the number of places in institutions and in the number of persons receiving home help.

Instead, there has been a substantial improvement in the quality of services during this period. Many new kinds of services were established and developed during the 1980s (e.g., night patrols, case management groups, day care for senile elderly, meals-on-wheels, alarm systems, and transport service). Opportunities for respite care were also created, and there has been an effort to improve conditions inside institutions for those who must live in them.

Another reason Sweden was able to cope with increasing demands during the 1980s was that the organizations and care services were actually in need of trimming back. The last decade has seen considerable reorganization of services and efforts to rationalize them. For example, many local efforts have been made to handle the problems with the system of divided responsibility for the care of the elderly (municipality/county council). There have been obvious, recurring problems, such as difficulties in cooperating, lack of continuity in visits to the elderly, and attempts to transfer main responsibility for an elderly person and all the associated costs to someone else.

Parliament, therefore, decided on a new system in 1992, whereby the municipalities were given the statutory responsibility for all types of institutional housing and care facilities for the elderly. The municipalities now also have the statutory responsibility for providing *health care* for elderly residents in institutional housing and care facilities. By agreement with the county council, the municipalities can also assume responsibility for home nursing care. Further, the municipalities are financially responsible for all other types of long-term institutional care, which include some patients in somatic general hospitals whose medical treatment has been completed.

However, much of the organizational slack in the Swedish system of care to the elderly has been reduced, and even if there is still scope for further rationalization, it is probably naive to believe that the "gains" achieved during the past 10 years can be repeated.

The predictable demographic changes will bring an increased demand for services and care for the elderly. Even though today's younger pensioners are, in many ways, healthier than those of yesterday it is difficult to see any signs that the total care needs of the elderly will diminish. The increase in life expectancy, even among the very oldest, will in the short run be accompanied by chronic illness and disability, which will need both medical care and social services.

The task in the years ahead will be to find answers to the central question of how to keep services and care up to standard, in both qualitative and quantitative terms, in face of restricted financial resources and rapid advances in medical technology. The 1990s will be characterized by the search for alternative solutions to care for the elderly and by continuous efforts to improve coordination and cooperation between different care providers.

Although private companies in the social sector have not been forbidden by law, there have been several impediments to the development of private initiatives. Some municipalities have contracted out services, such as cleaning, to private providers but have maintained responsibility for the services.

The 1991 elected liberal government in Sweden has tried to encourage the development of private alternatives to public services. By eliminating certain legal and economic barriers, the government wants to increase competition and stimulate private initiatives. Among other alternatives, possibilities are now being discussed for a system whereby individuals assessed as in need of care receive care vouchers. The individual then "buys" services from private providers. Such a system would stimulate development of care services and increase effectiveness, while providing the individual user a greater freedom of choice.

Another rather recent trend in the beginning of the 1990s is the emphasis on the care given by spouses, other family members, and friends and neighbors. There has been little research done to estimate the extent of this care or to find out what kind of support these people need to continue their caregiving role. It is clear, however, that informal care is extensive in Sweden. There is an increasing awareness of the essential role of informal care and the need to encourage and support caregiving relatives through financial incentives, social support, and respite care.

Previous to the 1992 reform, state subsidies to municipalities were earmarked to specific services, such as home care services, and were based on the number of personnel and services "produced." Currently, subsidies are given in a lump sum, related to the number of elderly in the municipality, the number of people with early retirement, the number of elderly living alone, and to the amount of rural area in the municipality. It is then up to the municipalities to direct funds where they are most needed.

This decentralization has the advantage of allowing for decision making at a local level. The municipalities have more freedom to assess and respond to the needs in their communities. The disadvantage is that there will be more variation in services and in their quality and availability among the municipalities. This presents a challenge to the policy, as stated in the Health and Medical Services

Act, of providing services to everyone on equal conditions. Another challenge is that, as yet, there are few controls established for quality of services.

To sum up, the increasing needs of services and care for the elderly will be met by efforts to rationalize and reorganize the public sector, by an increasing private for-profit sector, and by an increased burden for the families. It is, of course, not possible to foresee the degree of change in the different sectors. However, it is not likely that these changes will match the increased needs within the elderly population.

In the future it will be increasingly necessary to make decisions about service and care priorities. For the care of the elderly in Sweden, as for health care in general, no clearly formulated principles for setting priorities exist at either central or local levels, even if there has been some public debate in Sweden about how to establish criteria for the priority setting that will certainly be necessary in the future.

In practice, of course, decisions about priority have to be made all the time. The fact that the total number of people receiving home help has not increased is one example of decisions made by the local home help administrators to allocate restricted resources to certain consumers of help. This leaves those who previously received home help to manage without such assistance. Priority has also been given to people living alone.

There is also evidence that the medical care service agencies are giving priority to the very oldest. The fact that the proportion of medical care resources going to the elderly has increased during the last decade can only partly be explained by the increase of the numbers of elderly people. Another explanation is that ambitions in medical care have been raised and that even very old persons are now receiving treatment that was not given previously.

In times of plentiful resources, decisions about priority are usually based on careful and thoughtful consideration. When resources become scarce, decisions reveal certain assumptions and social prejudices, and the risk of inequality becomes greater. When, and if, more serious discussions about priorities are begun, they will probably deal primarily with questions about which patients should be given which types of medical treatment. Even if there is agreement as to which treatments can be discontinued, it is unlikely that the money saved will reduce the need for setting more general and consequential priorities.

BIBLIOGRAPHY

Calltorp, J. The "Swedish model" under pressure—How to maintain equity and develop quality? *Quality Assurance in Health Care* 1 (1), 13–22, 1989.

Gerdtham, U-G, and Jönsson, B. Health care expenditure in Sweden—An international comparison. *Health Policy* 19, 111–118, 1991.

Hokenstad, M. C., and Thorslund, M. Old age care in Sweden: Policy directives and program limitations. *Perspective on Aging,* 17–21. July/August and September/October 1991.

Johansson, L. Elderly care policy, formal and informal care. The Swedish case. *Health Policy* 18, 231–242, 1991a.

———. The national context of social innovation—Sweden. In R. J. Kraan, ed., *Care for the Elderly. Significant Innovations in Three European Countries.* Boulder, CO: Westview Press, 1991b, 28–44.

Johansson, L., and Thorslund, M. Care needs and sources of support in a nationwide sample of elderly in Sweden. *Zeitschrift für Gerontologie* 25, 57–62, 1992.

Malmberg, Bo, and Sundström, Gerdt. Fortsatt inventering av "seniorbostäder." *Planera Bygga Bo,* No. 6, 27–29, 1992.

Saltman, R. B. Emerging trends in the Swedish health system. *International Journal of Health Services* 21, 615–623, 1991.

Sjöberg, I. *Pensionärer.* Rapport 43, Levnadsförhållanden. Stockholm: Statistics Sweden, 1985.

Statens Offentliga Utredningar (SOU). 1956:1. Statens Offentliga Utredningar (Government White Papers), Åldringsvård. Ministry of Social Affairs, Stockholm 1956.

Statistics Sweden. 1992a. Ålderdomshem, servicehus, service-lägenheter, gruppboenden och dagcentraler 1991. *Statistiska Meddelanden,* S 23 SM 9201.

———. 1992b. Social hemtjänst 1991 samt social hemhjälp November 1991. *Statistiska Meddelanden,* S 21 SM 9201.

Sundström, G. *Caring for the Aged in Welfare Society.* Stockholm Studies in Social Work 1. School of Social Work, University of Stockholm, 1983.

———. Family and state: Recent trends in the care of the aged in Sweden. *Ageing and Society* 6, 169–196, 1986.

———. *Old Age Care in Sweden. Yesterday, Today... Tomorrow?* Stockholm: Swedish Institute, 1987.

Sundström, G., Berg, S., Branch, L., and Doyle, A. Local Variations in Old Age Care in the Welfare State: The Case of Sweden. *Health Policy* 24, 175–186, 1993.

Sundström, G., and Thorslund, M. Caring for the frail elderly in Sweden. In L. Katz Olson, *The Greying of the World; Who Will Care for the Frail Elderly?* New York: Hayworth Press, 1992.

Thorslund, M. The increasing number of very old people will change the Swedish model of the welfare state. *Social Science and Medicine* 32, 455–464, 1991.

———. *The Care of the Elderly in Sweden.* Fact Sheets on Sweden, No. 8. Stockholm: Swedish Institute, 1992.

Thorslund, M., Norström, T., and Wernberg, K. The utilization of home help: A multivariate analysis. *Gerontologist* 31, 116–119, 1991.

28

SWITZERLAND

Hans-Dieter Schneider

INTRODUCTION

Switzerland is a small country. With a surface of about 41,000 square kilometers, it has almost the same size as the Netherlands or only one-sixth of the size of the United Kingdom. The high mountains of the Alps mean not only that one-fourth of the surface cannot be used productively but also that there are many barriers to easy contacts within the country.

Due to these geographic conditions, the nation is largely subdivided into four linguistically different zones (German, French, Italian, and Romanish) and into 26 cantons with their own history and their own constitutions. Each canton is composed of similarly autonomous communities. The political system is a confederation of these cantons.

The differences between the cantons refer not only to the questions of past and present culture but also to the bases of the economy and wealth. The income per capita in the richest canton was, in 1989, more than twice the amount of that in the poorest canton (Bundesamt für Statistik, 1991). Altogether, Switzerland belongs among the richest countries in the world, with a per capita income of $28,200 in 1989.

Switzerland had a population of 6.8 million in 1990. The cantons differ again when one considers the population. The canton Zürich, with most inhabitants, has 1.2 million citizens, whereas the smallest canton, Appenzell, has only 14,000 citizens.

This background information points to the fact that the situation of the aged and the political solutions for their problems may be very different from community to community and from canton to canton. Only some solutions under the responsibility of the confederation refer to all inhabitants of Switzerland,

and additional regulations and contributions may occur on the level of the cantons and the communities.

The Role of the Elderly

The Problem of Defining Old Age

The elderly are defined in Switzerland according to the age when the pensions of old age and survivors' insurance (Alters- und Hinterbliebenen-Versicherung) begin to be paid. This age of retirement from gainful employment for most working people is 62 for women and 65 for men.

It is broadly discussed whether retirement should occur earlier or later. Currently, some leading enterprises retire their male and female employees at the age of 62. The staff of most federal, cantonal, and communal administrations can voluntarily leave earlier, up to the age of 60 years, at the cost of some percent of their pension as compensation for each advanced year. Political commissions discuss that the retirement age might be 65 for both sexes. An official deadline for work later than 65 has been proposed, but politicians seem to lack the courage to fight publicly for such a solution.

Because of the great difference in health, autonomy, and well-being between the young old and the old old, a subdivision is often made at the 75th or at the 80th year, when old age (*le quatrième âge*) begins.

Perception of the Elderly

There do not exist any national data concerning how the elderly are perceived. It may be supposed, however, on the basis of small and not representative studies, that there exists an age bias in Switzerland: a tendency to regard the elderly less positively than the young because of their age.

Although there do not exist formal prescriptions, most public functions, for example, as president of an association, have to be handed over to younger persons when retirement age is reached. There is even a discussion if politicians, too, should retire at 65. So by reaching the age of retirement, adults lose not only their power at their workplace but other bases of power, too. The remaining base of power in the hands of the elderly is their wealth (if they belong to the upper classes).

Mostly unnoticed by the population, the elderly exert a rather strong influence on political development by voting. Citizens not only vote for representatives in the parliaments but often vote on political questions at the ballot box. Because the elderly take rather conservative views, and because they participate frequently in voting, they sometimes make decisions that affect younger populations. Thus, the votes of the elderly were responsible for decisions that the young could not substitute civil service for military service, that the Swiss army should not be abolished, and that a proposed law protecting mothers-to-be should be rejected.

Table 28.1
The Presumable Partition of the Population in Switzerland According to Age until 2020

Year	\multicolumn{5}{c}{Class of Age}	N in million
	0-19	20-39	40-64	65-79	80+	
1980	28	30	28	11	3	6.335
1990	24	30	31	11	4	6.645
2000	22	28	34	12	4	6.830
2020	20	25.5	35	15	5	6.920

Source: Mathe, 1991, p. 79.

Demographic Data

In 1990, 14.5% of the population was 65 years or older. This portion rose from 5.8% in 1900 to 9.6% in 1950 and will continue to rise, as can be seen in Table 28.1.

According to a probable scenario, there will be about 20% of people over 65 in Switzerland in 2020. The number of the very old will increase from 245,000 in 1990 to 334,000 in 2020. This absolute growth in 30 years is only little more than the rise from 1980 to 1990, which totaled 76,000.

There are large differences concerning the portion of the elderly between the cantons and between the municipalities. For instance, at Lucerne the portion of elderly is 23%; in the surrounding communities it is between only 6% and 8%.

Life expectancy at birth is now 74.0 years for men and 80.9 years for women (Höpflinger and Stuckelberger, 1992). A person at 70 years still has a life expectancy of 12.1 years for men and 15.6 years for women.

History of the Elderly

The statistical data demonstrate that there were far less portions of aged in the last centuries than currently. One reason for this is the reduced reproduction rate, which diminishes the portion of the young in the population. Automatically, the portion of the constant number of the aged increases. A second reason is the increased life expectancy, which allows more people to experience old age. This change is largely due to reduced mortality in childhood as medicine acquired the means to combat children's diseases. So the population of Switzerland in the sixteenth century was, above all, a population of children and young and middle-aged persons. Old people were the exception.

According to Messmer (1990), one can differentiate three groups of older persons in the time from the seventeenth to the nineteenth centuries: the rich (composed of the noble, the patricians, and the clergy), those who possess means of production, and the poor. The first group, the rich, had so many servants that there was no lack of help, even in old age. As they did not know any shortage of nutrition, even in difficult times, their life expectancy was high after they had survived (even for them) a dangerous childhood.

Old people of property, farmers, craftsmen, and merchants could get remuneration from a son who used the production facilities. In order to prevent conflicts in times of shortages between the "retired" old and the young, it was usual to sign contracts that meticulously counted the rights of the elderly. The departing father lost his former status in the family, because the son was his judicial successor. Conflicts were not unusual, because the two generations lived generally in one household. The older craftsmen often sold their workshop and lived from the profit, or they lived in exchange for their business in a home or hospital (Verpfründung).

The members of the third group who had worked during their whole life could get a place in an asylum for the poor or were accepted as household members, for which the municipality paid the fees. During industrialization, life expectancy grew, and more and more have-nots became old and dependent. To pay these old people, cantons and municipalities introduced taxes for the poor. When the older population continued to grow, only private charity existed to keep the old and poor from starvation. Even after the foundation of savings banks for the working class, old age was—for the second and third groups—a life cycle with tremendous misery. There is no legitimation for romantic admiration of a common, happy living of three generations in one household; such a phenomenon was limited. The lot of the members of lower classes who lived until old age was to be a not-too-well-treated object of charity in institutions of the churches or the municipalities, especially when they lacked any family member who—by time and living space—could afford to care for them. The establishment of a modern system of old-age pensions, after World War II, was the beginning of better economic conditions for the aged of the lower classes.

The Formal Structure of Care of the Elderly

Swiss society is very traditional. Parties with traditional values and objectives could always preserve their majority because the more progressive Social Democrats received only about 25% of the votes since World War II. The liberal idea of individual freedom, which allows everybody to choose what one wants but which contains also the expectation that one bears the consequences of one's decisions, was gradually complemented by some elements of societal support, such as unemployment benefit or supplementary assistance for the poor elderly.

As Segalman (1986, pp. 59, 62) states: "One of the keys of the Swiss solution seems to be based upon retention of political power in the local and cantonal units rather than in the federal structure.... There is ... strong support for the principle of subsidiarity, which retains responsibility and authority for family, for community, and for cantons." This federalism anchors the individual, first of all, in the village or town, with the expectation of assistance from it when there is need. That means, for instance, that the local community (Bürgerort) has to pay the costs of help that exceed the contributions of health insurance and other bodies, even some years after the citizen has left it. And it means that the local social service is responsible for the well-being of all inhabitants.

The canton may give subsidies, and an old person in need will get support, first of all, at the local level. Federal aid is possible only by the old-age and survivors' pension system and juridically regulated additional aid.

Private organizations are ready to help persons who are without sufficient resources. Associations (like Frauenverein [Women's Association]), foundations (like Pro Senectute [old age]), and even enterprises (like Migros [largest retail organization in Sweden]) take responsibility to organize and finance help on the individual and local level. Since there exist hundreds of such organizations, it is often not necessary for the state to take action.

INCOME MAINTENANCE AND EMPLOYMENT

The Public Income Security Program: The Three Pillars

In 1980 Schweizer published a report on the economic situation of the retired in Switzerland. His conclusion, that the retired are economically almost as well-off as the working generations, was attacked by Gilliand (1983) and Lüthi (1983) for methodological reasons. The two latter authors proved that despite an almost comparable arithmetic mean of the retirees' income and an even better arithmetic mean of their fortune, many aged live in very restricted conditions.

Of all pensioners, the 10% with the lowest incomes receive 3% of all income for pensioners. Concerning the fortune, Lüthi (1983) points out that the 20% of retirees with the smallest fortune own 0.2% of all retirees' fortune; the richest 10% own 61.7%, however. We must conclude that, in general, pensioners in Switzerland are pretty well-off; but it must not be overlooked that 10% to 20% are in economic difficulties, a fact that is accentuated by recent research on poverty (Enderle, 1987; Mäder et al., 1991).

The Swiss social insurance system was introduced by the federation in 1948 (after being accepted by the people in 1947). Since then it has been regularly revised and supplemented. Currently, the economic situation of an old person rests on three pillars: the old-age and survivors' insurance (AHV), the compulsory professional pension system, and private provision (e.g., savings). Insurance is paid by all working persons, by their employers and—about 20%—by the federation and the cantons. The professional pension system is partly paid by the employer and partly by the employee.

The old-age and survivors' insurance provides a minimal income for every female in Switzerland who is 62 years or older and for every male 65 years or older. The maximum amount of 1,800 Swiss francs (US $1,200) per month for one person (1992) is twice the minimum amount. For married couples, the amounts are 1,350 and 2,700 Swiss francs, respectively (US $900 and $1,800). When the income of the two other pillars is added, it is hoped that a standard of living similar to that before retirement is possible.

Persons in extraordinarily difficult circumstances may apply for supplementary assistance (Ergänzungsleistungen). This support is calculated according to the earnings, the fortune, and the necessary expenses. If this assistance is not sufficient, the welfare services of the cantons and communities may provide further help.

The aged in Switzerland are, in general, economically well-off. For those 10% to 20% who need further assistance, local, cantonal, and federal institutions aid in securing a life of relative dignity for the aged.

Economic Benefits for the Elderly

There is discussion in Switzerland as to whether retirees should benefit from generalized special advantages, since most of them dispose of earnings comparably to the working population. Since this question will not be resolved soon, benefits will certainly remain for the aged until the next millennium.

Those benefits include, among others, reduced taxes, higher interest for savings, reduced transportation fees under some circumstances, reduced admission fees for cinemas, museums, popular universities, and so on, and reduced contributions to societies. There are even some hotels and restaurants where retirees may live or eat at reduced prices.

Working Beyond Retirement

The working career for most workers in Switzerland ends at age 62 for females and age 65 for males, when the national pension for the old-age and survivors' insurance is paid. The only exemptions are some self-employed, who may work as long as they wish, special professions such as university professors who—in some cantons—can work until 70, and pilots who go on pension at 55.

If retirees want to work in a new job, they are free to do so. In some regions, pensioners have created agencies to provide their peers with work. However, in economically hard times, it is very difficult to find jobs for them.

HEALTH CARE SERVICES

Membership in the health insurance system is obligatory for all. The health insurance funds are private, and their number have diminished from 1,154 in 1950 to 555 in 1980 (Müller, 1984). Because of steadily rising costs of the health system, there is much discussion on how to control patients, doctors, and pharmaceutical firms, so that they will reduce their demands. Since 1990, attempts with health maintenance organizations (Gesundheitskassen) have begun.

Contributions to the health insurance funds, which continue in retirement, are a heavy burden for the economically deprived elderly, even when the confederation contributes about 15% to the system. But basic health services, except dental care, are paid in the lowest insurance class. If extraordinary expenses arise, and if no fortune is at hand, they may be paid on request by supplementary assistance, welfare, or foundations.

The health system in Switzerland is based on private doctors and communal or cantonal hospitals. Private hospitals are possible in some cantons, but they are not numerous.

The Spitex Services

With two objectives in mind, to maintain the elderly in their private environment as long as possible and to lighten the financial burden of the health system, the so-called Spitex service was developed in 1960. This service comprises all forms of help brought to the elderly person living at home (such as home care, help with the household, meals-on-wheels, shopping, driving, visiting, going for a walk, pedicure and hairdresser, day care or night care in hospitals or in homes for the aged and so on) (see Eschmann, Kocher, and Spescha, 1990).

Currently, in almost every town and village, Spitex services have been established (often in cooperation with hospitals or homes for the aged). Explicit policies in many communities do not permit building or expanding homes for the aged, in favor of the development of these services.

The organizations responsible for Spitex are varied: the Red Cross, Pro Senectute (old age), women's associations, religious parishes, and social offices of the communities. Because dozens of organizations contribute to the support of the elderly at home, some towns (such as Lucerne or Basle) began to install coordinating offices to prevent duplication of services.

Institutions for the Aged

For those elderly persons who do not want to, or can no longer, live in their private household, there exist many institutions (Table 28.2).

Before 1970, homes for the aged were intended for those elderly persons who had difficulties in leading an autonomous household but who were physically in rather good condition. In the meantime, after the number of the very old had increased considerably, there began to develop installation of nursing departments in homes for the aged. Currently, each newly built home for the aged, that wants to profit from public subsidies must have such a department to satisfy the needs of residents who are in rather frail condition. Some nursing homes still accept only frail applicants (Pflege or Krankenheime). Generally these are big institu-

Table 28.2
Special Living Arrangements for the Elderly in Switzerland

Living Arrangements	Description
Apartments for the elderly	Apartments without special equipment, easily accessible
Specialized apartments for the elderly (Alters-Wohnungen)	Single or grouped apartments with special equipment for handicapped persons
Housing areas for the aged (Alterssiedlung)	Apartments for the elderly in one building, often with common rooms and basic services
Homes for the aged (Altersheim)	Rooms for older persons with common basic services (cleaning, organized leisure activities, and so on)
Homes for the aged with nursing departments	Combinations of general homes for the aged and nursing homes
Residences for older persons (Seniorenresidenzen)	Homes for the aged with particularly high standing, without or with nursing
Nursing homes for the aged (Pflegeheim)	Rooms for older persons with comprehensive support (nursing, simple medical treatment, rehabilitation, and so on)
Geriatric hospitals	Hospitals for diagnosis and treatment of older persons; stay from days to several months
Gerontopsychiatric hospitals	Hospitals for older psychiatric patients; stay from days to several months

Source: Altersfragen, 1979, pp. 251–253.

tions, often with more than 200 residents, whereas the other homes for the aged are far smaller, with, ideally, 45 residents (Frey and Schneider, 1988).

As shown in Table 28.3, 7.5% of the persons over 65 years of age are living in institutions, 4.8% are in homes for the aged, and 2.0% are in hospitals (from Bundesamt für Wohnungswesen, 1985, p. 117).

For those over 80 years, the portion is 20.1% in institutions, 14.2% in homes for the aged, and 5.1% in hospitals. In planning, the communities or cantons intend to guarantee 6% to 8% of the older population a place in a home for the aged. For about 2% more, the plans provide a nursing bed. The tendency is to reduce the places in homes for the aged and to increase the Spitex services.

For acute illness, the aged use the hospitals. Numbers from the canton Berne (Gesundheits-und Fürsorgedirektion, 1990) indicate that about 50% of beds in

Table 28.3
Housing for the Aged in Switzerland

Living Conditions	65 years and older (%)	80 years and older (%)
Private households	92.5	79.9
Collective households	7.5	20.1
Homes for the aged	4.8	14.2
Hospitals	2.0	5.1

hospitals are used by persons over 65 years. Psychiatrically ill elderly live either at home, in homes for the aged, in nursing homes, or in psychiatric hospitals.

Recently developed are "decentralized nursing stations," in six- to eight-room flats, where five to seven residents are cared for around the clock (Meister, 1992). They offer the advantages of a family-like atmosphere, a short distance from the former living area, and low investment costs. According to an evaluation study, these institutions are well accepted by old persons and by the staff.

HOUSING RESOURCES

Ninety-two percent of the older population live in private households. The married, compared with the unmarried and divorced, are found more often in such a setting. Older persons more often own their residence (38% compared with 30% of all households—Bundesamt für Wohnungswesen, 1985, p. 126). Yet the living comfort of the elderly is slightly inferior to that of younger households (Bundesamt für Wohnungswesen, 1985, p. 136). Of those who do not own their residences, rent represents a remarkable portion of the income: 32% of the elderly have to pay more than one-fourth of their income for their habitation, when the household comprises more than one person. For one-person households this high burden exists for 51% (Bundesamt für Wohnungswesen, 1985, p. 144).

The portion of older people in cities is significantly higher than in rural areas. As examples, the towns of Zurich and Basel had (in 1980) 19.8% and 19.9% inhabitants over 65, whereas in that year the overall portion for Switzerland was 13.9 percent. Thus, elderly in urban regions, with many new buildings, may have difficulty finding friends of their age in the environment.

Emerging Living Systems

There has been much discussion in print and at conferences about the best way to live for the single and the widowed elderly. Real experimentations are very limited, however.

Living communities for the elderly (Senioren-Wohngemeinschaften) are comfortable, one-family houses rented to groups of older persons in some towns. Despite great publicity, this form is not yet frequently used. The difficulties consist of finding groups who want to live together, resolving conflicts, and growing old and frail together.

Another new form of living is age-mixed apartments. In one big complex where an investigation was carried out (Wehrli-Schindler, 1989), about one-third of the apartments are for elderly residents, and rooms for common activities are available. In comparison to another building of the same owner, the residents were a little more integrated and satisfied.

When we turn to collective living, there are pilot projects of old-age homes organized in several groups of 12 to 20 residents, each with high autonomy, and old-age homes with many support functions for independently living older persons which integrates the home in the community.

SUPPORTIVE SERVICES

The foundation Pro Senectute offers nationwide services with the aim of helping the aged live their lives as independently as possible. (Some of these services were already mentioned as part of the Spitex services.) As Pro Senectute has, in every canton, its own organization with steering committee and local representatives, the services are especially applied to local needs.

Among special services offered are consultation in all questions concerning aging and being old, meals-on-wheels, homemaker services, home care, visiting programs, adult education, support in founding self-help groups, financial assistance, and celebrating anniversaries. In addition, there are training of experts and lobbying in federal and cantonal political institutions.

The Swiss Red Cross is also active in training housewives for working in Spitex and in old-age home services. Besides, many organizations (churches, enterprises, universities, charity groups, welfare services of the communities, and so on) support the elderly. In Winterthur, a town of 90,000 inhabitants, about 120 organizations are concerned for the aged.

LEISURE-TIME RESOURCES

Organizations for Self-Help

The elderly have always taken care of their own fate, individually and without specific organizations. In contrast to the present situation, such self-help in the past was directed at ameliorating one's own circumstances and not the situation of the elderly in general.

The creation of a group of older persons in order to stand up for the fate of all older persons in the town, canton, or federation began in 1949. It was then that the Union of the Old, the Invalid, the Widows and Orphans (AVIVO—Association suisse des Vieillards, Invalides, Veuves et Orphelins) was founded in Geneva to defend the material and spiritual interests of all old persons (and of the other groups mentioned in its name) in Switzerland. This organization presently has about 37,000 members and demands the elimination of several disadvantages of the pension system; additionally, it cultivates the social life of local groups.

Most of the other self-help organizations for the elderly were founded after 1970, like the Swiss Association of Pensioners (Schweizerischer Rentnerverband) with about 15,000 members. Its activities consist mainly of appealing to the parliaments or to individual politicians. Gray Panther movements were founded in several cantons with the aim of influencing the legislation and accomplishing individual help on the local level. Currently, the regional Gray Panthers have not yet organized into a national organization. There is also a union for pensioners (Rentnergewerkschaft) with several aims of ameliorating the standard of living of disadvantaged old persons. Efforts to be politically active, as members of cantonal parliaments, have not yet been successful, because the political groups of older persons have not yet obtained the necessary votes.

Besides these organizations with political intentions, many local self-help organizations have the goal of direct support to elderly in need (who are sometimes connected with social institutions), including Elderly for the Elderly (Senioren für Senioren), with employment agencies, shopping, visiting, and other services; clubs for the elderly that organize social gatherings; secondhand shops, which give their considerable profit to social organizations for the aged (Forschungsgruppe Gerontologie and Pro Senectute, 1988; Forschungsgruppe Gerontologie, 1987).

In 1989 several self-help organizations for the elderly formed a national association to better influence political and social life according to the interests of the aged: the VASOS (Vereinigung Aktiver Senioren- und Selbsthilfe-Organisationen der Schweiz—Pro Senectute, 1989).

Leisure-Time Services

Several studies on local or cantonal levels aimed at describing the living conditions of the elderly and their major conditions (see Höpflinger and Stuckelberger, 1992, pp. 60-62). The results indicate that the elderly use the media very often (about 55% to 85% use journals, television, periodicals, radio), often work in their household and like to take a walk (about 50% to 60%), and often attend religious services (about 45% to 50%). On the other hand, activities characterized by an important social component, such as visiting or being visited, helping other persons, and traveling, are less frequent (about 25% to 40%), as is reading books. Participating in associations, sports, working at home or for pay, and visiting restaurants are other forms of activities that are rather seldom utilized (about 10% to 20%). What the elderly do least is visit educational programs (about 6%). Another study showed that activities outside the home are more valued and satisfying than activities in the home.

There are so many possibilities for the elderly to spend their leisure time outside their home that only some will be mentioned. First of all, Switzerland has very many associations with different objectives that are open to older members. Though they are used by a large number of elderly, one must not forget that—especially for males—with increasing age, the number of associations one belongs to gets smaller. Two nationwide organizations (Intersport and Sport und Alter) offer opportunities for sports for the elderly. Their success demonstrates that it is possible to interest elderly in sports, even those who never thought of such activities in middle adulthood.

Churches offer social activities for their elderly, in addition to worship. There are, everywhere, possibilities to do voluntary work in homes for the aged or in Spitex services, but these activities are only seldom organized to develop the capabilities of aged workers.

Elderly Education

Most organized activities for the elderly have educational intentions. Towns have centers for the aged that offer lectures; discussion meetings; and courses in handicrafts, drawing, sewing, foreign languages, and other skills. At Winterthur, the Winterthur Assurances have established such a center. The Migros—the leading retail enterprise in Switzerland—offers adult education courses for the elderly in its school, as well as memory training courses (Stelle für Altersfragen, 1988).

The Popular Universities and other institutions of adult education not only accept older participants but offer courses on topics of special interest to them. All eight universities in Switzerland established universities for the elderly (Seniorenuniversitäten), after the first attempt in Geneva in 1975 proved to be very successful. The success persists. Lectures attract 500 participants and more. In most universities, however, there are only big lectures (with the possibility of posing questions at the end); seminars are installed only in some universities in the French-speaking part of Switzerland. Special training leading to new professional activities has not yet been established at the universities.

Preparation for retirement or for old age is another aim in Switzerland. According to yearly inquiries by Pro Senectute, there are about 350 organized courses with that aim each year. Most of the organizers are firms that try to prepare their aging employees, together with their spouses, during working hours. Other organizations active in this field are institutions for adult education and churches.

ADVOCACY AND PROTECTION

When older persons have difficulties, they may use the resources available for persons of all ages: lawyers, psychologists, or other consulting professions. For those who cannot afford such services, the communal welfare offices have social workers who may consult and help any elderly to satisfactorily resolve a problem. In addition, Pro Senectute, with about 85 consulting offices in Switzerland, offers the same service.

Other situations of concern in some countries (such as help when an older person is victim of a crime or when abuse of an elderly person occurs) are not met in Switzerland with special services. First, there exists a self-help organization, White Circle (Weisser Kreis), for persons of all ages; second, the usual legal steps would have to be undertaken. Some of the Gray Panther groups are available to assist older persons with special problems.

FUTURE PROJECTIONS

The population rate of the elderly will grow considerably in the future. Estimations go so far as to expect more than 21% to be over 65 and 5% to be over 80 in the year 2025. Since one-person households and families with very few children will increase, families will be less apt to help their aging members. Therefore, more needs will have to be met by public organizations after the year 2000.

Currently, in some parts of the country, it is difficult to find personnel to care for the elderly. Many of the caring personnel come from foreign countries: Spain, Croatia, Serbia, Turkey, and the Philippines. Some organizations have created a new job (Altenpfleger—carer of the old) needing less training than nurses. This job aims at housewives whose children have left the household. Another possibility is for young men who do not want to serve in the Swiss army but will, instead, do civil service to help people in need (such as the old).

When the portion of the very old further increases, after the year 2000, there will be very great difficulties to find the necessary personnel. One can speak of a state of emergency in the care of the elderly for the future. It may be that the solutions that will have to be worked out will considerably burden the younger generations.

The growing portion of the aged people in the whole population will be expensive, since they do not work, they pay small taxes, and they need highly priced health services. When this burden leads to more taxes and to higher contributions for the social and health assurances of the working population, social conflicts may arise. Sometimes the term *war between generations* has been used to describe possible future confrontations. If one wants to prevent such a development, new forms of conflict resolution must be accepted in the Swiss culture.

The old in the year 2020 will not be comparable to the old of today because they will be far more socialized to a high standard of living and profit from the rights of every citizen, so that they will not accept the poorer living conditions of the past. On the other hand, the "new old" will be better educated, more competent, healthier, more self-sufficient, and (perhaps) better prepared for their age. These new old will not need much help because they will be sufficiently integrated and competent to find their own solutions. One must expect other older persons, however, to be more dependent on social and health services. They will need official assistance, either by the communities or by private organizations.

In the past, many disabled died relatively early in life. As an example, one did not meet any gray-haired person with Down's syndrome; currently, these and other handicapped persons live longer. They get old, and the maintenance of these older handicapped persons is not yet discussed. Whether the handicapped elderly and normal persons who grow dependent in their old age should be cared for in the same or in different institutions also needs to be considered.

Currently, according to estimations, only one of five (or even of six) dependent old persons is cared for in or by institutions. Four to five of these old are nursed by their daughters, daughters-in-law, or other persons at home.

The diminishing number of children, the rising divorce rate, the growing working activities of females in positions of high responsibility, the growing geographical mobility, and other factors will certainly mean that families will be less likely to provide care for their elderly. If only 30% of those elderly cared for by relatives should need public help, a doubling of personnel would be necessary. One way out of this challenge might be the development of a feeling of responsibility not only for one's own family members but for people who live in the neighborhood.

Life of the elderly in Switzerland is easier than in many other countries. Financial means, supporting services, and activities for older people are available. These facts must not cover the fate of those 10% to 20% of the elderly in Switzerland who experience great difficulties. The mutual exchange by nations and cultures of ideas about how to ameliorate the problems of the aging process and methods of intervention may help all who are concerned with this interesting and challenging part of the population.

BIBLIOGRAPHY

Bundesamt für Sozialversicherung (ed.). *Die Altersfragen in der Schweiz.* Bern: Eidgenössische Druck- und Materialzentrale, 1979.

Bundesamt für Statistik (ed.). *Statistisches Jahrbuch der Schweiz 1992.* Zurich: Neue Zürcher Zeitung, 1991.

Bundesamt für Wohnungswesen (ed.). *Wohnen in der Schweiz.* Bern: Eidgenössische Druck- und Materialzentrale, 1985.

Enderle, G. *Sicherung des Existenzminimums im nationalen und internationalen Kontext.* Bern: Haupt, 1987.

Eschmann, P., Kocher, G., and Spescha, E. (eds.). *Ambulante Krankenpflege. Spitex-Handbuch.* Bern: Huber, 1990.

Forschungsgruppe Gerontologie (ed.). Selbsthilfegruppen der Senioren in der Schweiz. Forschungsgruppe Gerontologie: Freiburg/Switzerland, Report, 1987.

Forschungsgruppe Gerontologie. (Pro Senectute) (eds.). Selbsthilfeorganisationen in der Schweiz. Forschungsgruppe Gerontologie: Freiburg/Switzerland, Report, 1988.

Frey, W., and Schneider, H.-D. Was tun die Leiter von Alters- und Pflegeheimen? Forschungsgruppe Gerontologie: Freiburg/Switzerland, Report, 1988.

Gesundheits- und Fürsorgedirektion (ed.). Bern: Alterspolitik 2005. Gesundheitsfursorgedirektion: Bern: 1990.

Gilliand, P. *Rentiers AVS, une autre image de la Suisse.* Lausanne: Editions Sociales, 1983.

Höpflinger, F., and Stuckelberger, A. *Alter und Altersforschung in der Schweiz.* Zürich: Seismo, 1992.

Lüthi, A. *Die wirtschaftliche Ungleichheit im Rentenalter in der Schweiz.* Freiburg: Universitätsverlag, 1983.

Mäder, U., Biedermann, F., Fischer, B., and Schmassmann, H. *Armut im Kanton Basel-Stadt.* Basel: Social Strategies, 1991.

Mathe, H. L'âge des mutations. In O. Blanc and P. Gilliand (eds.), *Suisse 2000. Enjeux démographiques.* Lausanne: Réalités sociales, 1991, 71–87.

Meister, P. *Dezentrale Pflegestationen.* Zürich: Pro Senectute, 1992.

Messmer, B. Probleme des Alterwerdens in früherer Zeit. In H. Ringeling and M. Svilar (eds.), *Alter und Gesellschaft.* Bern: Haupt, 1990, 49–61.

Müller, S. *Schweizerische Sozialpolitik.* Bern: Lang, 1984.

Pro Senectute (ed.). 3. Selbsthilfe-Tagung der Senioren in der Schweiz (mimeographed). Bern, 1989.

Schweizer, W. *Die wirtschaftliche Lage der Rentner in der Schweiz.* Bern: Haupt, 1980.

Segalman, R. *The Swiss Way of Welfare.* New York: Praeger, 1986.

Stelle für Altersfragen (ed.). *Gedächtnistraining.* Rüschlikon: Gottlieb Duttweiler Institut, 1988.

Wehrli-Schindler, B. Überbauung Unteres Bühl (mimeographed). Winterthur, 1989.

THAILAND

*Malinee Wongsith and
Chanpen Saengtienchai*

INTRODUCTION

The Role of the Elderly

In Thai society, old age begins at 60 years. Age is still computed in 12-year (animal year) cycles, with the 60th birthday marking the completion of the fifth cycle and the beginning of the sixth (Chayovan, Knodel, and Siriboon, 1990, p. 3). After reaching this age, a person is addressed by younger persons with special terms of respect, the equivalent of the kinship terms *grandfather* or *grandmother,* even though the speaker may not be related to the older person in any way by kinship. In addition, 60 is the age of compulsory retirement in the civil service.

Thailand is currently experiencing a major decline in fertility, as seen by the recent proportionate reduction of very young persons and the increase in older ages. The number and proportion of older people (aged 60 years and over) in Thailand have grown steadily from about 1.2 million (4.6% of the total population) in 1960, to 1.7 million (4.9%) in 1970, to 2.4 million (5.5%) in 1980, and to 3.9 million (7.3%) in 1990. With substantial growth in the absolute number of the elderly, it is projected that the number of the elderly will increase to 9.9 million (14.1%) in 2020 (United Nations, 1993, p. 642). With the prospect of further declines in fertility and increasing life expectancy, it is to be expected that the future will witness even further aging of the population.

In view of age and sex structure, there are more Thai elderly women than elderly men, because female mortality continues to be lower than male mortality throughout older ages. It is believed that through socioeconomic development over the past two decades, longer life expectancy has improved, especially for females. However, increases of life expectancy at older ages do not guarantee better health for those who are living longer. Only a small proportion of Thai elderly consider themselves healthy and the proportion of those claiming good health decreases with age (Chayovan, Wongsith, and Saengtienchai, 1988, pp. 86–87).

The large majority of the elderly population in Thailand live in rural areas. The living arrangements of the elderly in the urban and rural areas are very similar. Old people are more likely to live in a three-person or larger household. The family has major responsibility for support and care of the elderly. They are looked after by their children, and at least one child coresides with them (Knodel, Havanon, and Pramualratana, 1984, pp. 297–328). Overall, elderly men are less likely to live alone than women but are more likely to live in collective households (primarily, temples). Only a small proportion of the elderly live alone. However, almost no married persons live alone, even though data from various sources show that very few elderly of either sex have never been married. There are more widowed women than men at older ages.

Regarding socioeconomic characteristics of Thai elderly, the results of the 1980 census indicate that the majority of women aged 60 and over and the majority of men aged 75 and over are illiterate. Only a minority of elderly Thai men and very small percentage of elderly women have primary education (Knodel, Chayovan, and Siriboon, 1990, p. 29).

The majority of the Thai population are engaged in agriculture, as well as in the informal sector. The official retirement age of 60 does not affect those who work in agriculture. Thai elderly continue to work as long as they are physically able. Based on the Labor Force Surveys conducted by the National Statistical Office (1981) from 1975 to 1980, the labor force participation rate during the agricultural season averaged 57% and 29% for elderly men and elderly women, respectively.

Traditionally, older members are well integrated and continue to play somewhat active roles in the economic and social life of their families. From generation to generation, the young are taught from a very early age to have respect for the old. Thais are taught both gestures and rituals that are appropriate to persons of different ages. Respect for one's elders is maintained throughout one's life. Within the family, the welfare of each individual member is always the primary concern of the family. The younger respect and support the elderly, as well as provide for their physical and psychological needs. On the other hand, the elderly serve as the cornerstone of the family. By virtue of old age, they are revered by the younger for their wisdom and resourceful experience. Thus, the family has major responsibility for support and care for the elderly until the end of their lives.

The Formal Structure of Care of the Elderly

The Thai government has, for a long time, realized the problems concerning the elderly. Accordingly, supportive programs for the aged have been carried out by various government agencies.

Public Welfare Programs

Homes for the Aged. The first public welfare institution in Thailand is Bangkae Home for the Aged, established in 1953 under the responsibility of the Department of Social Services, Ministry of Interior, with the main purpose of rendering residential care to needy persons who meet the requirements of being over 60 years of age for females and over 65 years for males, who are homeless, and who have no relatives to live with or who are not able to live happily with their own families. Three categories of programs are offered free of charge or for a fee for those who can afford hostels, private homes, and holiday homes. The services that have been provided to the residents are lodging and food, clothing, personal living effects, religious rites, medical services, physical exercise and therapeutic activities for physical rehabilitation, recreational activities, traditional festival activities, social work services, and traditional funeral services. Hobbies and vocational therapeutic activities are arranged, such as embroidery and handicrafts.

Elderly Social Services Centers. In addition to residential care for needy elderly persons, the Department of Public Welfare established the first Elderly Social Service Center in 1979 in the Compound of Bangkae Home for the Aged. The nine centers now functioning provide services to both males and females over 60 years who live in nearby areas, including the heads of households who shoulder the burden of having elderly in their responsibility. Services provided in these centers are therapeutic and rehabilitative care, recreation, day care, family assistance, and counseling, including an opportunity for social and community participation for nonresidents of the homes for the aged. Parallel to the service centers, home visits are made in the surrounding communities in order to give advice and primary medical treatment to elderly persons. The Elderly Social Service Centers have aided in promoting health conditions for the elderly in general and preventing and rehabilitating infirmity.

The government plan is to establish more Elderly Social Service Centers in various provincial areas in the future. The activities in these centers should enable the elderly to remain with, and be taken care of by, their families, thus reducing the need for additional homes for the aged.

Social Center for the Aged. In order to expand the coverage of services for the aged, the Department of Social Service has set up a Social Center for the Aged at Dindang in Bangkok. This center focuses its activities on various services, especially on educating the aged and providing social activities for them. The center also serves as a temporary home for the aged in time of urgent need.

Nonformal education programs. It is well known that education plays a very important role in keeping elderly persons alert and aware of the outside world and helps them to continue to be physically and mentally active. With this in mind, nonformal education projects have been initiated, including vocational interest groups, education through mass media, village reading centers, and audiovisual education, through the Department of Nonformal Education, Ministry of Education. Nonformal education is used not only to keep people abreast of current events and to promote understanding of, and preparation for, old age but to engage in appropriate activities and projects to keep them physically, intellectually, and mentally active.

Health Care. In view of the problems facing the aged due to deterioration of health, the Thai government included a program for prevention and cure of illness and provision of therapy for the aged as a part of the Fourth Five-Year Plan (1977–81). It was recognized that the demand for health care services increases with the growing number of the aged, and the Ministry of Public Health set up the Advisory Committee for Planning Health Care Programs for Aging in 1979. Several programs on health care for the elderly are augmented in general hospitals throughout the country. Up to now, many hospitals have operated geriatric clinics, and the rest are encouraged to render special care for the elderly. Moreover, the Ministry of Public Health has integrated preventive and curative services for the aged into the primary health care program.

Apart from these, in 1980 a Special Geriatric Health Service Program was initiated. Its main activities include training of personnel in health care for the elderly and widening public knowledge in this field through the mass media. One year later, a National Committee on Coordination of Health Care for the Elderly was formed as a planning and coordinating body.

In recognition of the emerging problems of an increasing elderly population and the importance of proper planning for the future, the government set up the National Committee on the Elderly of Thailand in 1982. Seven subcommittees were appointed to consider the various aspects of the aging.

Private Programs

It is well recognized that active participation of the private sector is an important element in the achievement of overall development. In the field of aging, as in other welfare and development fields, the private sector has played an active role through clubs, foundations, and associations, which offer services for the aged through various kinds of activities. Unfortunately, there are no complete records of such organizations, which operate on a voluntary basis.

Foundations for the Aged. Various foundations offer care for elderly persons. The most widely known is the Wai Wattana Nivas Foundation, which provides housing and services for homeless males over 60 years old. At present, under the responsibility of this foundation, there are about 500 elderly persons, most of whom are Chinese and almost half of whom are in poor health. The welfare services of this foundation include housing and food, physical and mental rehabilitation, vocational therapy, and so on. Other foundations that provide similar services are the Taranukraw Foundation and St. Louis Foundation. Their main activities focus on humanitarian and developmental aspects of the aging. Some private hospitals in Bangkok and the provinces provide free health care for the aged who are poverty-stricken.

Senior Citizen Clubs. Over 100 Senior Citizen Clubs have been established in 72 provinces in Thailand. Each club has its own activities, primarily concerned with health, religion, and recreation. There are also associations formed by elderly persons retired from the same organization or the same profession, such as the Retired Interior Officials Association and the Retired Militarian Association. These associations carry out activities similar to Senior Citizen Clubs.

In addition to the above organizations, welfare services can be found in private business. Some private firms have retirement and pension policies, while others do not. The range and coverage of services vary from one organization to another. The personnel of state enterprises and large-scale private firms are entitled to receive welfare services, while those elderly who are self-employed or work with small-scale establishments usually have to rely on their families.

All aspects of social and health services provided for the aged in Thailand are limited in coverage. The level of services for the aged is insufficient, and only a very small proportion of the elderly have used those services. For example, in 1990 the total number of persons aged 60 years and over was 3.9 million, while the government's homes for the aged could provide for only a little more than 1,000 persons. In addition, the criterion for acceptance to a home for the aged is a minimum 65 years for men and 60 years for women. This criterion contradicts the demographic fact that Thai females live longer than males. Men may not live long enough to qualify for the services. On top of that, most of the homes and centers for the aged are located in urban areas, while the majority of the elderly people live in rural areas.

In addition, the services provided by the government and the private sector have focused mainly on physical health care for the elderly. Needed are not only appropriate preventive and curative care and rehabilitative health services but also strengthening and maintaining the social values associated with care of the aged by their children.

INCOME MAINTENANCE AND EMPLOYMENT

Data from various sources indicate that a large number of the elderly had financial problems, even though about half of the elderly are supported by their children (Chayovan, Wongsith, and Saengtienchai, 1988; Chulalongkorn University, 1982, 1985; Kiranandana, 1985; Fry, 1980). Therefore, it is of interest to examine the old-age pension plan available in Thailand, which can be classified into three groups according to the categories of recipients of the benefits (Kiranandana, Wongboonsin, and Kiranandana, 1989, pp. 340–344).

Government Employees

Government employees receive benefits in the form of a lifetime pension or a lump-sum payment upon retirement. The compulsory retirement age is 60 years, but early retirement can be taken after age 50 or 25 years in service. Those who hold government jobs for 10 continuous years or longer are eligible to receive a lump-sum payment. Those who work for 25 years or longer can choose either a lump sum or monthly payments. The amount of the lump-sum benefit is calculated by multiplying the final monthly salary by the number of years in service. For those qualified for a pension, monthly benefits are equal to 2% of the final monthly salary multiplied by the number of years in services.

State Enterprise Employees

State enterprises contribute fixed percentages of the monthly total salary paid to the pension fund, and benefits are paid to the employees upon retirement in a lump-sum payment. The retirement age and early retirement are allowed in the same manner as for government employees, as well as lump-sum benefit calculation.

Private Enterprise Employees

Most of the pension plans for private enterprise employees are operated in the form of provident funds with contributions from both employers and employees. The Royal Decree on Provident Funds was issued in 1983 and became effective on 1 January 1984. Under this law, each employee contributes not less than 3% of the wage or salary earned, while the employer's contributions (taken as expenditure in the account period) should not exceed 15% of the wage or salary paid during that period. Benefits are paid to employees according to the terms specified in each employer's provident fund. However, only the large private enterprises are known to provide old-age or retirement benefits to their employees.

Only those who have worked with the government, state enterprises, or big, private enterprises are covered under existing pension plans. Besides those, a large number of Thai elderly have to rely on their own effort for economic security. Those who are engaged in agriculture or are self-employed and the able-bodied elderly can continue to work, on at least a part-time basis. For those who have access to a pension, income from the public or private enterprises seems to be rather unrealistic. Many are in need of financial aid. Unfortunately, there are no programs available on financial assistance, job training, reemployment services, or economic benefit programs. In addition, employment opportunities for the elderly are very limited. The elderly have to turn to their family for assistance, the major form of old-age security for Thai elderly. Thus, in 1993 the government set up a program on Welfare Promotion Funds for the Elderly and Family in the Community.

HEALTH CARE SERVICES

General Health Care System

The extent and use of health services are important indicators of the health care system. Although the care of those in ill health depends, in part, on how serious the ailment is, it is of interest to consider how people cope with their health problems and how health care services are provided to people.

The availability of government health centers in all subdistricts is the primary health service for the general population in rural areas. This is due to the improvement of public health services, under the Fifth National Plan (1980–84), and the increase and distribution of community hospitals and health centers at district and subdistrict levels. The services at health centers are based on a referral system for transferring patients from lower-level to higher-level service units. In practice, minor cases will be treated at local health centers and community hospitals, while serious cases requiring high-technology treatment will be transferred to urban hospitals and large medical centers. However, government health centers are least used in urban places, where other types of service, such as hospitals and private clinics, are much more available. Pharmacies and traditional medicine are other sources of health services, which are more often used in rural than in urban areas.

In view of the use of health services among Thai people, common places where the ill receive health services are hospitals, health centers, and private clinics. However, quite a number of people seek the services of pharmacies and traditional medicines. Use of pharmacies is a very common practice, even though it is inappropriate for diagnosis and prescription for medication. Generally, hospitals (or any type of service from doctors) are most common, particularly for urban people. Pharmacies and traditional medicine are second in popularity.

Like other, younger generations, the elderly tend to use government hospitals for health services, although a number of them prefer other sources. However, ill elderly, in some cases, may not use any service at all. This could be due to lack of knowledge and understanding that better health is possible, to difficulties in access to health service facilities, or to problems of affording the cost.

Financial support in public health services still depends on the government, with some help from other agencies. In general, a budget is allocated to health service tasks at all levels, in Bangkok and other regions, within and outside municipal areas. Services for low-income people, patients who need counseling, and drug addicts are included in the allocation. In 1990 and 1991, 4.8% and 5.3%, respectively, of the whole country budget was allocated to the Ministry of Public Health.

Even though health services are improving in coverage and availability, accessibility of health services is still a problem. A number of people, particularly in rural areas, do not receive adequate health care services. Public health services need to be more concentrated. The health card program in rural areas should be expanded to reach more people in more rural areas.[1] The quality and efficiency of medical care services in community hospitals and health centers should be improved.

Availability of Health Care Resources

Expansion of public health services has not been successful in coverage and availability. Most services are dispersed only through Bangkok and other urban places, while people in remote areas still have difficulties in accessing the services. Capability in providing health services facilities is shown in the following: in 1992, Thailand had 73 provinces and 704 districts, but only 15 regional hospitals, 74 general hospitals, 512 community hospitals, four medical and health centers, 7,460 health centers, and 403 community health centers (Thai Population Information Center, 1990).

The increase in number of beds in hospitals and other medical establishments can be seen from the fact that the ratio between population and beds for general service at the country level decreased from 1:793 in 1982 to 1:744 in 1985. However, the gap between Bangkok and other provinces is still large, as the ratio between population and beds for general services in Bangkok is 1:35, and that in other provinces is 1:862 (Thai Population Information Center, 1990).

Although the government has a policy to increase medical and health personnel, in order to reduce the ratio between population and health personnel, the increased number of personnel has not been sufficient. Particularly, health personnel in rural areas are not appropriately distributed. In 1985 and 1986, the ratio between medical doctors and population at the country level was 1:6,333 and 1:5,595, respectively. Similarly, the ratio between population and other types of personnel, such as dentist and nurse, is even lower when compared with that of developed countries (Department of Medical Services, 1990).

Use of Geriatric Clinics

Research findings indicate that medical treatment and health care are the basic needs of the elderly. In order to serve the needs of the aged, the Department of Medical Services in the Ministry of Public Health and related organizations from both government and private sectors have yearly campaigned for the expansion of geriatric clinics in general hospitals all over the country (Department of Medical Services, 1990).

According to the survey of health care programs for the elderly in all general hospitals conducted by the Department of Medical Services (1990), 225 hospitals operate geriatric clinics at least one to two times a week, some of them on a daily basis. Overall, about one-half of geriatric clinics are in community hospitals at the district level, and 62 of them are located in provincial and general hospitals. In Bangkok, only 12 hospitals and health service centers of Bangkok Metropolis Administration have geriatric clinics. Nine private hospitals have participated in the provision of special clinics for the elderly (Committee of Welfare for the Elderly and Social Development, 1991).

However, all health service centers, with or without geriatric clinics, have to serve elderly patients at least once a week. Treatments and services at hospitals or other health service centers that are provided to aged patients are similar to what other patients receive on the basis of free service or partly free service (depending on each case). Although it is a policy of the government to provide free service to the elderly, particularly to those who are homeless, disabled, or low-income, the elderly themselves still have to cope with costs of medical care. In general, the expense for inpatient care is higher than for outpatient care, because of the length of hospitalization.

In order to access the geriatric health services, the elderly in Bangkok are able to ask for services at the nearest hospital or health service center under the auspices of the Ministry of Public Health. In rural areas, however, one has to go to a health center in one's own subdistrict.

Health Services to the Elderly's Dwelling

The Department of Public Welfare has arranged a mobile unit to undertake home visits in the surrounding communities of the Elderly Social Service Center, in order to give advice and primary medical treatment to the elderly. Occasionally, some private organizations arrange mobile units or home visits on the same basis of health care services to the aged.

Health Services Within the Community

Besides health services provided through institutions, a strategy for solving health problems for the elderly is to encourage them to have social activities in their community. The Senior Citizen Club has been set up for this purpose in order to provide opportunities for the aged to participate in social, economic, health, hobbies, and promotion activities. As a result, the Senior Citizen Club indirectly provides knowledge of physical and mental health care to members in the form of lectures, meetings, and discussions. Meanwhile, participation in the club gives the elderly active and meaningful leisure time. Expansion of the elderly clubs is needed in order to increase the quality of the lives of elderly persons and to teach them knowledge of primary health care and treatment. An advantage of the elderly club is that the members will be able to help themselves, as well as other older persons within their community, in the matter of health care service.

HOUSING RESOURCES

Overall Policy and Program

Although support and care for the elderly are mainly provided by the family system, public policies and programs for the elderly have long been the government's concern, as seen in the five-year National Economic and Social Development Plans, from the first plan, starting in 1961, through the present seventh plan. Generally, emphases have been placed on welfare and health of the elderly population. Nevertheless, welfare programs for the elderly are still limited in coverage.

Regarding housing resources as a part of welfare programs, the government has realized a need to establish welfare institutions for the elderly since 1953, by operating the first Home for the Aged, Bangkae Home, in Bangkok. Eleven similar homes were subsequently set up in other parts of the country, and in 1992 there were 12 government Homes for the Aged throughout the country. The total number of elderly persons who receive residential care is 1,695, of whom 542 are male and 1,153 female.

As a result of an attempt of the government to encourage and promote the participation of the private sector in social services for the elderly, a number of private social organizations offer services for the elderly through various kinds of activities, including the provision of Homes for the Aged. By 1992 about 150 private organizations had been set up in the form of foundations, charities, and clubs to provide activities with a focus on humanitarian and developmental aspects of aging; however, only 19 of them operate housing services. The total number of elderly who receive residential care in these 19 homes (7 homes in Bangkok and 12 homes in other provinces) is approximately 1,500.

In order to cope with the residential problems of needy elderly persons, the government has formulated a five-year plan (covering 1992–96), entitled Housing Program for the Elderly, under the responsibility of the Department of Public Welfare, Ministry of Interior. The main objective of the five-year plan is to expand the housing services to the elderly at all income levels, in both urban and rural areas. By this plan, appropriate and convenient residences will be provided to the elderly who are homeless or who are not able to help themselves because of illness. Five types of institutional residences will be in operation to serve the elderly: nursing homes, homes for the aged, emergency homes for the aged, dormitories, and private homes. It is expected that 2,500 old people will be helped each year under the program.

The Department of Public Welfare is responsible for data on the housing needs of the elderly and cooperates with related government agencies, such as the Board of Housing Authority and Bangkok Metropolis Administration. Participation of private sectors in operating housing services for the elderly is encouraged. The department is the base of guidance and planning and consults with any organization that plans to establish residential services for the elderly. Financial support for programs will be drawn from the annual government budget, private organizations, and, occasionally, fund-raising activities.

Old-Age Community

To correspond with government policy for expanding housing services for the elderly, the Department of Welfare had set up an old-age community called Golden Age Village Program in 1991. The community is located in Chiang Mai province in the north of Thailand. The program aims to give a pleasurable housing environment, as well as convenience for the elderly to be able to live peacefully among those of the same age within the same community. Houses in the village are grouped in several clusters and in different designs and are surrounded by gardens, recreation areas, and a common building and religious hall.

The program seeks to be an ideal housing program; yet, on a private house basis, participation in the program is limited to only a small number of elderly persons who are financially able to own houses built in the village and conforming to the house designs of the Department of Public Welfare.

The private sector generally has limitations in its contribution to social services for the elderly. Some profit organizations have established communities for old age in Bangkok. Again, these programs serve a small number of elderly who can afford the cost.

Other Services

Community services that allow the elderly to remain in their own home are not formally set up. In reality, neighbors can assist the elderly who are in need of help in various everyday activities (such as preparing meals, visits, and home repair). Help and assistance from neighbors in urban areas seem to be less commonly found than in rural areas.

Other help for the elderly, like financial assistance, tax benefits, and other economic programs, are not available to maintain independent living in one's own dwelling.

SUPPORTIVE SERVICES

Besides residential care in an institution, other services outside the home (such as rehabilitative care, recreation, day care, counseling, and mobile units) are mainly provided by the government through nine Elderly Social Services Centers under the auspices of the Department of Public Welfare. These resources help the elderly develop their full capacities in personal and social relationships and also maintain a quality of independent living according to their own ability.

In the private sector, although services for the elderly are carried out by a number of foundations, charities, and clubs, assistance for the aged (in terms of day care and day hospital) is usually sponsored by profit organizations, such as private hospitals and nursing homes. Only the well-off elderly can seek these services, whereas the poor have to depend on the family system or government and nonprofit organizations.

In the event that the elderly need help, individuals can directly search for information on services for the elderly from relevant organizations, but, in fact, individuals are likely to find assistance from the Department of Public Welfare, which is responsible for all types of social services. The initial stage for seeking help and assistance is to go to either the center of help for all social problems, attached to the Department of Public Welfare in Bangkok, or the offices of public welfare in all 73 provinces.

Other forms of help for the elderly, regarding nutrition, homemaking, chores, and shopping, have not been formed.

LEISURE-TIME RESOURCES

More than any other institution, the family provides the central focus of social life for older people in Thailand. In the past, the predominant family structure was the extended family, with more than two immediate generations living together. In the extended family, the elderly could always find useful activities to carry out, such as caring for young children, cooking meals, and housekeeping, while younger family members were working outside the home. As the society gradually became less agricultural and more urbanized, the family structure also changed to the nuclear family, accommodating only the spouse and children. Several forms of in-kind assistance provided by the elderly have decreased.

Considering the activities outside the family, there are no formally organized leisure-time resources particularly available for the elderly. Most resources serve all age groups. Only senior citizen clubs organize various activities for members, such as dinners, short trips, and travel. The Thai elderly perform some functions according to their revered role as wise counselors or village leaders, are treated with respect, and remain important in decision making. Their long experience and seniority give them a significant participatory role in the community. The elderly often play ceremonial roles and are consulted on traditional issues and prominent ceremonies. For example, by tradition, only elderly persons are asked to pour lustral water over the hands of the bride and groom at a Thai wedding. Moreover, social involvement of the elderly occurs among those who have interpersonal relations derived from familiarity or common residence.

In addition, rural, rather than urban, Thai elderly spend their free time at the temple. The temple society serves as a social center for the community, offering a variety of social events and support groups that can enmesh a person in a comfortable network of acquaintances. They go (as individuals) to the temple to visit, make merit, perform religious ceremonies, and so on. These activities do not require joining a group, as Thai Buddhism emphasizes the role and responsibility of the individual. If they go to the temple with others, it is a matter of social preference or convenience, and religious participation is on an individual basis.

Regarding educational opportunities for the elderly, although the government has a policy for the lifelong education for the elderly and values formal and informal life education, little is actually done.

In brief, most Thai elderly are not members of any particular group. Their social involvement is informal, among relatives or neighbors. Recreational activities involve family members or age peers.

ADVOCACY AND PROTECTION

Advocacy groups and protective services for the elderly are not formed in Thailand. Traditionally, the family is the primary unit to take care of its members regardless of age. Whatever happens to the elderly is the task of the family, not the government or other private agencies. The government will provide care only as a last resort.

FUTURE PROJECTIONS

The future will witness further aging of the Thai population; an increase in the number and proportion of the aged. Combined with the rapid socioeconomic, technological, and cultural changes and limited number and coverage of government programs, there will undoubtedly be a serious burden for society. There is a growing concern whether the traditional family support system will continue to function effectively.

Attention should be paid to the elderly living alone and the very old elderly (persons aged 75 and over). By this age, it is unlikely that one would continue to work. As physical and mental impairments increase with age, the ability to function independently decreases, and families become more and more involved with their elderly relatives. In most cases, the family members are the major providers of health care for the elderly. The amount and type of assistance required by older people are determined by the state of their physical and mental health. However, caring for the elderly has many consequences for other family members, especially when the aged member suffers from senility, strokes, heart disease, or behavioral problems. Those who need special health care may require long periods of stay in a hospital or old-age institution. In this case, assistance from the government, both in cash and in-kind, is most needed. The government should spell out clearly its policy toward this special group so that responsible agencies will be drawn to work more efficiently for the well-being of the elderly.

With rather limited resources and no income maintenance program in existence, the elderly should be made more financially independent and be able to support themselves during old age. This is ideal for their self-esteem. The elderly population in the next decade will have to rely on their own efforts for economic security, since public or private pension plans are hardly sufficient. If older persons are aware of potential problems and prepare themselves before aging by saving and properly managing their savings, they will not have to face financial difficulties during their old age. Thus, it is the government's duty to promote public awareness of the aging problem through nonformal education and mass communications and to also endorse and supervise personal pension plans offered by authorized financial institutions (Kiranandana, 1985, p. 146).

Institutional residence is likely to be more important as an alternative home for a significant number of the aged population in the future. More homes for the aged are needed. It seems as if the government has operated only a small number of homes for the aged, while the private sector has had little or almost no participation in housing resources for the elderly. In addition, more attention should be given to the elderly who are dependent—homeless, disabled, or with low incomes.

However, as the most important fundamental unit in Thai society, the family should carry out a more supportive role. It is generally accepted that good family relationships are essential to the happiness of most elderly persons. Children should be providers of both economic and affectionate care for the elderly. The government has to assume the responsibility in facilitating the family to help the elderly, especially in terms of care for the very old.

NOTE

1. The health card program was initiated in 1983 by the Ministry of Public Health in order to provide more health care service to the people, particularly those who live in rural areas. To be covered in the program, one needs to be a member and purchase an inexpensive card for free medical care. Each card can be used for a maximum of six illness episodes a year and covers up to five persons in the same household.

BIBLIOGRAPHY

Chayovan, Napaporn, John Knodel, and Siriwan Siriboon. 1990. *Thailand's Elderly Population: A Demographic and Social Profile Based on Official Statistical Sources.* Ann Arbor: Population Studies Center, University of Michigan.
Chayovan, Napaporn, Malinee Wongsith, and Chanpen Saengtienchai. 1988. *Socioeconomic Consequences of the Ageing of the Population: Thailand.* Bangkok: Institute of Population Studies, Chulalongkorn University.
Chulalongkorn University Institute of Population Studies. 1985. *Kan Sammana Ruang Pho Sung Ayu Nai Prathed Thai.* Bangkok.
Chulalongkorn University Social Research Institute. 1982. *Khon Chara Thai.* Bangkok.
Committee of Public Health Development Plan. 1987. *Public Health Development Plan According to the Sixth National Economic and Social Development Plan (1987–1991).* Bangkok.
Committee of Welfare for the Elderly and Social Development. 1991. *Problems in Elderly and Strategies for Solution.* Bangkok.
Cowgill, Donald O. 1986. *Aging Around the World.* Belmont, CA: Wadsworth.
Department of Public Welfare. 1989. *Annual Report 1988.* Bangkok.
Department of Medical Services. 1989. *Long-Term Plan for the Elderly in Thailand (1986–2001).* Bangkok.
Department of Medical Services and World Health Organization. 1990. Second National Seminar on Health Care for the Elderly, 25–26 April, Bangkok.
Fry, Christine L. 1980. *Aging in Culture and Society: Comparative Viewpoints and Strategies.* New York: Praeger.
Kiranandana, Suchada. 1985. *Implications of Demographic Changes for Old Age Security in Thailand 1987–2021.* Bangkok: TDRI.
Kiranandana, Tienchay, Kua Wongboonsin, and Suchada Kiranandana. 1989. "Popula-

tion, Aspects of Development in Thailand: Health/Nutrition, Education and Old Age Security." In *Framework for Population and Development Integration,* Vol. 2, pp. 295–413. Bangkok: ESCAP, United Nations.

Knodel, John, Napaporn Havanon, and Anthony Pramualratana. 1984. "Fertility Transition in Thailand: A Qualitative Analysis." *Population and Development Review* 10 (June): 297–328.

National Economic and Social Development Board. 1988. *The Sixth National Economic and Social Development Plan (1987–1991).* Bangkok.

National Statistical Office. 1981. *Report of the Labor Force Survey, Whole Kingdom, July-September 1980.* Bangkok.

Thai Population Information Center. 1990. *Data Analysis on Population and Family Health.* Bangkok.

———. 1989. *Statistics of Population and Family Health.* Bangkok.

———. 1991. *Statistics of Population and Family Health,* Vol. 2. Bangkok.

United Nations. 1993. *World Population Prospects—the 1992 Revisions.* New York.

30

UNITED STATES

Abraham Monk

INTRODUCTION

Profile and Role of the Elderly

Like most industrialized and technologically advanced countries, the United States is undergoing a triple demographic revolution. First, life expectancy has gone up steadily from 46.3 years for males and 48.3 for females in 1900, to 71.9 and 77.6, respectively, in 1990, and it may yet continue this relentless ascent to an estimated 74.9 and 81.3 years, by the year 2020 (U.S. Bureau of the Census, 1989, 1991; National Center for Health Statistics, 1989). Second, the age cohort 75 to 84 years and especially the old-old cohort 85 and older are growing at a proportionally faster pace than the young old, that is, those under age 75. Lastly, there is a decline in fertility rates. Smaller families result from population control practices and incentives, coupled with aspirations for upward economic mobility among young people.

The obvious net effect of those three trends has been a substantial increase in both the number and the relative proportion of older persons within the total population. The elderly thus went from 3.3% of the population in 1900 to 6.7% in 1940 and to 11.1% in 1980. By the year 2000 they are expected to represent 12.7%. In absolute numbers the increase of the aged will be in the order of 400% between 1940 and 2000, climbing from 9,194 million to 35,276 million.

Despite the magnitude of this demographic revolution, the United States has not pioneered in the advancement of a forward-looking set of gerontological policies and programs. The first major policy breakthrough was the Social Security Act of 1935, passed in the aftermath of the worldwide depression, with the intent of assuring a floor of income for retired workers. It came about, however, decades after similar legislation was already adopted in several European countries. No other significant developments were to take place for the next 30 years until the enactment of both Medicare, a health insurance program, and Medicaid, its public assistance correlate for low-income persons not covered or unable to pay the premiums and coinsurance rates required by Medicare.

The mid-1960s proved to be a period of exceptional legislative productivity. Those were the "Great Society" years, when an activist government sought to introduce major social reforms. The Older Americans Act (OAA) of 1965 was one of its policy accomplishments, even if largely symbolic because of the limited fiscal resources allocated for its implementation. To a large extent this is the only piece of legislation in the United States exclusively targeted for the aged, given that all previously cited programs also extend their benefits to other vulnerable population categories, such as the blind and the disabled. The OAA especially signals the recognition that the federal government ought to proceed beyond its income maintenance and health insurance strategy and coordinate, as well as facilitate, the development of a wide array of community-based programs.

The creative momentum was not lost in the following decade. In the course of the 1970s, the U.S. Congress passed legislation that regulates and monitors private pensions. It also federalized public assistance and established a minimum floor of protection for all needy older persons through the Supplemental Security Income Program (SSI). The age of mandatory retirement was postponed from 65 to 70, but reference is made here to the age when a person must retire, not the age when a person could start collecting "full" benefits. The latter remained at 65.

The 1980s brought about some sporadic gains, such as the ultimate abolition of mandatory retirement in most occupational sectors. On the whole, however, the country experienced a slowdown and even a retreat from some of the policy gains of the past. This is attributed to many causes including a conservative administration in Washington that was largely adverse to embarking on new social welfare policies and the United States' losing its historical status as a creditor nation and becoming a debtor one. Because of the resulting budget deficits, the government opted for containing and even slashing the costs of many programs. It was also feared that younger generations of workers and taxpayers were no longer willing to foot the bill for the escalating costs of social insurance programs for the aged. There is no evidence, however, of such a generalized backlash in the U.S. population. Much to the contrary, survey upon survey, confirmed the prevalence of a positive disposition toward the aged and the concomitant acceptance of the fiscal responsibilities for their care and support (Harris, 1981).

The Formal Structure of Care of the Elderly

Notwithstanding the legislative accomplishments initiated in 1935, the United States lacks a unified and comprehensive policy on aging. There are, instead, about 50 major federal programs mandating the provision of services and benefits, but they have evolved incrementally and in response to specific public concerns. Funding those programs requires an increasingly larger portion of the federal budget. Thus, while 15% of the total federal outlays was spent on the aged in 1960, by 1991 these expenditures more than doubled, reaching the 31% level.

The federal government's budgetary participation is, however, dominated by social insurance programs that are contributory in nature. These funds consequently originate from prepayments made by the beneficiaries when previously employed and also by current workers. In the latter case, the funding of social insurance programs is a form of intergenerational transfer, whereby today's workers pay for those who preceded them.

In 1991, 54% of the aging-related expenditures was spent on retirement income, and an additional 26% covered the Medicare health insurance program costs. The funds for the remaining 20% were largely derived from general revenues and were spent, for the most part, on means-tested public assistance programs for needy or low-income elderly, such as Medicaid (health), SSI, subsidized housing, food stamps, low-income home energy assistance, social services to low-income persons, and so on. A smaller portion covers senior community service employment and OAA service programs.

The federal insurance programs and some public assistance programs, like SSI, have instituted uniform standards of eligibility and benefit rates for the entire country. It is different with most public assistance programs, because the federal government requires the fiscal participation of the states through their own tax levies. Furthermore, the federal government delegates both the administration and the definition of benefits and eligibility standards to each of the 50 state governments. As a consequence of this decentralized approach, there is enormous variation in benefit levels from state to state. Moreover, elderly persons often cannot obtain services or benefits for which they may be rightfully entitled, simply because these programs are too fragmented, inadequate, or simply just unavailable in their geographic immediacy. One of the main objectives of OAA is to precisely coordinate existing services and fill critical service gaps.

The Administration on Aging, a federal agency created to implement the mandate of OAA, consequently proceeded to establish offices on aging in each of the states. These offices oversee, in turn, a network of district offices called Area Agencies on Aging (AAAs). Nationally, there are about 600 such AAAs, responsible for implementing the coordinative mandate and also for facilitating access to services at the local level. The results of these planning initiatives have been, however, meager. According to an evaluative report of the General Accounting Office of the United States, service coordination can succeed only when (1) planning is done jointly by service providers and consumers; (2) services are established jointly by related state and local agencies; and (3) communities create clearly designated and visible single points of entry, or "one-stop" service centers where elderly persons can receive all services needed in one place, without having to shuttle from agency to agency, complete different forms and applications, wait for certifications of eligibility, and then wait for the actual provision of the service (U.S. General Accounting Office, 1991).

INCOME MAINTENANCE AND EMPLOYMENT

The cornerstone of income maintenance in retirement is the Social Security Act of 1935. It includes the Old Age Survivors Insurance Program (OASI), which provides monthly benefits for retired workers as well as their dependents and survivors. Age 65 is presently established as the "normal" retirement age for the collection of full benefits, but it is scheduled for postponement to age 66 in 2011 and to age 67 in 2022. Workers may opt to retire earlier, at age 62, but they will then experience a 20% lifetime loss of benefits.

Social Security is a compulsory program, and practically all working people (94%) participate through monthly deductions in their paychecks. Employers withhold 7.65% from a worker's earnings up to an income ceiling of $53,400 in 1991 and then match the same amount, for which they receive a tax credit. The maximum individual wage deduction is, consequently, $4,085 a year, but additional wages are withheld at the rate of 1.45% beyond the $53,400 limit and up to a maximum of $125,000 in earnings, as a contribution to the Medicare health insurance program (*Social Security Bulletin,* 1990).

Deductions are not fully proportional to wages, as high earners do not pay Social Security taxes for income exceeding the $53,400 limit. The OASI program has been criticized for these alleged regressive features, given that workers at the lower end of the income spectrum must (proportionally) part with a larger portion of their total income than their more affluent counterparts. The program is, however, progressive as far as its benefits are concerned. Thus, in 1990, the monthly checks for former low wage earners amounted to 58% of their average best preretirement wages. For higher earners the replacement rate declined to less than half: 24.5%.

On the whole, Social Security benefits return slightly over 40% of average preretirement earnings, a feature also often criticized by analysts advocating a more equitable rate, usually placed between 50% and 75% of average best previous earnings. Social Security had already reached a high of 54.4% in its average replacement rate in 1981, but it beat a retreat and cut back an assortment of benefits, such as a tax exemption on all Social Security earnings, when it was feared that the Social Security funds were spending more than they were taking in and would run the risk of depletion. Prospective retirees lacking other sources of income, such as private pensions, voluntary individual retirement accounts (IRAs), or savings, may face the possibility of a decline in their standard of living. Social Security benefits are, however, linked to the cost of living, as measured by the Consumer Price Index (CPI) of the Bureau of Labor Statistics and are automatically adjusted on an annual basis, thus offering a measure of protection against the risk of inflation.

Retirees who opt to continue working at the same time that they collect Social Security benefits may be subject to penalties. In 1991 the law authorized beneficiaries aged 65 to 69 to earn up to $9,720 without experiencing losses, but they have to return $1 of Social Security benefits for every $3 of earnings over that limit. This work disincentive provision, known as the "retirement test," does not apply, however, to working retirees over the age of 70.

The total number of retirees collecting Social Security benefits was 24,314,000 at the beginning of 1990, and their average monthly benefit was $567. Hailed as the most universal social policy in the United States, Social Security offers only a floor of protection but does not guarantee that all its beneficiaries will escape the risk of poverty. For older persons with limited income and resources, SSI may offer economic relief, provided they can prove need or hardship. Eligible applicants for SSI may also be entitled to Social Security payments, provided the latter do not raise them to the poverty threshold. In 1991, an individual's annual income had to fall below $4,844 to qualify for SSI. For a couple, the limit was $7,320. About 1,452,000 older persons received Supplemental Security Income benefits in September 1990, a figure that has been proportionately declining from a high of 2,307,000 in 1975. Applicants who qualify for SSI benefits are also eligible for other welfare or public assistance benefits that are means-tested, such as food stamps and Medicaid. The first of these programs enables needy people to buy certain categories of foods at reduced prices, while Medicaid covers a wide range of health care expenditures (especially nursing home care).

Social Security was intended to provide only a floor of income protection, not to fully replace earnings from wages. In addition, about half of the American work force is covered by employer-sponsored private pension plans. Although employers are not legally required to provide pensions, all such private pension plans must conform to funding and operational standards set in the Employee Retired Income Security Act of 1974 (ERISA). There are two major types of pension plans: "defined benefit" and "defined contribution" plans. Under the first one, employers make annual investments in a plan aimed to ensure that employees will receive a fixed and predictable amount of money at their retirement. Under a defined contribution plan, there is no assurance of a preestablished benefit, and the benefit collected by employees at retirement will, instead, depend on the volume of the employer's contributions, which may change depending on the economic success of the firm or corporation and also on the investment performance of the assets. In all circumstances, employees do not qualify automatically for pension benefits but must be "vested" or establish credit after a minimum number of years.

Following 1989, federal legislation requires pension plans to opt for one of two vesting methods. The "graded" vesting approach determines a right to 20%

of pension benefits after three years of service and then an additional 20% per subsequent year, thus attaining a full 100% after seven years of employment. The "cliff-vesting" approach requires a waiting period of five years before a worker may qualify for a 100% pension benefit (Regan, 1990).

HEALTH CARE SERVICES

Most older persons in the United States, about 71% of them, reported their health to be "excellent," "very good," or "good" in a 1989 Health Interview Survey conducted by the National Center for Health Statistics. However, given the higher survivorship rates, the acute care conditions that were prevalent earlier this century have given way to a more pervasive pattern of multiple chronic and disabling conditions (particularly in advanced old age). About 80% of the population age 65 and older are afflicted with at least one chronic condition. Arthritis leads among all chronic illnesses, and heart disease is both the leading predictor of short-stay hospital visits and the main cause of death, followed by cancer and stroke. Death rates from heart disease represent about 40% of all deaths among older persons, followed by cancer, which caused 21% of all deaths in this age population. It is noteworthy that deaths caused by heart disease and stroke have been declining since 1968, while the death rate from cancer is on the increase, a fact partially explained by the persistence of lung cancer. The number of older persons' visits to physicians is, on the average, 30% higher than for the general population, and their hospitalization rates are 300% higher than those of the population below age 65. Furthermore, their hospital stays are 50% longer (National Center for Health Statistics, 1990).

It is not surprising, therefore, that although the elderly constitute 12% of the U.S. population, they account for 35% of the total health care expenditures. In 1987, the average elderly individual's spending for health care was $5,400. The total national spending that year for health care by the elderly reached $162 billion, of which $61 billion, or 37%, came directly from the pockets of the elderly themselves. The balance of $101 billion, or 63% of the total, is covered largely by the nationwide health insurance program for the aged—Medicare, ($72 billion)—and by the public assistance program—Medicaid ($19.5 billion).

The Medicare program was established in 1965 as an addition to the Social Security Act of 1935 and consists of two subprograms: Part A, a mandatory hospital insurance, and Part B, a supplementary outpatient medical insurance, which is optional. In 1991, 30.3 million older persons were covered by Part A, and 29.8 million had elected to enroll in Part B.

Part A pays for all hospital expenses during the first 60 days, minus a deductible of $628 (in 1991) for each spell of illness or benefit. For days 61 to 90, the patient is responsible for a coinsurance payment equivalent to 25% of the hospital's daily costs. In the eventuality that more than 90 days may be needed in a single benefit period, the patient may utilize a lifetime reserve of 60 days, but the coinsurance amount increases to 50% of a hospital's daily bill, or $314 in 1991. Medicare will also cover up to 100 days of skilled nursing in a long-term care facility, but only for purposes of posthospital rehabilitation. After the first 20 days, a coinsurance rate of $78.50 must be shouldered by the patient. Home health care is reimbursed on a time-limited and intermittent basis for similar rehabilitation purposes, and hospice care is fully paid, up to a 210-day lifetime limit for Medicare-eligible beneficiaries determined to be terminally ill and with a life expectancy of six months or less.

Part B of Medicare pays 80% of charges for physicians' outpatient services, laboratory and diagnostic tests, ambulance services, and outpatient services at the hospital.

As of 1983, Medicare began reimbursing hospitals under a prospective payment system. This consists of a preestablished amount per case that is based on a classification of "diagnosis-related groups" (DRGs) and basically consists of a ceiling in reimbursement for the length of hospital stay for each of those DRGs. As a consequence, older persons stay, on the average, a shorter period in hospitals and may be discharged while still convalescing—a fact that produces a greater demand for home-delivered services (Isaacs and Swartz, 1992).

Long-term care services for functionally impaired and physically or mentally dependent older persons are offered in nursing homes, community-based care settings such as day-care programs, or the patient's own home. Nursing home (or institutional) care ranges, in turn, from highly skilled nursing facilities, certified by the Medicare program, to lower levels of nursing care (known as intermediate or custodial care) covered by the Medicaid public assistance program. Because the latter type does not lead to short-term rehabilitation, it does not qualify for Medicare reimbursements.

Nursing home care in the United States is very expensive. Medicaid will assume fiscal responsibility only for patients whose personal economic resources and assets have been "spent down" or exhausted. Retirement benefits of patients must also be applied toward the cost of institutional care. It is estimated that in any given day (in 1985), there were 1,490,000 residents in nursing homes, 88% of whom were over the age of 65. This constitutes less than 5% of the elderly population. However, given the relentless increase in life expectancy, particularly in the cohort 85 years of age or older, it is projected that by the year 2030 there will be 5.2 million older persons in dire need of nursing home care (Friedland, 1990). At present, 20% of the group 85 and older already reside in nursing homes and constitute 45%, almost half, of the elderly nursing home population.

Home care programs were developed as an alternative to the more costly institutional services delivered in nursing homes. Home care ranges from highly sophisticated technological and specialized nursing services to personal care and housekeeping or homemaker chore services. The number of home care agencies rose from 252 in 1966, to over 10,000 in 1986. About 6,000 of them have been certified by Medicare, the largest source of public funding for home care. Medicare reimbursement is very restrictive and time-limited, however. In order to be covered, home care must be justified medically, usually as a restorative sequence to recent hospitalization, and for no more than 38 days of care.

HOUSING RESOURCES

An assortment of program strategies helps older persons obtain, and live independently in, adequate housing. To begin with, low-income elderly may apply for rent supplement funds. In such cases, eligible persons, on their own, select an appropriate unit in the open private market, but they must apply up to 30% of their income toward the rental costs. The government then picks up the difference between that portion and the total rental price.

In the past there was also a greater emphasis on spearheading the construction of new housing units. Voluntary, nonprofit groups could become sponsors of special housing for the aged and disabled. They would then receive direct, low-interest mortgage loans from the federal government for such construction. Subsequently, the policy was directed toward subsidizing the interest rates charged by commercial banks for mortgage and construction loans, thus removing the federal government from acting as the main lender.

It is important to note, however, that the overwhelming majority of the aged in the United States are homeowners. In 1980, this was the case with 85.7% of aged families and 62.4% of unrelated older individuals. Poor families that included at least one older person owned their home in 69% of the cases. In comparison, 87% of aged nonpoor families also lived in a home they owned. Poverty does not appear to be a deterrent to home ownership, but many poor older persons find themselves unable to pay municipal taxes and cannot afford to properly maintain, heat, or cool their homes.

In addition to rent subsidies, the federal government began experimenting in the late 1970s with "congregate housing," which combines private, independent apartment living with optional supportive services. The latter may include homemaking, transportation, congregate meals, emergency response systems, and leisure and socialization activities (Monk and Kaye, 1991).

There is also a wide assortment of planned forms of residential dwellings organized for the aged, including group-shared housing, adult foster care, and adult homes. These resources aim at reducing the incidence of premature institutionalization in nursing home-type facilities and combine varying degrees of independent living with limited forms of assistance and supervision. Continuing Care Retirement Communities (CCRCs) offer, in a single site, the advantages of independent living and supportive services, including health care. Their most important feature is the contractual assurance of lifetime care, including the provision of intensive, round-the-clock skilled nursing care when needed. Because of their high costs of operation, due, in part, to the quality of the amenities and services provided, CCRCs are accessible only to a minority of affluent elderly.

SUPPORTIVE SERVICES

It is estimated that relatives dispense as much as 80% of all the support services needed by older persons. However, exclusive reliance on family care is no longer realistic, given the relentless increases in life expectancy and disability rates among the aged. Formal resources in the United States had to, therefore, step in and assume a supplementary role aimed at both relieving those overburdened relatives and ensuring the continuing residence of the older people in their natural communities.

Finding out what services are available, where they can be found, and whether one is entitled to get them could constitute an intimidating and exhausting job in its own right. Information and referral services (I & R) have been created precisely to facilitate access and entry to the service system. They operate in the area agencies on aging (AAAs) and also in community voluntary organizations, social service departments, public libraries, senior centers, hospitals, and so on. I & R services often do not passively wait for people to make inquiries but also reach out to the community and try to locate or identify shut-in, isolated, and despondent people in need of assistance. I & Rs also advertise their services, publish directories of services, conduct informational seminars, and keep computerized, up-to-date registries of waiting periods and vacancies (i.e., for nursing homes). They may also provide round-the-clock hot lines for crises and emergencies.

The function performed by I & Rs would be incomplete unless also supplemented by "case management services," which coordinate services at the individual client level. Basically these services start with an assessment and determination of the client's need. This diagnostic function is performed by a human services professional, usually a social worker, nurse, or a multidisciplinary team. Once it is established what services the person needs, a case manager negotiates access, obtains and coordinates the provision of those services (probably dispensed by several independent agencies), follows up and monitors the treatment and makes sure that it evolves according to plan, and periodically reassesses the client's needs. Case management services may be offered in area agencies on aging, hospitals, home care agencies, and specially designated freestanding agencies.

Multipurpose senior centers are probably the most frequently used community-based service. They were launched during the 1940s as social and recreational facilities for the relatively well and independent elderly whose major need was to overcome the risks of loneliness and isolation. They were originally grass-roots—rather than governmental—initiatives, but today they operate under both public—generally, municipal—and voluntary auspices. Estimates about the number of such centers range between 3,600 to over 14,000. An average center is attended by some 500 seniors per month, and the total membership probably does not exceed 5 million, or one in every six persons over the age of 65.

Typical center services fall in the following categories: (1) individual services, such as counseling, I & R, health maintenance, transportation and screening services for the homebound; (2) group services, like nutrition, education, recreation, and group activities; (3) community services, including advocacy, social action, and volunteering. Although initially created for the well aged, senior centers have gradually begun incorporating more frail and physically or mentally impaired, as well as chronically ill people. They are no longer self-contained organizations but are becoming focal points of entry to a wider range of services, and they reach out to the homebound and provide support and respite care to families.

Adult day-care programs appeared on the scene during the early 1970s as part of a federal demonstration project, precisely with the intent of providing respite care. They targeted ambulatory and semiambulatory frail older persons who did not require round-the-clock inpatient care. Services are provided during most of the daily hours and may include one or more meals, thus enabling relatives and other caretakers to work or meet other personal obligations without having to leave unattended their chronically ill and dependent family member. There are many types of day programs, depending on their location and programmatic thrust. Some are more socially or recreationally oriented. Others emphasize medical and rehabilitative services. Some are freestanding, while others are operational extensions of hospitals, nursing homes, or multiservice centers.

Initially hailed as the most viable alternative to institutionalization, adult day programs did not live up to their promise. Their growth in numbers has been slow, and public interest has remained limited or ambivalent, at best. There are about 2,000 day-care programs, serving fewer than 100,000 persons. The most commonly offered services are transportation, social services, nursing, personal care, physical therapy, and medical services. Centers, in general, and their transportation component, in particular, are costly to operate. The argument that day-care services are far more economical to deliver than nursing home care has repeatedly been questioned, once all expenditures are factored in. Public insurance reimbursement sources are not readily available to pay for this service.

LEISURE-TIME RESOURCES

Older persons, well into advanced age, remain affiliated with voluntary organizations. In fact, the largest membership organization in the United States is the American Association of Retired Persons (AARP), whose membership roster of 38 million members in 1991 grows at a relentless pace. Other age-centered organizations are the National Council of Senior Citizens, with about 8 million members who are mostly labor union retirees, and the National Committee to Preserve Social Security and Medicare, which is a more specialized policy-advocacy organization of over 500,000 dues-paying members.

Voluntaristic activism is, however, practiced only by a reduced proportion of this population, usually by those who already had a lifetime experience as volunteers. Starting in the later 1960s, the federal government sponsored several programs that recruit, train, and place senior volunteers. Among the best known are the following three. The Retired Senior Volunteer Program (RSVP) is active in the areas of education, housing, advocacy, information and referral, health education and assistance, and social services. Senior Companion Program (SCP) helps frail and isolated older persons in their own homes. The Foster Grandparent Program matches up seniors with multiproblem children and youth who reside, for the most part, in institutions for the physically and mentally handicapped and in correctional facilities.

Most of the recreation and socialization opportunities for older persons are found in their immediate communities, in the multiservice centers, unions or religious organizations (churches or synagogues), and civic and fraternal groups. Local colleges and universities are increasingly offering lectures and nondegree courses specifically adapted to the interests of older persons. There is also the possibility of auditing regular courses for no credit at a reduced nominal fee. The Elderhostel program has enlisted hundreds of institutions of higher learning, both in the United States and abroad, to offer a combination of short-term—usually one week—courses and housing for vacation-learning experiences at affordable costs.

ADVOCACY AND PROTECTION

No other age group in the United States is as dependent as the elderly upon public and private entitlements for their income maintenance, medical care, housing, health, transportation, institutional care, social services, and even nutrition. These benefits and services do not automatically arrive at age 65. Individuals must apply and prove they meet conditions for eligibility. Whenever discrepancies or uncertainties arise, negative determinations must be appealed. Services are often accessed only through complex bureaucratic and legal negotiations. These cumbersome and draining processes have better chances of succeeding when mediated by specialized legal aid.

Legal services for the elderly have already turned into a full-fledged professional specialty. This was partially the consequence of the 1975 amendments to the Older Americans Act, which introduced free legal assistance for people over age 60, although the actual provision of these services was rather modest and erratic because of limited budgetary backing. Private lawyers often accept cases without retainers and on a contingency fee; that is, they are paid between 25% and 33% of whatever compensation or benefit they obtain for their clients in a legal suit. Finally, professional bar associations, at the state or city level, are also known for providing pro-bono legal information and occasional services for low-income elderly.

A critical area of legal involvement is protective services for handicapped or mentally incompetent elderly. The most commonly used devices are durable powers of attorney, living wills, trusts, guardianships, and conservatorships. Under a "durable power of attorney," a person delegates power to an agent to act on his or her behalf in the eventuality of becoming mentally incompetent. Living wills constitute advanced directives to health care providers, relatives, and guardians with regard to the prolongation or termination of life in circumstances of persistent vegetative or irreversible comatose state. Guardians are appointed by courts to manage and make decisions of behalf of incompetent persons.

Conservators may be similarly appointed by courts to manage the property and assets of a person, even in the absence of mental incompetency. Conservatees do not lose, however, their legal or civil rights, as is the case under guardianship conditions. The office of "public guardian" has been established in several states to protect incompetent persons who have no relatives or viable support networks. There is also an emerging trend for the public sector to contract with private agencies for the purchase of guardianship services. It is assumed that this arrangement increases accountability and enables the public agency that awards the contract to stipulate explicit quality and performance requirements.

Federal legislation requires the provision of "ombudsman" services at the state and local level for residents of nursing home facilities. Local ombudsman programs are staffed by paid professionals or volunteers who respond to patients' complaints, investigate charges of possible abuse and neglect on the part of the nursing home, and negotiate a cooperative resolution of those grievances. Ombudsmen serve, in consequence, as advocates and mediators in conflict situations, their main objective being improving the quality of life of the institutionalized elderly (Monk and Kaye, 1984). The success of the nursing home ombudsman program led to its extension to other service areas, such as home care.

FUTURE PROJECTIONS

As more people will be reaching old age and living longer, their dominant and most critical need will be in the health care domain. In the absence of a national health insurance program that would include long-term care, older Americans will continue outlaying one-fifth of their income for medical expenses, while dreading the possibility of a catastrophic illness or nursing home placement that might wipe out all their assets. In addition to a total revamping of the health care system in order to make it more accessible and affordable, a future agenda addressed to this population will have to include:

1. More preventive care and community-based programs as essential components of a continuum of care. Home care, in particular, will have to be expanded.
2. More effective coordination of current networks of services. Health and social services will have to be better coordinated.
3. Greater ease in access to services.

4. More affordable congregate, or intermediate, service-enriched housing and more funds for rent subsidies.
5. More opportunities for regular, part-time, and flexible employment after formal retirement, without loss of retirement benefits.

BIBLIOGRAPHY

Friedland, R. B. (1990). *Facing the Costs of Long Term Care.* Washington, DC: Employee Benefit Research Institute (EBRI), Chapter 2.

Harris, L., and Associates. 1981. *Aging in the Eighties: America in Transition.* Washington, DC: National Council on the Aging.

Isaacs, S. L., and Swartz, A. C. (1992). *The Consumer's Legal Guide to Today's Health Care.* Boston, MA: Houghton Mifflin.

Monk, A., and Kaye, L. W. (1984). "Patient Advocacy Services in Long Term Care Facilities: Ethnic Perspectives." *Journal of Long Term Care Administration,* 5(10).

———. (1991). "Congregate Housing for the Elderly: Its Need, Function and Perspectives." In L. W. Kaye and A. Monk (eds.), *Congregate Housing for the Elderly* (pp. 5–20). New York: Haworth Press.

National Center for Health Statistics. (1989). *Health, United States, 1988.* DHHS Pub. No. (PHS) 89-1232. Washington, DC: DHHS.

———. (1990). "Current Estimates from the National Health Interview Survey, 1989." Vital and Health Statistics Series 10, No. 176, October.

Regan, J. J. (1990). *The Aged Client and the Law.* New York: Columbia University Press, Chapter 4.

Social Security Bulletin. (1990). Annual Statistical Supplement, Table 2.A1.

U.S. Bureau of the Census. (1989). "Projections of the Population of the United States by Age, Sex and Race: 1988 to 2080." *Current Population Reports Series,* P-25, No. 1018, January.

———. (1991). "1980 and 1990 Censuses of the Population." *General Population Characteristics.* PC80-1-B1.

U.S. General Accounting Office, Administration on Aging (1991). *More Federal Action Needed to Promote Service Coordination for the Elderly.* 23 April, GAO/HRD 91-45, Washington, DC.

31

USSR (Former)

Vladislav V. Bezrukov and Nina V. Verzhikovskaya

INTRODUCTION

The Role of the Elderly

In this chapter the term *the elderly* applies to those who are 60 years and over. In addition, some data will be provided of persons of retirement age: males 60 years and over and females 55 years and over.

Perceptions of the elderly in various parts of the former USSR differ greatly, depending on traditions, cultural values, place of residence, and so on. Higher authority and power belong to the elderly in Caucasus and Central Asia and in rural areas. In such areas, much more responsibility for care for the elderly is laid on the family and relatives. The same is true for rural areas of European republics of the former USSR (Ukraine, Byelorussia, Russian Federation, Baltic states), where institutional care is usually less tolerated by society.

According to the last census of 1989, the total population of the former USSR was 285.7 million, and those age 60+ numbered 40.6 million. In other words, the elderly were 14.2% of the total population. The percentage of the elderly in various republics of the USSR varied widely (from 6.1% in Tajikistan and Turkmenia to 17.9% in the Ukraine).

The rate of increase of elderly and old population exceeds the growth of the total population. In 1989 the increase of the total population of the USSR, compared with 1979, was 9%, and that of the elderly population was 20%. More pronounced changes were registered in higher age groups: the population age 75–79 years increased by 31%, 80–85 years by 50%, and 85 and over by 25%.

There were 480 males per 1,000 females aged 60 and over (this ratio for all ages was 892 to 1,000). This ratio was lower in rural (470 to 1,000) than in urban (486 to 1,000) areas. A greater deficit of males was in higher age groups:

the males to females ratio for the age group 85+ was 263 to 1,000. The above changes determine an ever-growing number of lone elderly, primarily among women.

Life expectancy at birth for both genders in 1989 was 69.5 years: 64.6 for males and 74.0 for females. Among the republics of the former USSR, the highest life expectancy at birth was in Georgia—72.1 years, and the lowest was in Turkmenistan—65.2 years.

With population aging in the former USSR, there has been an increase in the old-age dependency ratio. Thus, in 1979 there were 267 persons of retirement age (males 60+, females 55+) per 1,000 people of working age (274 in urban and 381 in rural areas).

The above demographic changes have a serious impact on the economy, expenditures of the state for pensions, medicosocial services, and so on.

Although elders prevailed in higher organs of the Communist party and government, not much was done for provision of care and protection of the rights of older people. For many decades, the state has proclaimed great concern about its old citizens, but at the time of disintegration of the USSR into independent states, the harsh reality was that no developed networks of medicosocial service, no extensive forms of self-care and voluntary assistance, and no adequate pension systems and gerontological policy existed for the elderly.

The Formal Structure of Care of the Elderly

In republics of the former USSR, medicosocial care of the elderly is provided primarily through separate systems of institutions of the Health Ministry and the Ministry of Social Welfare (the latter did not exist in the USSR but did, and does, exist in republics or independent states).

Medical aid to the elderly is delivered through the general health care system of the Health Ministry at inpatient and outpatient facilities. These services are public and free; expenses are covered mainly from the state budget.

Some specific forms of health care for the elderly exist, like geriatric consulting rooms at outpatient clinics and geriatric wards or units in some general hospitals.

The formal hierarchy of organizers of health care to the elderly includes republican geriatricians, regional geriatricians, municipal geriatricians (all unpaid), and physicians of geriatric units at outpatient departments at local levels (paid). Geriatrics as an official medical speciality has not been introduced in this country.

At institutional settings of the Ministry of Social Welfare, medicosocial care to lonely and frail elderly persons is provided at homes for the aged, nursing homes, and hospitals for veterans of war. Stays and services at such institutions are usually covered by the state, but some payment may be required from residents, their relatives, or some voluntary funds.

Some new developments have taken place during recent years: medicosocial territorial centers, day-care centers, and special housing projects with a complex of medicosocial services.

For many years the major source of financing institutions and services for the elderly was the state budget, divided among republics, regions, municipalities, and districts. A definite role in constructing and maintaining homes for veterans, nursing homes, and departmental hospitals was played by trade unions, enterprises, collective farms, and voluntary organizations.

Institutions for the elderly established and sponsored by religious organizations or groups are scarce but growing in number. There are few nursing homes and hospices sponsored by voluntary funds and private sources.

Institutions and services are provided mainly on the basis of need, not only by virtue of age. Target groups for receiving services are the disabled, handicapped elderly, single old persons or spouses, and other vulnerable groups at risk.

INCOME MAINTENANCE AND EMPLOYMENT

In accordance with the constitution (de jure), elderly people have a right to Social Security and social insurance. Along with this, many groups and layers of the population could not use their rights de facto (farmers and clergymen among them).

Laws on pensions are being discussed in the states and will correct any injustices and provide full coverage to the population of retirement age with pensions and allowances.

Major types of pensions include full old-age pensions, those granted due to the loss of breadwinner, and disability pensions. Increased individual pensions are provided to some categories of pensioners, like retirees receiving state prizes or awards, honored specialists, and former statesmen.

In the early 1990s, major events took place in the country: a state pensioning system for farmers was introduced, so-called social pensions were implemented for those who did not have enough length of service, and adjustment of pensions to the inflation rate was approved.

Social Security is largely formed from the state budget and allowances of enterprises and organizations that are mainly state-run. The social system, which has existed for many decades, envisaged nearly public ownership of land, resources, plants and factories, and equipment and means of production; only the state form of Social Security (including pension provision and insurance) excluded any private retirement programs.

It is believed that adoption and realization of the law on privatization and consideration of a new political economic situation in the new law on pensions will promote an implementation of new retirement schemes and regulations.

Social Security funds are also allocated for institutionalization, housing, low rent, other communal privileges, reduced transport fares, payments for other social and domestic services to the elderly, and tax benefits or exemptions for the elderly with minimum pensions. Local authorities and profitable enterprises, farms, and institutes have a right to use their funds for privileges to the elderly; still, these practices are not prevalent.

During the late 1980s and early 1990s, voluntary funds and foundations launched programs for needy and impoverished elderly people, like free meals and financial assistance in the form of lump-sum or regular payments.

Many elderly people (during recent years, up to 30–40% of all pensioners) continued working after reaching retirement age. (This is a result of legislative acts.) Due to limitations in the overall sum of pensions and wages, some of the elderly prefer to have a part-time job or other sources of income. Still, the recent crisis of economy, the production reduction, and transition to a market economy reduced employment opportunities for older workers and the elderly, decreased their income, and put them at the verge of poverty.

Job training programs for older workers exist in some enterprises (factories and mills), but reemployment services for the elderly are scarce and underdeveloped.

HEALTH CARE SERVICES

Provision and development of health services for older people are a component of the overall national health care program.

In many towns, the organizational-methodological and therapeutic-consultative provision of medical care for elderly and old people is carried out by physicians of geriatric rooms organized at territorial polyclinics (there is one physician per 100,000 adult people). The geriatric consulting polyclinics exist in a number of large towns. However, the central figure in the health care of the aged in the community is the district physician (family doctor).

The considerable need of old people for various kinds of medical care is related to the accumulation of chronic pathology with age (which is multiple, complex, and progressive) and changes for different organs and systems, as well as impaired physical abilities.

In the case of acute episodes or exacerbation and complication of chronic pathology, the elderly call an emergency phone number to a network of emergency medical stations throughout the country for urgent medical aid within homes, at work sites, or on the street. Requests for emergency medical aid for elderly people are 3–5 times higher than in the general population. For example, in Kiev, the number of emergency calls for people aged 60 and over is 1,254 cases per 1,000 population of this age group, while for people under 60 this value is 241. It appears that the increasing number of calls among the elderly indicates the need for improving the medical service of chronically sick, timely detection and treatment of pathology, and higher quality of a dispensary follow-up. One of the leading causes of emergency calls among elderly patients is cardiovascular diseases (which account for 70% of the calls).

Medical care for the chronically sick, who make up from 79.3% to 85.7% of the total number of the population aged 60 and over in different regions of the country (Bednij, 1975; Shilova, 1978; Sonin and Dyskin, 1984) is provided by district physician-therapeutists, specialists of ambulatory polyclinic departments, and inpatient hospitals. The need for inpatient hospital care in the elderly is very high, three times higher than in the adult population. Inpatient geriatric hospital care is carried out within general hospitals, geriatric units of multiprofile hospitals, and hospitals for World War II invalids. The need for inpatient medical care is not fully satisfied, especially for those requiring long treatment of chronic illness. At present, more than 20% of all beds in general inpatient facilities are occupied by old patients. In the therapeutic, neurological, and ophthalmological departments, very old patients make up 45–55% of all the hospitalized (Verzhikovskaya, 1985). The duration of treatment at such hospitals for old patients is, on average, 20–30% longer than for younger patients (Potekhina and Guseva, 1979).

There is a well-developed system of health care for invalids of World War II, who are now old people. Such hospitals function in all regions of the country. In general, they are well equipped with modern diagnostic and therapeutic instruments, provided with necessary facilities to carry out treatment and rehabilitation, and staffed with skilled medical personnel.

Geriatric units for long-term treatment of chronically ill patients began to be established within multiprofile hospitals only recently; they have eight beds per 1,000 population aged 60 and over. Such units, usually having the capacity of 30–40 beds, are meant to provide medical, social, and daily living services for the aged who are in need of treatment and long-term assistance. Each unit has a particular profile—therapeutic, neurological, surgical, treatment of bone and joints diseases—or is mixed.

In rural areas, elderly patients are admitted to village (district) hospitals for long-term treatment where they not only receive medical aid but also are given personal care. The elderly patients may stay, depending on their social situations, at these hospitals through winter and return home in summer. These hospitals are available in almost all rural areas of the Baltic republics, Ukraine, Russia, and so on. They are usually small with a capacity of 20–30 beds.

Day-care hospitals are an attempt to solve the problem of a large demand for geriatric hospital care and long-term restoration of health after illness. These are an intermediate, between hospital and ambulatory, form of geriatric care and are established on the premises of ambulatory polyclinic institutions, hospitals, and clinics of research institutes. They are used for the long-term treatment of chronically sick patients who are able to come to the hospital for treatment only in the daytime. Former inpatients who were treated at specialized hospitals may finish their treatment at such day hospitals. For each patient attending a day hospital, an individual course of treatment is planned.

Nursing homes are an essential part of medical care provided for chronic patients. Therapeutic aid is provided by the medical personnel of the home, while special medical care is provided by the medical personnel of the hospital. Homes have a therapist; large homes may have a therapist, neurologist, dentist, and so on, on their staff.

The first hospice in the country was established in St. Petersburg. Measures are now being taken to open hospices in Kiev and other towns.

During the last few years, there has been a movement to render medical care for elderly patients at home. Currently, 40–50% of patients receiving medical care at home are persons over 60. In this age group 80% suffer from cardiovascular pathology and receive medical aid at home (Verzhikovskaya, 1985).

By the time of retirement, 10% of elderly persons use a medical aid at home—one-third of those 70 years old and half of those 80 years old (Revutskaya, 1978). More than one-third of citizens over 70 years of age do not go to ambulatory polyclinic institutions. The data from investigations carried out in Georgia, Latvia, and Ukraine show that among town residents aged 70 and over who do not visit a polyclinic, 52.7% reported that it was difficult for them to visit a doctor, 15.5% practiced self-treatment, 7.9% were dissatisfied with the wait and organization of the polyclinic, and only 23.9% did not feel themselves ill. In rural areas, 37.6% of the interviewees said that it was difficult for them to visit a doctor, 14.6% found it a far distance to go, 13.4% practiced self-treatment, and 34.4% did not feel themselves ill (Verzhikovskaya, 1984).

Studies carried out in Byelorussia and Ukraine showed that in one year the number of home visits by physician per person over 60 years increased from 3.4 and 2.7 visits, respectively, to 7.3 and 4.7 visits within the last 15 years. The total number of ambulatory visits was equal to 10.1 and 9.0 per year but did not meet the needs of elderly people for ambulatory aid. In the specialists' opinion, there should be 18.2 physician visits per elderly person per year, both in polyclinics and at home.

Of all home visits, 90.2% are by district physicians, and 3.5% and 3.4% (and in some regions 13.0% and 8.1%) are home visits by surgeons and neurologists, respectively. A greater part of home visits (64.8%) is undertaken on the initiative of a district physician. As to the causes for a physician's visit, patients complain of troubles of circulation, respiration, and digestion and joint and muscle disease.

In-home hospitals are used in cases when the character of illness and home conditions permit such care. This offers a range of medical care made available at the patient's own residence. Patients are visited either by the district physician and nurse or by a special team from polyclinics that serve ill elderly at such in-home hospitals. The latter form has proved to be more effective. The team consists of one or two physicians, nurses, a physiotherapist, and a lab worker. If needed, all specialists of the polyclinic can be involved. Patients are cared for by charity nurses or social workers from the department of domiciliary care. In-home hospitals are effective and efficient. Although the average stay at in-home hospitals is longer, the cost of medical service is 2–5 times lower than at a usual hospital.

Table 31.1
Characteristics of Level of Amenities in Pensioners' Households (Percentage of total examined pensioners)

	Town	Village
Running water	69.0	9.0
Sewerage	67.0	8.0
Gas	69.0	20.0
Central heating	57.0	9.0
Bath, shower	43.0	6.0
Hot water	42.0	3.0
Telephone	13.0	3.0

Source: Kogan, 1986.

HOUSING RESOURCES

There is great variability in types of housing for the elderly in different regions of the country. Epidemiological investigations on the housing of pensioners in a number of towns and villages of Russia and Ukraine found that in towns, 66.8% of the elderly lived in state-owned separate flats, 20.4% in communal flats, and 22.8% in their own homes. For those living in villages, 10.3% of the elderly lived in state-owned separate flats, 13.9% in communal flats, and 75.8% in their own homes (Kogan, 1986).

A marked difference in level of amenities between urban and rural areas is also noted. Data illustrating this point taken from these investigations are presented in Table 31.1.

In large cities, the quality of pensioners' residential places (in terms of amenities) is somewhat higher than average data reported in Table 31.1. For example, 90% of pensioners live in accommodations with running water, gas, and sewerage, 85–90% with a bath (shower), and 80–87% with a telephone. Among the older people living in multistoried houses, only 40% live on the ground floor and 17% on the first. The level of amenities in households of elderly citizens living in rural areas is extremely low.

An important factor influencing the formation of types of housing and settings for elderly persons is their family status and presence of a spouse, children, and relatives. With increasing age, the number of persons living with a spouse decreases.

By the beginning of the 1990s, the proportion of elderly people and married couples living alone was 30% of the total elderly population of the USSR as a whole. It is noted that this process progresses over time: the data for Kiev indicate that, in 1970, 50% of persons aged 60 and over lived alone, while this percentage increased to 57% in 1980 (Barmashina and Verzhikovskaya, 1990).

The data from sociological investigations show that about 70% of members of two- and three-generational families prefer to live in separate flats (though in neighboring houses or in the same house) (Barmashina and Verzhikovskaya, 1990). Town builders discuss the planning of dwelling blocks that would provide a joint-isolated living of families consisting of two generations.

Analysis of the factors influencing the housing needs of older people and current world trends of residences focuses on planning two types of housing: specialized facilities and flats.

Traditionally, nursing homes for the aged and disabled in the USSR were an established form of institution for long-term residence of frail citizens. Such homes functioned within the social welfare system and provided their inhabitants with living accommodations, communal services, medical aid, and social and cultural services. As evidenced from sociological investigations, there is an urgent need for a revision of former practices of building large-sized nursing homes (with capacity of 300–500 places). Recent housing projects focus on building small nursing homes for 50–200 residents (Krundyshev, 1987).

SUPPORTIVE SERVICES

The foundation of special home services for incapacitated citizens within the social welfare system springs from an increase in the number of this group and in their need for care, as well as the impossibility to solve these problems by nursing homes for the aged. In 1987, a government decree focused on the provision of social care for citizens by developing domiciliary forms of medical, social, daily living, and cultural services and by an increase of home help for disabled citizens. Thus, a new system of social services was created to render differential assistance to elderly people who need outside guardianship and care.

The primary link of this network is home help units. The social workers of these units provide appropriate services for many old people (supply and delivery of food products, cooking and cleaning, other special services) to help them cope with loneliness. From 5 to 10 elderly citizens in towns and from 4 to 5 persons in villages are attended by one social worker. The units are provided with transportation.

In large towns, territorial social welfare centers have been established. The center is a medicosocial institution designed for a permanent or temporary residence of elderly and disabled people, under inpatient or day-care conditions, and for serving incapacitated old citizens at home. Centers provide medical care, various rehabilitation measures, and work therapy and guide the activity of home help units.

At present, some territorial centers include units for permanent and temporary residence, day care and home help, rehabilitation, and home help units, and some are organized on the basis of nursing homes for the aged (which include day care and home help units). It is assumed that each center may be supplemented with a residential house, providing its inhabitants with various kinds of social and domestic services.

As a rule, the territorial centers are organized either within existing municipal buildings or within special residential facilities for individuals. By early 1992, there were 46 territorial centers in the Ukraine, with 2,297 places for a daytime stay and 309 places in inpatient medical units. The designers worked up an improved project of territorial centers, and the Kiev city authorities have approved the construction of two new centers in the city.

Day centers are being created, both on the basis of territorial centers and within home care units. Many of them carry out rehabilitation measures, including work therapy. The goal of these day centers is promotion of physical and social activity of older people, particularly single persons, in terms of rational organization of free time and opportunities to establish friendly contacts. The work of such centers is run by a social worker. In some centers there may be an occupational therapist and a physiotherapist. Medical aid is given by a nurse, while skilled specialists from territorial polyclinics undertake visits on a special schedule and provide consultative assistance to older people. Church communities also establish day centers in which the elderly may obtain necessities such as food and clothes and also advice and consolation.

Social home care units were organized for the incapacitated aging, under supervision of local social welfare bodies throughout the country. State funds cover the entire cost of these units. In the Ukraine, at the beginning of 1992, there were 1,121 home care units, sponsored mainly by social welfare departments (872) as well as by boarding homes, territorial centers, and independent organizations.

By the beginning of 1992, not all needs of the elderly were satisfied by social home care. According to the Ministry of Social Security of Ukraine (personal data) about 70,000 elderly and disabled persons in Ukraine were registered as being in need of home care but never received it. The network of social home care continues to grow, and by January 1992 a total of 159,000 people received this kind of care. There were 19,500 social workers on the staff of day-care units, and still more were needed.

Nutritional programs for the elderly are part of the general state social care program for pensioners. Under supervision of social welfare departments, meals-on-wheels services have been organized. On the request of social workers, public nutrition and trade organizations take responsibility to arrange a delivery of food products and hot meals to homes.

Charity organizations, jointly with different local services and supported financially by fees, charitable donations, and so on, have set up free dining rooms to the needy and (primarily) frail aged citizens. It is difficult to estimate the national rate of this supportive care for the elderly. In the Ukraine, about 30,000 needy persons regularly receive free dinners or food products, at the expense of local authorities.

Social and domestic help is provided to elderly people with reduced independent abilities by social workers who give them assistance in cooking, cleaning house, and shopping or who simply visit them. In small towns and villages, a large share of help to elderly persons is given by neighbors. In villages, local authorities pay, in part or completely, small sums of money as a reward to neighbors looking after the elderly. They also pay for firewood, coal, and fuel and repair of houses of single older villagers and encourage the sale of food products at cost to the elderly.

Care of elderly people outside the home is carried on by day centers functioning within social welfare departments, territorial centers of social care for the pensioners, and boarding homes for the aged and disabled. Within the social welfare system, there is a network of sanatoriums of various profiles in which free spa treatment is provided for nonworking pensioners. The Ukraine has five such sanatoriums for patients suffering from cardiovascular, respiratory, gastrointestinal, and bone and muscle diseases.

The need for psychiatric care grows as the aging of population progresses. It is estimated that 15–20% of people aged 70 and over need ambulatory or inpatient psychiatric aid. Treatment of elderly mentally ill patients is performed at general mental hospitals or at geropsychiatric units within these hospitals. Such units incorporate geriatric physicians on staff.

For patients suffering from senile dementia and other mental diseases and needing constant care, a network of nursing homes for psychogeriatric chronically ill patients has been developed. The entire cost of their stay is paid by the state. They receive necessary medical care and aid and occupy themselves with work within their abilities.

Mentally disordered patients obtain both inpatient and outpatient medical aid in places of their residence, at ambulatory polyclinic institutions, and psychoneurological dispensaries. In some towns (Moscow, Tvor, and so on), day psychiatric units are organized on the basis of dispensaries in which rehabilitation measures are carried out under the supervision of scientists.

The need for giving support to families who care for their aging members has been recognized only recently. As a first step, a 1988 decision makes provision for the family to place an aging relative for a short period (up to three months) in a nursing home for the aged. This gives an opportunity for the family to go on a holiday or to use the time for other purposes. A new law provides a social pension to the relatives who care for an invalid.

Nursing homes for the aged and disabled can be subdivided, according to social status and health of their inhabitants, into homes of ordinary type for elderly and disabled, homes for labor veterans, and homes for mentally disordered patients who are to be isolated from healthy people.

Homes of ordinary type for single aging persons who require care and treatment and satisfactory housing are the most common. The average age of the inhabitants is 75–79 years. Only 10–15% of them are able to move and to satisfy their daily domestic needs, 60–70% of the inhabitants can partly serve themselves, and 20–30% are bedridden (Barmashina and Verzhikovskaya, 1990). The latter group is provided with a special unit. A greater portion of pension is spent to pay for living in the home. Expenses for room and board in the home are covered by the state.

Homes for veterans function in every republic, in accordance with appropriate laws. There are boarding homes for veterans having a 35-year (men) and a 30-year (women) length of service. In contrast to homes of ordinary type, where only therapeutic care can be obtained, homes for veterans have a well-equipped medical unit with a team of specialists comprising a geriatric physician, neurologist, stomatologist, physiotherapist, and an occupational and physical therapist. Presently, there is a move toward creating special boarding homes. For example, in the Ukraine, boarding homes have been established for persons who had previous convictions and were sentenced to long-term imprisonment.

In 1988, there were 1,772 boarding homes with 380,000 places in the USSR. By 1992, there were 213 boarding homes with a capacity of 46,339 places in Ukraine. The majority were for psychogeriatric patients.

In rural areas, small-sized homes for veterans with 10–30 places have been set up. Each worker of the home serves two to five persons. Collective farm funds cover the entire cost of such homes. Most of the inhabitants move to their own homes during the spring and summer and return in winter.

Residential houses designed for single and childless pensioners who are able to satisfy their daily domestic needs but require, at least partly, help in daily living seem to be a recent housing option for older people. These houses have a range of facilities for organizing medical and daily living services, nutrition, housekeeping work, and cultural services. By the beginning of 1988, more than 20 such residential houses had been built in the USSR.

Recently, the church has given help to the elderly. From funds provided by the Pochaevsky Monastery, a hospital in the Ukraine (with a capacity of 60 beds) was opened to accommodate bedridden patients. Church employees and parishioners help the staff of boarding homes in the care and nursing of the severely ill. They also assist social workers who look after single elderly persons who remain in their own homes and require everyday help in daily living.

LEISURE-TIME RESOURCES

A series of studies carried out at the Institute of Gerontology (Sachuk, Panina, and Romanets, 1986) showed that among nonworking pensioners, the level of social activity is higher for men and women former employees than for those currently working. Thus, among former employees, a high level of social activity was found for 57.1% of men and 47.2% of women, while among current workers a similar level of activity was noted for 18.8% of men and 17.0% of women. It was found that 50% of former male workers and 28.5% of current male workers helped their children in householding. For women, these figures were 60.7% and 63.8%, respectively. The percentage of pensioners taking an active part in the upbringing of grandchildren was very high: 31.3% and 35.7% in men, both former workers and current workers, and 42.9% and 58.3% in women, both former workers and current workers.

Social activity for people of retirement age is influenced, to the greatest extent, by educational level and, to a lesser degree, by income. In 82% of pensioners, a high social activity is combined with other kinds of activity (frequently, physical activity). A healthy life-style was found in every fifth pensioner. After retirement, the additional free time is spent to satisfy physiological needs—sleeping and walking. Involvement in intellectual activities (like attendance at various clubs, visiting museums and theaters) takes less time.

In this country, no special agencies deal with the organization of old people. Associations of war and labor veterans have, nowadays, become mass voluntary organizations of pensioners. The activity of these associations is aimed at social protection of pensioners, representation of their interests in all legislative and executive bodies, and participation in the formulation of gerontological policy in the country. Councils of veterans involve pensioners in sociopolitical, economic, and cultural life. They help pensioners to find an interesting occupation within their limited capacities. The councils participate in solving many questions pertinent to pensioners' daily living, housing, and medicosocial service. Mutual assistance is the main principle of these organizations.

Club and recreational activities have proved very popular among pensioners. The range of such activities varies from learning philosophy to dancing and singing. There are clubs for jogging, tourism, meditation, and so on.

"University of Health" is designed for health education for all people, irrespective of age. Unfortunately, public universities that educate pensioners on habits of a rational life-style have not developed.

ADVOCACY AND PROTECTION

For many years it was supposed that the rights of the elderly were sufficiently protected by the state and that all services were provided by the state and local communities to ensure a healthy and happy life for all. Unfortunately, lack of resources and distorted orientation and priorities prevented the actual implementation of these programs.

For many years there were no human rights-oriented policies toward the elderly. Formerly, there existed state-supported organizations of the elderly, like councils of veterans of war and labor, that were formed at local municipal, regional, republic (e.g., Armenia, Byelorussia, Ukraine) and all-union (USSR) levels. But their work was too formal and politically oriented. In fact, they were not advocacy groups for the interests of the elderly.

During the period of *perestroika* (restructuring) and *glasnost* (openness), places in some parliaments were given to representatives of organizations of veterans; commissions on issues of veterans and invalids were formed in parliaments, municipalities, and other agencies of power.

Some good drafts of laws were prepared, like on pensions and social protection of the elderly, but in the present political-economic situation these commissions are failing to ensure a better life and more opportunities for the elderly.

Legal assistance to the elderly is provided through a network of general legal consultancies, but services are limited. No special legal, victim assistance, or protective services (like an ombudsman) for the elderly at risk exist in this country.

Still, democratization of the country gives rise to hopes to attain a level of societal life where the elderly will be protected from maltreatment, victimization, and abuse.

FUTURE PROJECTIONS

When the USSR fell apart, the new states that appeared in its territory began seeking new societies, where rights of all groups of the population will be secured and the needs of aged people met. Currently, however, the projections are gloomy.

Institutions and services that exist in republics of the former USSR do not meet specific needs and demands of the elderly. Unmet needs include almost all areas of their lives. Income security is decreasing, and pensions cannot keep up with hyperinflation and skyrocketing costs of living.

Job opportunities are diminishing (during the transition to a market economy). Providing shelter and housing meets with difficulties: state housing programs are being curtailed; privatization and increasing prices for apartments and houses jeopardize (primarily) elderly people.

Medicosocial care and domiciliary assistance are insufficient, due to the lack of institutions, inadequate help to families, underdeveloped infrastructure of communal and social services, and so on.

The most important steps to be undertaken in the near future are to improve the quality of life for the elderly within an economic resurrection and the construction of a human-oriented democratic society.

NOTE

Although this is a description of the system of care and services in the country as a whole, the same also holds true about republics in the territory of the former USSR. Most recent developments in newly emerged independent states are not discussed.

BIBLIOGRAPHY

Barmashina, L. M., and Verzhikovskaya, N. V. *Urbanization and "Third Age."* Kiev: Budivelnik, 1990.

Bednij, M. S. *Sociohygienic Characteristics of Morbidity of the Urban and Rural Population.* Moscow: Meditsina, 1975.

Chebotarev, D. F., Sachuk, N. N., and Verzhikovskaya, N. V. Problems of health and position of the elderly in socialist countries of Eastern Europe. *Z. Alternsforsch.,* 36(6), 1981, pp. 437–472.

Dyskin, A. A., and Reshetjuk, A. L. *Health and Activities in Old Age.* Leningrad: Meditsina, 1988.

Gerontology and Geriatrics. *Gerontology and Geriatrics 1990 Yearbook.* Kiev: Institute of Gerontology, 1991.

Kogan, V. The single elderly—problems and ways of the social service. In *The Population of the Third Age,* D. I. Valentei (ed.). Moscow: Mysl, 1986, pp. 107–131.

Krundyshev, B. L. Social issues in housing for veterans. In *Medical and Social Problems of Aging,* D. F. Chebotarev and N. V. Verzhikovskaya (eds.). Kiev: Institute of Gerontology, 1987, pp. 80–85.

Potekhina, M. V., and Guseva, I. S. *Main Problems of Medical Demography.* Moscow: TsIUV, 1979.

Revutskaya, Z. G. Medicosocial care of elderly and old people. In *Life Conditions and Older Man.* Moscow: Meditsina, 1978, pp. 262–282.

Sachuk, N. N., Panina, N. V., and Romanets, A. V. Structure and factors of sociocultural activity of pensioners in the process of social adaptation. *Vestnik AMN SSSR,* 1986, No. 10, pp. 66–70.

Shapiro, V. D. *Social Activity of Elderly People in the USSR.* Moscow: Nauka, 1983.

Shilova, S. P. Sociohygienic characteristics of health of the elderly population in West Urals. *Sov. Zdravookhranenije,* 1978, No. 2, pp. 35–40.

Sonin, M. A., and Dyskin, A. A. *The Elderly in the Family and Society.* Moscow: Finansy i Statistika, 1984 (in Russian).

Verzhikovskaya, N. V. Health and medicosocial service of the elderly population. In *Gerontology and Geriatrics. 1982 Yearbook. The Elderly. Medical and Social Care.* Kiev: Institute of Gerontology, 1982, pp. 31–40.

———. The ways of development of social services for disabled members of society. Report of the Institute of Gerontology, 1984 (unpublished, in Russian).

———. Role of the district therapist in medical and daily living service of elderly population. *Zdravookhranenije Belorussii,* 1985, No. 1, pp. 22–24.

32

ZIMBABWE

Andrew C. Nyanguru

INTRODUCTION

The Role of the Elderly

Until the intervention of colonial rule in the country around 1890, respect for the elderly was a core value in the cultures of the people living in what had been called Rhodesia but is now (following independence in 1980) called Zimbabwe. Children were trained from an early age to obey and respect their parents and other elderly members of the community. There were few impoverished aged persons in traditional Zimbabwean society, and the elderly had productive roles to play. This was related to the elderly's ownership of scarce resources (land, livestock, ritual power), allocation of resources on the basis of need, and older husbands having several younger wives to aid in the maintenance of the family (Nyanguru, 1991; Nyanguru and Peil, 1991).

The situation in Zimbabwe has changed since the arrival of white settlers into the "colony" of Southern Rhodesia, the utilization of blacks as sources of cheap labor (Nyanguru, 1990, 1991; Hampson, 1990), and the assumption that rural areas of the country were "labor reserves" for the unemployed, temporary migrants, the sick, the destitute, and the aged.

The first line of defense for the elderly is the family. Most families want to look after their elderly relatives but do not have the means to do so. Many of the children of needy elderly parents are unemployed, young, or students. A study by Nyanguru et al. (1991) found that 48% of the elderly did not receive financial assistance from their children; 70% received less than $100 per year.

Many elderly persons have no one to look after them and are placed in institutions for the aged. There is a growing consensus among service professionals and community leaders and among the elderly themselves about the need for a residential care system in Zimbabwe. The demands for such a system are likely to increase over time as a result of the inability of families to provide care and the increasing number of homeless elderly, and can be seen in the growing waiting lists for homes for the aged.

In Zimbabwe, the official retirement age is 60 for most people and 65 for professionals; however, many people retire at 55.

Demographic Overview

The problems of an aging population have not been seen as important because the aged are such a small part of the population. However, life expectancy has increased, and the population and the number of elderly persons are growing. Life expectancy for males and females in 1983 was 52 years and 60 years, respectively (Hampson, 1985).

According to projections for the 1980–2025 period, Zimbabwe will experience one of the largest increases in numbers of persons aged 60 and over among Southern African countries (Hampson and Kaseke, 1989). As elsewhere in the world, there are more elderly women and elderly men in Zimbabwe, the largest group being widowed women (Tarira, 1983; Wilson et al., 1990; Nyanguru and Peil, 1991).

The elderly in Zimbabwe will mainly remain in rural areas of the country in the coming decades. Recent projections indicate that about 60% of Zimbabwe elderly will live in rural areas by the year 2000 compared with the present 80% of all elderly (Kasere, 1990).

There has been, and will continue to be, at least a 40% increase in the number of elderly in each decade in Zimbabwe (Adamchak et al., 1990), resulting from earlier high birthrates. The proportion of elderly will grow as a result of the acquired immunodeficiency syndrome (AIDS) epidemic, which has higher mortality rates for younger populations.

Similar to findings around the world, the elderly in Zimbabwe are the largest group living in poverty (Nyanguru and Peil, 1991). Impoverishment was true slightly more for elderly men than elderly women and for those without families, and destitution was found to be the major reason for African elderly persons to enter homes for the aged.

In Zimbabwe, as in other African countries, illiteracy is very high among the elderly (especially true for women) (Tarira, 1983). Relatedly, most African rural elderly are peasant farmers without much education; those in formal employment are unskilled laborers. By contrast, probably reflecting their educational backgrounds and discriminatory policies of colonial governments, the majority of Europeans have skilled and professional jobs.

Formal Structure of Resources

In an attempt to construct a comprehensive policy for the care of the elderly, the government of Zimbabwe has built upon the foundation laid by the colonial government. The old regime had established an efficient (and rather humane) system of care for the elderly in the European section of the country. Waterston (1982)—referring to the European population—indicated that Rhodesia (as it was known in the past) had the highest percentage of its elderly population in residential care in the world.

It has been hypothesized that "modernization" will break up families and leave welfare to the state. Zimbabwe is an interesting country in which to study this, both because the large white population should have made it easier to accept Western European norms of family and state responsibility and because a state with a socialist policy orientation should be more concerned than most African governments with the provision of welfare.

There was considerable development of state welfare during the colonial and Unilateral Declaration of Independence (UDI) periods in what was then Rhodesia—old people's homes, pensions, and health and unemployment benefits—but these were mostly for whites rather than for the population as a whole. Before Zimbabwe had attained independence and was a British colony, the Smith regime declared unilateral independence from Britain in 1965. It became an illegal regime and the U.N. issued sanctions against it. Social assistance for whites was widely available in the 1940s, but provision for blacks was very limited because they were (conveniently) seen as self-sufficient in their traditional societies. The Department of Social Welfare was established in 1948, but most assistance outside the extended family was provided by voluntary organizations (often affiliated with Christian churches).

The newly independent government was concerned with widening the provision of welfare, and the newly enfranchised voters were anxious that it should do so. However, there have been many problems translating official policy, with its emphasis on politics rather than economics, into reality.

The health service has been a major contribution, but the costs of maintaining it are considerable. Workmen's compensation, financed by contributions, is the main form of Social Security, and many of the African elderly with occupational disabilities would have made very few (if any) contributions and thus received no compensation. Personal social services (public assistance, old people's homes, old-age and disability benefits) are means-tested and mainly available in urban areas. There has been extensive drought relief (by way of food) in rural areas in the early 1980s and early 1990s. Public assistance is available only to those who can prove that they will receive no help from their families. The urban unemployed are encouraged to return to their villages.

INCOME MAINTENANCE AND EMPLOYMENT

Rhodesia has always been reckoned to be a country with one of the greatest inequalities in income distribution in the world. The income share of Rhodesia's lowest 40% of the economically active population has about 8.0% of the total income in the country. Although in terms of gross domestic product (GDP), per capita Zimbabwe is in the World Bank's middle-income lower group of countries, and although the glaring racial disparities in wealth in Zimbabwe are no longer so stark, the gap between rich and poor—12 years after independence— is still very wide. Minimum wage levels have been legislated, but the income gap has not narrowed much because of (1) the differential effects of inflation (12.1% for high-income urban dwellers in 1984, compared with 20.1% for low-income earners); (2) the wide gap in income levels (e.g., in 1981 in the civil service pay scale the highest level was 34 times the lowest); and (3) a regressive tax system (Hampson and Kaseke, 1989). The same authors suggest that in the rural areas the commercial farmers have better infrastructure and credit arrangements, which allow that group to capitalize on the prevailing producer prices to a greater extent than those in the peasant sector.

In Zimbabwe, until independence, pension coverage followed racial lines. Until 1980 all non-Africans who had reached retirement age and had assets less than a certain minimum or earned below a certain amount could receive a modest pension. Although the scheme has been discontinued, pensions that were in existence in 1980 continue to be paid. Government coverage for elderly Zimbabweans now consists solely of assistance by the Ministry of Public Service, Labour and Social Welfare through a public assistance for the destitute. The program is noncontributory but means-tested. Only a small fraction of the nation's elderly come within this coverage, especially those living in the rural areas. The department has been active in opening up a considerable number of rural offices, but public assistance continues to be an urban phenomenon, and the largest single category of public assistance applicants are elderly destitute.

As regards private pensions, Riddell (1980) noted that 70% of the European work force are covered by pension schemes, but the African work force, in general, is very poorly served. Only 17% of the agricultural work force and 44% of all Africans in formal sector employment are covered by pension schemes. Even those who are covered are not likely to receive substantial benefits. The study noted that only 1.3% of urban Africans in wage employment will receive pensions above the urban poverty datum line (PDL). The extent of destitution for black urban elderly is considerable.

A few farsighted efforts to provide financial security for urban workers upon retirement were met with opposition from various interest groups, including the so-called native commissioners. The assumption was that African workers were only temporary migrants in towns; urban life was for whites. When the "native" ended his period of employment, he was expected to return to his rural home.

The economic hardships of the elderly were, and still are, not fully appreciated by most African states. It is often supposed, for example, that the local community in Africa still provides old-age security, when, in fact, its economic role has been attenuated. Economic hardships are particularly acute for those workers who migrated from neighboring countries like Malawi, Zambia, Angola, and Mozambique. For the most part employed in commercial farms, mines, and domestic service, these workers had no rural home to return to in Zimbabwe once they ended their period of employment. The colonial policy of repatriation shifted the costs of retirement for these individuals onto the country of origin.

As a result of the declining rural economy and the lack of an adequate Social Security system in urban Zimbabwe, many of the nation's elderly face severe economic hardships. Most of the elderly interviewed in various studies were found to be destitute (Mucheua, 1978; Hampson, 1982; Nyanguru, 1987, 1990, 1991, 1992; Nyanguru and Peil, 1991; Adamchack et al., 1990). In particular, they were without the resources to pay rent or buy food, clothing, and other necessities.

For those elderly who were never in formal employment or who never received a pension, their usual source of subsistence is peasant farming. Seventy-five percent of elderly men and 83% of elderly women live in rural areas. Although evidence is scanty, it seems that rural households containing elderly are particularly poor, in comparison with elderly-headed urban households. Households with elderly members are undercapitated, with few or no cattle. Over half the rural households have no cattle, a serious deficiency when considering the economic, cultural, and productive significance of livestock. Many cattle in rural and commercial farming areas have died because of the recent 1992–93 drought—the worst in living memory. Previous reliance on household members' remitting cash to their rural homes seems to be becoming less common (Nyanguru, 1991; Hampson, 1990). In one study of rural elderly, fewer than 14% were in receipt of monthly remittances, and one-third of the elderly whose children were in paid employment reported never receiving remittances (Hampson 1985). During the drought year 1992, both government and voluntary agencies were deeply involved in the provision of drought relief throughout the country.

HEALTH CARE SERVICES

Before independence the gap between urban and rural health services (very closely paralleling the gap between white and black service) was extreme. The capital's main hospital (white) absorbed over 25% of the health budget, yet the capital's black hospital found that 31% of infant and child deaths were primarily caused by malnutrition (Hampson and Kaseke, 1989). Infant mortality in rural areas was estimated at 300 per 1,000. The national ratio of one hospital bed for every 452 people hid a rural provision that was three times as scarce. Urban workplace clinics and hospitals were well provided, but rural health care was mainly of an inferior standard and often voluntary agency- or mission-sponsored.

State health services are free for those earning less than $150 per month; yet availability is still rather uneven, with the cities well served at the expense of the rural population. State pharmacies are often short of many drugs, which can be purchased at considerable expense on the open market. Zimbabwe's access to health care professionals is highly skewed; with an average population per physician of 8,056, the rural population's average is 2,000 while the rural popultation is 33,000 per physician. The national average population per nurse and midwife is 1,190, but in the towns it is 320, while in rural areas it is 2,000. Many professionals have recently left the country for "greener pastures" in South Africa, Namibia, and Europe.

Municipal clinics charge small fees for services, as do mission health services, because they often find government financial assistance unable to cover their costs. The government spends around 1.4% of gross national product (GNP) on health services.

There are a few chronic care services, especially for the elderly. These are termed "C" schemes or nursing homes. Most of these schemes care for European elderly. For the African elderly, there are only two such homes, with only 100 beds for the entire African population. There has been a problem in many hospitals because elderly people stay there for long periods of time because they cannot be released to a relative or to an appropriate environment for their chronic illness.

There has been extensive use of institutional care, especially among the European section of the community. There is very little provision of health care to the personal dwellings of elderly persons living in the community. A few Europeans living in urban areas, at times, have the services of a district visiting nurse. Some church organizations have a visiting nurse for some of their elderly members.

With structural adjustment, people are now asked to pay for their medical treatment. In Zimbabwe, however, the Europeans have better access to health facilities than their African counterparts. Nyanguru (1991), in a study of old people's homes, found that 79% of the Europeans had personal doctors or were on private medical aid. None of the African elderly had these. Inequalities in health care are now by class, which could be termed the "reverse care law": the wealthy who need care least absorb the greatest expenditure on health, while the needy poor get the poorest care.

HOUSING RESOURCES

There is no policy in Zimbabwe to assist the elderly with housing (with the hope of keeping them in their homes). Most assistance is for the European community and is provided by associations (e.g., Masonic Association). There is no such function among the African elderly, especially in towns. Hence, a number of elderly are homeless because some of the houses they had lived in were tied to their employment. There is no shortage of accommodations for the rural elderly; however, they are of poor quality. Elderly people in rural areas often live in substandard houses. In a study by Nyanguru and Peil (1991), one-fifth of the houses in urban areas were inferior, while a third were judged the same in rural areas, and 41% of homes in urban areas were good, with only 24% judged the same in rural areas. The elderly in rural areas, whose homes are often thatched, have had problems in replacing thatch on their houses, (especially after the 1992 drought.)

In an attempt to have a comprehensive policy for the care of the elderly, the government of Zimbabwe has built upon the foundation laid by the colonial government. The old regime had established a very efficient and rather humane system of care for the elderly in the European section of the community. Waterston (1982), referring to the European population, writes that Rhodesia, as it was then, had the highest percentage of its elderly population in residential care in the world, over four times the comparable rate for the United Kingdom.

There are about 81 old folks' homes provided by the voluntary sector—housing over 3,000 residents. There are three types of homes. The sheltered or cottage type ("A" scheme) provides for the slightly frail population. The individuals live independently in their own homes but have access to a local warden in case of need. About 20% of the schemes are of this type and are occupied only by Europeans. The "B" scheme, or hostel accommodation, provides meals, a laundry service, and general care for residents, and 58% of the homes are of this type. These homes cater to Europeans, coloreds, and Africans. Finally, "C" schemes were instituted for the very frail and handicapped and provide nursing care and assistance with activities of daily living (such as use of the toilet and dressing). About 15% of the homes are of this type. However, the majority provide accommodations for Europeans and coloreds. There are only two such facilities for the total African population in the country. Most of the homes are found in the major towns and cities of Zimbabwe, with Harare (capital city) having 44%, Bulawayo 18%, Mutare and Marondera 7% each, and Masvingo 4%. The other smaller towns have one or two homes each; as has been mentioned before, there are more homes catering to European elderly than the African and colored elderly put together. This is because there has been the belief that the African elderly can still be looked after by their kin. However, there has been a very rapid increase in the number of old people's homes established soon after independence. Before independence, only three old people's homes cared for the African elderly. Even these were not full to capacity.

However, in 1992, there were 20 old people's homes, with more than four under construction. The reason for this high increase was that many African communities have felt the need to establish these homes for the many destitute, homeless elderly. One common feature of these homes is that they are not purposefully built. A number of dilapidated buildings have been renovated to accommodate these elderly. Also a number of international and national donor agencies have provided funds for the construction of such facilities.

The people occupying such homes have mainly been of foreign origin, from Malawi, Mozambique, and so on. However, there was an increase, after independence, of Zimbabweans' needing residential accommodations. The Zimbabweans include people who have been in jail for a long time and were released by presidential amnesty after independence, returnee elderly refugees who could not locate their relatives, ex-mental patients, and ex-migrant workers from mines in South Africa.

There has been no old people's home built for either the Europeans or coloreds since 1980. In fact, many homes have been closed due to lack of patronage. This is probably because a number of European elderly emigrated to South Africa, Australia, and Europe after independence. For the construction of old people's homes, the government provides 25% of the building costs, state lotteries match another 25%, and the balance comes from those building the homes. Most of the European homes have been built by local communities and associations and do not usually admit anyone except members. These homes tend to be a short distance from where the elderly persons used to live.

For the African counterparts, this has not always been the case. They have often been placed in homes far from their previous residence. Because of this and the fact that most are foreign, they do not have easy contact with friends and relatives. The Department of Social Welfare provides $100 per month per resident for homes of the destitute elderly. European homes are self-financing, and in most homes residents pay for their upkeep according to their ability. The poorer residents are subsidized by the richer. Most of these homes have money in trust, and they also get funds from legacies. The Ministry of Health pays bed grants for the elderly in "C" schemes. The amount has been very modest and was raised in 1991. One of the two African "C" schemes could not be open for six years due to the fact that the Ministry of Health failed to pay the bed grant.

SUPPORTIVE SERVICES

There are very few supportive services for the elderly in Zimbabwe. A few European elderly get meals-on-wheels, mainly offered by church-related organizations. The Salvation Army is very active in this area. There are no social work or counseling services for the elderly in the country.

LEISURE-TIME RESOURCES

There are no organized leisure-time resources, except for a few day-care centers for the European section of the community. Some of these centers are rundown due to lack of support, as a number of European elderly emigrated after independence.

ADVOCACY AND PROTECTION

With the Economic Structural Adjustment Program (recommended by the World Bank for greater efficiency) and the subsequent rise in prices and retrenchment of workers, the country has had a very steep rise in the crime rate.

The local newspapers have reported an increase in crimes against the elderly. Many elderly, especially elderly women living alone, have often been targets of thieves. Nyanguru (1990), in a study of old people's homes, found that the majority of European elderly women entered old-age homes for security reasons.

Some elderly people reported that they had built security fences around their homes, but this did not give them the security they needed. One elderly European reported that insurance companies had refused to insure her because she had had too many burglaries. She had become too risky to insure.

Yet, there are no formal advocacy and protection services in Zimbabwe. The elderly are not seen as a distinct group, and the elderly do not see themselves in that light.

FUTURE PROJECTIONS

The main problem with the elderly in Zimbabwe is poverty. For the majority in the subsistence economy, their livelihood depends on the vagaries of the weather, and the few who are formally employed receive no pensions when they retire. This has significance for their quality of life in that they have difficulties in meeting their basic needs (shelter, food, health, transportation).

The situation has been worsened by the introduction of the Economic Structural Adjustment Program, which is likely to make the elderly poorer. By implementing the program, workers have been involuntarily retired from government and the private sector. So far over 8,000 workers have been forced to retire, mainly because of their age.

The most important impact is that older workers are unlikely to be considered for retraining for another job. Because they are in low-paying and unskilled jobs, they are not likely to get a pension. If they do get one, it is not inflation-related. They are likely to be frustrated and to see the pension as not being adequate.

Because the elderly have little money, they suffer malnutrition, leading to depression and mental confusion. The most vulnerable elderly in Zimbabwe are widowers who have never been involved in food preparation.

AIDS

Zimbabwe has been affected by the epidemic of AIDS, and the highest incidence of human immunodeficiency virus (HIV) infection and AIDS occurs at young ages in both males and females; a quarter of the diagnosed AIDS cases occur in babies and young children. Because of this, it is easy to regard the problems of the elderly as relatively unimportant. Yet, the impact will affect none more than the surviving grandmothers.

A number of young people, because of the effects of the Structural Adjustment Program (and the recession) will engage in prostitution, contract AIDS, and become ill (at times for very long periods). They will need nursing care, which usually comes from the elderly, who have few resources at their disposal. Also, in view of the tendency for older men to marry younger additional wives in a community where mobility of partners is accepted, some of the older husbands will also develop AIDS, probably much more frequently than the sexually inactive senior wives. Thus, the grandmother's future existence is compounded by grief and struggle with an unknown disease of terrible potential. It is not uncommon for grandmothers to look after eight or more grandchildren and great-grandchildren who are AIDS victims.

Policy Suggestions

The first line of defense for the elderly is the family. Most families have an obligation and want to look after their elderly relatives, but they do not have the means to do so—many are too young or are unemployed. There is need for policies to keep the family intact, perhaps through the introduction of a cash disability allowance or constant attendant allowance for family members or neighbors (at a cost less than that of care by a trained professional and less than that for the institutional care of an older person).

With the introduction of the Structural Adjustment Program in Zimbabwe, elderly people are going to be squeezed out of the formal sector by the younger, more educated, retrenched workers who have capital and training. There is need to give resources to the elderly.

The elderly should be encouraged to stay within their own communities. One suggestion is the creation of old people's cooperatives where the residents establish surrogate kinship (or *sahwira*) with another older person.

It is also suggested that supplementary feeding schemes be developed for the elderly (especially in rural areas). Relatedly, geriatric dentistry needs to be expanded in the country. Also, a crop levy for rural elderly farmers could be developed, so that the government could buy surplus food from the elderly in good times and provide them with financial assistance in times of drought based upon the earned credit.

Finally, it is suggested that national planning for the elderly involve them at all stages of planning and implementation. Planners need to remember the full potential of the elderly and remember that their conceptual thoughts and logical reasoning do not suffer with age if they have continued opportunities to cultivate these abilities.

BIBLIOGRAPHY

Adamchak, D., Nyanguru, A., Hampson, J., and Wilson, A. (1991). "Aging and Support Systems: Intergenerational Transfer in Zimbabwe." *Gerontologist* 31 (4):505–513.
Bledsoe, C. (1980). *Women and Marriage in Kpelle Society,* Stanford, CA: Stanford University Press.

Clarke, D. (1977). *Economics of African Old Age Subsistence in Rhodesia.* Gweru: Mambo Press.
Gelfand, M. (1965). *African Background: The Traditional Culture of the Shona-Speaking People.* Cape Town: Juta.
Hampson, J. (1982). *Old Age, a Study of Aging in Zimbabwe.* Gweru: Mambo Press.
―――. (1985). "Elderly People and Social Welfare in Zimbabwe." *Aging and Society* 5:37–67.
―――. (1990). "The Marginalisation of the Rural Elderly." *Journal of Social Development in Africa* 6(2):7–24.
Hampson, J., and Kaseke, E. (1989). "Social Welfare in Zimbabwe." In J. Dickson, *Social Welfare in Africa.* London: Croom Helm.
Kasere, C. (1990). Speech delivered by the director of social welfare at the completion of Sick Bay at Melfort Farm Project. 4 July.
Mucheua, O. (1978). *Africa Aged in Town,* Harare: School of Social Work.
Nyanguru, A. C. (1987). "Residential Care for the Destitute Elderly: A Comparative Study of Two Institutions in Zimbabwe." *Journal of Cross-Cultural Gerontology* 2:345–357.
―――. (1990). "The Quality of Life of the Elderly Living in Institutions and Homes in Zimbabwe." *Journal of Social Development in Africa* 5(2):25–43.
―――. (1991). "The Health Problems of the Elderly Living in Institutions and Homes in Zimbabwe." *Journal of Social Development in Africa* 6(2):71–89.
―――. (1993). "A Home That Is Its Community." In K. Tout, *Elderly Care: A World Perspective.* London: Chapman and Hall.
Nyanguru A. C., Hampson, J., Adamchack, D., and Wilson, A. (1991). "Family Support for the Elderly in Zimbabwe." Paper presented to the Board of Directors, Help Age Zimbabwe.
Nyanguru, A. C., and Peil, M. (1991). "Zimbabwe Since Independence: An Assessment." *African Affairs* 90:607–620.
Peil, M. (1988). "Family Support for Nigerian Elderly." Paper presented at the ASA Conference on the Social Construction of Youth, Maturation, and Aging.
Riddell, R. (1980). *Report of the Commission of Enquiry into Incomes, Prices and Conditions of Service.* Harare: Government Printers.
Tarira, J. (1983). "Helping the Aged in Their Rural Environment." B.S.W. diss., School of Social Work, Harare.
Waterson, L. (1982). "Medical Problems Associated with Ageing." In J. Hampson, ed., *Old Age: A Study of Ageing in Zimbabwe.* Gweru: Mambo Press.
Wilson, A., Nyanguru, A. C., Hampson, J., and Adamchak, D. (1990). "A Study of Well-Being in Three Elderly Communities in Zimbabwe." Paper presented at Workshop on Geriatric Care of the Elderly. University of Zimbabwe Medical School, Harare.

SELECTED BIBLIOGRAPHY

Barrow, G. M. (1986). *Aging, the Individual, and Society.* 3d ed. New York: West.
Brody, E. M. (1981). "Women in the middle" and family help to older people. *Gerontologist,* 21(5), 471–480.
Chan, P. H. T. (1985). *Report of Elderly Abuse at Home in Hong Kong.* Hong Kong: Council of Social Service and Hong Kong Polytechnic.
Chappel, N. L. (1990). Aging and social care. In *Aging and the Social Sciences,* 3d ed., ed. R. H. Binstock and L. K. George. New York: Academic Press, 438–454.
Chow, N. W. S. (1988). *Caregiving in Developing East and Southeast Asia Countries.* Tampa, FL: International Exchange Center on Gerontology, University of South Florida.
Clark, M., and Anderson, B. (1967). *Culture and Aging.* Springfield, IL: Charles C. Thomas. (Also in Barrow, 1986.)
Cowgill, D. (1986). *Aging Around the World.* Belmont, CA: Wadsworth.
Cowgill, D., and Holmes, L. (1972). *Aging and Modernization.* New York: Appleton-Century-Crofts.
Garrett, W. W. (1979–80). Filial responsibility laws. *Journal of Family Law,* 18, 793–818.
Gibson, M. J. (1983). Family support of the elderly mentally ill: An international overview. Paper presented at the World Congress for Mental Health, Washington, DC.
———. (1984). Family support patterns, policies, and programs. In *Innovative Aging Programs Abroad: Implications for the United States,* ed. C. Nusberg. Westport, CT: Greenwood Press, 159–195.
Greengross, S. (1981). Caring for the carers. In *Care in the Community: Recent Research and Current Projects,* ed. F. Glendenning. Stoke-on-Trent, England: Beth Johnson Foundation, 18–30.
International Institute on Aging. (1989). Preliminary findings of survey on training needs in developing countries. Report prepared for the Expert Group Meeting on Short-Term Training in Social Gerontology, Valletta, Malta.

Keith, J. (1990). Age in social and cultural context: Anthropological perspectives. In *Handbook of Aging and the Social Sciences,* 3d ed., ed. R. H. Binstock and L. K. George. New York: Academic Press, 91–111.

Kosberg, J. I. (1988). *Family Care of the Aged in the United States: Policy Issues from an International Perspective.* Tampa, FL: International Exchange Center on Gerontology, University of South Florida.

———. (1990). Assistance to crime and abuse victims. In *Handbook of Gerontological Services,* 2d ed., edited by A. Monk. New York: Columbia University Press, 450–473.

Kosberg, J. I., and Garcia, J. L. (1991). Social changes affecting family care of the elderly. *Bold* (Journal of the International Institute on Aging), 1(2), 2–5.

Lewis, J., and Meredith, B. (1988). Daughters caring for mothers. *Ageing and Society,* 8, 1–21.

Myers, G. C. (1990). Demography of aging. In *Handbook of Aging and the Social Sciences,* 3d ed., ed. R. H. Binstock and L. K. George. New York: Academic Press, 19–44.

Tauber, C. (1990). Diversity: The dramatic reality. In *Diversity in Aging: Challenges Facing Planners and Policy-Makers in the 1990s,* ed. S. Bass, E. Kutza, and F. Torres-Gil. Glenview, IL: Scott, Foreman.

Tout, K. (1989). *Aging in Developing Countries.* New York: Oxford University.

United Nations. (1980). *Selected Demographic Indicators by Country, 1950–2000: Demographic Estimates and Projections as Assessed in 1978.* Ser. R 138. (Also in Barrow, 1986.)

———. (1988). *Economic and Social Implications of Population Aging.* (ST/ESA/SER.R/85). New York: United Nations. (Also in Myers, 1990.)

INDEX

Aged and Disabled Persons Hostels Act (1972)(Australia), 20
Aged or Disabled Persons Homes Amendment Act (1988)(Australia), 26
Aged Persons Homes Act, (1954)(Australia), 20, 26
Aging, statistics on, xv–xvi
Argentina: economic characteristics, 3–4; future projections, 11–14; gender differences, 2; Gerontological Conference (1989), 1; government, role of, 4–5; health care services, 6–8, 13; health status, 3; housing resources, 8–9, 12–13; income maintenance and employment, 5–6; legal assistance, 11, 13–14; leisure-time resources, 10–11, 13; life expectancy in, 3; status of elderly in, 1–4; supportive services, 9–10
Association of Retired Officers of the Services and Education (AROSE) (Barbados), 63
At-home facilities/services: in Argentina, 8, 9; in Austria, 40; in Malaysia, 258–259; in Norway, 327–328; in Spain, 379; in Sweden, 405, 406; in Switzerland, 421; in Thailand, 438; in the United States, 451–452
Australia: Aborigines and Torres Strait Islanders (ATSI), 19; educational resources, 29; future projections, 31–32; gender differences, 17, 18, 19, 22–23; government, role of, 19–21; health care services, 23–25, 31–32; health status, 19; housing resources, 25, 31; income maintenance and employment, 21–23, 31; legal assistance, 30–31; leisure-time resources, 29; life expectancy in, 30–31; status of elderly in, 17–19; supportive services, 25–28
Austria: demographic overview, 35–36; educational resources, 45; expansion of social services, 36–37; future projections, 48–49; gender differences, 35, 39; government, role of, 37–38; health care services, 40–41; housing resources, 41–42; income maintenance and employment, 38–40; legal assistance, 46–47; leisure-time resources, 45–46; life expectancy in, 46–47; status of elderly in, 34–37; supportive services, 43–45

Barbadian Organization of Retired Nurses (BORN)(Bardados), 63
Barbados: economic assistance, 54–55; educational resources, 63; future pro-

jections, 64; government, role of, 52, 53, 60; health care services, 56–58; housing resources, 58–59; income maintenance and employment, 53–56, 60; legal assistance, 63–64; leisure-time resources, 62–63; life expectancy in, 63–64; status of elderly in, 51–53; supportive services, 60–62
British North American Act (Canada), 67

Canada: educational resources, 74; future projections, 78–77; gender differences, 67, 72; government, role of, 67–68; health care services, 70–71; housing resources, 71–73; income maintenance and employment, 68–70; legal assistance, 75; leisure-time resources, 74–75; life expectancy in, 75; status of elderly in, 66–67; supportive services, 73–74
Canada Health Act, 68
Canada/Quebec Pension Plan, 69
Charities Act (1979)(Barbados), 62
China: demographic characteristics, 81–83; educational resources, 90, 91; future projections, 92–93; gender differences, 81; government, role of, 83–85; health care services, 86–87; health status, 82; housing resources, 81–82, 87–88; income maintenance and employment, 81, 82–83, 85–86; legal assistance, 91–92; leisure-time resources, 90–91; life expectancy in, 91–92; status of elderly in, 80–83; supportive services, 88–90
China National Committee on Aging, 88–89
Clubs/associations: in Argentina, 10–11; in Austria, 45; in Barbados, 62–63; in China, 90–91; in Czech and Slovak Federal Republic, 102; in Ghana, 150; in Israel, 208–209; in Japan, 240; in Malta, 282–283; in the Netherlands, 301; in New Zealand, 316; in Poland, 351; in South Korea, 365–366; in Spain, 384–385; in the Sudan, 398; in Switzerland, 426; in the United States, 455; in the USSR, 469

Comité National des Retraités et Personnes Agées (National Committee of Pensioners and Elderly Persons) (France), 122
Czech and Slovak Federal Republic (CSFR)(Former): educational resources, 102; future projections, 102–103; government, role of, 96–97; health care services, 98–99; health status, 96; housing resources, 99–100; income maintenance and employment, 97–98; legal assistance, 102; leisure-time resources, 101–102; life expectancy in, 102; status of elderly in, 95–96; supportive services, 101

"Declaration of the Rights of the Elderly" (UN), 1
Direccion Nacional de Ancianidad (DNA) (Argentina), 4, 5, 9

Economic Structural Adjustment Program (Zimbabwe), 479, 480, 481
Educational resources: in Australia, 29; in Austria, 45; in Barbados, 63; in Canada, 74; in China, 90, 91; in Czech and Slovak Federal Republic, 102; in France, 122; in Germany, 135; in Great Britain, 171; in Hong Kong, 184; in India, 195; in Israel, 209; in Italy, 221; in Japan, 240–241; in Malaysia, 265; in Malta, 283; in the Netherlands, 301–302; in New Zealand, 316–317; in Norway, 333; in Poland, 351; in South Korea, 366–367; in Spain, 385; in the Sudan, 398; in Sweden, 409; in Switzerland, 426; in Thailand, 441; in the United States, 455; in the USSR, 469
Elizabethan Poor Law (1601)(Great Britain), 158
Employment: in Argentina, 5–6; in Australia, 21–23, 31; in Austria, 38–40; in Barbados, 55–56; in Canada, 70; in China, 81, 85–86; in Czech and Slovak Federal Republic, 97–98; in France, 112–115; in Germany, 127–129; in Ghana, 143, 144–146; in Great Britain,

156, 160–162; in Hong Kong, 179; in India, 190–192; in Israel, 199, 201–203; in Italy, 216–217; in Japan, 228, 232–233; in Jordan, 244–245, 246–247; in Malaysia, 253, 256–257; in Malta, 273–274; in the Netherlands, 293–294; in New Zealand, 308; in Norway, 325–327; in Poland, 344–346; in South Korea, 358–361; in Spain, 375–377; in the Sudan, 395–396; in Sweden, 403–404; in Switzerland, 420; in Thailand, 434–435; in the United States, 448–450; in the USSR, 461; in Zimbabwe, 474–476
Established Programs Financing Act (1977) (Canada), 68
Euthanasia: in Austria, 47; in Canada, 75; in the Netherlands, 302
Exceptional Medical Expenses Act (1968) (AWBZ)(Netherlands), 295

Family care of the elderly, changing views toward, xvi–xvii
Federal Social Welfare Act (1961) (Germany), 127, 128, 129
Federation of Austrian Social Insurance Institutes (1955), 38
Financial assistance: in Argentina, 3–4; in Barbados, 54–55, 60
Food programs: in Argentina, 9; in Australia, 29; in Austria, 43–44; in Barbados, 55, 61; in Canada, 72, 73; in Czech and Slovak Federal Republic, 101; in Germany, 132–133; in India, 193–194; in Israel, 207; in Malaysia, 262; in Malta, 281–282; in Norway, 331; in Poland, 349–350; in the USSR, 466; in Zimbabwe, 479
France: educational resources, 122; future projections, 122–123; gender differences, 105, 113; government, role of, 110–112; health care services, 115–117; housing resources, 117–119; income maintenance and employment, 112–115; legal assistance, 122; leisure-time resources, 121–122; life expectancy in, 108; status of elderly in, 104–110; supportive services, 119–120

Gender differences: in Argentina, 2; in Australia, 17, 18, 19, 22–23; in Austria, 35, 39; in Canada, 67, 72; in China, 81; in France, 105, 113; in Germany, 126; in Ghana, 141, 142; in Great Britain, 155–56; in Hong Kong, 175; in India, 189; in Israel, 199; in Jordan, 245; in Malaysia, 253; in Malta, 272; in the Netherlands, 291; in New Zealand, 306; in Norway, 323–324; in Poland, 341, 343; in Spain, 374; in the Sudan, 394, 396; in Sweden, 402; in Switzerland, 417; in Thailand, 430; in the USSR, 458–459; in Zimbabwe, 473
Germany: educational resources, 135; future projections, 136–137; gender differences, 126; government, role of, 127; health care services, 129–131; housing resources, 131–132; income maintenance and employment, 127–129; legal assistance, 135–136; leisure-time resources, 134–135; life expectancy in, 126; status of elderly in, 125–127; supportive services, 132–134
Ghana: demographic characteristics, 140–141; future projections, 151–152; gender differences, 141, 142; government, role of, 143–144; health care services, 146–147; housing resources, 147–148; income maintenance and employment, 143, 144–146; legal assistance, 150–151; leisure-time resources, 149–150; life expectancy in, 150–151; status of elderly in, 139–143; supportive services, 148–149
Government, role of: in Argentina, 4–5; in Australia, 19–21; in Austria, 37–38; in Barbados, 52, 53, 60; in Canada, 67–68; in China, 83–85; in Czech and Slovak Federal Republic, 96–97; in France, 110–112; in Germany, 127; in Ghana, 143–144; in Great Britain, 158–160; in Hong Kong, 177–178; in India, 190, 192; in Israel, 200–201; in Italy, 214–216; in Japan, 229–231; in Jordan, 245–246; in Malaysia, 254; in Malta, 274–277; in the Netherlands,

291–292; in New Zealand, 307; in Norway, 324–325; in Poland, 343–344; in South Korea, 357–358; in Spain, 374–375; in Sweden, 402–403; in Switzerland, 418–419; in Thailand, 431–434; in the United States, 446–448; in the USSR, 459–460; in Zimbabwe, 473–474
Gratuity Act (1972)(India), 191
Great Britain: educational resources, 171; future projections, 172; gender differences, 155–156; government, role of, 158–160; health care services, 162–165; health status, 157; housing resources, 165–167; income maintenance and employment, 156, 160–162; legal assistance, 171–172; leisure-time resources, 170–171; life expectancy in, 171–172; status of elderly in, 154–158; supportive services, 167–170
Guaranteed Income Supplement (GIS)(Canada), 69

Health and Medical Services Act (1983)(Sweden), 402–403
Health care services: in Argentina, 6–8, 13; in Australia, 23–25, 31–32; in Austria, 40–41; in Barbados, 56–58; in Canada, 70–71; in China, 86–87; in Czech and Slovak Federal Republic, 98–99; in France, 115–117; in Germany, 129–131; in Ghana, 146–147; in Great Britain, 162–165; in Hong Kong, 179–181; in India, 192–193; in Israel, 203–205; in Italy, 217–218; in Japan, 233–234; in Jordan, 248–249; in Malaysia, 257–259; in Malta, 279–280; in the Netherlands, 294–297; in New Zealand, 308–312; in Norway, 327–329; in Poland, 346–347; in South Korea, 361–363; in Spain, 377–379; in the Sudan, 396–397; in Sweden, 405–406; in Switzerland, 420–423; in Thailand, 435–438; in the United States, 450–452; in the USSR, 461–463; in Zimbabwe, 476–477
Health Reform Law (1989) (Germany), 130

Health status: in Argentina, 3; in Australia, 19; in China, 82; in Czech and Slovak Federal Republic, 96; in Great Britain, 157; in Israel, 199–200; in Italy, 214; in Japan, 233; in Malaysia, 254; in Malta, 274; in New Zealand, 306; in Norway, 324; in Poland, 343; in South Korea, 361; in the Sudan, 396; in Sweden, 402; in Thailand, 430–431; in the United States, 450; in Zimbabwe, 480–481
Help Age Ghana, 148, 149
Home and Community Care Act (1985) (Australia), 27–28
Home Help Service (Barbados), 59–60
Home Help Services (Sweden), 407–408
Home Nursing Subsidy Scheme (Australia), 20
Hong Kong: educational resources, 184; future projections, 185–186; gender differences, 175; government, role of, 177–178; health care services, 179–181; housing resources, 181–183; income maintenance and employment, 178–179; legal assistance, 184–185; leisure-time resources, 184; life expectancy in, 184–185; status of elderly in, 175–176; supportive services, 183
Hospitals: in Argentina, 7; in Barbados, 57; in Canada, 71; in China, 86; in Czech and Slovak Federal Republic, 98–99; in France, 116–117; in Germany, 130–131; in Great Britain, 163; in Hong Kong, 179–180; in Israel, 204; in Malaysia, 257–258; in Malta, 279–280; in the Netherlands, 296–297; in New Zealand, 309–310; in Norway, 327; in Poland, 346–347; in South Korea, 362; in Spain, 378–379; in Sweden, 405; in Switzerland, 422–423; in Thailand, 436–438; in the United States, 450–451; in the USSR, 462; in Zimbabwe, 477
Housing resources: in Argentina, 8–9, 12–13; in Australia, 25, 31; in Austria, 41–42; in Barbados, 58–59; in Canada, 71–73; in China, 81–82, 87–88; in

Czech and Slovak Federal Republic, 99–100; in France, 117–119; in Germany, 131–132; in Ghana, 147–148; in Great Britain, 165–167; in Hong Kong, 181–183; in India, 193; in Israel, 205–206; in Italy, 218–219; in Japan, 234–237; in Jordan, 249; in Malaysia, 259–261; in Malta, 280–281; in the Netherlands, 297–299; in New Zealand, 312–313; in Norway, 329–330; in Poland, 347–349; in South Korea, 363–364; in Spain, 379–382; in the Sudan, 397–398; in Sweden, 406–407; in Switzerland, 423–424; in Thailand, 438–440; in the United States, 452; in the USSR, 464–465; in Zimbabwe, 477–479

Income maintenance: in Argentina, 5–6; in Australia, 21–23; in Austria, 38–40; in Barbados, 53–56; in Canada, 68–70; in China, 82–83; in Czech and Slovak Federal Republic, 97–98; in France, 112–115; in Germany, 127–129; in Ghana, 144–146; in Great Britain, 160–162; in Hong Kong, 178–179; in India, 190–192; in Israel, 201–203; in Italy, 216–217; in Japan, 231–232; in Jordan, 246–247; in Malaysia, 254–256; in Malta, 274, 277–279; in the Netherlands, 292–293; in New Zealand, 307–308; in Norway, 325–327; in Poland, 344–346; in South Korea, 358–361; in Spain, 375–377; in the Sudan, 395–396; in Sweden, 403–404; in Switzerland, 419–420; in Thailand, 434–435; in the United States, 448–450; in the USSR, 460–461; in Zimbabwe, 474–476

India: educational resources, 195; future projections, 196–197; gender differences, 189; government, role of, 190, 192; health care services, 192–193; housing resources, 193; income maintenance and employment, 190–192; legal assistance, 195–196; leisure-time resources, 194–195; life expectancy in, 195–196; status of elderly in, 188–189; supportive services, 193–194

Inter-American Development Bank (IADB) study, 58

Israel: educational resources, 209; future projections, 210–211; gender differences, 199; government, role of, 200–201; health care services, 203–205; health status, 199–200; housing resources, 205–206; income maintenance and employment, 199, 201–203; legal assistance, 209–210; leisure-time resources, 208–209; life expectancy in, 209–210; status of elderly in, 198–200; supportive services, 206–208

ISTAT (Italian National Institute of Statistics), 217, 218

Italy: educational resources, 221; future projections, 223–225; government, role of, 214–216; health care services, 217–218; health status, 214; housing resources, 218–219; income maintenance and employment, 216–217; legal assistance, 221–223; leisure-time resources, 220–221; life expectancy in, 221–223; status of elderly in, 213–216; supportive services, 219–220

Japan: demographic characteristics, 227; educational resources, 240–241; future projections, 241–243; government, role of, 229–231; health care services, 233–234; health status, 233; housing resources, 234–237; income maintenance and employment, 228, 231–233; legal assistance, 241; leisure-time resources, 240–241; life expectancy in, 241; status of elderly in, 227–229; supportive services, 237–240

Jordan: future projections, 250–251; gender differences, 245; government, role of, 245–246; health care services, 248–249; housing resources, 249; income maintenance and employment, 244–245, 246–247; legal assistance, 250; leisure-time resources, 249–250; life expectancy in, 250; status of elderly in, 244–245; supportive services, 249

Knights of Saint John (Malta), 270, 274–75

Labor Protection Regulations of People's Republic of China (1951), 85
Law for the Health of the Aged (1982) (Japan), 230, 233, 234
Law for the Welfare of the Aged (1963) (Japan), 228–229, 230–231, 233–237
Law of National Assistance (1961) (Germany), 127
Legal assistance: in Argentina, 11, 13–14; in Australia, 30–31; in Austria, 46–47; in Barbados, 63–64; in Canada, 75; in China, 91–92; in Czech and Slovak Federal Republic, 102; in France, 122; in Germany, 135–136; in Ghana, 150–151; in Great Britain, 171–172; in Hong Kong, 184–185; in India, 195–196; in Israel, 209–210; in Italy, 221–223; in Japan, 241; in Jordan, 250; in Malaysia, 265–267; in Malta, 283–284; in the Netherlands, 302; in New Zealand, 317–318; in Norway, 333–335; in Poland, 352; in South Korea, 367–368; in Spain, 388–389; in the Sudan, 399; in Sweden, 410; in Switzerland, 427; in Thailand, 442; in the United States, 455–456; in the USSR, 469–470; in Zimbabwe, 479–480
Leisure-time resources: in Argentina, 10–11, 13; in Australia, 29; in Austria, 45–46; in Barbados, 62–63; in Canada, 74–75; in China, 90–91; in Czech and Slovak Federal Republic, 101–102; in France, 121–122; in Germany, 134–135; in Ghana, 149–150; in Great Britain, 170–171; in Hong Kong, 184; in India, 194–195; in Israel, 208–209; in Italy, 220–221; in Japan, 240–241; in Jordan, 249–250; in Malaysia, 263–265; in Malta, 282–283; in the Netherlands, 301–302; in New Zealand, 315–317; in Norway, 332–333; in Poland, 350–351; in South Korea, 365–367; in Spain, 384–388; in the Sudan, 398; in Sweden, 409–410; in Switzerland, 424–426; in Thailand, 441; in the United States, 454–455; in the USSR, 468–469; in Zimbabwe, 479
Life expectancy: in Argentina, 3; in Australia, 18; in Austria, 35–36; in Canada, 67; in Czech and Slovak Federal Republic, 96; in France, 108; in Germany, 126; in Hong Kong, 175; in India, 189; in Israel, 199; in Italy, 213–214; in Japan, 227; in Jordan, 244; in Malta, 272; in the Netherlands, 291; in New Zealand, 306; in Norway, 323–324; in Poland, 341, 343; in South Korea, 356; in Switzerland, 417; in Thailand, 430–431; in the United States, 445; in the USSR, 459; in Zimbabwe, 473

Malaysia: demographic characteristics, 252–253; educational resources, 265; future projections, 267–268; gender differences, 253; government, role of, 254; health care services, 257–259; health status, 254; housing resources, 259–261; income maintenance and employment, 253, 254–257; legal assistance, 265–267; leisure-time resources, 263–265; life expectancy in, 265–267; status of elderly in, 252–254; supportive services, 262–263
MALBEN (Israel), 200
Malta: demographic characteristics, 271–272; educational resources, 283; future projections, 284–286; gender differences, 272; government, role of, 274–277; health care services, 279–280; health status, 274; housing resources, 280–281; income maintenance and employment, 273–274, 277–279; legal assistance, 283–284; leisure-time resources, 282–283; life expectancy in, 283–284; status of elderly in, 270–274; supportive services, 281–282
Medicare/Medicaid: in Australia, 23–24; in the United States, 450–452
Mental health: in Argentina, 9–10; in Barbados, 61–62; in Canada, 74; in China, 89–90; in France, 121; in Great Britain, 169; in Hong Kong, 181; in Is-

rael, 207–208; in Malaysia, 263; in Norway, 324, 328–329; in Poland, 350; in Spain, 383; in the USSR, 467
Municipal Health Service Act (1982)(Norway), 325, 327
Municipalidad de la Ciudad de Buenos Aires (MCBA), 9, 10;

National Aid Fund (Jordan), 247
National Assistance Act (1948) (Great Britain), 159
National Assistance Board (NAB)(Barbados), 59, 60, 61, 62, 63
National Better Health Program (1987)(Australia), 29
National Commission on the Aged (1982)(Ghana), 144
National Committee on the Elderly of Thailand (1982), 433
National Council for the Aged (Norway), 324–325
National Council on Aging (Barbados), 63
National Health Act (1953)(Australia), 26
National Health Act (1964)(Australia), 20
National Health Service (NHS)(Great Britain), 159, 162–163; and Community Care Act (1993), 164
National Health Service (Spain), 377
National Housing (NHC)(Barbados), 59
National Housing Policy (1988)(India), 193
National Institute of Social Services for Retirees and Pensioners (INSSJP), 1, 4, 6, 7–8, 9, 10, 11, 13
National Insurance Institute (NII)(Israel), 201–202, 205, 208
National Insurance Scheme (NIS)(Barbados), 53, 54
Netherlands: demographic characteristics, 290–291; educational resources, 301–302; future projections, 302–303; gender differences, 291; government, role of, 291–292; health care services, 294–297; housing resources, 297–299; income maintenance and employment, 292–294; legal assistance, 302; leisure-time resources, 301–302; life expectancy in, 302; status of elderly in, 288–291; supportive services, 299–301
New Zealand: educational resources, 316–317; future projections, 318–319; gender differences, 306; government, role of, 307; health care services, 308–312; health status, 306; housing resources, 312–313; income maintenance and employment, 307–308; legal assistance, 317–318; leisure-time resources, 315–317; life expectancy in, 317–318; status of elderly in, 305–307; supportive services, 313–315
Norway: demographic characteristics, 323–324; educational resources, 333; future projections, 335–339; gender differences, 323–324; government, role of, 324–325; health care services, 327–329; health status, 324; housing resources, 329–330; income maintenance and employment, 325–327; legal assistance, 333–335; leisure-time resources, 332–333; life expectancy in, 333–335; status of elderly in, 321–324; supportive services, 330–332
Nursing Homes Assistance Act (1974)(Australia), 26
Nursing homes/long term care: in Australia, 25; in Austria, 40–41; in Barbados, 57; in Czech and Slovak Federal Republic, 99; in France, 117; in Great Britain, 163–164; in Hong Kong, 180; in Israel, 204–205; in Japan, 234, 236; in Malaysia, 258; in Malta, 280; in the Netherlands, 296–297; in New Zealand, 310–312; in Norway, 328–329; in Poland, 347; in Spain, 378–379; in Sweden, 405–406; in Switzerland, 421–422; in the United States, 451; in the USSR, 462–463

Old Age Security (OAS)(Canada), 69
Old Age Survivors Insurance Program (OASI)(U.S.), 448
Older American Act (OAA)(1965)(U.S.), 446, 447
Old Foundation of China (1986), 89

Pension Act (1871)(India), 190
Pensioners' Union (Czech and Slovak Federal Republic), 101
Poland: educational resources, 351; future projections, 352–354; gender differences, 341, 343; government, role of, 343–344; health care services, 346–347; health status, 343; housing resources, 347–349; income maintenance and employment, 344–346; legal assistance, 352; leisure-time resources, 350–351; life expectancy in, 352; status of elderly in, 340–343; supportive services, 349–350
Programa de asistencia medicas (PAMI)(Argentina), 6–7
Provident Fund Act (1991)(India), 190

Registered Nurses Association (Barbados), 57
Retirement/retirement pensions: in Argentina, 4, 5, 12; in Australia, 20, 21; in Austria, 38–39; in Barbados, 53–54; in Canada, 69–70; in China, 85–86; in Czech and Slovak Federal Republic, 97–98; in France, 112–115; in Germany, 127–129; in Ghana, 144–146; in Great Britain, 160–162; in Hong Kong, 177–178; in India, 190–192; in Israel, 201–203; in Italy, 216–217; in Japan, 230, 231–232; in Jordan, 246–247; in Malaysia, 254–256; in Malta, 274, 277–279; in the Netherlands, 292–293; in New Zealand, 307–308; in Norway, 325–327; in Poland, 344–346; in South Korea, 358–361; in Spain, 375–377; in the Sudan, 395–396; in Sweden, 402, 403–404; in Switzerland, 419–420; in Thailand, 434–435; in the United States, 448–450; in the USSR, 460–461; in Zimbabwe, 474–476

Sauvy, Alfred, xiii
Senior Citizen Employment Promotion Act (1991)(South Korea), 360–361
Senior Citizens' Welfare Act (1981)(South Korea), 357, 359, 362, 364

Silver Age Club, in Argentina, 10, 11
Social Care Act (1991)(Norway), 325
Social Security: in Argentina, 4, 5; in Australia, 21–22; in Austria, 37–38; in Barbados, 52; in China, 85; in France, 110–111; in Ghana, 144; in Great Britain, 158, 162; in Hong Kong, 178–179; in Israel, 201–202; in Japan, 229–230; in Jordan, 247; in Malaysia, 255–256, 257; in Malta, 275, 277–278; in the Netherlands, 289; in Norway, 321; in Poland, 345; in Spain, 375–377; in Sweden, 402, 404; in the United States, 446, 448–350; in the USSR, 460–461
Social Services Act (1982)(Sweden), 402, 406
Social Tenancy Law (Germany), 131
South Korea: educational resources, 366–367; future projections, 368–370; government, role of, 357–358; health care services, 361–363; health status, 361; housing resources, 363–364; income maintenance and employment, 358–361; legal assistance, 367–368; leisure-time resources, 365–367; life expectancy in, 367–368; status of elderly in, 356–357; supportive services, 364–365
Spain: educational resources, 385; future projections, 389–391; gender differences, 374; government, role of, 374–375; health care services, 377–379; housing resources, 379–382; income maintenance and employment, 375–377; legal assistance, 388–389; leisure-time resources, 384–388; life expectancy in, 388–389; status of elderly in, 373–374; supportive services, 382–384
Spitex service (Switzerland), 421
States Grant Paramedical Services Act (1969)(Australia), 20
State's Grants Home Care Act (Australia), 20
Sudan: educational resources, 398; future projections, 399–400; gender differences, 394, 396; health care services,

396–397; health status, 396; housing resources, 397–398; income maintenance and employment, 395–396; legal assistance, 399; leisure-time resources, 398; life expectancy in, 399; status of elderly in, 393–395; supportive services, 398

Supportive services: in Argentina, 9–10; in Australia, 25–28; in Austria, 43–45; in Barbados, 60–62; in Canada, 73–74; in China, 88–90; in Czech and Slovak Federal Republic, 101; in France, 119–120; in Germany, 132–134; in Ghana, 148–149; in Great Britain, 167–170; in Hong Kong, 183; in India, 193–194; in Israel, 206–208; in Italy, 219–220; in Japan, 237–240; in Jordan, 249; in Malaysia, 262–263; in Malta, 281–282; in the Netherlands, 299–301; in New Zealand, 313–315; in Norway, 330–332; in Poland, 349–350; in South Korea, 364–365; in Spain, 382–384; in the Sudan, 398; in Sweden, 407–409; in Switzerland, 424; in Thailand, 440–441; in the United States, 453–454; in the USSR, 465–468; in Zimbabwe, 479

Sweden: educational resources, 409; future projections, 410–413; gender differences, 402; government, role of, 402–403; health care services, 405–406; health status, 402; housing resources, 406–407; income maintenance and employment, 403–404; legal assistance, 410; leisure-time resources, 409–410; life expectancy in, 410; status of elderly in, 401–402; supportive services, 407–409

Switzerland: demographic characteristics, 417; educational resources, 426; future projections, 427–428; gender differences, 417; government, role of, 418–419; health care services, 420–423; housing resources, 423–424; income maintenance and employment, 419–420; legal assistance, 427; leisure-time resources, 424–426; life expectancy in, 427; status of elderly in, 415–418; supportive services, 424

Temporary Law of the Retirement and Resignation of Workers (China), 80

Thailand: educational resources, 441; future projections, 442–443; gender differences, 430; government, role of, 431–434; health care services, 435–438; health status, 430–431; housing resources, 438–440; income maintenance and employment, 434–435; legal assistance, 442; leisure-time resources, 441; life expectancy in, 442; private programs, 433–434; public welfare programs, 432–433; status of elderly in, 430–431; supportive services, 440–441

Third Age, use of term, xv

United States: educational resources, 455; future projections, 456–457; government, role of, 446–448; health care services, 450–452; health status, 450; housing resources, 452; income maintenance and employment, 448–450; legal assistance, 455–456; leisure-time resources, 454–455; life expectancy in, 455–456; status of elderly in, 445–446; supportive services, 453–454

Universal Declaration of Human Rights, 399

USIAMAS (Malaysia), 266

USSR (former): educational resources, 469; future projections, 470; gender differences, 458–459; government, role of, 459–460; health care services, 461–463; housing resources, 464–465; income maintenance and employment, 460–461; legal assistance, 469–470; leisure-time resources, 468–469; life expectancy in, 469–470; status of elderly in, 458–459; supportive services, 465–468

Victim assistance: in Argentina, 11; in Australia, 29–30; in Austria, 47; in Barbados, 64; in Canada, 75; in Germany, 135–136; in India, 196; in Jordan, 250; in Malta, 284; in the Netherlands, 302; in New Zealand, 317; in Norway, 333–334; in Spain,

388; in Sweden, 410; in the USSR, 470
Volunteerism/voluntary organization: in Argentina, 11; in Australia, 29; in Barbados, 62; in Canada, 74; in China, 89; in Czech and Slovak Federal Republic, 102; in Ghana, 148–149; in Great Britain, 167, 170–171; in India, 194–195; in Israel, 201, 208; in Italy, 221; in Malaysia, 261, 263–264; in Malta, 283; in the Netherlands, 301; in New Zealand, 315–316; in Norway, 332; in Poland, 351; in South Korea, 364–365; in Spain, 387–388; in Sweden, 403, 409–410; in the United States, 454–455;

Women's World Banking Ghana (WWBG)(Ghana), 149
The World Ageing Situation 1991 (UN), xvi

Zimbabwe: AIDS, 480–481; demographic characteristics, 473; future projections, 480–481; gender differences, 473; government, role of, 473–474; health care services, 476–477; health status, 480–481; housing resources, 477–479; income maintenance and employment, 474–476; legal assistance, 479–480; leisure-time resources, 479; life expectancy in, 479–480; status of elderly in, 472–473; supportive services, 479

ABOUT THE EDITOR AND CONTRIBUTORS

JORDAN I. KOSBERG is the Philip S. Fisher Professor and Director of The Centre for Applied Family Studies in the School of Social Work at McGill University in Montreal, Quebec. Formerly, he was Professor of Gerontology at the University of South Florida. He has authored many articles on applied social gerontology and edited several books pertaining to aging and old age in the world.

ABDULLAH MALIM BAGINDA was Director-General of the Department of Social Welfare and is presently Visiting Fellow in the Caring Society Program of the Institute of Strategic and International Studies in Kuala Lumpur. He is the founding president of the Gerontological Association of Malaysia and president of Usiamas, an advocacy and service organization for elderly persons in Malaysia.

ROBERTO E. BARCA is Director of Postgraduate Education in Gerontology, School of Public Health, College of Medicine, the University of Buenos Aires. He is the founding member and first president of the Gerontology Association of Buenos Aires and of the Gerontology Association of Argentina.

EVA BEVERFELT has been Research Director at the Norwegian Institute of Gerontology since 1973. Author of many books and articles, her research interests include the areas of coping behavior, older workers, and policy on aging.

She has served as the Norwegian representative on the World Health Organization Committee on Aging.

VLADISLAV V. BEZRUKOV a physician and Director of the Institute of Gerontology of the Academy of Medical Sciences (formerly of the USSR, presently of Ukraine) in Kiev and Chief of the Institute's Laboratory of Social Gerontology. He serves as president of the USSR Gerontology and Geriatrics Society, has over 160 publications (many on geriatrics), and serves as editor-in-chief of *Problems of Aging and Longevity*.

FARLEY S. BRATHWAITE is a Senior Lecturer in Sociology at the University of the West Indies. His research and teaching interests are in the areas of social problems, social planning and policy, and social gerontology in the Caribbean, and he is author and editor of several publications on the elderly in Barbados.

CAI WENMEI, formerly a Professor in the Institute of Population Research at Peking University, is currently vice-chairman and general secretary of the Sociology Association of Beijing and editor-in-chief of *Sociology and Social Survey*. She has published articles in the area of gerontology in China.

CHARLES K. BROWN is a sociologist and Director of the Centre for Development Studies at the University of Cape Coast. He has undertaken extensive field research on vulnerable groups in Ghana and has published in the area of services to the elderly.

CHO KAH SIN, formerly with the Institute of Strategic and International Studies in Kuala Lumpur, Malaysia, is presently Senior Officer for Social Development, Drugs, Culture and Information at the Association of South East Asian Nations in Jakarta, Indonesia. A member of the executive committee of the Gerontological Association of Malaysia, he has written on caregiving to the elderly.

NELSON W. S. CHOW is a Professor in the Department of Social Work and Social Administration at the University of Hong Kong and has served for many years as an adviser to the Hong Kong government on matters relating to the provision of social welfare services to the elderly. He has written widely on efforts to meet the needs of the elderly in East and Southeast Asian countries.

CHANDRA DAVE, a sociologist and social worker, has studied the psychosocial aspects of aging and old-age homes. Presently, she is involved in voluntary social work, is Joint Secretary for the Indian Association of Gerontology, and is a member of the editorial board for *International Social Work*.

About the Editor and Contributors

AMAL H. EL-FARHAN, an Associate Professor of Public Administration at the University of Jordan in Amman, has coauthored four books and published many articles. She serves on boards of many national and voluntary associations.

CRISTINA GAGLIARDI is a researcher in the Department of Gerontological and Geriatric Research at the Centre for Economic and Social Studies in Ancona. She has a degree in the political sciences.

MARIO D. GARRETT, a psychologist, currently is a member of a task force created by the Maltese government to recommend future policies for the well-being of the elderly. He formerly worked as a Program Officer for the UN International Institute on Aging (located in Malta). He has published papers in the areas of economics, management, and psychology and has progressively specialized in international gerontology.

S. D. GOKHALE is president of the International Federation on Ageing and Chairman of the International Leprosy Union, Rehabilitation Coordination-India, and the Centre for Research and Development. He has a long history of participation in activities of the United Nations, has directed many research projects, and has widely published books and articles (many translated into international languages).

LADISLAV G. HEGYI is Director of the Research Institute of Gerontology and primarius in the Department of Internal Medicine and Geriatrics in Malacky. He is vice-president of the Slovak Gerontological Association and has written widely in the areas of gerontology and geriatrics.

JEAN-CLAUDE HENRARD is a Professor and Head of the Department of Health and Aging at René Descartes University in Paris. He has served as a technical adviser to the Secretary of State of the Elderly and to the Secretary of State for Health. He has authored and edited several publications.

JIANG LEIWEN is a sociologist and Assistant Professor in the Institute of Population Research, Peiking University. He has published several papers on family issues within China.

JOSEF HÖRL is an Associate Professor of Sociology and Social Gerontology at the University of Vienna. Author and researcher on the family and other informal groups, he is a member of the Austrian Family Ministry's Advisory Panel on the Elderly.

MALCOLM L. JOHNSON is Professor of Health and Social Welfare and Dean of the School of Health, Welfare and Community Education at the Open University in Milton Keynes. Founding editor of *Aging and Society,* he has published widely in many areas of sociology and gerontology and has served on many public and professional boards.

FRED KARL is a sociologist and an Academic Lecturer for Social Aspects of Aging with the Department for Social Work at the University of Kassel. As a member of an Interdisciplinary Working Group for Applied Social Gerontology and the German Association for Gerontology and Geriatrics, he has published several articles on applied gerontology.

PEGGY G. KOOPMAN-BOYDEN is the Chief Executive of the New Zealand Institute for Social Research and Development Ltd. in Christchurch, and former Senior Lecturer in the Sociology Department at the University of Canterbury. Currently, she is president of the New Zealand Gerontology Association and a Council Member of Age Concern (Canterbury). Her research interests include family care, retirement life-styles, and income support.

GIOVANNI LAMURA is a researcher with the Department of Gerontological and Geriatric Research Department at the Centre for Economic and Social Studies in Ancona. He holds degrees in economics and social sciences.

NIEMAT A. LATIFF MURSI works in the Ministry of Social Welfare and Development in Khartoum. She has been involved in various workshops and seminars dealing with disadvantaged populations—the elderly, the handicapped, AIDS victims, the homeless, and women—and she has presented papers on aging and old age in Sudan.

HOWARD LITWIN is Associate Professor at the Paul Baerwald School of Social Work of the Hebrew University in Jerusalem, where he serves as Chairman of the Master of Social Work Program. He is the author of many articles, chapters, books, and research reports in the areas of community work and social services for the elderly.

LUO XIAOYUI is Professor of Cardiovascular Surgery at the Capital Medical Institute and the Deputy Director of the Xuan Wu Hospital and the Beijing Geriatric Center. He has authored numerous articles and books in his areas of medical and geriatric interests.

JOHN McCALLUM, a sociologist, is Senior Research Fellow at the National Centre for Epidemiology and Population Health at the Australian National University in Canberra. He is author of many articles, reports, and books on aging and old age in Australia and in various countries in Oceania and the Far East.

MUHSEN A. MAKHAMREH is Professor and Chairman of the Business Department at the University of Jordan in Amman. He has published three books and many articles and is a member of many charitable organizations.

VICTOR W. MARSHALL, a sociologist, is the Director of the Centre for Studies of Aging and Professor of Behavioral Science at the University of Toronto. He is the former editor-in-chief of *The Canadian Journal on Aging* and current Director of the Canadian Aging Research Network. His research and publication areas of interest include the family, long-term care, and health policy.

MASSIMO MENGANI is Senior Researcher at the Department for Gerontology and Geriatrics Research in the Centre for Economic and Social Studies in Ancona. He holds a degree in economic sciences and has authored many books and articles on the problems of the elderly (especially the disabled elderly).

ABRAHAM MONK is Professor of Social Work and Gerontology and Director of the Institute on Aging, at the Columbia University School of Social Work in New York City, and he has authored many books, articles, and chapters in the fields of aging, social policy, social planning, and evaluative research. He has conducted extensive research on intergenerational relations, social and health settings for the aged, pre- and postretirement issues, and policies and services for the aged.

RICARDO MORAGAS MORAGAS is Professor of Sociology and Director of the Master of Gerontology Program at the University of Barcelona. He has held positions in the public and private sectors and in several universities and has been a Principal Researcher with the International Red Cross in Geneva.

ANDREW C. NYANGURU, formerly in the School of Social Work at the University of Zimbabwe in Harare, is presently Senior Lecturer in the Department of Social Anthropoloogy and Sociology at The National University of Lesotho in Roma, Lesotho. His publications focus upon social settings for the elderly, the quality of institutional care, and migration and aging in Zimbabwe.

CHANPEN SAENGTIENCHAI, a demographer, is a researcher at the Institute of Population Studies at Chulalongkorn University in Bangkok. She has authored or coauthored publications on the socioeconomic consequences of an aging population in Thailand and living arrangements of the Thai elderly.

MARISA SCERRI is an Administrative Officer in Research and Planning Section within the Malta Secretariat for the Care of the Elderly. She has been involved in gerontological training and planning activities.

HANS-DIETER SCHNEIDER is Professor of Applied Psychology at the University at Fribourg (Switzerland). He directed his efforts in the areas of adult education and organizational psychology, and his present research and writing interests are in social psychology and social gerontology.

THEO N. M. SCHUYT is Senior Researcher on Social Work and Social Policy in the Department of Sociology and Social Gerontology at Vrije University in Amsterdam. A sociologist, he has many publications in the area of social gerontology.

YUTAKA SHIMIZU, a sociologist, is Director of the Department of Social Welfare Research at the Tokyo Metropolitan Institute of Gerontology. He has published articles on family care of the elderly and the need for family support.

SONG YUHUA is the Director of the International Department, China National Committee on Aging, and Adviser of the China International Conference Center for the China Association of Science and Technology. She has carried out research and has written on the elderly in China.

GERDT SUNDSTRÖM is a Senior Researcher at the Institute of Gerontology in Jönköping and an Assistant Professor in Social Work at the University of Stockholm. He has published and lectured widely in Sweden and abroad on old-age care, family sociology, and related fields.

KYU-TAIK SUNG is Professor and Director of the Center for Social Welfare Research in the Department of Social Work at Yonsei University in Seoul. He has published many articles on filial piety, family caregiving of the elderly, and cross-cultural comparisons of parent care, and he is the president of the Korean Gerontological Society.

BRUNON SYNAK is Professor and Head of the Department of Sociology, Institute of Philosophy and Sociology, at the University of Gdańsk. He has published widely in the areas of formal and informal care of the Polish elderly.

MATS THORSLUND is a sociologist and Professor in the School of Social Work at the University of Stockholm. He has held several academic and research appointments and has published numerous articles, chapters, and books on care of the elderly, the family, and the elderly themselves.

MICAELA TONUCCI is a researcher in the Department of Gerontological and Geriatric Research at the Centre of Economic and Social Studies in Ancona. She has degrees in economics and social sciences.

GERARD H. VAN DER ZANDEN, a social scientist, is an Associate Managing Director at the Dutch Center for Health Promotion and Health Education. He has worked as a researcher in social welfare and aging, directed the first Dutch research program on aging, and was executive managing director of the Netherlands Institute of Gerontology. He has published in such areas as policy on aging, attitudes toward aging, and social participation of the elderly.

NINA V. VERZHIKOVSKAYA works at the Institute of Gerontology of the Academy of Medical Sciences in Kiev.

JUNKO WAKE, a social worker, is an Assistant Researcher in the Department of Social Welfare Research at the Tokyo Metropolitan Institute of Gerontology.

BLOSSOM T. WIGDOR is a psychologist and the former director of the Centre for Studies of Aging at the University of Toronto (where she continues to work). She is the immediate past chairperson of the National Advisory Council on Aging and has published two books and numerous articles on retirement and aging.

MALINEE WONGSITH is an Associate Professor at the Institute of Population Studies at Chulalongkorn University in Bangkok. Her publications focus upon the impact of the living arrangements of the elderly on government programs, attitudes toward family values, socioeconomic consequences of the aging of the Thai population, and family care of the elderly in Thailand.

ISBN 0-313-28338-9

HARDCOVER BAR CODE